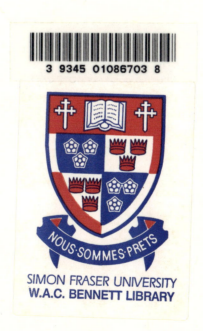

Play

as a
Medium for
Learning and
Development

Contributors

Irene Athey, Graduate School of Education, Rutgers University, New Brunswick, NJ 08903

Inge Bretherton, Department of Human Development and Family Studies, Colorado State University, Fort Collins, CO 80523

Arlene Brewster, Northside Medical Center, Family Practice Center, Youngstown, OH 44501

Nancy Curry, Department of Child Development and Child Care, University of Pittsburgh, Pittsburgh, PA 15213

Rheta DeVries, Laboratory School, Department of Human Development and Consumer Sciences, University of Houston, Houston, TX 77004

Michael Ellis, Department of Physical Education and Human Movement Studies, University of Oregon, Eugene, OR 97403

Beverly Fagot, Department of Psychology, University of Oregon, Eugene, OR 97403

Laura Gaynard, Phoenix Children's Hospital, Phoenix, AZ 85006

Evelyn Hausslein, Graduate School, Wheelock College, Boston, MA 02215

Constance Kamii, Department of Curriculum and Instruction, University of Alabama at Birmingham, Birmingham, AL 35294

Margot Kaplan-Sanoff, Graduate School, Wheelock College, Boston, MA 02215

Sherri Oden, High/Scope Educational Research Foundation, Ypsilanti, MI 48197

Anita Rui Olds, Olds and Associates, Cambridge, MA 02138

Stephanie O'Neill, La Frontera Center, Tucson, AZ 85713

Anne E. Porter, Department of Reading, Language Arts, and Computer Literacy, Oakland University, Rochester, MI 48063

Patricia Ramsey, Department of Psychology and Education, Mount Holyoke College, South Hadley, MA 01075

Rebecca Reid, Division of Early Childhood, SUNY Agricultural and Technical College at Cobleskill, Cobleskill, NY 12043

Annemarie Roeper, Consultation Services for the Gifted, Oakland, CA 94618

Kenneth Rubin, Department of Psychology, University of Waterloo, Waterloo, ON N2L 3G1, Canada

Olivia Saracho, Department of Curriculum and Instruction, University of Maryland, College Park, MD 20742

Dorothy G. Singer, Department of Psychology, Yale University, New Haven, CT 06511

Jerome L. Singer, Department of Psychology, Yale University, New Haven, CT 06511

Kenneth Smith, Department of Teacher Education, University of Nebraska at Omaha, Omaha, NE 68182

Bernard Spodek, College of Education, University of Illinois, Urbana, IL 61820

Jim Stillwell, Department of Health, Physical Education and Recreation, Pittsburg State University, Pittsburg, KS 66762

Brian Sutton-Smith, Graduate School of Education, University of Pennsylvania, Philadelphia, PA 19104

Play
as a
Medium for
Learning and
Development

A Handbook
of Theory and
Practice

Edited by
Doris Bergen

Department of Psychology and Counseling
Pittsburg State University

Heinemann
Portsmouth, New Hampshire

Heinemann Educational Books, Inc.
70 Court Street   Portsmouth, NH   03801

London • Edinburgh • Melbourne • Auckland
Singapore • New Delhi • Ibadan • Nairobi
Johannesburg • Kingston • Port of Spain

10 9 8 7 6 5 4 3 2 1

The following have generously given permission to reprint copyrighted material in this book:

Section 1, Introduction: From G. A. Sheehan (1975), *Dr. Sheehan on running*, pp. 182–84. Mountain View, CA: World. Reprinted by permission of *Runner's World Magazine.* Copyright 1975. Rodale Press, Inc. All rights reserved.

Chapter 2: Play observation scale and summary of play and non-play behaviors from K. H. Rubin (1985), *The Play Observation Scale (POS)*, pp. 7, 10. Waterloo, Ontario, Canada: University of Waterloo. Reprinted by permission of the copyright holder, K. H. Rubin.

Section 2, Introduction: "Binker," from *Now we are six* by A. A. Milne. Copyright 1927 by E. P. Dutton, renewed 1955 by A. A. Milne. Reprinted by permission of the publisher, E. P. Dutton, a division of New American Library. First stanza of "Hoppity," from *When we were very young* by A. A. Milne. Copyright 1924 by E. P. Dutton, renewed 1952 by A. A. Milne. Reprinted by permission of the publisher, E. P. Dutton, a division of New American Library.

Chapter 5: Chart adapted from P. Hesse and D. Cicchetti (1982), "Perspectives on an integrated theory of emotional development," in D. Cicchetti and P. Hesse (eds.), *Emotional development*. San Francisco: Jossey-Bass. Copyright © 1982 by Jossey-Bass. Reprinted by permission of publisher and authors.

Chapter 6: Adaptation of figure 3.2, p. 42, by permission of Macmillan Publishing Company from *Understanding motor development in children* by David L. Gallahue, originally published by John Wiley & Sons, Inc. (New York: Macmillan, 1982). Two figures from Bryant J. Cratty, *Perceptual and motor development in infants and children*, © 1979, pp. 17, 18. Reprinted by permission of Prentice-Hall, Inc., Englewood Cliffs, New Jersey.

Chapter 9: Vignette reprinted from "Some properties of social play," *Merrill-Palmer Quarterly* 20 (3) (1974), p. 174—example 4, by Catherine Garvey, by permission of the Wayne State University Press and the author. Vignette in K. H. Rubin, "Fantasy play: Its role in the development of social skills and social cognition," in K. H. Rubin (ed.), *Children's play*. San Francisco: Jossey-Bass, Inc. Copyright © 1980 by Jossey-Bass. pp. 75–76. Reprinted by permission. Figure 9–1 from Nancy Rambusch (1982), "Organization of environments." In D. T. Streets (ed.), *Administering daycare and preschool programs*, pp. 71–87 (Boston: Allyn & Bacon). Reprinted by permission of D. T. Streets.

Chapter 10: Excerpts from I. Opie and P. Opie (1959), *The lore and language of school children*. London: Oxford University Press. Reprinted by permission of I. Opie. Figure 10–3 from A. Taylor and G. Vlastos (1975), *School zone, learning environments for children*. New York: Van Nostrand Reinhold. Reprinted by permission of Anne P. Taylor. Figure 10–4 from A. Taylor and W. F. Preiser (n.d.), *Activity-based design of applied learning classroom environments*. Albuquerque, NM: Institute for Environmental Education, University of New Mexico. Reprinted by permission of Anne P. Taylor.

Chapter 11: From Dylan Thomas, *Quite early one morning*. Copyright 1954 by Dylan Thomas. Reprinted by permission of New Directions Publishing Corporation.

Section 3, Essay: From Margery Williams Bianco, *The velveteen rabbit: Or how toys become real.* New York: Doubleday, 1926. Reprinted by permission of the publisher.

Library of Congress Cataloging-in-Publication Data

Play as a medium for learning and development.

Bibliography: p.
Includes index.
1. Play. 2. Learning. 3. Child development.
I. Bergen, Doris.
LB1137.P553 1987   155.4'18   86-31858
ISBN 0-435-08432-1

Chapter-opening photo credits: Holly Andrecheck—Introduction, chapter 6; Ellen Creager—chapters 1, 2, 4, 5, 7, 8, 9, 10, 11, and epilogue; James Sponseller—chapter 3.
Front-cover photo by Ellen Creager.
Figures by Holly Andrecheck and Maria Szmauz.
Designed by Maria Szmauz.

PRINTED IN THE UNITED STATES OF AMERICA.

Contents

Preface

When my first book on play was published (Sponseller, 1974), I was an assistant professor of early childhood education at Oakland University and was actively involved in an innovative teacher training project designed to bring the philosophy of play as a learning medium into the mainstream of public school and early education. Our project was one of many at that time; we were part of a consortium of early childhood training institutions that were engaged in translating early childhood theory into curricular practice.

The authors who wrote chapters in that book, *Play as a Learning Medium*, were from universities that were members of the consortium. They shared the belief that play is a basic factor in learning, and they agreed that the stress on structured academic skill learning, which was being emphasized by some theorists during the seventies, was threatening to crowd play out of the early school curriculum. The value of play was also being questioned by many parents who were concerned with their children's academic progress. These parents were being encouraged to teach rote skills at home and to organize most of their children's out-of-school time.

In the preface to that book I stated:

When early learning is defined as being only academic learning, play is often taken out of the curriculum to achieve these goals. The elementary school years have traditionally valued "work" in the classroom and have relegated play to recess time only. Kindergarten teachers are reporting that with increasing emphasis on accountability for reaching early academic objectives, there is now less time for play in their classrooms. And often the movement toward "educational" content in the preschool is interpreted in ways which cause downgrading or even abandonment of play time in the preschool as well.

Parents are now told that their job is not to play with their child but to teach him. The free and easy play interaction between parent and child at play has been an important part of early learning about self,

family, and society. In an effort to develop "teachable" activities for parents, play behaviors have sometimes been utilized for structured lessons. If this unstructured play is replaced by conscious efforts on parents' parts to be "teachers," much of the spontaneity and delight of parent/child play may be lost. (pp. 1–2)

During the 13 years since *Play as a Learning Medium* was published, the pressures on children to achieve academically in a worklike (or workbook-like!) school environment have not diminished. Moreover, many school-aged children have pressure-filled lessons schedules that monopolize their after-school time as well. The growing success of day-care and early education programs that stress structured academic learning and omit free playtime is also evidence that upwardly mobile parents are choosing environments for their very young children in which the value of play is minimized. Thus, there is a continuing need for educators to study the value of play for learning and to know how to translate their knowledge into educational practice.

Despite these pressures, there are many researchers and educators who view play as an important part of learning. Some of them are the colleagues who contributed to *Play as a Learning Medium*; in the years since then, I have come to know many more colleagues who share similar views. One of the joys for me in planning this new book has been to call upon some of them to be authors and essayists. As I have worked on this book with these colleagues, I have had this purpose: to create an integrated, conceptually sound and relevant book that explains how play acts as a learning medium and that unites play theory, research, and practice to make it useful for those who desire to use play to enhance learning in both traditional and nontraditional educational environments.

Acknowledgments

In addition to the authors who are listed as contributors, a number of others have made the writing and editing of this book possible. They include the following persons whose help and expertise I have greatly valued:

Joel Fink, who critiqued many sections of the manuscript and who provided me with moral support on many occasions. Ellen Creager, who edited a number of chapters of the manuscript. Holly Andrecheck, who drew the figures and environmental plans. Gail Sponseller, who provided me with one of my favorite vignettes.

The perceptive students from Oakland University and Pittsburg State University who allowed me to share their observations of children's play and their own childhood play experiences with the readers.

The educators and/or administrators from Lakeside School, Pittsburg, KS; the Matthew Lowry Early Childhood Center, Oakland University, Rochester, MI; the Gorse Child Study Center, Mount Holyoke, South Hadley, MA; the Cobleskill Campus Child Care Center, SUNY Agricultural and Technical College, Cobleskill, NY; the Phoenix Children's Hospital, Phoenix, AZ; and the the Alfred I. DuPont Institute, Wilmington, DE, from which many of the ideas presented in the environmental models were adapted.

Sandy Oliver, Ellen Dailey, Leah Bevin, and Cynthia Pfannenstiel, who provided bibliographic and library resource assistance. Debbie Amershek, who did much of the technical manuscript preparation, and Rosalie Zlomke and Jody Billiard, who assisted with technical preparation.

Introduction

Play and Learning: Questioning Current Ends and Means

● Are learning goals too narrow?

Play has been undervalued as a curricular tool by educators and by parents because society has defined the goals of learning, especially school learning, very narrowly. Learning goals have been stated primarily in terms of mastering basic academic skills. Educators have been required to focus on these narrow learning ends even though the knowledge needed by adults in a complex technological society is much broader than the competencies promoted in a basic skills approach. This emphasis on basic skills has been increasing even at the preschool level, where the learning of letters, numbers, words, and colors has been stressed. These learning ends, however, represent only a small subset of the essential learning elements that must be incorporated into early education. Play, which allows children to choose their learning focus and which fosters a broad range of developmental goals, should be included as an essential learning element. If attaining a narrow set of academic skills as quickly as possible is the end endorsed by society, however, then play, which requires extended time periods, is likely to be undervalued.

Part of the educational stress on lock-step, efficient production of learners who can perform a narrow set of standardized skills comes from the influences of the value system promoted by the industrial society, which has been dominant during this century. According to Toffler (1980), the technological advances that have been made in the past few decades predict that the society of the future will require citizens who have adaptive, creative, and complex cognitive and communication abilities. Instead of promoting skills needed for a standardized,

1

mass-produced, rigidly time-regulated society, educators will need to focus on helping children develop individualistic and versatile competencies. Future learning goals are likely to be ones that can be promoted particularly well by a rich diet of play opportunities in the early years of school.

In the past decade there has been an explosion in the body of research on the relationship of play to children's development and learning. Researchers from many disciplines and theoretical perspectives have demonstrated the existence of these relationships. As reflected in the increase in articles on play in research journals, the study of play is now considered respectable. This book draws upon a rich research base that was not present at the time of my first book on play. The result of this increased research effort has been to make clear the many learning ends that are related to play. The importance of play for emotional, social, physical/motor, gender/sex role, language, and moral development as well as its relationship to complex aspects of cognitive development, is being documented in this research. Research describing how play affects the development and coping skills of children with special needs also serves to expand our view of appropriate learning goals and to emphasize the role of play in learning.

● How has play been used to promote learning?

Given the evidence that play is related to development and learning, and that the technological age may require citizens with qualities that are promoted by play, the next question is whether play has been used effectively to promote learning. Educators have usually responded in one of three ways to the idea of using play as a curricular tool. First, many have continued to ignore the need for play in educational settings. In some cases, even those who value play have diminished the amount of playtime available for children in the school or preschool environment because of immediate pressures to concentrate on basic skills.

Second, because many educators have not understood what play is or how to use it as a medium for learning, they have used it in an ineffective, distorted, or manipulative way. The value society places on competition, production, and exploitation has in-

fluenced the way play has been used by some educators and parents. For example, undue emphasis has too often been placed on educational toys, workbook games, and competitive sports, while child-initiated free play has been eliminated.

A third response has come primarily from those adults who truly value play and who teach in environments that effectively promote learning through play. Their tendency has been to cling determinedly to traditional materials and standard activities, without attempting to incorporate appropriately new technological materials such as computers into the play environment. Some have been afraid that these new play materials would crowd out valuable traditional materials, while others have included new equipment but not promoted its use in play. Educators need to evaluate the play value of these new technologies carefully. The long-term effects that specific areas of technology will have on development and learning are as yet unclear. For example, research on effects of various types of television program viewing has produced mixed results, but two general effects have been clearly demonstrated: (1) Television viewing decreases the time available at home for free play, and (2) the content of children's symbolic play at school reflects the television world. Even though television is no longer a new technology, many educators have yet to examine the potential of television as an enhancer of play environments.

The potential effects of computers on play also seem unclear, with the possibility of both positive and negative influences. Research suggests that although computer game playing may promote stereotypic and rote behaviors, the interactive nature of computer play may enhance creativity and problem solving. The concept of the computer as a playmate seems likely to open up a wider range of cognitive content fields to playful activity for children.

If the competencies needed in the society of the future are ones that rely on adaptive, playful, and individualistic responses, as Toffler (1980) suggests, play should no longer be ignored. Educators should cease to exploit play as a means of reaching narrowly defined learning ends; instead, they should value play as an important medium for learning the competencies essential for success in the society of the future.

Play as a Medium

All human beings are active seekers of knowledge; play is an integral facet of this ongoing quest. Play development is best explained through a theoretical framework incorporating Piagetian, information-processing, social learning, psychoanalytic/psychosocial, psychobiological, and ethological theories. Each of these theoretical perspectives answers certain questions about play, and each is useful in explaining some types of play. Educators should be able to draw upon many models that have usefulness for learning and teaching. The pedagogical value of play does not lie in its use as a way to teach a specific set of skills through structured activities called "play." Rather, play is valuable primarily as a medium for learning. The word *medium* can be defined in a number of ways; a discussion of five definitions given by Webster (1980, p. 708) can help us see why play can be viewed as a medium.

1. A *medium* is "a condition in which something may function or flourish." Play can be thought of as a condition in which a broad range of learning may flourish. It supports elaborative functioning of the cognitive structures of the mind, thus promoting the development of intelligence. Because play is a condition that promotes optimal functioning, it can enhance other learning goals as well.
2. A *medium* is "a means of effecting or conveying something." Play serves to enhance children's self-awareness and sense of effectance because it assists in the translation of their experiences into internal meaning. Since they are less able to use language as a means of understanding their own thoughts and feelings, the play medium provides them with a way to gain an internal sense of mastery over the environment and to communicate within themselves, giving them a feeling of effectance.
3. A *medium* is "a channel of communication." Language provides adults with their prime channel of social communication. Until children have that language facility, play acts as a prime channel by which children's thoughts and feelings are communicated to others. Many of children's misconceptions and incomplete understandings are conveyed when adults observe children's play. Through observation of play adults can also understand the level of complexity of children's thought processes and the intensity of children's feelings.
4. A *medium* is "a surrounding or enveloping substance." Observers of children are often aware of how enveloped children are in their play. Playing children show an intensity of concentration and involvement that seems to enclose them in a special world. Play acts as a surrounding environment that can temporarily soften realities of the world, provide a filter through which unpleasant experiences can be faced, and allow children to try out actions within a risk-free world of their own.
5. A *medium* is "a material or technical means of artistic expression." Adults use a variety of media for artistic, creative expression; play serves as a primary medium for the artistic expression of children. It acts as a technical medium for exploring materials from many perspectives, enabling children to explore (a) the range of possible uses of objects, (b) different ways to deal with social situations, and (c) how their own bodies can best function. Children combine the medium of play with drama, art, music, dance, and literature in their active pursuit of knowledge.

Overview of the Book

This book discusses the present state of knowledge of the medium of play, how play is related to children's physical, cognitive, language, moral, social, emotional, and gender/sex role development, and how environments can be designed to facilitate learning through play.

The authors of this book speak to a wide range of issues concerning play as a learning medium. These issues are presented in two formats: (a) in 11 chapters that discuss major aspects of play, its relationship to development, and its place in educational practice; and (b) in a series of 12 essays that focus on specific themes identified by their authors as crucial for understanding play.

The first section addresses how play has been defined, studied, and explained. In chapter 1, Spodek and Saracho present an overview of the historical role of play, the theory and research that define play as an educative experience, and the implications for practice that the challenge of educational play suggests. In chapter 2, Bergen reviews methods used to study play, presents criteria that can guide play research, and provides some models that can be used as guides for studying aspects of play. In chapter 3, Bergen describes the universal stages of play development and discusses differences in play that are influenced by individual and cultural factors.

The essayists in the first section speculate about the role of play in human survival (Ellis); raise questions about the appropriate balance between educational and festive play (Sutton-Smith); and discuss implications of the developmental stages of social play (Rubin).

In the second section, three chapters describe the relationship of play to other areas of development. Athey, in chapter 4, examines the role of play in relation to cognitive, language, and moral development. In chapter 5, Curry and Bergen review emotional, social, and gender/sex role development in relation to play. In chapter 6, Kaplan-Sanoff, Brewster, Stillwell, and Bergen discuss the relationship of play to physical/motor development and to the development of children with special needs (i.e., handicapped, hospitalized, and environmentally at-risk children).

The essayists in this section discuss the role of imagination in play development (Singer and Singer); explore moral development in play (DeVries); raise questions concerning play environments as settings for sex role stereotyping (Fagot); and point out the role of play in the development of gifted children (Roeper).

Section 3 brings together the research literature on social and environmental effects on play and provides suggestions for designing play environments. In chapter 7, Bergen describes how a schema for play and learning can assist educators in planning ways to use play as a curricular tool. Bergen, Smith, and O'Neill, in chapter 8, discuss environmental factors in regard to infant and toddler play. Ramsey

and Reid review the research and give guidelines for play environments for preschoolers and kindergartners in chapter 9. In chapter 10, Bergen and Oden look at the implications of the design of play environments for elementary children. In the final chapter, Bergen, Gaynard, and Hausslein discuss special play environments (i.e., those in the larger community and those for severely multihandicapped or hospitalized children).

The essayists in this section give a perspective on the essentials of environmental design for children (Olds); point out the significance of symbolic play development (Bretherton); suggest linkages of symbolic play with later academic learning (Kamii); discuss the unique effects of the computer on play and learning (Porter); and speculate on the future of play and human players in a technological world (Bergen).

Defining, Explaining, and Studying Play

To play or not to play? That is the real question. Shakespeare was wrong. Anyone with a sense of humor can see that life is a joke, not a tragedy. It is a riddle and like all riddles has an obvious answer: play, not suicide. . . . In play you realize simultaneously the supreme importance and the utter insignificance of what you are doing. You accept the paradox of pursuing what is at once essential and inconsequential. In play you can totally commit yourself to a goal that minutes later is completely forgotten.

Play, then, is the answer to the puzzle of our existence. . . . It is not, as we believed, simply a method of relieving tension and providing relaxation. Nor is it a service activity preparing us for the more serious and important everyday world, the real world.

Play, as the true player knows, is the most real thing that he does. Indeed, one must play with a passionate involvement, play as if his life depended on it, if play is to mean anything at all. (Sheehan, 1975, pp. 182–84)

The paradox of play, described so eloquently in Sheehan's (1975) *Dr. Sheehan on Running*, has been defined, explained, and studied for over 150 years. Many of the attempts to answer questions about play raise as many questions as they answer. Because of the nature of play—a concept that everyone understands and no one understands—researchers may never unravel all of its mysteries. For play often seems to be a "puzzle" or a "riddle," and those who study play are also "players" (Lorenz, 1976, cited in Johnson, 1984, p. xi).

Why has play become a topic of so much current research interest? According to Johnson (1984), there have been advances in the way play is conceptualized and improvements in methodologies that have made play research "more empirically manageable" and "more scientifically respectable" (p. xii). A basic body of research has also been collected during the past 20 years and this now serves as a catalyst for extending play research in new directions.

Many conceptual and methodological problems remain and there are numerous gaps in the empirical and theoretical research literature. However, a momentum has been achieved that promises to further expand the body of knowledge about play development and consequently to provide information that will significantly influence educational practice.

Chapter 1 gives an historical and definitional overview of the concept of play. It also summarizes the ways play is used in early education programs. Chapter 2 describes the methods used in play research and the decisions that researchers must make in order to conduct studies of play. Chapter 3 describes the stages of play development and the trends in that development throughout the life span. The essayists in this section share their ideas about the purposes and paradoxes of play.

CHAPTER ONE

The Challenge of Educational Play

BERNARD SPODEK ● OLIVIA N. SARACHO

One of the interesting characteristics of early childhood educators is their need to justify the use of play in programs for children, as well as their need to justify themselves as professionals whose prime concern is children's play. It is difficult to justify a serious concern with play in a culture that is still rooted in puritanism. Too often the basic concern with play is denied by suggesting that play is really something else, such as "play is the work of the child!" By calling play work, it becomes serious and scholars can be serious about it and maintain their professional self-esteem.

The problem with such statements is that they obscure real differences and deny valid concerns. A concern with play should not be hidden but should be seriously considered. Play is legitimate; it needs to be accepted in its own right for it to be used wisely.

The first activity-oriented program in the history of early childhood education was begun about 150 years ago when Frederick Froebel created the kindergarten in Germany. Froebel observed children, abstracted the essential ingredients of their activities, creating an educational program from this. He called the educational materials he designed "gifts," and the educational activities "occupations." The gifts were sets of objects, such as balls, wooden blocks, and other materials. The occupations included paper weaving, paper folding and cutting, and many of the arts-and-crafts activities that are offered to children in kindergarten today. These materials symbolized the key ideas that Froebel viewed as essential to an understanding of the unity of the world and of the individual, God, and nature. Even though Froebel (1887) uses the word *freedom* extensively in his writing, the activities he designed were highly prescriptive. Because the children had to do what they were told with the materials, the activities cannot really be termed play.

In Italy, more than a half-century later, Maria Montessori developed a very different program of early childhood education. She also observed children's play and abstracted activities from her observations. Her activity-based program became known as the Montessori Method (Montessori, 1965, 1973). Even though children were involved in manipulating materials, the prescribed way they were required to use these materials precluded play.

In both these approaches, observations of play were the source of program ideas, but the observations were interpreted through different theories, and the resulting programs included activity, but not play.

Beginning with the development of the nursery school movement in England in the early 1900s and the reform kindergarten movement in the United States at about the same time, play began to be accepted as a legitimate educational activity. These educators observed children and realized that what children do in play is real, is vital, and has within it the potential for learning. They saw how children use play to test ideas, abstract information, and operate on this information. The natural play activities of children were valued, supported, and nurtured in these early childhood programs. Housekeeping areas, blocks, and outdoor play activities were provided for children. Recent research has added to knowledge about children's play and has permitted educators and researchers to elaborate upon the possibilities of play activities that promote learning.

The puzzle of play has been one that many theorists have attempted to solve in the last 150 years. They have grappled with problems in defining play, and they have disagreed with one another about its definition. They have provided many explanations for why play occurs and how to tell when it will occur. They have also suggested how it functions in the processes of education and development and have argued about whether adult interventions in children's play help or hurt these processes.

Practitioners who work in educational settings with young children have also been concerned with the topic of play. They have proposed numerous educational approaches that use play (as they define it) to promote children's development. They, too, have debated the appropriateness of specific play interventions that have been suggested.

This chapter sets the stage for further discussion of many of these theoretical and practical issues. It gives an overview of the definitions of play that have been offered in the past and that are currently suggested, reviews rationales provided for children's play, and discusses the educational functions of play in the lives of children. A brief discussion of methods for promoting play as a medium for learning and development in early childhood education concludes the chapter.

Definitions of Play

Play is difficult to define accurately. There are 59 definitions of play in *Webster's New World Dictionary* (1972). The word *play* is used in many ways in everyday life. For instance, a play is a dramatic performance, and one can play a musical instrument; this conveys a sense of performance. Kidding around is also considered play. A pun is a play on words. A car is taken into the service station to be repaired because the steering wheel had too much play in it. Because it is used in so many ways, attempting to define the word *play* in everyday use presents a challenge.

When play began to be accepted in education, a variety of definitions were developed. Educators and philosophers developed a range of definitions of play, which included the following (Mitchell & Mason, 1948):

- Seashore: Free self-expression for the pleasure of expression.
- Froebel: The natural unfolding of the germinal leaves of childhood.
- Hall: The motor habits and spirit of the past persisting in the present.
- Groos: Instinctive practice, without serious intent, of activities which will later be essential to life.
- Dewey: Activities not consciously performed for the sake of any result beyond themselves.
- Schiller: The aimless expenditure of exuberant energy.
- Spenser: Superfluous actions taking place instinctively in the absence of real actions. . . . Activity performed for the immediate gratification derived without regard for ulterior benefits.

- Lazarus: Activity in itself free, aimless, amusing, or diverting.
- Shand: A type of play directed at the maintenance of joy.
- Dulles: An instinctive form of self-expression and emotional escape valve.
- Curti: Highly motivated activity which, as free from conflicts, is usually, though not always, pleasurable. (pp. 103–104)

Each definition suggests different consequences for understanding and interpreting play.

Often play is defined as distinct from work. An activity is play, if it is not work. However, the same activity can be identified as work under some conditions and as play under other conditions. When children play football on Saturday morning, it is play. When Joe Montana participates in a football game on Sunday afternoon, there is little that is playful about it. It is very serious business. Similarly, a person hired to build a cabinet is working; someone creating a cabinet in his or her home workshop, would be playing, even though it would be serious cabinet-making.

It is not the activity itself, but the reasons for the activity, that seem to determine whether it is play or work. The criteria for play are not observable. Whether an activity is play or not play is inferred from the sources of satisfaction in the activity. Activity done for its own sake is seen as play; activity done for external reward, salary, or pay is seen as work.

The degree of seriousness of the activity can also be used as a criterion for distinguishing work from play. Using this criterion, anything that is frivolous can be considered play. But when children engage in dramatic play activity, it is often hard to find anything frivolous about it. Children's play is often as serious as anything that can be observed.

In the absence of a consensus regarding a definition of play, many researchers continue to investigate play (Schwartzman, 1978). They often suggest using paradigm cases of the phenomenon, presenting examples and counter examples while postponing dealing with definitional problems (Matthews & Matthews, 1982). The problem of defining play cannot be put off indefinitely, however, because definitional problems seriously hamper efforts to distinguish among various kinds of play.

Researchers on play vary in academic backgrounds; therefore, studies on play come from many disciplines, including the natural and biological sciences, social sciences, and humanities. Efforts to define play range from presenting structural definitions (e.g., delineation of typical gestures or movements) to offering functional or causal definitions (e.g., delineation of enjoyable activities without considering the purposes of the activities). Play has been considered to affect almost every human achievement and to be the basic foundation of human culture (Huizinga, 1950). Such assumptions have probably led some to assume that "the category 'playful activity' is so loose that it is almost useless for modern psychology" (Schlosberg, 1947, p. 215) or that play refers to "an artificial category" and a "stimulus seeking behaviour to which we cannot ascribe a preponent motive" (Ellis, 1973, p. 109).

Smith and Vollstedt (1985) suggest identifying play through analyzing the many characteristics of an activity that might be considered play, instead of using a single attribute as the criterion that determines whether a behavior is play. Using additional criteria may provide the best assurance that play behavior will be classified as such (Sokal, 1974). Recent literature has proposed several criteria of play (e.g., Rubin, Fein, & Vandenberg, 1983; Neumann, 1971; Lieberman, 1965; Spodek, Saracho, & Davis, 1987). However, there is little empirical support for selecting one set of characteristics over another to classify an episode as play. For example, the criteria suggested by Krasnor and Pepler (1980)—flexibility, positive affect, intrinsic motivation, and nonliterality—have been questioned by Sutton-Smith and Kelly-Byrne (1984). The latter contend that some forms of play are not voluntary or flexible and that play may sometimes be described by negative affect.

In reviewing the literature on play, Rubin et al. (1983) identify six criteria that have been used to define play as a dispositional factor: (a) intrinsic motivation; (b) orientation toward means rather than ends; (c) internal rather than external locus of control; (d) noninstrumental actions rather than instrumental actions; (e) freedom from externally imposed rules; and (f) active engagement. They indicate that play has also been defined in terms of the behaviors that are observed and the contexts in which these behaviors are elicited.

Neumann (1971) suggests that an activity can be determined to be play according to three criteria that lie on a continuum from work to play. She indicates that many activities fall somewhere in the middle of the continuum. The three criteria are:

1. *Control.* There is a difference between internal control and external control of activities. To the extent that control is internal, an activity is play. To the extent that control is external, it is work. In most cases, the control is neither totally internal nor totally external. The only time people can totally control their own play activities is when they are playing alone. As soon as more than one player is involved, control is shared, and this involves a move from internal to external control for each individual.
2. *Reality.* There is a differentiation between internal reality and external reality. One of the criteria of play is the ability of the player to suspend reality, to act "as if," to pretend, to make believe, to suppress the impact of external reality, to let the internal reality take over. To the extent that an activity is tied to the real world, it stops being play. To the extent that one can act in an "as if" way, one is acting in a playful manner. Most play, however, maintains some tie with external reality.
3. *Motivation.* To the extent that an activity is internally motivated, it is play. As soon as the motivation is external it stops being play. Seldom is the motivation entirely internal or entirely external.

Lieberman (1965) suggests yet another set of criteria for what she considers to be "playfulness." She believes that a quality of playfulness is part of all activities. Playfulness, she asserts, is related to divergent thinking: The more creative thinker is also the more playful thinker. Lieberman's five criteria for playfulness are physical, social, and cognitive spontaneity; manifest joy; and sense of humor.

Motives for engaging in an activity provide clues to determine whether it is play. The goals, materials, rules, and other elements used in play activity suggest that play can be identified according to the following criteria (Spodek et al., 1987):

1. Play is personally motivated by the satisfaction embedded in the activity and not governed either by basic needs and drives, or by social demands.
2. Players are concerned with activities more than with goals. Goals are self-imposed and the behavior of the players is spontaneous.
3. Play occurs with familiar objects, or following the exploration of unfamiliar objects. Children supply their own meanings to play activities and control the activity themselves.
4. Play activities can be nonliteral.
5. Play is free from rules imposed from the outside and the rules that do exist can be modified by the players.
6. Play requires the active engagement of the players.

Smith and Vollstedt (1985) attempted to examine empirically which criteria most individuals use to characterize an activity as play. For their study, they selected intrinsic motivation, nonliterality, positive affect, flexibility, and means/ends distinctions. Their results showed that observers used three of these criteria to judge an activity as play. Most observers did not evaluate on the basis of intrinsic motivation. Smith and Vollstedt conclude that a combination of nonliterality, positive affect, and flexibility is most useful for making a judgment of play because more than half of the episodes rated by most observers as being playful had these characteristics. This conclusion implies that observers see play as enjoyable, flexible and, most typically, as "pretend."

Smith and Vollstedt suggest that these criteria be accepted as forming a tentative definition of play, although they indicate that criteria other than those studied may also be related to play. Specifying criteria can help identify play behavior but can also lead to rejection of some important play episodes. If research studies indicate that play is important for development and/or education, then researchers and practitioners need to have a basis for identifying play behavior. Acceptable definitions must be related to developmental theories rather than only conforming to ordinary usage.

Definitions and criteria may create problems in distinguishing work from play, because they are used by research and practitioners in an all-or-none fashion. Activities may be defined as being either work or play and these may be considered mutually exclusive. That is, if something is work, it cannot be play and vice versa. Schwartzman (1978) differentiates play from work as follows:

Play is not work; play is not real; play is not serious; play is not productive; and so forth. . . . [Yet] work can be playful while sometimes play can be experienced as work; and likewise, players create worlds that are often more real, serious and productive than so-called real life. (pp. 4–5)

As this scholar suggests, distinguishing work from play is not an easy task. Play is a phenomenon that has been difficult to define, explain, understand, and observe in all of its different forms. Children, adults, and nonhuman animals engage in play; therefore, it continues to be a phenomenon that must be considered in the individuals' development and education.

Rationale for Children's Play

The work of Neumann (1971), Rubin et al., (1983), Spodek et al., (1987), and others provides useful criteria that assist in defining play more clearly and communicating more accurately about play. Unfortunately, clearer criteria and definitions do not help in understanding *why* people play and especially why *children* play, a challenge that psychologists have encountered for literally hundreds of years.

Gilmore (1971) identified the various theories of play, many of which deal with the reasons why people play. He categorized the theories into classical and dynamic theories of play. The classical theories, which try to explain why people play, are older. The dynamic theories accept the fact that people do play; these theories attempt to explain the processes of play. The classical theories of play include the surplus energy theory, the relaxation theory, the pre-exercise theory, and the recapitulation theory. Many of these theories have been around for a long time, and educators continue to use them in their commonsense discourse about play.

The surplus energy theory postulates that there is a quantity of energy available to the organism and a tendency for the organism to expend that energy either in goal-directed activity (work) or in goalless activity (play). Play occurs any time the organism has more energy available than it needs to expend for work. Within this theory, the energy that people have is expended somehow, and if it is not expended at work, it is expended at play. The content of play activity is not important; one form of play can easily be substituted for another.

There is commonsense support for the surplus energy theory. When children are constrained, energy seems to build up until they are ready to explode, and all manner of activity seems to burst forth. But this theory cannot account for all the many situations in which play occurs.

According to the relaxation theory, play is used to replenish expended energy. It is a recreational form that allows people to gather additional energy to be used for work. The relaxation theory is more difficult to ascribe to young children's play than is the surplus energy theory because young children do not typically engage in work activities from which they must relax. In fact, there is no "real" work for children in society.

The pre-exercise theory suggests that play is instinctive behavior. Children instinctively involve themselves in play activities that are in essence forms of a more mature behavior they will later have to assume. The content of children's play is, therefore, determined by the content of mature, future adult activity. Play is seen as a preparation for future work. For example, historically the play of little girls with dolls has been viewed as preparation for an adult mother role.

Again, there is commonsense support for this theory. In preliterate societies, for example, male children run and shoot with bows and arrows, which parallels the activity of adult male hunters. The play of the boys could be explained as preparation for the male adult world. However, in present-day society few adult roles parallel the play of young children. Indeed, the fact that many present-day vocational roles were not even conceived of during childhood would raise serious questions about the validity of this theory.

The recapitulation theory suggests that rather than anticipating activities that will be essential in later life, play allows the individual to recapitulate the activities of earlier stages in the cultural development of the race. By allowing individuals to rid themselves of primitive and unnecessary instinctual skills, play prepares them for the elaborate sophisticated activities of the contemporary world. The play of children more closely resembles the activities of primitive people than those of modern adults, according to this theory.

These four classical theories, each of which attempts to explain the reason for the existence of play in human activities, seem to be composed of opposing pairs. The surplus energy theory provides an explanation of play that is contradicted by the relaxation theory, for one activity cannot provide both a means for sloughing off excess energy and a means for creating new energy. Similarly, while the pre-exercise theory explains play in terms of preparation for the future, the recapitulation theory sees the roots of child's play in the past, again a contradiction. None of the classical theories of play provides an adequate base for explaining the causes of play in all situations, nor do they adequately explain the existence of any content or thematic materials in the play of children.

Gilmore (1971) also identified two dynamic theories of play, one derived from psychoanalytic theory and the other from Piagetian theory. Psychoanalytic theory considers play a cathartic activity that allows children to express feelings they cannot handle rationally and thus master difficult situations. They can play out personally painful occurrences, and by mastering pain in fantasy play, come to grips with their pain in reality. Such activity also allows children to cope with the affective elements of more positive life situations.

Murphy (1962) describes the use of play activities as a means for coping with the problems of living, such as starting nursery school or going to the hospital. Other difficult experiences (such as having a new baby within the family, having a fight with a friend, or even going through a harrowing Halloween experience) can be played out until children master them, cope with them, and internalize whatever has been learned. They can then move on to deal with other problems.

The psychoanalytic theory of play has had a major influence on early childhood education during the past half-century. The role of the preschool teacher was seen as that of a stage setter who did not interfere with the play activities of children. Play activities were to serve as catharsis, thus allowing children to avoid fixation and adult neurotic states. While children played out their problems, the teacher recorded copious notes in order to understand—but not interfere with—the children's behavior. The role of the preschool teacher was very close to that of a child therapist.

More recently the works of Piaget (1962) have been used to understand play dynamically. He viewed the development of human intellect as involving two related processes: assimilation and accommodation. In the process of assimilation, individuals abstract information from the outside world and fit that information into the organizing schemes representing what they already know. They also modify these organizing schemes when they do not fit adequately with their developing knowledge. This latter process is called accommodation.

Fein and Schwartz (1982) refer to assimilation as the way children impose their own way of thinking on the world. Children apply their previously acquired action patterns to solve current problems. Accommodation allows children to adapt their own internal organization to meet the demands of the world; for example, adjusting their behavior in order to solve a problem.

Play, according to Piaget (1962), is a way of abstracting elements from the outside world and manipulating them so that they fit the person's present organizational scheme. As such, play serves a vital function in a child's developing intellect and continues to some extent in adult intellectual behavior. Theory development, for example, is a form of play. The theorist must suspend reality and deal with hypothetical situations, assimilating and accommodating in the process.

Piaget defined three distinct stages in the development of play. The first is the sensorimotor stage of infancy, which is based upon reflexive patterns of physical behaviors. The second is a level of symbolic play, the stage of dramatic or pretend play that is characteristic of most preschool and kindergarten children. In the third stage, playing involves games that have rules; this play is typical of older children. As children mature through the early childhood period and enter the primary grades, they become more oriented towards games and less towards dramatic play.

Dramatic or symbolic play can be considered a form of representation. Once children are able to represent the outside world, they can manipulate the elements within it, using the processes of assimilation and accommodation. When children reach the stage of representation, play becomes an intellectual activity.

Beginning in the second stage—symbolic play—assimilation tends to predominate over accommodation, which permits children to modify reality in their own way without the constraints imposed by objective reality. In the first stage–sensorimotor play—accommodation is more pronounced (Saracho, 1986).

The joy of symbolic play is derived from children's ability to manipulate and change meanings (Piaget, 1962). Children develop a variety of action patterns without a specific purpose. They engage in play as a form of enjoyment, at the same time adapting to difficult situations and mastering new concepts, skills, and feelings. Thus, play provides a unique challenge that children create for themselves, and offers opportunities to develop.

Ellis (1973) adds another dimension to the theory of play. He characterizes as modern theories of play those that view play as a function of competence motivation, and those that view play as arousal-seeking. Traditionally, psychological theories have conceived of the natural human state as passive; such theories need to account for activity. However, White's (1959) theory of competence motivation suggests that people receive satisfaction from developing competency, regardless of whether external rewards are gained in the process. Play is one means for developing competency because it enables children to act on their environment, becoming more effective in their actions and thus receiving personal satisfaction.

Arousal-seeking theory suggests that human beings normally need to be continually involved in information-processing activities. The absence of stimuli in a person's environment will cause discomfort, leading the individual to increase the amount of perceptual information available, either by seeking it externally, or by creating it internally. Too much stimulation will cause individuals to "turn off"

their environments by attending less. Play is a vehicle through which children mediate the amount of stimulation available to them in order to achieve an optimal arousal level.

Arousal-seeking theory explains children's tendency to create interesting and exciting environments through play, and Piagetian theory explains the ways in which children act upon these stimuli through play to achieve knowledge. Together, these theories provide a rationale for the use of play as an educational tool.

Educational Functions of Play

The preceding theories and definitions suggest that play serves an important function in the education and development of young children. Play helps them learn about their world, express their ideas and feelings, and develop social relationships with their peers.

Play is initiated as early as infancy, with the infant's sensorimotor and social experiences in the crib; it extends to adulthood, with games characterized by sophisticated rule structures. In particular, children's play experiences during their first 6 years assume an important role in their development of knowledge. Play helps them to gather the information needed to create new ideas, compare and contrast this information with their old knowledge, and then reject, confirm, expand, or modify their ideas accordingly.

Early childhood programs involve children as active learners by providing them with play experiences that enable them to develop and accumulate their own knowledge. The educational functions of play relate to areas of cognitive, creative, language, social, and physical development. (Saracho, 1986).

● Cognitive play

In cognitive play, children create objects and roles. Although they may use an object to stand for something else, they are aware of the original identity and purpose of the object.

Young children develop an awareness of both the imaginary use and the real use of an object or role. Such awareness is best learned in symbolic play, in which children are able to use objects and roles in imaginary and realistic ways. Although they do switch back and forth from imaginary to realistic play, it is difficult to observe this reversibility in children's play.

When teachers can identify the play factors that relate to children's understandings, they can design environments that are more likely to encourage play in support of children's cognitive growth. Lunzer (1959) believes that the degree of organization found in children's play determines their play maturity, which in turn is related to their intelligence. Rubin and Maioni (1975) agree that the least mature level of play is unrelated to the children's ability to classify and to understand other persons' points of view. Children express their point of view when they take on various roles in pretend play, which often occurs in the housekeeping and block areas (Christie, 1980a, 1982). In these roles they interact with other children and process a range of information, including their peers' points of view. This interaction can create incongruent responses and the differences that emerge must be resolved; in the process of working out these differences, children develop a more mature level of logical thinking.

● Creative play

Creativity is the process through which imagination is given full rein; it is inventing and not imitating. Creative individuals disregard the common to produce the novel. According to Wallach and Kogan (1965), creativity develops a sufficiently unique content and integrates a playful and permissive attitude. Play and creativity, which, in their view, share the same basic structures, are therefore integrated.

Creative children are usually physically, cognitively, and socially spontaneous, as well as humorous and joyful (Lieberman, 1965). Three- and four-year-old children develop their creativity in play situations that require them to use their imagination (Singer, 1973). Play materials should elicit children's novel reactions to the objects (Dansky & Silverman, 1973) used in fantasy play.

Pretense/fantasy play enhances the development of children's cognitive and social skills (K.H. Rubin, 1980). For example, they use cognitive and social skills when they play "Pretend You Are Sick" (Garvey, 1974). Children who engage in fantasy play situations must use the cognitive skills that are in-

trinsic to pretense and that facilitate the perspective-taking involved in such play. Since pretense is usually based on children's daily lives and the day-to-day problems they confront, it supports young children's perspective-taking (Matthews, Beebe, & Bopp, 1980). The association of play situations to real-life situations varies among children. Their play activities range from those that approximate the immediate day-to-day situation, such as playing house or games, to activities that are remote from real-life situations, such as playing pirates, cops and robbers, cowboys, or cartoon characters. The total environment can be employed and a wide array of problems can be explored.

● Language play

Language ability is one characteristic that differentiates humans from nonhumans. Young children communicate through the symbolic use of objects (e.g., they use a doll to represent a baby or use a piece of paper to represent a blanket) and words (e.g., they substitute sounds for objects). Both language and pretend play are used to represent reality and convey meaning.

At first, children use objects to transmit thoughts; later, they play several roles to differentiate meaning from real objects (Vygotsky, 1962). During a play event, young children often employ speech play in exploring and manipulating the many components in their language, shuttling between actions and verbal descriptions of actions. Speech play fosters the development of metalinguistic awareness, which generates literacy as young children become cognizant of language rules.

Children experiment with words and manipulate their use, meaning, and grammar. They do not necessarily emphasize the meaning or value of words; rather, they experiment with rhythm, sound, and form (Johnson, 1928). They manipulate the phonological, syntactic, semantic, and pragmatic elements of language when they participate in speech play (Pellegrini, 1981). Children may use double meanings in speech play as they explore the consequences of changing the elements in words (Chukovsky, 1963). Certain elements of speech play, such as linguistically transforming roles and props, can help young children reconstruct situations in the appropriate sequence (K.H. Rubin, 1980; Sachs, 1980).

In thematic-fantasy play, young children have to verbally encode play role transformations and object transformations (Pellegrini, 1982b). Sachs (1980) questions this transformation process, because such a transformation is assisted by the use of roles and props. Roles and props can become a crutch in children's communication, but they can also serve to convey new understandings of concepts. Young children need to interact with others through language, such as discussing events in the past, in order to develop narrative language performance. Play and language foster children's development of flexible and expressive tones, as well as their perception of the rules underlying the use of voice or conversation patterns of whatever role they have assumed.

● **Social play**

The socialization process requires children to learn to get along with others. In social play, they learn a wide range of verbal and nonverbal communication skills for dealing with their peers' feelings and attitudes. When children play with their peers, they discover points of view that differ from their own. They must either assimilate others' points of view and revise those perspectives to fit with their own, or adapt to different perspectives by accepting as many different points of view as possible and considering the social atmosphere (Rubin & Hayvren, 1981). In social play young children learn to become responsive to their peers' feelings, to be patient, to wait for their turn, to be cooperative, to share materials and experiences, and to obtain instant satisfaction when others value (i.e., like) them. In sharing and cooperating they also learn to use their own resources and those of others. Thus, peer play affects young children's social and cognitive development.

● **Manipulative play**

Play materials can stimulate young children to participate in a variety of play situations. Play materials that appeal to young children can promote both non-representational (manipulative) and representational

(pretend) play. Toys are considered the tools of play as they serve particular purposes in the development of the child. The development of play is gradual and continuous. Children employ play materials based on their age (Kawin, 1934; Westby, 1980). DeLoache, Sugarman, and Brown (1985) found that during manipulative play, 1½- and 3½-year-old children attempted to arrange a set of five nesting cups by size with little or no prompting. In similar studies (e.g., Greenfield, Nelson, & Saltzman, 1972; Sugarman, 1983) young children employed increasingly complex methods (i.e., composition procedures) to combine the cups. DeLoache et al. (1985) documented the existence of a developmental sequence in young children's strategies for correcting their errors in manipulating a set of nesting cups. The increasing scope and flexibility of the strategies observed have parallels in other realms of cognitive development.

Children's use of toys depends on their age. Therefore, age should be considered in selecting toys. The preschool setting, for example, typically contains categories of toys that are appropriate for young children, including miniature sets of toys that represent objects (e.g., dolls, doll furniture, wagons, engines) characteristic of life around children. These toys (a) facilitate children's role taking or dramatizations of adults' serious and meaningful experiences; (b) provide young children with knowledge, meaning, standards, and skills of their world; and (c) guide children to understand life, to play different roles, and to perceive others' feelings. The value of play materials depends on the extent to which they help young children learn specific skills or concepts.

Promoting Educational Play in Early Childhood

When young children play, they learn to understand the world around them. Observing children's play can help teachers to understand children's perceptions of their world and can offer teachers ideas about how to facilitate learning. Teachers must become facilitators of learning by becoming supportive rather than directive with their teaching.

Many teachers discourage young children's play

Arguing { because they perceive supervising play as baby-sitting. They may belittle children's imaginative and playful reactions in solving problems and may view playful social interactions with peers as misbehaving. If teachers believe that children need to learn complex concepts to be able to live successfully in modern society, then they must understand that young children have to use a variety of play experiences to assimilate and accommodate knowledge.

1 { Teachers must also become aware of the developmental and learning outcomes of a play curriculum. A well-designed curriculum can allow teachers to help young children learn social roles and understand the adult world. In designing a play curriculum for young children, educators need to know about using play as an educational medium.

Almost all early childhood curricula include play. To be most effective, teachers must (a) offer a supportive environment with sufficient play areas, materials, and equipment; (b) foster positive social interactions; and (c) extend (i.e., make more productive) children's play. It is essential for teachers to understand the uses of particular types of play that are appropriate for young children. Spodek, Saracho, and Davis (1987) suggest that teachers should be active in initiating and extending children's play.

● Initiating children's play

Play activities are often initiated simply by making play materials available to children. These materials should be attractive, provide reasonable play opportunities, and offer some novelty. Involving children in a short planning period before playtime can help them anticipate what they can do in their play period; further, such a planning session provides an opportunity to introduce new pieces of equipment or new toys. The purposes, uses, and limitations of the materials can also be discussed during the planning period.

Variety and novelty arouse children's interest in play activities. Sometimes novelty can be achieved by presenting existing materials in new forms. Teachers can rearrange the block area, display some new signs in the dramatic play area, or introduce new materials to transform an old activity into an attractive new activity.

A new play activity needs to stimulate children's imagination. Enriching their store of information will

often do this. Teachers can take children for a walk through the neighborhood, read them a book on a specific play topic, or show a film or filmstrip.

● Extending children's play

Teachers need to guide young children's play, extending it or helping it become more productive. At times teachers may find it necessary to participate with children in their play. However, teachers must encourage children to become independent, intervening as little as possible in order not to structure the play too much. They must be careful not to make themselves the focus of attention or the major source of play ideas since this will discourage children's play initiatives. Careless intervention can keep the activity from becoming a positive, productive play experience. Teachers must evaluate the consequences of their verbal and physical actions; they have to be sensitive to the play situation. If they go too far, they can pull back without causing too much discomfort; but they should not abstain completely from intervention.

Teachers may extend children's play by adding or deleting materials from the play area. If children play supermarket, for example, the teacher may make available a range of props that will enable children to assume different roles: a doll carriage, a wagon, or other wheeled toy to serve as a supermarket cart; boxes and empty food containers to serve as merchandise; and tables to serve as shelves. Signs can be written to label the different foods as well as the prices. A toy cash register and some play money can be added later. The teacher can ask the children what they need, suggest materials, or display some things from which the children might select what they need (Spodek, Saracho, & Davis, 1987).

Teachers can also extend children's play by suggesting new roles. Questions like "Who is doing the shopping?" or "Who is the supermarket clerk?" suggest new roles. Or the teacher may join the play activity briefly and assume the role of shopper, purchasing items and raising questions about prices. Children can thus become aware of the variety of roles that can be taken in playing supermarket.

When children are blocked in their play, the teacher might take them on a field trip to a supermarket. A few purchases can help children learn the shopping process and stimulate their imagination for future play periods. Children need to be encouraged to observe the way the store is arranged. The teacher might take children to the different areas in the supermarket, such as the storage area, butcher area, bakery, or other areas, which the children can then relate to their play situation in the classroom.

Evaluating Play Intervention Strategies

Because the basic goal of education is to help young people become something different than they might become if left alone, children are enrolled in artificial, contrived situations called "schools," where educators intervene in their lives to modify their development. This intervention is called "education." Teachers intervene in children's behavior and development, as do parents, and even nondirective therapists. Sometimes these interventions are explicit, sometimes they are implicit; sometimes they are direct, and sometimes indirect. But no matter how people intervene, they ought to do it consciously. If intervention is conscious, it can be done carefully, it can be done well, and it can be evaluated and improved upon.

The question is, can intervention (i.e., education) and play take place at the same time? Neumann (1971) suggests that teachers must judge the extent to which the child (a) retains a degree of control over the play situation, (b) determines its degree of reality, and (c) provides motivation for the activity, that activity is play. In the educational environment, the teacher—to some degree—has control, influences the child's motivation, and imposes a measure of reality on the play of children. The activity is no longer play when the intervention goes too far.

Using Neumann's criteria, Ellis (1973) suggests asking (a) whether the child is seeking external or experiential rewards; (b) whether the child's behavior is controlled by outsiders or by the child; (c) whether the child is forced to recognize the constraints of reality or is permitted to suspend those constraints; (d) whether the setting imposes consequences on the child's behavior or choices are left to the child; and (e) whether the setting imposes connections between events and consequences or relaxes such connections.

These questions determine the extent to which children can be characterized as working or playing. While no setting will be arranged so that children are totally free from external constraints, unnecessary constraints can be removed to increase the probability that children will play.

White and Carew-Watts (1973) reported a study of the family influences that seem to help young children become more competent. Based on this study, White and his associates presented some of their best guesses about most effective childrearing practices: Mothers talk to their children at a level they can handle. They show interest in their children's activities and provide them with appropriate materials. They encourage their children and demonstrate and explain things to them. When they prohibit certain activities, they do so consistently and firmly. These parents are imaginative and skillful as they strengthen their children's motivation to learn. They also give their children a sense of task orientation. Such parents serve as designers and consultants, creating an environment that nurtures children's curiosity—one that is filled with manipulable, visually detailed objects, including toys and other materials. White has suggested that these parents provide a world for children to play in. Rather than teach directly at prescribed times, they can do a lot of it "on the fly."

Effective teachers of young children use the same model: They, too, serve as designers and consultants, creating a world in which children can learn through play opportunities that increase the educational value of play.

Krown (1974) has described such a model of teaching in her report on a program for what she called "disadvantaged children" in Israel. In the beginning, play activities were highly stereotyped. Two years later, the children who had gone through this program had modified their play. The quality of richness within the play is evident in Krown's descriptions. In order to effect this change, the teachers supported purposive activity by inviting themselves into children's play. They sometimes added new materials or asked questions to stimulate detailed observations and play, often helping children to recall and associate prior experiences. Often teachers developed discussions, took children on field trips, or introduced books to provide children with additional information to use in their play.

In this setting, children were allowed to control their world, maintain a sense of suspended reality, and motivate their own play activities; the teachers' actions helped the play become more educational.

Tizard, Philips, and Plewis (1976a, 1976b, 1976c) examined the differences in teachers' behavior in relation to children's activities in three different preschool settings. The children's play in the traditional nursery schools was significantly different both from play in nurseries without qualified teachers and play in schools with language programs. In these nursery schools, the least amount of symbolic play and the greatest amount of "appropriate" play (e.g., play that exploits the properties of the materials and fails to engage in the development of symbolic themes) were found.

Many educators assume that the intrinsic motivation of self-initiated play offers the type of serious absorption that assures learning. Tizard et al. (1976a, 1976b, 1976c) argued that in practice other elements of free play alter this absorption. In their study, most of the observed children's play was assessed as being at a low level. Children usually played brief and simple games and moved from one activity to another. Although 3- and 4-year-old children can be persistent, some elements in the free-play nursery setting may work against developing longer attention spans. Tizard and associates attribute their results to the wide range of alternative play material available, the teachers' lack of pressure on the children to work to their maximum capacity, and the large group of other children who provided distractions. In only 2% of the observations were staff members observed playing with the children. They hardly interacted with children in their activities and did not stay with them long enough to help initiate and sustain a complex game or construction. Such teacher behavior may have resulted from a belief that self-initiation is of prime importance.

Tizard et. al (1976c) assumed that the direction of the teachers' activity probably influenced the degree of symbolic play among children. In the traditional nursery schools teachers directed most of their energies to providing a variety of "creative" activities for the children to explore daily, such as collage making, finger painting, and leaf painting. The chil-

dren used the materials the way the teacher intended, but symbolic play hardly developed. In comparison, both the nursery schools with language programs and those that were not staffed by qualified teachers offered fewer such activities. Teachers spent their time providing language instruction and conversational exchanges with the children in the language-oriented type of program, while in the other type the teachers exhibited less educational interest and expertise.

Young children's play behavior changes socially and cognitively as they grow. Teachers can observe children's play behavior in the classroom to gain a sense of the level at which children are playing in the different play areas. They can develop play interventions, modifying the setting, adding new materials, asking children questions, moving into the children's play long enough to guide their play, and immediately moving out of the play situation. They must be careful that the activity continues to be play when they intervene, taking care, for example, not to make children become conscious of reality or of their authority.

Teachers can support young children's play by accepting children's existing play patterns, gradually inviting children to join a small group involved in new activities without forcing anyone. Those children who prefer not to engage in group activities should be excused and provided with an alternative activity. Play activities demand that children consider the feelings of others, cooperate, conform, and be assertive without being aggressive. Children engage in different forms of play, such as playing alongside a friend, playing together with other children, and playing by themselves, exploring the properties of play materials to develop themes.

Children who play alone should not be forced to participate in cooperative play. Teachers can encourage these children to cooperate by asking them to help clean up after snack time. They can extend young children's play to enrich their social experience. Intervening appropriately in the play of young children helps them develop their social skills. Play intervention may require a suggestion, a supportive comment, or the addition of accessories to encourage children to engage in a play activity.

Children's play sometimes fails to be productive. If a play activity bogs down, or if it becomes overly repetitive and fails to move anywhere, it can create conflict among children and lead to destructive behavior. Teachers may need to intervene in the children's play for it to become educationally productive by using a number of different intervention strategies: instruction, praise, maintenance, conversation, demonstration, redirection, and participation (Spidell, 1985). Instruction is a strategy teachers use to tell children a fact or concept that will move the play along. Teachers praise children's play behavior to show their approval and support of a specific behavior so that other children will imitate this play behavior. Maintenance strategies are used to help children cope with problems arising from a crowded space, insufficient materials or equipment, disagreement about rules, and so forth. Teachers use conversation to engage children in a dialogue about their interests and activities, demonstration to show children the way to do something, and redirection to suggest alternative activities. Finally, teachers engage in participation when they join the play activity for short periods of time.

Teachers vary in their choice of strategies for play interventions; some, of course, have particular favorites. Spidell (1985) reported that not all of the strategies described above were equally effective in moving the children's play along. In most cases, teachers in this study combined the different intervention strategies to enhance the dynamism and productivity of children's play.

The most powerful strategy teachers employ as a play intervention is never observed in the early childhood classroom because it takes place before the children initiate play. This strategy is preparation: setting the stage for play before children arrive in school. The teacher intervenes most effectively by organizing the physical setting so that space and materials conducive to productive play and proper classroom behavior are available in each play center. Once the stage is set, the teacher can suggest play activities and offer resources that permit play activities to develop. Teachers can share information with children about play themes by reading books to them, holding discussions, inviting resource persons, or taking children on a field trip. These experiences permit children to extend their play and expand on what the teacher originally provided.

When should teachers intervene? How far should they go in extending play? This can only be judged situationally. The judgment must be based upon a knowledge of children in general and the children in a particular play situation, as well as a knowledge of the kinds of play activities that might be productive at a given time. Too much intervention inhibits play. At the same time, the absence of intervention can keep play from achieving its potential. Teachers have to strive continually for a balance that avoids either of these extremes.

Conclusion

The challenge of play for teachers, parents, and recreational workers is to intervene in order to optimize the educational consequences of play without sacrificing its essence. Children can be seduced into games for adult purposes. They can mouth phrases far beyond their ability to comprehend. They can repress their needs, their desires, even their intellectual ability in order to please adults. All activities in children's schools and homes need not be play and should not be play, just as all activities in home and school need not be educational. Teachers can distort play activities if they intervene too much. They can also miss opportunities for promoting learning if they do not intervene. Without some help, children's activities can become repetitive, stereotyped, and devoid of educational consequences.

The key, then, is balance. Sensitive and provocative balance, design, and consultation can help move children's activities along so that their thinking moves along as well. Learning can occur in a context of playfulness. The essence of good teaching and good parenting lies in this ability to think about the needs of young children, to respond, to intervene without unnecessary interference and distortion. Perhaps this requires adults who themselves bring a quality of playfulness as well as respect to their relations with children.

In summary, the challenge of play may be as much the adults' challenge as the children's. An understanding of the reasons for children's play as well as its consequences may help educators to perceive play as a potential rather than as a challenge.

Questions for Discussion

1. Discuss the similarities and differences between work and play.
2. What roles do children assume in pretend play? How do they test and operate on their ideas within their play activities?

Play Activity Problems

1. Record the play of young children in an early childhood educational setting. Categorize the children's play activities using theories of play discussed by Gilmore (i.e., surplus energy theory, relaxation theory, pre-exercise theory, recapitulation theory).
2. Interview three teachers. Ask them to identify their criteria of play. Compare their criteria with those criteria presented in the chapter.

Suggestions for Further Reading

Garvey, C. (1977). *Play*. Cambridge, MA: Harvard University Press. Provides an overview of types of play and ways play has been studied and describes Garvey's research on social and linguistic play.

Rubin, K. H. (1980). Fantasy play: Its role in the development of social skills and social cognition. In K. H. Rubin (Ed.), *New directions in child development: Children's play*. No. 9, pp. 69–84. San Francisco: Jossey-Bass. Compares the influences of fantasy play and peer play in relation to children's development of social skills and understanding.

Sutton-Smith, B. (Ed.). (1979). *Play and learning*. New York: Gardner Press. Describes the views of a number of major play theorists and researchers. Reports on their work and discusses their ideas.

Weininger, O. (1979). *Play and education: The basic tool for early childhood learning*. Springfield, IL: Charles C Thomas. Provides a basic overview of the ways play has been used in educational practice.

Recommended Films

Children's play. (20 minutes, color). CRM McGraw-Hill Films, 1011 Camino Del Mar, Del Mar, CA 92104. Discusses the importance of play in children's growth and development.

Child's play and the real world. (18 minutes, color). Davidson Films, 165 Tunstead Ave., San Anselmo, CA 94960. Shows the intimate, colorful world of children's play and the importance of play in development.

Facilitation of children's dramatic play. (29 minutes, color). Campus Film Distributors, Inc., Two Overhill Rd., Scarsdale, NY 10583. Presents a number of examples on ways teachers can encourage dramatic play.

Play and the Origin of Species

MICHAEL J. ELLIS

Our actual beginning as a species is lost in the mists of time. However, as we gaze backward toward our origins, we see some clues as to why and how we are now as we are. Usually the attempts to picture our evolution are restricted to physical form, mostly because it is only the bony structures and stony artifacts of some of our precursors that remain. From those hard objects, we derive stories of our beginnings. Rarely do we take another approach—first trying to imagine the behavior of our precursors and then speculating on how their form was determined by their behavior.

This essay takes the latter approach and considers the evolutionary significance of a behavior, play. It postulates that in the grand design of things, play was a requirement for the evolution of mammals. Play, and the pro-

pensity for it, was necessary for our evolution. Our ancestors were playful and because of it, they survived. Although the behavior itself is complex, the underlying rationale for its existence is simple. Some early people survived because every now and again one of them, in going beyond the narrow habits and conventions of the time, stumbled across a new idea or practice. When these findings or inventions were beneficial, they tended to survive.

Survivors in a competitive situation had to be relatively more successful than their competitors. Variations in the capacity to exhibit tried and true behaviors with greater power and endurance were rewarded. Individuals with more power and endurance survived to breed and so eventually stabilized the beneficial variation in the gene pool of the species. In the same way, successful behavior in the form of skills, attributes, and propensities stabilized the related forms that permitted their expression. Thus, variation in the central nervous system and the capabilities and behaviors it produced were also subject to selection and stabilization.

Of course these organizations that are bred into the soft tissue of the central nervous system have not survived in the sense that the bones of our ancestors have. But their effects have survived in two forms. One kind of evidence is the playful nature of some of the hard artifacts that were made by our precursors. Some cave paintings, in which early artists recorded their observations of the important and the sacred, reveal a playful nature. We can recognize and appreciate these touches to this day. The other form of evidence lies in our gene pool, the source of our current playful propensities and capacities. The process of natural selection preserved and accentuated those earlier playful characteristics, and they live to be examined in ourselves today, albeit in exaggerated form.

Our behavioral propensity to play has intrigued us. For many generations, we have pondered the role that play has in our existence. In a materialistic and direct sense, play seems to be unnecessary for immediate survival. There do not seem to be immediate and critical consequences that permit the pressures of a competitive environment to select for this behavior and stabilize the soft tissue structures that permit or encourage it. Play somehow lies outside the normal explanations for the shape of our other features; it is seen as enigmatic. This has given rise to many fanciful explanations that go beyond those used to explain the other forms and functions of our existence. However, play can be explained using exactly the same theories used to account for the evolution of other characteristics.

One of the principal characteristics of the mammals is that they are behaviorally adaptable. They learn readily. Their biobehavioral "ace in the hole" is their ability to change at a faster rate than can be driven by the gradual evolution of the gene pool. In fact this characteristic behavioral plasticity is a most powerful evolutionary advance and is responsible for the enormous success of the mammals. While there are narrow and stable niches occupied by mammals, many mammals, and particularly the recently evolved species, make a speciality of not being specialized. The mammal that is highly predictable, or that does not notice the opportunities or challenges presented by change in its niche, does not last for long. Whenever the environment is changing it selects for playful individuals. The underlying reward mechanisms for playing that exist in the soft tissues will be selected for and enhanced over the generations. Playfulness is thus stabilized and enhanced from generation to generation by the genes.

The propensity to play is a biological system for promoting rapid adaptation to threats to survival that cannot be predicted. Playfulness, then, is characteristic of animals that make a specialty of being adaptable, and is a prime capability in changing and changeable settings. Playfulness is well developed in the pack hunters and scavengers, bears, and of course the anthropoids. Naturally, we would claim that humans are the most playful and most adaptable of all.

Playfulness as a behavioral propensity is at the center of the evolution of mammals. Seeking change for the rewards inherent in asking and answering questions about the physical and social environment is the characteristic that has set mammals, and particularly humans, off on their evolutionary path as a species. This same propensity also launches and sustains the explorations of the individual. Learning results from play and forms the basis for subsequent forays into the unknown.

The propensity for play is in fact the learning mechanism applied to the unique and unpredictable elements of each individual's existence. In his book, *Design for a Brain*, Ashby (1960) put it well:

Its peculiarity is that the gene-pattern delegates part of its control over the organism to the environment. Thus it does not specify in detail how a kitten shall catch a mouse, but provides a learning mechanism and a tendency to play, so that it is the mouse which teaches the kitten the finer points of how to catch mice. This is regulation, or adaptation, by the indirect method. The gene-pattern does not, as it were, dictate, but puts the kitten into the way of being able to form its own adaptation, guided in detail by the environment. (p. 234)

I believe that the above arguments prove convincing; play is never "just play." The lesson is clear. Some substantial part of each day should be devoted to play. For it is during play that humans are most human. They learn to extend the limits of human experience and to develop the capability to deal with the unknown. No matter what the imperatives of the known present, educators should accord equal weight to the imperatives of the unknown future of the individuals and the species. Playfulness is a critically important characteristic of humans. Its behavioral correlate, play, should be both prized and encouraged. It brought us to where we are now both as a species and as individuals and will be the basis for our future adaptation to the unpredictable future.

CHAPTER TWO

Methods of Studying Play

DORIS BERGEN

A dramatic increase in the volume of research literature on play has occurred. Britt and Janus (1941) reported that at the end of the nineteenth century there were 10 empirical studies of play; in the 1930s there were 70 published. In their recent comprehensive review, Rubin, Fein, and Vandenberg (1983) list 450 play research citations. Over 50% of all play research studies have been published in the last 10 years (Pepler & Rubin, 1982). These studies arise from a variety of theoretical and conceptual bases. Researchers differ in the definition of play they accept, the questions they ask, the assumptions they make, and the data collection and analysis methods they use. Their interpretations of results and the implications for practice that they draw from the results are also diverse and, in some cases, conflicting.

In planning studies of play, researchers have to consider two levels of design. First, they must meet the methodological standards that are accepted practice in social science research, and second, they must address some special research issues that are related to the nature of their topic—play. As Vandenberg (1982) remarks,

In some ways, "play" is a clown in the realm of psychological phenomena. It has eluded precise formulation, and at times seems to be playing hide-and-seek with us. We respond by either dismissing it as an unimportant prankster, or by trying harder to find it. (p. 15)

One of the reasons for the marked increase in the study of play is advances in methods for studying it; it is now possible to investigate questions of play development that previously seemed to be inaccessible. Play research is still in its infancy, however, and attention to research methods is of major importance if knowledge of play is to continue to grow.

This chapter describes the decisions that researchers must make in planning and conducting their studies, presents typical models used for studying play, and reviews some questions of current research interest. Three research studies that can serve as prototypes of play research design are presented and ways of adapting these designs for the use of educational practitioners are suggested.

Decisions on Theoretical Questions

The major theories of play proposed by theorists over the past 150 years have been described in chapter 1. The purpose of a theory is to conceptualize knowledge into a systematic structure that can then serve as a guide for explaining phenomena and solving problems. Theories cannot really be true or false; they can be useful or not useful. Useful play theories assist researchers in identifying problems for study, determining the methods to be used, and interpreting study results. The theoretical viewpoint of the researcher guides the planning and implementation of the research design; thus, the first steps in planning research on play are to clarify the assumptions on which the theory rests and to identify testable hypotheses that can explain the phenomena in question from that particular theoretical perspective.

As the discussion of theories in chapter 1 has demonstrated, researchers have yet to agree on a common theoretical paradigm for play. Those who wish to study play must first make some decisions about the theoretical perspective they will embrace. They must decide (a) whether play is a phenomenon that can be productively studied; (b) whether the study will focus on play as an individual or as a cultural phenomenon; (c) on what portions of the theory of play their research will focus; and (d) what assumptions underlying the theory will influence their research plan.

● Deciding whether play is a researchable phenomenon

Although the question of whether play is a possible or desirable topic of study has been answered with a resounding "yes" by many present-day researchers, in the not too distant past this question was a prominent one. Because determining precise classifications of play has been difficult, play has often been conceptualized as "what is left after all other behavior is explained" (Sponseller, 1982, p. 227). Gilmore

(1971) calls this the "wastebasket" definition of play. This perspective would lead to the decision not to study play as a separate phenomenon but to study all other phenomena until there is nothing left to be called play. Schlosberg (1947) espouses the view that the concept of play is not useful for research and should be discarded. Obviously, researchers who decide to study play will not agree with that viewpoint.

● Deciding whether play is an individual or a cultural phenomenon

Once researchers have decided to study play, they plan their studies from theoretical vantage points that are usually determined by their own professional disciplines. Sutton-Smith (1979b, 1980) indicates that there are two major "play theory paradigms" (p. 3) for studying play. One of them, which he calls primary, is focused on individuals. It is used primarily by psychologists and educators. They view play as a voluntary activity that is under the player's control and through which the player may gain cognitive, creative, or other developmental organization. The secondary paradigm is that used by anthropologists, folklorists, and sociolinguists. In this model, play is seen as a way of organizing collective behavior and communicating with others. Play reflects and influences the culture and social structures of the larger society, which are of interest to these theorists. Although some researchers combine an individual and a cultural focus, usually they operate within one or the other of these paradigms.

● Deciding on the specific theoretical focus of the phenomenon

Researchers must also decide on the focus of study within a particular theoretical perspective. According to Sutton-Smith and Kelly-Byrne (1984), this can be difficult because play theories often have a bipolarity. That is, they have features that suggest play leads both to equilibrium and disequilibrium and promotes both conservation and innovation in human beings. For example, Huizinga (1950) asserts both that play is a voluntary and fun-filled activity and that it involves bloody, fatal contests. Piaget (1962) states play leads to cognitive consolidation but that it also is characterized by the distortions of assimilation. Singer (1973) stresses both the problem-solving and creativity-enhancing features of play. Bateson (1956) describes both the metacommunicative and the paradoxical communicative functions of play. Thus, researchers must decide on whether they wish to focus on "rational or irrational," "civilized or uncivilized" aspects of the play phenomenon (Sutton-Smith, 1985).

● Identifying the assumptions that underlie the theory

Ellis (1973) outlines the assumptions that underlie various theoretical explanations of play. These assumptions both inform and limit the way play research may be conducted. For example, a researcher who accepts the theory of Schiller (1954), who defined play as an energy-release mechanism, would assume that children's excess energy cannot be stored but must be expended through play. One who agrees with arousal-seeking theory (Berlyne, 1960; Shultz, 1979) assumes that children need an optimal level of arousal and must meet this need to seek stimuli through their exploration and play. Researchers from these two theoretical perspectives might have very different studies, because the set of assumptions underlying their theoretical frameworks will influence the researcher's plan. The hypotheses or questions of interest will also be affected by these assumptions.

Decisions on Research Definitions

After researchers have decided on their theoretical orientation, they must move on to specify the operational definitions under which their research will be conducted. That is, play must be defined in behavioral terms that will enable the researcher to collect information about the phenomenon. There is no one set of behaviors that are always play. Almost any type of behavior can be playful, depending on the intentions of the subjects engaged in it. Blurton-Jones (1972) notes, for example, how adult observers can easily confuse fighting and play-fighting because the observable behaviors are so similar. Also, as Neumann (1971) points out, the elements that signify

play may be present in varying amounts in different behaviors that could be called play. There are points along this continuum of behaviors that might be categorized as play or not.

Although behaviors are sometimes difficult to define, Rubin et al. (1983) state that defining play in behavioral terms is easier than defining play in theoretical terms. A range of behaviors have been defined as play and have been studied with methods that draw upon a number of useful research models. Definitional decisions that researchers must make involve: (a) deciding whether to focus on behaviors related to the motives of play or to the content of play and (b) specifying the operational definitions (i.e., the precise categories or global qualities of play that are to be observed and recorded).

● Deciding on motive or content

Ellis (1973) subdivides play into two categories that are determined by the kinds of questions researchers ask. Some focus on motives (i.e., asking why and when play occurs); others on content (i.e., asking what are the constituent elements of play). Questions oriented toward motives include those from early classical theorists and those from modern researchers concerned with external and internal motivational conditions (Berlyne, 1966; Ellis, 1973; Hutt, 1971; Shultz, 1979).

Dynamic theorists of the psychoanalytic school (e.g., Erikson, 1963; Freud, 1920/1961; Klein, 1955) also focused on the motives for play. They saw play as a means for ameliorating experiences that have been unpleasant or that are out of the child's control and stress the role of play in mastering emotional experiences.

Although Piaget (1962) described a motivational rationale for play, he primarily focused on problems of content, such as organizing structures, stages of development, and transitional processes. Theorists from the secondary play theory paradigm (e.g., Bateson, 1956; Schwartzman, 1978; Sutton-Smith, 1985) have also been primarily concerned with questions of content and structure.

Those researchers who focus on motives typically ask questions about the antecedents or the consequences of play and the conditions that elicit it. For example, Lepper and Greene (1975) and Perry,

Bussey, and Redman (1977) are interested in effects of extrinsic reinforcement on play behavior. They have studied whether providing external rewards for play behavior increases or decreases children's playfulness. Their work is based on the assumption that play requires inner motivation and control. Their results, indicating that spontaneous play in playful children decreases if it is first rewarded and then the reward is withdrawn, are explained by the hypothesis that external reward turns the play into work.

The majority of Piagetian-based researchers focus on content questions (e.g., Bretherton, O'Connell, Shore, & Bates, 1984; Fein, 1975b; Fenson & Ramsay, 1980; Garvey, 1977a; McCune-Nicholich & Bruskin, 1982; Nicholich, 1977; Sinclair, 1970). They try to answer questions about the structure of pretense, the nature of its transitions, and the relationship between its development and cognitive, language, and social organizing schemes. Some of these researchers also draw assumptions from the communication theory of Bateson (1956).

An example of this type of research is that of Bretherton et al. (1984), who examined three levels of role representation (i.e., child as agent, doll as active recipient, dolls as both agent and recipient) in toddlers' free and elicited pretend play with realistic, ambiguous, and counterconventional objects. They described how the nature of pretense is affected by the age of the children, the level of role representation, and the realistic qualities of the objects; and they related these findings to relationships between language and symbolic action.

Ethnographic researchers (e.g., Aldis, 1975; Schwartzman, 1978) also ask content questions. For example, Schwartzman analyzed both the content of children's sociodramatic play and their social status within the preschool classroom and described how the classroom social structure (i.e., the context of play) influences the pretend play roles (i.e., the text of play). Aldis observed children's play in naturally occurring settings and described categories of play-fighting in detail. He suggests that research priority be given to collecting descriptions of the naturally occurring content of play. Researchers who study games (e.g., Roberts, 1980; Roberts & Sutton-Smith, 1962; Sutton-Smith & Rosenberg, 1961) also focus on content questions. For example, Sutton-Smith and Rosenberg (1961) looked at the changing of children's games over a 60-year period.

Because the specific operational definitions of the play behaviors to be studied are based on whether the questions to be answered focus on motive or content, researchers must choose their orientation early in the planning stage in order to further define the processes or the structures to be studied.

● Deciding on the operational definitions

Rubin et al. (1983) outline the three approaches typically taken in defining play behaviorally: (a) listing psychological dispositions or sets marking its occurrence; (b) describing observable behaviors; and (c) specifying the contexts in which play behaviors are likely to be exhibited. The six characteristics included as psychological dispositions are described in chapter 1. They include factors such as self-imposed motivation, control, goals, and rules; active engagement; and nonliterality or playfulness.

Although a number of specific components of psychological dispositions (e.g., inner control) have been identified (Lieberman, 1965; Neumann, 1971; Rubin et al., 1983); these components are not discrete variables. The amount of the characteristic present in a particular behavior determines whether it is play. Researchers, therefore, must define at exactly what point the behaviors they observe will be categorized as play and must specify these categories in operational terms.

These categories are defined differently by various researchers. For example, Hutt (1979) and Hutt and Hutt (1977) have distinguished between the dispositions present in exploration as compared to play. Hutt (1971) separates behaviors into (a) epistemic behaviors, which are used to acquire information (i.e., "What does this object do?"); and (b) ludic behaviors, which are playful uses of past experiences (i.e., "What can I do with this object?"). Her work is devoted to studying temporal and physiological differences to clarify this distinction. Henderson (1984) indicates that other researchers do not emphasize this separation and consider "exploratory play" as an appropriate category of study.

Wohlwill (1984) discusses similar definitions, specifically in regard to object play. He characterizes exploration of objects as information extraction and play with objects as transformation (i.e., either reality or fantasy transformation). He proposes a three-stage model: undifferentiated exploration, transitional play, and pretense. McGhee (1984) further characterizes exploratory play as interesting but not funny and playful play as having humorous incongruities, determined by the child's playful frame of mind.

Researchers who describe play in terms of observable behaviors also use a variety of categories. Piaget classifies play into three categories: practice, symbolic, and games-with-rules (Piaget, 1962). Piaget categorizes imitation and play as distinct, whereas Millar (1968) includes some behaviors in a category of imitative play. The categories studied by Garvey (1977a) include play with language, motion, objects, and social materials. Parten (1932) identifies levels of social play: onlooking, solitary, parallel, associative, and cooperative. Smilansky (1968), Rubin, Maioni, and Hornung (1976), and Sponseller and Jaworski (1979) have combined Piagetian and Parten categories of social play to develop their taxonomies.

Researchers on pretend play also attend to categorizing observable behavior. Pretense is variously defined by its levels of cognitive and language complexity (Nicolich, 1977); object and agent characteristics (Fein, 1981); social and cognitive elements (Smilansky, 1968); and thematic content (Saltz, Dixon & Johnson, 1977). Many theorists and researchers do not include the category of games under the rubric of play (e.g., Rubin et al., 1983) whereas others consider play as a global category that covers all ludic activities throughout the life span (e.g., Herron & Sutton-Smith, 1971).

Definitions by context specify as play those behaviors that occur in settings designed for play. Rubin et al. (1983) describe the methods used in controlled research settings to elicit play behaviors. The settings designed to elicit play usually include (a) familiar peers and interesting toys and/or materials; (b) adult permission for children to choose what they wish to do; (c) minimally intrusive adult behavior; (d) an atmosphere of friendliness and safety; and (e) a schedule ensuring that children are rested, fed, unstressed, and healthy. Rubin et al. state that from this perspective, play is defined as what occurs in these settings.

Contextual elicitors of play may be culture specific, however. Schwartzman (1984) indicates that ethnographic literature cites instances of imaginative play in which the contextual requirements—access to play props, space and time for play, encouragement and modeling by adults—are not evident. She concludes that in many cultures children use whatever is available for play and have self-designed toys.

Because of the problems inherent in stating specific operational definitions, Matthews and Matthews (1982) suggest using a paradigm case approach that involves making judgments of play on the basis of global information. Observers are asked to identify pretense on the bases of their judgment that, "This is a case of fantasy play if anything is!" (p. 26), and the concept of fantasy play is not defined in specific behavioral terms. They report that naive observer judgment of cases of play has high reliability. Because this approach does not specify the discrete behaviors that are the components of play, it may not be useful for investigating some of the questions of research interest.

Decisions on Research Methods

All researchers must address a common set of methodological questions. The characteristics of subjects and methods of selection, specific data collection procedures, methods of data preparation and analysis, and plans for reporting results must meet the criteria of each researcher's own discipline. Researchers must decide on the reliability of their measures, (i.e., whether their data collection methods provide similar information across times and settings). They must resolve validity problems (i.e., whether their research really measures what they intend it to measure). They must also face issues of generalizability, (i.e., whether they have used methods that permit application of their results to other settings, conditions, or populations). Often they must also evaluate the educational significance of their results, (i.e., whether their findings have implications for educational practice). A detailed discussion of these methodological issues and of general research design and analysis procedures is beyond the scope of this book. Suggestions for further reading on research methodology are given at the end of this chapter.

In addition to resolving the methodological concerns of all scientists, researchers on play have some additional methodological problems because of the nature of the topic. Careful attention to the methods selected for the study of play are required if the researcher is to have reliable, valid, and generalizable results.

● Deciding on methods for studying play

Methodological decisions include (a) choosing the specific testable hypotheses or questions of interest; (b) selecting the subjects who are likely to exhibit the behaviors to be studied; (c) determining the context in which the behaviors may be found; (d) specifying the procedures and/or instruments that will be used to collect information about these behaviors; and (e) choosing the appropriate methods for analysis and reporting of this information.

Typical methods used for studying play include (a) naturalistic observation; (b) experimental manipulation and observation; and (c) self-report/performance measures, such as interviews, questionnaires, and psychological or informational tests. Most studies of young children's play conducted in the 1920s and 1930s used naturalistic observation of play in home or nursery school settings. The play of older children was primarily studied with interviews or questionnaires. Although naturalistic and survey methods are still used, experimental approaches have become common. Not all methods are appropriate for all studies. For example, the laboratory or home observational methods appropriate for the study of pretense in toddlers may not be effective for studying this type of play in first-grade children. Similarly, an interview approach used to study middle childhood game playing may be less useful for studying emergent games of preschoolers.

Each of these methods and the specific characteristics of hypotheses, subjects, settings, and procedures are described in Tables 2–1, 2–2, and 2–3. Examples of researchers who use the various approaches are also presented.

Naturalistic observation studies typically have these characteristics:

1. The hypotheses usually focus on types of play that may be observed in particular settings, relationships between types of play and other areas of development, stages of play development that occur naturally, ecological factors that influence play, and the nature of the playful social interactions of familiar adults and children.

2. The subjects are predominantly in the age range of infancy to kindergarten age, although a few observational studies have been done with older children.

3. The settings are typically the children's homes, day-care centers, preschools, or kindergartens. Sometimes play is observed in playground or community settings as well.

4. The procedures usually consist of event sampling (i.e., recording instances of the behavior of interest), time sampling (i.e., recording behavior at specified time intervals), or recording of cases (i.e., describing individual behavior over a longer time span). Observational coding instruments or narrative "running account" descriptions that are later coded are methods used to collect data. Videotape or audiotape recording of the entire episodes of study are often made. Analyses may be quantified (i.e., with frequencies of behaviors recorded, comparisons of means or percentages, and statistical analyses as appropriate) or qualitative (i.e., narrative descriptions of the behaviors observed, case studies, or reports based on specific ethological models).

5. Suggestions for using these methods effectively include (a) becoming knowledgeable about the historical body of literature on observational research and the typically used coding schemes and instruments that might be adapted to promote comparability with other studies; (b) determining the level of analysis appropriate for communicating clearly the results from a large body of data; and (c) specifying as many contextual variables as possible to enhance generalizability and clarify distinctions between developmental and contextual factors.

Characteristics of *experimental studies* of play are as follows:

1. The hypotheses address cause-and-effect questions, such as the effects of training or other interventions designed to improve children's play, or they explore questions of developmental stages in object exploration, pretense, peer play,

TABLE 2–1 ● Naturalistic Observation Methods of Studying Play

Questions of Interest	Age of Subjects	Settings	Procedures	Researchers
Social/cognitive play dimensions	Toddler/preschool/ kindergarten	Classroom	Time samples, social/cognitive dimensions compared	Rubin et al., 1975, 1976, 1978; Sponseller et al., 1974, 1979
Pretense/language relationship	Infant/toddler	Home	Sequence of events, sensorimotor/ language relationships explored	Nicolich, 1977
Recess play/games	Elementary	School playground	Event samples, social/cognitive dimensions compared	Eiferman, 1971
Adult/peer social play	Infant/toddler/ parent	Home/center	Sequence of events, social play interactions described	Hay et al., 1979, 1983; Bruner et al., 1976, 1982
Peer social play	Toddler	Center	Event, time samples, social play interactions described	Mueller et al., 1975, 1977
Physical/social play	Elementary	Parks, playgrounds	Events recorded on film, play fighting categories described	Aldis, 1975
Sociodramatic play	Preschool	Center	Sequence of events, text and context described	Schwartzman, 1978, 1979
Language/game play	Elementary	Streets, playgrounds	Game events, language samples collected and described	Opie & Opie, 1959, 1969
Physical outdoor play	Preschool/primary	Playgrounds	Time, event samples, social/ cognitive types of play recorded	Frost et al., 1985

or adult-child interaction. Antecedents and consequences of play processes are also studied with experimental methods, as are physical environment effects (e.g., influences of play space or object placement).

2. The subjects are primarily children from infancy through kindergarten age, with emphasis on the toddler and preschool ages. Few experimental play studies of older children's play have been reported.

3. The settings are usually homelike or playlike laboratory settings. Day-care centers and preschools where specified environmental variables can be controlled have also been used in experimental studies.

4. The procedures for studies that train children to

TABLE 2–2 ● Experimental Methods of Studying Play

Questions of Interest	Age of Subjects	Settings	Procedures	Researchers
Levels of object transformation in pretense	Toddler/preschool	Laboratory/testing room	Conditions varying by realism, responses to conditions recorded	Fein et al., 1975, 1979; Golumb, 1977
Fantasy/cognitive relationships	Preschool	Center/training room	Pretest, training in fantasy play, posttest	Saltz et al., 1974, 1977; Rosen, 1974
Pretense development	Toddler/preschool	Laboratory/testing room	Modeling, eliciting of pretense under varied conditions, responses recorded	Bretherton et al., 1984; Fenson, & Ramsey, 1980
Sociodramatic play intervention	Preschool	Center/in class	Pretest, sociodramatic play intervention, posttest	Smilanski, 1968
Activity level/ environment interactions	Preschool	Laboratory/testing room	Camera recorded activity/movement/ play under varied physical environment conditions	Ellis & Scholtz, 1978
Social/language pretense interactions	Toddler/preschool	Center/testing room	Peer dyads in settings with varied materials, interactions recorded	Garvey, 1977
Elicitors of exploration/play	Preschool	Laboratory/testing room	Responses in presence of objects of varied novelty and complexity recorded	Hutt, 1971, 1979
Play/problem solving relationships	Preschool/ kindergarten	Laboratory/testing room	Conditions varying in directness of problem solving suggestions/play, responses to novel problems recorded	Sylva et al., 1976
Fantasy play/ television relationships	Preschool	School center/ home	Pretest, television intervention, posttest	Singer & Singer, 1978, 1984

engage in specific types of play include pretest, intervention, and posttest; for developmental or ecological studies a set of play materials or a particular play setting is designed to elicit the play behaviors that are the object of study. Many of these sessions are also videotaped, and behav-iors are coded and recorded. Analysis is usually quantitative, but often also includes descriptions of play events or language sequences, with explanations tied to the theoretical model of the researcher.

5. Suggestions for using these methods effectively

TABLE 2-3 ● Self-Report or Self-Performance Methods of Studying Play

Questions of Interest	Age of Subjects	Settings	Procedures	Researchers
Game and play preferences	Elementary	School/home	Play preference list, self-report	Rosenberg & Sutton-Smith, 1960; Wolfgang, 1985
Imaginative play predisposition	Preschool/ kindergarten	Center/school/ home	Interviews with children/parents	Singer & Singer, 1973, 1978
Game and play knowledge and preferences	Elementary	Neighborhood	Questions on game knowledge	Roberts, 1980
Friendship/play relationships	Elementary	School classroom	Sociometric techniques	Hallinan & Tuma, 1978
Games/play	Elementary	University classroom/ neigborhoods	Retrospective reports, collectors' reports, published works	Abrahams, 1962; Brewster, 1953
Favorite play experiences	Eementary	University classroom	Adult retrospective accounts	Bergen, 1985, 1986
Basis of friendship (including play-related)	Elementary/adult	Varied	Interviews	Berndt, 1981, 1982, Selman, 1981; Youniss & Volpe, 1978
Expectations for friendship (including play-related)	Elementary	Classroom	Essays	Bigelow, 1977

include (a) monitoring the behavior occurring in the designated play setting to ensure that the characteristics signaling it as play are present and that factors of novelty or stress are not affecting the quality or quantity of the play being observed; (b) extending experimental approaches over time and varying conditions systematically so that more complex types of play that are less easily elicited in an experimental setting can be observed; (c) using videotape or other procedures that allow subsequent observation of factors not initially the focus of the experiment; and (d) making the setting as similar as possible to the natural setting (which increases generalizability of results).

Self-report/performance measures (i.e., interview, questionnaire, and testing methods) usually have these features:

1. The hypotheses are oriented toward content (i.e., they are related to types of play or games and comparisons between respondent groups) or toward traits (i.e., they assess cognitive, personality, language, or other traits, such as imaginativeness).
2. The subjects are children of preschool age and older, ranging to middle childhood. Adults (parents, teachers) are also often subjects of study; in many cases they provide data to be related or compared to data collected from children.
3. The settings are varied and depend on where respondents are. Typically they include school, playground, home, or neighborhood settings.
4. The procedures usually involve the use of a standardized or a specially designed questionnaire, assessment instrument, or interview technique, which is then analyzed according to methods appropriate for that instrument. It may

yield quantitative or qualitative information and may include comparisons of groups or correlations of a number of measures taken on the same individuals.

5. Suggestions for using these methods effectively include: (a) providing children with the opportunity to gain familiarity with the tester or interviewer to increase the likelihood of optimal and accurate performance, (b) using the accepted practices of interview or survey research in selecting or designing the instruments so that results will be valid and generalizable, and (c) selecting a sampling method that will include representatives of all groups and ensure a high response rate.

Combinations of the naturalistic, experimental, and self-report approaches are also used. For example, observations in both a natural and a controlled experimental setting may be compared. Or, interviews with parents or children, as well as observational data, may be collected. Singer (1973), for example, combined interviews, projective measures, and naturalistic observations; Eiferman (1971) combined naturalistic observation and interview; and Smilansky (1968) combined naturalistic observation, experimental intervention, testing, and interviews.

● Methods for studying certain types of play

A number of researchers have discussed methodological issues that must be addressed in studying a particular type of play. For example, Henderson (1984), in a discussion of research on exploratory play, stresses that although this type of play is strongly influenced by the novelty of the objects in the environment, the social context is also an important variable. According to Henderson, three major approaches to studying exploration and exploratory play have been used: (a) controlled laboratory studies of perceptual (primarily visual) exploration of two-dimensional stimuli; (b) naturalistic studies of children's manipulation of and questions about novel objects; and (c) collections of exploratory/curiosity trait data from parent, teacher, or peer responses to questionnaires or rating scales. Methodological decisions include determining what objects to use (e.g., deciding what an object of moderate novelty looks like); selecting the categories of behavior to be ob-

served (e.g., determining what is to be called exploration and what is to be called exploratory play); and planning the involvement of adults or peers, (e.g., deciding whether adults will provide information, model behavior, or observe).

In a discussion of methodological issues related to the study of pretense, McCune-Nicolich and Fenson (1984) cite two paradigms that have been used for studying this type of play. Nicolich's (1977) study exemplifies a naturalistic observation method, conducted in the home or a homelike setting. In studies using this approach children typically have a range of toys from which to select. Adult roles usually include those of mother as a play participant, and researcher as a minimally intrusive observer rather than an elicitor of play. Play is observed over an extended time period.

The other method, exemplified by a study of Fenson and Ramsay (1980), is designed to elicit a particular set of pretense skills through adult modeling and play suggestions. This type of study is usually in a laboratory in which a set of play objects designed to elicit selected play behaviors are present. Adults are required to take specified roles in different conditions of the study. Observation of play episodes is typically for shorter time periods than in naturalistic studies. Elicitation procedures include having the experimenter present toys, model actions, give verbal suggestions, or combine actions. Mothers are usually involved as minimal participants or as observers.

McCune-Nicolich and Fenson (1984) indicate that, whether the setting is the home or laboratory, the sessions are usually videotaped. In addition to deciding on the paradigm to be followed, researchers must address problems regarding how their methodological decisions will affect children's behavior. For example, level of parent participation, degree of children's familiarity with setting and experimenter, and categories of play selected for analysis will affect the reports on level and content of children's pretend play.

Imaginative and thematic fantasy play have been studied in preschoolers and early elementary children with other methodological models. A model incorporating assessment of individual differences and correlations of levels of imaginative play with other variables has been used by Singer and Singer and colleagues (e.g., Singer, 1973, J.L. Singer & D.G. Singer, 1978; Singer & Rummo, 1973). Singer

(1973) indicates that this model requires observational records from two independent observers, obtained over at least a two-day period. Interview procedures must follow a specific protocol, and reliable independent judgments on rating scales must be obtained on the variables of interest.

Thematic fantasy play training studies (e.g., Freyberg, 1973; Saltz, Dixon & Johnson, 1977) involve assessing children's fantasy play skills before and after training. Saltz and Brodie (1982), in a critique of pretense training studies, note that the increases in some types of cognitive functioning reported may be due to interacting factors not explored in present research designs. They indicate that changes observed after brief training do not necessarily mean that basic cognitive structures have been altered. They suggest that study of stability of effects over time and careful attention to the contextual elicitors of play is needed.

Studying games with rules involves its own set of methodological problems. Although observational methods have been used (e.g., Piaget, 1932; Eiferman, 1971), these methods are more difficult to employ with the older children who are the prime subjects for studying games. Because the children who play games with rules do not usually play in the school setting (as preschoolers do), it is problematic to plan unobtrusive ways to study them at play (Roberts, 1980). It is difficult to decide if the play observed in a public setting (i.e., school, street, playground) is a valid representation of the level or content of play during middle childhood. Methods typically include questionnaires (Sutton-Smith & Rosenberg, 1961); tests of game knowledge (Roberts, 1980); and observation/interview combinations (Opie & Opie, 1959, 1969). The development of young children's pre-game playing strategies have been studied with experimental methods (DeVries, 1970).

Three Models of Play Research

Three play research models are presented that can be adapted by practitioners who are interested in studying children's play. The first is a two-dimensional naturalistic observation model that has been used to study whether the types of play described by Parten, Piaget, and Smilansky follow developmental sequences (e.g., Rubin, 1985b; Rubin, Maioni, & Hornung, 1976; Rubin, Watson, & Jambor, 1978; Sponseller & Lowry, 1974; Sponseller & Jaworski, 1979). The second model is an experimental one used to study the development of object substitution in the transformations occurring in early pretend play (e.g., Fein, 1975b; Fenson & Ramsay, 1980; Golomb, 1977). The third model, a self-report survey method for studying the games of elementary-age children, has been used by researchers in a variety of cultures, times, and places (e.g., Nadelman, 1970; Rosenberg & Sutton-Smith, 1960; Terman, 1926).

● A naturalistic observation model

The version of the naturalistic observation model to be described in detail is that developed by Sponseller and colleagues. This model features the social play categories of Parten (i.e., solitary, parallel, associative, cooperative) and the cognitive play categories of Piaget (i.e., practice, symbolic, games with rules). It includes Parten's "onlooking" category to record the amount of time young children spend observing other children's play. The coding instrument is two-dimensional, with one dimension being the Parten social play categories (on the vertical axis) and the other being the Piaget cognitive play categories (on the horizontal axis). The model combines the social and cognitive categories into "play complexity" cells. For example, in the first cell, behavioral instances of children watching peers' practice play (onlooking-practice) are recorded. Similarly, sociodramatic play (cooperative-symbolic) is recorded in cell 14. The Sponseller et al. observational coding instrument is shown in Figure 2–1 with examples of play behavior that might be recorded in each cell. The Sponseller et al. model was designed to be used with toddler-age children whose play includes few examples of product oriented (constructive) play but numerous examples of brief social interactional (associative) play.

The objective of the Sponseller and Jaworski (1979) study was to observe the developmental trends in social quality of play, as described by Parten (1932), and cognitive types of play, as outlined by Piaget (1962), in the same group of children at toddler and preschool age. The major hypotheses were that (a) the spontaneous play behaviors observed in the children at toddler and preschool age would follow the sequences described by Parten and Piaget and (b) the complexity of early play, as mea-

	Practice	Symbolic	Games
Onlooking	1	2	3
Solitary	4	5	6
Parallel	7	8	9
Associative	10	11	12
Cooperative	13	14	15

Child _____
Age _____
Date _____
Observer _____

● **Examples of play coded by cell**

Cell

1. **Onlooking-Practice:** Slowly walking through gross motor area, observing children going up and down slide and rocking in boat.
2. **Onlooking-Symbolic:** Observing another child "feeding" popcorn to a puppet.
3. **Onlooking-Games:** Standing, intently watching teacher and two children play Ring-Around-the-Rosy.
4. **Solitary-Practice:** Walking alone on tiptoe over pillows, carpet, tile, up and down stairs.
5. **Solitary-Symbolic:** Making animal puzzle pieces "walk" around and "talk" to each other.
6. **Solitary-Games:** Arranging cars in special order in line, selecting them according to self-designed rule, moving them in certain sequence so that one will "win."
7. **Parallel-Practice:** Painting with fingers on table beside other children, all of whom are focused on their own play.
8. **Parallel-Symbolic:** Setting table and "feeding" doll in house area, while other children are engaged in similar but separated play.
9. **Parallel-Games:** Running along with other children but not racing against them, only with self.
10. **Associative-Practice:** Rolling on pillows with another child, laughing and escalating activity in response to other child's action.
11. **Associative-Symbolic:** Building a "barn" with another child, helping by handing blocks, suggesting how to make the roof, adding to the wall, but also doing some independent building.
12. **Associative-Games:** Playing a "turn-taking" game with another child, such as pulling child in wagon, then sitting in wagon as other child pulls, then pulling child, then being pulled.
13. **Cooperative-Practice:** Throwing ball back and forth to another child for an extended time period.
14. **Cooperative-Symbolic:** Engaging in sociodramatic play as "mother" or "daddy" and demonstrating appropriate role actions for extended time period.
15. **Cooperative-Games:** Participating in a game of tag or hiding and finding, following rules for an extended time period.

FIGURE 2–1 ● Two-Dimensional Play Observation Form

sured by the combined dimensions, would be predictive of later play complexity.

The subjects were a group of normally developing children who first attended the laboratory toddler program and then the preschool program. The setting was the university school, during the regularly scheduled children's programs. No attempts were made to change the setting or activities; the videotape equipment used was introduced prior to actual recording and was present in the setting on a daily basis, so that it was not a novel element.

The procedures included collecting videotaped samples of the free play of randomly selected focal children. After the instances of each child's play were recorded (i.e., by time sampling at 30-second intervals), the behavior was coded, frequencies of play in each category were tabulated, and percentages of play types were calculated. A complexity score, based on the combined dimensions of play, was also derived. The hypotheses for evidence of developmental trends were supported; however, the social quality dimension, rather than the cognitive dimension, accounted for the predictiveness of the model. That is, the level of social play at toddler age was predictive of the complexity of play at preschool age.

Results showed that when the children were toddler age, solitary (31.2%) and parallel (22.6%) play predominated in the social dimension while practice (53%) was predominant and symbolic was secondary (12.2%) in the cognitive dimension. The most common type of play was solitary practice, with parallel practice a close second. The largest proportion of symbolic play was at the solitary level. At the preschool level, the same children's solitary play decreased (from 31.2% to 16.7%) while their parallel play increased slightly (from 22.6% to 30.6%). Increases in associative and cooperative play were evident, with associative going from 6.5% to 10.9% and cooperative from 1.9% to 9.1%. Practice play decreased (from 53% to 44.2%), while symbolic increased (from 12.2% to 32.3%). Onlooking also increased slightly (from 9.4% to 12.8%).

The Sponseller et al. model can be used by practitioners who wish to observe children at play in child-care centers, schools, hospitals, playgrounds, stores, and other settings. It is suitable for most age ranges, but different categories of play will be the focus of observation depending on the age of the children. The coding instrument can also be used as a diagnostic tool to observe the play of one child (e.g.,

if a child seems to be having problems becoming engaged in play or seems to be operating at lower levels than age would indicate are appropriate).

Two cautions must be observed with this model. First, for studies of play in naturally occurring settings, the setting itself may influence the kinds of behaviors observed; systematic variation of materials can clarify the extent to which the play observed is indicative of children's developmental level and the extent to which it is influenced by setting variables. Second, because solitary play has been shown to have different qualities at younger and older age levels, categorization of solitary play into a less mature (i.e., solitary practice/functional) and a more mature (i.e., solitary/constructive) form may be especially important when studying children of later preschool and kindergarten age (Barnes, 1981).

A model that has been used extensively with children 4 to 7 is that of Rubin et al. (1976, 1978, 1985b). This model draws on the categories of cognitive play developed by Smilansky and the Parten social categories. It also includes some non-play categories. The four Smilansky cognitive play categories are: functional, constructive, dramatic, and games with rules. The Parten social categories of solitary and parallel are used, but the model combines the associative and cooperative play categories into one category, called "group play." The Rubin et al. observation scale and a summary of play and non-play behaviors to be observed is shown in Figure 2–2.

● **An experimental model**

Fein (1975b) employed the experimental model described here in an investigation of young children's ability to transform objects in their pretend play. Many researchers have applied variations and elaborations of this method of studying pretense to the exploration of the stages of symbolic play (e.g., Bretherton, O'Connell, Shore, & Bates, 1984; Golomb, 1977; Fenson & Ramsay, 1980; O'Connell & Bretherton, 1984). Typically, the procedure of presenting pretense-eliciting objects is combined with various adult facilitation strategies such as modeling and suggesting pretense themes. This type of study is usually conducted in a homelike laboratory setting.

Fein (1975b) hypothesized that, within a given relationship between pretend objects and acts, young children's ability to perform transformations in pre-

Child_____ School_____

Date_____ Sex_____ Minute_____

						Solitary						Parallel						Group							
Transition	Unoccupied	Onlooker	Aggression	Teacher Conversation	Peer Conversation	Functional	Exploratory	Reading	Constructive	Dramatic	Games	Functional	Exploratory	Reading	Constructive	Dramatic	Games	Functional	Exploratory	Reading	Constructive	Dramatic	Games	Affect (+ or −)	
T	U	O	AG	T/C	P/C	F	E	R	C	D	G	F	E	R	C	D	G	F	E	R	C	D	G	A	Names

Anecdotal Notes and Comments:

								Solitary						Parallel						Group						Affect		
T O T A L	T	U	O	AG	T/C	P/C	F	E	R	C	D	G	F	E	R	C	D	G	F	E	R	C	D	G	+	o	−

● **Summary of play and non-play behaviors**

Behavior	Goal or Intent		
Solitary	To engage in an activity entirely alone, usually more than three feet away from other children.	Games with rules	To engage in a competitive game-type activity following pre-established rules and limits.
Parallel	To engage in an activity beside (but not with) other children, usually at a distance of three feet or less.	Exploratory	To seek sensory information.
		Reading	To receive cognitive information from books, records, etc.
Group	To engage in an activity with another child or children, in which the cognitive goal or purpose is shared among all group members.	Unoccupied	There is a complete lack of goal or focus during this behavior.
		Onlooker	To watch (or listen to) the behaviors and activities of other children.
		Transition	To prepare for, set out, or tidy up an activity, or to move from one activity to another.
Functional	To experience sensory stimulation through simple, repetitive muscular movements.	Conversation	To communicate verbally with others.
Constructive	To create or construct something.	Aggression	To express displeasure, anger, disapproval through physical means.
Dramatic	To dramatize life situations or bring life to an inanimate object.	Rough-and-tumble	Playful physical activity.

FIGURE 2–2 ● The Play Observation Scale Coding Sheet

tend play (i.e., permit one object to be used as if it were another) varies as a function of the number of substitutions required. She predicted that double substitutions would be more difficult for toddlers than single substitutions.

The subjects were children of 22 to 27 months and the setting was a testing laboratory with a one-way window. Two experimenters were involved; one was in the room with the children presenting the objects and actions and one was behind the window scoring responses. (Many similar studies collect data on videotape for later analysis.) The children's mothers sat in the room away from the testing table.

The objects used in the experiment were at two levels of representational realism: (a) a plastic cup and a cup-shaped shell and (b) a realistically detailed plush horse and a metal horse shape. Fein predicted that the more prototypical, or realistic, objects (i.e., cup and plush horse) would be transformed more readily than the less prototypical objects (i.e., cup-shaped shell and metal horse shape).

Procedures included a baseline trial period in which all children were presented with three conditions and given 10 seconds to respond. First, the realistic objects were displayed; then the experimenter modeled pretense by using the realistic cup to pretend to feed the realistic horse. Finally, the experimenter asked the child to pretend the realistic horse was hungry and to feed it. This baseline period was meant to ensure that the children understood pretending. Those children who did not were excluded from the study.

The substitution trials were then conducted, following the same three steps: (a) display, (b) modeling, (c) suggestion; but the children were randomly assigned to different object substitution conditions. Children were asked to pretend either with (a) a single substitution of the shell with the plush horse; (b) a single substitution of the metal horse shape with the cup; or (c) a double substitution of the cup-shaped shell with the metal horse shape.

Results supported Fein's hypothesis. For the cup-only substitution, 79% of the children pretended; for the horse-only, 61% pretended; but for the metal horse shape and cup-shaped shell (i.e., the double substitution), only 33% pretended. Even when the adult modeled pretending, the children pretended less in the condition requiring two transformations. Fein concluded that children's ability to pretend varies as the play objects vary and suggested

that future research explore how transformational ability changes with age and environmental conditions. The numerous subsequent studies of pretense have employed similar experimental models to explore these differences in children from toddler through kindergarten age.

Because home and school settings usually have objects that are at varied levels of realism, this model can be readily used by practitioners to explore object transformations in the pretend play of children from age 2 to 6. Bretherton (1984b) provides a number of adaptions of this model that are appropriate for exploring specific aspects of pretense. These models can be utilized to assess the pretend play abilities of mentally retarded and learning disabled children as well. Researchers must keep two caveats in mind: (a) The prototypical level (i.e., the level of realism) of the objects must be reliably categorized and (b) the adult must follow standard procedures (i.e., the same words and actions for each child), so that extraneous clues or prompts do not inadvertently influence children's responses.

● **A self-report/performance model**

Interview, questionnaire, and testing methods are useful primarily with older children because they can provide reliable information at that age level. Some studies supplement or replace self-report measures with parental report. Self-report performance methods were developed early in this century. Coury and Wolfgang (1985) describe the three major self-report/performance methods: (a) written checklists of play preference items (e.g., Terman, 1926); (b) forced dichotomous choices between toy photographs or objects (e.g., Vance & McCall, 1934); and (c) photo cards or toys that must be ranked in order (e.g., Nadelman, 1970, 1974). Coury and Wolfgang recommend that researchers make sure their survey items reflect contemporary play activities and toys.

The model described here is that of Rosenberg and Sutton-Smith (1960), who adapted their play categories from the earlier lists of Terman (1926) and Lehman and Witty (1927). After initially collecting ideas from children and comparing them to the early lists, the researchers selected 180 play activity items. The final list included (a) games with formal rules, such as tag or baseball; (b) general play activities, such as climbing or collecting; and (c) dramatic play activities, such as cowboys or house.

The objective of the study was to compare males' and females' preferred play activities. Subjects were children in fourth, fifth, and sixth grade from five midwestern townships. Procedures involved administering the list to the children and asking them to find the play activities in which they had engaged and to indicate whether they liked or disliked that type of play by marking L or D. After children had responded, the 115 items that were preferred by at least 50% of the children were used in the analysis.

The researchers reported that girls had selected many more activities than boys and that more items differentiated their play. That is, many of the girls' selections were not chosen by boys, but some of the boys' selections were also chosen by girls. Forty activities differentiated girls' play; only eighteen activities differentiated boys' play. Examples of preferences that differentiated between boys and girls are as follows:

1. Boys preferred active pretense activities such as bandits, bows and arrows, building forts, cars, cops and robbers. They also enjoyed structured games such as football and marbles and quiet activities such as making model airplanes and using tools.
2. Girls preferred active play such as cartwheels, seesaw, dancing, and pretend play such as dress-up, dolls, store, and school. Girls also included many active traditional games in their list of preferences, such as blindman's buff, crack the whip, farmer in the dell, fox and geese, hopscotch, jump rope, red rover, and stoop tag. They enjoyed quiet games such as clue, pick up sticks, and jacks.

When Rosenberg and Sutton-Smith (1960) compared their list to the early Terman (1926) list, they found that only 8 of 27 items that had differentiated boys' play remained differentiated in their study. They concluded that girls' interests have broadened but that boys' interests have narrowed. Even games such as baseball and basketball were named often enough by girls that they no longer differentiated between boys and girls. The researchers state that their results point to a broadening of female role perception but a narrowing of male role perception.

With this method, practitioners can explore the play of children of 5 to 12 years who are able to respond to questions, checklists, or other rank-ordering directions. Some self-report methods (i.e., picking toy photos) may be used with children younger than elementary age. The methods can also be combined with observational data collection methods. Researchers must be careful to (a) ensure that the response items are representative of children's present-day interests; and (b) make directions clear so that all children follow the procedures correctly. Coury and Wolfgang (1984) also suggest organizing the categories according to a theoretical perspective (e.g., using categories of a particular theorist) so that the results can be explained in terms of the theory.

Some Research Questions Needing Further Study

A number of researchers have identified questions that need further study. These questions can serve as a guide for future directions in play research:

1. For those who have been studying exploratory play, the major question is still that of determining where the line between play and exploration should be drawn. McGhee (1984) states that answering the questions of whether exploratory acts can be referred to as play is the "major unresolved issue" in exploratory play research (p. 223). Other questions are related to the contexts in which exploration and exploratory play are exhibited (e.g., the different social influences of home and group settings). Questions about object properties and physical settings that elicit exploratory play continue to be of interest, and methods to explore these questions are becoming increasingly sophisticated.
2. According to McCune-Nicolich and Fenson (1984), the major questions for those studying the development of pretense are (a) what are the experiences or internal developmental factors that account for specific changes in pretense? (b) what are the interrelationships among the structures of play stages (e.g., decentration, integration, decontextualization) and the processes of transition of higher stages? and (c) what are the interrelationships among trends in pretense development and other developmental trends (e.g., language or social and emotional

development)? An important question is the role of language in enhancing pretense development. There is currently little focus on the symbolic play of the elementary-age child; methods for exploring the nature and developmental trends of symbolic play after early childhood should be of interest to some researchers. Cross-cultural studies are also needed.

3. Researchers on the games of middle childhood are particularly concerned with answering questions on how present sociocultural forces and technological advances affect game development. There are conflicting viewpoints regarding whether the number of games played, the time spent in play, and the content of game play is changing more rapidly and substantively now than it did in the past (e.g., Roberts, 1980). Another point of controversy mentioned by Roberts is whether adults should teach or try to facilitate the playing of traditional or innovative games. The effects of adult involvement on middle childhood game playing have not been systematically studied. Replications of historical and cross-cultural research on game pervasiveness and content are sparse as are observational and experimental research approaches for studying the game playing of the elementary-age child. These are questions that might be productively studied. Cross-cultural studies of games have become a topic of increasing research interest; these will continue to be a focus of ethnographic research.

4. In a summary of the views of several leading researchers on play, Sutton-Smith (1979b) identifies five major play research issues: (a) antecedents of play (i.e., how it arises and develops); (b) transitions into play (e.g., boundary behaviors, play frames); (c) play structures (e.g., routines, formats, stereotypes, games, flow); (d) developmental changes over small time spans (i.e., synchronic) and long time spans (i.e., diachronic); and (e) consequences of play (e.g., for social, cognitive, or language development).

5. Future directions identified by Rubin et al. (1983) include the study of play as an assessment tool and its relationship to language, cognition, and socialization. Improvement in and more attention to studies of play in special needs groups have also been recommended. For example, more study is needed of the play of children who are handicapped (Quinn & Rubin, 1984), culturally different (Schwartzman, 1984), and physically or environmentally stressed (Cicchetti, 1985a). Additional study of the potential of training to enhance play development is also needed (Saltz & Brodie, 1982).

Conclusion

It is evident that research on play is thriving and that many directions for study are open to the researcher. The planning of research requires decision making on theoretical questions, on research definitions, and on research methodology. There are guidelines for naturalistic, experimental, and self-report/performance methods; many studies are available to serve as models for research. Practitioners can draw upon the play research literature not only for ideas for planning learning activities for children, but also for suggestions about how they can be better observers and recorders of children's play.

Play research has increased greatly during the past 25 years, and in the process has generated enough additional questions to keep researchers busy for the next 25 years. As the body of research has increased, the methods employed and the hypotheses tested have become more sophisticated. Rubin et al. (1983) summarize the state of research:

There remains a plethora of unanswered questions concerning the study of play. However, after a dearth of research in the area, we appear to have turned the corner. Now, perhaps researchers can derive as much pleasure from their serious investigative efforts as children do from engaging in this mutual topic of interest—play! (p. 759)

According to Mead (1934), play helps children to make their lives meaningful. Play research can give educators and other practitioners information they need to develop optimum learning conditions for children. Ultimately the significance of play research relates to its perceived usefulness for understanding children's development and for planning environments that facilitate that development through the medium of play. Play research also has meaning for adults, however, and indeed for the society as a whole, because efforts to unravel some of the mystery surrounding "that clever fool, play" (Vandenberg, 1982, p. 15) can enrich adults' as well as children's lives.

Questions for Discussion

1. What questions might be asked by researchers coming from two different theoretical perspectives (e.g., motive versus content, or individual versus cultural)? How would they be likely to plan their research projects to answer those questions?
2. How would researchers who preferred a naturalistic, an experimental, or a self-report/performance method go about a study of pretend play? What questions might each one ask, what subjects might each select, what hypotheses might each test, and what procedures might each follow?

Research Replication Exercise

Select one of the models described in the chapter (i.e., Sponseller & Jaworski; Rubin; Fein; or Rosenberg & Sutton-Smith). Following the procedures of that model, collect data on at least two children. Compare your results to the results reported by the researchers.

Suggestions for Further Reading

Brown, F. L., Amos, J. R., & Mink, O. G. (1975). *Statistical concepts: A basic program.* New York: Harper & Row. Presents a programmed instruction approach to understanding the basics of descriptive and inferential statistics that can be completed in about five to eight hours of study time. Includes practical formulas for statistical analyses typically employed in studies designed by practitioners.

Coury, K., & Wolfgang, C. (1984). An overview of the measurement methods of toy and play preference studies. *Early Child Development and Care, 14* (3–4), 217–232. Critiques the types of play preference instruments and methods developed during the past 60 years; includes samples of instruments and descriptions of methods.

Fein, G. G. (1975). A transformational analysis of pretending. *Developmental Psychology, 11,* 291–296. Reports method and findings of the study that served as an example of the experi-

mental model in this chapter.

Gay, L. R. (1976). *Educational research: Competencies for analysis and application.* Columbus, OH: Charles E. Merrill. Gives a basic introduction to the major principles of educational research, including problem definition, research plan development, sample and instrument selection, research procedure implementation, data analysis and interpretation, and results presentation. Writing style is nonthreatening, clear, and even enjoyable to read.

Pellegrini, A. D. (1984b). Training teachers to assess children's play. *Journal of Education for Teaching, 10*(3), 233–241. Explains one way that the Rubin (1985) scale has been used.

Rosenberg, B. G., & Sutton-Smith, B. (1960). A revised conception of masculine-feminine differences in play activities. *Journal of Genetic Psychology, 96,* 165–170. Describes study that served as an example of the self-report questionnaire model in this chapter.

Rubin, K. H. (1985). *The play observation scale (POS)* (Revised ed.) Waterloo, Ontario: University of Waterloo. Contains complete protocol for using the Rubin observation scale; includes explanation of scale development, definitions, and a bibliography.

Rubin, K. H., Maioni, T. L., & Hornung, M. (1976). Free play behaviors in middle and lower class preschoolers: Parten and Piaget revisited. *Child Development, 47,* 414–419. Describes one of the Rubin et al. observational studies, with Smilanski categories derived from the work of Piaget and Parten.

Sponseller, D. B., & Jaworski, A. (1979). *Social and cognitive complexity in young children's play: A longitudinal analysis.* Paper presented at the meeting of the American Educational Research Association, San Francisco. Presents detailed results of the naturalistic observation study described in this chapter.

Sponseller, D. B., & Lowry, M. (1974). Designing a play environment for toddlers. In D. B. Sponseller (Ed.). *Play as a learning medium* (pp. 81–106). Washington, DC: National Association for the Education of Young Children. Describes the conceptual model used in this chapter and gives results of the researchers' pilot study employing the model.

The Struggle Between Sacred Play and Festive Play

BRIAN SUTTON-SMITH

In many tribal cultures festival play is sacred play. Excesses of behavior are decreed as appropriate to certain seasonal or religious ritual occasions (Turner, 1984). In modern civilization, however, we tell ourselves that play is not a sacral and an obligatory performance whether it is excessive or not; rather, it is a profane and optional one. At least that has been our general message since the advent of industrialism. When in 1695 John Locke discouraged his readers from allowing their children to play in the streets and urged that they were better off inside the house with their alphabet blocks away from the company of raucous children, he initiated what was to become a new distinction. Now there was to be educational play. In the course of the next few centuries, and in the hand of Pestalozzi and Froebel and their successors, this was to become a new kind of sacralized play at least amongst a minority of educators, particularly those concerned with preschool children. In the present century social science studies have gone way beyond this by suggesting that educational play is directly related to how children learn, how they solve problems, and how they become creative. The present book is itself an illustration of the emergence of the research-based view that schools have a great deal to gain by basing their curriculum on children's play. What we are left with then in modern life is the notion, not of one kind of play that serves to unify the tribe, but of two kinds of play, an educational one that is somewhat sacred, or fast becoming so, and another more festive kind that we hope to confine to the playground, but that often has a tendency to sneak into the school and upset our lessons, whereupon it is termed "illicit" play (King, 1982a).

The contemporary situation is complicated further by the fact that even this distinction is too simple. Modern organized sports have also achieved a kind of international sacralization in this century. And given the rapid and massive expansion of the toy market in the past two decades, together with its accompanying literature assuring us of its educational value, one can assume that it too might in time acquire a similar odor of virtue. When one considers the agitation against war toys, it is quite possible to envisage a time when the toy industry is completely domesticated by conservative public opinion and can take on the ideal status that already is granted by us to such "educational" activities as number games, word games, and game simulations of everything from geography to the marketplace. One can see that even the cartoons today are much more domesticated than those of just 20 years ago. Whereas Bugs Bunny and Road Runner were quite violent characters who were constantly undergoing transmogrifications of their bodies and identities, the typical modern cartoon (e.g., G.I. Joe), though it is full of massive explosions and property violence, carefully veils from us the death or dismemberment of particular individuals, and the cast of characters always displays a proper balance of the sexes and minorities. The cartoon is on the way to the kind of idealization that the jigsaw puzzle has had for 100 years.

So we are left a puzzle. If the history of play within our own century has been one of increasing rehabilitation from its earlier status as idleness and triviality or even bestiality, and now its increasing educational idealization, will there be any scope left for festive play? Will there be an echo of the bacchanalian revelry spoken of by Rabelais in 1530? My own guess is that there will be. That in a more modest way festival play is still all about us, but it is more diffuse and private than it was in the time of the full-scale Mardi Gras, the Black Mass, the Boy Bishop, or the Lord of Misrule. One hears it in the shouting crowds at sports, in the shouting children at recess, and in the noisiness of taverns, as well as at Atlantic City. In the nursery school one finds it more often in that sort of play in which the children never seem to settle down to any coherent effort but go on from one thing to the next with a kind of revelry and nonsense in their behavior. They may chase one another round and round the room but never seem to catch up with one another and never seem to mean to catch up with one another, but all the time are yelling, "I am going to catch you," or "No you are not," neither of which ever truly happens. This is a game of chase in which they only pretend to chase. Or in another piece of playful nonsense, as fast as they set the table with plastic dishware they sweep it onto the floor, laughing loudly as they do so. This hilarity and disorder persists amongst the very young except in very strictly governed environments, and even in the latter cases it persists more secretly and more perversely.

The point of these remarks is to remind us that while we are discussing play "as a learning medium" we need to remember that it has a long history also as a learning medium that is not strictly school oriented. It has always been a learning medium as in the acquisition of skill at chess, at mancala, at mock physical warfare, and in physical play-fighting or rough-and-tumble. It has always been central to learning the social principles of dominance and submission and one's place in the social group, which includes the learning of child politics. In the past we could take for granted these kinds of social learning that were afforded through play. But in many modern families, in which street play is either not allowed or not possible and much time is spent in solitary play in front of the television, there is a need to make plentiful recess time at school so children can go about their own political education. I have recently had the thrill of observing some preschools in which the children arrive at 7 a.m. and leave at 6 p.m., and in which the period before 9 a.m. and after 3 p.m. is devoted entirely to group self-initiated play. The levels of play and the children's love of their exciting day at school are absolutely remarkable.

The examples of "nonsense" play mentioned earlier illustrate that play is a learning medium with a destiny outside the classroom. These examples also illustrate that play is a medium of impulsivity and impulse control. This hilarity and nonsense is not so generally appreciated by adults, but it is a part of adult behavior and it is a part of universal human behavior. Despite the appearance of noise and nonsense, this kind of play involves highly controlled patterns in the strict imitation of others and in the traditional forms of the games, as in Ring-a-Round the Roses, in which the players collapse upon the ground

in disorder after a period of strict unison. I would suppose that the great freedom for license in such behaviors as shouting and running is what makes them so rejuvenating to their participants. Understandably most teachers would be happier to tolerate them out of doors.

In sum, I argue that while play can be educational in the school sense, we should never forget that its much more vital role in learning has to do with child culture, not with adult culture; and furthermore, it has a festive role to perform that is often the very antithesis of our own educational concerns.

CHAPTER THREE

Stages of Play Development

DORIS BERGEN

In every culture and in every time, children have played. Since the early 1800s theorists from a multitude of disciplines have attempted to answer questions of why play occurs and what functions it serves for human beings and their societies. The information that has been collected in the last few decades on how play develops and what environmental conditions promote, delay, or change its developmental course has begun to provide a picture of the universal stages of play development. This research also indicates that individual and cultural differences may affect the timing of onset, the extent, and the varieties of play development observed.

This chapter gives an overview of the stages of play development from infancy through middle childhood as they have been reported by researchers and theorists who have used a variety of taxonomies, observational methods, and analytical models. The waxing and waning of various stages and the types of play observed at each stage are described and trends in play development are outlined. Characteristics of play at later life periods are briefly discussed in order to provide a life perspective on play development. Individual differences that affect expression of these stages of play and cultural factors that may influence the timing, quantity, or quality of play development are also reported.

Play as a Developmental Phenomenon

According to Rubin (1982a), the idea that play develops in orderly stages is rooted in the qualitative categorizations of types of play that were proposed by early theorists. For example, Schiller (1875), Spencer (1873), Groos (1901), and Buhler (1935) all described ways that play could be organized into stages. Hall's (1920) theory of recapitulation, which linked the changes over time in types of play children exhibit to the history of the human species, also gave support to a developmental view of play.

In the 1930s Parten's examination of social development in preschool children, which outlined a taxonomy of social play levels, made educators aware that there were stages of social play development. Her classification scheme (Parten, 1932, 1933) has been used in many studies of social play. Piaget (1962), who carefully observed the play of his own children, was very influential in initiating present interest in play as a developmental phenomenon. His research led him to identify a sequence of play stages that has provided a framework for much of the current research on play development.

As study of the universal stages of play has progressed, much has been learned about the sequence, transitions, and content of the stages of play development, and about individual and cultural differences in the developmental progression and range of play behaviors. The conceptualization of play as a developmental construct containing sequentially observed categories of behavior has: (a) encouraged the systematic study and analysis of developmental trends in play, (b) made explicit the fact that play behaviors that usually occur at certain times do not always appear automatically, and (c) prompted research on methods of promoting play development at all age levels.

The Play Development of Infants and Toddlers

During the past 20 years, infant and toddler play development has been studied extensively. In this early period, exploratory/sensorimotor play is primary. However, the beginnings of symbolic play and the emergence of reciprocal social games or routines are also evident. These early play behaviors form the basis for the development of the wide and complex range of playful activities that human beings exhibit throughout their lives.

● Exploratory/sensorimotor play

The initial play of infants grows from sensorimotor exploratory behavior, which consists of visual and motor actions upon the objects and people of the environment and experimentation with their reactions. Piaget (1962) identified the sensorimotor stages of development that occur during the first 2 years of life. The earliest stage is reflexive and the second, called primary circular reactions, involves coordination of reflexes. That is, a reflex, such as sucking, can be coordinated with movements of hand and arm, so that a thumb can be sucked. By 6 months of age (i.e., sensorimotor stage 3) infants try to make interesting experiences occur or continue by their goal-oriented actions. For example, infants will hit or kick to make a toy continue to twirl. In the fourth stage, during the latter half of the first year, infants can coordinate their sensorimotor schemas. The last two stages, which occur during the second year of life, involve inventing new sensorimotor schemas (e.g., trying to solve a puzzle through a variety of trial-and-error actions) and, finally, engaging in mental or imaginary exploration (e.g., trying to solve the puzzle by looking for a certain shape that is kept in mind). This final stage marks the transition to representational (i.e., symbolic) thought. According to Piaget, children are able to assimilate their experiences and construct knowledge first through their exploratory/sensorimotor (i.e., practice) play and then through their symbolic play (i.e., pretense).

The sensorimotor action schemas used by infants and toddlers have been categorized by Uzgiris and Hunt (1975). At first, the same action is applied to all objects; for example, mouthing or shaking actions are used on food, rattles, books, and people. As exploration continues, infants learn to differentiate actions according to the appearance of the object; they shake rattles, put bottles in their mouths, visually inspect books, and touch gently or pat people. The final action schemas show the influence of social transmission of knowledge. Books are brought to adults to be read, beads are put around the neck, and small cars are pushed along on their wheels.

As these action schemas are mastered and the objects explored, the learning is consolidated through play in which infants practice variations of motor actions. Rubin, Fein, and Vandenberg (1983) describe sensorimotor play as "repetition with deliberate complication" (p. 700) in which adaptive behaviors are consolidated and reorganized. Sensorimotor play is called practice play by Piaget because of its repetitive nature. Sensorimotor play has also been called functional play (Buhler, 1935). Because of the pleasure infants appear to experience in exercising their existing sensorimotor schemas, this early play provides "function pleasure." It is the form of ludic (i.e., playful) activity that has been characterized as the least mature because it predominates during the earliest age levels. Sponseller and Jaworski (1979) found that toddlers spend more than 50% of their time in practice play. Practice play with objects is the primary type of play that infants initiate, although they respond to adult-initiated symbolic and social play.

The relationship between exploration and exploratory (i.e., practice) play has been studied by a number of researchers (e.g., Berlyne, 1960, 1966; Hutt, 1971, 1979; Hutt & Hutt, 1977; Fenson, Kagan, Kearsley, & Zelazo, 1976; McCall, 1974). McCall (1979), who has studied the relationship between exploration and play during the first 2 years of life, states that he is "not concerned about the fuzziness of the distinction between exploration and play" (p. 36). He indicates that young children vacillate between these two modes because they use exploration to acquire information and play to influence the environment.

A number of researchers (e.g., Fenson et al., 1976; Inhelder, Lezine, Sinclair, & Stambak, 1972; McCall, 1974) have studied the stages of sensorimotor play. First, infants engage in exploratory and playful visual and motor transactions. Then motor and visual transactions are combined. By 9 months of age, infants are more likely to select novel objects for exploration and play. They especially enjoy objects that are responsive (e.g., noisemaking or bouncy). By 12 months, making things work and exploring cause and effect begin to be of interest. Toys that perform when children act upon them have special appeal.

In the second year, as children begin to understand the social meaning of objects, their play demonstrates this awareness. They playfully explore relationships between functions of objects, combining and coordinating objects in various spatial and causal relationships. As they play, they begin to classify objects that are alike, putting them in piles or collecting them, although they cannot yet verbally express the criteria they use for classification. They may collect cars or blocks in a basket, dump them all out and then arrange them in rows by color or stack them by size.

The manipulations of practice play, in which means rather than ends are important, gradually give way to purposeful manipulations. By late toddler age, practice play often has elements of constructive and symbolic play. For example, instead of stacking and restacking the blocks (i.e., practice play), children are more likely to build a structure and label it as a "garage." McGhee (1984) states that a distinction between exploratory play and "playful" play is exhibited by 2-year-olds. Exploratory play is interesting but not humorous; playful play is associated with incongruity and has humorous elements. For example, 2-year-olds will engage in incongruous actions such as "drinking" from a shoe or giving inappropriate labels to objects, such as calling dogs "cows." When they find these deliberate incongruities funny, they are giving evidence of their cognitive development and beginning ability to play with ideas (i.e., symbolic play).

● Pretense/symbolic play

The first instances of symbolic play, which Rubin et al., (1983) characterize as "assimilative manipulation of symbols" (p. 700), can be observed during the second half of the first year of life. Between 9 and 30 months of age, children increase their abilities to use objects in symbolic play. They learn to transform objects (i.e., substitute them for other objects and to act toward them "as if" they were these other objects) during this age period. Using a block as if it were a "sandwich" and pretending to eat it is an example of a transformation.

Numerous researchers (e.g., Elder & Pederson, 1978; Fein, 1975b; Fein & Apfel, 1979; Lowe, 1975; Nicolich, 1977; Sinclair, 1970; Watson & Fischer, 1977) have studied the development of symbolic play. During infancy there is a systematic shift toward pretense that does not seem to be affected by cultural influences (Rubin et al., 1983). Nicolich (1977) describes the stages of pretense during the second and third years of life. At about 12 months, infants seem to make a strong move to pretend play, operating in the "as if" mode first by replicating details of real life with realistic objects. Gradually, pretend play becomes separated from specific contexts, outcomes, or needs, and becomes less dependent upon realistic materials.

Researchers have studied children's pretense during the second and third years of life to pinpoint the various levels that children go through in developing representational abilities. These include (a) decontextualized pretense, (b) self-other relationship, (c) object substitutions, and (d) sequential combinations. The first of these, decontextualized pretense, is shown by children's emerging ability to engage in pretend actions out of context. For example, by 12 months they "eat" without food or "sleep" when they are not tired and they perform these behaviors out of the settings where the real behaviors typically occur.

During the second year of life, there is also a change in the self-other relationship. A typical pretend play action at 12 months is for the infant to pretend to drink from an empty cup—a self-referenced action. At 21 months the infant is likely to feed a doll with an empty bottle—an other-referenced action. Initially children are the symbolic actors; later children manipulate objects as as though the objects were the actors. The third process, object substitution, begins in the second half of the second year. According to Watson and Fischer (1977), by 24 months about two-thirds of children demonstrate transformational behavior. Realistic objects are more likely to be used before 19 months, but substitute objects become increasingly employed by 24 months. Combining and coordinating the objects and actions into sequenced and multi-schemed pretense (i.e., sequential combinations) and giving evidence of planning and of language use in symbolic play are achieved between the ages of 2 and 3 years (Nicolich, 1977).

● **Social play and games**

Even very young infants are responsive to social stimulation (Brazelton, Koslowski, & Main, 1974; Clarke-Stewart, VanderStoep, & Killian, 1979) and in the second half of the first year are capable of engaging in reciprocal social games (Bakeman & Adamson, 1984, Bruner & Sherwood, 1976; Lewis & Rosenblum, 1974; Stern, 1977).

Stern (1974b, 1977) reports that eye contact between mother and infant serves to maintain and break the flow of interaction during the early months of the infant's life. Mother and child interactions change when the child reaches about 8 months; both mother and child can focus on an object other than

each other. Stern concludes that learning about the social world precedes learning about the object world. The view that the precursors of play originate in social relationships is also held by El'konin (1966), Lewis (1979), McCall (1979), Sutton-Smith (1979a), and Vygotsky (1967). Piaget, on the other hand, asserts that interaction with objects is the primary play mode.

McCall (1979) characterizes the stages of social play as follows: from 2 to 7 months, infants explore their social influence through playful interaction. By 13 months, infants intentionally elicit social responses through play, and by 21 months they engage in symbolic social play. Thus, even young infants are aware of social contexts. McCall (1979) states that symbolic play has a major exploratory element because it is "fantasy exploration of social influence" (p. 37). Sutton-Smith (1979a) points out that pretend play is never totally solitary; it always has an element of "performance," before a real or an imagined audience.

Hay, Ross, and Goldman (1979) describe infant games as having the qualities of all social interactions: mutual involvement, alternation of turns, and repetition of sequences, as well as the playful quality of nonliterality (i.e., pretense). These early games, such as peek-a-boo or hiding objects, are often called exchange routines or rituals because they do not have true competitive elements (Kirschenblatt-Gimblett, 1979). Many theorists believe that early social games provide the basis for all later social rule-governed behavior.

Preschool and Kindergarten Children's Play

The play development of children age 3 to 5 has been studied more extensively and continuously than that of any other group. This age period is one in which major changes in play occur and the development of different kinds of play can be readily observed. Piaget (1962) states that play during this age period serves an assimilative function, enabling children to consolidate their experiences. The means by which specific processes and structures of play are developed during this age period have been of major interest to researchers.

● Exploratory, practice, and constructive play

Preschool and kindergarten children engage in exploratory play, but they spend less time exploring than infants and toddlers do. Ellis (1979) found that 3- to 5-year-olds spent an average of only 30 seconds in exploration before beginning to play with a novel object. As children grow older, practice play is most often observed when novel materials, objects, or actions are presented. Practice play constitutes about 33% of the play of 3- to 5-year-olds, but less than 15% of the play of 6-year-olds (Rubin et al., 1983). This type of play also begins to contribute to the development of coordinated motor skills needed for later game playing.

Gradually practice play is replaced by constructive play, in which children engage in self-regulated creation or construction of a product or in problem solution. For example, instead of moving their fingers around and around in the finger paint, children are more likely to draw the outline of a house or person in the paint. Constructive play is the most common activity (40%–50%) among preschool and kindergarten children (Hetherington, Cox, & Cox, 1979; Rubin, Maioni, & Hornung, 1976). Constructive play is not considered play by all researchers (e.g., Piaget, 1962) because it falls between the assimilative and accommodative modes. It is commonly called a play activity in school settings, however, and its relationship to problem-solving ability is of special interest to some researchers (e.g., Forman & Hill, 1980; Pepler & Ross, 1981; Sylva, Bruner & Genova, 1976, Vandenberg, 1981b).

● Symbolic/pretense, dramatic, sociodramatic play

According to Singer and Singer (1979), who have extensively studied imaginary play, the preschool years are "the golden age of socio-dramatic and make-believe play" (p. 195). The early solitary or dyadic symbolic play of infants and toddlers is gradually expanded into increasingly social and complex symbolic play, reaching full flower in children of 4 and 5. It then begins a gradual decline, at least in overt manifestations. The development of dramatic and sociodramatic play during preschool years has been the focus of study of many researchers (e.g., Connolly, 1981; Emmerich, 1977; Hetherington,

Cox, & Cox, 1979; Johnson & Ershler, 1981; Miller & Garvey, 1984; Rubin et al., 1976; Rubin et al., 1978; Sanders & Harper, 1976; Smilansky, 1968; Sponseller & Jaworski, 1979).

Although group pretense becomes more popular during this age period, solitary pretense is still an important part of symbolic play. Children pretend with replica objects (e.g., miniature versions of people, cars, houses), with realistic or nonrealistic normal-sized objects, or without objects. The developmental trends in object use during pretense have been studied by Wolf and Grollman (1982); Wolf, Rygh, and Altshuler (1984); and Overton and Jackson (1973). Children in the preschool and kindergarten years are more adept at using imaginary objects than toddlers are. Preschoolers and kindergartners use nonrealistic objects frequently and increase the diversity of their pretense themes (Pulaski, 1973). They can also employ substitute objects that are ambiguous (i.e., having the potential of many uses). Further, in pretend, they can use objects in counterconventional ways (i.e., use an object with a commonly identified use for another purpose). However, they may protest that the counterconventional object lacks resemblance to the real object. When the object substitution becomes too inappropriate, children comment on the absurdity and often "rename" the object or task to indicate their awareness of the inappropriateness. For example, when children were asked to substitute fruit for the "head" piece in a puzzle, they renamed the picture "fruit man" (Golomb, 1977).

Role taking with replica objects is exhibited in both solitary and peer play. Wolf et al. (1984), reporting on a longitudinal study of play with replica objects, indicate that as children reach preschool age they play both narrator and actor roles during pretend play with replica objects. Shantz (1975) defines role taking as the covert understanding of role attributes and role enactment (i.e., role-playing) as the ability to enact those attributes. Shantz (1975) and Garvey (1977a, 1979) have demonstrated that the development of role taking and of role enactment abilities, which are essential for pretense, follow predictable sequences. For example, children of 2½ years can act the mother role with the caregiver acting as baby, but not until age 3 can they assume reciprocal social roles with peers, enacting mother, father, and baby roles (Miller & Garvey, 1984). The ability to frame the play in terms of role expectations, to coordinate roles, and to communicate within and out of the play frame becomes greater as children's age and experience with social pretense increase.

Miller and Garvey (1984) report that in pretend play with dolls, girls exhibit mature role-play by age 3. Mature role-play requires the ability to set up the context for play (i.e., the play frame) and to make the pretense acts congruent within that frame. Children use language to communicate within the play frame as well as to communicate about the play frame. Within the play frame they speak "motherese" to the dolls, exhibiting slow, repetitive, simple speech, nursery "tone," and euphemism. In negotiating the play frame, they issue play invitations, assign identities, improve the play production, and terminate the play performance.

The roles girls portray toward dolls include affection, nurturance, control, and teaching. Roles toward peers usually do not include affection but do include the other three elements. By age 3 the pretend play may have multi-schemed sequences prefaced by explicit plans. Verbal role taking is possible in two registers, with the child speaking both for the mother and for the baby. Boys are less likely to demonstrate their ability to be "mother"; however, they are also adept at employing appropriate social language, expressive tone, and voice patterns in pretend play (Martlew, Connolly, & McLeod, 1978).

Garvey (1977b), who has studied how social play and language are related, stressed that, in play, relationships are transformed within social systems; thus role enactment skills reflect children's role taking ability. Garvey describes four types of roles typically taken in group pretense play: (a) functional roles, which are organized according to the objects or an action plan (e.g., doctor, fireman); (b) relational roles, which are complementary and usually familial (e.g., mother and baby); (c) character roles, which are fictional or stereotypic (e.g., superman, witch); and (d) peripheral roles, for which no alternate identity is assumed (e.g, giving a prop to a role player).

Because of the many levels of interaction in group pretense, communication is a central part of the play process. Children must be able to understand and apply the structural properties of play communication in the same way that they apply those of

language. As is true for language, play competence is essential for play performance, and metaplay awareness (i.e., being able to think about play) is for play as important as metalinguistic awareness is for language. In negotiating the play frame, children must both set up a context for play and then use play as the text within that framework (Garvey, 1977a; Bretherton, 1984a).

Smilansky (1968) indicates that language serves five "framing" functions in group pretense (i.e., sociodramatic play): (a) to change personal identity; (b) to change object identity or action; (c) to substitute words for actions; and (d) to describe the context of the pretend action. Kirschenblatt-Gimblett (1979) states that application of language in these ways helps children gain an awareness that "This is play" (Bateson, 1956).

In preschool and kindergarten, sociodramatic play appears to follow an inverted U trend. Hetherington et al. (1979) found that, compared to pretend play at other ages, the highest percentage (71%) of group pretense occurred at age 5, with 6-year-olds having the next highest level (65%). Four-year-olds and seven-year-olds showed lower levels of pretense. Researchers who have charted the course of all forms of social play find that the solitary play curve appears to follow a U trend, not an inverted U, with solitary play being at its lowest level at age 5 as compared to age 4 and age 6 (Rubin et al., 1983). These results are congruent with the findings of high levels of sociodramatic play during this age period.

Saltz and colleagues (Saltz & Brodie, 1982; Saltz, Dixon, & Johnson, 1977; Saltz & Johnson, 1974) have been particularly interested in preschool and kindergarten children's development of thematic fantasy, which is pretense with fictional characters. Some evidence implies that thematic fantasy is a more mature form of group pretense than sociodramatic play. The latter draws upon events in children's everyday experiences, whereas thematic fantasy play uses themes from children's literature and the media.

In a study of play among children who were unfamiliar with one another, Stockinger Forys and McCune-Nicolich (1984) concluded that the most typical social interaction at preschool-age level is pretend play. Pretending seems to assist unfamiliar peers by providing a means by which children can find common ground for interaction.

● Social play and games

During the preschool and kindergarten years, all forms of social play with peers become increasingly evident. In addition to group pretense or sociodramatic play, which has its own set of rules related to role enactment, social play takes two other forms: (a) rough-and-tumble play and (b) emergent games with rules.

Although rough-and-tumble play continues during the elementary years, it is initially manifested during early childhood (Aldis, 1975; Blurton-Jones, 1972). The movement patterns of rough-and-tumble play are similar to those of hostile behavior (e.g., running, chasing, wrestling, jumping, falling, hitting), but these behaviors are accompanied by signals (e.g., laughter, exaggerated movement, open rather than closed hands and faces) that indicate "This is play" (Bateson, 1956).

Blurton-Jones (1972) speculates that preschool may be a critical period in which this type of play is learned and states that it is important for children to learn to distinguish rough-and-tumble play from aggression. Some children, especially many girls, do not learn how to engage in rough-and-tumble play or to recognize the signals that indicate it is play, not aggression.

Aldis (1975) observed similar types of rough-and-tumble play and described the play signals (e.g., laughter, play screams, open and smiling mouths) that distinguish play and that increase the general arousal effect and thus the playfulness. This type of play is often hard for adults to allow, both because they are not always able to distinguish it from aggression and also because the increasing levels of arousal that it promotes may cause an escalation that is difficult to control. It is a very common type of play, however, in the early and middle childhood years.

Preschoolers also engage in social game play involving simple rules of reciprocity or turn taking. Kamii and DeVries (1980) have been particularly interested in the way young children play games with rules. Piaget (1932, 1962) has stated that truly competitive games cannot be played by children until they reach elementary age. He classifies play as "egocentric" among 2- to 5-year-olds and as characterized by "incipient cooperation" from age 5 to 8. Young children's game playing does not involve strict adherence to rules or competition. Rules of games

are followed but the purpose is for everyone to enjoy the game, not to win.

Kamii and DeVries suggest that playing games with rules is useful for young children because they learn to decenter; that is, to consider other viewpoints. Kamii and DeVries (1980) describe how a typical game invented by children of 4 might be one in which every child follows the same set of actions or rules (e.g., putting marbles in a container) but the children take turns doing the action by themselves rather than playing cooperatively or competitively.

DeVries (1970) found five stages of competitive game playing in 3- to 7-year-olds, ranging from (a) viewing the opponent as a cooperative partner, (b) following the rules as a pattern rather than with the intent of winning, (c) following rigid patterns but having an attitude of competition, (d) trying to win but using transparent strategies, and (e) playing competitively. She reports that children become able to play both complementary role games and competitive role games when they reach 5 or 6 years old. This type of play becomes a major component of the play of middle childhood.

Elementary Children's Play

Roberts (1980) notes that, although the play of elementary-age children drew research attention earlier in this century, the play of children from 7 to 12 years is not of major current research interest. He cites two reasons for this lack of attention. First, theorists hold the view that play does not have as central a role in the accommodative learning mode of middle childhood as it does in the assimilative mode of the early childhood years (Piaget, 1962; Fein & Schwartz, 1982); therefore study of play in children of elementary age has not been considered as crucial for understanding children's development and for application to educational practice.

Second, it is less convenient to study middle childhood play because much of it occurs outside the school setting, and these other settings (e.g., home, playground, neighborhood) do not lend themselves to the use of the direct observational methods commonly used in research on early childhood play. Roberts (1980) comments, "Once a child enters school . . . and certainly by the time he enters middle childhood, play is pushed to the edge of life" (p. 97). That is, play occurs primarily outside of school.

Although evidence on play in middle childhood has not been analyzed as extensively as that in early childhood, sufficient studies do exist to provide a general overview of certain types of middle childhood play. There is debate on the question of whether children in this age period are playing less than they used to or whether they are merely engaging in different types of play. Roberts states that although patterns of play have changed, games of middle childhood still are varied and extensive. The major play type commonly reported during middle childhood is that of rule-governed games. However, practice, constructive, and symbolic play can also be observed.

● Practice and constructive play

Eiferman's (1971) studies of recess play show that many elementary-age children still engage in unstructured motor practice play. Running, jumping, sliding, twirling, and throwing balls or other objects are activities frequently observed on playground and street. Although it appears similar to the repetitive practice play of early childhood, this practice play differs from earlier practice play because much of it appears to be ends rather than means related. That is, children engage in it for the purpose of enhancing motor skills that are needed for competence in games or sports. According to Eiferman, there is an increase in practice (i.e., exploratory) play in the later elementary years.

Constructive play is a primary play mode in middle childhood, both in and out of the classroom. Partially this is because it is one of the few play-like activities allowed in work-centered classrooms. For example, building a diorama or creating a play about a social studies topic allows children to engage in constructive play. Whether it is considered play by children appears to depend on whether they choose to do it or see it as imposed by the teacher (King, 1979) and whether the task is enjoyable (King, 1982b, 1982c).

Play with materials solely for the sensory experience rather than for the construction of a product is less common than in earlier years; however, out-of-school constructive play and sensorimotor play are popular (Allen, 1968; Berg & Medrich, 1980). Construction activities can range widely over the continuum of play to work depending on how many of the elements that signal playfulness are present.

● Symbolic play

There are few studies of the changes that occur in pretense during the elementary years. Informal observations suggest that sociodramatic or group pretense continues to decline after the age of 6 or 7 but the trend of the decline has not been described. Because of the paucity of research data, it is not possible to indicate how much of the decline is general and how much is context specific. That is, these play behaviors seem to be less frequently observed in school and playground settings but they may continue in less public environments.

Eiferman's (1971) comparative study of middle class and working class children's recess play suggests that, although middle class and working class children follow a similar sequence in their play development, the age of highest incidence of particular types of play varies between the two groups. In both groups sociodramatic play reaches a peak and then begins to decline as games with rules increase. However, the peak of pretend play for working class children occurs at a later age (6 to 8 years) than in middle class children (5 to 6 years). Middle childhood may be an especially important age for group pretense development for children of working class families. Only further study of pretend play in middle childhood can answer the question of what really happens to it as children grow older.

Although evidence from empirical studies is sparse, informal observation suggests that symbolic play evolves in a number of directions during the middle childhood period. One change is that much symbolic content is integrated into games with rules. Opie and Opie (1969) report that much group fantasy play is evident in British children's game playing. Other examples of symbolic games of middle childhood include fantastic challenge games such as Dungeons and Dragons and competitive board games such as Monopoly.

Another way symbolic play changes is that it becomes abstract, being transformed into mental games and language play. Middle childhood is an age of verbal invention, and verbal play seems to peak at age 8 or 9. Roberts (1980), Sutton-Smith (1976), and the Opies (1959) describe the many ways language becomes a plaything in children's riddles, puns, tongue twisters, insults, chants, and rhymes. Sanches and Kirschenblatt-Gimblett (1976) maintain that sound play is especially important to children in elementary grades. The development of secret codes, which involve playing with the syntax and semantics of language, is also especially popular with this age group. Children's riddles serve the purpose of parodying adult emphases on rote learning and oral interrogation (Roberts & Foreman, 1971; Sutton-Smith, 1976). McGhee (1984) reports that the humor older children experience in verbal play is a result of their more complete understanding of the meaning of lexical incongruities.

Symbolic play also becomes appropriately socialized. It is either practiced in private places (e.g., one's own room or in one's own head) or it is exhibited in publicly approved forms (i.e., on a theater stage). Although scant research data describe this transition, adult retrospective self-reports (Bergen, 1985, 1986), children's self-reports, and parental reports (J.L. Singer & D.G. Singer, 1978, 1983), as well as the popularity of miniature toys, suggest that much dramatic and fantasy play occurs in the more private spaces of home environments. Elementary-age children may spend hours playing detective, or engaging in other fantasy activities of which adults are hardly aware. They often have secret clubs that restrict membership to those who take similar fantasized worldviews. Rubin et al. (1983) include daydreaming, which they characterize as "playing with ideas," as "one of the developmental successors to the young child's active involvement" (p. 700) in overt pretend play. Reading mystery or adventure stories and watching television dramas provide other means of living in a pretend world.

In Roberts' (1980) study of children in Scotland, the typical child interviewed spent an average of three hours a day viewing television. Roberts concludes that this time reduces the amount of time children spend in outdoor play. Television may serve as a substitute for observably active pretend play. Organized activities, such as after-school lessons, adult-directed clubs and sports participation, reduce the time available for pretend. Thus, pretend play may

decline in amount as well as change in character. Children differ greatly on this play dimension, as studies of imaginative play demonstrate (Singer, 1973).

● Social play and games with rules

In the early part of the century, there was great interest in the games of middle childhood. As a result of the child study movement (Hall, 1920), a number of surveys of children's games were conducted in the years between 1900 and 1920 (these have been reviewed by Roberts, 1980, and Schwartzman, 1978). Since the 1960s the playground and street games of elementary-age children have again become a topic of research interest. Many of these recent studies have been conducted by anthropologists, linguists, and folklorists rather than by psychologists (e.g., Abrahams, 1962, Von Glascoe, 1980).

Research conducted in England (Opie & Opie, 1959, 1969), Scotland (Roberts, 1980), France (Caillois, 1961), Israel (Eiferman, 1971), and the United States (e.g., Abrahams, 1969; Brewster, 1953; Fischer & Fischer, 1963; Sutton-Smith & Rosenberg, 1961) has indicated that child-initiated game playing is not disappearing; however, some traditional games are no longer being played by elementary-age children, and sports-related games are very popular.

Opie and Opie (1959, 1969) were particularly interested in the language children used in their traditional game playing and the pervasive culture of childhood that preserved these games in numerous versions throughout the country. The Opies indicate that middle childhood games often involve a large element of luck so that the competitive element is blunted. This allows more children to enjoy the game, a particularly important point when games are played in neighborhoods or playgrounds where choice of players is limited.

In Scotland, Roberts (1980) surveyed children's knowledge of traditional and nontraditional games, language play, and sports. He found that children are familiar with a wide range of games but that girls still play more traditional games while boys focus on ball games and sports. Sutton-Smith and Rosenberg (1961) reported similar findings, indicating that girls' choices of games had increased over the past century while boys' choices had narrowed.

In recess observations, Eiferman (1971) found that the highest incidence of game playing is during the age period from 10 to 12. After age 12, games decline in popularity, to be replaced by unstructured practice play, conversations, and organized sports. Eiferman identifies four types of games observed on the playground: (a) steady or constant games, such as tag, which are played consistently; (b) recurrent or cyclical games, such as marbles or hopscotch, which seem to follow cycles of popularity and decline; (c) sporadic games, which are played rarely, and (d) one-time games, such as hula hoop contests, which rise once to popularity and then disappear. Eiferman also stresses that after age 12, interest in sports rather than games is emphasized; she attributes much of the practice play observed with older children to the desire to increase motor skill performance for playing sports. Comparing play and sports, Roberts (1980) declares, "Sport is hostile to play" (p. 30) although "the spirit of fantasy pervades even the elaborate structures of competitive sport" (p. 7).

Eiferman (1971) states that in middle childhood the games played feature the "meaningfulness of a challenge" (p. 287). This challenge is present if children possess both the skills needed to play and an understanding of the rules of the game. The level of skill and understanding must be sufficient to play well but not so great that the outcome of the game is predetermined; that is, there must be challenge. All structured rule-governed games have the intellectual challenge of rule mastery and the motivational challenge of consistently conforming to the rules.

Piaget (1932) studied games with rules by observing the way boys aged 7 to 13 played the game of marbles. He concluded that boys of 7 to 10 played very differently from boys of 11 to 13. The younger boys followed differing, contradictory, but rigidly held rules that seemed to be arbitrarily accepted. The older boys arrived at rules by consensus. They were clear about the rules but also could intervene and change the rules when they decided to do so. Piaget constructed a theory of moral development that drew upon this study of marble playing. He was unable to find a girls' game that was as complex and so did not investigate the differences among girls' game playing and their moral development.

Competitive games require an additional challenge of winning and receiving prestige or material rewards, and group competitive games have the additional challenge of coordinating one's actions with those of other participants in the group (Eiferman, 1971). This latter challenge is also present in cooperative group games. Unstructured or free play also poses challenges of physical, mental, or social effort; and many kinds of practice play involve the challenge of skill improvement. Eiferman believes that the preparation for challenge or the participation in challenge provide the underlying motivation for much play in middle childhood.

● Play with academic skills and problem solving

In the early elementary classroom, the use of play to foster problem solving, thinking skills, and academic skill learning has been of interest (Pellegrini, 1980, 1982a, 1984a; Vandenberg, 1980, 1981a). Usually this type of play has been labeled "discovery learning" activity (Bruner, 1966). The open classroom and learning center classroom approaches have been partially built on two factors that have been identified as essential for play: (a) allowing children to feel internal control over their activities and (b) allowing them to use their internal motivation to initiate their learning activities. Rather than promote the assimilative reality-bending characteristics of play, however, the use of discovery learning through playlike activity is planned to meet accommodative purposes. That is, playful approaches in the classroom usually are ends rather than means oriented. For example, instead of engaging in free play with the texture and other physical properties of water, children may hypothesize how fast an object will float as water is poured down different widths of tubing and then experiment playfully by practicing the actions over and over while writing down what happens and then coming to conclusions.

Many educators plan classroom activities that include elements of humor, encourage playing with ideas, and promote creativity. Learning centers encourage practice play, assist mastery of academic skills through games, and provide playful problem-solving and inventive thinking activities. Educators also support the performance of plays, the writing of imaginative stories, the expression of artistic abilities, and the playful exploration of computers and other technological equipment.

Distinctions between work and play begin to blur at this age level when means and ends elements may both be present in classroom activities (King, 1982b, 1982c). Although research evidence is mixed, playful discovery approaches seem to foster certain types of higher-level learning (Christie & Johnson, 1983; Vandenberg, 1980).

Play in Adolescence and Adulthood

Theorists have disagreed about whether play serves similar purposes for adults as it does for children (Herron & Sutton-Smith, 1971) or even whether play exists in adults (Piaget, 1962; Csikszentmihayli, 1979). Herron and Sutton-Smith (1971), who define play as "an exercise of voluntary control systems with disequilibrial outcomes" (p. 344), contend that play is pervasive throughout life, but that it takes different forms at various ages. Although play may be phenotypically different (i.e., taking different forms) at later ages, it may be genotypically similar (i.e., serving basic human needs) at all ages (Singer & Singer, 1976). The tendency to playfulness seems to be inherent in human beings, but its manifestations vary, not only because of the changes in behavior that come with various developmental stages, but also because of cultural expectations of appropriate behaviors at various age levels. For example, it is not usually appropriate for adults to wear dress-up clothes and engage in sociodramatic play. However, adults do participate in role simulation exercises, belong to community theater groups, hold brainstorming sessions, join liars' clubs, attend political conventions, and engage in work roles requiring sociodramatic-like behaviors. Many adult rituals communicate a sense of playfulness and nonliterality. Older children and adults are also more adept at appearing to be working when they are actually playing—for example, by doodling during a boring lecture or by daydreaming while appearing to attend.

Thus, as people grow older, play's outward manifestations continue to change, becoming further miniaturized, socialized, and abstracted. Symbolic board games in which pawns (e.g., knights) are manipulated instead of the players using their own bodies to be the pretend protagonists and in which paper symbols (e.g., thousand-dollar notes) are treated as real money are examples of this trend, as are mental games in which language takes the place of objects and people. Herron and Sutton-Smith (1971) ask, "Is the 'reality' of chess or football more real than the reality of 'bogeyman?' Or is it simply that as adults we are more familiar with our own ludic forms?" (p. 301).

Csikszentmihayli (1979) contends that adult ludic behavior is better characterized as "flow" rather than play. Although flow has elements similar to those of play, it need not be voluntary. It is a condition, in either a work or play setting, in which the challenges match one's skills. People who enjoy their work, he states, describe it in ludic (i.e., playful) terms: It takes their full concentration, they feel in control, they lack self-consciousness, and they have goals that lead to immediate feedback. He maintains, "Play is the experience of flow in a setting or frame of action in which the activity is perceived to be voluntary or autotelic; that is, the goal is in the activity itself and unrelated to 'real-life' consequences" (p. 268). Although many adult activities involving flow would not be characterized as play by Csikszentmihayli, he sees "play as a training ground for the more adequate adult life of flow in any kind of experience (work or play)" (p. 275). Play is a culturally or individually structured form in which one can experience flow (i.e., living at optimal capacity).

Researchers are only beginning to explore the course of development of flow during middle childhood and adolescence. It is possible that research on the middle childhood years, when the distinctions between work and play become more defined as well as more overlapping (King, 1982c) could explain how in adults one person's work becomes another's play and vice versa. Eiferman's (1971) contention that challenge is a major factor in play during the later elementary years would predict that the condition of flow, in which challenge matches skill, can be experienced in either play or work at that age.

It is clear that the qualities children exhibit in play are ones that adults continue to seek, even though the question of whether these activities should be labeled work or play is unanswered. Sutton-Smith (1979c) believes that "play may lead ultimately to the capacity for 'flow' in adulthood; that those who have learned to engage in autotelic play behaviors when young will show more capacity for finding 'flow' possibilities in their adult lives" (p. 313).

Lewis (1979) reminds researchers that "in adults the range of activities we want to call play, from symbolic play to exploration to sports to the whole gamut, is so broad that I believe we would be naive to assume that there was a single developmental course for them all. They may have somewhat different developmental histories" (p. 33). It remains for researchers to determine those histories.

Individual and Cultural Differences in Play Development

Although uncovering universals of play development has been the major focus of psychological play research, many studies have also focused on identifying individual and cultural differences. Stable individual differences have been observed in play activity levels, cognitive styles, and personality traits. Sex, ethnic, and socioeconomic differences have also been noted frequently.

Anthropologists rather than psychologists have been the major researchers of children's play in other cultures. Psychologists and anthropologists have often focused their studies on different play forms. Psychological studies are typically directed at sensorimotor or symbolic play development, whereas many anthropological studies have explored organized games rather than unstructured play (Schwartzman, 1979). Kirschenblatt-Gimblett (1979) states that play takes different forms in different cultures and adds, "Which activities count as play is culture specific" (p. 220). Cultural differences in onset of play stages, elaboration of specific types of play, patterns of adult modeling or facilitating of play, and attitudes toward play/work distinctions have also been reported.

Even when psychologists and anthropologists study similar play types, because their questions of interest and research methods differ, their data are not usually directly comparable. It is also difficult to interpret reports of individual or cultural differences because they are often in studies in which several variables are confounded. For example, activity levels or cognitive styles may be confounded with

sex, social class, or ethnic distinctions. Reported sex differences, in particular, may be explained by influences of both individual and cultural factors. Results from a wide range of studies have indicated that individual and/or cultural differences in play are apparent in a number of areas.

● Activity levels

The amount of energy used in play, the physical and motor behaviors exhibited, and the level of sustained play activity differ among children from their earliest months of life. Infants exhibit differing tempos of play by 6 to 9 months (Kagan, 1971; Longo, Harvey, Wilson & Deni, 1982; McCall, 1974; Wenckstern, Weizmann, & Leenaars, 1984). Some infants play at a slower, more focused tempo and exhibit less repetitive motor behavior. Others show a faster tempo and a wider range of sensorimotor actions. Toddlers also show variation in tempo of play, especially in regard to the number of different actions and objects used in pretend play (Fein, 1979b). Children can be identified as "high arousal" and "low arousal" types by preschool age (Hutt, 1979).

Ellis and Scholtz (1978) report that physiological factors affect activity patterns. For example, Down's syndrome children operate at a slower pace than normal children (Linford, Jeanrenaud, Karlsson, Witt, & Linford, 1971). A number of studies show higher activity levels for boys than for girls (DiPietro, 1981; Pulaski, 1973; Smith & Daglish, 1977). Preschool females have been reported to be more sedentary and males more active in dramatic play (Rubin, Watson, & Jambor, 1978). Preschool males are more active motorically during exploratory play than females and 5-year-olds are more active than 4-year-olds. (Ellis & Scholtz, 1978). However, activity levels also fluctuate as a function of context (Wade, Ellis, & Bohrer, 1973) and of cultural expectations (Blurton-Jones & Konner (1973).

● Cognitive styles

Researchers have also reported differences in the ways children understand and think about problems and in their methods of perceiving, remembering, and judging information (e.g., Saracho, 1983, 1985). These cognitive style differences are evident in young children's object and pretend play and in their social play. Wohlwill (1984) reports that there are individual differences in the propensity to use exploration or play as a primary mode of orientation toward the world.

Children who have been identified as field dependent (i.e., gaining their information from people) or field independent (i.e., focusing on information in the inanimate object world) show differences in play styles (Saracho, 1985). Saracho suggests that a strong relationship exists between play and cognitive styles, with those children who are field dependent being more likely to engage in parallel, associative, and cooperative play and those who are field independent being more likely to prefer solitary play. Lewis (1979) agrees that at an early age some children are more object oriented, while others are more socially oriented.

In studies of early symbolic play by Harvard University Project Zero researchers, distinctive play styles have been observed: Some children are "dramatists"—interested in sequences of interpersonal events and feelings, while others are "patterners"—interested in configural uses of materials and curious about the object world. These differences become evident by 18 to 24 months. By 3 years, children become able to use both play styles, even though many show a strong preference for one or the other initially (Shotwell, Wolf, & Gardner, 1979). The researchers conclude that these observed styles "represent fundamentally different, but equally valid, routes toward general symbolic competence—routes originating both in children's overall personalities and in their underlying mental structures" (p. 130).

Individual differences in disposition to fantasy play are evident by age 3 or 4 (Singer, 1973; D.G. Singer & J.L. Singer, 1978). High and low fantasy children do not differ by sex or IQ but do differ on ability to delay gratification and on measures of creativity. More firstborns and only children are high in fantasy. In 5-year-olds, high fantasy predisposition is related to originality, spontaneity, verbal fluency, ideational fluency, and flexibility (Pulaski, 1970).

There are also individual and cultural differences in the way language is used in play. Individual styles of language ability affect levels of pretense. Referential (i.e., object-oriented) and expressive (i.e., feeling-oriented) speakers show different levels of pretend play, with expressive children showing more pretense (Fein, 1979b). Children of different socio-

economic and cultural backgrounds have different levels of ability to use language in sociodramatic play (Smilansky, 1968). In children's speech play and riddling there are cultural differences in form and content of speech as well as in the style used to express imaginative play (Kirschenblatt-Gimblett, 1976).

● **Personality traits**

Social orientations exhibited in play are related to cognitive styles (Coates, Lord, & Jakabovics, 1975; Halverson & Waldrop, 1976; Rubin & Maioni, 1975; Rubin et al., 1978). For example, children who engage in solitary play often are field independent (Saracho, 1985).

There are also personality differences in the dimension of "playfulness" (Lieberman, 1965). Teacher ratings of children indicate a factor of playfulness in kindergartners (Lieberman, 1965) and in boys (Singer & Rummo, 1973). Intelligence levels appear to be a confounding factor, however. Characteristics of the home environment also appear to be related to children's playfulness (Barnett & Kleiber, 1984). Studies of adolescents and adults suggest that playfulness may be identified at these levels although its manifestations are much more varied in older subjects (J.N. Lieberman, 1977).

● **Gender/sex roles**

Gender differences in play development are cited by many researchers. Whether these differences are due to innate traits of each gender or to cultural expectations regarding sex roles that elicit and support differences is as yet unclear. There is evidence to support both hypotheses.

Gender differences reported include higher activity levels for preschool boys (Maccoby & Jacklin, 1974); more sedentary activity for girls (Rubin et al., 1976); different toy and play preferences (Fagot, 1974; Fein & Robertson, 1975; Roberts, 1980; Sutton-Smith & Rosenberg, 1961); and different thematic content in pretense (Connolly, 1981; Pulaski, 1973; Singer, 1973).

It is evident that sociocultural factors begin to influence sex role play interactions at a very early age. For example, women who interacted with unfamiliar infants whose gender had been labeled arbitrarily by researchers selected stereotypic male or female toys on the basis of the gender label (Smith & Lloyd, 1978). Their levels of verbal encouragement and responsiveness to gross motor play were significantly different for perceived boys and perceived girls; they showed more verbal encouragement to girls and more gross motor response to boys. Other studies show that parents of both sexes interact differently with sons and daughters (Arco, 1983; Bright & Stockdale, 1984; Crawley & Sherrod, 1984; Lamb, 1977; Power & Parke, 1980, 1983) and give children of different sexes different play environments and materials (Rheingold & Cook, 1975). These differences in play interaction in the home also relate to later peer popularity (MacDonald & Parke, 1984).

Peers also support sex stereotypes in play. Male peers are particularly likely to ridicule or punish other males for perceived inappropriate sex role play (Downs & Langlois, 1977; Fagot, 1978b; Pitcher & Schultz, 1983). Studies of play in other cultures also show differences in parent and teacher attitudes toward appropriate play for boys and girls (Ammar, 1954; A.B. Smith, 1983).

Play and games become even more differentiated between boys and girls as children reach middle childhood. Roberts (1980) and Sutton-Smith and Rosenberg (1961) report that more girls play traditional games during middle childhood while more boys channel their play into sports. Further, girls spend more time at home rather than in the neighborhood and play more quiet symbolic board games. Sutton-Smith and Rosenberg report that girls' play choices have broadened during the past half-century, whereas boys' choices have narrowed. Apparently cultural expectations for girls have changed to allow a greater range of appropriate behaviors without a similar broadening of appropriate behaviors for boys.

● **Stages and types of play**

In studies of the play of children from low income and/or minority groups and of children in non-Western cultures, differences in the onset and timing of stages in the development of pretense (Eiferman, 1971; Mead, 1975) or in its frequency and quality (Feitelson & Ross, 1973; Freyberg, 1973; Smilansky, 1968; Smith, 1977) have been observed. Many play

training studies have focused on ameliorating the "developmental lags" in pretense of children in low income or minority groups (Freyberg, 1973; Saltz, Dixon, & Johnson, 1977).

In a discussion of the research of Shotwell, Wolf and Gardner (1979), Gardner concludes, "Symbolic play is something that we take for granted as developmental psychologists in the United States, but it may be an irrelevancy as far as other cultures are concerned" (p. 148). Schwartzman (1984) and P.K. Smith (1983) contend that these differences are not necessarily deficits. Researchers agree that form, content, and amount of pretense vary widely depending on the context in which they are observed. Because the settings, props, and time available for play differ in various cultural contexts, types of play observed in cultures other than that of the American white middle class are also likely to be different.

Schwartzman (1984) states that the ethnographic literature gives evidence that imaginative play exists even when the typical contextual elicitors and props are not present. Children use whatever materials they find and design their own toys. She also disputes the assumption that play cannot occur if children are required to work. She cites Fortes (1976), who reports evidence of an integration of play and work within the same context. For example, while Talesi children are working at their assigned tasks, they are exhibiting the behaviors that signal that they are playing. Bloch (1984) found that children in Senegal engage in representational play using the materials that are available in their environment.

Black urban children are introduced early into the street culture of the city and have long play interaction periods with peers and with street adults (Ogbu, 1981). The peer and street culture provides an important educative environment and many skills are developed in street play (Foley & McGuire, 1981). Children play action games that explore their physical capabilities (e.g., climbing fences, throwing rocks at targets). They also experiment with available materials (e.g., cardboard boxes, iron bars, discarded wheels) and construct buildings (e.g., using material from abandoned houses). Children also engage in role-playing (e.g., "racing" abandoned cars), and they engage in many varieties of language play such as "signifying" or "playing the dozens" (i.e., engaging in verbal insult contests) (Foster, 1974). These play activities promote the competencies of physical agility, adaptability, verbal skill, and role-playing abilities needed by urban children and youth.

Although cross-cultural studies of older children's play have given pictures of childhood cultures in various countries (e.g., Abrahams, 1969; Caillois, 1961; Eiferman, 1971; Opie & Opie, 1969; Roberts, 1980), comparisons of the similarities and differences between play in other cultures and in the United States have been sparse. In one cross-cultural study, Roberts and Sutton-Smith (1962) identified three basic types of games requiring different competitive styles: (a) physical skill, (b) strategy, and (c) chance. They suggest that the predominant types of games observed depend on the cultural values of the society and that participating in a certain type of game assists children in handling conflicts and in learning the competencies needed in their particular culture. They conclude that play variety increases as complexity level of the culture increases. Eiferman reports failure to confirm this "enculturation" hypothesis in her observations of Israeli children's play.

● **Adult-child patterns of interaction**

Cultural differences in adult-child interaction patterns as influences on the course of play development have also been reported. Working class parents in Israel do not place as much value on play and provide less support for pretend play in the home than do middle class parents (Smilansky, 1968). The Singers (1979) report that in the Aymara Indian culture, adults prevent imaginary play although games are allowed.

Early adult-child interaction patterns differ among various ethnic groups in the United States. For example, Mexican-American mothers engage in more nonverbal interactions and ask fewer questions than do other American mothers (Laosa, 1977). Differences in socioeconomic status are often more influential than ethnic differences, however.

Laosa (1977) concludes that the modes or rules for interacting are learned at home and thus children may learn different interaction styles. Moreover, even the meaning of interactions that appear to be similar may differ across cultural or economic groups. Because adult modeling of play interactions influences the course of play development (El'konin, 1966; Smilansky, 1968; Sutton-Smith, 1979a), children

from various cultural backgrounds may exhibit different play developmental levels because of the interaction styles they have learned.

Ogbu (1981) argues that patterns of adult-child interaction in urban black families differ from those of middle class families because the competencies valued for survival differ. For example, adults exhibit abundant nurturance of infants but engage in adult-child contest relationships using verbal and physical rebuffs with children after infancy. Ogbu maintains that such combinations may help children learn to manipulate people and to fight back; thus, these interactions are adaptive for the urban environment. The differences in minority children's play may be influenced by these early social interactional patterns.

Because play serves as a form of communication of the shared understandings of a culture, the play transformations and paradoxical statements learned by children in a particular culture are influenced by the categories of that culture. Bateson (1956) contends that in play children learn what these cultural categories are; thus through play children learn frames for behavior. Communicating about play across cultures may be doubly hard because the behaviors that signal paradoxical meanings in one culture may have different meanings in other cultures. For example, humor is often difficult to translate from one culture to another because the meanings embedded in the humor are not shared.

Huizinga (1950), who was one of the first to study the "play-element in culture," contends that play is older than culture and is the root of culture. According to Huizinga, not only is play the prerequisite for language, literature, and art, but it is also the base from which law, ritual, and even war have developed. In his view, play is an essential element of life and thus, the development of play and the development of culture are always related.

Charting Developmental Trends

Although many of the trends in play development remain to be explored, a simple conceptual model that outlines the general trends of development can be drawn. It is based on trends identified by research, informal observation, and self-report information. Figure 3–1 gives these trends in play development.

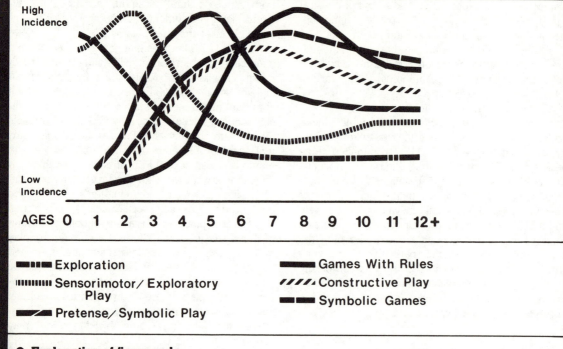

● **Explanation of figure code**

■■▮▮Exploration: This begins in early infancy and continues throughout life when new physical and social environments are encountered. Sensorimotor exploration becomes less observable, with more visual inspection, talking and question asking and verbal rule-seeking substituting for direct physical manipulation. Exploration is a life-long activity although modes of exploration change and amount of time devoted to exploration diminishes with experience.

▮▮▮▮▮ Sensorimotor/practice play: This begins during the second quarter of the first year of life and continues as the prime mode of play in infancy and early toddler years. It continues throughout life when new skills are being learned; when physical or mental mastery and coordination of skills are required for effective performance of games or sports (e.g., playing baseball); or when consolidation of specific learning skills is desired (e.g., manipulating computer programs).

◢◣◤ Pretense/symbolic play: This begins in the last quarter of the first year of life. Overt manifestations reach a peak in preschool through kindergarten years. Although elementary age children still engage in overt symbolic play, especially in non-

public environments (at home or in outdoor after-school play settings), their symbolic play begins to change character by becoming more "miniaturized," with small objects representing symbolic actors (e.g., paper dolls or toy soldiers); "abstracted," with ideas and language substituting for physically observable symbolic actions (e.g., writing secret codes); and "socialized," with redefinitions of appropriate settings or labels for playing actions (e.g., performing in "skits").

■■■■Games with rules: These begin with infant participation in adult initiated one-rule gamelike reciprocity play. Precursors appear in toddlers' spontaneous one-rule social reciprocity games. During preschool and kindergarten simple rule games, usually those previously adult initiated, are observed during spontaneous play. From these beginnings, games with rules increase in quantity and complexity during early elementary years and reach a peak in the middle elementary years. In later childhood they change character similarly to the way symbolic play changes; i.e., become "miniaturized" into board games; "abstracted" into paper and pencil or guessing games; and "socialized" into sports and other formal rule-driven games.

FIGURE 3–1 ● Trends in Play Development

////. Constructive play: As sensorimotor/practice play wanes and symbolic play increases, constructive play, which combines physical/motor repetitive activity with symbolic representation of objects and ideas, becomes a major play mode. Although concrete experiences are represented in constructions of young children (i.e., building a block "house"), older children begin to represent abstract concepts in their constructive play (i.e., painting what "war" or "peace" looks like), and these behaviors continue into adolescence and adulthood, although they may then be called art, craft, or construction rather than play.

■■ ■ Symbolic games: Although many early games have symbolic elements and much symbolic play has gamelike rules, during elementary age symbolic games become a prime mode of play. This type of play combines the games with rules structure with symbolic or pretense content. The rules of symbolic games make sense only within the play frame of pretense. Symbolic games are popular throughout adolescence and adulthood. The basic structure remains the same but the symbolic content is that which is relevant for each age, sex, or cultural group (e.g., Dungeons and Dragons, Monopoly, chess).

Note:

Adult festivals, craft shows, parades, pageants, fairs, performances, rituals, and contests combine elements of these various types of play. The means/ends distinction is blurred and the identified ends usually have symbolic meaning rather than realistic meaning. They include the qualities of playfulness: positive affect, exaggerated motor or verbal signals, suspension of reality, voluntary control, and internal motivation, although they are usually not labeled as play.

FIGURE 3–1 CONT'D ● Trends in Play Development

Conclusions

This chapter has given an overview of play development from infancy to adulthood. Although more empirical evidence describing developmental trends is available for some types of play than for others, a general picture of play development across the life span can be outlined. Play development parallels that of many other areas. For example, representational thought, language, and symbolic play begin at about the same time and ability to play games with rules coincides with concrete operational thought and physical coordination of complex movements.

While parents, educators, and other adults do recognize the importance of play in children's lives, they rarely think about it as a developmental phenomenon that follows an orderly, sequenced growth process similar to the processes of cognitive, language, moral, social, emotional, physical, or gender/sex role development. They often do not evaluate home, school, community, or cultural factors that can promote or hinder play development. Nor do they think about how their actions may influence its development. Thus, they may dismiss play as something that need not concern them.

If adults view play as a developmental phenomenon, however, they will be concerned with its development in childhood and will give attention to the factors that can enhance or limit its full expression. Also, if adults are aware that play is not just a childish phenomenon but that it is transformed into other ludic forms in adult life, they will be better able to find the "player" in themselves and to relate their playful experiences to the play of children.

Questions for Discussion

1. How might developmental problems in the earlier stages of play development affect later stages? Give an example, using at least three age periods.
2. What are some of the potential interactions between individual and cultural differences that might affect play development in the infant/toddler, the preschool, and the elementary-age period?

Research Replication Exercise

Select one of the types of play described in this chapter and charted in Figure 3–1, Trends in Play Development. Using a research method described in chapter 2, collect data on one or more children at three of the age levels where this type of play is likely to be exhibited. Describe your results in comparison with the information about stages of play development presented in this chapter.

Suggestions for Further Reading

Bruner, J. S., Jolly, A., & Sylva, K. (Eds.) (1976). *Play: Its role in development and evolution.* New York: Basic Books. Contains seminal articles, both classic and recent, that explore characteristics of animal and human play.

Schwartzman, H. B. (1978). *Transformations: The anthropology of children's play.* New York: Plenum Press. Provides an overview of the study of play from the anthropological perspective.

Herron, R. E., & Sutton-Smith, B. (1971). *Child's play.* New York: Wiley. Gives a range of perspectives on the study of play, including psychoanalytic, learning, cognitive, and ethological.

Rubin, K., Fein, G., & Vandenberg, B. (1983). Play. In E. M. Hetherington (Ed.), & P. H. Mussen (Series Ed.), *Handbook of child psychology. Vol. 4: Socialization, personality, and social development* (698–774). New York: Wiley. Summarizes the current research on play from the psychological perspective.

Some "Good News" and Some "Not-So-Good News" About Dramatic Play

ESSAY ON PLAY

KENNETH H. RUBIN

Play is the veritable "stuff" of childhood. It fills children's hours with joy, interest, and newfound creative experiences. Play serves parents with non-guilt-ridden "leave-time"; to be told, "Go play" is a reward not a punishment.

Now it seems that we all know what play is . . . it's fun, knowledge laden, non-punitive. But, for a phenomenon so easily recognized, it strikes me as being so surprising that play has a long-standing reputation of being impossible to define. Indeed, in our lengthy review of the literature of children's play written for the most recent edition of *Handbook of Child Psychology* (1983), Greta Fein, Brian Vandenberg, and I spend countless words and pages dealing with the difficulties of defining play.

In the following paragraphs, I will endeavor to provide a relatively brief definition of play. I will then describe some recent findings, freshly derived from The Waterloo Longitudinal Project, suggesting that all is not well for play advocates. Play, as defined herein, will be shown to be associated with positive childhood characteristics only in some social settings and only at certain ages.

Play Defined

The shortest and perhaps most reasonable definition of play is simply, "it's just pretend." Ask any two adults (i.e., preferably adults who are familiar with children or who have good memories of their own childhood) to

67

visit a preschool, a playground, or a neigh-borhood backyard. Request these adults to note any incidence of "just pretend." There is really no need to supply your observers with lengthy observation training sessions. My prediction is that "just pretend" is sufficient information to produce readily identifiable and reliable codings of "play." Matthews and Matthews (1982) have argued convincingly for the paradigm case approach to the study of play.

But as we peek into the infrastructure of play, we discover that there is much more to it than "just pretend." The critical definitional characteristics are as follows:

1. Play is intrinsically motivated; it occurs because the child is moved to pursue a given activity, not because it is forced on him or her or reinforced by others.
2. Play is its own "means" and "ends"; it is a behavior that is not goal oriented. If any goal exists, it is simply to enjoy the activity and have fun.
3. Play is non-rule-governed. There is no set number of guidelines passed on from generation to generation or from child to child regarding the rules for this or that type of play. In this regard, play is distinguished from *games* that are rule governed, competitive, and often not enjoyable!
4. In play, children impose their own meanings on objects. They are past the "stage" of discovering what a given object does (i.e., they are finished exploring object properties). During play, children are fueled by the question, "What is it that I can do with these things?" and not by the question, "What's this object all about?"

5. Play involves some element of nonliterality. It involves, as Fein (1985b) puts it, "denotative license," in that children invent new meanings for real world objects and activities. Objects are transformed and decontextualized (e.g., a piece of cardboard becomes a "magic mirror"), and people assume nonliteral identities (e.g., 4-year-old Jason becomes Prince Adam, holder of the "magic mirror"). In short, play involves pretense.

To summarize, play is an enjoyable, intrinsically motivated behavior that is non-rule-governed, non-goal-oriented, and "just pretend." Rubin et al. (1983) give a more refined version of this definition.

The "Good News" About Play

Given these characteristics of play, it seems reasonable to ask, "What's so good about it?" To those who are serious students of play (a contradiction of terms), the answers seem obvious. In infancy and toddlerhood, when objects are substituted for the real things (e.g., a stuffed Paddington bear is "baby"; an empty slipper is "Paddington's glass of milk") or when activities are transformed and decontextualized (e.g., the 4-year-old protagonist with clenched teeth is playing the role of Daddy when he's angry), there is more to the behavior than "it's just pretend." Pretense designates mental representation. It is a marker of cognitive maturation; things can substitute for other things and activities don't have to be taken literally. Furthermore, play as representation indicates that children recognize and remember things and people not in present view, and they can act out these recognitions in play. So just as language and words are taken as representational substitutes for the real things, so too is play. Interestingly, language and the onset of representational (i.e., pretend) play appear to arrive in the human repertoire at approximately the same time (e.g., McCune, 1985). The good news, then, is that in infancy and toddlerhood, pretend is a marker of cognitive (i.e., representational) development and the enactment of play allows the practice of representational skills.

More good news: In the preschool and kindergarten years, pretend becomes more sociable. Children begin to share the nonliteral meanings of their pretend worlds with parents, siblings, and perhaps most important, peers. They can create or borrow new roles for themselves (e.g., "I'll be He-Man, you're Skeletor, she's She-Ra"). They can deliberate and negotiate over who will play these roles and at what times (e.g., "O.K., I'll be Skeletor this time, but next time I get to be She-Ra"). Children can plan numerous creative scenarios for their social-fantasy activities (e.g., "Remember, She-Ra only rescues He-Man if he's in real danger; otherwise, it'll be two against one and Skeletor will always lose!")

The bottom line is that sociodramatic play allows young children to create and adopt new roles and changeable rules. It allows them to practice persuasion, negotiation, cooperation, and even assertion/defense (e.g., in rough-and-tumble activities), all within a nonliteral framework. As such sociodramatic play has been viewed by many psychologists as a means by which children learn to communicate, negotiate, create, problem-solve, and understand social roles, rules, and perspectives.

So far the news is all good. Indeed, the extant literature indicates that young children who engage in high frequencies of sociodramatic play are (a) more popular among their peers, (b) more intelligent, (c) more creative, and (d) better social-cognizers and perspective takers than their age mates, who are less inclined to participate in social-pretense (see Rubin et al., 1983, for a relevant review). What then could possibly be wrong with play?

Some "Not So Good" News About Play

Given all the good news, it is important to reveal some new findings that suggest that when play as defined above is found in high frequencies in certain social contexts, or when it is found at certain ages, it may warrant the raising of a red warning flag. It may be a convenient index of "something not quite right."

First, with regard to the social context, it is interesting to note that from ages 3 to 5, classroom or playground pretend occurs mainly when children are interacting with others (Rubin et al., 1983). In our research, we have discovered that preschoolers and kindergartners who engage in relatively high frequencies of classroom or outdoor solitary pretense and in pretense near, but not with others (i.e., parallel-pretense), are disliked by peers and are perceived by teachers as socially incompetent (Rubin, 1982b). Furthermore, these nonsocial pretenders are less able to understand other people's perspectives and they are less able to produce many solutions to common interpersonal dilemmas (e.g., obtaining a desired toy from a peer) than their more sociable pretending counterparts (Rubin, 1985a). Finally, our data indicate that the frequent display of nonsocial classroom pretense in kindergarten is predictive of social skills deficits when children are in grade two.

Taken together, these data suggest that high frequencies of nonsocial pretense, when children are in formal group settings (i.e., not when they are home alone in their rooms), reflect a lag in the development of social skills. The implication is that not all forms of dramatic play are "good for" young children. Sociodramatic play is clearly productive; nonsocial pretense, in group settings, is far less beneficial and perhaps reflects some developmental lag.

The other news about dramatic play concerns the age at which it is exhibited. In our recent studies concerning the development of social skills and peer relationships, we have found that the frequent display of sociodramatic play becomes an increasingly less important marker of competence with age. Thus for example, in grade two, the frequent display of sociodramatic play in group settings does not correlate significantly with teacher and peer assessments of social skills and positive peer relationships. By grade four, children who spend much of their time in sociodramatic play are actually disliked by peers and rated as aggressive by peers and

teachers. Furthermore, they are more likely to display immature social behaviors and play patterns when in groups (e.g., more sensorimotor play and more solitary play). The play-like behavior in grade two, and especially in grade four, that appears to take the place of sociodramatic activity as a marker of social competence is group games with rules. This type of activity involves the simultaneous understanding of rules, cooperation, competition, turn taking, and perspective taking.

To summarize, with development, children's play becomes increasingly symbolic and sociable. The 2- and 3-year-old who spends a good deal of time pretending while alone or near others is demonstrating maturity and cognitive competence. From ages 4 through 6, children who share their pretend world with their peers are viewed as socially and cognitively skilled and creative. The nonsocial pretender appears to evidence both social and cognitive difficulties. Finally, during the concrete operational years (i.e., 6 or 7 through 10 or 11, social and cognitive prowess is associated not with sociodramatic play, but with formalized, rule-governed cooperative/competitive games. Indeed, the frequent display of social pretense at age 10 is as strong a marker of immaturity and developmental lag as nonsocial pretense at ages 4 and 5.

The good news? Play appears to serve children well through the early years of childhood. The bad news? Childhood is fleeting; by the time children reach the mid-elementary school years social pretense is not enough. Children are expected to exhibit all the real world competencies representative of "success" in middle class North America. They must be able to attend to and abide by rules, they must willingly and competently take turns, and they must demonstrate a strong working knowledge of the double-edged concept of cooperation/competition. To be a "creative game player" (e.g., "four strikes and you're out; you get one turn, I get three") is only acceptable until such time that the concept of "game" is understood. After that time (i.e., in concrete operations), the bending of rules and the abandonment of the real world for the world of fantasy becomes increasingly associated with peer rejection and the lack of social skills. The really bad news then is that the glorious play worlds of Care Bears, He-Man, Princess Leia, and Optimus Prime appear to crumble within the first 10 years of childhood. The really good news is that the skills developed in their social fantasy worlds probably help children immeasurably to become competent game players and citizens in their real worlds of North American society.

SECTION TWO

The Relationship of Play to Other Areas of Development

In his poems, A. A. Milne (1924, 1927) gives a picture of the many ways that play relates to the development of the child. For example, he speaks of the imperatives of motor development:

> Christopher Robin goes
> Hoppity, hoppity,
> Hoppity, hoppity, hop.
> Whenever I tell him
> Politely to stop it, he
> Says he can't possibly stop. . . .

and of the ways that play serves the imagination and meets social and emotional needs:

Binker—what I call him—is a secret of my own,
And Binker is the reason why I never feel alone.
Playing in the nursery, sitting on the stair,
Whatever I am busy at,
Binker will be there.

> Oh, Daddy is clever, he's a clever sort of man,
> And Mummy is the best since the world began,
> And Nanny is Nanny, and I call her Nan—
> > But they can't
> > See
> > Binker . . .

As demonstrated by the words of Milne, the relationship of play to thinking, to feeling, and to acting is clear.

One of the major interests of play researchers has been to explore how play development affects children's cognitive, language, moral, emotional, social, gender/sex role, and physical/motor development. As Vandenberg (1982) observes, those who study play have often tied their questions to other developmental research topics because play has not always been seen as a respectable topic of research. Researchers reason that demonstrating a relationship between play and cognitive, language, or other development may foster recognition of the importance of play research and of the role of play in education.

Researchers have also been interested in observing how the development of children with special needs might be helped through the use of playful educational methods. The results of these studies have implications for special needs environments, such as hospitals, because play is more likely to be allowed in the hospital setting if research demonstrates a linkage between play and physical or emotional health.

The number of studies related to specific developmental areas varies in proportion to how important those areas are as current child development issues. For example, there are many more current studies relating play to cognitive development than to physical/motor development. In the twenties and thirties, when physical/motor development was of great interest, more studies of play related to that area and few were focused on cognitive development.

Chapter 4 reviews the theoretical and research literature on play and cognitive, language, and moral development. The relationship of play to social, emotional, and gender/sex role development is discussed in chapter 5, and links to physical/motor development are described in chapter 6 which also reviews the relationship of play to the development of children with special needs.

The essayists raise a number of issues concerning the educational implications of these relationships.

Imaginative Play and Human Development: Schemas, Scripts, and Possibilities

JEROME L. SINGER ● DOROTHY G. SINGER

Play Viewed From a Cognitive-Affective Perspective

We are presently in an era, reflecting no doubt a scientific "paradigm change," in which our conception of human beings presents them as information-processing creatures, seeking continuously to organize and to give meaning to stimuli from the physical and social environment, from their own memory store or from the ongoing machinery of their bodies, forming such information into organized meaning structures (Kreitler & Kreitler, 1976; Singer, 1973, 1984). Indeed, following upon the great insights of Silvan Tomkins (1962–1963) and the supportive empirical research of Izard, Ekman, Schwartz, and others (Singer, 1984), we today view humans as individuals whose differen-

tiated emotional response patterns are closely intertwined with the novelty, complexity, and other structural properties of the information they confront from moment to moment. A major task of childhood is the organization of the complex and varied stimuli presented to the infant or toddler into structures that can provide anticipatory sets and expectations as each new environmental situation is confronted. Faced with new situations of information that cannot be matched against previously established schemas, the child will at first be startled and even frightened. As the child begins to assimilate (Piaget, 1962) new material with established schemas, the emotion may change from fear to interest and even excitement, and further exploration may occur. As matches are made and well assimilated, the child may experience the emotion of joy (Singer, 1973; Tomkins, 1962–1963).

From this perspective, we can understand symbolic or imaginative play in early childhood as a major way in which the child learns to develop new schemas and script structures that can become the basis for a continuous exploratory and adaptive interaction with the changing environment. The child's attempt to assimilate the complex novel material, whether from the physical or from the social environment, is extremely difficult and complex because the child approaches each situation with such a limited repertory of preestablished schemas or action-oriented scripts. It is at this juncture that we probably see beginnings of symbolic and fantasy or make-believe processes (Singer & Revenson, 1978).

The efforts at imitation of adult behaviors by the child are impeded on a number of counts: There is inadequate verbal capacity, as yet insufficiently differentiated motor skill, and, in addition, only a very limited experiential base of comprehending the nature of the adult action or of the large objects that move around (e.g., in one's environment in a public street). Children can in effect control these novel and strange experiences by creating a miniature environment in which they attempt to assimilate their previously imitated actions or overheard sounds or phrases by reducing them to the manageable proportions of floor games with blocks or toys. By moving blocks up and down and imitating the sound effects of cars or trucks or by introducing snatches of adult phrases that are often not well understood, the child rehearses and experiments in the formation of new schemas. To the extent that adults or other older children occasionally offer corrective suggestions for the naturally faulty assimilations that constitute the "cuteness" of children's play, the child may gradually correct many of the schemas-in-formation and emerge with reasonably socialized private schemas and action scripts that will function effectively in new social situations.

Fears, Frightening Images, and the Origins of Transference

One must of course understand play as a form of schema formation in relation to the different age levels and the cognitive capacities or environmental demands at the various stages of development. For the preschool period, and even for the somewhat later phases of childhood, there are many events and experiences particularly difficult to assimilate and to match with already established schemas. Consider the situation of the young child lying in bed at night and seeing the shifting play of shadows on the wall. Perhaps flashes of lights from passing automobiles cast different patterns on the wall. There are many noises one discerns at night that take on figural properties compared with the normal background din of the daytime. The difficulties the child faces in trying to assimilate these into an established schema certainly must arouse negative affects such as fear. In addition, in the quietness of presleep children experience an upsurge of their own memories and fantasies and awareness of unfulfilled plans or partially assimilated material (i.e., what Freud has termed the *day residue*), which we might call simply *unfinished business*—the various unresolved issues or incompletely assimilated materials of the child's day-to-day life. Klinger (1970) has elaborated on the notion of the "current concerns" that are the major characteristics of adults' as well as children's dreams and fantasies and the ongoing stream of thoughts. Breger, Hunter, and Cane (1971) have called attention to the role of unresolved stress in generating dream and fantasy content.

Children may make efforts to form schemas based on what they already have available as organized structures. Such efforts include remembering tales of faraway places, religious and supernatural plots that adults have already made available to the child. Nowadays new thoughts are related to the considerable material based on television and film. In an effort to form these viewed experiences into play structures and make-believe, the child may develop sets of relatively private "mythologies," schemas or

scripts about the unknown or novel in interpersonal relations that are not necessarily subject to later correction because of the private way in which they have been developed. One might argue that it is this type of formation, growing out of the child's efforts at play, that builds at least some of the basis for what in adult life can be seen as the transference phenomenon, that is, the attribution to adults in ordinary social situations of expectations and beliefs derived from childhood or early life experiences (Singer, 1985).

The complexity of symbolism available to us today is built into our language and our communication media. One need really make no assumptions of a genetic coding or archetype to explain the multilayered symbolism that emerges in psychotherapy and mental imagery techniques. With advertising writers actively providing us with phallic automobiles and symbolic mistresses perched within them, what need do we have of the notion of racial unconscious to account for metaphors in our dreams or fantasies? Symbolism pervades our lives as part of our cultural heritage and as part of the very metaphorical characteristics that human beings lend to their schemas in social settings. That these should emerge from the child's efforts at creating manageable play forms should not be so surprising. Thus, the make-believe play of the child, while certainly essentially an adaptive function and critical for the formation of schemas about the environment, also creates the possibility, particularly in the earlier years, for the formation of expectancies about human interaction.

The Role of Parents as Mediators

Our own recent research has focused on the special ways in which parents or other adult caregivers in the family play a critical role in mediating the complexity of the child's physical and social environment (Desmond, Singer, Singer, Calam, & Colimore, 1985; Singer & Singer, 1984; Singer & Singer, 1985). There is considerable evidence that children's ability to use their own imaginative skills and make-believe for effective assimilation functions and schema formations depends in

part on the extent to which adults interact with them. Such interaction may be evident when adults label aspects of the environment, and/or tell children stories so that the youngsters can learn to frame complex events within organized structures. By tolerating imaginative play and overt verbalization by the preschooler, parents also foster self-development of these skills.

In our own research we have found that a score developed from parent questionnaires, which we have called *discussion versus prescription/discipline*, identifies those parents who engage in labeling, explaining, and storytelling. The children of parents who score higher on this dimension tend to be more capable of self-control in waiting situations, show less overt aggressive behavior, show better general knowledge assimilation from the environment, and tend to be less susceptible to some of the more negative effects of heavy television viewing. Our studies also indicate that heavy viewing of television by children can preclude the opportunities for practicing make-believe play that give the child an independent ability to organize and control new information and form it into schemas. Instead, heavy viewers tend simply to become dependent on television and seem to show less general ability to organize and comprehend new material, including plots from television plays (Desmond et al., 1985; Singer & Singer, 1983). Indeed, we have evidence that children who engage in extensive viewing of television at the preschool and early school-age years show less imaginativeness in their play during the following years as measured by block play, interviews with the children, and their responses to projective techniques (Singer, Singer, & Rapaczynski, 1984).

In summary, we propose that imaginative play functions to enhance the child's need for organizing environmental complexity into meaningful schemas and scripts about possible future actions. It also aids children in experiencing control over the environment and in expressing more positive affective responses. In make-believe play, children are exposed to the world of the possible, a major dimension of human experience; but children confront this world on their own terms.

Too often, adults' neglect and failure to engage the child in storytelling or to read books to the child, as well as parents' occa-sional direct humiliation of the child's efforts at imagination, may hinder the natural evolution of the child's use of make-believe for schema formation. Our data show again and again that constructive parental interaction as well as ample opportunities for practice by the child of make-believe games leads not only to improved cognitive performance by the child, but also to greater control over aggression and restlessness and to evidence of the positive emotions of interest-excitement and joy.

The Relationship of Play to Cognitive, Language, and Moral Development

IRENE ATHEY

Early childhood educators have long cherished the belief that spontaneous play can nourish children's intellectual and social development (Isaacs, 1933). This belief has been supported by theorists writing from Freudian and Piagetian perspectives (Erikson, 1977; Piaget, 1952, 1962). During the past 10 to 15 years, a new trend has become evident; play has increasingly become the subject of empirical research by developmental psychologists, as may be seen from an examination of the relevant journals, national conference programs, and recent reviews (Christie, 1980b; Fein, 1981; Levy, 1984; Rubin, Fein, & Vandenberg, 1983; Smith, 1977).

This chapter will discuss the theoretical and research-based evidence that describes ways in which play contributes to cognitive, language, and moral aspects of child development. The exposition will draw primarily upon Piagetian theory and research (1926, 1932, 1952, 1962), but also from work

in learning theory (e.g., Gagne, 1977) and information processing (e.g., Klahr & Wallace, 1970). Throughout the course of the discussion it will be necessary to keep in mind the distinction between ways in which particular forms of play *reflect* corresponding developmental stages and ways in which the play behaviors themselves *contribute* to the evolution of these stages. The former is easier to document than the latter. Indeed, certain theorists, such as Piaget, overcome this difficulty by integrating their accounts of play into broader theoretical formulations of cognitive development. Demonstrating that play in general or any form of play in particular is a necessary or sufficient condition—or even a contributing factor—to development in general or to the emergence of a particular aspect such as development of a single concept, is necessarily more speculative but also offers a fertile field for research. A question less frequently asked, but equally intriguing, is that posed by Rubin et al. (1983) as to whether and to what extent other skills such as problem solving in turn facilitate play.

Generic and Specific Aspects of Mental Growth

Human beings differ most markedly from other species in the levels of abstraction they attain in their thinking and language. This achievement is possible because humans, by virtue of their neurological structures, are able to develop mechanisms and strategies for dealing with a barrage of information that is often confusing and sometimes overwhelming. These strategies include ways of organizing, storing, and retrieving information, and are the end product of a continuous, lifelong process of learning that starts at birth. This process makes possible not only advanced intellectual operations but also symbolic systems such as language and higher orders of reasoning pertaining to the social and moral sphere. It can be argued

---

TABLE 4–1 ● Generic and Specific Aspects of Mental Growth

Generic Function	Specific Process
(1) Discriminate between relevant and irrelevant information	a. Selective attention (ignoring or filtering incoming stimuli; being alert to novel or potentially noxious stimuli) b. Categorization (grouping incoming stimuli in different ways) c. Generalization (transferring relevant cues to new situations) d. Hypothesis testing (postulating and testing relationships between events) e. Problem solving (identifying relevant aspects of problems and suggesting appropriate solutions) f. Creativity (generating original solutions to old or new problems)
(2) Generate more information from fewer cues	g. Association (developing expectations of regularly occurring events in the environment) h. Object identification (making inferences based on past experiences) i. Symbolic representation (using images, symbols, signs, etc., to represent objects or events) j. Memory (using increasingly complex stategies to re-create experience) k. Concept learning (organizing physical events in terms of space, time, number, order, relationships, cause-effect, probability of occurrence) l. Class inclusion (organizing concepts in hierarchies of classes and subclasses) m. Rule learning (inferring scientific principles, social and moral codes based on regularity of relationships between objects, persons, events, or concepts) n. Logical operations (using logical operators, e.g., identity, reversibility, etc.)
(3) Attain increasingly higher levels of abstraction	o. Representational thought (using language, writing systems, etc., to represent objects) p. Reasoning (making hypothetical-deductive chains of inference) q. Metacognitive and metalinguistic awareness (reasoning about one's own intellectual and linguistic functioning)

with some plausibility that, in this cumulative and reiterative process, play makes both direct contributions at given stages and also a long-range, indirect contribution by providing a basis for further learning.

Developmental psychologists, whose business is to chart the course of learning, do not always agree about the route that is followed or the major landmarks along the way. They do agree, however, that cognitive growth involves many factors. Among the most important of these are: (a) greater ability to discriminate between information that is relevant or irrelevant to a given purpose, (b) increased adeptness in using fewer cues to generate more information, and (c) higher levels of abstraction. Each of these three aspects of growth involves a large number of more specific functions, the more important of which are presented in Table 4–1.

This classification scheme can be used to illustrate some of the ways play interacts with and promotes development of specific functions, thereby contributing to more global aspects of human growth. Some of the specific processes enumerated in Table 4–1 can be used to illustrate the relationship of play to cognitive, linguistic, and moral development. For example, concept development (2–k) and problem solving (1–e) are presented as primary components of cognitive development; categorization (1–b) and generalization (1–c) are treated as necessary precursors of concept learning (2–k), while class inclusion (2–l) is viewed as a special case of concept learning. Under problem solving are subsumed reasoning (3–p), logical operations (2–n), hypothesis testing (1–d), and creativity (1–f) as a special case of problem solving. Language development includes, for purposes of this discussion, elements of the phonological (e.g., Table 4–2, 1–b, 2–d), syntactic (e.g. Table 4–2, 3–g), semantic (e.g. Table 4–2, 5–m, 6–n), and pragmatic (e.g., Table 4–2, 8–p) systems, with emphasis on symbolic representation. Finally, moral development is considered as a subclass of rule learning (2–m) combined with an unusual measure of metacognitive awareness (3–q). It should be clearly understood, however, that these functions have been selected for illustrative purposes only, and that operation of any of the higher mental processes involves a complex interplay of many different abilities.

Cognitive Development and Its Relationship to Play

H. (2 years, 6 months) is playing with the plastic connecting beads. She takes two beads out of the box and connects them, then takes another one. While trying to attach it, she looks up at people talking in the hallway, but never stops her attempt to connect the third bead. H. finally connects it and places the three connected beads next to the group of three that she had previously put together. H. stares at the pattern of the first group (yellow, yellow, blue), then at the pattern of the second group (yellow, red, red). She takes out a blue bead, placing it next to the other blue bead in the first pattern. Then she takes out a red bead and connects it to the other red ones. H. takes a yellow bead, and after looking at both patterns intently, adds the yellow bead to the yellow ones in the second group. She then connects the yellow ends of the two groups, making one long pattern. And then she smiles.

Two of the major areas related to cognitive functioning at all ages are the network of concepts and the ability to solve problems. Early experiences are important in establishing the foundation for these processes both in terms of content and method. For example, modes of categorization learned in the formative years may influence the concepts of later periods and the flexibility with which the person learns new categories.

● The development of concepts

Essential processes for concept development are categorization (Table 4–1, 1–b), generalization (1–c), concept acquisition (2–k), and class inclusion (2–l). Each of these processes is enhanced by play; they also further development of play itself.

Categorization (1–b). Categorization of objects and events is important in its own right and also as a foundation for some other types of learning such as concept and rule identification. The infant's preference for certain types of objects or events over others shows that a primitive type of categorization evolves early in life. How events are categorized thereafter appears to be a function of children's ability to impose their own structure in a way that is meaningful for them. This ability is manifested in the process Piaget calls *assimilation*, that is, the integration of any sort of reality into a structure, a process that is fundamental to learning. Play, he further maintains, is pure assimilation (i.e., the need to modify behavior to fit reality is suspended). In Piaget's theory, infant play provides the foundation for later learning of categorization skills. (For examples of categorization behavior, see Piaget's descriptions of his daughter Jacqueline's play).

Children construct categories that are meaningful to them and appropriate to their developmental level. Often this construction is not the result of adults drawing attention to the category, but evolves through children's spontaneous activity and observation. Indeed, there is some evidence that they are resistant to training on adult-based categories. Tenney (1973), for example, found that when asked to generate a category in response to a familiar stimulus word, kindergarten children tended to produce rhymes (e.g., blue: "boo-clue-glue"), whereas third- and sixth-grade children could utilize structures for generating categories under a self-planned condition (i.e., in which the category was not suggested by the experimenter). Training procedures designed to induce children to use cognitive structures do not appear to have long-term success (Scribner & Cole, 1973). Inhelder and Piaget (1964) also point to the young child's tendency to categorize on the basis of spatial considerations (e.g., objects that happen to be close together), subjective preference (e.g., "Because I like them"), or other irrelevant criteria.

The significance of play in this regard lies in the fact that it not only brings the child in contact with a whole range of stimuli designed to induce categorizing behavior, but that this behavior develops in pace with the child's ability (DeLoache, Sugarman, & Brown, 1985). The categories are induced from within, not imposed from without, and are thus assimilated into the child's existing mental structures. The subjective groupings give way to broader, but more functional, categories, such as things to eat, or objects found in certain rooms of the house, or big toys and little toys.

As with other kinds of learning, children seem to benefit most from exposure to behavior that is slightly above the level at which they are operating. Kuhn (1972) found that if children are allowed to observe a model performing classification tasks, they tend to imitate classificatory behavior that is at the same level or slightly higher than their own. Play situations in which children are exposed to other children who are operating at a slightly higher level is therefore optimal for encouraging imitation that leads to growth. For example, more mature play in preschoolers is positively correlated with their classification skills (Rubin & Maioni, 1975).

Some learning of categories occurs as the result of instruction, but a good deal comes about through the child's own leisure activities, such as reading or social games like 20 Questions. Many of the games of elementary school children seem to involve collecting and categorizing large assortments of objects, including stamps, license numbers, badges, rocks, pressed flowers, or newspaper clippings. Occasionally, the collection of a certain class of objects becomes very popular among children of this age. Trading among collectors is brisk, and competition for the best specimens may become quite fierce.

Although research evidence is, as yet, sparse, it appears that play enhances categorization skills, leading to better discrimination and greater attention to relevant cues at all developmental levels.

Generalization (1–c).   Generalization refers to the transfer of concepts or principles to new situations. Such transfer implies discrimination of those aspects in the original situation that are relevant to the new situation. Transfer is promoted by exposure to novel situations, but the nature and degree of novelty are important. Stimuli that are too novel or too complex lead to disorganized behavior and transfer does not take place. The new situation must be sufficiently similar to the old in ways the child can perceive, yet possess clearly discriminable novel aspects so that generalization can occur. For the young baby, surrounding events appear to be a succession of disconnected sense perceptions rather than meaningful and organized sequences. The smiling face of a parent appearing above the crib at a certain time may seem to have little connection with the serious or worried face appearing at some other time. Gradually, however, the infant learns to generalize across situations and to ignore irrelevant cues such as a hat worn on the head. Continuous periods in which parents engage in prolonged play with their baby are particularly valuable in this regard, for under these conditions, the infant can see the changing facial expressions and associate them with the rhythm and intonation of the voice. This generalization may serve as the prototype of understanding the identity and continuity of all objects, physical and social.

Another generalization that the infant learns in the course of random, playful activity is that of self-as-cause. A hand moving through space may strike an object, causing it to swing or rattle. At first, the child perceives no connection between these two events, but with repeated occurrence, the child is able to generalize and hence to engage in the purposeful activity required to set these events in motion (Piaget, 1952).

The generalizations learned by young children through play are many and varied (Kamii & DeVries, 1978). They learn that blocks are heavy, while feathers are light, that corks float, while marbles sink. They find that Bobby does not seem to mind when his toy is snatched from him, but Andrew retaliates with his fists, and Sally cries and screams to get the teacher's attention. Play situations may be particularly conducive to learning generalizations if only because the child tends to have greater control over the situation than is often the case in other kinds of events. While a wealth of anecdotal evidence is available to support the contention that play provides optimum opportunities for children to draw generalizations (e.g., Isaacs, 1930/1966), systematic research on this issue is needed.

During the years from 2 to 7, the child is in the preoperational stage of intelligence. According to Piaget, this means that the child's thinking is egocentric (i.e., limited to one perspective) and unidimensional (i.e., concentrating on a single aspect of an object or event). Children's generalizations at this age are rather simple, based on particular features of the situation that strike their fancy, or on an incomplete understanding of the complexities involved.

Elementary school children, on the other hand, have reached the stage of concrete operations, when simultaneous attention to two or more aspects becomes possible. Play with physical objects now has

an important role in the acquisition of more complex generalizations. Children of this age are much more aware of the properties and limitations of physical objects, and of ways in which they can be reformed or regrouped to suit different purposes. Games of skill become possible, because children are now able to take into account a number of factors such as the trajectory and speed of a ball, the weight of a bat or racket, the direction of the wind, and the opponent's tactics. Advanced levels of motor coordination require not only coordination of one's own body but also coordination of self with the movements of objects and other people (Keogh, 1977). Although very young children can acquire skills such as swimming or ball throwing and catching, it is at the elementary school level that attention to such factors as coordination and style becomes possible, because children are now able to make generalizations about the relative positions of various parts of the body as a particular movement is made. Although some of these generalizations may be transmitted through verbal instructions, the surest way to learn them is by engaging in the activity itself. In the social sphere, generalizations are also becoming quite sophisticated, incorporating more than a single factor. For example, in communal games, rules may be changed if the parties concerned agree that this would make the game more interesting. Fair play, which in the earliest years meant equal treatment for everybody, now includes consideration of handicaps or other factors.

Thus, at all levels of infancy and childhood, play contributes to generalization.

Concept learning (2–k). Concept learning requires the interaction of discrimination and generalization. Infants are capable of some discriminations soon after birth, and children a little over a year old can form their own simple generalizations. Labeling of objects precedes concept learning, but gradually, through exposure to a variety of instances, the child is led to discriminate those salient features of an object that define it as a member of a class, and to generalize this insight to new exemplars. Negative instances are also valuable in defining the limits of the concept.

Concepts are acquired gradually, involve a long period of hypothesis testing and are subject to the errors of faulty discrimination and overgeneralization. Exploration and manipulation of objects in play provides the conditions that promote concept learning in young children. Not only do the materials themselves reinforce or disconfirm the child's hypotheses, but feedback from other children provides cognitive stimulation to broaden and deepen the conceptual repertoire (Piaget, 1952). The child's store of concepts increases geometrically during the early childhood years.

Apart from the concepts of familiar objects, there are the more fundamental, abstract concepts of space and time, cause and effect, probability and number, which provide the basis for all thinking about objects and events. It strains the imagination to think of a universe in which objects are not extended in space or events do not occur in temporal sequence. Although children are born with predispositions to perceive the world in certain ways (Bower, 1982; Fantz, 1966), these structures are modified through learning. Piaget's series of books on children's concepts emphasizes how gradually children pass through stages or successive approximations to eventual attainment of the adult view.

Play is a medium for testing out and revising children's immature concepts. For example, in moving around in large, open spaces or in smaller interior rooms, children are learning about space, about cues received in depth perception that signal the distance of an object, the relative size of near and remote objects, which objects can be pulled through the narrow space between two trees or tables, and many other dimensions that together constitute the concept of space. Time is a more difficult concept, but soon expressions such as "in a few minutes," "in a little while," or "tomorrow," come to have meaning when children must take turns with their toys, or anticipate a popular activity. Although children frequently collapse time intervals (e.g., in their domestic play), they do learn much about time sequences in this manner.

The notion of cause probably originates in the discovery of self-as-cause, which begins when the baby discovers that a noise can be made by striking the rattle against the crib. When infants become mobile, the range of objects over which they can exert this power vastly increases (Piaget, 1952). About the same time, they discover the power of producing effects in the people around them. Objects, including other people, are also perceived as causative agents, possessing a will of their own (i.e.,

Piaget's stage of animism). In their preschool years, children begin to learn about specific cause-effect relationships. As they play with large and small toys, sand, water, clay, and other materials, by pushing and pulling, stretching and squeezing, patting and stroking, sucking and blowing, and watching adults and other children do the same, associations that undergird the concept of cause and effect are learned through hundreds of such relationships (Dansky & Silverman, 1973).

Through observation of events, young children also learn about probabilities. Probability as a mathematical concept is still imprecise in young children's thinking, but children may be able to make fairly accurate predictions about certain kinds of events that they have observed regularly.

In the elementary school years, play and games continue to have an important role in the development of concepts. Based on their research into the nature of children's concepts in the concrete-operational period, Furth and others (e.g., Furth & Wachs, 1974) have developed several series of "thinking games" for the specific purpose of promoting children's understanding and reasoning. Some schools have adopted simulation games to develop concepts such as democracy or capitalism. Commercial games like Monopoly may also serve a similar purpose.

Class inclusion (2–1).   Class inclusion (i.e., the ability to understand sets and subsets) is a more difficult form of concept learning that occurs at about the age of 7. Inhelder and Piaget (1964) found that preschool children have formed many concepts, but seem to be unaware of the fact that concepts may be grouped hierarchically. For example, they tend to use a class term such as "bird" interchangeably with a member of a class such as "robin," and are unaware of more abstract categories such as mammal or vertebrate. The differentiation into a superordinate and subordinate class system probably comes about through social interaction with peers who have already moved to the stage of class inclusion, but this kind of concept learning often proves resistant to overt instruction. Games such as 20 Questions, which emphasize the set-subset relationship, or games in which opposing teams take turns to think of a member of a class or species would seem to be very valuable in this regard, fostering cooperation and teamwork as well.

● Play and the development of higher order thinking

Higher order thinking requires the ability to solve problems. Some of the processes involved in higher order thinking are reasoning (Table 4–l, 3–p), logical operations (2–n), hypothesis testing (1–d), problem solving (1–e), and creative thinking (1–f). Play is related to all of these processes.

Reasoning (3–p). Reasoning (i.e., mentally operating on symbolic objects) is basic to problem-solving ability. According to Berlyne (1970). "reasoning and thinking are highly specialized and intricate ways of manipulating and responding to symbols" (p. 940). The sensorimotor intelligence of the infant cannot properly be called reasoning by this definition. Nevertheless, Piaget would maintain that sensorimotor activity is an essential precursor of later reasoning and that by engaging in sensorimotor play, the infant is laying the foundations of thinking and reasoning. Certainly, much behavior at this stage conveys the impression that some thinking is going on. It is "as if" reasoning were taking place without the use of symbols. However, symbolism does begin to appear at about 18 months of age, at which point children are able to reason about concrete reality even in its absence.

Research on the symbolic play of preschool children gives evidence of great strides in reasoning ability (Bretherton, 1984b). Within certain limits, prediction of events, estimation of probabilities, reasoning about cause and effect, and conclusions about the nature of things are possible. Play both promotes and reflects these expanded capabilities. On the other hand, thought is still egocentric with children being incapable of dwelling simultaneously on two aspects of a situation. However, the experiences gained through play and games lead to the progressive decentering of young children's thought (Kamii & DeVries, 1980).

With the advent of concrete operations, children are able to deal with symbols and operations upon symbols at successively higher levels of abstraction. They can think about the same entity from different perspectives (e.g., as a whole or as a number of parts). They can also mentally reverse an operation upon objects or quantities to return to the point of departure and perform other transactions requiring a higher degree of abstraction than during the preoperational period. As might be expected, this leads to games that deal less with manipulation of concrete objects, and call for a greater degree of reasoning ability (e.g., games of strategy, commercial and computer games).

In middle childhood, children are also capable of more cogent thinking about psychological causality, that is, why people behave the way they do and the psychological defenses they use, such as rationalization and projection (Whiteman, 1967). No doubt this ability may be attributed to the "decentering" that has taken place, enabling children to adopt the perspectives of other people. The sociodramatic play of the preschool period assists this particular aspect of decentering. Saltz and Brodie (1982), for example, discuss the role of fantasy play training in developing perspective taking skills in young children.

Logical operations (2–n). Logical operations refers to the area of knowledge dealing with the formal aspects of thought, as opposed to that which pertains to knowledge of the physical world. Examples of such operations are identity (A = A), negation (A ≠ B), conjunction (A + B), implication (A implies B), and transitivity (A > B > C). A primitive understanding of these operations is seen even in the small child. For example. the fact that the baby looks with anticipation for a rattle thrown from the crib to reappear, or for a person who has disappeared behind a screen to emerge from the other side, suggests the beginnings of a concept of identity. Piaget describes the incipient understanding of transitivity demonstrated by his young son in seeking a watch placed under a hat. In playing with manipulable objects and materials, preschool children have many opportunities to observe these principles. A doll remains the same through many changes of clothing. A ball keeps its identity, even when its shiny new colors have worn off. The seedlings planted are the same, even when they begin to grow rapidly. Through such experiences, the child learns to identify the core of continuity and sameness that persists through successive changes in size and appearance. Similarly, the universal truth of other relationships such as transitivity dawns on children through their own perceptions and other children's discussions. For example, children often play games that involve arranging people or things in order from largest to smallest or tallest to shortest. In such contexts, the relationship of transitivity becomes very obvious.

Games during the elementary school years continue to reinforce the learning of logical operations. Rules of games may stipulate that a player may choose either A or B, but not both. To choose A implies certain things and to choose B implies certain other things. For example a person or team that wins the toss must figure out the consequences of choosing one alternative over the other.

Hypothesis testing (1–d). Hypothesis testing, an ability often tied to scientific thinking, in reality occurs in all forms of thought. Generalizations do not burst fully formed into consciousness, but are frequently the end product of a long period of induction and testing. The person makes tentative hypotheses on the basis of a few examples, and revises the hypotheses as they are refuted by experience. People are able to form hypotheses only by virtue of the order and uniformity of events in the universe.

The newborn infant first experiences this order in the rhythms of sleeping, feeding, and bathing, and the collateral feelings of pleasure and pain. Gradually these experiences give rise to expectations (e.g., hunger followed by food and in turn by diminution of the hunger pangs), but the expectations are at a preverbal level. Some of these early, unverbalized expectations form the core of what later becomes a system of beliefs and assumptions about the universe that are extremely resistant to change. As children's command over language increases, expectations about objects and events are more likely to be verbalized, and hence become accessible to the processes of logic and reasoning. At this stage, although unverbalized assumptions are still likely to be the end product of the inductive process, explicit hypotheses are also formulated.

In *Intellectual Growth in Young Children*, a book packed with insightful observations of children's thinking during play, Isaacs (1930/1966) relates the ability to construct fruitful hypotheses directly to the ability to reconstruct past events in play: "The ability to evoke the past in imaginative play seems to me to be very closely connected with the growth of the power to evoke the future in constructive hypotheses" (p. 104, examples on pp. 112–113).

As Piaget suggests, children formulate tentative hypotheses, which they then communicate with more or less confidence to their peers. When these hypotheses are discredited, dissonance is aroused; the hypothesis is discarded, or new evidence is sought. Sometimes lack of experience or misinterpretation of experience may lead to invalid hypotheses.

Isaacs' (1930/1966) examples illustrate the importance of social context in formulating and testing hypotheses. Play is a vital ingredient of this context, because the child is playing with ideas that are roughly at the level at which they can be assimilated (K.H. Rubin, 1980). The cognitive conflict induced by the rejection of these ideas impels the child to rethink the hypothesis and seek a resolution of the conflict at a time when the problem is meaningful. The new evidence forces the child to modify the hypothesis and hence to attain a higher level of equilibrium (Piaget, 1952).

Problem solving (1–e). Problem solving is a term that is used broadly in the literature, running the gamut from simple tasks requiring a novel response to intellectual endeavors calling for the application of complex logical and scientific principles (Gagne, 1977). Simple problem solving has been demonstrated in infants under 1 year old (Buhler, 1935). Piaget (1952) also notes some forms of problem solving occurring in the infant's play. For example, if the infant sees an adult place a watch under a blanket, then remove the blanket to find only a hat, the infant will look for the watch under the hat. Many similar problems are encountered by young children in the course of trying to obtain objects they desire or do things they want to do. Their often remarkable persistence in the face of problems is presumably due to the fact that the problems are self-generated and not imposed from without.

Play has been shown to be an important vehicle for teaching problem-solving skills (Simon & Smith, 1985). Based on earlier findings that disadvantaged Israeli children engaged in less sociodramatic play than middle class children (Smilansky, 1968), Rosen (1974) conducted a study in which training and practice in sociodramatic play for the disadvantaged children resulted in significant improvement in posttest group problem-solving skills compared to two control groups. Still, as Saltz and Brodie (1982) point out, it would be premature to conclude that the lack of such skills in disadvantaged school-age children is attributable to their meager experience with socio-dramatic play in the preschool years, since one cannot rule out the possibility that interaction with adults is the crucial variable.

Problem solving is enhanced through play in three other ways. First, play encourages cognitive flexibility in the solution of problems (Pellegrini, 1981, 1984a). Parental attitudes toward problems may engender the belief that there is only one right way to approach a problem. Or, punishment for errors may reduce children's willingness to take risks. In either case, the discovery that there are alternative ways to view problems, and different—or even better—ways to solve them, is a major learning experience. It is precisely the lack of such flexibility, as demonstrated in the experiments on functional fixedness (Luchins & Luchins 1968; Wason & Johnson-Laird, 1972), which has been shown to impede problem solving in adults. Play is preparation for life, not in the sense that it trains specific behaviors, but because it promotes a general cognitive flexibility in preparation for coping with problems that are as yet unspecified. Play is "preparation for the unknown" (Ellis, 1973, p. 120).

A second important aspect of play is that for children it can serve the same symbolic function in solving a problem as thinking or talking through a problem does for adults (Vygotsky, 1967). Children may often be observed repetitiously working through a problem in their play (e.g., attempting to deal with the fact that the mother has gone to hospital by playing hospital all day long). Such coping mechanisms are an attempt to assimilate some information, especially of an anxiety-arousing nature, which is imperfectly understood (Curry & Arnaud, 1974). Yet parents and teachers frequently discourage fantasy play on the grounds that the child must learn to cope with the "real world," and must not be a "dreamer." In so doing, adults ignore the fact that such play may be the best vehicle for learning to cope with the "real world." As Millar (1968) remarks: "The pretense of make-believe is not a cloak for something else, or behavior intended to mislead, but thinking (recoding and rehearsal) in action with real objects as props" (p. 256).

The attempt to assimilate experiences that are frightening for children, or that they have witnessed as having frightening effects on adults, may account for the many games containing an element of the macabre. Some of these have been documented by the Opies (Opie & Opie, 1969), for example, the reenactment of an assassination, war games, and even a game, played in the Auschwitz concentration camp, called "going to the gas chamber."

A third way in which play functions to enhance problem solving is that it leads to the discovery, even the generation, of new problems. Maier (1940) calls this the "problem-solving attitude," and Mackworth (1965) emphasizes that finding problems is more important than solving problems. Guilford (1967) identifies sensitivity to problems as one of the important components of creative thinking. Play situations in which children are allowed to structure their own activities and to choose which problems to solve are perhaps the most conducive to fostering this sensitivity to problems. The intrinsic motivating forces of exploration and curiosity drive children to seek novel stimulation, thereby increasing the chances that they will come to recognize problems new to them. For example, a 6-year-old girl who had saved her pocket money to buy a small cactus plant, on seeing a picture of a very large cactus of the same variety asked, "What can I do to make mine as big as that?"

Problem solving is inherent in the games of older children, too. Usually the problem consists of thinking of strategies to eliminate the competition. Competitive play reaches a peak in the elementary school years (Eiferman, 1971), as children sharpen their skills in thinking of ways to outwit their rivals. Team spirit is high. Even leisure time reading may be about the competition between teams or gangs. At the same time, there is a strong cooperative element in children's play at this age. Sometimes a group will spend weeks on a project such as creating Halloween costumes. Play provides a medium in which problems may be identified, investigated, and solved by children of all ages.

Creativity (1–f). Creativity is the highest form of problem solving. A creative solution is one that is new to the individual who produces it, and possibly also to society at large. Presumably, most of the infant's problem solving would fall into this category, since many of the child's problems are being encountered for the first time. Many psychologists and educators (e.g., Caplan & Caplan, 1973) have remarked on the creative aspects of young children's play.

Torrance (1966), who has explored the subject of children's creativity in some depth, finds that it peaks in early childhood and seems to decline around fourth grade. Since the years in which creativity is at its height are those in which a larger proportion of the child's time is spent in play, there should be a substantial correlation between amount of play and measures of creativity. Lieberman (1965) found a relationship between the quality of playfulness (i.e., spontaneity, joy, and humor) in kindergarten children's behavior and certain measures of divergent thinking (e.g., ideational fluency, spontaneous flexibility, and originality). In a similar vein, Pellegrini (1984a) concluded that young children's associative fluency can be facilitated by encouraging them to explore objects and answer descriptive questions about these objects.

Torrance's (1966) tests of creativity include the kinds of tasks that are frequently observed in the self-imposed spontaneous play of children. For example, the Just Suppose subtest requires the child to consider an improbable situation and think of all the events that would follow as a result of its occurrence. Children particularly enjoy such games as What If, which consist of entertaining suppositions, often of a fantasized nature. The Picture Construction test presents the subject with an egg-shaped piece of green paper that the child may attach anywhere on a blank sheet of paper and incorporate into a picture he or she creates. Children often perform this kind of activity in painting. They do not seem to have an image of the picture they will create in their head before starting to paint. Rather, they take a full brush, splash the paint on the paper in a somewhat random fashion, and proceed to create a picture from the resulting blob of color. In fact, the kinds of activities that Torrance uses to measure creativity bear a strong similarity to those the young child engages in spontaneously. Scores on the creativity battery are improved significantly by training on similar tasks (Cartledge & Krauser, 1963), and are known to correlate substantially with certain aspects of elementary school achievement. Hence, the activities children engage in freely in the course of their play are likely to promote both creative thinking and school performance.

The question as to whether the decline in creativity scores around fourth grade (Torrance, 1966) is related to the comparative lack of opportunities for spontaneous play in the elementary school should be explored. School programs such as the "integrated day" (Murrow & Murrow, 1972), which encourage in elementary children the same approach to problem solving found in young children's play, might be expected to prevent this observed decline in creativity, but there is no empirical evidence on this. Another possibility is that teachers may exert considerable influence on creativity decline. As a facet of his work on creativity, Torrance (1965) conducted a study to determine student behaviors valued most and least by teachers. In their perceptions of the "ideal pupil," teachers as a group believed that children should be discouraged from being intuitive, being good guessers, regressing occasionally, being visionaries, and always asking questions, all qualities that have been reliably shown to discriminate persons of high and low creativity. Similarly, creative adults have been shown to have the capacity to transcend the here-and-now and to play with ideas that do not necessarily correspond closely to reality.

● Summary

Cognitive development encompasses a broad panoply of simple and complex abilities. The growth of cognitive development is highly dependent on conceptual development and on the development of problem-solving abilities. Specific skills contributing to each of these aspects of cognitive development can be subsumed under three generic abilities: the ability to (a) discriminate between information that is relevant versus irrelevant to a given purpose; (b) use fewer cues to generate more information; and (c) attain higher levels of abstraction. In this section, claims concerning the contributions of play to particular skills subsumed under each of these abilities have been supported by the extant research evidence. Processes of categorization, generalization, concept learning, and class inclusion, as factors in conceptual development, have been shown to bear a relationship to play. Factors in the development of problem-solving ability (e.g., reasoning, logical operations, hypothesis testing, simple problem solving, and creativity) are also promoted by play. In effect, play may be seen to contribute to the development of *all* the skills listed in Table 4–1 and hence to cognitive development in general.

Language Development and Its Relationship to Play

Acquisition of the primary language is a developmental achievement that is remarkable not only for its universality but for the speed with which it occurs. It requires the mastery of two reciprocal modes of performance, comprehension and production, which develop concurrently. Comprehension presupposes the ability to differentiate language stimuli from other forms of auditory input and to infer meanings by virtue of hypothesized rules of language usage. Production requires the ability to select and organize the sounds of the language in ways that produce meaningful words and sentences in the relevant language environment.

Both the comprehension and production modes presuppose mastery of four separate but related systems: (1) the phonetic or sound system, (2) the syntactic or generative rule system, (3) the semantic or meaning system, and (4) the pragmatic or contextual system. Table 4–2 suggests what *some* of the components comprising each of these four systems might be.

The infant rapidly learns enough about each of these systems to be able to communicate intelligibly and intelligently by the age of 2 and has a basic mastery of all of them by the age of 6. The disputes relating to the mechanisms by which this learning takes place are too lengthy to discuss here, and have been reviewed elsewhere (Athey, 1971). However, the roles of imitation, reinforcement, and other mechanisms are not irrelevant to the relationship of language and play.

The cursory treatment accorded the phonetic, syntactic, and pragmatic systems in the present discussion should not be construed as suggesting that these systems are not important in their own right or that play makes no contribution to their development. On the contrary, each of these systems has

been studied extensively by numerous researchers (e.g., Anisfeld, 1984; Cazden, 1968; Garvey, 1977a, 1977b; Weir, 1966). Because the essence of a language lies in its use as a means of communication, this discussion emphasizes the relationship of play to the semantic system.

● Phonological system

Activities that are precursors both to language and play can be identified during the sensorimotor period. For example, infants' responses to sounds in the environment exhibit the same features of internal motivation and repetition that characterize their interaction with visual and tactile objects in the environment. By the age of 6 months, infants differentiate language from nonlanguage stimuli and seem to be aware of the rhythms and intonations of speech (Condon & Sander, 1974; Eimas, 1974; Morse, 1974). Studies of early infant-parent interaction suggest that infants' responses to parents' language play involve communicative intent and serve as signals for the parents to continue (Brazelton, Koslowski, & Main, 1974). In effect, infants appear to select and manipulate auditory stimuli (i.e., to play with language) in ways that provide for repetition and enjoyment in both their reception and production.

Repetition is an intrinsic element of play at the sensorimotor stage and appears to enhance mastery of specific skills both in exploration and in language. As Zaporozhets and El'konin (1971) note: "Just as the mastery of objective reality is not possible without formation of activity with objects, exactly in the same manner is language mastery not possible without formation of activity with language as the material object with its concrete form" (p. 141). Hence, the onset of babbling, which has all the earmarks of repetitive play, appears to be a critical milestone in the acquisition of language. Lewis (1963) further comments on the pleasurable aspects of this activity as the infant gains mastery over the production of sounds, which forms the basis for complex skills necessary for language production. Infants also seem to take particular delight in such words as "splash" or "click," which reproduce qualities of objects or events (Jakobson, 1968). Sanches and Kirschenblatt-Gimblett (1976) describe how the sound elements of language are still a major focus of play in the elementary years.

TABLE 4–2 ● Generic and Specific Aspects of Linguistic Development

Generic Function	Specific Process
Phonological System	
(1) Comprehend incoming verbal communications (2) Produce meaningful verbal sounds	a. Discriminate between language and nonlanguage stimuli b. Discriminate elements of phonetic system c. Isolate words from incoming stream and attach meanings d. Produce languagelike sounds e. Combine sounds in linguistically acceptable groupings
Syntactic System	
(3) Comprehend grammatical structures (4) Produce syntactically correct sentences	g. Isolate words from stream of communication h. Identify functional elements (e.g., nouns) i. Learn sentence structure and acceptable positions (e.g., verbs) in sentences j. Identify structures of complex sentences (e.g., relational clauses, embedded sentences) k. Combine parts of sentences in acceptable ways l. Combine sentences in increasingly complex ways
Semantic System	
(5) Understand communicative intent in others (6) Understand referential quality of symbols, signs (7) Respond to others appropriately	m. Attend to gestures, verbalizations of others n. Associate symbols with objects, events, concepts o. Produce sounds, gestures, words, sentences; engage in meaningful dialogue
Pragmatic System	
(8) Develop awareness of social functions of language	p. Use language appropriate to situation and context

Bruner (1970) suggests that with repetition some of the sensorimotor sequences become smoother and more automatic, thus freeing up attention for their expansion or integration with other sequences. This analysis has some parallels with the concept of automaticity invoked by LaBerge and Samuels (1974) with respect to later cognitive tasks such as reading. Further, Bruner's analysis reinforces the idea that play leads to mastery of subskills, which in turn permits attention to be directed to learning higher-level abilities.

Repetitive play is not confined to the babbling stage. As the ability to use words and short sentences develops, young children exhibit obvious delight in rhyme and alliteration, stringing together sounds that clearly mimic adult intonational patterns (Menyuk, 1974). Playing with sounds is a primary activity during the first five years and continues to be manifested in the games that characterize the period from 7 to 12 years of age.

● Syntactic system

In the same way that young children play with sounds, they also play with the syntactical aspects of language. Some linguists have even detected implicit knowledge of syntax in the child's early one-word sentences. Brown and Bellugi (1964) suggest that three processes, each of which may be seen in children's play, are at work in their acquisition of syntax: imitation, expansion, and hypothesis testing. Parents' comments are first imitated in reduced form, but later, as the adult expands on the child's statements, these expansions are also imitated. Additionally, through language play, hypotheses about the rule system are developed and tested. As was the case with aspects of cognitive growth, repetitive play has a crucial role in the development of syntactic competence.

● Semantic system

The evolution of a semantic system is possible only by virtue of the ability to use symbols to represent objects and events. The development of symbolic or pretend behavior, which Shotwell, Wolf, and Gardner (1980) define as "the ability to represent actual or imagined experience through the combined use of objects, motion, and language" (p. 176), has been documented in the literature (Fein, 1981; McCune-Nicolich, 1981; Piaget, 1962). Piaget (1962) traces the intimate link during the period of preoperational intelligence between symbolic play and the development of representation. The growth of the symbolic function throughout the sensorimotor period is described in detail to illustrate the "progressive differentiation between 'signifier' and 'signified'" (p. 101). Infant behavior during the first year of life is concrete and presymbolic. Sensorimotor behavior in the presence of objects does not continue once these objects are out of perceptual range. As perceptions of color, shape, taste, and feel become coordinated through repetitive activity into the perception of objects, they give rise to the idea of object continuity. The infant gives evidence of expecting an object to reappear (e.g., Piaget's example of the in-

fant looking expectantly at the point where the object will reappear from behind a screen). Such behavior suggests that the infant has, at least to a limited extent, grasped the notion of object permanence. Before long, a single aspect of the object may come to signal this reappearance (e.g., the infant becomes excited at the sound of the mother's voice in an adjoining room). Eventually, language cues (e.g., the word "mother") will elicit the same behavior.

Although the relationship between play and symbolism has received some attention (Nicolich, 1977), its exact nature is not entirely clear. Piaget maintained that both language and play are manifestations of the symbolic ability that emerges toward the end of the sensorimotor period. As soon as the infant is able to form mental images of objects, and thus reconstruct them in memory, symbolic representation in the form of images or words becomes possible. According to Piaget (1962), the symbolic function is the bridge between the sensorimotor activity of the infant and the operational intelligence of the school-age child, for "there is functional continuity between the sensorimotor and the representational, a continuity which determines the construction of the successive structures" (pp. 2–3). The ability to use a symbol to represent an object or another symbol is the essence of operational thought. For Piaget, the symbolic function is the basis for all forms of adult intelligence, including thought and language.

Since the dual processes of language and pretend play both have their roots in the sensorimotor period and reflect the growth of the symbolic function, one might expect a general relationship in their subsequent development, and indeed, such a correspondence of stages has been corroborated in a longitudinal study of infant play (McCune-Nicolich, 1981, p. 791). Symbolic play is a type of representation that promotes the development of the symbolic function. For example, playful repetition of the names of familiar objects consolidates learning of the associations between signifier and signified. The results of Goodson and Greenfield's (1975) study suggest a parallel between certain structural principles in children's play and dimensions of language. Similarly, Ungerer and Sigman (1984) found functional play with dolls and with other persons to be related to receptive and expressive language at 13½ months and again at 22 months. Additionally, symbolic play and several measures of relational play were associated with language at the older age level.

In Piaget's theory, play is the form of adaptation in which the balance of assimilation and accommodation is tilted almost entirely in favor of assimilation. The growth of symbolic representation is clearly seen in the way the infant's play changes. Piaget recounts how one of his children, Laurent, first began to use action schemas, such as pretending to go to sleep, outside the context of his bedtime routine. Next the schemas became detached from the child's own actions and were transferred to some other object, such as putting the doll to sleep. Finally, the entire schema became interiorized, so that images, gestures, or partial events could be used to represent and anticipate future events. Learning to use fewer or partial cues to represent objects and events is accomplished with great rapidity and evidence of pleasure by the child. Some months later, words rather than actions are used for this purpose.

The transition from sensorimotor to symbolic behavior is first seen in the reenactment of familiar activities, such as grooming or sleeping, outside the daily routine. According to McCune-Nicolich and Fenson (1984, p. 86), "this early form of appropriate use out of context can be observed as early as 9 or 10 months of age and corresponds to the fifth sensorimotor stage." Symbolic play proper emerges around the end of the first year. Its earliest manifestations take the form of familiar actions or sequences that unfold as if they were taking place in "real" situations (e.g., drinking from an empty cup). Pretend play at this age relates to appropriate objects present in the immediate environment, is confined to familiar actions involving the child's own body, and may be accompanied by language.

Between 15 and 18 months there is a dramatic increase in symbolic behavior regardless of situational or cultural variations (Rubin et al., 1983). Moreover, this behavior becomes increasingly "appropriate" to the specific function of the object (Rosenblatt, 1977). The involvement of other persons or person substitutes such as dolls marks an important step in the progress of the child's symbolic play, and one in which language plays an increasing role, for it is at this stage that the young child begins to realize the power of language in facilitating attainment of goals. In fact, it has been suggested (Watson & Fischer, 1977) that pretend play may be the mecha-

nism whereby preschool children move from egocentric to "decentralized" thought when make-believe behavior originally directed toward the self becomes other-referenced. The first "other" is typically the mother, but subsequently a doll or stuffed animal may fill this role (Shimada, Kai, & Sano, 1981). This surrogate first serves as a passive recipient of the child's action, but at a more advanced level is manipulated as if it were an active agent (McCune-Nicolich & Fenson, 1984; Rubin et al., 1983, p. 718). However, the former authors caution that it is difficult in practice to ascertain whether the child truly attributes human qualities to the surrogate object.

Recent research has raised additional questions pertaining to (a) the basis on which the child selects the object used in symbolic play (Matthews, 1977), (b) the similarity of the object to its referent (Elder & Pederson, 1978), and (c) the child's judgements about the correspondence between referent and substitute object (Copple, Cocking, & Matthews, 1984). The latter authors conclude that "the use of objects in make-believe play is not only a mentally initiated activity . . . but one in which the children's awareness of their own mental processes and representational criteria is increasingly explicit" (p. 122). Again, language use associated with such play is instrumental in the development of this awareness.

Toward the middle of the second year, pretend play begins to take on several new dimensions. Whereas the earlier symbolic behavior is observed only in the presence of appropriate objects and is confined to reproduction of familiar activities, at this stage it becomes "decontextualized" (i.e., dissociated from these objects). The simpler behaviors exhibited earlier may become embedded in more complex units. Children begin to imitate the actions of others and to project symbolic schemes previously reserved to the self onto others. Moreover, children of this age have also been observed to take the initiative in involving parents in the simpler behaviors observed previously, and to use language to this end.

According to Rubin et al. (1983), " a large number of psychologists and educators have proposed that the growing amount of time that pretense activities occupy, from the toddler to the early elementary school years, plays a significant role in children's lives [and] has been viewed as partially responsible for the development of a plethora of skills" (p. 716). In commenting on the large amounts of time children spend in pretense activities, (Singer 1973) suggests that such activities are closely linked to the growth of symbolic representation. Vygotsky (1967) also believes that pretense assists in the development of representation by separating meanings from objects.

Fenson and Ramsay (1980) suggest that the capacity for integrating symbolic play acts into longer, more sophisticated sequences and for spontaneously involving other participants with accompanying verbal commentary may presage the later ability to plan play activities. Planning as a separate variable in symbolic play has been studied by Nicolich (1977) and Field, DeStefano, and Koewler (1982). Singer (1973) advances the possibility that make-believe play allows "for a greater range of trial selves and tentative imagined excursions into the future which ultimately become the basis for effective planning" (p. 207). Imagined practice can lead to greater overt proficiency. It also seems likely that

one consequence of make-believe play for the child is an increasingly differentiated self-concept or awareness of self. In effect, by practicing a variety of make-believe selves and roles, a child gradually differentiates himself out from the field around him and sees many options within himself that are not automatically called for by the external situation. (p. 206)

Singer is cautious, however, about drawing the inference that make-believe play serves a specific developmental function, preferring to view the capacity to generate and practice imagery and the associated linguistic skills of elaboration as fundamental capacities with which humans are "wired."

In a similar vein regarding the planning function of symbolic play, Rubin et al. (1983) advance the interesting notion that this "as if" behavior may presage the learning of "scripts" as described by Schank and Abelson (1977). Scripts involve cognitive and linguistic material that is stored in memory for ready retrieval upon the presentation of certain cues. Recently, under the general heading of "schema theory," scripts have been hypothesized as representing background knowledge that plays a large role in reading comprehension (Anderson & Pearson, 1984). If this is the case, the argument might be advanced with some plausibility that a rich diet of pretend play promotes listening, and later, reading, comprehension.

The important role that symbolic activity assumes in children's play during the preschool years has been amply documented (Isaacs, 1933). At this stage, symbolic activity takes on a variety of forms. In the stimulating environment of the preschool, children can give full rein to fantasies. Any and every object may be used to symbolize another, without regard to the nature and function of either. A block may represent a train, a house, or a baby with equal facility; conversely, a person may be called upon to represent an object. One outcome of this type of play is that, through their own activity, children learn about the properties of represented objects and how to apply labels to these names and properties. Especially when the object is novel or puzzling, this manipulation of both objects and symbols (words) may be an effort to make sense of the world. Or it may be a rehearsal of something the child has experienced and is attempting to assimilate, or simply an attempt to reaffirm that the event did indeed occur.

Piaget's view, encompassing as it does the exploratory, manipulative, confirming, and labeling activities of young children, demonstrates the importance of symbolic play as the undergirding structure for all later operations, both cognitive and linguistic, involved in processing information. In this sense, fantasy is constructive as opposed to compensatory, as it is seen from the psychoanalytic viewpoint. It is not necessary to conclude, however, that these two positions are mutually exclusive. Fantasy both in thought and play is a most useful vehicle for learning intellectual and social skills and language as well as for solving emotional problems.

Pretend play involving more than one child is usually referred to as sociodramatic play. A number of investigators have explored the facilitative effects of sociodramatic play on cognitive problem solving (Saltz et al., 1977; Smilansky, 1968; Smith & Dutton, 1979) and flexible, unusual, or novel actions (Bruner, 1972; J.N. Lieberman, 1977; Singer, 1973; Zammarelli & Bolton, 1977). Research is needed to investigate the question of whether either spontaneous or induced sociodramatic play leads to increased verbalizations or more sophisticated uses of language.

Around the age of 7, according to Piaget, symbolic play tends to disappear, and a balance of assimilation and accommodation occurs. The child begins to think in terms of concepts rather than perception and fantasy. Vygotsky sees this decline in fantasy as a reintegration of the thought processes in which the free assimilation of play is now internalized as part of the creative thinking process. Although the language system will continue to undergo elaboration, all its essential elements have been mastered by this age. As thought becomes progressively "decentered," language is increasingly used in preference to action as a vehicle for expressing meanings. It should be noted, however, that fantasy play does not disappear entirely from the child's repertoire, but tends to be "miniaturized" in the form of paper dolls, electric trains, and similar toys.

The growth of language permits children to associate things that could not otherwise be linked together in many different ways that they enjoy exploiting through their games. Hence the popularity of such games as I spy or competitions to think of the most birds or animals beginning with a certain letter. The games of elementary school children call for more complex types of associations, and language permits children to clarify these associations verbally and to think about them either critically or playfully. Unusual associations or double meanings also provide the basis for the humor found in the jokes, riddles, puns, and word games that abound at this age.

Reading, which has been defined as the extraction of meaning from written language, involves playing with different interpretations, especially where the text is vague or ambiguous. The world of imagination is laid open for the child's entertainment and edification, including life in other parts of the globe, unfamiliar modes of transportation, foods, occupations, foreign languages, and so forth. Through stories about other children's experiences, young readers learn to associate feelings and reactions with new forms of behavior. Play consolidates such learning and, in turn, reflects it.

● Metalinguistic awareness

Perhaps the highest form of abstraction of which human beings are capable is the ability to think about their own actions and inner states. Humans alone, of all species, possess this capacity, possibly as a result of their highly developed symbol system. How this capacity comes about is described by Vygotsky (1967) as follows: It does not exist at all in the infant. When language first appears in the young child's repertoire, it is not used for purposes of self-examina-

tion, but is either purely expressive or is directed toward meeting immediate needs and desires. Through experience, children learn to speak or respond to others in ways designed to elicit their attention and help. Gradually, children's responses take the form of "inner speech," or talking to themselves as well as others. Hence language that began as a means of social control becomes a means of self-control. Through such verbalizations, children come to understand their own actions, to plan them, to be critical of them, and to consider alternative courses of action. Their burgeoning language abilities are instrumental, if not essential, to this metacognitive awareness.

Similarly, during middle childhood, children begin to recognize correct and incorrect uses of language. They begin to notice accents and phonetic aberrations. They understand the grammatical functions of words and sentences, and the semantic choices available to them for communication purposes. Finally, they become aware of their own uses of language as a tool that may be used adroitly for purposes of self-expression, persuasion, and so forth. Metalinguistic awareness appears around the age of 10.

Language is a higher form of abstraction than concrete experience, because it enables us to talk about objects and events in their absence. But not all language is equally abstract. Linguists are essentially in agreement that there is a hierarchy of linguistic forms representing a succession of degrees of abstraction from objects. Children acquire an understanding of this hierarchy only gradually. Probably the first abstraction the infant makes is the conditioned response or "expectation" of an event following a signal (e.g., the mother's voice). Even at this stage, some form of utterance, such as a gurgle of delight, may become part of the response. Some months later words are used to represent objects, but the words do not have the abstract quality they do for adults. They are as real to the child as the object they symbolize. This "nominal realism" dominates the preoperational period, giving way only by degrees to the realization that names are arbitrary conventions.

Piaget and others have performed a number of experiments to demonstrate that, for the preschool child, a name is an inherent quality of its object and cannot be changed at will. Papandropoulou and Sinclair (1974) found four stages of successive abstraction in children aged 4 years, 5 months, and 10 years, 10 months. Below 5 years of age, no distinction was made between words and things. By the age of 10, words had acquired a clear autonomy, and not only had become meaningful units in themselves, but also had been integrated into a linguistic system in the sense that they were now seen as grammatical constituents of higher order units such as sentences and paragraphs. Hence, by middle childhood, the arbitrary, or conventional, nature of words is fully realized, and the child can play with these new-found abstractions in jokes, puns, riddles, and the like. Stories also become more removed from the immediate reality of the child's environment. Tales of mythical creatures, children of other lands, and aliens from other planets are high in popularity. Games also use more abstract language to symbolize a situation.

In the early years of the preoperational period, play tends to be solitary. Even solitary play, when accompanied by soliloquy, permits extensive practice of language skills. Later, the proportion of solitary play declines in favor of the social variety, which is directed by individual or mutual planning. Social play, in which children's attention is drawn to their own actions by the remarks of peers, is undoubtedly a powerful vehicle for learning about actions and motivations.

Metalinguistic awareness, or consciousness of one's own use of language, develops more slowly. Downing (1969) has shown that, even in first grade, many children do not have the concept of a spoken word. The study by Papandropoulou and Sinclair (1974) and one by Meltzer and Herse (1969) report similar findings for the written word. The former authors conclude that metalinguistic awareness develops in stages along with the general cognitive structures described by Piaget. No doubt much of this awareness comes about through direct instruction, especially in the language arts. On the other hand, popular games that involve name calling, rhymes, or chants, also make a substantial contribution. Elkind (1981) suggests that elementary school children are becoming conscious of themselves as manipulators of a linguistic system.

● Pragmatic system

Concurrent with the development of awareness of their own language, children learn through play with adults and other children the social conventions governing the appropriate use of language. These conventions include giving appropriate answers to questions, keeping the conversational ball rolling, inferring unstated information from context, and many others.

● Summary

Language development involves the growth and interaction of four complex systems: the phonological, syntactic, semantic, and pragmatic. Play contributes to all of these systems. Play is intimately related to the development of symbolic representation, both reflecting and facilitating that development.

Moral Development and Its Relationship to Play

There are many criteria by which to judge the usefulness of a theory. One of the most important is the breadth of natural phenomena the theory is capable of explaining. Although other theoretical systems (e.g., social learning) are important contenders in explaining moral development, Piaget's theory has the advantage of being more comprehensive, encompassing every aspect of cognitive development, including morality. Some of his earliest works deal with applications of the theory to particular aspects of human thought, such as scientific concepts like space, time, and probability. At the same time, Piaget was becoming intrigued with the idea of subjecting moral reasoning to the same type of analysis. In *The Moral Judgement of the Child* (Piaget, 1932), he suggests that the stages of cognitive development proposed for other concepts are equally appropriate to describing the growth of moral reasoning. These stages, with additional ones suggested by Kohlberg (1976), are described briefly:

- *Stage One:* "Punishment-and-obedience" orientation in which the child defers to the power of the adult.
- *Stage Two:* "Instrumental-relativist" orientation in which rules are followed in return for some expected benefit.
- *Stage Three:* "Good boy-nice girl" orientation in

which the child seeks approval and conforms in order to please.

- *Stage Four:* "Law-and-order" orientation in which rules are followed for the sake of maintaining social order; concern for wider community (Kohlberg, 1976).
- *Stage Five:* "Social-contract, legalistic" orientation in which justice flows from a contract between governor and governed that assures equal rights for all.
- *Stage Six:* "Ethical-principles" orientation in which justice, universality, and consistency prevail.

The theories of Piaget and Kohlberg have given rise to a number of studies (e.g., Bull, 1969; Graham, 1972), but there is little research exploring the relationship of play to moral development. While it would be difficult under these circumstances to assert that play contributes to a child's movement from any one of these stages to the next one in the hierarchy, some speculation on the relationship of play to moral development is possible particularly as it relates to rule learning and metacognitive awareness (see Table 4–1).

● Rule learning (2–m)

Rule learning includes two types of rules: scientific and conventional rules. The former refer to laws about the physical universe, and have been discussed to some extent under the section on generalization. The latter refer to the arbitrary rules formulated and enforced by individuals or groups representing the larger society. Both children and adults learn much about this kind of rule through their play.

Even tiny infants must begin to have some perception that there are constraining forces at work in the world when their demands are not met with immediate satisfaction. Perhaps the first intimation comes when children hear the word "No!" delivered in a firm tone when they reach out to touch something. At all events, by the time they reach the age of 2 or 3 years, children have a clear notion that a system of rules exists. Piaget (1932) tried to determine the nature of children's ideas on this subject by asking them how the rules applied in the games they were playing. Young children believed the rules for a game such as marbles to be eternal and unchange-

able, and infringement open to immediate and severe punishment. In their dramatic or fantasy play, children of this age are often very severe in laying down rules and punishing miscreants. Actually this kind of play is very valuable in helping children to comprehend a confusing and often inconsistent moral code. Similarly, children's reasoning about morality reaches a new level in middle childhood, when their concepts of rules, punishment, and justice become more complex and sophisticated, reflecting progress toward "moral relativism." Even the most casual observer of children can witness moral dilemmas associated with these concepts being worked out in the course of sociodramatic play.

Between the ages of 7 and 12, children begin to move away from the "moral realism" of early childhood, and to understand the arbitrary and conventional nature of rules. This is the age at which rule-governed games come into their own. Most of these games cannot be played unless there is complete understanding and acceptance of the system of rules. Hence rules assume a great deal of importance in the eyes of the contestants. Children who break rules, causing the team to be penalized or disqualified, are censured by their teammates. Sometimes an unfair or "stupid" rule will be changed by mutual consent. In a sense, games are a microcosm of the larger society, with its system of rights and penalties, and thus a form of socialization into the moral code and traditions of the culture. In their play, elementary school children also act out the exploits of their heroes, this being another way to learn the social code of behavior and to internalize its rules.

● Metacognitive awareness (3–q)

Finally, metacognitive awareness (i.e., the ability to think about one's own thinking and reasoning processes) is essential for moral development. It allows children to realize how their thinking differs as situations change, to analyze the logic of their reasoning processes, and to compare their thinking with that of others.

The arguments over game rules, the negotiations arrived at in play, and the "what if" solution generation arising from hypothetical premises (e.g., Piaget's question, "What if coal were white?") are evidences of ways play gives children opportunities to develop metacognitive awareness.

Implications for Education

The major conclusion to be drawn from this discussion is that play can, and should, have an important role in a curriculum for young children. The view that play is in some way superfluous or unimportant is a gross misunderstanding of the nature and value of play.

One implication of this review is that, to contribute to learning, play need not be an all-group, teacher-centered, product-oriented activity. Because every child develops at a different rate, materials that are sufficiently unstructured and projective, so that children can impose their own structure on them, are preferable to formal toys that require "right" answers or "correct" usage. During play periods, the choice of activity should be the child's, with the teacher playing an encouraging and supportive role. Adults can assist by being on the alert for the many opportunities for growth inherent in all kinds of materials: growth in powers of discrimination, in ability to remember and use information, in reasoning and problem solving, in symbolic representation, and in moral inference. This growth is possible because the young child's mental structures are at that stage of development where they are optimally stimulated and challenged by the possibilities inherent in play situations.

To be convinced of the value of play in fostering cognitive, linguistic, and moral development is to be equally convinced that play must be a mainstay of the early childhood curriculum. It should not be necessary to ask the question "structured or unstructured?" or even "how much structure?" Play carries its own structure, and the alert adult can recognize how and when to inject a question, a comment, some new material, or other device to maintain or reorganize the existing structure.

The tendency to extend elementary curriculum downward into the early childhood years might well be reversed in deference to young children's need to play (Elkind, 1986). The child's need for play does not dissipate overnight when the child first enters kindergarten. An equally good case may be made for the extension of preschool—upward. For example, there have been several articles in recent years recommending that formal teaching of reading be postponed until the child has the cognitive structures to understand its meaning and purpose in the larger frame of experience (Furth, 1969; Rohwer, 1971).

A second implication relates to the need for greater use of the outdoors for purposes of play. Children need space to develop their imaginative projects, and more simply, to move around if they are to develop coordination, muscle strength, and spatial perception. Too often, the possibilities of available outdoor space are not fully exploited, while groups of children remain cooped up and frustrated in small classrooms, for no particular reason except lack of imagination on the part of the supervising adults. Similarly, the community at large appears to have little conception of the value and use of outdoor space for purposes of play. Ellis (1973) has written a scathing indictment of playground planning in the United States, showing its limited potential for challenging or sustaining the interest of children of any age.

Finally, the importance of individual record keeping in schools cannot be overemphasized. The teacher must be aware of children's interests, the kinds of projects each child has chosen to work on, the problems being encountered, the potentialities and limitations of the materials, and other important information. Only by careful observation and conscientious record keeping can the teacher hope to provide the optimal stimulation that play can offer, both in the present situation and in terms of contributing to long-term development.

The value of play is not confined to the years of early childhood. Sutton-Smith (1967) cites a number of studies showing that games fulfill a similar function for school-age children. The energy and enthusiasm of children of this age, and their expanding repertoire of concepts and skills, make it especially beneficial to embed routine types of learning in the context of broader plans and projects. Erikson (1963) calls this the age of "industry versus inferiority," during which lifelong work patterns are established. Surely, then, it is important to make "work" as pleasurable as possible, in other words, to discard the work-play dichotomy, instead of emphasizing it as most schools do, in the mistaken notion that more will be accomplished by "buckling down" to the "task" of learning.

Conclusion

This chapter has reviewed some of the theoretical and research literature with examples that illustrate the role of play in cognitive, linguistic, and moral development. Cognitive growth in humans may be viewed from three perspectives: (a) the developing ability to identify and use information relative to a given purpose and to ignore or suppress that which is irrelevant; (b) the increased capacity to generate greater amounts of information from fewer cues; and (c) the ascent to higher levels of abstract thinking. Within each of the above perspectives, several of the cognitive processes related to play were discussed. These processes ranged from simple associative learning to the creativity involved in the solution of complex problems. Play was seen to make a powerful contribution to cognitive growth by providing access to more information, thereby enriching the content of the child's thinking; and consolidation of mastered skills, practice in the use of these skills in new situations, and pleasure in their deployment. Further, play was seen to promote and sustain creativity through the playful use of ideas in problem-solving as well as effective functioning of the intellect through its continuous operation on a broad range of content.

But play provides more than the "mere content" of thought. Play *is* intelligence, problem-solving, and creativity in action: "the child's play is the infantile form of the human ability to deal with experience by creating model situations and to master reality by experiment and planning" (Erikson, 1963, p. 222). Placed in a challenging environment, with freedom to explore and express, children acquire a large repertoire of novel associations that may be used adaptively in new situations. Such learning must, of necessity, have value for later learning even though direct causal connections have not been demonstrated. According to Sutton-Smith (1967), a direct link need not be shown; rather, the fact that play promotes the expression of a wide range of behaviors permits human beings to have behavioral choices that are adaptive for changing conditions. These "large response repertoires" are the content on which the higher processes draw. Hence, we may say that play is a medium—in young children, *the* medium—by which these higher processes evolve.

Questions for Discussion

1. How can play assist the development of concepts and higher order thinking in infants and toddlers? In preschoolers? In elementary-age children? Give an example at each of these age levels.
2. What is the relationship between the development of language and symbolic play? What are some of the ways this relationship can be observed? How can it be enhanced?
3. How does play assist in the development of metacognitive and metalinguistic processes?

Play Activity Problem

Select three of the processes outlined in Tables 4–1 and 4–2 to observe in the play of children of preschool age. Collect at least five play examples and describe how the three processes were involved in the play. Observe these same three processes in the play of elementary-age children and compare the ways these processes were demonstrated in the two age groups.

Suggestions for Further Reading

Furth, H. G., & Wachs, H. (1974). *Thinking goes to school.* New York: Oxford University Press. Using a Piagetian theoretical base, the authors describe how to create a "thinking" environment in the elementary school. Gives practical curricular suggestions for extending children's thinking by active, playful means.

Jacobs, L. B. (1965). *Using literature with young children.* New York: Teachers College Press. This classic book by one of the deans of language arts education has many good suggestions for enhancing language, reading, and knowledge of literature. Suggestions can apply to children of ages 3 through 9.

Kamii, C., & DeVries, R. (1978). *Physical knowledge in preschool education*. Englewood Cliffs, NJ: Prentice-Hall. Describes many play activities that allow children to experiment with the physical world. The discovery model of teaching and the range of activities are based on Piaget's theory. The ideas can also be adapted for older and younger children.

Kohlberg, L., & Mayer, R. (1972). Development as the aim of education. *Harvard Educational Review, 42*, 449–496. Presents a statement of educational theory based on cognitive developmental theory.

Wolf, D. (Ed.) (1979). *New directions in child development: Early symbolization*, No. 3. San Francisco: Jossey-Bass. Contains articles that relate symbolic development in play, language, singing, metaphors, drawing, and counting, to the meaning of early symbol use.

Yardley, A. (1973). *Young children learning series: Discovering the physical world; Senses and sensitivity; Exploration and language*. New York: Citation Press. A series of books providing ideas for children's learning through play, from the perspective of British informal education. The philosophy of this approach to education is embedded in the many suggestions.

Moral Development in Play

RHETA DeVRIES

Social play is a medium for moral development because children have opportunities for decentering—recognizing and taking account of the behaviors and psychological states of others (that is, their desires, feelings, ideas). Inevitably, conflicts arise, and children must cope with opposition. Interpersonal conflicts of all sorts are an important part of a constructivist program of education because children are forced (sometimes painfully) to confront the opposed behaviors of others. With sensitive teacher guidance, children can begin to take account of the opposed desires lying behind opposed behaviors, and develop methods of cooperation—of coordinating their desires with those of others.

To test the hypothesis that cooperative teaching promotes children's social-cognitive development, Goncu and I compared the interpersonal negotiation strategies of pairs of 4-year-olds from constructivist and Montessori classrooms in a situation where they played a game without a teacher. Using a coding manual developed by Selman and his colleagues, each interaction could be characterized and scored at a developmental stage from 0 to 3. While behaviors at stages 0, 1, and 2 were found in both groups, Montessori children had significantly more level 1 interactions in which they expressed a one-way understanding—only the needs or wishes of the self. Constructivist children had significantly more level 2 interactions in which they expressed awareness of the other as planful and having feelings, opinions, and behaviors that must be taken into account. Within conflict segments (perhaps the real test of social-cognitive competence, when self-interest is threatened), Montessori children had significantly more level 0 behaviors in which they expressed raw will (for example, grabbing, hitting) without any reflection on the other's point of view. No differences in occurence of level 1 behaviors were found, but constructivist pairs had significantly more level 2 behaviors. The findings of this study suggest that constructivist teaching fosters children's progress in sociomoral development.

Consider the following example of a play interaction that gives us insight into this process. Two 5-year-olds, Yousef and Christopher, both want to be first in a game of Concentration. In this situation, occurring at the Human Development Laboratory School at the University of Houston, competing clearly depends on successfully achieving cooperation—agreeing upon a rule, abiding by it, and accepting its consequences.

T (Ms. Rebecca Krejci): Who should go first?

Y: Me.

C: Me.

T: You both want to go first.

Y: Bubble gum, bubble gum . . . (*Begins rhyme, to himself and Christopher alternately.*)

C: I don't like to do "Bubble gum, Bubble gum."

Y: Let's take a vote.

C: No, there aren't enough people who want to vote.

The moral atmosphere of the classroom is reflected in Yousef's response to this conflict situation. Teachers had worked hard to give children methods of settling disputes through the use of impartial procedures such as voting and rhymes that designate players successively and accord a privilege to the last player designated. Yousef's practical reasoning is thus above a bald insistence upon what he wants. Christopher, too, focuses on the method for deciding rather than just on what he wants. The teacher moderates to help keep the discussion going.

T: O.K., so far we've talked about "Bubble gum, Bubble gum" or voting, and you don't like either of those. What do you think, Christopher?

C: I think that I'll just pick who goes first.

T: Yousef, do you like that idea?

Y: No.

T: No?

C: I'll just pick.

Y: No, I said that first. And then you came and speaked when I was speaking. So, I'm just gonna do "Bubble gum, Bubble gum."

C: O.K., but that sure does disturb me.

Christopher's insistence on what he wants brings another impasse, with each child repeating his solution. Christopher grudgingly agrees to go along with Yousef, but expresses his unhappiness. The problem for the teacher is to respect Christopher's feelings, but try to get him to consider the idea of fairness.

T: Do you think "Bubble gum, Bubble gum" would be all right with you, Christopher?

C: It's not all right with me, but if he wants to do it (*shrugs*).

T: Do you think your picking would be fair, Christopher?

Y: No, I don't think Christopher should pick.

With the impasse reasserted, the teacher continues to give the responsibility to the children for coming to agreement, but upholds the value of mutual agreement. By respecting the ideas of both children, she expresses the idea that conflict resolution should consider everyone's feelings.

T: Let's see if y'all can decide on something that you both like.

C: I just wanta' pick somebody. I don't like "Bubble gum, Bubble gum."

Y: All right. (*He decides to try voting.*) Who says to do "Bubble gum, Bubble gum?" (*He raises his hand.*)

C: Nobody. I don't.

Y: (*Turns to teacher.*) Do you wish to do "Bubble gum?"

T: Well, if I vote, then whatever I say will happen because you both disagree.

C: It's O.K. with me if you do whatever you want because you're the adult.

Christopher's response is at Kohlberg's Stage 1 because it identifies fairness with whatever the adult authority wants. The teacher tries to move the children's thinking beyond this level by upholding the idea of the importance of agreement among players.

T: But y'all are playing the game, too. I think y'all should decide, too.

C: Well, I'd just like to pick.

T: Do you have any other ideas, Yousef?

Y: Well, you need to vote, too.

C: Well, Yousef, the only thing that doesn't disturb me is "Eeney, Meeney, Miney, Mo." You can say that, but not "Bubble gum, Bubble gum."

Y: O.K. Eeney, meeney, miney, mo. Catch a tiger by the toe. If he hollers, let him go. Eeney, meeney, miney . . . (stops as he realizes that "mo" will land on Christopher.) Wait a second.

C: No, no. You can't just stop.

Y: Wait. Let me pick somebody now.

Yousef's acceptance of a procedure agreeable to Christopher as well as himself turns out to be rooted in the expectation that a rhyme procedure will get him what he wants. When he miscalculates, it is Christopher's turn to defend the rhyme procedure when it suits his self-interest. The teacher tries to uphold the agreement made between the two boys on using a rhyme procedure to resolve the the conflict.

T: How did that work out? What happened with "Eeney, Meeney, Miney, Mo?"

Y: He was gonna' get first.

C: Wait, now let me do it. (Repeats the rhyme and "mo" lands on the teacher.) You can go first.

T: That's what you want me to do?

C: Yeah.

Y: Yeah.

Letting the teacher go first is an acceptable solution to both boys, so the teacher goes first.

Such is the stuff of which early socio-moral development consists. Even though the eventual agreement in this situation is based on what Kohlberg (1976) would call Stage 1 deference to the teacher's authority, it is a solution arrived at through a process of exchange of viewpoints and autonomous decision making of the two children.

Sometimes educators think that children at Kohlberg's (1976) Stage 1 require the use of firm authority and discipline. Even at Stage 1, however, children are open to exchange and agreement seeking, exchange that fosters movement to the next stage.

Piaget viewed conflict, both intraindividual and interindividual, as one of the general mechanisms of the construction of knowledge and intelligence. It is intraindividual conflict that is a particular source of progress in Piaget's dialectical constructivism. He further explicitly stated that social interaction is necessary for the development of logic. Interindividual conflict in play can provide the context for intraindividual conflict and efforts that lead to new social-cognitive adaptation.

Teaching in terms of conflict rests within a general conceptual framework emphasizing cooperation. Conflict is cooperative in the sense that individuals think or "operate" in terms of one another. The constructivist teacher practices cooperation with children—for example, by consulting them, helping them listen to one another, giving them the opportunity to propose solutions to conflicts, and upholding the value of mutual agreement, as shown in the play example above. This teaching attitude is in contrast to an authoritarian attitude in which the emphasis is on obedience. Piaget hypothesized that the first of these attitudes (that is, autonomous or cooperative) promotes children's development and that the second attitude (heteronomous or coercive) retards their development. Autonomy defined as self-regulation is at the heart of Piaget's theory of both intellectual and sociomoral development. When teachers consistently promote children's autonomy in play situations involving interpersonal issues, children make progress both in sociomoral and intellectual development.

CHAPTER FIVE

The Relationship of Play to Emotional, Social, and Gender/Sex Role Development

NANCY CURRY ● DORIS BERGEN

The recognition that emotions color our view of and approach to the world is at the heart of art, music, drama, and literature. Theories of emotional or affective development have been proposed by ethologists, psychoanalysts, psychologists, and anthropologists, and these theories have informed practice in educational and therapeutic endeavors. The primacy of emotions in the learning process was stressed in the progressive period in education during the 1930s and 1940s. Play had a key role as a curricular tool, since educators viewed play as an avenue for releasing and enhancing emotional expression. Again in the protest period of the 1960s (Glickman, 1984), the advocates of the open school and the British Infant School used play as a central mode for learning and recognized the role of emotions as they hindered or facilitated the educative process. The amount of attention given by researchers and educators to social development has followed a similar historical sequence, fluctuating as various theoretical viewpoints

waxed and waned. Many of the same influences that have determined the level of interest in emotional development have affected social development research and practice. For example Dewey's (1916/1966) progressive school curriculum stressed social development, and it is integrated into the goals of the British Infant School (Schools Council, 1971; Yardley, 1973). Psychoanalytic, social learning, and ethological theories have been influential in providing perspectives through which to view effects of parents' caregiving, teachers' instructional methods, and peers' interactions on children's social development. Since the era of Sputnik, early childhood educators have been impelled to investigate the cognitive payoffs in play activities in order to justify using play as a curricular tool. Thus theories of cognitive development have had an impact on study of emotional and social development. It is clear that learning is multifaceted and includes cognitive, social, and emotional aspects. Further, gender/sex role development exerts a strong influence on play styles, motivation, and expectation. Theory and research have recently focused on this aspect of development as well.

This chapter reviews theories of play from the perspective of emotional, social, and gender/sex role development. In the first section, on emotional development and play, a central organizing principle is the process of development of the sense of self. The emotional environment that helps shape the self and the role of play in enhancing and reflecting the emerging sense of self are discussed. The second section focuses on theories of social and gender/sex role development and the way in which play influences those aspects of development.

Emotional Development and Its Relationship to Play

In the fall, K. went off to kindergarten. Her parents, excited by this landmark in their lives, prepared her as best they could by talking of the teacher whom they had all met, by tracing the bus route, and by reminding her of the children whom she already knew who would be in her class. She was well launched on the first day with encouraging words from both her parents, who took time off from work to share in her new adventure, and with welcomes from her neighborhood cohorts as she climbed onto the bus. On her return home, her face was flushed; she reported a triumphant morning, but a near-fiasco on the returning bus. The driver had taken an alternate route on the way home from school. Her seatmate, an erstwhile nursery school friend, had burst into tears, so that the driver had driven out of his way to deliver the distraught child first. Thus, he had to use yet another road unfamiliar to K. before depositing her at home. Her mother sympathized and then asked gently "And did you cry too?" K. responded reflectively, "No, but my face was *very* sad."

● Theories of emotional development

How does a 5-year-old come to have the ability to feel, express, label, and handle emotions? It appears that this ability has a history of its own, as do other

lines of development (Freud, 1965). The study of how emotions develop over time has a history, too, with its roots in theories of evolution and in psychoanalysis. Darwin (1872/1965) originally proposed a biological basis for emotional development; this proposal has been the impetus for studies of such theorists as Tomkins (1962–1963), Izard (1971), and Ekman and his colleagues (Ekman & Friesen, 1975; Ekman & Friesen, 1978; Ekman, Friesen, & Ellsworth, 1972; Ekman, Roper, & Hager, 1980). Freud's medical training included studying Darwin; he, too, used a biological approach and placed affective development at the core of his theorizing (e.g., Freud, 1923–1924, 1926).

In comparison with the rich history of psychoanalytic exploration of *affects* (a term psychoanalysts interchange with "feelings" and "emotions"), there has been a comparative lack of attention to emotional development in the psychological literature. In their review of some prominent textbooks in child psychology, Lewis and Michaelson (1983) note that a small percentage of pages is usually allocated to emotional development (usually less than 10%). Recently, however, there has been a spate of books and journals devoted to this topic, probably as a result of new methods of observation and the increased focus on infant development (Emde, 1980). In the past decade, researchers have begun to develop instruments to measure emotions (Ekman & Friesen, 1978; Emde, Gaensbauer, & Harman, 1976; Field & Fogel, 1982; Izard, 1982; Lewis & Michaelson, 1983; Plutchik, 1983). This lag in developing assessment instruments attests to the difficulty in defining and measuring emotion in contrast to measuring cognition.

In a review of the controversy over which domain (cognition or emotion) has primacy over the other, Cowan (1982) points to the intertwining of both domains. Referring to research in infant development, he states, "The data here supports the hypothesis that cognitive achievements are necessary for emotional experience; I have suggested that it is also possible to interpret the data as implying that emotional experiences are necessary for cognitive growth" (p. 77).

With the current recognition that the two domains of emotion and cognition interact and are dependent upon each other, there seems to be an agreement about the importance of positive emotional interchanges between caregivers and infants for propeling, enhancing, and enlivening development. The psychoanalytic, ethological, and psychological literature gives the following view of the process of emotional development.

Psychoanalytic theory. While the early psychoanalytic literature tended to present affects from a highly theoretical point of view, there was the implicit assumption that interpersonal relationships, particularly between parent and child, were essential. Rapaport (1953), in one of the numerous theoretical articles on the psychoanalytic theory of affects (e.g., Arlow, 1977; Basch, 1976; Brenner, 1974; Brierly, 1937; Emde, 1980; Green, 1977; Rangell, 1967; Schafer, 1964; Schmale, 1964), used the term affect synonomously with emotion and feeling. He noted that the development of theory of affect paralleled the development of psychoanalytic theory in general. In early psychoanalytic theory, affects were equated with the drives (i.e., sexual and aggressive) and therefore, the unconscious. In the later theory, affects served as signals to guide as well as drive behavior.

Hartmann (1958) introduced the importance of autonomous ego functions and indicated that they are biologically prepatterned affective channels. More recently, many psychoanalysts have focused on object-relations theory, which considers affective interchanges between the self and other as essential for the development of interpersonal relationships and of the ego functions in general (e.g., Jacobson, 1964; Kernberg, 1975, 1980; Kohut, 1971; Mahler, Pine, & Bergman, 1975). Psychoanalytic theorists, then, have seen affects as biologically based and discreet entities that develop and differentiate through meaningful interpersonal transactions and that serve adaptational functions (Emde, 1980).

Social learning theory. Building on the historical tradition of Skinner (e.g., 1974) and Watson (e.g., 1914), social learning theorists such as Bandura (1969; 1977) and Sears and colleagues (e.g., Sears, Maccoby, & Levin, 1957) added a new dimension to ideas about what transpires within persons as they respond to incoming stimuli. In terms of emotional development, social learning theorists stress the importance of social variables, focusing on the interactions of people. Bandura introduced the concept of modeling in interactions between parents and chil-

dren; this included the modeling of emotions and how one handles them. Sears, too, emphasized the importance of the emotional and social environment, which initially involves parent-child interactions, moves to family-centered learning, and finally encompasses the social world of neighborhood and people outside the home (Maier, 1969). Sears' research included studies on various aspects of emotional development such as identification (Sears, Rau, & Alpert, 1965), aggression (Sears, 1950, 1961; Sears & Whitney, 1953), and dependency (Sears & Whitney, 1953); he summarized the influence of parents on their children in these and other areas in a seminal book (Sears, Maccoby, & Levin, 1957). Social psychologists such as Lewis (Lewis & Brooks-Gunn, 1979; Lewis & Michaelson, 1983) have had a strong interest in both emotional development and self acquisition and believe that these are learned in a manner similar to the way other learning occurs.

Ethological theory. Utilizing Darwin's (1872/1965) studies of animals and their survival skills in natural environments, ethologists have begun to apply the ethological approach to the study of child behavior (e.g., Blurton-Jones, 1972; McGrew, 1972). This theoretical perspective posits that, just as animals have innate action patterns that have been adaptive for their survival, so infants are programmed to exhibit behavior that will elicit the caregiving essential for their survival. In terms of emotional development and parent-child relationships, Bowlby (1969, 1973) introduced the concept of human attachment. In the process of obtaining and giving care, the mother-infant bond is established. This bond develops into attachment (i.e., a relationship to the mother, or other caregiving person, that is shown by the infant's active seeking of the presence, touch, and comfort of the person to whom he or she is attached).

Bowlby's emphasis on the importance of attachment has generated much research (e.g., Ainsworth, 1969, 1972, 1973, 1974, 1979; Sroufe, 1979). Strong attachment in infancy has been related to later competencies such as empathy (Zahn-Waxler, Radke-Yarrow, & King, 1979), sympathy (Waters, Wippman, & Sroufe, 1979), problem solving (Arend, Grove & Sroufe, 1979; Matas, Arend, & Sroufe, 1978), ego resiliency (Block & Block, 1980), high fantasy predisposition (Singer, 1973), play

skills (Pepler & Ross, 1981; Sylva, 1977), and sociability (A.F. Lieberman, 1977).

Self psychology.   Currently there is in the literature
remarkable concordance about the importance of the
first 3 years of life, with the recognition that a major
developmental task during these years is the establishing of a sense of self that is marked by both object
and self constancy. A recent comprehensive review
of the self-system by Harter (1983) describes the
current state of the field from a variety of perspectives. In general, psychologists view the self as a
cognitive structure (e.g., Kegan, 1982; Lewis &
Brooks-Gunn, 1979; Sarbin, 1962), while psychoanalysts tend to focus on the emotional aspects. Harter
(1983, p. 291) summarizes the positions taken by
psychologists such as Lewis and Brooks-Gunn
(1979), by psychoanalytically oriented writers such
as Mahler et al. (1975) and Sander (1975) and those
influenced by ethology (e.g., Ainsworth, 1969, 1972,
1973, 1974, 1979; Bowlby, 1969, 1973). There is
agreement among most authors that the self has two
intertwining aspects: the self as subject and the self as
object (Harter, 1983), with developmental changes
occurring over time and through relationships with
other people.

The emotional aspects of self-development as an
intrapsychic developmental task are described by
psychoanalysts in terms of both object (i.e., meaning
the primary caregiver) constancy and self-constancy.
Jacobson (1964), Kernberg (1975, 1980), Kohut
(1971, 1977), and Mahler et al. (1975) have provided the impetus for looking at the apparent stability
of those personality characteristics associated with
the establishment of the self or identity and the individual management of self-esteem. These characteristics arise from a complex intertwining of
constitutional factors and the child's life experiences,
especially through meaningful emotional relationships, and may be the clearest behavioral evidence
there is to support theoretical psychoanalytic concepts such as the "cohesive self" (Kohut, 1971), the
"integrated self" (Kernberg, 1975) and the self "on
the way to object constancy" (Mahler et al., 1975), all
of which are theorized as being established in the first
3 years of life.

The view, then, that adult-child interactions are
essential for self-development and that emotions facilitate that development has support from the psy-

chological, the psychoanalytic, and the ethological
literature. Emotions are important in these interactions; the ways emotions arise, are differentiated, and
influence development throughout childhood are
thus important to consider.

● Characteristics of emotional development

Differentiation of emotions.   The view that primary
emotions are innate has been proposed by Darwin
and elaborated by Tomkins (1962–1963), Tomkins
and McCarter (1964), Ekman and associates (1972,
1975, 1978, 1980), and Izard, (1971, 1972, 1980,
1982). The child brings into the world a prepatterned
analogue of emotional responsivity that is nurtured
and expanded through meaningful interactions with
caregivers, usually the mother. Infants are not the
helpless passive receivers of this caregiving; contemporary psychologists perceive them as active participants in interactions from birth. Constitutional factors
that contribute to individual differences have been
noted (Benjamin, 1961; Escalona, 1968; Escalona &
Heider, 1959; Thomas & Chess, 1977). These individual differences inevitably influence parental responses to children (Bell, 1971). Further, the
organization of the newborn's behavior in terms of
sleep/wakefulness and rest/activity points to the biological readiness of children to produce differentiated
behaviors that will call forth differentiated responses
from caregivers (Capella, 1981; Emde, Swedberg, &
Suzuki, 1975; Gaensbaur & Emde, 1973; Moss &
Robson, 1968; Sterman & Hoppenbrouwers, 1971;
Stern, 1971, 1974a; Wolff, 1969).

"Affective reciprocity" (Emde, 1980) begins in
these early infant-caregiver exchanges and continues
to be an essential ingredient in all human relationships. Children's prepatterned affective responses
(e.g., smiling, crying, facial grimacing, drawing up of
the limbs, flailing of the arms and legs) elicit emotional responses from their parents; adults' readings
of children's affective states are essential in the differentiation of emotions as well as in helping children
learn the communicative value of affective expressions. Depending on whether or not caregivers meet
children's needs in a predictable, loving fashion,
children begin to perceive a world that may alleviate
or may extend discomfort.

As emotions differentiate, at least 10 universal
primary discrete emotions seem to develop during

the first year of life (Ekman et al., 1972; Gaensbauer, 1982; Izard, 1971; Plutchik, 1983; Sroufe, 1979). The differentiation of these emotions and self-definition continue to flourish through the nutriment of the mother-child dyad. Mahler and her colleagues (1975) have proposed a four-stage developmental progression in the separation-individuation process during the first 3 years of life in which children move toward individuality and separate intrapsychically from parents. Mahler et al.'s formulations are paralleled by Sander's (1975) seven adaptational issues, which parent and child must negotiate in self- and other- awareness during the same time span. Greenspan and Greenspan (1985) have delineated six emotional milestones of the first 4 years of life that fit well with the Mahler et al. and Sander models.

Such authors agree that toward the end of the first year of life, well-developing infants are securely attached, which is evidenced by a discernible, differentiated response to a standard measurement of attachment (Ainsworth, 1969, 1972, 1973, 1974, 1979). By now, the foundation of basic trust has been established (Erikson, 1963). If emotional interactions have not gone well during this first year, infants will have a pervasive feeling of mistrust of their caregivers and of themselves.

Infants have become upright, have developed intense relationships with their families, and are beginning to demonstrate empathy for others, which is another indication of the burgeoning sense of self and an awareness of their separateness from other people. This dawning empathy for others is enhanced by caregivers who themselves are empathic and display a wide range of emotional expressions (Barnett, King, Howard, & Dino, 1980; Eisenberg-Berg & Mussen, 1978; Hoffman, 1982; Strayer, 1980, 1983).

Table 5–1 incorporates Hesse and Cicchetti's (1982) summary of various perspectives on emotional development and Greenspan and Greenspan's (1985) milestones in emotional development.

Widening of emotional range.   The designation of 18 months as a developmental crossroads has support from numerous sources (Erikson, 1963; Greenspan & Greenspan, 1985; Mahler et al., 1975; Piaget, 1962; Sander, 1975; Sroufe, 1979). As Table 5–1 indicates, Spitz' (1959) third reorganizer, negativism, corresponds to Sroufe's (1979) seventh stage, emergence of self, which in turn corresponds to

Greenspan and Greenspan's (1985) fourth milestone, the emergence of an organized sense of self. The emergence of the sense of self as conceptualized by these researchers parallels Piaget's (1952, 1962) final stages of the sensorimotor period. Mahler et al.'s (1975) rapprochement stage and Erikson's (1963) stage of autonomy versus shame and doubt also focus on children's emotional and cognitive recognition of the separateness of self from others and the attendant ambivalence that arises from pitting oneself against the wishes of beloved adults whom one both yearns for and struggles against. The stormy period of toddlerhood is notorious; emotions are strong, differentiated, complicated, and reciprocal. Some of the predominant feelings toddlers experience are shame and doubt (Erikson, 1963), love, hate, pride, self-esteem, jealousy, rage, and envy, all in the context of intensifying and broadening social relationships.

In terms of the development of the sense of self, Mahler et al. (1975) posit that the toddler, having negotiated the first three subphases of separation and individuation, now moves into the final subphase, the emergence of libidinal object constancy. Now, the feelings of goodness and badness about oneself and others need to become integrated into a perception of self and others that is stable in spite of shifts in feeling states. Once the sense of self- and other-constancy is achieved, preschool children are freer to test out that self in relation to peers, parents, and meaningful adults. An expanded view of the self includes identification with important adults. Bad dreams, phobias, and aggressive outbursts characterize the preschool years, as well as the capacity to show deep and abiding affection (Fraiberg, 1959; Josselyn, 1955). In terms of affective development, Erikson (1963) points out the danger of the intense guilt children can feel because of destructive wishes and fantasies toward beloved or feared adults and other children; they may retreat from the initiatives they are capable of taking in the areas of play, learning, and social relationships.

As children enter the late preschool years, advancing cognitive sophistication, social awareness, and changing physical appearance (e.g., knobby knees, lost teeth, lanky arms and legs) all render kindergarten children prone to fluctuating self-esteem. If all has gone well in the earlier stages, they are enthusiastic about learning, intensely curious about their widening world (especially about birth

TABLE 5–1 ● The Development of Social Emotions from Various Perspectives (adapted from Hesse & Cicchetti, 1982)

Developmental Level	Spitz (1959)/Emde, Gaensbauer, & Harmon (1976)	Sroufe (1979)	Erikson (1950)	Greenspan & Greenspan (1985)
Infancy/ sensorimotor development		1) *Absolute stimulus barrier*: endogenous smile, startle/ pain distress due to covering face, physical restraint, extreme discomfort	1) *Trust vs. mistrust*: sadness, depression, anxiety, rage, pain, pleasure	1) *Self-regulation and interest in the world*: birth to 3 months
	I. *First reorganizer*: social smile	2) *Turning toward*: obligatory attention distress same as before 3) *Positive affect*: pleasure, rage (disappointment), delight, active laughter, wariness 4) *Active participation*: joy, anger		2) *Falling in love*: 2 and 3 months
	II. *Second reorganizer*: fear of strangers	5) *Attachment*: fear (stranger aversion) 6) *Practicing*: elation, anxiety, immediate fear, angry mood, petulance	2) *Autonomy vs. shame/doubt*: shame, doubt, love, hate, pride, self-control, self-esteem, jealously of siblings, shame as precursor of guilt, rage turned against self, defiance as a precursor of sense of justice	3) *Developing interactional communication*: 3–10 months
	III. *Third reorganizer*: negativism	7) *Emergence of self*: positive valuation of self-affection, shame, defiance, intentional hurting		4) *Emergence of organized sense of self*: 9–18 months

Developmental Level	Spitz (1959)/Emde, Gaensbauer, & Harmon (1976)	Sroufe (1979)	Erikson (1950)	Greenspan & Greenspan (1985)
Early childhood/ intuitive or preoperational thought		8) *Play and fantasy*: pride, love, guilt	3) *Initiative vs. guilt*: curiosity, interest, jealousy, pleasure in attack, conquest, enjoyment of competition, goal-directedness, hope	5) *Creation of emotional ideas*: 18–36 months 6) *Emotional thinking*: basis for fantasies, reality and self-esteem: 30–48 months
Middle childhood/ concrete operations			4) *Industry vs. inferiority*: competence, achievement, motivation, enjoyment of work, self-esteem, guilt, pride, enjoyment of new locomotor and mental power, resignation, anxiety, terror, despair, frustration, pleasure, hope, rage	

and death), and eager to socialize. But the cognitive capacities that serve them so well also make them vulnerable to negative self-perceptions and widely fluctuating self-esteem. They range from bombast to blubbering; they compare themselves and are compared to other people. They recognize themselves as vulnerable and small as they become aware of the wider world, which is filled with all varieties of people with higher expectations. The kindergarten year is thus full of triumphs and tragedies. During this period, children need the support of parents and teachers; adults serve as mirrors who can enhance or crush the fragile self-esteem of the 5-year-old.

Consolidation of emotional patterns. Erikson (1963) notes the school-age child's task of negotiating the opposing feeling states of industry versus inferiority. Sarnoff (1976) describes school-age children as calmer, more educable, and more pliable than their preschool counterparts due to the lessening of the aggressive and sexual drives, but notes that emotions continue to exert a strong influence on children's capacity to learn. Adults continue to play an important role in arousing, shaping, and helping to modulate those emotions. Positive emotions are embedded in children's wish to please adults at home and school, to compete yet ally themselves with the now exceedingly important peers, and to satisfy the urgent drive to learn by applying themselves with the industry that marks that period. It is important to recognize that negative emotions also can permeate children's lives. If parents and teachers do not respond to these, they can interfere with the learning process. For example, children may experience shame and doubt when they cannot meet family and school standards, guilt for harboring feelings of jealousy and envy towards higher achieving age mates and siblings, fluctuating self-esteem, and noxious reactions from too many experiences with hated and feared adults.

The school years are generally viewed as the latency period in terms of emotional development, yet children continue to experience the whole range of emotionality and to confront the developmental task of learning to channel these emotions into acceptable, rewarding, and productive outlets. They may also have some emotional and cognitive sophistication to assist them in consolidating a sense of themselves as partners and participants in the wide world of school and community and to enable them to apply themselves industriously to learning the tools of our culture (Erikson, 1963).

● **Relationship of play to emotional development**

The richness of play, especially dramatic play, has always intrigued theorists and clinicians. Throughout the historical development of play theories, the social and emotional facets of play, in particular, have captured the attention of such theoreticians as Schiller (1875), Spencer (1873), Groos (1901), Freud (1920), Peller (1954), and Erikson (1963).

The psychoanalytic view of play takes the position that play is a projection of the individual's emotional or inner life. Play, in this framework, is theorized as serving compensatory (Capell, 1967; Menninger, 1942; Peller, 1954; Robinson, 1920); mastery (Erikson, 1963; Freud, 1920); cathartic (Isaacs, 1933; Menninger, 1942); and assimilative

(Waelder, 1933) functions, which are all closely linked to emotional development.

Both psychoanalysts and psychoanalytically oriented educators (Griffiths, 1935; Isaacs, 1930/1966; Lowenfeld, 1935; Piers, 1972) have developed the concept that play is a bridge between the child's inner life and external reality, an important aspect of ego development. The role of play in ego development is strongly supported by Erikson (1950/1963), Alexander (1958); Freud (1965), and Kardos and Peto (1956). According to Erikson, "I would look at a play act as, vaguely speaking, a function of the ego, an attempt to bring into synchronization the bodily and social processes of which one is a part even while one is a self" (1950, p. 184).

In Piaget's (1962) discussion of the play of the child in the preschool years, he is also partially in agreement with psychoanalytic writing concerning play and games. He describes the symbolic games of the representational stage of intellectual development in much the way the psychoanalysts describe play. "Compensation, fulfillment of wishes, liquidation of conflicts, etc. are continually added to the pleasure 'of being the cause' inherent in sensori-motor practice" (Piaget, 1962, p. 112). He further agrees with the psychoanalytic veiwpoint as to the function of symbolic play, "which is to assimilate reality to the ego while freeing the ego from the demands of accommodation" (p. 134).

The relationship of play to the emotions is made explicit by many of these authors; the relationship to the sense of self is usually implicit. Play mirrors and enhances the child's progress through self-definition during the preschool years and assists the tasks of self-consolidation during the school years. The importance of affectively laden interchanges with meaningful adults (first parents and/or caregivers, later teachers) and peers to the development and content of play also is seen in play.

Infant play. Most authors agree with Piaget that sensorimotor or practice play typifies the play of infancy (Piaget, 1962). Caregivers and their infants engage in playful interchanges, which are first initiated by the caregiver. In the first 3 months of life, a period labeled variously as relative autism (Mahler et al., 1975), initial regulation (Sander, 1975), naive synchrony (Foley, 1986), and self-regulation and interest in the world (Greenspan & Greenspan, 1985), infants begin to learn to live with others. Their awareness of what comes from inside and what comes from outside is gradually evoked by parental attention to physical needs that also involve playful encounters. The content of mother-infant play includes playful vocalizations, tactile and visual stimulation, and playful manipulation of the arms and legs (Crawley et al., 1978; Power & Parke, 1980; Sroufe & Wunsche, 1972; Stern, 1977; Watson & Ramey, 1972). Brazelton and Als (1979) have noted that in these very early playful sequences between parent and child, the parent not only respects the child's need to withdraw from too much stimulation in caretaking game playing, but also recognizes value in challenging and interesting the baby in prolonging the attention states that make possible a play dialogue. They propose four sequences in the developing play interactions of mother and child that culminate in beginning object play, which they feel demonstrates a true test of attachment at 3 to 4 months: (a) physiological motor orientation and state regulation during which the baby alternatively shuts out and reaches for stimuli; (b) orientation in which the child begins to prolong attention states; (c) play dialogue; (d) beginning object play.

During the period of symbiosis (Mahler et al., 1975), a play platform is beginning to build through child-adult play encounters that are laden with affect. With the onset of meaningful smiles (Emde, 1980; Spitz & Cobliner, 1965), the infant gives evidence of positive affect, which helps elicit ever more positive play responses from parents (Watson & Ramey, 1972). Greenspan and Greenspan (1985) call this the period of falling in love.

Mahler et al. (1975) label the period of 4 to 9 months as the differentiation subphase, when children are both differentiating themselves from others and beginning to recognize the parents as special. Mahler et al.'s subphase corresponds to Sander's (1975) stages of reciprocal exchange and initiative and the Greenspans' (1985) developing interactional communication. This process is facilitated by differentiating games with the manual, tactile, and visual explorations of one's own body parts as well as those of parents and of the inanimate environment. Several researchers report that fathers are more likely than mothers to play physical games with their infants during this period (Lamb, 1977; Smith & Daglish, 1977; Weinraub & Frankel, 1977); in these vestibular experiences the child's body is invested with emotional tones of pleasure and potency. The baby's beginning individuality is highlighted by the traditional games of babyhood (e.g., peek-a-boo; this little piggy, where's baby's nose), which are symbolic vehicles for parents to delineate for their babies, "This is you and this is me."

One of the earliest instances of the baby's beginning symbolization of the deep emotional meaning of parental caregiving and soothing is the use of the security blanket and other "transitional objects" (Tolpin, 1971; Winnicott, 1971), which seem to represent certain physical attributes of mother (e.g., the touch of her skin, a smell associated with her caregiving functions.)

As children move from being babies-at-the-breast to babies-at-mother's-feet in the differentiation period, to crawling and then walking, their view of and access to the world expands. Practice play (Piaget, 1962) is exemplified by the child's capacity to walk. Thus begins the practicing period, a subphase (Mahler et al., 1975) of separation-individuation in which most children seem to exude a sense of potency in discovering themselves as active players and explorers of the animate and inanimate worlds. Their increasing awareness of themselves and others as both physically and emotionally separate is indicated in the beginnings of imitative pretend behavior at approximately 1 year (Fein & Apfel, 1979), in which the actions of meaningful others are understood well enough to be imitated. Run-and-chase games, which children initiate by taunting adults into chasing them (Speers, 1975), demonstrate children's reaching out for independence with the concomitant need to be reassured that their caregivers will retrieve them. In negotiating the adaptational milestone of focalization (Sander, 1975) at 10 to 13 months, children intensify their focus on parents and seek them as play companions. The need for mirroring approval of parents at this age is essential and provides the launching pad for children's beginning imitative play; through play, children involve their primary caregivers and their activities and themselves as both recipient and initiator of caretaking functions.

Toddler play. As children near the end of the sensorimotor period, cognitive and symbolic capacities enlarge. With cognitive awareness of separateness, the rapprochement period (Mahler et al., 1975) begins, during which children are confronted with awareness of both physical and intrapsychic separateness from their parents. The urgency with which children move toward self-definition is expressed in the autonomous assertions (e.g., "No," "Mine," and "Do it myself"). The capacity to symbolize becomes a tool for negotiating through this period. Games of disappearance and reappearance are of great appeal and help the children cope with this burning development issue of separation and autonomy. Sorting and discriminating tasks (Freud, 1965) also serve as symbolic vehicles for differentiating what/who belongs to what/whom as children attempt to find their place in the scheme of things.

Research on decentralized and self/other role taking supports this progression in self-awareness, awareness of others, and definition of self and other. In their comprehensive review of the current research on play, Rubin, Fein, and Vandenberg (1983) summarize the literature that traces the developmental progression of decontextualized and self/other role taking that begins in the second year and becomes elaborated in the preschool years. Fein (1984), for example, discusses the self-building aspects of pretend play. She has developed a chart (p. 127) describing the basic structures in Mead's (1934) model of role-playing and role taking with four components that seem to progress developmentally with cognitive and emotional growth: (a) self in pretend activities; (b) generic role transformation (i.e., without complementarity), with single perspective taking; (c) generic role with complementarity, with double perspective taking; and (d) generic role with complementarity and reversal, with double perspective taking and perspective switching.

Symbolic role taking, as described by Fein (1984) and others, demonstrates children's perceptions of both self and others as being more clearly defined; such clarity enables children to take part in beginning representational individual play acts. Studies by Belsky and Most (1981), Fein and Apfel (1979), Inhelder, Lezine, Sinclair, and Stambak (1972), Lowe (1975), and Watson and Fischer (1977) demonstrate that "self-referenced behavior declines between 12 and 30 months, whereas doll-referenced behavior increases" (Rubin et al., 1983, p. 718). They further report increases in the use of a substitute object between 19 and 24 months and the

beginning of coordination and sequencing of pretend acts during the second and third years (p. 719).

Children's continued movement toward separation-individuation as they near the age of 3 is reflected in their abilities in rudimentary representational play to take distance from themselves through self-pretend (e.g., pretending to be a defiant baby who won't go to bed) and through pretending to be another person (e.g., putting on father's shoes and clomping around, speaking in a deep voice).

Preschool play. Most research findings agree with Piaget that sociodramatic play increases markedly between ages 3 and 6 (e.g., Corsaro, 1979; Emmerich, 1977; Hetherington, Cox, & Cox, 1979; Iwanga, 1973; Rubin & Krasnor, 1980; Rubin, Maoni, & Hornung, 1976; Rubin, Watson, & Jambor, 1978; Sponseller & Jaworski, 1979). Using the framework of the self, children are on their way toward libidinal object consistency (Mahler et al., 1975) and have an internalized, stable image of themselves and of the important others in their lives that is maintained regardless of the others' presence or absence. These internal representations of self and of meaningful others become externalized through dramatic role-play, which becomes less imitative of physical attributes and has more elements of identification with others in terms of their feelings and functions as well as of children's own feelings about these relationships.

Psychoanalytically oriented authors have made the greatest contribution to study of thematic content of pretense. From her carefully recorded observational records of preschool children during three years in a group setting, Isaacs (1933) noted the prevalence of hostility and aggression in the children's play and attributed this to the "surface" motives: (a) possession, (b) power, (c) rivalry, (d) feelings of inferiority, superiority, or general anxiety. She noted the absorption her pupils had in the basic themes of birth and death and proposed an intriguing theory around these interests to explain why children are fascinated with creating "cozy places." Her contemporary Griffiths (1935), in studying the imaginative development of 5-year-olds in London and Brisbane, Australia, also noted her subjects' preoccupation with birth and death, as well as their interest in power, autonomy, and independence, which was dramatized in play and other imaginative vehicles (e.g., art, stories, dreams) through themes full of hostility and aggression. In 1946, Bach also wrote of the wild and weird content of ordinary children's play. Levin and Wardwell (1962) summarized the doll play research studies dealing with aggression, doll preferences, effects of separation from parents, and reactions to racial and religious differences. At that time the number of aggression studies (31) far outweighed those in the other categories. All of these themes point to self issues concerning basic human themes of birth and potential death, caring and conflictual relationships with other people, desires to be seen as an individuated person, and intense struggles with feelings of both love and aggression.

Following in this tradition, Peller (1952, 1954) described in depth what roles children play and why they play them. In a seminal paper, she (1954) charts the developmental progression of play activities from infancy through school age according to categories: (a) the central theme as related to current object relations; (b) the deficiency anxiety; (c) the compensatory fantasy; (d) the style, social aspects, and play materials; and (e) secondary gains. In another paper (1952) she describes a number of models of play activities with children's choices of and motivations for roles: (a) love and admiration, (b) fear, (c) the wish to portray the losing party (incognito indulgence), (d) clowning, (e) deflected vengeance, (f) anticipatory retaliation, (g) happy ending, (h) magic (no risk), and (i) manipulative and playful repetition.

Since Peller, the two major contributions to the thematic content of children's play have come from Gould (1972) and Curry and Arnaud (1974, 1982). Gould specifically focuses on representations of the self as demonstrated in play roles. Both the context of play episodes (i.e., the style children demonstrate when depicting the role) and the text (i.e., content) of the role are considered. Gould's thesis is that children reflect their earlier experience in nurturance and provision with their primary caregivers. Identification with these meaningful people, as well as the attitudes primary caregivers consistently demonstrate toward them, become part of their self-representations, which can be observed in the style children use in fantasy play and the content of that play. Gould points out that children's roles display primary iden-

tification with the nurturant/provider, the aggressor, or the victim. Consistently positive experiences with nurturance result in children's predominant identification with the provider and is evident in their role-play, even those roles with highly aggressive content (e.g., Superman, policeman, and doctor) are played with a strongly nurturant, rescuing aspect.

Children who have had primarily negative experience in nurturance portray a prominent identification with either the aggressor or victim and manifest a rigidity in this defensive depiction of victim or aggressor representations (Gould, 1972, p. 266). Such children are unable to take distance from themselves in play and tend to *become* the role, have "fluctuating certainty" in terms of distinguishing reality and fantasy, and demonstrate "global self-condemnation" toward themselves, inferring that they do not have a sense of entitlement.

Curry and Arnaud (1974, 1982) also see developmental progression in both the style and content in children's role-playing, and propose a developmental sequence in terms of (a) symbolic elaboration of the role, (b) thematic content, (c) integration of intellectual affect, (d) distinction between reality and fantasy, (e) modes of interpersonal transaction, (f) enactment of the good in idealized self. They have proposed a developmental sequence in thematic content that appears to reflect children's growing ability to portray themselves and others with greater accuracy at the same time as they color those self-views with the emotional tones surrounding meaningful interpersonal interactions.

This developmental sequence for thematic content is exhibited by children who are encouraged by invested adults to use play by being given (a) play periods, (b) appropriate props, and (c) permission to express emotions freely. Who or what the children choose to portray in role-play and how they play those roles show their cognitive and emotional perceptions of themselves and others.

By age 3 there is an amalgam of self-representations, representations of primary caregivers now internalized, and the emotional meanings carried in the representations. In portraying their view of self and significant others, 3-year-olds, if all has gone well in early childhood caring experiences, engage predominantly in nurturing themes of caregiving dyads: father or mother/baby, nurse or doctor/patient, big sister/

little sister, animal parent/animal baby. In general most 3-year-olds prefer the more powerful role of caregiver as if they are still too close to babyhood to perpetuate that status in pretend play. Themes of separation, loss, and return are enacted through roles such as runaway baby or puppy; concerns about the body are depicted in beginning medical play.

Aggressive imagery appears in the play of most young preschoolers in unmodulated, barely disguised, stereotypic depiction of monsters or wild animals with focus on teeth and claws. Such outright aggression causes many 3-year-olds to lose "distance from self" (Gould, 1972) and frighten themselves or their playmates. However, some children tend to use such imagery without distancing themselves through the guise of pretend, and *become* the role in a perseverative, driven fashion. Such modulated wild animal or superhero play becomes the bane of the preschool teacher's existence.

The relatively placid bucolic play of 3-year-olds gives way to the more aggressive emotion-packed play of older preschoolers. While themes of nurturance, power, and body integrity continue, other concerns take center stage. For example, with their more stable sense of who they are and an increasingly clearer view of who others are, 4-year-olds develop an intense curiosity about adults, whom they tend to glorify. The depiction of parents beyond-nurturance, the glamorous view of mother (e.g., Barbie dolls), and the powerful view of father and other males (e.g., He-Man) come into play. Triadic roles of mother/father/child or doctor/patient/nurse appear, and the emotional essence of the role is portrayed (e.g., the exasperated mother who punishes fractious children; the distracted father who banishes his children from the TV area). In their playing out of masculine and feminine roles they want outward manifestations of the role (e.g., high heels, gloves, purses, jewelry, hats, frilly skirts; or capes, hats, magic wands, and other accessories). Relational roles (Garvey & Berndt, 1977) predominate, but character roles are a close second, perhaps because of the strong influence of television, but more likely because of the permission such roles give to children to project their fantasies of idealized and aggrandized adults into "safe," distant-from-parent representations.

Dyadic roles continue but now represent good and bad (e.g., policeman/robber; He-Man/Skeletor), as children struggle with their heightened aggressivity along with their wish to be good. Dichotomous human themes of birth and death, escape and rescue, body image and intactness, loss and return, power and weakness, and interpersonal negotiations enliven the play of 4-year-olds.

In all these roles, children's primary identifications with nurturer/aggressor/victim are even more easily observable than at age 3. Preoccupation with aggressive imagery may be intensified in children with negative self-perceptions. Children who have more stable, positive self-views are still fascinated by the aggressive roles, but are able to portray them more comfortably through the themes of rescue, body repair, and caretaking (e.g., firemen who put out fires, examine the injured, and call for an ambulance to take the ailing to the hospital).

By age 5, children can dramatize every aspect of their widening world; roles are as varied as are children's experiences (e.g., teacher, school principal, storekeeper, librarian, soldier) and fantasies (e.g., royalty, spacemen, superheros, and TV characters). The heightened interest in romance as well as the stereotypic definition of oneself as male or female is depicted in play, often with fairy-tale elements (e.g., kings and queens, princes and princesses, the good and persevering winning out over forces of evil). Struggles to come to terms with a self-view of goodness and badness continue to be played out both in fantasy and in stylized battle scenes (e.g., wild versus tame animals; knights versus dragons) at a greater distance than such roles are portrayed by younger preschoolers. In this play, children seem to be indicating a stronger awareness of themselves as members of a system that extends beyond family and includes others who people the world of reality and of fiction. This higher level of awareness demonstrates a fairly cohesive view of a self attempting to be effective in and on the personal and impersonal environment.

Elementary play.   While most authors agree with Piaget's delineation of games-with-rules as typifying the play of school-age children (Freud, 1965), pretend play does continue, as evidenced by Eiferman's (1971) study and by Peller (1952, 1954). Arnaud and Curry (Arnaud, 1971; Arnaud & Curry, 1974; Curry & Arnaud, 1974, 1984) have noted the thematic content of the play of school-age children when they are given encouragement and permission to continue such play. Children are confronted with the many expectations of an intriguing world that cannot always be comprehended or dealt with competently in all its complexities. This attempt to make sense of the world and how they fit into it is demonstrated in dramatic play, in which school-age children test out many fearful fantasies under the safe guise of play. They can take distance from their frightening speculations and fantasies and feel more in control by attempted mastery through staged dramas and written stories, as well as dramatic play. As Arnaud describes,

The most gleefully invested play and role enactments—and remember, they are over developed by *normal children*—are usually blood and thunder melodramas, dripping with gore, featuring ambush and attack, killing and death. They are peopled by ghosts, statues that come to life, grisly folk heroes (e.g., Dracula), vampires, and people who turn out to be very different from what they purport to be. (Arnaud, 1971, p. 11).

Arnaud further describes the absence of parents in role-play; parentless bands of peers and siblings take center stage, and adults are often depicted through cultural symbols of danger (e.g., Mr. Hyde, vampires). The self-views of school-age children include their anticipation of future gender/sex roles that carry with them fears, fantasies, and speculations. In play, interest in the relationship between males and females is often "treated in hostilely joking, disparaging terms; danger is implicit in them" (Arnaud, 1971, p. 11).

The emotional aspects of daydreams, sports, games, and hobbies are important as well. Gump and Sutton-Smith (1955) and Redl (1959) have written about the symbolic meaning of roles assigned or chosen in organized sports and games.

It is clear that the style in which children enact dramatic play roles (e.g., dyadic play at 3 years, triadic play at 4 and 5; parentless peer play at school age) and the basic thematic content (e.g., caregiving at 3; aggression and romance at 4 and 5) reflect developmental preoccupations that absorb children at various ages. Individual children's choices of roles (e.g., victim, aggressor, nurturer) within that developmental context gives us a picture of how they view the world and the self within that world.

● Play therapy

Play therapy has been provided for children who are not able to handle their fears, fantasies, and emotions with the flexible defenses and identifications seen as necessary to be a solid player, group member, and efficient learner. According to Erikson (1950, p. 195), "to play it out" is one of the most natural self-healing measures childhood affords.

Traditionally, the techniques of play therapy fall roughly into three main schools: the English (Klein, 1932), the Viennese (Freud, 1928, 1965), and the nondirective (Axline, 1947). Freud (1928) was one of the first psychoanalysts to attempt the analysis of children through the use of play rather than free association. Her techniques, which diverge from classical psychoanalysis by allowing for the child's immature psychic structure (Freud, 1965), have been further developed and advocated by such child psychoanalysts as Erikson (1950/1963, 1951), Solomon (1951), Waltman (1955). The therapist becomes an auxiliary ego for the child, whose fluid personality state permits therapy to open new channels for development. Interpretation is used to highlight, release, and alleviate emotional conflict, but play itself is seen as being therapeutic (Erikson, 1950/1963). An offshoot of Freudian analysis is the English school, headed by Klein (1932). She likened child analysis to adult analysis and advocated constant interpretation of symbolism as it appeared in play.

The nondirective therapy of Axline (1947) extended Rogers' (1942) client-centered therapy to work with children. The therapist gives the child undirected use of the toys; the resultant play expresses the child's personality and releases feelings and attitudes. Rather than being an auxiliary ego as in Freudian therapy or being a constant interpreter of symbolic meanings in the Kleinian manner, the nondirective therapist reflects the child's feelings without being interpretive or judgmental. A form of transactional therapy for adults (Berne, 1964) has utilized a theory of games as a diagnostic tool and operational premise.

In the past decade there has been a proliferation of multiple approaches to therapy. This is documented by Schaefer and Millman (1980), who describe a wide variety of frequent behavioral problems of childhood for which techniques using a number of specific approaches (e.g., art therapy, behavior modification, behavior therapy, desensitization, dynamic therapy, family therapy, psychoanalysis, relaxation therapy, and visualization and imagery). Many of these modes of treatment utilize play as adjunct to a primary technique such as behavior modification.

● **Implications for educational practice**

Since emotions enhance, propel, and occasionally impede development, they deserve careful consideration and nurturing on the part of adults who have chosen to work with children. It is clear that play can be a window to children's emotional lives and that it serves as a diagnostic as well as a curricular tool. Both the context (i.e., style) and text (i.e., thematic content) of dramatic play can tell teachers (a) where children are developmentally; (b) what they might be grappling with emotionally; and (c) where there could be emotional interferences. Adults then can use those communications to further children's emotional growth.

The process and content of in-depth play episodes serve emotional development in terms of mastery, catharsis, and self-definition. However, if children are to be free to express their feelings through play, they need an environment that facilitates expressiveness. Such an environment is created by adults who allow for play unhampered by time constraints, and who provide props, space, and developmentally appropriate peers, as well as keen approval of expressive activities. Teachers need to recognize that emotionally tinged play often deals with the less pleasant aspects of children's daily and fantasy lives (e.g., death, destruction, evil figures such as witches, monsters, and ghosts). Such content can make many adults uncomfortable and they may terminate or prohibit such play for their own comfort, unaware of the emotional value it can have for children. Well-timed suggestions and clarifications from invested adults can provide the structure and support children need to deal with emotional issues in play, so that they do not become frightened by or flooded with emotion that may seem unmanageable without adult buffering. Voicing fears and fantasies, trying out alternative strategies in dealing with them, and discovering solutions are steps children can negotiate in play that will have emotional, as well as cognitive, payoffs.

Social and Gender/Sex Role Development and Its Relationship to Play

One vignette:

T. (a 4-year-old-girl) is sitting by the teacher and by S. (a boy age 3 years, 6 months) at lunchtime in the day-care center. T. tells the teacher that she has a doll. S. says, "I play with my doll." T. responds, "Just girls play with dollies, not boys." Mrs. H., the teacher, asks T. why only girls can play with dolls. T. says, " 'Cause they's Mommies." S. then says he has a truck he plays with at home. T. answers, "I play with trucks too." Mrs. H. asks T., "If you play with trucks why can't boys play with dolls?" T. emphatically finishes the conversation, "Girls can play with dolls *and* trucks, boys can't play with both."

Another vignette:

The boys (age 9) have been playing baseball for about an hour. They are approached by J., an 8-year-old girl, who asks to play with them. She is told "no" by L., one of the boys, very distinctly. She asks again in a few moments and is again told "no" by the same boy. Another boy about his same age and build says, "Ah come on, L., what are you, a male chauvinist?" "No," replies L., "only when it comes to baseball." J. is not allowed into the game.

Emotional, social, and gender/sex role development arise from similar sources and are influenced by many common childhood experiences. For example, social adjustment and gender role acceptance have been linked to the psychosexual stages of Freudian theory (Freud, 1923–1924), and socialization processes affecting both emotional and social development have been described by learning theorists (Sears, Maccoby, & Levin, 1957). Because the processes promoting children's social and emotional development are complementary, some theorists and researchers have held the view that these areas of development are so intricately intertwined as to be inseparable. Certain theoretical and research perspectives have intentionally integrated the two (e.g.,

Erikson's (1963) theoretical model of psychosocial crises). However, as the first section of this chapter demonstrates, theorists concerned with emotional development have identified distinct characteristics and processes. Social development research has provided some unique perspectives as well.

Theory and research on social development have focused primarily on family and on peer relationships, although the roles of teachers and of the media have also been studied. Because so much of children's social interaction involves play, research on social development has been a prime source of information about play development as well (e.g., Parten, 1932; K.H. Rubin, 1980).

Theorists and researchers focusing on cognitive development, especially on social cognition (i.e., understanding of the social world) have also explored how play development affects and is affected by children's thinking about social relationships. Some of these studies (e.g., Damon, 1977) have explored children's understanding of friendship and issues such as fairness and rule following, which are often reflected in play and games.

The study of gender/sex role development has been a focus of separate study only in the last 15 years. The now classic work of Maccoby and Jacklin (1974), which surveyed the research literature on gender-related developmental factors, called attention to the need for focused study of gender similarities as well as difference. Although earlier researchers collected data and reported results in which gender differences were found, they sometimes focused only on the results for boys. For example, if effects of differing childrearing methods on social behaviors were found only for boys, these might be reported as explanations for *children's* development, with only a brief accompanying statement that the (different) results were unexplained for girls.

Sometimes differences were noted, but were interpreted to mean that female development was problematic. For example, studies of moral development initially characterized female responses as immature rather than as indicating that females have different moral concerns (Gilligan, 1977). Reported differences in academic or skill abilities were routinely interpreted to be biologically based and appropriately sex-typed (e.g., Garai & Scheinfield, 1968). Few studies showing no gender differences were reported;

Maccoby and Jacklin (1974) speculate that researchers' emphasis on gender differences rather than similarities may have resulted from the attitude of journal reviewers that studies showing no differences are not worth publishing.

Researchers from social learning, cognitive-developmental, and feminist theoretical perspectives have been especially interested in gender/sex role development. Many of these studies have drawn heavily upon the rich data source of children's play.

● Theories of social and gender/sex role development

Because many of these theories are discussed elsewhere in the book, this discussion will center only on the aspects of the theories that have been useful for studying social and gender/sex role behaviors.

Psychoanalytic theory. During the 1950s and 1960s, psychoanalytic theory, described earlier in this chapter, was influential in formulating the view that the parents (i.e., usually the mother) were salient in children's social development. According to this theoretical view, the nature of the relationship of the mother to her male or female child, as the child proceeded through the early psychosexual stages (i.e., oral, anal, Oedipal) and psychosocial stages (i.e., trust, autonomy, initiative) is crucial to social development because it sets the pattern for social adjustment in later childhood and adulthood. Few empirical studies have attempted to document characteristics of psychosexual or psychosocial stages, but, because of the theoretically posited importance of feeding, elimination, and sexual behaviors for later social adjustment, the relationship of social development to childrearing practices has been studied extensively.

Differences in gender/sex role development are explained by psychoanalytic theory as being biologically predetermined and based on the physical attributes of males and females (Erikson, 1951). For example, in a replication of an early Erikson study, Cramer and Hogan (1975) report that boys' block building continues to be outerdirected, thrusting, and erect, while girls' structures are internally focused, have gates or other entries, and are enclosing.

These theorists have used the concept of "identification" with the same-gender parent to explain social and gender/sex role development. Freud and other Freudian theorists (e.g., Erikson, 1963) maintain that during the Oedipal period, children are attracted to the opposite-gender parent and feel in competition with the parent of the same gender. To resolve the anxiety generated by these feelings, they incorporate aspects of the same-gender parent's personality, and may also demonstrate them in play. The concept of identification has been used to explain aggressive play behavior and "feminized" play in males (i.e., qualities of nurturance or compliance that have been stereotypically attributed to females). When fathers were absent or socially and emotionally unavailable, boys' problems with "feminization" in play were explained as due to poor individuation from their mothers and lack of identification with their fathers. Girls' identification has been judged to be a simpler process, not requiring them to individuate themselves as fully from their mothers; thus, nurturing "mommy" play has been encouraged for girls. Some researchers, however, suggest that girls' social development may be hindered by the expectation of close identification with their mothers because they may have difficulty later gaining independence (e.g., Baumrind, 1980; Chodorow, 1974).

Social learning theory. This theoretical perspective, as conceptualized by Bandura (1977) and Mischell and Mischell (1976), has strongly influenced the study of children's social and play development. It draws upon some basic tenets of learning theory (e.g., operant conditioning); but also stresses the importance of observational learning of social behaviors exhibited by models (i.e., parents and other adults, peers, and the media).

Operant conditioning is a means of shaping behavior. That is, by contingently reinforcing behaviors that are somewhat like the behaviors that are desired, adults can shape children's behavior, making it resemble the social behavior they have identified as appropriate. Studies in which children's social play is contingently reinforced (e.g., Peck, Apolloni, Cooke, & Raver, 1978) are examples of operant conditioning to achieve social development goals. Much of the verbal feedback given to children during play results in the shaping of their behavior to conform to social standards.

Observational learning is the process by which children who watch models of behavior acquire novel responses, combine these with elements of their existing behavior repertoire, and learn what the consequences of reproducing selected aspects of observed behaviors will be. Children select from modeled experiences those they wish to imitate, and their future social performance reflects those behaviors (Perry & Bussey, 1979). Factors such as power, nurturance, gender, and age of the models influence the selection process, and environmental conditions elicit or suppress these behaviors (Yando, Seitz, & Zigler, 1978). Because parents exhibit both nurturance and power, they are the most important models; thus, social learning theory has stressed the importance of the home environment on socialization and of the parent as the prime socialization agent. Because perceived similarity to a model also influences imitation (Feshbach, 1978), peer behavior, too, provides salient models, especially during social play.

Children may learn social behaviors through observation but not perform them until environmental conditions elicit the behaviors. In play, children may demonstrate behaviors such as nurturance or aggression, but they may not perform their entire repertoire of play behaviors if these are perceived as not congruent with peer, adult, or media models of behavior expected of males or females. Playing a range of roles may consolidate social learning; however, learning occurs even if the modeled behaviors are not immediately imitated or incorporated into play. For example, although boys may perform few nurturing behaviors, such as caring for dolls, in their play, they do learn how to nurture through observing parents nurturing and thus can perform a nurturing role when conditions elicit it. Similarly, girls are able to engage in rough-and-tumble play when the setting encourages them to do so. Social learning theory posits that the human ability to perform a range of roles as adults results from observational learning in childhood.

Social learning theory has provided a major theoretical base for many studies of gender-related behavior. These studies report that adults differentially reinforce boys' and girls' play (Block, 1979; Langlois & Downs, 1980; Serbin, Tonick, & Sternglanz, 1977); provide different environmental elicitors such as toys and room decorations (Fein, 1975b, Rheingold & Cook, 1975); provide different role models in books (Ashton, 1983); and model different behaviors when playing with children (Dunn & Wooding, 1977; Miller & Garvey, 1984). Peers and siblings also model and contingently reinforce stereotypic gender sex/role behaviors in play (Dunn & Kendrick, 1981; Fagot, 1978b, 1984a).

Ethological theory. Ethological theorists have been interested in the social quality of those infant care-eliciting behaviors that promote their survival, and in caregiver responses and initiations of social interaction. This theoretical view has been the impetus for numerous studies of social interactions such as infant-caregiver play observed in the early bonding process (e.g., Shultz, 1979). One study of innate factors in social smiling development during infancy indicated that infants in institutional, kibbutzim, and family-reared environments all showed a high level of social smiling at 4 months, giving support to the biological base of social smiling (Gewirtz, 1965). Only the family-reared infants continued to smile at a high level by 18 months, however, buttressing the view that environmental influences are crucial for social development.

Studies focusing on social aspects of attachment report that securely attached infants are more socially outgoing, more cooperative and compliant, and more independent (e.g., Arend, Gove, & Sroufe, 1979; Clark-Stewart & Hervey, 1981). Infants who are maltreated by caregivers are likely to be insecurely attached (Schneider-Rosen & Cicchetti, 1984). Children do not need to spend all their time with their parents in order to be attached to them; infants in day-care are similar to home-reared infants in that they exhibit primary attachment to their parents (Kagan, Kearsley, & Zelazo, 1978). Studies indicate that attachment may predict social adjustment (Matas, Arend, & Sroufe, 1978); that children become attached to other persons as well as to their parents (Schaffer & Emerson, 1964); and that play seems to enhance the development of attachment (Shultz, 1979). Ethologists have also studied the relationship of the peer group to social development; for example, social play with peers has variations across cultures (Blurton-Jones & Konner, 1973).

Cognitive developmental theory. Because much of Piaget's work (e.g., Piaget, 1952) reported stages of logico-mathematical thinking, researchers and ed-

ucators initially did not focus on his description of how the processes of social interaction influence cognitive development. However, Piaget (1926, 1952) has emphasized the importance of social interaction with peers as a way to overcome egocentric thought, to foster communicative competence, and to force cognitive adaptations. Most of children's early peer social interactions occur during play; thus, studies of social cognition have often focused on social play interactions. In play, perspectives of other children are encountered (Damon, 1977); social comparisons are made (Chafel, 1984); concepts of friendship are developed (Asher & Gottman, 1981); and differences between social conventions and moral rules are highlighted (Turiel, 1977).

Drawing on the theoretical constructs of Piaget, Kohlberg's (1966) theory of gender/sex role development attempts to explain how and why sex typing (i.e., stereotypical gender/sex role development) occurs. The steps in this theoretical formulation are (a) establishing gender identity (i.e., self-categorization as boy or girl); (b) understanding gender constancy (i.e., knowing gender is not changeable by transforming irrelevant criteria); and (c) adapting to the fact of gender class membership by taking on the behaviors that appear to be qualities exhibited by members of that class. Block's (1979) adaptation of cognitive theory, which is based on Loevinger's (1976) ego development theory, states that all young children exhibit agency (i.e., self-assertiveness); they must then temper that with communion (i.e., conformity to group welfare and opinion). The paths to communion are different for boys and girls because social forces have required each gender to show different behaviors to achieve communion.

The concept of androgyny has also been important for gender development theory. There are two definitions of the term; the more common one is that androgyny means that one has both male and female characteristics and behaviors (Hall & Halberstadt, 1980). For example, a child might be good at playing ball (a "male" quality) and at jumping rope (a "female" quality). Bem (1976, 1981), however, considers androgyny to be the ability to have self-identity determined by criteria other than gender. That is, children might decide to engage in a social behavior, such as playing ball or jumping rope, by assessing whether they have the skills needed or interest in the play rather than judging whether to engage in it because of its appropriateness for their gender. Bem describes how children form schemes of both genders as organizers of information and use those schemes in judging appropriate behaviors. She stresses that the course of gender/sex role development, as well as play development, could be changed if gender were not such a culturally salient organizing scheme. Since most societies use gender as a primary classification mode the type of androgyny Bem describes may be difficult to achieve. Conscious societal effort would be required in order to do so.

Feminist theory.   Although feminist theory does not discount the fact that there may be hormonal or other biologically based differences in males and females and that environmental factors shape and demonstrate differentially to male and female children what their behavior should be like, the basic assumption of this viewpoint is that traditional roles can be explained neither as a result of biology nor of simple environmental adaptation. Feminist theory stresses that sex role differences, including those expressed in play, are a function of the socially determined power and dominance position of males, which requires subordination of females to maintain its social power base (Birns & Sternglanz, 1983).

From this theoretical perspective, fathers' strong insistence that their sons exhibit stereotypical gender/sex role behavior in play, and the pressure of male peers for conformity to male play stereotypes, both of which have been documented in many studies (e.g., Fagot, 1984a), can be explained by the higher status of the male. Lower status group members are expected to want to move higher but higher status group members are pressured to stay in their group so that the status of the entire group is not threatened. Feminist theory predicts that changing the way children are socialized to help them gain a more androgynous (i.e., gender balanced and integrated) social identity and self-identity will depend on changes in the male/female power and status balance of the larger society. Those changes will then be reflected in children's play.

Huston (1983), in a review of sex typing, discusses a feminist rethinking of psychoanalytical theory suggesting that women rather than men may be seen by children as the powerful ones because they are the primary caregivers who control children's lives. According to this view, children fear and envy the powerful caregiver and learn to devalue women in order to gain autonomy from that power. Males, in particular, devalue women's power because of their desire to distance themselves from early caregiving experiences; this explains why boys shun caregiving play. According to these theorists (e.g., Lerner, 1974), male/female shared caretaking of young children would redistribute some of this anger and envy against women to men. Huston summarizes this theoretical view as follows: "Males must be important caregivers to produce a substantial change in societal views about male and female roles" (p. 401). Because societal roles are reflected in play, changes in views would also be reflected in play.

Family systems theory.   Theorists who study family structures also have explanations for gender/sex role development. Drawing on the work of Parsons (1970), who categorized the family as having an instrumental-expressive dichotomy, Johnson (1975) posits that because the father is typically the instrumental one in the family, his interactions with female children put them in the expressive role. He conveys to them that females are sexually attractive, nurturing persons; thus they learn to fill the traditional expressive gender role. Observations of the differences between fathers' play with boys and girls also support this hypothesis (e.g., Power & Parke, 1983). Studies of effects of father absence on females show that, although young girls do not seem as affected by father absence as young boys, in adolescence these girls may have difficulty relating to males (Hetherington, 1972).

Family systems theory also stresses the total family system as the socializing unit and the context in which behaviors of family members must be viewed, including children's gender/sex role behaviors. This view stresses the interrelationship of all system members; roles are reciprocal and changes in behavior of one member will change the system (Satir, 1967). Changes may be resisted by the system members because systems are biased toward maintaining stability (Barnard & Corrales, 1979). Changes in play expectations or behaviors would consequently affect all members of the family system.

● Characteristics of social and gender/sex role development

Research on the characteristics of social and gender/sex role development has focused on three themes: (a) children's understanding of their social world (i.e., social cognition), (b) the development of prosocial behaviors, and (c) the relationship among social cognition, prosocial behavior, gender identity, and sex role development. Many of these studies have relevance for the study of play development.

Understanding the social world. According to Damon (1977), social knowledge includes the categorizations and concepts used to organize social experience. Three areas of social knowledge are (a) adult and peer roles, the characteristics of those roles, and the rules and schemes for playing those roles (i.e., scripts); (b) understanding of the nature of relationships between persons (e.g., authority/obedience, friendship); and (c) knowing how to regulate, maintain, and transform those relationships (e.g., by sharing, showing kindness, or being aggressive). Social development is thus the process of acquiring social knowledge.

Because research on social cognition is drawn from a Piagetian perspective, assumptions are that qualitatively different stages exist and appear in invariant order, although there may be differences in rate of appearance. For example, friendship, sharing/fairness, obedience to authority, and social convention/moral development all seem to be stage related. Although sequenced stages of social cognition have been described by some researchers (e.g., Berndt, 1982; Bigelow, 1977; Selman, 1981; Youniss, 1978), the research has not provided as clear a picture as the stages outlined for logico-mathematical knowledge development. Social knowledge seems to follow a more varied time interval pattern, probably because the nature of children's social experiences are less predictable than are their encounters with the physical world.

Even very young children exhibit some understanding of the social world. Infants become upset if parents stop responding in social play/exchange routines (Trevarthen, 1977); show awareness of peers (Hay, Nash, & Pedersen, 1983); and respond differentially to "personalities" of other infants (Lee, 1973). Toddlers exhibit preferences for play with certain children although these "emergent" friendships are unstable and situational (Bergen, Gaynard, Torelli, 1985; Vandell & Mueller, 1978). Toddlers also show sensitivity to variations in adult interaction patterns, altering their distance from parents and the nature of their play (Fein, 1975a); showing empathy

(a form of perspective taking) by sharing objects (Mueller & Lucas, 1975); and providing help and comfort to siblings (Dunn & Kendrick, 1981). There is controversy over whether these early instances are truly examples of perspective taking because they do not involve abstracting and anticipating others' thoughts or feelings (Borke, 1971; Chandler & Greenspan, 1972).

By the age of 3, children show the ability to differentiate objects and people by attributing emotional/social intent (Keil, 1979). For example, they recognize that people can act sorry for their actions but that objects cannot. Young children are aware of physically perceivable ethnic differences but do not discern more abstract differences, such as religious views (Fagot, 1974). Three-year-olds are well aware of social scripts (i.e., mental event schemas for social roles and sequences of behavior) and demonstrate these both in their rigid adherence to routines of caregiving and in their pretend play (Nelson, 1981; Nelson & Seidman, 1984).

Preschool children of 4 years can make social comparisons in their play, comparing their behaviors or characteristics with those of peers (Chafel, 1984). They think of sharing and fairness primarily in terms of their own needs (Damon, 1977). That is, they believe that they should have what they want, just because they want it, which is one reason why sharing play materials or waiting turns is often difficult. Major changes in social cognition occur between the ages of 4 and 7. Children under 5 usually equate their own desires with those of authority figures (i.e., they do not separate adult perspectives from their own). By 5, they know their wishes may differ from those of adults but they obey because they believe adults have an inherent right to be obeyed (Damon, 1977). Five-year-olds are also able to differentiate between social conventions, such as following game rules or rules about manners, from standards of moral behavior, such as not hurting others or stealing property (Damon, 1977; Turiel, 1977, 1978). They rehearse many of these social conventions in their play scripts (Nelson, 1981).

Five-year-olds can also describe their understanding of friendship (Selman, 1976, 1981; Youniss, 1978, 1980; Youniss and Volpe, 1978). They define friends primarily as playmates and give concrete reasons for the friendship (e.g., "he lets me play with his trucks"). From the early childhood period through middle childhood, children's understanding of friend relationships changes from being primarily based on the sharing of play (5 to 7 years) to being characterized as including the sharing of resources and being especially kind or nice to each other (8 to 11) to being primarily based on abstract and general personality attributes (after age 11) (Damon, 1977; Gottman & Parkhurst, 1980; Youniss & Volpe, 1978).

For example, children younger than 9 report that friends are those they play with and share with while 9- and 10-year-olds say friends are those who like and help each other (Berndt, 1981b). First- and fourth-grade children describe their friends differently, with the younger children indicating that their friends are very similar to themselves and the older children being aware of both similarities and differences. Younger children prefer friends with whom they are likely to have few conflicts, but as children's egocentrism diminishes, they become more capable of friendship that includes working out ways to cooperate (Youniss, 1980).

Oden, Herzberger, Mangione, and Wheeler (1984) state that the work on children's understanding of friendships is unclear because of the lack of precise categories of peer relationships. They propose a four-celled model that could be used to explore children's social understanding: close friends, social friends, activity partners, and acquaintances. These categories differentiate between levels of liking, sharing of activity, sharing of personal information and problems, and help giving. For example, close friends may include all of these dimensions, social friends may share only play activities, while activity partners may share only task-related activities. Oden (1987) urges more precise exploration of these dimensions and also suggests that the category of "enemy" might be fruitfully explored.

In a review of peer relationship problems, Oden (1987) cites studies reporting that between 8% and 17% of elementary children indicate they are lonely or feel "left out of things" most of the time in the school environment. There is a correlation between poor self-esteem and low peer acceptance (Hartup, 1983). Children can be assisted in learning ways to change their behavior to gain acceptance; in particular, they can be helped to learn social skills that can improve their social play (Oden & Asher, 1977).

Besides having more sophisticated understanding of friendship, children at the concrete operational stage exhibit greater perspective-taking ability and higher levels of understanding of authority relationships, distributive justice, and morality (Damon, 1977). According to Damon and colleagues, 6- to 8-year-olds are able to use social information in role taking to see others' viewpoints (i.e., Stage 2), and 8- to 10-year-olds exhibit self-reflection—that is, they can imagine what they would think or feel in similar conditions (i.e., Stage 3). Children also become aware that other people hold opinions about them. Thus, they can negotiate game rules and resolve disputes in play.

Elementary children's views of authority also change, with 8-year-olds being able to reason that authority figures should be obeyed because of past assistance they have given, rather than because of their inherent right to obedience. Once the legitimacy of authority is based on other than inherent right, however, children can progress to the belief that obedience is voluntary and requires a mutually cooperative basis (age 9 and above). This belief system underlies the game-playing behavior of older children (Piaget, 1932).

Children of 4 to 6 are already beginning to distinguish social conventions from moral judgment; thus, their obedience to adult authority is influenced by the moral nature of the situation. For example, children at all ages in Damon's (1977) study said mothers could not tell you to steal or do something to harm yourself. Turiel (1975) reports that children under 4 think social conventions conform to their desires. Although children from 5 to 11 years obey social regulations to avoid aversive consequences, they distinguish between rules that represent social conventions and those that represent moral issues. The delight that elementary children have in following complex rules, in arguing over the fairness of rules, and in making judgments about the goodness or badness of opponents, is a reflection of this growing ability to distinguish between conventional and moral issues.

Damon (1977) indicates that distributive justice progresses in a similar developmental pattern: Fairness is first justified by concrete reasons (at age 5 a child might give more toys to a friend); then strict equality (everyone gets the same number of toys); then reciprocity (awarding the best toy on the basis of merit); then relativity (different persons may have more or less claim to toys); and then coordinating equality, reciprocity, and relativity (by age 9, taking many factors into account).

Social cognition in general goes from surface to depth, simple to complex, rigid to flexible, self-oriented to other-oriented, immediate to future oriented, and unsystematic to well organized (Damon & Hart, 1982).

Learning prosocial behavior.   Children's observed social and play behavior gives evidence of what they have learned about social roles, conventions, and relationships. Studies of socialization (i.e., the process by which children learn culturally sanctioned behaviors) have focused on behaviors such as sharing, cooperation, compliance, nurturing, and dependence and on the parental, teacher, peer, media, and other societal influences that affect this learning. Mussen and Eisenberg-Berg (1977) and Radke-Yarrow, Zahn-Waxler, and Chapman (1983) have reviewed the processes involved in the development of prosocial behaviors, which have been a focus of study since the 1960s. Much of this research has used play or games in laboratory settings where children were required to cooperate, share or help; naturalistic observation of children in peer play has also been a major source of information.

Because parents have been viewed as the major socializing agents, much research has focused on how childrearing practices affect social behaviors such as aggression and dependency (e.g., Baumrind, 1966, 1971, 1973; Bandura, 1973; Feshbach, 1974). These studies have shown relationships between certain "profiles" of childrearing (e.g., those described by Baumrind) and children's social behavior. For example, parents classified as authoritative by Baumrind combine warmth and support with control, inductive discipline, and encouragement of maturity and autonomy. These parents had boys who were more socially responsible and girls who were more independent than children whose parents had other profiles.

According to Radke-Yarrow et al. (1983), young children are basically prosocial and intrinsically rewarded by exhibiting these behaviors, even though they may experience some personal cost. Evidence of cooperation in play with parents is seen by 6 to 9 months (Hay, 1979); of sharing objects by 18 months (Rheingold, Hay, & West, 1976); and of spontaneous "helping" with laundry and other home tasks by 2 years (Rheingold, 1979). Two-year-olds will try a number of strategies to relieve their mothers' distress (Zahn-Waxler, 1980; Zahn-Waxler et al., 1979), and

they show concern for siblings' problems (Dunn & Kendrick, 1981).

However, not all behavior is prosocial; by 12 months children exhibit both instrumental (i.e., to gain ends) and hostile (i.e., to harm others) aggression. Gender differences in aggression in play appear at about 18 months (Fagot, Hagan, Leinbach, & Kronsberg, 1985). Although 2-year-olds have social skills, there is mixed evidence as to the positive and negative quality of early social interactions (Bronson, 1981; Eckerman, Whatley, & Kutz, 1975; Vandell & Mueller, 1980). Radke-Yarrow et al. (1983) cite studies indicating that parental reinforcement promotes and maintains prosocial behaviors and that parental hostility and laxness is related to aggression.

Preschoolers show responsiveness to the distress of other children by seeking aid from adults, directly consoling the distressed child, and threatening children who have caused the distress (Sawin, 1980). In Sawin's study, about 75% of the children responded to peer distress. Preschoolers also cooperate to attain goals in sociodramatic play (Parten, 1932; Rubin et al., 1976, 1978).

Prosocial and aggressive behaviors may go together in some preschoolers (Radke-Yarrow & Zahn-Waxler, 1976). Those who exhibit the most prosocial behaviors often show a high level of aggressive behaviors (Friederich & Stein, 1973). Children with both these characteristics are more socially active in general and the aggression that is observed is instrumental rather than hostile aggression. Four-year-olds with high levels of hostile aggression seem to lack perspective-taking ability; that is, they see others' actions as hostile to them even when the actions are not. Preschoolers who are above average in aggression in play are more likely to be influenced by aggressive television programs (Stein & Friederich, 1972, Friedrich & Stein, 1975).

After reviewing the evidence on prosocial behavior in preschoolers, Radke-Yarrow et al. (1983) state, "Children of these ages are not only egocentric, selfish, and aggressive; they are also exquisitely perceptive, have attachments to a wide range of others, and respond prosocially across a broad spectrum . . . " (p. 484).

Evidence of prosocial behavior in elementary-age children comes primarily from laboratory studies, and many of these report inconsistent results. For example, older children do not always show more comforting behavior than younger children do

(Radke-Yarrow & Zahn-Waxler, 1976). Girls are more likely to show increases in nurturance as they grow older than are boys (Berman, Stoan, & Goodman, 1979), and cooperation in play may decrease as competition increases (Radke-Yarrow et al., 1983). Although laboratory studies usually show that older children share more, sharing with peers in natural settings is less consistently exhibited (Dyson-Hudson & Van Dusen, 1972).

Radke-Yarrow et al. (1983) caution that because research on elementary children's sharing, helping, and other prosocial behaviors is still so limited, the data do not permit conclusions about the age-related frequency of prosocial behaviors. They suggest that more attention should be paid to research design and they stress that the linkages between social cognition and prosocial behaviors need clarification. They also urge coordinated study of affective, cognitive, and socialization factors on prosocial behavior.

Gender/sex role behaviors. A most intriguing question is how gender/sex role development influences the relationship between the development of social cognition, which seems to be relatively similar for boys and girls, and prosocial behavior, which seems to differentiate boys and girls increasingly during the age period from infancy to 12 years. That is, although all children may develop similarly in their understanding of the social world, their prosocial behavior development may not be the same because of the socialization messages that they receive.

According to cognitive developmental theory, gender identity is achieved by age 3; gender constancy develops from 4 to 7; and, for girls, acceptance of sex-typed gender class membership follows a curvilinear pattern. Preoperational thinking influences the development of gender constancy; during that period children adopt rigid interpretations of gender/sex role stereotypic behaviors. Concrete operational thought provides the ability to think more flexibly about gender/sex roles.

Research on social development shows that children begin to exhibit gender identity at about age 2 but base that identity on nonessential perceptual evidence such as clothes or hair length (Marcus & Overton, 1978). Children as young as 2 or 3 can give the sex role stereotypes for common activities and objects (Kuhn, Nash, & Brucken, 1978), choose toys on the basis of gender appropriateness (Fagot, 1974;

O'Brien, 1980), and classify themselves with others of the same gender (Thompson, 1975). By 4 or 5 they know stereotyped responses regarding appropriate occupational choices (Nemerowicz, 1979).

In an observational study of gender/sex role development in children ages 2 to 5, Pitcher and Schultz (1983) observed the trends in same- and opposite-gender play: (a) There were more same-gender contacts at age 4 and 5 but cross-gender play did not increase; (b) boys showed cross-gender play at 3 but showed little of this at 5; (c) girls increased their initiations of cross-gender play at 5, but these attempts were rarely successful. Some studies show that teachers can increase the instances of cross-gender play if they notice and reinforce it (e.g., Serbin, Tonick, & Sternglanz, 1977).

Whether adherence to rigid and stereotypic gender roles in the preoperational period is necessitated by children's perceptually based classification abilities, as cognitive developmental theory suggests, or whether it is a function of adult and societal signals that make children focus on irrelevant criteria (e.g., boys play with trucks; girls play with dolls) rather than relevant criteria (e.g., the presence or absence of male or female sex organs), is a question of major interest (Bergen, 1984). Bem (1983) points out that gender is often used as a classification category when it is irrelevant. For example, teachers often divide their classes by gender for activities such as lining up, playing games, taking turns, or using materials. Parents also use gender as an irrelevant criterion. Their actions are often influenced by other societal institutions. For example, toy manufacturers may make toys of the same basic design but have pink ones designated for girls and brown ones designated for boys.

Children gradually achieve gender constancy (i.e., they know their gender will not change by making changes in appearance or behavior or by wishing that it were different) during the period from 4 to 9 years (DeVries, 1969). After they are in the concrete operational period, they are able to acknowledge that stereotypic gender/sex roles are arbitrary (Meyer, 1980). Socialization pressures toward conformity and the cultural definitions of appropriate behavior for each gender influence whether they adopt more or less stereotypic behavior (Block, 1983). Although girls and boys are at a similar cognitive gender role stage at age 5 (i.e., adhering to play behaviors identified as appropriate to their gender label), during elementary years girls broaden their range of play behaviors while boys continue to narrow theirs, excluding many ambiguously labeled behaviors. The messages children receive from the media, peers, and adults about the value placed on each gender may be related to these trends.

In a study of children's perceptions of the changes that would occur in their lives if they were the opposite gender, elementary-age children included changes in socially appropriate behavior, activity level, amount of freedom, and amount of time that would be spent with fathers (Baumgartner, 1983). Girls expected to be more assertive, self-reliant, and active, to have more freedom, and to spend more time with fathers if they were boys, and boys thought they would lose those same qualities if they were girls. Research also indicates that parents of elementary-age children have different expectations about work and play for boys and girls. They define good/bad and appropriate/inappropriate behavior for each sex differently (Bacon & Ashmore, 1982) and have different expectations about whether and when boys and girls should be able to bake a cake, fix a bicycle, write a letter, and build something of wood (Zill & Peterson, 1982). They also allow boys to range farther from home (Roberts, 1980). Exploration of the complex interactions of social cognition and socialization factors with regard to gender/sex role development is only beginning.

● The relationship of play to social and gender/sex role development

The relationship of play to social and gender/sex role development is pervasive during the early years. Social play begins at birth and exists in various manifestations throughout the life span. Infant-parent social games, toddler peer parallel play, preschoolers' sociodramatic and thematic fantasy play, and elementary children's elaborate game playing all require social skills and at the same time assist in the development of those skills. The patterns of play of boys and girls have also been well documented, and many of the environmental factors that interact with children's emotional, social, and cognitive readiness levels and individual personality differences that influence play have been described.

Chapters 8, 9, and 10 discuss in detail age-spe-

cific relationships among play, social, and gender/sex role development. Some of the major aspects of these relationships are as follows:

Infant and toddler play.   During the first year of life parent and child social games and routines build a basic pattern of social and communicative interaction, and infants learn the social rules of reciprocity and cooperation (Hay, 1979). Children learn what play is (i.e., a nonliteral activity) from parents' early communication that "This is play" (Bateson, 1956). In play children learn not only role behavior but "learn that there is such a thing as a role" (Bateson, 1956, p. 148).

Toys serve as social play facilitators; parallel play with objects and materials is a prime play mode during the early years (Mueller & Brenner, 1977; Mueller & Lucas, 1975). Early play with parents, siblings, peers, and toys also communicates about gender-appropriate behavior. For example, mothers' differing responses to their 6-month-old boys' and girls' play predicted gender differences in their children's play at 1 year (Goldberg & Lewis, 1969).

Preschool play.   In the preschool years children make major strides in social development through the medium of play. Play affords opportunities to share objects and materials in practice, constructive, and pretend play; to rehearse scripts and cooperate in sociodramatic play; and to take turns and follow rules in gamelike play, all of which enhance social learning and the development of social cognition. Fantasy play, in particular, seems to increase perspective taking and cooperation (Connolly & Doyle, 1984; Rosen, 1974; Saltz & Johnson, 1974). Peer-oriented social skills are fostered by social fantasy play because it serves "as a mediator between peer experience and social competence" (Connolly & Doyle, 1984, p. 805).

Preschool children's elaboration and performance of social scripts provides clear evidence of children's understanding of behaviors appropriate to social roles and the sequences of actions that make up organized and integrated social behaviors (Bretherton, 1984a). To be successful players, children must be able to operate in the larger social context as well as in the play text and to communicate about their roles as well as about the broader social structure (Schwartzman, 1978). According to

Schwartzman, in play children learn about the various kinds of social relationships. The play texts serve children as "formats for commentaries on their own relationships to each other" (p. 244) and suggest "the possibility of reinterpretation, challenge, even change in relationships" (p. 245).

During play, preschool children also demonstrate their increasing knowledge of the social expectations that are attached to their gender label (Beeson & Williams, 1985; Fagot, 1981; Fling & Manosevitz, 1972; Liss, 1983). This knowledge is enforced increasingly over the preschool period by the peer group, especially the male peer group (Eisenberg, Tryon, & Cameron, 1984; Fagot, 1984a). According to DiPietro (1981), rough-and-tumble play, frequently observed in preschool boys, is conducive to boys' social development because it requires at least two consenting partners and gives them practice in reading quasi-threatening social cues, in regulating levels of physical exchange, and in dealing with dominance hierarchies.

Preschoolers exhibit stereotypic toy and activity preferences, even in families where their mothers have nontraditional out-of-home work roles, possibly because the parents continue to perform gender-stereotypic tasks in the home (Wolfgang, 1985). However, positive social reinforcement by teachers can be effective in increasing cross-gender cooperative play (Gershner & Moore, 1985).

Social play behaviors in the preschool years can predict level of comfort and success at later ages; for example, preschoolers who seem stuck at solitary or parallel practice levels of play or who seem to have difficulty moving freely into the social world of cooperative dramatic play may later experience discomfort and difficulty in social situations (Rubin, 1982b). Thus, efforts to increase preschoolers' social play ability may be useful.

Elementary age. The diverging of boys' and girls' play in the elementary years serves many social functions that have been related to traditional gender/sex role expectations. Although older children are more aware of play stereotypes, they also know that these stereotypes can be changed. In their play behavior, however, boys and girls of 8 and up usually become more and more separated and even hostile to one another in play. Whether this situation serves positive developmental needs is a question that present research does not answer.

In any case, Sutton-Smith and Savasta's (1972) study of play in middle childhood clearly point to a cleavage between the games of boys and girls. Sutton-Smith and Savasta list strength, body contact, active interference with other players' movement, well-defined winners and losers, personal initiative, continuous motor activity, simultaneous movement of many players, and movement over large spaces as characteristics of boys' games. They indicate that these dimensions are characteristic of most types of sports. In contrast, girls' games show ordered turn taking, rhythm, songs, rhymes and other talk, well-defined stages in the game, indirect competition, numerous precise rules, competition between individuals rather than groups, partial body movement, and solitary practice time.

Lever (1976, 1978) asserts that fifth-grade boys' games show a more complex style (e.g., playing in larger groups; competing more vigorously; having more rules, role differentiation, and team formation) than do girls' games, which often promote individual skills and are sequenced in unvarying patterns. Even the same playful actions may be exhibited differently by boys and girls; for example, 7- and 8-year-old boys chase aggressively and physically while girls chase in a teasing, asserting/withdrawing pattern (Robinson, 1978). It may be that these differences in play serve as preparatory activities for male and female life in the larger society. Lever suggests that boys' complexly organized hierarchical games may prepare them for adult work in business and governmental organizations. For example, in Little League games boys learn the skills of negotiation, such as trading favors, threatening, and reasoning (Fine, 1980, 1981). It is likely that elementary children rehearse social scripts through game playing in much the same way that preschoolers learn social skills through acting out their pretense scripts.

● **Implications for educational practice**

Recent research on social play calls into question some of the assumptions about appropriate educational practice that adults have traditionally held. For example, adults may need to re-examine their belief that infants and toddlers do not need opportunities for peer play in the light of research on early peer play interactions. The pervasive encouragement by parents and teachers of same-gender, rather than cross-gender, peer play may also need re-evaluation if egalitarian social goals are to be furthered. Educators may even need to consider the potential benefits of promoting social play and friendship development opportunities as part of the "basic skills" curricula of the elementary school.

Schools have been entrusted with promoting the socialization goals that a particular society values. How these goals can be fostered by educators has often been a matter of debate. When teachers do include social goals in the curriculum, they often focus on having children learn social conventions rather than giving them the opportunity to confront moral issues such as fairness or equality.

Educational goals should include helping children to (a) understand and deal with the diverse values of other social groups, (b) gain skill in making and keeping friends and relating effectively to adults, (c) perform a range of required social roles, and (d) select appropriate social strategies. Because so much of social development can be enhanced through play, educators should build play experience into all curricular areas.

In play, children try on the social conventions of the larger society as well as try out variations and elaborations of those conventions. Play enables children to identify the arbitrary aspects of social conventions, which they can choose to accept or to discard, thus promoting the development of higher levels of social cognition. Play often provides the testing ground for learning about conflict resolution, negotiation, fairness, and both cooperative and competitive social strategies. The social patterns practiced in play are patterns of social interaction that children will use subsequently in their encounters with the broader social world.

Play is an especially powerful learning medium for gender/sex role development. Therefore, teachers must carefully consider what gender/sex role messages are being communicated in classroom and playground play and determine whether those messages are congruent with the educational goals of optimizing all children's potential and helping them develop the competencies needed in both present-day and future society. Often messages about gender appropriate behaviors are conflicting; they may even prove disfunctional for children growing up in a culture that is technologically rich, that abounds with information, and that values egalitarianism.

Play can serve as an important means of broadening social knowledge and enhancing prosocial behavior. It can also give children opportunities to try nonstereotypic gender role behavior. However, it may also promote social learning and elicit social behaviors that adults do not wish to encourage. In the chapters in the following sections, specific suggestions are made for accomplishing some of these social developmental goals. If teachers and other adults who work with children can bring to conscious awareness the social learning that is occurring in the play they observe and/or encourage, they may be able to use that knowledge to assist children in developing positive social understanding, skills, and gender identities through their play.

Conclusions

Emotional, social, and gender/sex role development have often been considered only as peripheral goals of education. Thus, almost by default, these areas of development have been promoted by informal means rather than by formal curricular decisions. Because adults often have ignored the emotional and social messages conveyed and elaborated in play, they have hardly been aware of the powerful influence play has on these areas of development. By understanding the developmental and learning processes involved in these areas and their relationship with play, adults who are concerned about promoting expanded human self-concepts can plan play environments that permit and encourage a "well-developed self" in every child.

Questions for Discussion

1. What are some of the early life experiences that may affect emotional development? How do they relate to experiences that affect social development? Gender/sex role development?
2. What is the difference between the text and the context of play? Give an example of each and tell how a teacher could use text and context features in implementing a play curriculum that promotes emotional, social, and gender/sex role development.
3. How does play serve as a means of expanding children's emotional and social options? Of restricting those options?

Research Replication Exercises

1. Observe a child for 15 minutes during a sociodramatic play episode. From the content and structure of the play diagnose if the child is engaging in developmentally appropriate play.
2. Select two children from a preschool group that the teacher has designated as displaying (a) predominantly nurturant play and/or (b) predominantly aggressive play. Using Gould's (1972) framework of behavioral characteristics, note where the children are in relation to her categories.
3. Interview three children, one of 4 years, one of 6, and one of 8. Ask each child 10 questions about his or her knowledge of friendship (e.g., Who is your best friend? What is your friend like? How many friends do you have?). Analyze whether the answers the children give fit into the stages of friendship described in the chapter.

Suggestions for Further Reading

Curry, N. (1986). *The feeling child: Affective development reconsidered.* New York: Haworth. Reviews the major aspects of emotional development in children and gives suggestions for enhancing that development.

Damon, W. (1977). *The social world of the child.* San Francisco: Jossey-Bass. Reviews the research and theory on social cognition, discussing children's development of friendships, ideas of justice and fairness, views on moral law and social convention, and reactions to authority. Describes research study results that outline stages of development of social cognition.

Gould, R. (1972) *Child studies through fantasy.* New York: Quadrangle Books. Presents research on fantasy play and relates these studies to children's emotional development.

Greenspan, S., & Greenspan, N. T. (1985). *First feelings: Milestones in the emotional development of the child.* New York: Viking. Gives an overview of the stages of emotional development and integrates a number of theoretical positions.

Hetherington, E. M. (Ed., & Mussen, P. H. (Series Ed.). (1983). *Handbook of child psychology: Vol. 4. Socialization, personality, and social development.* New York: Wiley. Includes chapters by Hartup on family social relationships, by Radke-Yarrow, Zahn-Waxler, and Chapman on prosocial behavior, by Huston on sex-typing, and by Minuchin and Shapiro on school socialization.

Liss, M. B. (Ed.). (1983). *Social and cognitive skills: Sex roles and children's play.* New York: Academic Press. Provides a comprehensive look at contemporary research and theory on play and the development of gender/sex roles.

Oden, S. (1982). Peer relationship development in childhood. In L. G. Katz (Ed.), *Current topics in early childhood education (Vol. 4,* pp. 87–117). Norwood, NJ: Ablex. Gives an overview of the major ideas on peer relationship development that would be of interest to early childhood educators. Includes suggestions for curricula.

Shantz, C. U. (1983). Social cognition. J. H. Flavell, & E. M. Markham (Eds.), P. H. Mussen (Series Ed.), *Handbook of child psychology: Vol. 3. Cognitive development* (pp. 495–555). Provides an overview of current research on the development of children's thinking about their relationships to peers, family, and the larger society.

Toddlers' Play and Sex Stereotyping

BEVERLY I. FAGOT

From an early age, boys and girls engage in different styles of play. Block (1983) suggested that differences in early play styles lead to differences in intellectual and emotional development. Girls utilize existing cognitive and social structures that are modified by incremental steps. They are given toys that encourage the learning of rules and imitation of behaviors and are encouraged by adults to keep in close contact. Boys, on the other hand, are given toys that force them to develop their own schemas and to find out how the toys work. Boys are also encouraged to engage more in activities with peers and not with adults. Block hypothesized that, as a consequence of these differences in play styles and differences in interactions with adults and peers, girls' development is more stable than boys because girls can draw upon adults for help. Boys' development is less stable because they do not use adult help as effectively, but they are forced to restructure more often and to produce their own unique solutions.

Are there data to support Block's hypothesis, or is it merely intriguing theorizing with no real-world foundation? For the past 15 years in the University of Oregon Psychology Department Child Laboratory, my colleagues and I have been studying just this question. What evidence is there for differences in play styles of boys and girls from 1 to 5 years of age? When do such differences begin? How do the reactions of teachers and peers help initiate boys' and girls' differences in play styles? Finally, is there any indication that such differences in play styles have the kind of long-term consequences for social and emotional development predicted by Block?

The first question is the simplest to answer. Yes, there are differences in play styles of boys and girls, and the differences have

133

not really changed over the last 20 years. Girls engage in more doll play and domestic rehearsal, more art activities, and dressing up. Boys play more with transportation toys, with blocks, and with carpentry toys. Boys also engage in more aggressive activities and play more in larger peer groups. Girls spend more time talking and spend far more time with teachers than do boys (Fagot, 1984a; Fagot & Patterson, 1969). As they grow older, both boys and girls increasingly spend more time in same-sex play groups and actively avoid the opposite sex (Fagot, 1985; Fagot & Patterson, 1969).

When do sex differences in play styles begin to appear? In our laboratory, we do not see differences in play styles in 12- to 18-month-old boys and girls, either in terms of toy choices or interactive styles. A group of children was brought into infant play groups when they were 12 to 14 months of age. They were observed over a period of three months, and two styles of interaction were observed: assertive behaviors (e.g., hitting, pushing, shoving, grabbing for another's toys) and communicative behaviors (e.g., gesturing, babbling, or talking). There was no difference in the occurrence of these behaviors between boys and girls. The adult caretaker's reactions to the child's initiations, however, was

highly dependent upon the sex of the child. If a boy produced an assertive behavior, he received a response from the teacher 41% of the time, but if a girl produced the same behavior, she received a response from the teacher only 10% of the time. If a girl produced a positive type of communicative behavior, she received a response from the teacher 65% of the time, while a boy initiating the same behavior received a response 48% of the time. On the other hand, boys who demanded attention negatively by whining, crying, screaming, or by pulling at the teacher received attention 55% of the time, while girls performing similar acts received a response only 18% of the time.

When we looked at these same children approximately one year later, we found sex differences in the children's behavior. Boys performed more aggressive acts, while girls spent more time talking and interacting with the teachers (Fagot, Hagan, Leinbach, & Kronsberg, 1985). We found that sex differences in play styles and in interactive styles began to appear from 20 to 24 months of age and were well established by the time the children were 36 months old.

In a study with slightly older children (Fagot, 1985), I found that girls changed their behaviors when either teachers or other girls reacted to them, while boys reacted only to the responses of other boys. In addition, girls' peer groups tolerated play with many more play materials than did boys'. Boys' peer groups responded negatively to boys who played with "girls'" toys and to boys who played with girls, so that boys were being given constant feedback on both appropriate play styles and appropriate playmates. Girls were given feedback on appropriate playmates only. When we combine this with the tendency of boys to ignore teacher feedback and to spend much less time interacting with teachers than did girls, we start to see that, indeed, the same play group or preschool environment does not provide boys and girls with the same socialization experiences.

Finally, is there any indication to support Block's ideas that differences in intellectual and emotional development arise from these early differences in play and interactional styles? So far, such data are only correlational. We know that boys lag behind girls in their ability to deal with school-like tasks and that they show more emotional problems during early childhood. Also, boys who show extreme aggressiveness and girls who show extreme dependency as young 2-year-olds continue to have the same problems for as long as two years (Fagot, 1984b). The relation to intellectual development is less well documented, but girls who show extreme feminine play preferences are less likely to do well in math and science (Fagot & Littman, 1975). Our conclusion is that children should be encouraged to try out as many play behaviors as possible without regard to sex, and that teachers need to examine their response styles very carefully to avoid reacting to children in ways that perpetuate stereotypes.

CHAPTER SIX

The Relationship of Play to Physical/Motor Development and to Children with Special Needs

MARGOT KAPLAN-SANOFF ● ARLENE BREWSTER ● JIM STILLWELL ● DORIS BERGEN

Young children first approach their world from a sensorimotor perspective and learn about the environment through their sensory and motor actions. They demonstrate their physical/motor development in play and their play enhances that development. Healthy growth and competent motor ability, facilitated through play, make a major contribution to development. However, not all children develop their physical and motor capacities to an optimum level. In particular, young children with handicapping conditions that make it difficult for them to relate to the environment in a physically active and motorically skilled manner may be profoundly affected by diminished capabilities for sensorimotor interactions.

Children who have specific physical disabilities are not the only ones whose handicaps present problems that may prevent development to optimum capacity. Children handicapped by cognitive, language, emotional, and social deficits caused by biological factors or specific environmental trauma face a host of developmental problems. But also, there are children whose environments put them at general risk for developmental delay or social and emotional problems and those who are chronically or intensely ill. Whether special needs children's problems are the result of specific deficits that interfere with normal development (e.g., cerebral palsy, spina bifida, mental retardation) or whether the problems are precipitated by events that may cause intense or prolonged stress, (e.g., hospitalization, abuse/neglect, family dysfunction or dissolution), such children face serious impediments to optimal development. Heavy demands on their coping skills as well as a diminution of their psychic resources add stress to the already challenging task of growing up. Special needs children can be helped to make the most of their abilities and to cope with their environments through play; however, their play abilities may be affected by handicap, illness, or other kinds of problems.

This chapter first reviews some basics of physical growth and describes aspects of motor development theory and research. Then the relationship of play to physical growth and motor development is briefly discussed. The second section of the chapter focuses on how play is related to the development of children who have a variety of special needs: (a) physical and other developmental limitations imposed by their handicapping conditions, or (b) stresses in family or broader social environments that impinge on their ability to develop within normal limits.

The theoretical and research literature related to the play of special needs children as well as how play relates to their development is examined. Possibilities for using play to assess and intervene in that development are also suggested.

Physical/Motor Development and Play

● Theory and research on physical growth and motor development

Because early researchers believed that maturation was the major factor in development, many research studies in the twenties and thirties focused on describing milestones of physical growth and motor skill as these were exhibited in the play of normally developing children. These studies were usually not based on a particular theory of development; rather, they described the normative stages in motor behaviors, such as climbing, running, and throwing (e.g. Ames, 1937; Bayley, 1935; Shirley, 1931), and compared effects of various environmental factors on specific motor skills such as roller skating or tricycle riding (Johnson, 1935; Jones, 1939; McGraw, 1935).

In the late fifties and early sixties a number of studies of motor development emerged (e.g., Espenschade, 1960; Glasslow & Kruse, 1960; Rarick & Larsen, 1958). Commenting on the dearth of recent studies of motor skill development, Keogh (1977) reports that a review of motor development studies by Eckert (1973) contains 37 studies done before 1950, 18 done between 1950 and 1960, and only 2 done since 1961.

Because the revival of interest in motor development research initially arose from concerns for children with learning disabilities, many studies of the past 10 years have come from this perspective, which

attempts to find links between movement, perception, and cognitive development (e.g., Kephart, 1960). Keogh (1977) states that often these studies have been methodologically flawed and thus a "decade of research in this area has provided little of theoretical and empirical value" (p. 78).

At the present time, the research literature on the relationship of play to the physical/motor development of normally developing children is sparse. Even the recent emphasis on adult play and physical fitness has been only sporadically reflected in the research on children's physical/motor development (Brown, 1980). Keogh urges that motor development research should build on the normative data accumulated through earlier studies describing children's physical growth and motor development. He suggests observational research methods, but also that analysis should go beyond description to "identifying organizational processes and inferring underlying qualities of movement mechanisms and their functioning" (p. 79). The relationship of play to children's physical growth and motor development can be viewed within the context of present information on physical growth and motor development.

Physical growth. Because physical growth has a strong maturational component, most of the research in this area of development is atheoretical; that is, it is not tied to a theoretical view that attempts to interpret and explain the development. Normative data amassed from many observational studies indicate that developmental trends in physical growth are universal and orderly, although there are individual differences within the range of normal development (Ausubel, Sullivan, & Ives, 1980).

Different organ systems show different patterns of growth. For example, neural growth is almost complete by about age 5; skeletal growth spurts occur in infancy and late childhood; growth of the heart and other visceral organs usually keeps pace with skeletal growth; genital growth occurs at puberty. Consequently, body proportions also change over time, with the head becoming proportionally smaller as children mature. Unless nutritional deficits occur, height and weight also follow predictable growth trends. These physical growth factors have many implications for children's (a) body image (i.e., mental picture of themselves); (b) ability to perform coordinated motor actions (e.g., when body proportion or height changes, motor coordination must be readjusted); and (c) competence in performing certain types of play or games (e.g., early maturing children may be better at basketball). Elements of physical and motor development essential for physical fitness have been identified by a number of researchers. For example, Brown (1980) lists strength, muscular endurance, flexibility, and cardiorespiratory endurance as necessary for physical fitness. Most studies indicate that school-age children often have poor levels of physical fitness (e.g., Sarner, 1978).

Research suggests that children with handicapping conditions or those with unusually late, early, or extreme patterns of physical development may have both deficient motor skills and disadvantaged social interactions (Ausubel et al., 1980). Both adults and children may devalue or reject children whose physical appearance and/or motor skills are different from the norm (Dion, 1973; Richardson & Royce, 1968). Although the physical growth of individual children is strongly affected by genetic factors, their optimum physical growth depends on good nutrition, sufficient rest, consistent access to health care, and opportunities for active play. The interaction between the innate aspects of physical growth and the environmental experiences children encounter will greatly affect their motor development as well as many other areas of development.

Motor development.   The ideas of a number of developmental theorists (e.g., Erikson, 1963; Havighurst, 1972; Piaget, 1952) have influenced current motor development theory. Erikson's view of development as a series of stage-related crises influenced by both biological and environmental factors has focused attention on children's need for movement experiences and mastery-oriented play. Children's motor interactions seem to reflect and to be affected by the psychosocial crisis of each Eriksonian period. For example, infants' establishment of basic trust involves being able to move closer, reach for and grasp the objects in the environment, and predict what actions will cause various reactions. The toddler stage of autonomy coincides with the increased autonomy of motor skill, in which children move away from caregivers to explore the environment, control their bodies, master objects, and influence people through their motor actions. Later stages—preschool (i.e., initiative) and elementary years (i.e., in-

dustry)—also reflect increasing motor competence. According to Gallahue (1982), Erikson's theory implies that play assists mastery of movement-related concepts such as laterality, directionality, and spatial awareness.

Havinghurst's (1972) developmental task model posits that children achieve particular developmental tasks during specific time periods. Achievement of developmental tasks not only leads to feelings of pleasure but also increases possibilities of success with later tasks, while task failure leads to frustration and difficulty in achieving later tasks. The cumulative nature of motor task achievement is evident in many areas of motor development. For example, children's abilities to control their body processes, an early developmental task, is dependent on coordinated motor skills. Tasks of middle childhood (e.g., developing a wholesome attitude toward one's physical growth, achieving the ability to care for and to enjoy using one's body) are also influenced by earlier motor competence.

Piaget's (1952) theory, in which sensorimotor action is viewed as the precursor of representational thought and cognitive development, implies that children's engagement in motor, visual, tactile, and auditory action on the objects in their environment is essential for optimum development. Piaget viewed early movement experiences both as indicators of cognitive development and as a means of enhancing that development. According to cognitive developmental theory, sensorimotor activity is especially important for developing concepts of space and ability to use spatial language terms, such as "in" and "over" (Cratty, 1982; Piaget & Inhelder, 1956). Piaget's view that thought springs from action has influenced motor development research and theories of movement education, although not all researchers agree that infant thought is dependent on motor action (Cratty, 1982).

The recent work of theorists and researchers studying the neurological structures of the brain points to potential directions of interest for study of motor development (Tipps, 1981). For example, researchers are investigating neurological factors influencing body control (Crothers & Paine, 1960) and relationships between early brain growth spurts and sensorimotor stages (Epstein, 1978). At the present time, however, this work has influenced the field only minimally.

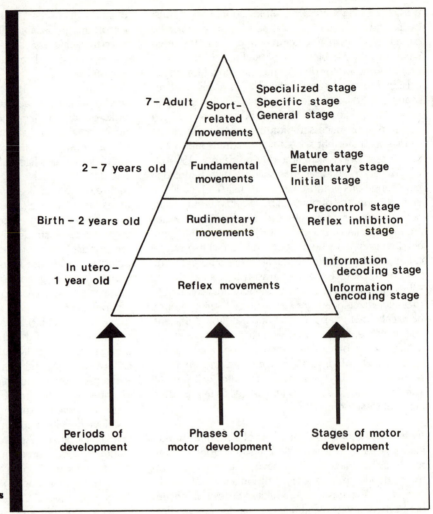

FIGURE 6–1 ● The Phases of Motor Development

Three writers in the field of motor development have identified theoretical issues or described movement development models. Drawing on the work of a number of other theorists, Gallahue (1982), for example, has outlined a model consisting of four phases: (a) reflex movements, (b) rudimentary movements, (c) fundamental movements, and (d) sport-related movements. The model is shown in Figure 6–1.

Reflex movements (i.e., involuntary movements, such as sucking, blinking, and grasping) begin during the fourth month of fetal life; some remain throughout life but others disappear as the neurological structures mature. Chapter 3 describes changes in reflexive movement that occur as children move through the sensorimotor period.

Rudimentary movements (i.e., early voluntary movements such as control of head and neck, learning to grasp and release voluntarily, creeping, crawling, sitting, standing, and walking) are primary during the first 2 years of life. These motor skills follow the sequential principles of cephalocaudal (i.e., head to tail) and proximodistal (i.e., close to distant) development.

Fundamental movements (i.e., voluntary coordination movements such as jumping and running, pulling and stretching, and throwing and kicking) involve exploring variations and coordinating patterns of movement. These movements, predominant from age 2 to 7, are not totally maturationally determined because environmental factors such as children's play habits, opportunities to practice, and environmental elicitors influence their development.

Sport-related movements, which begin at about age 7 and continue throughout life, include locomotor, nonlocomotor, and coordinated patterns. They are outgrowths of fundamental movements and are used as a means to an end rather than as an end in themselves. For example, the fundamental locomotor movement of sliding is used in games of tag or baseball; jumping is used for hopscotch, jump rope, dancing, and track and field events. The level of development of these complex coordinated movement skills is highly related to environmental opportunities.

Several writers have separated the fundamental movement category into discrete, age-related stages (e.g., Jewett & Mullan, 1977; McClenaghan & Gallahue, 1978; Stanley, 1969). For example, McClenaghan and Gallahue (1978) propose three internal stages: (a) initial, when attempts lack coordination (typical of 2-year-olds); (b) elementary, when attempts show some coordination, smoothness, and refinement (typical of preschoolers); and (c) mature, when movements are well-coordinated, process oriented, efficient, fluid, and aesthetically pleasing (typical of elementary children). Gallahue (1982) suggests that children should begin the mature stage by age 6. He points out that, if children have not had ample time, space, and equipment for play, or do not have motivation to improve, they will not become well-coordinated and efficient in their movement. Then, they will have difficulty learning complex motor games and sport-related movements. Individual differences among children often become evident at about age 6 or 7.

Cratty's (1979) multidimensional scheme focuses on the interrelationships of complex motor skills and encompasses the four components of motor, perceptual, cognitive, and verbal development. He sees motor development as arising from a biological base, then branching into differentiated attributes, becoming coordinated and integrated into complex activities that require a coordination of movement in all four areas of development. For example, learning to write requires postural control, eye-hand coordination, symbolic understanding, and language skill. Complex play behaviors such as tumbling, catching balls, and swimming also require multiple coordinations.

Cratty (1979) defines an attribute as an ability trait demonstrated by a motor test score. Attributes emerge and mature at different rates, proliferate and overlap, can be bonded to form complex skills, and can be selected as needed to be combined with other attributes. Examples of the motor development strand of Cratty's model are shown in Figures 6–2 and 6–3.

Keogh (1977, p. 79) has stressed the importance of studying the "organization of sequences of movement elements or subroutines." He identifies movement skill development as the process of learning to control movement and lists two control problems that children must learn to solve: (a) developing movement consistency and (b) developing movement constancy. Consistency refers to a repertoire of motor skills that can be reliably used (e.g., walking, catching). Constancy refers to the ability to use these consistent movements flexibly in a variety of situations (e.g., walking on varied surfaces, catching both a ball and a piece of paper). Consistency of movement is required before flexibility of movement can occur. According to Keogh, play is important for developing these abilities because "a child at play repeats a movement many times (consistency), then 'plays' with the movement by doing it in different and unusual ways (constancy)" (p. 80).

Keogh (1978) indicates that two processes are essential for developing effective movement: (a) coordination of self and (b) coordination of self in relation to others. Children must learn to coordinate the movements within their own bodies (e.g., eye-hand coordination, locomotor, and postural control), and they must learn to coordinate their movements with the movements of objects and other people (e.g., catch a ball when it is thrown high, low, slow, fast; or predict the speed and direction of another child and move appropriately in order to tag the child). Keogh points out that these relational coordinated movements are essential for playing complex games and sports.

The label "clumsy" has often been applied to children whose movements are not well coordinated

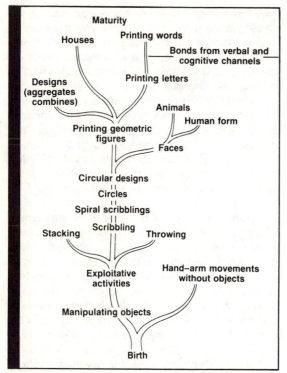

FIGURE 6–2 • Model of One Strand of Motor Development

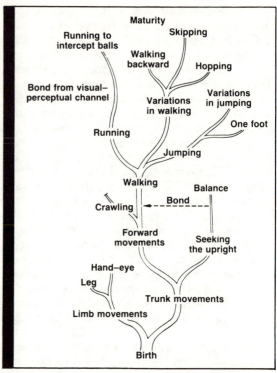

FIGURE 6–3 • Model of One Strand of Motor Development

(Keogh, 1978). Motor dimensions used to identify the specific problems of children with "clumsy" movement include body control (i.e., coordinating discrete motor skills within a more complex movement pattern); body/spatial awareness (i.e., understanding the placements, boundaries, and relationships between the body and other objects in space); and motor planning (i.e., anticipating needed motor responses, remembering past motor responses, and responding motorically with appropriate timing) (Zeller, 1985). Between 8% to 15% of first-grade children, primarily boys, have been described as having clumsy movements, due to either organic causes or "learned helplessness" (Cratty, 1982). During the elementary years, these children may be excluded from peer play because it requires coordinated complex movement.

Keogh (1978, p. 326) indicates that children labeled as "hyperactive" (i.e., "ones who move too soon, too often, and at the wrong time") may have

skilled motor abilities in spite of apparent deficits. He concludes that both hyperactive children and those identified as having "perceptual-motor" problems must be assessed carefully to ensure that their underlying competence is measured as well as their performance.

● Relationship of play to physical/motor development

The four boys (ages 6 through 8) ride their bicycles almost every afternoon. They have learned to ride with a great deal of skill, and now enjoy stunts such as lifting the front wheel, to ride on only the back wheel. These stunt routines have been fairly well mastered by now. Today, they park their bikes and go into the garage, emerging with two pieces of 1' by 2' plywood and a few bricks. They use the materials to build a ramp and begin riding bikes up and over the ramp, with the oldest boy leading the way. At first they proceed cautiously, then repeat with more and more abandon. Finally they remove one board to make a narrow ramp and build it with a higher slant. They ride up the ramp and jump the bikes off. Laughter and shouts accompany the play, as they point out to each other the particularly good jumps. The play continues throughout the week.

Play as a medium for promoting physical/motor development may seem to be so obvious that it needs no systematic study. Many writers have stressed the importance of play opportunities for motor skill development during the early childhood years (Coleman & Skeen, 1985; Corbin, 1976; Cratty, 1979; Ellis, 1973; Gallahue, 1982; Keogh, 1978; Siedentop, Herkowitz, & Rink, 1984). However, research on these relationships has not been extensive. Many of the studies addressing motor development through play are described in section three of this book, which focuses on play environments for children of various age levels. The research literature includes (a) descriptions of the types of motor play; (b) comparisons of motor play of different groups (e.g., boys/girls, older/younger children); and (c) comparisons of play materials and contexts as elicitors of motor skill development. A few examples are provided here to indicate the range of questions being studied.

An example of a descriptive study of motor play is that of Aldis (1975), who has categorized various types of "play fighting." Through analysis of films of children in natural settings, he has identified a number of types of wrestling, chasing, hitting and kicking, as well as types of swimming pool play. He points to one type of motor play especially enjoyed by children under 7: that which provides "vestibular reinforcement" (i.e., stimulation of the sense organs of the inner ear where balance is maintained). This play involves deliberately causing oneself to be out of balance. Play such as swinging, sliding, and acrobatics allows children to test and retest their vestibular balancing system.

Examples of studies reporting differences in boys' and girls' motor play are numerous. In a study of recess play, Beth-Halachmy (1980) found that primary-age boys and girls did not differ in their level of motor activity, but boys and girls in the later elementary grades did differ. The older boys played active sport-related games in large groups; the older girls' play was more passive and included much time spent sitting, walking, and talking in small groups. Although the younger children were all similarly active, the content of the play differed; primary-age boys' play was with balls, while girls divided their activity between ball games and active games that did not use balls.

Because of the importance of balls in motor play of elementary-age children, a number of studies have looked at the influence of the characteristics of balls as play objects. Isaacs (1980) found that for 7- and 8-year-olds, a smaller ball promoted more mature catching (i.e., catching that uses only the hands, not the body to "trap" the ball). Earlier studies showing that larger balls were easier to catch (e.g., Morris, 1976) did not measure maturity of catching skill. Isaacs also reports that children more easily caught balls of a color they preferred, possibly because the preferred color was a more salient attentional cue. Boys were generally better at catching maturely than were girls; whether this is due to faster reaction time of boys or to lower levels of play experience with ball catching by girls is unclear.

In addition to influences of characteristics of specific play objects, the general context in which the motor play occurs also influences its quantity and quality. For example, in a comparison of kindergartners' motor activity in physical education classes and in free play, children showed more motor and locomotor activity and spent more time in play in the free-play condition (Myers, 1985). They spent more time unengaged in play during the structured class time. There were no differences in activity level or type of play between boys and girls, but during free play, children with higher levels of motor skill played more.

The general recess environment affects the quantity and type of motor play. In observations of recess play, Hovell, Bursick, Sharkey, and McClure (1978) report that only 60% of children's recess time was spent actively engaged in play. The rest was spent waiting for turns. They attributed this to the lack of equipment, which meant that the most available play was ball and other game play. They estimate that the children's activity level was about half what would be needed to meet aerobic requirements; thus, aerobic fitness was not promoted by recess play in that setting.

These research examples point to a variety of interesting directions for future research on play and physical/motor development. Keogh (1977) states, "We need to use play environments more as our research setting. . . . Within these environments and experiences are the primary opportunities of children for development of movement skills" (p. 84). If researchers follow Keogh's suggestion to relate their studies to theoretical constructs, the next decade may show major strides in understanding how play can enhance motor skill development.

● **Implications for education**

Because play is a primary medium through which physical and motor development are promoted, providing opportunities for gross and fine motor play has always been important in early education (Schurr, 1980; Graham, Holt-Hale, McEwen, & Parker 1980). Equipment that encourages motor skill development during free play is included in most early education classrooms and on most school playgrounds. The chapters in section three describe many of the ways that environments can be designed to enhance physical/motor development. There is much evidence to indicate that environmental design can affect the types of motor play that occur. As Hovell et al.'s study (1978) points out, the environment may provide inadequate or limited play opportunities.

Educators who understand the basic components of effective movement can plan programs that include movement education experiences that build on play-oriented techniques. A number of movement education models have been developed to give children systematically planned opportunities to experience a wide range of movement. One of the most influential of these is Laban's theoretically based model (Laban, 1948; Laban & Lawrence, 1947). In this model, children are taught to use their whole bodies as well as specific body parts in a wide range of movement activities that vary in intensity of effort, levels and arrangements in space, and coordinated interrelationships. Teachers of the Laban method of movement education use games, dance, and gymnastics as vehicles for these movement experiences.

During the sixties, movement education models were widely advocated as a means of promoting movement skills thought to be related to cognitive development and academic learning (e.g., Delacato, 1959; Radler & Kephart, 1960). Studies of the effects of these approaches have not demonstrated clear relationships between movement education experiences and perception or cognition, although there seem to be some common attributes necessary for both motor and cognitive functioning (Keogh, 1978; Zeller, 1985).

Although most writers in the field of movement agree that providing opportunities for children to exercise their movement skills in play improves motor performance and competence, there are differences of opinion about the degree of structure or direction teachers should use in planning these play opportunities. Stillwell (1987) agrees that free play is important but states that structured play is also needed if children's motor performance and fitness are to be improved. He adds that this has never been more true than it is today, when much of children's playtime is comprised of sedentary activity such as watching television and playing computer games.

Children with Special Needs

This section focuses on the special needs of (a) children with identified physical, emotional, cognitive, and/or other deficits; and (b) children who experience environmental stresses such as hospitalization, abuse/neglect, or family dysfunction/dissolution. Play can often enhance the ability of these children to cope with their life situations.

Handicapped children include those identified as mentally retarded, physically impaired, developmentally delayed, learning disabled, and/or emotionally disturbed. Handicapping conditions may be limited to development in one specific area, or the handicap may affect several areas of development in an overlapping fashion. For example, spina bifida, which is a physical defect in the spinal column, may create limitations in movement ranging from minimal to severe; it can also affect language and social interaction patterns. Quinn and Rubin (1984) state that "all handicapped children show the similar disadvantage that the condition interferes with, and sometimes alters, the expected pattern and rate of development" (p. 66).

Many children, including some of those with identified handicaps, may face environmental factors that may place them at risk for less than optimum development. Optimal environments in which children can flourish incorporate the following basic support systems: (a) physical care; (b) social/emotional support from a group of interested, emotionally healthy, consistent adults; and (c) environmental balance between nurturance and risk (i.e., support for development toward independence and maturity that both stimulates and protects). Although this "ideal" environment provides positive stress and stimulation for children to develop without being overwhelmed (i.e., demands do not exceed their ability), in actuality, many children do not have this optimum combination. As members of families, communities, and societies, children are subject to the disruptions, setbacks, and trials that are part of human existence. If these situations are chronic or acute, they are likely to have a major impact on children's development, including play. Play can, however, also serve to ameliorate the impact of such stressors.

● Theory and research on handicapping conditions

L. (age 4 years, 10 months) is a Down's syndrome child who is in a day-care program for toddlers. He spends much of his time playing alone with the many toys and materials in the setting. One of his favorite activities is to pull the wagon around and around. Sometimes he puts blocks or dolls in the wagon but today, the wagon is empty. L. stops his pulling to watch intently as two other children drive the trucks past him. He hears a noise behind him and turns just in time to see R. (age 2 years, 9 months) climb into the wagon. R. says "give me a ride." L. smiles delightedly and quickly picks up the handle of the wagon. He pulls R. around and around until R. says loudly "stop, stop, stop." R. jumps out of the wagon and motions to L. to get in, saying "your turn to ride, I want to pull." Seeing L.'s look of bewilderment, R. says again, "get in," motioning to L. L. finally climbs in slowly and settles himself; then he beams as R. pulls him around the room.

Extensive bodies of theory and research on children with handicapping conditions have been amassed during the past 30 years. However, the amount of research focusing on play has been very limited, primarily due to the theoretical perspectives that have dominated the field until very recently. The traditional training of educators who work with handicapped children has been influenced by behaviorist and social learning theory, which emphasizes the role of reinforcement, imitation, and teacher-directed instruction (e.g., Bereiter & Englemann, 1966). Recently the developmental approach, which emphasizes the active role of learners in creating their own knowledge about the world, has been promoted (Hunt, 1981; Iano, 1971). Theorists from these two perspectives have viewed the role of play in the learning process very differently.

Behaviorist and social learning theory. The behavioral approach, influenced by the research of Bloom (1964) and Kirk (1958), countered the earlier view that genetic endowment determined the potential of handicapped children. These researchers reported that, although outer limits of potential are determined by heredity, rate of intellectual development can be altered by changing the environment. For example, Kirk reported acceleration in young retarded children's intellectual development when a stimulating preschool environment was provided. Behaviorist theory views learning as the acquisition of successive chains of behaviors, with these behaviors being acquired through a stimulus-response paradigm.

The behavioral model in special education (e.g., Allen, Turner, & Everett, 1970; Baer, 1967; Bereiter, 1972; Johnston, Kelley, Harris, & Wolf, 1966) recommends analysis of skills children need and systematic teaching of these skills through behavioral techniques such as reinforcing and shaping. Child-initiated play is not usually promoted because learning is considered to be more efficiently taught through adult-directed reinforcements. Teachers use play as a reinforcer, with the promise of later playtime insuring children's compliance with work demands. For handicapped children, teachers may even omit play as a reward, because they believe the children have to work continuously to "catch up" with peers. Although adult-directed techniques may incorporate "playlike" activity, spontaneous play is not a major part of these programs.

The social learning approach (Bandura, 1977) is based on assumptions similar to those of behavior analysis, but it focuses more on the learning of social interaction patterns than on cognitive skill development. Teachers and peers serve as models of appropriate behavior. Using role-playing or other modeling formats, teachers demonstrate social situations and model appropriate responses. This modeling may also include directing children to give particular verbal responses.

Play research done from the behaviorist and social learning perspectives includes studies on increasing specific playlike social responses in retarded children (e.g., Peck, Apolloni, Cooke, & Raver, 1978); developing social play in socially isolated children (e.g., Allen, Hart, Buell, Harris, & Wolf, 1964); and supporting prosocial play in overly aggressive children (e.g., Pinkston, Reese, LeBlanc, & Baer, 1973).

Developmental theory. The developmental approach conceptualizes learning as an interaction between the child and the environment (Kohlberg & Mayer, 1972). In these interactions between children's own thought processes and the responses they receive from people and objects in the environment, children actively seek to make sense out of their world and, in the process, construct their own knowledge (Piaget, 1952). This theoretical view, which posits a learning process with invariant, sequential stages and assumes that children are intrinsically motivated to move to the next state, has very different implications for the education of handicapped children.

Developmental theorists stress the importance of assimilation in the development of intelligence as well as adaptation. Modification of behavior that occurs without reference to internal mental structures may result in the appearance, but not the actual achievement of, task mastery (Simeonsson, Grunewald, & Scheiner, 1978). Yet if the behavior is not integrated meaningfully, this apparent mastery is likely to be lost within a few weeks. Simeonsson et al. indicate that this happens frequently when handicapped children's behavior is shaped without concern for assimilation and knowledge construction.

Because developmental theorists see intelligence as dependent upon experiences with and feedback from the environment, they consider play an excellent vehicle for facilitating cognitive growth. At the present time, research on handicapped children's play from a developmental perspective is still limited. However, this research is beginning to show that the play of handicapped children is similar to that of normally developing children in many ways (Cicchetti, 1985b; Field, 1982; Hill & McCune-Nicolich, 1981; Wing, Gould, Yeates, & Brierley, 1977).

● **Research on play of handicapped children**

Results reported in the research literature on handicapped children's play have often been difficult to interpret because of a number of factors, including the researchers' differing conceptualizations of play and their varied theoretical perspectives which influence what areas of disability they study and what methodology they use. In addition, there have been many methodological problems with this research (Quinn & Rubin, 1984).

Some of these differences in conceptualization, theoretical perspective, and methodology are evident in comparisons of behaviorist and developmentalist research approaches. For example, the behaviors studied as play by behaviorists may not be considered play by developmentalists. Sponseller (1982) and Rubin, Fein, and Vandenberg (1983) have discussed some of these definitional problems.

Play studies may lack comparability because the research paradigms used to study specific disabilities differ. Quinn and Rubin (1984) state that intellectual impairments have usually been researched from a psychoeducational paradigm; emotional disturbance from a clinical psychological and/or psychiatric perspective; and physical disabilities from a medical/physical therapeutic viewpoint. Because few studies have employed developmental theory as a base, comparability with studies of normally developing children has been limited. Furthermore, although many children are multihandicapped, research has usually focused on one disability area.

Methodological problems include (a) small, nonrandom, inadequately defined, and/or heterogeneous samples; (b) failure to control for confounding variables such as sex, age, or institutional status; (c) observer categories that are not drawn from a theoretical base; and (d) unfamiliarity of researchers with developmental norms. Thus, Quinn and Rubin (1984, p. 66) conclude that many of these studies have been "methodologically flawed and/or conceptually vacuous."

They believe this is unfortunate because research on play of handicapped children can be very beneficial for several reasons. First, by observing the developmental progression of handicapped children's play and comparing it to developmental norms, "useful nonlaboratory indices for assessing and diagnosing young children" (Quinn & Rubin, 1984, p. 64) can be gained. Second, comparisons of sequences of play for handicapped and nonhandicapped children can provide information for further validation of developmental scales that have demonstrated initial validity for normally developing children (e.g., Nicolich, 1977; Rubin, Maioni, & Hornung, 1976; Rubin, Watson, & Jambor, 1978). Third, intervention treatments used with nonhandicapped children (e.g., sociodramatic training or social skills training) may be adapted for use with handicapped children.

Given the methodological and theoretical problems inherent in play research on handicapped children, reports on play of handicapped children must be interpreted cautiously. However, recent developmentally based studies (e.g., Crawley & Chan, 1982; Guralnick, 1980, 1981; Guralnick & Groom, 1985; Guralnick & Weinhouse, 1983, 1984; Lombardino & Sproul, 1984) indicate that comparisons between the play development of handicapped and non-handicapped children and of children with different levels of handicaps can be made. Due to the wide range of severity levels and systems affected by handicaps, ability to initiate play varies greatly among handicapped children. For example, a child who has physical/motor disabilities may not be able to move toward or manipulate potential play objects, and a child who is visually impaired may be less likely to initiate social interactive play that depends on visual cues. Thus, research indicating differences in play competence level may be influenced by environmental constraints on the play performance of the children. A review of research-based characteristics of handicapped children's play reported for functional/practice/constructive play, symbolic play, and social play, including social games and routines, follows.

Functional/practice/constructive play. There are numerous descriptions of functional/practice play in the literature because it is a commonly observed play in handicapped children. Mentally retarded, developmentally delayed, emotionally disturbed, and sensory impaired children engage in functional play. Their level of play seems to follow developmental sequences based on their mental age rather than their chronological age. For example, Switzky, Ludwig, and Haywood (1979) report that 4-year-old Down's syndrome children with a mental age of 2 play in ways that are similar to toddlers (e.g., dumping and filling containers with toys). They also engage in less exploration and more play when they are repeatedly exposed to the same toys and they do more exploration, rather than play, when toy complexity is high. These behaviors are typical of nonhandicapped children also (Hutt, 1979). Fait and Kupferes (1976) report that young Down's syndrome children can follow directions for simple motor actions such as jumping, but they have difficulty following complex, sequential directions; such sequences also seem to be less frequent in their play.

Weiner and Weiner (1974) report that functional play of 6-year-old mentally retarded children, with a mental age (MA) of 3 had some similarities to that of 3-year-old nonretarded children (e.g., push-pull toys were used similarly), but that the nonretarded children did more combining of toys in complex actions. These differences in complexity have not always been found by researchers, however (e.g., Hulme & Lunzer, 1966).

A study of older children found that retarded children (MA of 7) preferred more structured, concrete, and constructive materials than did nonretarded children of 7 years (Horne & Philleo, 1942). This may be due to the increasing sense of helplessness and dependency that is commonly observed in retarded children as they grow older (Zigler, 1966).

Visually impaired children use their hands more in functional and exploratory play than do nonimpaired preschoolers (Olson, 1983). Visually impaired boys and girls show toy preferences that are similar to those of nonimpaired preschoolers, and boys use more varied actions, a finding similar to that for normally developing children. Olson speculates that school improved the visually impaired children's exploratory play abilities because their levels of exploration were related to the time that they had been in a school program. Tait (1972b, 1972c) reports that blind children also tend to show "learned helplessness" and thus, the school experience may have countered some of that. Tait (1972a) found that visually impaired children of 4 to 9 years engaged in more functional play than did nonimpaired age mates, who engaged in more symbolical and social play. Almost two-thirds of the blind children did engage in symbolic play, however.

Although few studies of hearing impaired children are available, Higginbotham and Baker (1981) found that hearing impaired children spent more time in noninteractive constructive play than in social and symbolic play. Guralnick and Groom (1985) also found that, for developmentally delayed children, constructive play serves as a type of social play (i.e., it is engaged in with other children present).

The functional play of autistic children has also been studied. Tilton and Ottinger (1964) found that the stereotypic, repetitive play that has been considered symptomatic of this condition does not characterize the behavior of all autistic children. Almost half of their subjects did not exhibit these behaviors with play objects. Autistic children rarely combine objects in functional play, however (Wing et al., 1977).

Severity of handicaps greatly affects children's levels of exploration and functional play. Switsky, Rotatori, Miller, and Freagon (1979) state that self-initiated functional play is not seen in severely impaired children. In a study of constructive play, Guralnick and Weinhouse (1984) categorized the play of severely, moderately, and mildly handicapped toddlers and preschoolers into inappropriate, exploratory, constructive, and pretend/games types of behavior. In the younger group, the majority of play was exploratory; this did not change over a two-year period. Because about half the toddler group were severely handicapped, much of their time was spent in unoccupied behavior. In the older group, which contained only 8% severely handicapped children, constructive play was the typical type of play observed.

Symbolic play. Recently the symbolic play of handicapped children has become a topic of research interest; many of these studies build on the developmental research linking symbolic play and language development in normally developing children. For example, Casby and Ruder (1983) compared the language and symbolic play of trainable retarded and nonretarded young children. In both groups their mean length of utterance (MLU) was related to their ability to play symbolically. In the normal group, both chronological age (CA) and mental age (MA) were

related to performance; in the retarded group MA was related to performance but CA was not. This finding agrees with Wing et al.'s (1977) finding that an MA of 20 months and language competency are required for symbolic play in retarded children.

Other studies of this relationship have found that language impaired children have lower levels of symbolic play (Williams, 1980), and hearing impaired children show less symbolic play with objects (Kretschmer, 1972). Older language impaired children show symbolic levels more advanced than their linguistic skills would predict (Terrell, Schwartz, Prelock, & Messick, 1984).

An interesting study by Rogers and Puchalski (1984a) indicates that about half the developmentally delayed children studied exhibited pretense by 26 months although they were less able to perform symbolic sequences than 20-month-old normally developing children. The crucial factors in both groups' ability to play symbolically were presence of the word "No" in their speech, ability to make two-word combination utterances, and sensorimotor play skills.

Symbolic play is present in sensory impaired children's play although it is often less well developed (e.g., Kretschmer, 1972; Singer & Streiner, 1966; Tait, 1972a). Lombardino and Sproul (1984) examined the relationships among receptive language, expressive language, and symbolic play. They state that symbolic play is usually exhibited by retarded children when both receptive and expressive language are present; by nonvocal or minimally vocal children when receptive language is present; and in hearing impaired children when both receptive and expressive language are delayed. They note, however, "A pattern in which symbolic play is less well developed than language has not been observed" (p. 11).

The study of autistic children's play also indicates that there is a relationship between level of play and receptive language (Ungerer & Sigman, 1981). Autistic children have difficulty using language meaningfully; they also do not usually differentiate themselves from the objects in their environment, a requirement for symbolic play. In an adapted replication of Fein's object transformation study, Riguet, Taylor, Benaroya, and Klein (1981) were able to elicit autistic children's imitation of symbolic play acts although their ability to use objects in transformations did not reach the level of the compared retarded and normally developing subjects. Down's syndrome children showed fewer different symbolic substitutions than normally developing children in both the free-play and the structured conditions; autistic children showed fewer different substitutions in the structured conditions but not in the free-play condition, due to the Down's syndrome children's tendency to repeat the same actions. However, the authors conclude that "the content of symbolic play is impoverished in autistic children and demonstrates less symbolic fluency than symbolic play of other children of similar verbal mental age" (p. 447).

Social play.   Children with handicaps often seem to have major difficulties in social development. Research has not fully explored the question of whether this is a function of (a) the handicap per se (e.g., lack of social communicative ability/responsiveness, or presence of physical deficits that prevent active peer play); (b) lower social acceptance levels and negative social judgements (e.g., peer avoidance of handicapped children in mainstream programs); and/or (c) lack of opportunities to learn social skills (e.g., parents' overprotectiveness and confinement of the children at home). Recently, however, several studies based on developmental theory have focused on the social play of handicapped children.

One direction of study has been that of describing developmentally delayed or retarded children's social play in segregated and mainstream settings. For example, Guralnick and colleagues (Guralnick, 1981; Guralnick & Groom, 1985; Guralnick & Weinhouse, 1984) have used the categories of social/cognitive play designed by Rubin and colleagues to investigate the play development of mildly, moderately, and severely retarded young children. Guralnick and Groom found that handicapped preschoolers played more like toddlers, with solitary play predominating (39%); only 11% of play was social. The children spent 37% of their time not engaged in any type of play, however, which is not typical of normal toddlers. One-fourth of the subjects played alone over 50% of the time. In an integrated setting, Guralnick (1981) found that the less severely handicapped children did engage in social play with non-handicapped children but that the social play of severely delayed children did not increase when they were put in an integrated group. However, their level

of "inappropriate" play did decrease in the integrated setting.

In a longitudinal study, Guralnick and Weinhouse (1984) found that peer-related social play increased over a two-year time period for the moderately and mildly retarded children but not for the severely retarded. The less severely retarded children's increase in social play was still slight compared to that of normally developing children during the two-year period. Those children who did engage in social play still played less often. Normally developing 3-year-olds engaged in social play at least 25% of the time, but the handicapped children with an MA of 5 years showed only 10% of time in associative play and 0% in cooperative play. Moreover, 20% of the retarded children accounted for over 60% of the social play instances observed. The researchers conclude that the "vast majority of developmentally delayed preschoolers fail to engage in sustained social interaction" (p. 824).

Other studies using Parten, Smilansky, Piaget, or Rubin categories report results that are congruent with those of Guralnick et al. For example, handicapped preschoolers interacted more with adults than peers and spent more time looking and listening than playing (Brophy & Stone-Zukowski, 1984); unoccupied time and teacher-child play decreased over time while solitary and parallel play increased for mildly and moderately retarded children; however, peer play increased only for mildly retarded children (Crawley & Chan, 1982). Moderately handicapped preschoolers showed less associative play than normally developing peers, and severely handicapped preschoolers showed the least social interaction (Beckman, 1983). Developmental age (DA) and social play scores were correlated in preschool children (Odom, 1981); and elementary children with learning disabilities spent more time playing alone during recess, although the cognitive type of play observed did not differ from the play of other children (Levy & Gottlieb, 1984).

Studies of children with sensory impairments also indicate that severity of handicap greatly influences social play and adjustment. For example, teacher ratings of hearing impaired preschoolers' social adjustment were related to whether the children were multiply handicapped. Those children with no other handicaps were rated similarly to normally developing children, but multiply handicapped children were rated lower (Meadow, 1984). Meadow speculates that at preschool age hearing impairment alone is not as great a social handicap as it is at later ages when verbal communication has a greater role in social interaction. Higginbotham, Baker, and Neill (1980) also found that hearing impaired preschoolers' language and social play levels were related.

Developmentally based studies of handicapped children's peer play are beginning to provide baseline information that may be useful in planning interventions that will increase the level of handicapped children's social play. For example, Beckman and Kohl (1984) found that the presence of "social" rather than "isolate" toys encouraged more social play in both integrated and nonintegrated preschool settings. Quilitch and Risley (1973) indicated that the types of toys given to older handicapped children also influence their social interactions. Behaviorists concerned about increasing social interaction have not often used social play techniques (Li, 1983). However, pleasurable play can be used as a reinforcer (Wehman, 1977) and play-based interventions are being used by behaviorists. For example, a planned teacher-directed sociodramatic play intervention increased social play levels in handicapped preschoolers (Strain, 1975; Strain & Wiegerink, 1976).

Recent research on handicapped children's social play has also focused on the social play routines of parent and child. Because these early social games have been hypothesized as crucial for attachment, later social adjustment, and even for understanding what play is, the patterns of social play of handicapped infants and their parents may be especially predictive of their later development. In a study of the social interaction patterns of blind infants and their mothers, Fraiberg (1974) pointed out how the infant's lack of visual regard and responsiveness affected the social interaction. For example, mothers perceived their blind infants as unresponsive because of the absence of differentiated facial expression and "eye language." Techniques used by mothers to engage their infants in social play include much gross motor and tactile stimulation as well as vocalizations. However, even vocalization may be sparse because of the absence of the usual eliciting visual stimuli.

In a recent study of mothers and their visually impaired infants at play, Rogers and Puchalski (1984b) reported that visually impaired infants used fewer vocalization and had fewer social interactions, with more ignoring and negative affect. Mothers were less "enfacing" and showed fewer positive vocalizations. There were no differences in mother-child play patterns between the partially sighted and the blind infant groups. The authors conclude, "Both partners in the visually impaired dyads are deprived" (p. 55). The social play of mother/retarded infant dyads is also different from normal social play interactions. With retarded infants, mothers take a more directive and "managerial" role (Bailey & Slee, 1984; Stoneman, Brody, & Abbott, 1983), and both mothers and fathers use more physical contact and parental positive affect (Stoneman et al., 1983). These researchers suggest that the lower level of responsiveness of retarded children influences the parenting play style. Play styles of parents of high-risk infants also are affected by their children's lower response levels (Field, 1979).

Attempts to ameliorate the problems in the play of adults and handicapped infants have been directed toward teaching social games to parents and giving them suggestions for interactive approaches that may encourage social play (Hodapp & Goldfield, 1983; Li, 1983; Linder, 1982).

● Assessing handicapped children's development through play

Numerous assessment instruments have been designed to measure and identify deficits in children's motor, language, and general cognitive development. Although formal diagnostic assessment using standardized instruments can provide useful information about the abilities and problems of many handicapped children, these measures may not give a picture as complete as educators or therapists would like. Also, children with physical or language impairments are often unable to demonstrate their abilities because they cannot produce the specific motor and/or linguistic responses required by traditional norm-referenced tests, which typically focus on a set of specific behaviors to be elicited by an examiner. Many emotionally disturbed children are also unable to perform to their capacity in formal testing situations.

The potential use of play as an assessment tool for evaluating the sensorimotor, social, cognitive, and language development of nonhandicapped children has been described recently by a number of researchers (e.g., McCune-Nicolich & Fenson, 1984; Pellegrini, 1984b; Rubin, 1982b, 1985; Rubin, Daniels-Beirness, & Hayvren, 1982). Enslein and Fein (1981) and Rubin and Krasnor (1980) have reported reliability and stability of the Rubin et al. scale. Pellegrini points out that although there are still some psychometric questions about the hierarchic structure of social/cognitive observational matrices, this method can be applied productively in most classroom settings.

Quinn and Rubin (1984) suggest that some of the play scales that have demonstrated validity in assessing the play development levels of nonhandicapped children (e.g., Nicolich, 1977; Rubin, 1985b, Rubin & Krasnor, 1980) might be adapted for use with handicapped children. In particular, assessing handicapped children's development through observing spontaneous play may be appropriate for children whose handicapping condition calls into question the validity of conventional test results. The use of multiple data points, collected through observation of play in a variety of settings and over a number of time periods, could give a better overall assessment of potential for many children. Play can provide the diagnostician with the opportunity to observe and analyze a variety of behaviors as children freely manipulate the events and the objects in their environment (Weiner, Ottinger, & Tilton, 1969).

Psychoanalytic clinicians have long used observations of children's play to assess their emotional health (e.g., Axline, 1947; Klein, 1955), but these approaches have not been psychometrically validated. Many researchers working with autistic children suggest play as an assessment tool (e.g., Clune, Paolella, & Foley, 1979; Ungerer & Sigman, 1981; Wing et al., 1977) because it is particularly difficult to assess these children with traditional testing methods.

Higginbotham, Baker, and Neill, (1980) have reported validity for an adapted version of the Parten (1932) and Rubin et al. (1976, 1978) methods in the assessment of the social/cognitive play of hearing impaired children. Higginbotham et al. (1980, p. 269) state that this revised scale may have "considerable application for the assessment of individuals with communication disorders . . . [and results] . . . may then be compared to normal preschool free-play behavior." They urge caution in interpreting these comparisons because the instruments have not yet been standardized.

In a review of 54 nonclinical and clinical peer interaction assessment measures, many of which involve observations of play, Guralnick and Weinhouse (1983) indicate that many of these instruments have psychometric problems. For example, on the peer-related items, "only 21% of these tests were considered standardized, only 33% reliable, and only 21% valid" (p. 270). They conclude that concerted efforts should be directed toward development of psychometrically sound social play assessment measures because of the many problems handicapped children have in developing social relationships; however, they point out that, given the complexity of the task, "this will not be very easy to accomplish" (p. 270).

Although these psychometric questions remain, play as an informal assessment tool may yield important information about handicapped children's level of functioning, ability to compensate for the handicap, and the ways their environment helps or hinders their development. Just as a single test is not used to diagnose handicapping conditions, no single play behavior is sufficient to determine children's skill levels; however, patterns that emerge from play observations can be examined and measured against other information that has been gathered in order to plan appropriate interventions (Brooks-Gunn & Lewis, 1982; Newson & Newson, 1979; Wing et al., 1977). Suggestions for developmental areas that may be informally observed during play are in Table 6–1.

Such observations can yield information in a variety of developmental areas. For example, observers of children in a free-play setting can determine children's motor skill level by watching them manipulate toys, do puzzles, use drawing materials, and navigate the obstacles in the environment (Clune et al., 1979). Observers can also encourage children to participate in a range of play activities that require different motor abilities (Newson & Newson, 1979). In addition, techniques for collecting and analyzing spontaneous language samples of normally developing children can yield information about the form, content, and use of handicapped children's language (Bloom & Lahey, 1978; Hubbell, 1977; McCune-Nicolich & Carroll, 1981; Warren & Rogers-Warren, 1980). Observations of parent-child social play at

TABLE 6–1 ● Developmental Areas to Observe Through Play (from Kaplan-Sanoff)		
Motor:		
Gross motor:	Balance Locomotion Coordination Body image Body boundaries Ability to cross midline	
Fine motor:	Hand dominance Dexterity Grasping	
Visual- peceptual:	Attending Following, scanning Eye-hand coordination Visual memory Visual discrimination Drawing skills Constancy Figure-ground	
Language:	Attending Listening Auditory memory Auditory discrimination Information processing Semantics—concepts, labels, actions Syntactics—word order, plurals, negatives, possessives, questions, prepositions Articulation	
Cognitive:	Discrimination/matching—objects, pictures, objects with pictures Sorting Seriating Sequencing Counting, one-to-one correspondence Basic concepts—color, number, shape, letters Problem solving Object permanence Conservation	
Social:		
Self-concept	Perception of others/world view Motivation Response to praise Recognition of success Knowledge of body parts	
Self-help skills:	Toileting Dressing Washing/grooming Feeding	
Socialization:	Interaction with peers, parents, other adults Approach/withdrawal Managing anger—tantrums, emotional controls	
Play level:	Use of symbolic roles Flexible or perseverative and rigid Fantasy Aggressive/passive balance Prosocial skills	

home can identify dysfunctional patterns of interaction and aid educators in helping parents to improve these social play experiences (Linder, 1982; Olson, 1983; Rogow, 1984).

● Implications for education

Special educators who are aware of the value of play for learning will be able to find many ways for handicapped children to learn through play. Because play can serve as a medium for skill development, specific skills that handicapped children need to learn or strengthen can be practiced within the context of play. For example, children can use fine motor skills by preparing and serving make-believe clay food or building a garage of blocks. Social and language skills can be enhanced as children learn to interact with adults, peers, and fantasy figures (Hill & McCune-Nicholich, 1981; McCune-Nicholich & Carroll, 1981; Taenzer, Cermak, & Hanlon, 1981). Children can even learn self-care skills such as handwashing playfully if opportunities for water play and washing are available.

Those children with physical/motor handicaps or sensory impairments may experience frustration because of their inability to move freely. Although these restrictions are a reality of their handicap, an environment designed to give them access to play materials and that promotes opportunities for peer play can reduce this frustration (Hohman, Banet, & Weikart, 1979; McGuinness, 1982; Olds, 1979). Often children with severe physical disabilities are judged as not interested in or unable to play when actually the constraints of the environment are preventing engagement. For example, a child in a wheelchair cannot play with blocks if the blocks are on the floor. Either the blocks must be brought to the appropriate height or another support system must be used to enable the child to play on the floor. Chapter 11 discusses further ideas for adapting environments to allow physically handicapped children to play.

Similarly, children with learning disabilities that make it difficult for them to process information and language efficiently or accurately may experience the frustration of being unable to communicate (Levy & Gottlieb, 1984). Traditional speech and language therapy consisting of adult modeling of language that the child is required to imitate may result in a parrotlike, rigid use of specific phrases (Hubbell, 1977);

adult facilitation of spontaneous language during play activities can result in greater language facility and use (Taenzer et al., 1981). Children who may not answer direct questions or repeat phrases upon request may talk when manipulating a puppet, "driving" a pretend car, or caring for a doll.

Program planning for play differs from the traditional special education approach (Odom, 1981; Odom, Jenkins, Speltz, & DeKlyen, 1982). In play programs, educators teach specific skills within the context of play rather than breaking the skills into sets of small steps that do not promote generalization. For example, having children match circles and squares by imitating the adult's action of putting them in piles is not likely to support broader concept development (Kaczmarek & Dell, 1981). Play programming promotes opportunities to classify, order, and organize play materials and experiences. Because children's handicaps may prevent them from engaging in a wide range of play, experiences designed to meet specific goals must still be carefully arranged and monitored (Wolfgang, 1977); when children are taught within the context of play, however, they are likely to feel more in control of their learning.

Developmental play programs, encompassing a wide variety of motor play and games, have demonstrated that generalized motor development of mildly handicapped children can be fostered (e.g., Roswal & Frith, 1980). Promotion of symbolic play to help children deal with the stresses of their handicaps has assisted children who are emotionally disturbed (Guerney, 1976), learning disabled (Guerney, 1979), and retarded (Ginsburg, Sywulak, & Cramer, 1984). Various training studies using modeling and reinforcement have also shown that specific play skills can be fostered (e.g., Peck, et al., 1978; Wehman, 1975). Sociodramatic play training techniques have increased the level of retarded children's social play (Strain, 1975).

Attention to the social play development of handicapped children is especially important in both mainstream and segregated program settings, especially for those children with moderate or severe handicaps. Techniques for encouraging nonhandicapped children to learn social skills can be adapted for handicapped children as well. For example, social skills training has helped retarded children learn how to join in play, defend or share space and toys, and ask for help (Combs & Arezzo-Slaby, 1977).

Facilitating play in severely handicapped children is much more difficult; however, these children can still experience the pleasure of adult-child interactive play, manipulate play materials with whatever physical or sensory modalities are available to them, and engage in play in the company of other children. Although a behavioral approach may be most appropriate for teaching specific self-help and communication tasks (Bushell, 1973), play can help children achieve these developmental tasks by allowing them to use the skills in a variety of ways. Children can enjoy practice of even the simplest skills if they can learn about the pleasure of play.

Adults must not expect the play of handicapped children to be like that of their nonhandicapped age mates, nor should they discourage play that may seem immature for children's chronological age but that is appropriate for their mental age. Adults should encourage the development of more mature play, however, and provide opportunities for play development at home and at school for every handicapped child.

● **Theory and research on hospitalization**

One vignette:

> W. (8 months) is lying on his back in the narrow metal crib, staring intermittently through the bars, at his hands, and at the faded picture on the wall high above the crib. He has been in the hospital for a week now; at first he screamed constantly, but now he seems to be calm and the staff believes he has "adjusted" to his hospitalization. The only time he seems upset is when his mother comes; the staff is thinking of suggesting she come less often.

Another vignette:

> B. (8 months) has been in the hospital for a week. He is playing with a busy box attached to the crib. He manipulates the box for about 10 minutes, then yells loudly to a staff member passing by. He is carried down to the playroom, where the child life worker places him on a mat with a number of toys. He rolls around, exploring the objects until his mother comes into the room. She sits down and plays with him for a while.

For the past 30 years, there has been a great deal of research devoted to the impact of hospitalization on children, because this experience combines several elements that may adversely affect children's healthy development. These stress factors include (a) separation from the patient's family and other emotionally significant figures, (b) infliction of painful procedures and the fear of the outcome of the illness, and (c) enforced physical confinement and disruption of routines. Since the late sixties, research on the effects of hospitalization has included efforts to (a) further delineate the sources of stress, (b) document effects of different technological procedures on children's hospital experience, and (c) develop and assess play programs and other methods of ameliorating the stress. Concerns about the effects of hospitalization on children have come from a number of theoretical and research perspectives including medical, ethological, cognitive-developmental, and family systems perspectives.

Medical perspectives on hospitalization. Before the 1940s, pediatric wards were designed primarily for the purpose of limiting the possibility of infection; the environment was designed to be as sterile as possible, and children were isolated from their families. Often this meant that children were physically restrained in bed to prevent them from coming in contact with germs. Although the discovery of antibiotics ameliorated the necessity for dealing with rampant infections, these isolation procedures remained intact. During the late forties and fifties psychiatrists and psychologists began to point out the deleterious effect of these practices (e.g., Prugh, Staub, Sands, Kirchbaum, & Leniham, 1953; Robertson, 1958, 1961; Spitz, 1945). A classic study of this period was that of Spitz, who coined the term "hospitalism" to describe the lethargy, depression, and marasmus afflicting infants who were raised in physically and emotionally barren institutional environments. The condition can be fatal to infants.

Two other classic studies of the period were Robertson's (1961) film, which documented the pathos of a young child separated from his parents by hospitalization, and Prugh et al.'s (1953) study of effects of various hospital environments. One scene of the Robertson film showed a small child isolated in bed, desperately clinging to his shoe, the only familiar thing left to him. The film, which marked the first public attention given to the emotional needs of hospitalized children, was initially met with anger and disbelief by the medical community.

Prugh et al., (1953) studied the behavior of two groups of children while they were in the hospital, shortly after discharge, and six months later. The control group had traditional hospital care; the experimental group had increased parental visiting hours, early ambulation, and play programs. All children showed adverse reactions to hospitalization up to six months after the experience, and the stress was greatest among the youngest children. Those children who experienced a play program were less adversely affected by hospitalization. This documentation of benefits of play programs in hospitals provided the initial impetus for program development.

Studies have focused on the different treatment experiences children have as a result of their diagnosis. Hospitalization has changed over the past generation, from dealing primarily with acute, usually infectious diseases, to dealing with chronic illness and conditions that require complex long-term procedures (Barbero, 1984). For example, recent orthopedic advances to correct birth defects or repair serious accidents can mean that children are immobilized in a full body cast for almost a year. Children's play needs must be met in the hospital setting if they are going to play at all; special arrangements must be made to give them choices and a sense of control over their experience.

Similarly, cancer treatments have advanced to the point that the children's cancer that was fatal 10 years ago now may be controlled. This prognosis and treatment brings unique psychological problems because children may show radical changes in appearance as a result of procedures, and their involvement and that of their families may last for years. In long-term treatment cases, night terrors and magical thinking often accompany the illness (Katz, Kellerman, & Siegal, 1980). There are also often extended grief periods because of a long terminal stage, which brings problems that are different from those that occur when death comes quickly (MacCarthy & MacKeith, 1985). Thus, stress is prolonged and there is little closure for families (Barbarin & Chesler, 1984). A play program can provide diversion and support especially for these patients, who must return again and again to the hospital.

Ethological perspectives on hospitalization. The literature on attachment and separation (Bowlby, 1973) has greatly influenced hospitalization practices because long and enforced separation from parents and other emotionally significant people has been shown to have harmful effects on the subsequent personality development of young children. Bowlby's documentation of the process of young children's adjustments to separation (i.e., stages of protest, withdrawal, despair, and subsequent readjustment at a more guarded level of personality organization) points out a particular concern for hospitalized children. The stage of subsequent readjustment, when children may appear to be adjusted to the hospital, may be evidence that they have lost a sense of trust in other people's ability to meet their needs consistently and predictably, thus impairing their ability to enter into subsequent trusting relationships. The younger the children are at the time of hospitalization, the more affected they are by the experiences. This is due to the great dependence children have on their parents and their limited ability to understand separation. If they are able to play out separation experiences, as well as have the diversion offered by play, they can make these effects less severe.

Cognitive developmental perspectives on hospitalization. Painful procedures are a routine part of the hospitalization experience. Everyone who enters the hospital is subjected to anxiety-provoking procedures such as the drawing of blood, being given IVs and injections, and having surgery. Adults are able to deal with the anxiety of hospitalization with the knowledge that these procedures are being done for the purpose of curing or ameliorating their condition. Children's lack of understanding of the reasons for these procedures compounds their impact. The cognitive understanding of the *cause* of hospitalization and the *intent* of medical protocols are beyond the ability of the young child. Thus young children do not have the coping devices of adults.

The work of Piaget (1952) has demonstrated that the cognitive understanding of cause and effect, and the understanding of people's intentions and roles, is an ongoing developmental process. Children's stage of cognitive development influences the way they comprehend illness and the reasons for medical procedures. For example, children in the preoperational stage view themselves and their actions and wishes as causing the events around them and they have difficulty taking another person's point of view.

A study by Brewster (1982) shows that chronically ill, hospitalized children's understanding of the cause of illness follows a developmental sequence. Preoperational children (i.e., under age 7) see their illness to be a result of something that they did. They report as causes such things as "eating a rotten sandwich," "going out in the snow without your coat," or "bumping into someone with a bike," as causing their hospitalization. Children at the concrete operational stage (i.e., between 7 and 10 years) can identify an outside agent as causing their illness. At this stage, children conclude that all illnesses are caused by a single factor: germs. This is true no matter what illness they have or reason they are hospitalized. As they begin the formal operational stage (i.e., age 10 or 11), they can begin to comprehend multivaried causes of illness, such as congenital defects, viruses, or faults in the immune system. Children's misunderstandings are often reflected in their play; their play can help them to explore the cause/effect relationships as well as give staff members insight into their thinking processes.

A parallel developmental sequence occurs in children's understanding of people's roles and intents (Brewster, 1982). Children under 7 think nurses and doctors perform painful procedures to punish them because they have been bad. Children from ages 7 to 10 are able to comprehend that procedures help them get well, but they do not think doctors and nurses know the procedures are painful unless children give visible signs of pain, such as crying. For example, one 7-year-old diabetic child said that adults could understand his pain "only if they took an X-ray," because "then they could see the crying inside." Children over 10 or 11 are able to comprehend the intent of medical personnel and know adults can understand their point of view, even if the children give no visible signs. They say "they were kids once" or "they know me well." Play opportunities are valuable both to allow children to express these fears, anxieties, and feelings of pain and to give adults an opportunity to give children a sense that they are aware of their feelings.

There are also developmental and gender differences in children's demonstration of anxiety. A study by Katz et al. (1980) documented that children undergoing bone marrow aspirations in an oncology clinic showed universal anxiety, regardless of age. They also found that young children show more variety of anxious behaviors over a longer period of time, while older children are more inhibited in their expression of anxiety (i.e., they may show increased muscle tension and withdrawal). The Katz et al. study further indicated that children do not become used to the procedure, and that females at all ages show more anxiety. Chesler and Barbarin (1984) suggested that parents of older children have a great number of conflicts with medical staff because older children have greater awareness of their health status and greater anxiety over their disease outcome, as well as a tendency to engage in more protracted power struggles with the staff. Play programs for older children may help them deal with these high levels of anxiety. As Gibbons and Boren (1985) point out, hospitals must provide stimulation, exercise, and social interaction on a routine basis to promote children's normal development. The hospital must see to this because the children are not in a position, either emotionally or physically, to provide it for themselves.

Family systems perspective on hospitalization. The family's responses to hospitalization can affect the level of stress children feel. Families often cannot offer children the support, or even the physical presence, that they ideally need. Burns (1984) writes about the particular vulnerability of the single parent family at the time of hospitalization. These families usually have less financial resources, and the mothers have lower self-esteem. Burns adds that often parents who have had bitter divorces use their children's illness as battlegrounds for their continuing conflict.

Mothers and fathers often play different roles when children are hospitalized. Fathers may see their role as being a passive support to their children and thus they may have limited contacts with medical staff and participation in hospital preparation for their children (Knafl & Dixon, 1984). The minority of fathers who take an active role in the preparation and decision making dealing with their children's care seem to be less trusting and more difficult for staff to deal with than mothers are (Barbarin & Chesler, 1984; Knafl & Dixon, 1984). Well-educated and high socioeconomic families have more conflict and difficulty and report less satisfaction with medical staff, leading to greater defensiveness on the part of the medical staff. Robinson (1985) states that medical staff give conflicting messages to parents with chronically ill children. Although the parents had assumed tremendous responsibility for the care of their sick children at home, they reported feeling devalued and looked upon as ancillary and non-competent personnel when they entered the hospital setting.

Siblings of children who are hospitalized are often affected. In a survey by Craft, Wyatt, and Sandell (1985), siblings reported that they felt their parents were less lenient and had less time for them. Siblings also reported being afraid of catching the illness that their hospitalized siblings had, even though it was not contagious. In a review of the research on the impact of chronically ill children on siblings, McKeever (1983) indicates that these families have less personal and material resources to devote to siblings, and communication patterns are often disrupted. Siblings may have academic problems, behavior or adjustment problems, and negative self-images. They often do not have a clear understanding of the illness. Because hospitalization has a major impact on the family, which also influences the ill children's stress and the stress on siblings, it becomes a circular phenomenon in which each member contributes and reacts to the stress of this experience.

Play programs in hospitals certainly cannot alleviate all of the many stressors on hospitalized children and their families, but because such programs promote mastery and enjoyment, they can do much to involve parents and children in more normal interactions. All family members, including siblings, can benefit from the opportunity to have a place and time for play in the hospital.

● The relationship of play to hospitalization

Although many methods to ameliorate the psychological trauma of hospitalization for children have been used (e.g., increased visiting hours for parents, facilities for parents to stay overnight, pre-hospital visits, preparation of children for procedures, and relaxation training), the provision of play programs has been one of the major ways hospitals have tried to help children better cope with the experience of hospitalization. Four distinct functions of play for hos-

pitalized children have been identified: (a) preparation, (b) diagnosis, (c) mastery and coping, and (d) stress reduction. Play often incorporates two or more of these aspects, but studies typically focus on a single function.

Play can help *prepare* children for medical procedures. Aids such as miniature medical equipment, puppets and dolls playing the role of physician and patient, or other adult-directed interactions have been shown to prepare children. Because of the high level of adult direction, this type of activity is not always considered play because children do not control the transaction. In any case, such activities seem to help children.

For example, a study by Cassel (1965) showed that children prepared with three sessions of puppet play showed less emotional upset during cardiac catheterization than those who did not receive this therapy. Puppet play was defined as the therapist and child acting out the cardiac catheterization procedure; the therapist first played the doctor and the child played with the patient puppet, and then the roles were reversed. Post-hospitalization behavior of the experimental and control groups was not significantly different, however. Children undergoing hospitalization for dental surgery had less disturbed behavior when they engaged in related play before and after the procedure (Schwartz, Albino, & Tedesco, 1983). The study showed that the group that engaged in play related to the procedures benefited more than the group that engaged in unrelated play.

Johnson and Stockdale (1975) demonstrated that familiarizing children with procedures through puppet play lowered their anxiety as measured on the Palmar sweat test of anxiety. These studies consistently indicate that play can function effectively in hospitalization as a way of preparing children for painful and unknown procedures by lessening some of the anxiety.

Children's attitudes toward play and play objects can provide clues about their level of anxiety and coping. Gilmore (1966) showed that children with moderate levels of situational anxiety chose toys that were related to the anxiety-provoking experience to help them work through their anxiety. If their anxiety was too overwhelming, however, children withdrew from toys that were associated with anxiety or frightening experiences. Thus, play can serve as a coping mechanism if the child is not too traumatized.

Using a model designed by Janis (1958), Burstein and Meichenbaum (1979) studied the effects of anxiety and hospitalization. Janis' curvilinear model proposed that denial of anxiety or overwhelming anxiety was associated with poor post-surgical adjustment in adults. Burstein and Meichenbaum found that highly defensive children who would not play with surgically related toys before surgery did not do as well after surgery as children who did play with such toys. The children also showed more post-surgical anxiety and did not remember preparation information that parents had provided. McTigue and Pinkham (1978) also found that children's avoidance or use of dental-related toys predicted their reactions to dental surgery.

These studies suggest that by observing children's play, adults may be able to identify children who are more likely to be at risk for post-hospital disturbance. Observation of play may also contribute to the *diagnosis* of situational anxiety or long-term emotional problems in hospitalized children (Pfeffer, 1979). By engaging suicidal children in play, Pfeffer identified aspects of their emotional trauma as well as methods they might use in suicide attempts.

Therapeutic literature indicates that play may enhance children's coping abilities and sense of *mastery*. For example, play can help children to master frightening situations (Axeline, 1947; Erikson, 1963; Freud, 1920; Moustakas, 1953/1973; Piaget, 1952). One of the underlying tenets of play programs in hospitals is that children need time, space, and adult encouragement to play out their experiences. Although empirical studies with control groups have rarely been done because of methodological difficulties, the role of play in aiding mastery has been documented by case studies (e.g., Frick & Deplo, 1984). Children can integrate their hospitalization experiences; work through their feelings of anger, helplessness, and desire for vengeance; and they can gain an understanding of their identification with the medical staff.

Play also serves as a means of general *stress reduction*. Play programs encourage social activities among children and adolescents, which make their experience of illness and hospitalization less isolating and boring. Gibbons and Boren (1985) describe various types of social and physical play activities for pediatric oncology patients (e.g., ski trips for child amputees, pizza parties, games, and contests).

Adult-initiated play activities may be essential because children who face body image problems brought on by treatments (e.g., loss of hair, amputation, pallor) often withdraw from peers. Play activities can give these children a social life and help them accept their capabilities that still allow them to lead a normal life. Because they often lack energy and ability to overcome their isolation through their own efforts, adults must help them through the medium of play.

● **Implications for education and therapy**

Play can be a multidimensional tool during hospitalization—for diagnosis, preparation, mastery, and for helping children to have fun even under stressful circumstances. Hospital play activities must be planned as integral parts of the hospital treatment, not as peripheral activities. Play can ameliorate the emotional trauma of hospitalization and contribute to a total atmosphere of support. As Hughes (1982), the designer of a special group therapy and activity program for chronically ill children, explains, "When care, sustenance, affection, play, pleasure, and gratification are available, the future may be seen as less threatening" for these children (p. 710).

● **Theory and research on environmental stress**

Much of the theory and research relevant to the needs of children who are at risk for impaired development due to severe environmental stress is drawn from the psychoanalytic and social learning literature on emotional/social development, which is reviewed in chapter 5 (e.g., Erikson, 1963; Isaacs, 1933; Sears, Maccoby, & Levin, 1957). Maccoby and Martin (1983) have reviewed the many factors that influence parent-child interaction in the socialization process. Some of these may put children at risk for impaired development in a number of ways. Honig (1986) has reviewed children's major stress factors and coping strategies; this section addresses only those aspects that relate to two types of environmental stress : (a) abuse/neglect and (b) family dysfunction or dissolution. Although the research literature relating these stresses to play is sparse, play does seem to have an ameliorating role as well as a diagnostic role in relation to the developmental needs of these children.

Psychosocial theory. According to Erikson, young children must resolve basic psychosocial issues during their first years of life. Children living in chaotic households may be at risk for developing psychosocial problems because the environment does not help them to resolve such developmental crises as trust versus mistrust or autonomy versus shame and doubt (Erikson, 1963). Cicchetti (1985a) cites evidence of five recent studies showing insecurity of attachment in maltreated infants. Later adaptation may also be affected because many maltreated children develop strategies for coping with an unpredictable environment that are maladaptive. They may cope with fear of abandonment or lack of trust by putting their trust in objects rather than people, investing their emotional energy in "security" objects that they carry around with them. They may have difficulty trusting new or changing events, either being frightened by new toys or activities or by displaying false bravado to surmount their fears. While they may appear confident about their abilities to handle an event, they may become over-excited or out of control, thus confirming their inability to trust themselves. Their behavior may tend to polarize at extremes: They may seem both tough and vulnerable, aggressive and fearful, aloof and needy (Kaplan-Sanoff & Kletter, 1985).

The intricate process of autonomy development also affects children's self-worth and capacity to handle stress (Mahler, Pine, & Bergman, 1975). If this process becomes confused, with children needing to meet their parents' needs rather than their own, the children's development may be delayed. Children who are expected to be mature at an early age to ease family stress often develop precocious self-help and motor skills (e.g., walking, talking, toileting, dressing) but show immaturity in other areas, reflecting the pressure under which they are performing (Koplow, 1985). They may seem to lack energy for play, with all of their energy directed toward meeting unrealistic parental expectations, caring for siblings, or needing to be on guard for unexpected negative events (Simon & Larson, 1985).

Social learning theory. In homes where children are abused or neglected, the models parents provide, the reinforcements they give, and the socialization practices they encourage differ from those of parents in other homes. Some of these behaviors may make playful parent-child interactions unlikely. For example, abusive parents are likely to exhibit more authoritarian control, anxiety-induction, guilt-induction, inconsistent discipline, and overprotectiveness. They may show less rational guidance, discourage independence and openness to new experiences, and express less positive affect toward their children (Susman, Trickett, Iannotti, Hollenbeck, & Zahn-Waxler, 1985). These behaviors are most apparent in parents who use physical abuse. Susman et al. conclude that "child abuse is part of a much larger constellation of parenting problems that pervade the entire socialization system" (p. 247).

In general the literature indicates that parents in abusive homes are under great stress themselves (e.g., Daniel, Hampton, & Newberger, 1983; Hughes & Barad, 1983). Abusive punishment in single parent families is double that in two parent families (Sack, Mason, & Higgins, 1985). However, children who witness extensive marital violence in two parent homes are also likely to have behavioral and emotional problems (Hershorn & Rosenbaum, 1985). They may exhibit both overcontrolled (i.e., passive) and undercontrolled (i.e., aggressive) behavior. One study of children from families with marital violence found that preschoolers had below-average self-concepts, elementary-age boys were aggressive, and elementary-age girls were passive and withdrawn (Hughes & Barad, 1983). Children who are social isolates at school seem to be more likely to come from families where the parents are also isolated and without a friendship support system (Oden, 1987). These stress factors may all impinge on children's play development.

Cognitive developmental theory. Studies of parents who abuse children indicate that they may be lacking the ability to comprehend the effects of their mistreatment on their children. Differences between abusive/neglecting and nonabusive parents in levels of social cognition were found in both urban and rural parent groups (Newberger & Cook, 1983). These authors suggest that helping parents develop higher cognitive levels of awareness could be an approach to help ameliorate child abuse. Abusers often have less realistic expectations of what children's behavior should be (Kravitz & Driscoll, 1983). Thus, the noise and clutter of normal child play may be negatively perceived.

Children's understanding of separation and divorce appears to be related to their cognitive developmental level (Wallerstein & Kelly, 1981). Wallerstein (1983) has characterized six psychological tasks that children must face in coming to terms with separation and divorce. These tasks extend over many years, must be reworked at different age levels, and roughly parallel the stages of grief (e.g., denial, resolution of loss, accepting permanance). Although some children seem to cope well with divorce (Wallerstein & Kelly, 1981), the age of the child at the time of divorce influences the coping strategies. Preschoolers seem to have difficult adjustments initially, but their later adjustment may be more complete and integrated, while elementary-age children may seem to cope better initially but they carry more memories that are difficult for them to face and resolve (Wallerstein, 1984). Although play may help children cope, their play may also be reduced or distorted by these stressors.

● The relationship of play to the development of environmentally at-risk children

Children's patterns of play often reflect the environmental stress that they have encountered. For example, the play of abused/neglected children may give evidence of how they have learned to survive in their world (Simon & Larson, 1985). Aggression may serve as a coping device during play, or themes of power or orderliness, through which children attempt to control events, may dominate their play (Simon & Larson, 1985). They may show hypervigilance, making it difficult for them to relax enough to become involved with play materials or symbolic play themes.

Play of children undergoing family separation and/or divorce often reveals boundary problems (Wallerstein & Kelly, 1981). Children may be unable to differentiate other boundaries when the family boundaries have been disrupted. For example, they may have trouble doing puzzles that were formerly easy for them or need to be reassured about which toys go together or what rules apply in the play situation. Play may also provide a major means of coping with problems of separation; in one study about 20% of the children engaged in fantasy play extensively to deal with separation issues (McDermott, 1968).

Hetherington, Cox, and Cox (1979) found that the stressful experiences of young children immediately after divorce and during the two-year period after divorce were reflected in their play. Initially both boys and girls exhibited less mature play. At the end of two years, although girls' play was again similar to the play of other children, boys' play still reflected immaturity and less acceptance by peers. Thus boys still spent more time in solitary play. The male peer group, which may have labeled these boys as unacceptable playmates during the period immediately following divorce when they were exhibiting high levels of aggression, apparently continued to reject the boys even though their observed behavior two years later was not aggressive. Those boys who had moved to other schools were accepted more readily; they did not continue to experience difficulty in social play.

● Implications for education

Although play may not enable children under stress of maltreatment, family dysfunction, or family dissolution to abandon their concerns, careful attention to play environment factors can help these children play more successfully. Space can be well organized and play materials systematically arranged to encourage children to engage in appropriate play behaviors and to help them organize their own behavior (McGuinness, 1982).

Many children under stress survive by becoming suspicious and wary; they cannot allow themselves to play because they are distracted by every sound or social interaction within their proximity. Quiet play spaces with low but defined boundaries that allow maintenance of eye contact with adults can promote their play (Scott, 1985). Structured play materials such as puzzles or sorting boxes can allow children to enjoy success in play and can provide a sense of order and mastery (Kaplan-Sanoff & Kletter, 1985).

Play can help these children gain a sense of mastery over their traumatic environment by letting them feel in control, even if temporarily, through pretend play about their life events (Ginsburg, Sywulak, & Cramer, 1984; Guerney, 1976, 1979). Play materials such as water and other fluids (Wolfgang, 1977) or blocks (Scott, 1985) can help these children gain a sense of mastery. Fluids support their need for permissible messy play; blocks give them an opportunity to control timing and structure. Specific social play skills may also be taught through social skills training (Stocking & Arezzo, 1979), teacher-directed activities (Wolfgang, 1977), or sociodramatic play training (Strain & Wiegerink, 1976). Reinforcement through adult attention for appropriate social interactions can increase social play in children who are socially isolated (Allen, Hart, Buell, Harris, & Wolf, 1964); aggressive (Pinkston, Reese, LeBlanc, & Baer, 1973); or disruptive (Cooper, Ruggles, & LeBlanc, 1979). O'Conner (1972) has demonstrated that showing withdrawn children films depicting playful social interaction can increase their social participation.

Conclusion

Play is of major importance for those children who have physical/motor or other handicapping conditions, who must undergo hospitalization, or who must face other stressful life situations. It is also vital as a means of promoting healthy physical/motor development in every child. The research literature relating play to these developmental areas has only begun to be collected. The increased sophistication of play research techniques and the more precise theoretical information on play development should provide direction and impetus for further study. This chapter has pointed out some of the problems in doing research in these areas; however, it has also emphasized the many ways that play can aid development, and it has provided suggestions for translating present theory and research into practice in ways that will benefit children with special needs.

Questions for Discussion

1. What are some of the major physical/motor developmental tasks that can be promoted by the play of nonhandicapped children? Of physically handicapped children? Of children with other handicaps or special needs?
2. What similar developmental needs can be met through play for handicapped children, hospitalized children, and environmentally at-risk children? What different needs do they have that play can help to provide?

Research Replication Exercise

Using one of the three play research models described in chapter 2, collect data on three special needs children. Compare your results to play developmental norms and play patterns of normally developing children.

Suggestions for Further Reading

Brewster, A. (1982). The chronically ill child's conception of illness. Pediatrics, 69(3), 355–362. Describes the study discussed in this chapter.

Curtis, S. R. (1982). The joy of movement in early childhood. New York: Teachers College Press. Describes components and stages of motor development and gives play activity ideas to improve fundamental movement abilities.

Golden, D. B. (1983). Play therapy for hospitalized children. In C. E. Schaeffer & K. J. O'Conner (Eds.), Handbook of play therapy. New York: Wiley. Gives suggestions for ways to use play within the hospital environment.

Kaplan-Sanoff, M., & Kletter, E. F. (1985). The developmental needs of abused children: Classroom strategies. Beginnings, 2(3), 15–19. Provides a framework and gives teachers ideas on how to identify and help abused children.

Stillwell, J. L. (1987) *Making and using creative play equipment*. Champaign, IL: Human Kinetics. Describes 49 pieces of homemade equipment and a variety of movement experiences for children that are designed to promote development of fundamental movement skills and fitness.

Stillwell, J. L., & Stockard, J. R. (1983) *Fitness exercises for children*. New York: Leisure Press. Gives a series of play and movement exercises designed to enhance development of physical fitness in young children.

Play and Gifted Children

ANNEMARIE ROEPER

Play has a special place in the process of growth for the young of humans and many other animal species. It takes many forms; it has many purposes. Play can be one of the best tools for learning because it fosters active processes of seeking knowledge about the world. It also involves ownership; play is owned by the persons involved in it. It serves to create a sense of mastery, without the pressure of striving for success. Play helps children develop strategies for being alone as well as for getting along with others; it also promotes academic and physical skills. In all of these ways, play has special meaning for the gifted. I would like to concentrate this essay on a discussion of the impact of play on the emotional and social development of gifted children.

The significance of play is different for the gifted than for others because gifted children have some different emotional and intellectual characteristics. One of the consequences of their unusual characteristics is a vague feeling of not belonging. Even very young gifted children feel separate from their peers and perceive themselves as outsiders. They often have this feeling in relation to their teachers and even sometimes in relation to parents. This feeling is particularly difficult for young children who cannot put it into words but who just have feelings of discomfort.

Another outstanding characteristic of most gifted children is their creativity. They seem to overflow with imaginative ideas; they often do amazing things with their hands and they think of alternative ideas and activities that no one has thought of before. They will do this thinking at any time, in any place (e.g., even in school). Their inner life, exem-

163

plified in their daydreaming, often distracts them from the required activities at hand. Daydreaming is considered by many adults as an undesirable habit. For many gifted children, however, it is a necessity. It is the only way they can cope with their creativity and their imagination.

They also have insatiable curiosity about many things. They want to know and to understand everything, even in topic areas where necessary adult guidance and help is not available. For example, even the most capable young readers may not have access to adult libraries where the information on the subjects of their interest is kept. This sometimes forces them to think and dream by themselves. Because imagining is more acceptable to most adults if it is accompanied by play activity with objects, children take their animals or other toys and play with them. In play they express their love, anger, power, and imagination. All of this expression is legitimate and even supported by adults when it is done in the context of play.

Many gifted 3- and 4-year-olds have one to three imaginary companions who are their closest friends and playmates. This is especially common for children who do not communicate well with others. The imaginary companion serves many functions. Often they represent the "bad" side, the angry side in children. If children do something their mothers disapprove of, they can say that they did not do it but the imaginary companion did it. This is particularly important for those who have highly developed consciences, which is a common characteristic among the gifted. These highly developed consciences exist at an age when the children are not really ready to live within the demands of that level of conscience.

Gifted children often do not give themselves permission to have any negative feelings (e.g., to be jealous of the baby). They might be overcome with unbearable guilt if they hit another child. But if Co-Ra, the imaginary companion, hits another child, the real child can be excused. (These companions often have strange names.) It is important that gifted children learn the line between reality and fantasy and receive help in dealing with their perfectionism and guilt. Pretend play allows the safe expression of feelings within a clearly distinguished "not-real" framework.

Another characteristic of gifted children is their sense of being powerless. They are keen observers and they have a well-developed sense of justice. They see what is wrong in the world around them and often feel strongly that there is nothing that they can do about it, at least at their young age. In the real world, they feel unable to make a difference, but in play they can become very powerful, pretending to be the boss and changing those things that they don't find fair. They make things happen the way that they would like them to be and create a world that is acceptable and dependable and on which they can make an impact.

For gifted children, even more than for other children, the line between play and work or learning hardly exists. Play, work, and learning serve the same purpose: mastery. These children have a desire to be in charge of their destinies, to master the world, and to learn all the skills for meeting self-imposed challenges. These desires motivate their activity. They play what they learn and they learn what they play. It is clear that the difference between play and work has been created by adults, not children. Play and work also serve the purpose of helping gifted children develop their self-image. The self-image is the vision that children have of their own unique personality; it is the way they feel themselves to be. Playing helps gifted children integrate and expand their sense of self as they react to and relate to parents, teachers, playmates, and the larger social and physical world.

Much of the time, in their social world and interactive relationships, children have to subordinate their needs to rules and regulations of others. These rules and regulations do not always fit children's needs but in their play they can make them fit. In play, aggression and hostility are allowed, as long as it is in pretend (e.g., in roles as witches or space invaders). Playing with peers in sociodramatic play develops gifted children's social skills and the tolerance they need to live with others who may not have the same view of the world. These skills are often more difficult for gifted children because they have different interests and conceptions of the world than their peers. Thus play is particularly helpful for them in understanding and relating to their social world.

Competition plays a different role for them also. They often have goals that are not shared by others; that is, they "follow their own drummer." Competition forces them to pursue the same goal as others and therefore they are not usually interested in competing. If they do compete, they have a very hard time accepting the fact that they might lose. In playful competition, however, losing is more acceptable and they learn something about how to lose and to give up some of their need for perfection. Play and recreational activity are important for gifted people of all ages because they have a tendency to put themselves under great stress. When they set goals for themselves that are hard to attain they may feel burdened because they are so sensitive and aware of problems that others hardly see. Often they feel the social environment is unresponsive.

Gifted children are often "loners," especially if they have no access to children with similar skills and interests. They can be helped by play because learning to relate to other children in at least one area of their lives can be very important. Even though they may have little in common with the neighborhood children, they may share one interest (e.g., playing baseball). Play then is a vehicle that builds a bridge between the gifted and other children.

Many gifted children seem to learn with their whole bodies, and all their senses seem intensely alive. Often their great *joie de vivre* and outstanding sense of humor are expressed in their physical and verbal play. The tension release of physical play and the sense of power that comes with increased physical skill contribute to their well-being. They are also especially adept at "playing with words"; in fact, an early evidence of their cognitive development is their special ability to use language in riddles, jokes, puns, and other playful ways.

Gifted children are fascinated with games of all sorts because they can use their mind safely in games. A case in point is the interest of older gifted children in games such as Dungeons and Dragons. Many adults are amazed at the concentration and accomplishment that grow out of symbolic games such as Dungeons and Dragons. Children who may not participate in school, or at least are not motivated to do much routine work, will cover pages and pages with original creative writing and thinking, do math that no one knew they were able to do, and get along with other children in a much better manner than they exhibit in other settings. All of these behaviors appear within the context of this game. Gifted children's fascination with fantasy games seems to originate from an inner need for integration of their abstract conceptual abilities and their desire to control their world.

One of the greatest misunderstandings of the needs of the gifted is the belief that their time should be highly structured and directed, rather than "wasted" on play. Adults sometimes think that gifted children need less playtime than other children. In reality, depriving them of play removes them from one of their greatest resources for growth and well-being.

"What is an elephant?" the blind men asked. When they approached the huge beast, each one of them took hold of a different part. The one who touched the tail said, "Why, an elephant is long and thin and wiggly, just like a snake." The one who touched the leg said, "No, no, an elephant is sturdy and round, similar to a tree," while the one who touched the ear stated that, "The elephant is exactly like a big, floppy leaf." Of course, those who touched the elephant's side, tusk, and trunk had other descriptions. All of the men were equally sure, however, that their conception of an elephant was the correct one.

Play as a Curricular Tool

Those who have studied play and learning have encountered a similar dilemma. There are many definitions and descriptions, each of which may be accurate for the portion the theorist or researcher has chosen for the focus of observation. The chapters in previous sections have described play, its relationship to development and learning, and the major theoretical viewpoints that have been studied. In this section, the role of play as a curricular tool will be examined.

A major theme of this section is that all children can benefit by being in environments designed to foster play. Through the medium of play, these environments can further the achievement of a wide range of learning goals. In addition, they can further play development—the ability to become creative, confident, autonomous, lifelong players. Educators' skill in using play as a curricular tool is based on three factors: (a) knowing about the relationships between play and learning, (b) knowing how to design environments that enhance those relationships, and (c) valuing play abilities in children, in themselves, and in other adults.

Chapter 7 presents a schema for play and learning that can be used as a framework for planning play activities and designing play environments that encourage various types of learning. Chapters 8, 9, and 10 discuss how these activities and environments can be developed for children of different ages. Chapter 11 demonstrates how these principles and techniques can be adapted to enhance learning in special play environments. The essayists in this section raise issues about the interaction of the environment with children's play development.

Using
a Schema
for
Play and Learning

DORIS BERGEN

Because there are numerous activities that may be labeled play, educators and other practitioners who wish to plan for play as a learning medium for children must be consciously aware of the attributes that distinguish these various activities that are called play. They also need to understand the processes that are involved in learning and they must be adept at selecting play experiences that will help children to meet learning goals. This chapter provides a schema that can assist educators in making distinctions and connections between play and learning.

First the categories of behavior that educators usually call play and those they usually consider not to be play are discussed. The major learning processes that occur in educational environments are also defined. The schema for play and learning, which demonstrates the potential complementary relationships between various types of play and the range of learning processes, is presented, and examples of the application of the schema are given. A brief overview of factors in the physical and social environment that influence play and learning is also included.

In order to use play effectively as a curricular tool, adults must have an intellectual understanding of the connections between play and learning. In addition, they must have personal experience of the power of play to enrich their own lives. Play has value throughout life and serves many purposes for adults that are similar to those for children. Those adults who are in touch with their own playful qualities and who value the play potential that all human beings have will be more successful in fostering children's play development than those who see play as an immature, inconsequential, and limited activity confined to the less powerful members of society. The schema for play and learning can enhance understanding of the play of adults as well as children, and can facilitate planning for the use of play as a learning medium at any stage of life.

Categorizing Play and Not Play

Theorists and researchers who have studied play usually define the term play to mean only those behaviors that are child initiated and that involve cognitive assimilation rather than accommodation processes. Fein and Schwartz (1982), for example, indicate that assimilation dominates accommodation in play and that, therefore, in play the challenge is not "presented by the environment nor . . . sought in the environment." Rather, it "represents challenge produced by the child" (p. 96). Similarly, Hutt (1971) distinguishes between exploration and play by pointing out that in exploration children discover what objects do, but that in play they discover what they can do with objects. Some researchers also distinguish play from games because, although both are rule governed, the function of play is for the satisfaction of playing, while the function of games is "to compete to win and to achieve some specified goals" (Rubin, Fein, & Vandenberg, 1983, p. 728).

Educators, on the other hand, often term many types of activities play. In their definition of play they may include activities that are freely chosen by children and ones that require all to participate. They may also call many games by the name play, including ones directed by children and those that are directed by adults; those that have a low level of stress on winning and a minimal risk of failure; and those that have high levels of competition and include judgment of success or failure. Thus, educators' definition of play may include behaviors with accommodative as well as assimilative aspects.

Although play theorists and researchers may deny that some of these behaviors are play, this broader definition of play has been useful in educational practice. How educators can translate the findings of research and the logic of theory into educational practice continues to be a question of major importance because the applications are not usually obvious or direct. For example, although research findings indicate a relationship between pretend play and cognitive growth, the educational application of this finding is unclear. Should educators provide space, materials, and time for children to engage in pretense? Should they provide adult or peer modeling of pretend behaviors? Or should direct teaching of how to pretend be included in the curriculum?

In planning ways to translate research and theory into practice, educators must also be careful that they do not turn play into not play (i.e., work). The schema for play and learning, first developed for *Play as a Learning Medium* (Sponseller, 1974), has been found useful by many educators for evaluating types of activities called play and for determining which types of educational environments are most likely to elicit and develop various types of play and learning. The schema makes explicit the fine line between play and work and the distinctions among various learning processes that relate to the types of play that are planned as curricular tools.

A basic premise of the schema is that play includes both observable and nonobservable behavior. The study of play as an observable phenomenon has provided the substance for most of the information in this book. However, play in its broadest sense is not always observable. All people have engaged in mental play—playing with ideas, creating scenarios with action and conversation, and imagining the unknown. Although these activities are not usually labeled play and are not the subject of much research, some nonobservable behaviors have the essential elements of play as defined by Neumann (1971): internal control, internal motivation, and internal reality.

Watching others play (i.e., onlooking) or engaging in other seemingly passive behaviors, such as television viewing, may include elements of mental playfulness that are not observable. Some children may appear to be uninvolved in play, but educators need to be aware that children who are watching other children play may be engaged in cognitively playful activity and that their later observable play behaviors may reflect learning achieved during these onlooking periods. For example, studies of television viewing show that preschoolers' themes of pretense reflect the content of the programs they have watched (James & McCain, 1982). Many children silently watch peers sing or play games at school and subsequently exhibit those same playful behaviors at home. Perhaps they are playing "inside their heads" when they are observing others' play. Chaille and Young (1980) point out the importance of this play as well as the problems involved in studying it.

The categories used in the schema for play and learning are based on the following attributes (Neumann, 1971):

1. Degree of internal/external control (i.e., the amount of choice children have about what activities to engage in, where and how to do them, and who will interact with them).
2. Degree of internal/external reality (i.e., the range of possibilities for children to bend or alter real conditions, take risk-free challenges and try difficult skills, or fail without facing lasting consequences).
3. Degree of internal/external motivation (i.e., the level of opportunity for children to initiate, escalate, change, or withdraw from activity in response to their own optimal arousal needs).

The schema is an interrelated two-level continuum ranging from behaviors having the greatest internal control component (i.e., child initiated) to those having the greatest external control component (i.e., adult initiated). Those with the highest internal control component have the least overt adult direction and those with the highest external control component have the most obvious adult (or societal) direction. The assimilative component is highest at the left (i.e., high internal) end of the continuum and the accommodative component is highest at the right (i.e., high external) end.

The play and learning schema is shown in Figure 7-1. The play/not play component ranges from free play to work. The learning process component moves from discovery learning to drill and practice.

The five points on the play/not play continuum are as follows:

1. *Free play* has the greatest degree of internal control, reality, and motivation.

The player chooses whether to play, what to play, how to play, and when to play. The player also determines whether to play alone or with other players. The choice of which other players to play with is also freely determined. Free play has some external restrictions imposed by the physical environment—for example, block towers fall if not properly balanced—and by the player's physical or mental abilities, such as verbal skill or eye-hand coordination.

In an educational setting, there are also rules based on freedom within minimal externally imposed limits, such as a time span and a designated space in which to play. During free play, however, children are least bound by environmental constraints because

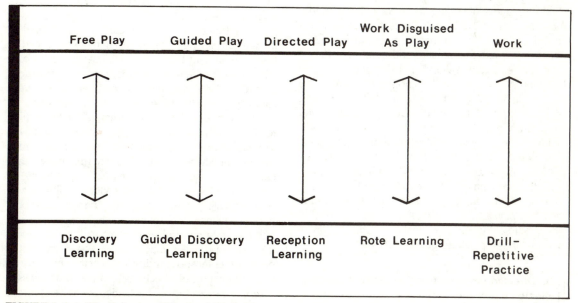

FIGURE 7-1 • The Schema of Play and Learning

they are operating in an assimilative mode. Although free play can occur in any environment, some environments promote a richer set of free-play behaviors than others. For example, a wider range and higher level of social and pretend play usually occur in settings where large equipment with many action options is located.

2. *Guided play* occurs within a loosely defined framework of social rules, requiring children to give some attention to externally imposed control, reality, and motivation.

Although the players continue to have a wide choice of play activities and the environment is still conducive to freely chosen play in which children can create their own challenge, more social rules regarding appropriateness of choices, safety, sharing, or motor constraints are present. Features of the physical environment may be more regulated than in free play. There may also be a specifically limited number of choices for play or children may be expected to engage in a specified number of play activities during a particular time period.

Adults monitor the play more closely and may step in often to redirect, present challenges, and provide materials. Although for long periods of time children may be operating in the assimilative mode, the guidance of adults sets limits that require accommodation as well. It may be necessary to adjust play to meet external realities and adult-determined rules. For example, a workbench for pounding and hammering play might be monitored closely by adults. Guided play with frequent adult restatement of rules for tool use would be appropriate with workbench materials. Adults may also encourage children to engage in social rather than solitary play. The design of the physical environment may be planned to provide most of the guidance for play. Specified rules may also be imposed by other players. The role of the adult is usually a more active one than in a free-play situation. What is called free play in preschool settings is often really a combination of periods of free play and guided play.

3. *Directed play* has many externally imposed elements that are defined by adults and the play is often led by adults.

Children may still have some opportunities to exercise internal control, reality, and motivation, but only within the limits directly specified by adults. The appropriate range of behaviors is clearly directed by the adult leaders and enforced by both adults and peers. Game playing in most kindergarten and early elementary classrooms falls into the directed play category. Many group activities in the early education setting have playful or gamelike qualities in which the adult provides an initial stimulus such as a story or fingerplay.

In directed play children do not usually have a choice about whether to play, what to play, how to play, or when to play. Everyone in class participates, there are constraints on what games can be chosen, adult-specified rules are enforced, and the time allotted for play is designated narrowly. For example, the adult may designate three educational games that can be played at the back table by no more than two people, after they have finished their workbook lesson. Or the entire class may play a symbolic game such as Dog and Bone or participate in a relay race. Children are not usually permitted to choose the other players, although at times they are allowed to choose their own partners or team members. Accommodation processes provide the basis for these activities, although within the play experience itself, the assimilative mode may be present for brief periods.

Children enjoy much directed play, particularly if it has a sufficient level of interest to be experienced as truly playful. But because activity ceases to be play when children have no internal control, motivation, or reality, the adult must choose directed play very carefully in order to preserve some elements of choice in spite of external parameters. Children must retain the desire to be involved in play and the ability to bend reality. The elements of the social environment in particular are crucial in determining whether children will experience directed play activity as playful. Conveying respect for children's differences, showing willingness to adapt or change rules, promoting a climate that minimizes risk and failure, and offering children choices can retain the essence of true play in directed play. Adults' knowledge of the developmental and learning levels of the children and their adaptation of directions to meet these levels is essential if these types of activities are to be correctly categorized as play.

4. *Almost play or "work disguised as play"* describes task-oriented activities that are not inherently playful but that can be transformed into directed or guided play activities if the potential for internal control, motivation, and reality can be tapped.

Educational settings in which basic skills learning is stressed may require a sizable portion of time for rote memorization, repetitive practice, and other work activities. Although many aspects of basic skills learning are learned well during free play, guided play, and directed play, educators often believe that some learning goals may require children to spend a certain amount of time on rote learning.

Educators who work in settings that require children to learn much rotely memorized information often devote a significant portion of their educational planning to making these tasks become "almost play." Singing an alphabet song to learn the alphabet sequence, playing a spelling game, or having an "addition facts race" are examples of work disguised as play.

Although it may be confusing to children to have these activities labeled as play, and although children may experience them as boring or fear inducing, this technique has long been applied in classrooms as a means of increasing repetitive practice and promoting learning of materials that children may have little interest in learning. Children are usually aware that these adult-imposed activities are not play and they label them work even though adults may have given them a playful sounding name (King, 1979).

How great a place these activities should have in educational settings is debatable. Children do seem to find some of them enjoyable and sometimes repeat them in their own free-play time. Rather than arbitrarily disguising this type of work as play, educators can discuss with children how work can sometimes be made more interesting by treating it as play and can allow the children to decide how they can do this. Since creating a challenge is something children know how to do, they can decide on playful ways to learn required tasks. However, they must have some internal control, motivation, and reality if children are to consider these activities play.

5. *Work* is activity that is engaged in to reach an externally defined goal and for which mo-

tivation is external. There is no opportunity to bend the reality of the work situation; thus work is totally in the accommodation mode.

Because much of children's time is spent in the assimilative mode, the line between work and play has always been difficult to draw. Indeed, one of the favorite lines of theorists of earlier times was "Play is the child's work." The distinction between work and play is a clear one, however, if the criteria of external versus internal control, motivation, and reality are applied. In work, children do not decide when to work, how to work, where to work, or what to work at. Moreover, if they attempt to take control and turn this work into play, adults are usually displeased (King, 1982a). Many educators believe that children should find all learning tasks playful while others believe that children should find out early that there will be times when they will need to work hard at goal-oriented tasks even if they do not wish to. Children can also learn that activities called work can be enjoyable and satisfying (King, 1982b, 1982c).

Labeling some of children's self-directed activities work is considered important by practitioners of some theoretical viewpoints. For example, the activities in the Montessori program are labeled work rather than play. In the definitional framework described here many of those activities would be labeled guided or directed play, because children have some internal control and motivation as they operate within the structured materials and environment.

In summary, researchers and theorists might draw the line between play and not play at a different point on a continuum than practitioners would.

Categorizing Learning Processes

How do human beings learn? Before educators can use the schema of play and learning, it is necessary to understand the range of learning processes that have been identified by theorists and researchers who have studied learning and cognitive development. Most learning theorists have rejected the idea that development of higher cognitive processes, such as problem solving, can be explained by simple reinforcement models of learning. These complex learning processes have internal control components and motivational complexities that make them similar to the components of play.

For example, Polya (1971, pp. 197–198), in his outline of the steps in problem solving, discusses the role of the subconscious in helping to solve difficult problems. During these "moments in which it is better to leave the problem alone for a while," ideas are mentally combined and recombined informally, and then "a bright idea appears and you solve the problem easily." This mental incubation process is internally controlled and motivated and has assimilative, as well as adaptive, qualities. Gagne's (1968, 1977) hierarchy of learning processes places problem solving at the highest level, requiring mastery and coordination of many other types of learning. Studies examining the characteristics of adults who are good problem solvers present evidence that adults are hampered in solving problems if they have had narrow fixed experiences with an object or have learned by rote a particular method for solving problems (Wason and Johnson, 1968).

Information processing theorists have been particularly interested in the cognitive processes of perception, memory, rule learning, problem solving, creativity, evaluation, and metacognition (i.e., thinking about thinking). Their work points to the complexity of these processes even in young children's thinking. Flavell (1976, 1977, 1981, 1982) has identified the metacognitive processes that are essential for higher order thinking. They include having the ability to activate cognitive rules and strategies; control distraction and anxiety; and monitor the solution process. Metacognition also entails flexibility of thought, a desire for an "elegant" solution and a belief that thinking can result in solutions (i.e. "faith in thought"). All of these abilities increase as children grow older and they are influenced by environmental factors. For example, exposure to events that challenge beliefs (e.g., predicting that objects will float or sink and observing what happens) may increase metacognitive development.

For the purposes of the schema of play and learning, the learning processes occurring in educational settings are categorized according to internal/external dimensions of control, motivation, and meaning. The schema does not imply that meaningful learning cannot occur when children are in goal-oriented work settings. It does suggest, however, that play environments can facilitate certain types of learning and assist children in their construction of knowledge.

The range of learning processes that make up the points on the schema are as follows:

1. *Discovery learning* occurs through the spontaneous manipulation of the objects in the physical environment and through informal social interactions with adults and peers. Knowledge grows as these interactions are mentally organized.

Bruner (1966, 1979) and Piaget (1972) have stressed that cognitive development must involve discovery learning, in which children develop strategies for problem solving and receive feedback from the environment. The alternation of assimilation and accommodation that occurs in these interactions results in intellectual adaptation, which Piaget calls the construction of knowledge. He asserts that concepts cannot be given to children, but instead must be constructed by each person. If answers are provided to children or if children are forced to make quick, adult-defined correct responses, the concept development process is impeded rather than assisted. Discovery learning allows children the opportunity to generate their own concepts as they actively manipulate and interact with the environment.

2. *Guided discovery learning* has many elements of discovery, but the experiences are carefully structured so that certain discoveries are more likely to occur. Open-ended questions asked by adults channel the concept development process.

Guided discovery is often used in educational settings because, although discovery learning processes may eventually lead to a richer conceptual base, they also require longer time spans than may be available in school. Also, adults often have learning objectives that they want all children to achieve, but the discovery learning process may not lead all children to that objective at a particular time. Thus, some children may not discover the particular concept that educators identify as an important learning objective. Guided discovery learning can help children focus their activity and thought on a certain set of questions that can assist their construction of certain kinds of knowledge.

Often, guided discovery learning proceeds by the process called proleptic instruction (Wertsch, 1979), in which the learner performs after the adult informally models performance. This type of instruction involves mutual negotiation with a balance of observation and guided trials, primarily with the learner in the help-seeking role and the adult in the respondent role. Social and cognitive interactional systems developed between learner and teacher that allow the learner to define the task have also been called scaffolding (Hodapp, Goldfield, & Boyatzis, 1984; Wood, Bruner, & Ross, 1976). Teacher and learner interact to build the conceptual structure.

Guided discovery learning can also proceed through the structuring of the materials and equipment in the physical environment, with the cues for the direction for learning coming from these structures. Opportunities for both discovery learning and guided discovery learning are usually present in the same educational environment.

> 3. *Reception learning* is meaningful learning that occurs primarily through verbal means; either by adult instruction, by reading, or by discussion. In order to be meaningful, the learner must have a base of concrete experience that can be related to the verbal learning.

Ausubel (1968), who has described the reception learning process, states that discovery learning accompanied by concrete materials is important for young children because they have not yet developed cognitive structures that can apprehend meaningful verbal learning. He agrees with Piaget that the verbal skill of young children sometimes conceals the fact that they lack sufficient concrete experiences to make verbal learning meaningful. Piaget has called these examples of using words without underlying knowledge "verbalisms." Much of what children repeat from television commercials falls in the verbalism category (e.g., "40% off the cover price," "shaves incredibly close"). Ausubel contends that meaningful verbal learning, which he terms reception learning because the learner is able to receive it without having had immediate concrete experiences, is an efficient mode of learning for children once they are about 6 years old.

To Ausubel, verbal learning is meaningful when the cognitive structures are sufficiently developed so the information can be mentally organized or subsumed by the learner. Ausubel believes this occurs at about the same age (i.e., 6 or 7) that Piaget expects to find concrete operational thought. Some adult-directed activities can promote meaningful verbal learning at the preschool level as well if a base of concrete experiences is provided. If educators consistently assess children's experiential readiness level before providing directed verbal activities, they will be able to select those activities that will promote reception learning. For example, a trip to a fire station before reading about or discussing fire fighting might provide the needed experiential base for reception learning.

> 4. *Rote learning* is verbal learning that is not inherently meaningful but that may be assisted by memory strategies such as rehearsal, association, clustering, detecting patterns, and counting. Rote learning may later be used in the service of other learning or may be related to meaningful learning if the learner has the experiential base needed to transform it into knowledge.

Rote learning can either be verbal or motor learning. It is achieved through motor repetition or conscious efforts at verbal memorization. Because the segments of the material to be learned and/or the material as a whole do not have immediately relevant meaning, the learning occurs primarily by verbal or motor chaining (Gagne, 1968). That is, the elements are linked together by association in time, sequence, or by other arbitrarily imposed linkages so that they can be remembered. Often the elements are not remembered if the sequence is broken or the elements are separated and put in other contexts. Research on memory indicates that young children's recognition memory is better than their recall memory but that neither type of memory is as efficient as that of older children or adults. Theorists believe this is because children have fewer cognitive units in which to store memories (Newcombe, Rogoff, & Kagan, 1977). Thus, young children are less able to make rote learning meaningful, even though they are adept at repeating strings of information they have learned in a rote fashion.

> 5. *Drill/repetitive practice* has no inherent meaningful elements and is difficult for children to relate to any meaningful experiences.

When learning is so removed from meaningful experience that the motivation for learning must come entirely through expectations of external reward or punishment, it is reduced to what is commonly called by the pejorative name "drill." At some point this learning may be usable in relation to a meaningful activity. However, recall of the information is usually poor and understanding of the reason for learning it is lacking. Unless the learner can see the necessity for this repetitive practice in furthering desirable long-range goals, there may be negative side effects of reduced motivation for learning and interference with the development of metacognitive processes. Young children who learn multiplication or word recognition—or older children who learn algebra or a foreign language—by repetitive practice without connecting it to a meaningful mental scheme will be unlikely to recall much of it when they are adults. Although some activities called work may also be enjoyable and may foster many kinds of learning, both adults and children usually label as work those activities that are required, repetitive, and without inherent meaning to the person.

Using the Schema for Play and Learning

The previously described behaviors called play and those called learning are arranged on the schema to reflect a continuum of internal/external elements and to point to the interrelationship of play and learning processes. The left end of the schema highlights play and learning processes that require educational planning, observation, and facilitation of play and learning by adults but that do not require obtrusive adult direction. At the right are processes that have a high level of adult direction or task setting; children may not be motivated to engage in them unless there

are external sanctions or rewards. Educators can evaluate their environments in terms of the dimensions on the schema.

Depending on the theoretical perspectives of the educator, the range of play encouraged will vary. There are many educators who would agree with the researchers who define only free play as true play. Other educators use guided and directed play as well, especially in the preschool and kindergarten. In general, as the age of children in the educational setting increases, educators allow less free-play time and devote more of their energies to using play in the service of work. Because elementary-age children are able to learn much from play, they can still benefit from an environment that includes activities from the playful end of the continuum. Educators' effectiveness in curricular planning and environmental design depends on the play and learning balance within the educational environment. Figure 7–2 gives examples of the typical spread of play and learning in some educational environments.

In many educational settings, learning activities are under a high level of adult control. Adults in those settings consider "work disguised as play" a valuable curricular tool, but rarely encourage other types of play. Because children are adept at turning dull but required activities into play, they can understand the value of making this transformation. If children have no control over transforming work into play, however, they may consider teacher-imposed tasks to be work even if they are called play (King, 1979). With young children, there may be confusion about the message of what play is because the signals for the play/work distinction may be unclear. Older children, however, can distinguish between enjoyable or playful work and "real play" (King, 1982c).

Activities that are in the center of the continuum may or may not be playful, depending on what elements essential for play are present in the setting. To be playful for children, these activities must grow from children's experiences and serve purposes of reception learning, consolidation, and mastery. That is, children must already possess a level of ability to perform the activity and be ready to "play around" with the idea. If the activity is primarily adult directed or if external reinforcement is necessary to get children to participate, children will not perceive the activity as play.

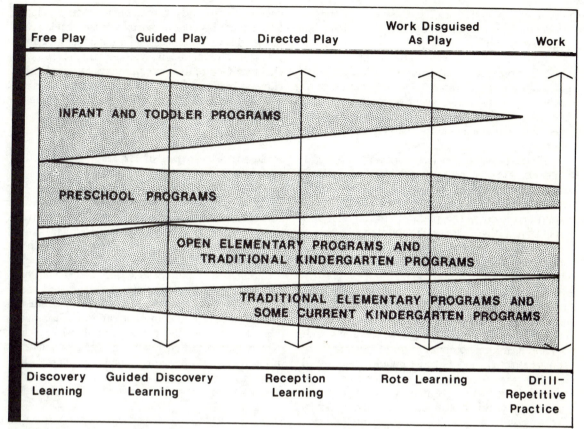

FIGURE 7–2 • The Schema of Play and Learning: Four Environmental Patterns

Those who plan to use play as a curricular tool must evaluate the activities typically called play in educational settings and must determine whether these activities have the right qualities to make the behavior playful. To plan play that is most likely to facilitate the goals of knowledge construction, educators should be aware of how these types of play are linked to learning goals. In designing educational play environments, careful thought should be given to the appropriate mix of types of play, and a high proportion of this playtime should be devoted to free play and to guided play. Although educators may employ directed play and work disguised as play as curricular tools, they should not be the only activities labeled as play in the educational environment. For children who have not yet reached formal opera-

tional thought levels, the development of metacognition is most likely to be promoted through play. Moreover, enjoyment of learning is most likely to be fostered in play environments.

The Physical and Social Environment as Design Variables

According to Piaget (1952), the processes that interact to promote the growth of intelligence are fourfold: (a) maturation (i.e., the unfolding of biologically based growth processes); (b) physical interaction with objects in the environment; (c) social transmission of knowledge through experiences with people; and (d) equilibration (i.e., the child's internal efforts to construct knowledge by organizing and relating experiences).

Educators can directly influence only two of these four processes. They can affect the world of physically perceivable knowledge (i.e., the physical environment) and the world of socially transmitted knowledge (i.e., the social environment). Both of these environments influence children's play development.

Physical environment factors include the types of materials and equipment available; the quality, quantity, and arrangement of space; the amount and sequencing of time; and sensory elements such as sound and texture. The physical environment also includes ecological factors in the educational community, and natural settings. For example, educational environments differ in important respects if located in city or rural areas.

The social environment factors to be considered in planning play environments include the social interaction patterns of the adults and children in the particular setting, the influence of the children's families and their local community, and the influence of ethnic, regional, and national cultural values and practices. For example, ratio of adults to children, ages of peers and their numbers, extent of parent participation, and involvement levels of community people all will affect the play environment. Particular cultural attitudes toward play as a facilitator of learning and the competencies that the culture values will also influence the extent and nature of play. Because the society's cultural expectations have a major impact on the developmental competencies that are encouraged (Ogbu, 1981), play ability may be seen as a factor leading to success in the society or as an unimportant behavior that does not need to be encouraged. These values will affect support for the design of play environments in educational settings.

In planning play environments, educators and other practitioners can draw upon available research information on physical and social environmental factors that affect play development. They can relate that information to their knowledge of child development and to their personal knowledge of play as a medium for learning.

In addition to understanding children's play and learning development processes and general factors in the physical and social environment, educators need to understand environmental design principles, which must be considered in planning settings for play and learning. Specific information about principles of environmental design is given in the following chapters. One of the basic principles that provides a criterion measure for environmental planning is the principle of "load," which is described by Mehrabian (1976).

A Basic Principle of Environmental Design

According to Mehrabian (1976), *load* refers to the rate of information flow and the quantity and intensity of stimuli that are present in an environment. Some of the factors that make a high or low load environment are listed in Table 7–1.

Since all of the characteristics that define load can be related to dimensions of novelty and complexity, *load* is sometimes referred to as the combination of novelty and complexity in an environment. Novelty refers to the degree of unfamiliarity and uncertainty in the environment; it affects ability to predict what will happen. Complexity refers to the combination of the number, variety, and variability of elements. People react to environments either with

TABLE 7–1 ● Characteristics of High- and Low-Load Environments (from Mehrabian, 1976, pp. 12–13)

High Load	Low Load
Uncertain	Certain
Varied	Redundant
Complex	Simple
Novel	Familiar
Large scale	Small scale
Contrasting	Similar
Dense	Sparse
Intermittent	Continuous
Surprising	Usual
Heterogeneous	Homogeneous
Crowded	Uncrowded
Moving	Still
Rare	Common
Random	Patterned
Improbable	Probable

approach or avoidance. Exploration, affiliation, and high performance are approach behaviors while lack of exploration, distancing, and operating below performance level are avoidance behaviors.

A particular environment may have the right balance of factors and thus the appropriate level of load for some people but not for others. Both children and adults vary in their sensitivity and reactions to environmental stimuli (Mehrabian, 1976; Thomas & Chess, 1977). Also, environments with different combinations of high and low load features may elicit different behaviors. For example, the research on factors predicting when children explore and when they play indicates that high novelty and complexity environments may elicit exploration rather than play, while environments with a moderate level of novelty and complexity are more likely to elicit play (Collard, 1979; Ellis, 1979; Hutt, 1979; Wohlwill, 1984).

Conclusion

In order to use play as a curricular tool, educators must be able to identify the kinds of learning that they wish to encourage and to evaluate the playful quality of their planned activities. Overall curricular plans can be reviewed to determine the appropriate balance of play/learning types and to predict the impact of the physical and social environment on curricular goals. Principles of environmental design can be used to create and enhance environments that foster play as a learning medium.

Good designs for play environments must be based on knowledge of the developmental characteristics of the children who will play in that setting; their individual differences and any cultural factors that may influence behavior in the play environment must also be considered. This knowledge can then be combined with information about environmental design principles so that the play environment will have the optimum degree of novelty and complexity for the play development of those children.

Questions for Discussion

1. What are the elements common to free play and discovery learning; guided play and guided discovery learning; directed play and reception learning; work disguised as play and rote learning; and work and drill/practice?
2. How might a physical environment focusing on repetitive, task-oriented, teacher-directed learning differ from one stressing creative, playful, child-directed learning? How would they be the same?

Play Activity Problem

Pick one of the age level models on Figure 7–2 and plan the curriculum for a typical day in a program at that age level. Identify the sequence of educational activity, the balance between play and learning types, and the physical arrangement of the space and equipment.

Suggestions for Further Reading

Coates, G. (1974). *Alternative learning environments*. Stroudsburg, PA: Dowden, Hutchinson, & Ross. Provides examples of environmental designs appropriate for children's learning in a variety of settings, including ones in the larger community.

Cohen, U., Moore, G. T., & McGinty, T. (1978). *Environments for play and childcare*. Milwaukee: University of Wisconsin, Milwaukee Center for Architecture and Urban Planning Research. Discusses the essentials of good design for group environments for young children.

David, T. G., & Wright, B. D. (Eds.). (1975). *Learning environments*. Chicago: University of Chicago Press. Contains articles by a number of environmental designers concerned with school environmental designs that foster active learning.

Mehrabian, A. (1976). *Public places and private spaces: The psychology of work, play, and living environments.* New York: Basic Books. Gives views of environmental design from a psychological perspective. Includes chapters on basics of environments and how people's feelings and personalities are affected by and affect environments.

Walberg, H. J. (Ed.). (1979). *Educational environments and effects.* Berkeley, CA: McCutchan. Discusses evaluation, policy, and productivity issues related to a variety of learning environments. Includes articles on microenvironments (home, sociopsychological, and instructional) and macroenvironments (community, state, and nation).

Places of Beauty

ESSAY ON PLAY

ANITA RUI OLDS

Recently, I have come to think of settings for children not only as play, child care, and educational spaces, but also as environments for healing. By this I do not mean that children are physically or emotionally ill. Rather, the process of growth in our culture requires the establishment of an individual identity that in many ways conflicts with the underlying sense of unity and connection to all life that children know instinctively and that we all require in order to feel whole and fully ourselves.

In addition, the pursuit of goals and purposes, so fundamental to success in our culture, inevitably creates blinders; awareness of the whole is submerged by a focused and narrow vision to free consciousness for the performance of tasks. With age, accordingly, is an increasing tendency to be unaware of many subtle aspects of the physical world

and its impact on work, moods, feelings, and well-being. Whereas children are exquisitely sensitive to *all* qualitative aspects of the environment, adults tend to absorb stimulation mechanically, without real attention. Eventually, such "distancing" from the environment leads to feelings of alienation, isolation, and separateness.

To counter this process of acculturation, the physical environment has an important role to play as a healing agent. To heal means "to make whole." A well-designed environment that forms a unifying thread, that both relates and harmonizes people and parts, can help to heal the breech between self and other that accompanies acculturation. To do this, the environment must mirror and support change, as well as create a sense of cohesiveness and aesthetic unity. Aesthetics, I believe, is the key.

Beautification of the dwelling preoccupies many a homemaker, yet comparable consideration is rarely given to the urban landscape, the work place, or play spaces for children. Instead, these settings, by virtue of their communal ownership, become aesthetic no-man's lands, designed more to assist the custodians who maintain them than the users who must grow and heal with them. It is considered fortunate if child-care spaces are large and clean. Aesthetic considerations beyond the basics are thought to be "luxuries," which invariably rank last or are ignored, frequently on the basis of expected cost alone.

But it is both illusory and possibly harmful to assume that an environment is suitable merely because it is lacking egregious faults of design and safety and can pass rudimentary safety and cleanliness standards. Environments, like all aspects of life, are potent purveyors of stimulation, information, and affect, and their effects are *always* felt and incorporated in some way. Children live according to the information provided by their senses, and feast upon the nuances of color, light, sound, touch, texture, volume, movement, visual and kinesthetic vibration, form, and rhythm, by which they come to know the world. Their play is largely a response to variations in the environment. As the Hindus claim, "Sarvam annam," everything is food. Environments must be consciously and lovingly created to uplift the spirit and honor children's heightened sensibility. It is not sufficient that a setting be adequate. It must, instead, be beautiful.

Beauty is powerfully regenerative. The embrace of physical wholeness and harmony in a beautiful space transmits psychic wholeness and tranquility. By inviting one to pause, attend, and be nourished by the world's richness, a beautiful place helps the inhabitants to feel connected yet free, and closer to personal sources of vitality and well-being. Far from being a luxury, one must question whether today's children, bombarded by chaotic, artificial, poorly integrated, and ugly settings can afford *not* to be given more aesthetically pleasing play and learning spaces. To do so requires attention to at least three factors: the quality of light, the presence of nature, and the character of interior finishes.

Quality of Light

Natural light changes continuously. It enables us to experience the passage of time, to estimate the time of day without recourse to mechanical devices, and to enjoy an implicit form of variety as our perception of objects and spaces changes under different conditions of illumination. It therefore provides many components of healing, including motion, change, difference-within-sameness, variety, information, and orientation.

According to Richard J. Wurtman, a neuroscientist at MIT, "it seems clear that light is the most important environmental input, after food, in controlling bodily function" (quoted in *The New York Times*, October 19, 1982). Experiments have shown that differently colored lights affect blood pressure, pulse, and respiration rates, brain activity, and biorhythms, and can be used to cure neonatal jaundice, psoriasis, and herpes sores (Wurtman, 1975). Sadly, the younger and more wounded an individual in this society is, the more likely it is that he or she will be placed in dark, poorly illuminated settings.

Research (Ott, 1973; Spivack & Tamer, 1981) suggests that the trend for people to spend increasing hours behind windows and windshields, eyeglasses and sunglasses, in front of TV and display terminals, and under the partial spectrum of fluorescent bulbs affects the incidence of headaches, arthritis, stunted growth, hormonal imbalances, and many other disorders. A healthy body seems to require that full-spectrum light enter the eye and strike the retina, thereby affecting the production of melatonin, a neurotransmitter that controls sleep, mood, and carbohydrate assimilation. Time spent outdoors, or in the presence of sunlight streaming through an open window, may not only be healthful and educationally sound, but critical to our overall well-being.

For biological and aesthetic reasons, lighting must become a part of architecture, and a variety of forms—natural and artificial, general-ambient and task-specific—must be provided. Varied sources of lighting (e.g., floor, desk, ceiling, wall) can be easily added to most child spaces. Wall-mounted, reflected-light fixtures, in place of overhead fluorescents, simulate the experience of light in nature by "washing" the light down a wall and up over the ceiling. Most importantly, full-spectrum lights, which approximate the range of wavelengths provided by sunshine, should replace standard bulbs as a means of reducing disturbances caused by inadequate exposure to the ultraviolet and infrared ends of the spectrum. Accordingly, every means possible should be found to give play spaces an abundance of natural light; indeed, even to require that no space without windows be used for educational purposes whatsoever, is not too stringent!

Access to Nature

When a setting provides rhythmic patterns of predictable sameness, combined with moderate diversity, the senses are able to maintain optimum levels of responsivity and we experience what is known as "comfort." The standard for environmental comfort and well-being is set by nature itself. Natural elements such as blazing fires, babbling brooks, and gentle breezes are always in motion, undergoing fairly predictable yet varied transformations that prevent boredom and withdrawal by periodically reawakening the nervous system. Nature is perceived as both aesthetically pleasing and as a healer because of such soothing qualities of "difference-within-sameness."

Childhood is traditionally the period when subconscious images of nature as a primal source of nourishment and rejuvenation are laid down. Yet the absence of nature in many child-care spaces and in the urban setting, along with dense building proximity, and the tendency to locate child-care centers near target populations, public transportation, and energy sources rather than near sites with an abundance of natural features (i.e., woods, grass, open bodies of water, beautiful areas for walking) makes it increasingly difficult for children to have these kinds of primary experiences. Biofeedback studies show that merely imagining a healing space can have a strong regenerative effect. How much more powerful then might be the experience of being physically located in a natural, outdoor setting?

The beauty and tranquility experienced in natural settings is essential to healthy development. This suggests a new vision for play and child-care environments that must include not only "playgrounds" but the entire outdoors as a part of any program. It should also incorporate natural features, as much as possible, into interior spaces. Ultimately, gardens, lawns, woods, ponds, and hills, where children could wander as part of their play, would become required elements for child-care environments; and buildings would be designed to incorporate and take advantage of unique views, perspectives, and relationships to the out-of-doors. Eventually, these features need to be seen to be as critical to site selection as square footage and other locational criteria. In the meantime, every attempt must be made to enhance those natural features that do exist at any outdoor site, and to create interiors with a profusion of natural elements. Moderate structural changes such as balconies, porches, courtyards, window wells, lowered window sills, windows that can be opened, greenhouses, and clerestories (i.e., windows above eye level) could all assist in providing vital links between the indoors and the outside.

Finishes

The monotonous character of many child-care settings exacerbates feelings of dis-ease, isolation, and separateness. This monotony must be replaced by the quality of difference-within-sameness so exquisitely manifest in nature, which enables the senses to maintain optimal levels of responsivity. Variety is the best guideline for creating aesthetically pleasing interiors. This means that, in addition to an abundance of natural light and nature-related elements, the finish materials used on floors, walls, ceilings, windows, and furniture need to be chosen for their capacity to create not just clean and safe, but meaningfully rich, interiors. Finishes have a more powerful impact on users and the overall ambience of a facility than any other single factor. The textures and colors applied or not applied to the surfaces of interiors—perceived visually as well as tactually—are the close-at-hand aspects of the environment with which children come into contact most often, and "read" continually as they experience any space. Finishes affect what is seen, heard, touched, and smelled, and therefore have a direct effect on how people feel in a setting. While often the last design decision to be made—and often given short shrift where finances are limited—the choice of finishes must be an essential part of the design of any environment from the outset.

It is important to realize that all materials have texture. No one texture is better than any other, except in terms of purposes and aesthetics. Problems arise when all or most surfaces have the same textural quality. The experience of texture is a complex interaction of the nature of the surfacing material—its depth, color, the way it reflects or reacts to light—and the nature of the light sources around it. Meaningful richness is the result of a variety of textures, each appropriate to the function, desired mood, and aesthetic feel of a particular space.

Modern human-made materials such as plastic, aluminum, gypsum, and concrete tend to show wear and tear and do not age gracefully. Wood, on the other hand, shows the marks of use and time in ways that enrich and mellow the material. Messages of newness, modernity, and efficiency must be balanced by materials that convey a sense of history, timelessness, experience, permanence, and maturity. Neither is right nor wrong; rather it is the balance and variety that are critical.

Finishes chosen for surfaces may have two additional effects: they may emit odors or have a special "institutional" smell, and they may emit small quantities of noxious gases (Sterling, Sterling, & McIntyre, 1983) that cause headaches, respiratory and eye discharges, and nausea. In general, the effects of man-made materials on human health are not fully known. In the best interest of everyone, designers should try to utilize natural fabrics and substances (e.g., wood, brick, cotton, wool) wherever possible.

The Torre

Japanese architecture features an arch called a "torre" to signal the transition from profane to sacred territory, from that which is spontaneous and ordinary to that which is spiritually and aesthetically integrated. I have often thought that every child space should be framed by such an arch, and that the space should be designed to fulfill its meaning. Passage beyond the torre would then surround each child with beauty, wholeness, and care, proclaiming that each belongs to the sacred domain and, by his or her presence in it, is graced with inner and outer loveliness.

CHAPTER EIGHT

Designing Play Environments for Infants and Toddlers

DORIS BERGEN ● KENNETH SMITH ● STEPHANIE O'NEILL

One has only to observe an infant repeatedly putting measuring spoons in and out of a pan from the cupboard or a toddler taking that same pan and spoon to feed a teddy bear to know that very young children engage in exploratory/practice play and in simple symbolic play with any materials that are available, no matter what the setting. A good starting point for environmental design is to review what researchers have learned from observing the play of infants (i.e., children age 1 year to 18 months) and toddlers (i.e., children age 18 to 30 months.)

Research on the environmental factors that influence infant and toddler play has been extensive during the past 10 years. The information describes how infants interact with objects and other physical properties of the environment and what roles adults and other children have in facilitating play development at home and in group settings.

This chapter gives a brief overview of the types of play exhibited by children in their first 2½ years of life, then presents research findings on how the physical environment affects play. The chapter also discusses the important roles that parents and other adults have in early play experiences, as well as the ways in which other children affect play development. This information is then applied to practice, with examples demonstrating how these characteristics can facilitate play and learning in the home and in out-of-home group settings. One setting is described in detail to serve as a model for environmental design.

Play Development of Infants and Toddlers

Looking and listening are the first methods of exploration. Infants gaze for long periods of time at different objects and human faces. They turn their attention to various sounds and respond especially to their mothers' voices and visual cues (Henderson, 1984; Lewis & Rosenblum, 1974; Yarrow, Rubenstein, & Pedersen, 1975). This first visual and auditory curiosity (i.e., distal exploration) precedes infants' ability to initiate motor actions directly upon the objects of their world (i.e., proximal exploration).

As their physical capacities increase, infants begin to engage in sensorimotor exploration of the environment, coordinating visual and motor actions with their bodies and with the objects and the people in the environment. During the latter half of the first year symbolic play (i.e., pretense) begins. Infants also engage in the precursors of games with rules, first by responding to rule-governed exchange routines initiated by adults and later by participating in brief games with other children that are patterned after these adult-child games. The play behaviors exhibited by infants and toddlers during the sensorimotor period include exploratory/practice play, symbolic play/pretense, and social routines/games.

● Exploratory/practice play

Children's sensorimotor actions consist of exploratory behaviors, through which information is gained, and exploratory/practice play, which is repetitive playful interaction with the environment. Exploration and play behaviors alternate frequently in this age period, and are often difficult to distinguish (McCall, 1979; Wohlwill, 1984). Sensorimotor play includes fine motor practice play, gross motor practice play, and coordinated combinations of the two.

Infants begin their sensorimotor exploration by grasping, shaking, or mouthing objects and parts of their own bodies, such as their hands and toes. These action schemes (i.e., patterns) are elaborated into dropping, throwing, putting objects into and out out of other objects, pushing and pulling objects, and using other repetitive trial-and-error manipulations. Exploratory/practice play begins as soon as infants demonstrate enjoyment in trying repetitive variations and novel combinations of actions. These vignettes give examples of practice play:

T. (9 months) is sitting in the playpen looking bored with the numerous toys that are piled about him. He suddenly smiles; then slowly and deliberately throws his clown doll through the bars, watching it sprawl on the floor. The ball,

three rattles, a jumping jack, and the busy box follow; as each lands, T. squeals with delight. He is enjoying the exercise of his throwing scheme.

Fortunately, T.'s father knows this is a naturally occurring form of practice play; otherwise he might consider it "naughty" behavior.

W. (19 months) observes the teacher put a ball in the clear plastic chute and watches intently as it comes out the other end. He grabs the ball and climbs the platform to reach the top of the chute. As the teacher watches, he tries to put the ball in the chute and, after a few unsuccessful attempts, gives an excited crow when the ball rolls out the bottom of the chute. All of the other objects on the platform that can fit in the chute are sent down to the bottom by W., as he shouts with increasing pleasure.

As W. manipulates the various objects, his teacher provides a verbal overlay of comments about his actions; the teacher's comments on this trial-and-error play assist the child in realizing the connection between cause and effect relationships.

M.'s (23 months) eyes slowly look up at the teacher as she carefully touches a container of pudding; she slides it toward her on the table and dumps some of it on the cookie sheet. "Don't help me," she insists. As she watches the other children, she begins to scribble in the pudding, wiggling her fingers, then mixing two kinds together to get another color. She scribbles faster, then slowly lifts a finger to her mouth, tasting the pudding. She lifts her pudding-covered fingers in the air, wiggles them and laughingly says to another child, "You have bumps in yours, bumps." She quickly tastes the pudding again, using one finger, then takes four fingers and scrapes up pudding into her mouth. Cheerfully she says, "I'm done!"

These examples of fine motor practice play illustrate the pleasure children experience and the learning that occurs during practice play with objects and with sensory materials. Other play experiences they enjoy are spreading mud and sand; rubbing materials like cotton or fur against their bodies, and playing with their food. Mashed potatoes, pudding, and ice cream are favorite sensory playthings. As toddlers use their physical skills to explore and discover, they seem to be having a love affair with the world.

Children of 8 months to 24 months especially enjoy practicing gross motor skills with their bodies (i.e., crawling, pulling up, walking, running, climbing). Toddlers like to carry bulky things, throw lightweight balls, and hang on shelves. They climb just because something is there to climb, even though adults don't consider it climbing equipment, and enjoy getting into and out of containers, no matter what their size. They also combine fine and gross motor play in coordinated sequences, as these examples illustrate:

L. (8 months) has learned to sit up and to roll over. She is just beginning to crawl and is enjoying alternating these skills. She sits on one of the carpeted levels on the center floor, then rolls to her stomach, crawls up to another level, sits up, rolls again, crawls to the uncarpeted area, sits up, rolls over and over until she reaches the platform near the mirror. She crawls up on the platform, looks in the mirror, pats it and smiles, sits up and begins babbling to her image in the mirror.

R. (20 months) has mastered the basic skill of walking; now he has begun to add playful variations on his walking skill. He is walking around the table, gradually going faster and faster; suddenly his attention is caught by some children walking on pillows. He runs across to them, observes briefly as their laughter escalates, then runs to the area where the trucks are. He sits on one of the big moving trucks and, using his feet and leg muscles, makes a complete circle of the active area. Maneuvering the truck through the block area, he encounters M. (27 months), who pushes him off the truck. He lands on the floor, distressed but not crying. M. sees his distress and points out another smaller truck for R. He drives his new truck after M., following wherever M. goes.

Children select only those actions for play that they are ready to consolidate; when a specific skill is mastered to a level that makes playful variations

challenging but enjoyable, those skills are then objects of play. L. and R. selected the challenges that were at the right level for their motor skills. R.'s play also unexpectedly provided him with an opportunity for peer interaction. Although many early peer contacts may seem negative to adults, children often resolve conflicts in a socially satisfying way, even at this early age.

S. (17 months) is fascinated with little things. She picks up tiny pieces of lint from the carpet and deposits each in her empty cup. Then she puts some cereal pieces from her bowl, one piece at a time, into the cup. She transfers the cup of little things to her wagon, includes some other small toys and some puzzle pieces. As she pulls the wagon around the kitchen, occasionally she stops and unloads some of her objects onto a chair, talking softly to herself. She repeats the sequence of loading and unloading until mother calls her to get dressed. Then she picks up her cup of little things and carries them into the bedroom.

Filling and emptying containers requires coordination of fine and gross motor skills; often the containers are dumped and, after observing the effect, the toddler may move on to dump others. Stacking and knocking down are also favorite forms of practice play requiring coordinated action.

● **Symbolic play/pretense**

Symbolic play begins during the second six months of life. As infants observe the people in their environment and their activities, they begin to imitate their actions. From this early imitation, the ability to initiate pretend play with objects, actions, and verbal symbols develops. Although much early pretense is solitary, it often includes adults and, at later toddler ages, other children.

The first transformations of objects in pretense involve realistic objects and actions that are focused on the self. For example, children of about 12 months may pretend to drink "milk" out of an empty cup. The ability to suspend reality and transform objects increases dramatically during the 12- to 30-month age period. The following illustrates an advanced stage:

B. (27 months) walks to the housekeeping stove and picks up a purple cup. She takes it to the table, puts a wad of Play Dough in the cup, then looks for a round block. She takes the dough out of the cup, puts it on the block, and rolls the block. As the teacher walks by, B. says "I makin' pancakes." B. puts the pancake in the cup, walks to the stove and puts it in the oven. She takes more dough and makes another pancake, depositing it in the oven also. The teacher asks if the pancakes are ready to eat and B. opens the oven and takes them to the table. The teacher has placed a stack of plates on the table. B. "sets" the table, putting one plate by each of the four chairs. She still has more plates in her hand. After a brief glance at the ones she has already placed, she deposits the other plates one by one on the same side of the table. She puts her pancake on a plate, then looks at T., who is sitting at the table and says, "He can have one."

B. is able to look for items she needs for her play (i.e., plan), use objects that are not exact replicas (i.e., transform) and, aided by the adult, engage in pretend sequences (i.e., use multischemes). She is not playing with T., however, even though he is allowed a pancake. An interesting glimpse of B.'s intuitive understanding of one-to-one correspondence is also provided in this example.

Although early pretense involves one action or object (e.g., feeding the doll or putting the doll to sleep), coordinated sequences occur by about 24 months. More than one action is performed with the same object (e.g., the doll is fed, rocked, put to bed, and awakened) or more than one object is acted upon (e.g., all of the dolls are fed or put to bed). Planning of the pretense also becomes evident, with the play organized in a sequence demonstrating mental intention. Often this pretense is accompanied by verbalizations. For example, toddlers may say they are "going shopping," then collect the doll, put the doll in the wagon, and leave the house area.

By the end of the first year, infants respond to and begin to produce language. By 9 to 12 months, they can be observed playing with language sounds, repeating and varying the sound combinations. Because toddlers are mastering the basics of language, they engage in a great deal of language play with the sounds, structures, and meanings of language. They may accompany action play with sound play (e.g., driving cars while saying "brumm, brumm"); repeat rhymes and phrases while varying the words or sounds (e.g., "cookie monster, gookie monster, gookie mooster"); and engage in verbal routines with other children (e.g., "I'm making cake"; "I'm making pie"; "I'm making pie-cake"). Materials that may provide the impetus for language play include books and television, as well as the language of adults and other children. Toddlers' first demonstration of humorous response to incongruity often grows from "mis-labeling" (e.g., chanting that the dog says "meow"). This child is especially tuned in to language play:

C. (30 months) has loved to hear stories and look at books since her first year of life. She is fascinated with a set of magnetic letters; first manipulating the letters and, as her mother labels them, repeating those names in the same manner she used to learn the names of animals in books and objects in her home. She arranges the letters on the magnetic board in a random order, asking her mother what they say. Her mother puts three letters in order and says "Mom"; C. repeats the name. For the next few days, she enjoys finding those three shapes, putting them together on the board, and repeating "Mom." During the next few weeks, she asks how to make "Dad" and her own name. The sound of the name for the letter "W" is especially appealing; she repeats "dubba-you," "dubba-you" as she is engaged in other play.

Toddlers exhibit the same playful approaches to language, reading, and numbers that they show toward all objects in their environment. They explore and play with symbolic material in a trial-and-error fashion until representational connections are made. Then they enjoy manipulating these arbitrary verbal signs as another kind of symbolic plaything.

A. (30 months) says, "I'm a farmer; give me some milk." The teacher gives him a wooden milk bottle. A. gives a wooden cow a drink of milk from the bottle. He makes the cow say "Yum, yum." He continues a conversation with the cow, asking "Want some chocolate milk? Yeh, this one's chocolate milk. Want some hay?"

His cow's answers sound moo-like. He joins the other children in "eating food" represented by blocks, labeling the food as he eats it. Then he turns to his cow and asks in a nurturing tone, "Want some of my bite?" He makes the cow answer with a mooing "yes." Other children try to feed his cow but he warns, "No, he's had his."

In their pretense, older toddlers use the tone and language appropriate for the roles they are playing. A. is able to state his role (i.e., the farmer); play the role of the object (i.e., make the cow speak and eat); and operate both in and out of the play frame (e.g., speaking nurturingly to his cow; warning other children to stay out of the play frame).

Symbolic play with other children is still difficult for toddlers. Although much of it occurs in the presence of other children, it differs from the sociodramatic play of preschoolers because there is rarely a differentiation of roles and there are no sustained plots. For example, children playing in the house area all engage in similar pretense scripts; everyone is setting the table, taking care of the dolls, or fixing dinner. The play is primarily of a parallel nature, although some associative sequences do occur. If older children are directing the play, toddlers may be assigned roles as "baby" but they rarely tailor their actions to fit a specific role.

● Social routines/games with rules

Infants respond to games initiated by adults, such as pat-a-cake, peek-a-boo, and catch me/chase me. In self-initiated individual games and peer social games, toddlers exhibit beginning ability to observe rules in simple games. These gamelike activities are often called routines because they do not have a competitive element. They include one-rule action games, such as social turn taking, and parallel action games, such as parading.

When playing alone toddlers invent rituals that have a rule they must follow but, because toddlers cannot explain the rule, it is difficult for adults to recognize that a rule-governed ritual is taking place. These rules are not stable; toddlers cannot hold an invariant rule in mind for long. Often adults realize there is a rule when the child cries after the rule has been inadvertently broken by the adult. Advanced levels of practice play frequently follow such rules; for example, the toddler may require puzzle pieces to be put back in a certain sequence. Examples of social games follow.

Every day for the past week, P. (24 months) and his dad have played the same game at noontime. As dad's car comes up the drive, P. runs to hide. Dad comes in the door, saying "Where's P.?" He looks under the table, behind the sofa, in the closet, accompanying his looking with a running commentary about where P. must have gone, all the while ignoring P.'s giggles. Finally, when the play has escalated to an almost unbearable level for P., dad looks under P.'s chair (i.e., the place P. always hides) and, with exaggerated surprise, dad says, "I'm so glad I found you."

The play of P. and his dad illustrate how adults monitor the social game to fit the child's level of game playing skill. Dad knows what level of arousal P. can handle. He also knows that their attachment bonds are firm enough to mock a loss and separation experience, and that the end result of the play is a strengthening of that attachment bond.

K. (28 months) is on the "mountains and caves" climber platform. As N. (29 months) walks past on the ground level, K. sticks his fingers through the holes in the side of the platform and yells to get N.'s attention. When N. looks up, L, wiggles his fingers in the holes, daring N. to catch hold of them. N. grabs for them, misses, grabs again, and catches one. Giggles ensue as they struggle. The "catch the finger" game goes on for some time.

Early peer games are usually versions of the games children have played with adults, in which there are reciprocal roles with a governing rule. Toddlers enjoy chasing games and other taglike routines. They have many games with the rule of "turn taking," such as taking turns riding and pulling the wagon. The reciprocal element is important; and the presence of another child enhances and sustains the game. A game that has parallel rather than complementary roles is that of "parading" or other follow-the-leader types of play, the type engaged in by B. and M. with the trucks.

As all of these examples of infant and toddler play illustrate, the objects and structures in the physical environment (e.g., what toys are available and whether play occurs at home or at school) can influence the play that is exhibited. The social environment (i.e., the various interactions of parents, teachers, and other children) also may make a difference. Although many of the factors that could affect play development have not been studied, there is information gained from research on some of these factors. This information, which can assist adults in designing play environments for infants and toddlers, is reviewed in the following sections.

Characteristics of the Physical Environment

While infant and toddler development has long been the subject of research and speculation, the natural environments in which that development takes place have not been so well examined. More is known about infant and toddler behavior in laboratory settings than in the natural settings of the family, home, and child-care center (Belsky, 1977; Parke, 1978). Information is particularly sparse about the natural environments of children of minority/ethnic groups. Although laboratory studies have provided useful data, especially on infants' and toddlers' interactions with objects, studies set in natural environments may help to answer questions of particular interest to practitioners.

Few researchers would deny the impact of children's natural physical environments on play development. The role of the physical setting in providing stimulation for children's established and emerging skills and for giving a motivational context for the exercise of those skills cannot be overstated. The nature of the interaction between children and the environment has profound consequences for play development and all other areas of development.

Factors in the physical environment that have been the focus of research include (a) global and structural features, such as familiarity/unfamiliarity of total setting, spatial and structural characteristics, social density and other social context effects; and (b) the availability of toys and other play objects, including object attributes such as responsiveness, size, and realistic quality.

● Global and structural features

Studies indicate that novelty, density, and space arrangement affect young children's play.

> 1. Studies of effects of environmental novelty on the exploration and sensorimotor play of infants and toddlers show mixed results; this may be due to interactions with other variables.

Mobile infants and toddlers generally remain closer to their mothers in unfamiliar physical environments than they do in more familiar surroundings (Castell, 1970), which results in a decrease in their exploration of the environment. The novelty of the environment does affect children's reactions to novel stimuli in that setting, but the direction of the effect is unclear. In some cases the novel environment seems to increase exploratory play (Rheingold & Eckerman, 1970); in other cases the unfamiliarity of the setting results in an increase of anxiety and wariness, thus decreasing the level of exploratory play (Castell, 1970; Parry, 1972).

In a study designed to clarify this question, Ross (1974) found that 1-year-olds explored unfamiliar toys in a novel environment more than they did in a familiar environment. Ross concludes that the impact of objects on infants is related both to the physical context in which the objects are encountered and to the stimulus features of the objects themselves.

> 2. High social density (i.e., ratio of number of people to size of space) may interfere with infant exploratory play.

A number of studies have been conducted in the home setting to explore the effects of social and spatial density on young children's behavior. Schoggen and Schoggen (1985) report that a high density of people in the same room with an infant may interfere with the infant's ability to discriminate sounds associated with caregivers and complicate the infant's visual exploration and pursuit of interesting stimuli. High density also seems to disrupt exploratory play, especially for mobile children, by interfering with their ability to use the caregiver as a "safe base" (i.e., a psychologically reassuring figure who can be seen and heard everywhere in the environment) when moving out to explore (Goldberg & Lewis, 1969; Rheingold & Eckerman, 1970). This may be a stressful situation for children (Schoggen & Schoggen, 1985). Crowding and high noise levels disturb child-parent interactions; male and high-risk infants are most negatively affected by noise (Wachs, 1976; Wachs & Chan, 1985; Wachs & Gandour, 1983).

Low income and/or minority children may be particularly at risk because these crowded conditions occur often in low income and/or minority family homes. On the other hand, differences in cultural values or expectations may lessen negative effects of crowding. Research on density and noise effects in these homes is needed.

3. Toddlers use the structural features of the environment (i.e., spatial arrangement, closed and open space) in their social play.

In a study comparing toddler play in a child-care center and in family day-care settings, Howes and Rubenstein (1978) found that toddlers in family day-care used the spatial arrangements of the home as play structures. Toddlers used hallways, corners, and connecting rooms for interactive play in the same way that the toddlers in the center played on the non-portable climbing structures. The researchers conclude that nonmovable elements of the physical environment, such as spatial arrangement and structure of rooms, must be considered part of the play environment. If equipment specifically designed for interactive play is not available, toddlers apparently can find a substitute.

● **Availability and attributes of play objects**

Toys and other objects for play that infants and toddlers encounter in the environment have a significant impact on their play behavior.

1. Availability, variety, and responsiveness of toys positively affect infant play behaviors.

In a series of studies on infant exploratory behavior, McCall (1974) found that exploratory manipulation increased as infants played with more responsive objects (e.g., objects that made a noise or reacted when touched or pulled). He lists the key characteristics of toys that stimulate infants to spend more time manipulating and exploring: (a) degree of contingent responsiveness of the toy (i.e., how much of what the toy does depends on what the child does to it); (b) the potential of the toy to produce an interesting sound; and (c) the plasticity of the toy (i.e., the ease with which the infant can manipulate and change the shape of the object).

Wachs (1985) indicates that availability of many toys has a positive effect on younger (6 mo. old) infants, but variety (i.e., frequent changing of a smaller set of toys) is most important for older (12 mo. old) infants. These attributes of availability and variety, together with the quality of responsivity, were combined into a classification of "high affordance" objects (i.e., objects having stimulus properties that prompted interactions). Although presence of high affordance objects was related to high levels of parent interaction with infants at 12 months, it was not related at 6 months (Wachs & Chan, 1985; Wachs & Gandour, 1983). The researchers conclude that parents may provide sufficient objects of this type for younger infants even when they do not engage in high levels of social interaction.

2. Objects can promote toddler peer play; however, they are more important at some ages than at others.

A number of studies have provided information on how objects promote peer play (e.g., DeStefano & Mueller, 1982; Garvey, 1977a; Mueller & Brenner, 1977; Mueller & Lucas, 1975; Vandell & Mueller, 1978; Vandell, Wilson, & Buchanan, 1980). Mueller and colleagues report that object play precedes play with toddler peers, and conclude that parallel play with objects is a necessary stage of social play development. Garvey (1977a) agrees that "objects are the prime currency of exchange for toddlers" (p. 51) because many early social acts are showing, exchanging, taking, or giving objects to peers.

However, Vandell et al., (1980) found that nonsocial object play was not a precursor of social play in 6-month-old-infants. They observed more social play in the absence of objects. Hay, Nash, and Pedersen (1983) agree that when objects are not available, there is an increase in infants' peer touching and action reciprocity. Because their results showed no correlation between explorations of toys and interest in peers, they state, "it would be a mistake to assume that infants view their peers as just another set of toys" (p. 561).

> 3. Toddler social play is influenced by the availability of play materials and the size of play objects in the environment.

Although toddlers often are drawn together by shared interest in the same toys, both positive and negative interactions increase when toys are absent (DeStefano & Mueller, 1982; Eckerman & Whatley, 1977; Mueller & Brenner, 1977). Both Mueller and Brenner and Eckerman and Whatley report that toddlers show more and longer interactions when toys are not present.

DeStefano and Mueller (1982) found that when small objects are present, toddlers have more struggles for possession and more negative affect. When large structures are present, the quality of activity is more positive because there are multiple opportunities for concurrent activity. Large objects keep the toddlers from physically interfering with each other.

> 4. Toddler pretend play is influenced by the attributes (i.e., realistic or nonrealistic) of objects.

Toddlers' ability to engage in object substitution is affected by the level of realism of the objects (Fein, 1975b). Most studies of pretend play use a set of typical experimental toys (e.g., blocks, dolls, pots) to elicit this behavior. They often also use less realistic objects as well. Initially, transformation of objects in pretend play is easier when the objects are prototypical, looking like the real object (e.g., toy phone to be used for a real phone). Ambiguous objects (e.g., block to be used for a phone) can be transformed more easily than counterconventional objects that are definitely inappropriate (e.g., car to be used for a phone), even when adults model the pretend behaviors (Bretherton, O'Connell, Shore, & Bates, 1984). Older toddlers are especially resistant to inappropriate object substitution (Garvey, 1977a). Pretense with imaginary objects occurs by age 2 years and 6 months (Elder & Pederson, 1978).

Characteristics of the Social Environment

The major sources of information about the factors in the social environment that influence the development of play are studies of parent-infant playful interactions, of specific play facilitation strategies used by adults, and of components of peer and sibling play. Cultural factors related to early play have also been explored in some of these studies; however, studies of some cultural groups in the United States (e.g., Mexican-American) are needed.

● Adults' roles in fostering play development

Although El'konin (1966) and Vygotsky (1967) theorized that adult modeling and language interactions are essential for children's play development, Piaget's (1962) studies of his own infants focused primarily on their interaction with the object world. Researchers have only recently begun to focus on what Sutton-Smith (1979a) calls "the role of Mrs. Piaget as mother" (p. 307). Recent studies provide support for the importance of adult facilitation of play and point to several conclusions; these are discussed below.

> 1. Infant-caregiver playful interactions provide infants with knowledge of the rules and play signals that provide a frame for social play. Through these early social games infants learn to distinguish play from not play and how to interact with others within the play frame.

Infants' early responsiveness to playful social stimulation (Brazelton, Koslowski, & Main, 1974; Bruner, 1982) provides the basis for social play. Bruner and Sherwood (1976), who analyzed the structural patterns of infant-mother interaction in the game of peek-a-boo, suggest that the rule pattern of contact-withdrawal-recontact is a prototype of later games with rules.

Not all researchers agree that this early rule-governed play should be called games. Some prefer to call them exchange routines or rituals (Sutton-Smith, 1979d) because they do not have competitive elements. This type of play seems to provide the basis for a wide range of later rule-governed and symbolic play behaviors. McCall (1979) states that early interactive play allows infants to explore their social influence. Stern (1977) also reports that these caregiver-infant interaction patterns are primary for learning social skills.

Adults (i.e., usually mothers) communicate "this is play" (Bateson, 1956) to infants by providing a play frame that is safe and that teaches the play signals (Stern, 1974b; Sutton-Smith, 1979a): (a) a proxemic bubble (i.e., close facial contact); (b) a play face (e.g., open eyes and mouth and exaggerated features); (c) a play gaze (e.g., infatuated); (d) play vocalizations (e.g., a high pitch, long vowels, and slow speech); and (e) a play setting (e.g., occurring after meals or in the crib).

There are differences in father-infant and mother-infant play (Clarke-Stewart, 1977; Lamb, 1977; Power & Park, 1980). Research suggests that fathers and infants initiate about the same number of play actions; mothers are more initiating and responsive than fathers. Fathers are more likely to engage in active, high arousal play when they do interact with infants. Parents also play differently with boys and girls. Parents of high-risk infants and parents who have abused their children have lower levels of play interaction and more difficulty keeping the play routine going (Beckwith, 1985; Beckwith, Cohen, Kopp, Parmalee, & Marcy, 1976; Frodi & Lamb, 1980).

In social games, infants learn what actions are signals for play, that play is fun, and that it is nonliteral (i.e., it has nonrealistic elements). Garvey (1977a), who has analyzed play as communication, states, "a nonliteral orientation to experiences is probably communicated to an infant within the first months of life" (p. 8). According to Sachs (1980), adult-child play involves "the construction of narrative" (p. 39), with story lines imposed by the adult on the play.

|| 2. Early social play enhances and supports
|| caregiver-infant attachment.

In a study of tickling games, Shultz (1979) concludes that infants respond more positively when the tickler is the mother and enjoy more vigorous tickling from mothers than from strangers. This behavior is especially evident in boys. Shultz believes that play strengthens attachment bonds not only with parents, but with all members of the social group. It may have major implications for the development of trust (Erikson, 1963).

The more fun that mothers and infants have when playing, the more securely attached the infants seem to be (Blehar, Lieberman, & Ainsworth, 1977). Those infants who are judged to be securely attached also seem to have more fun when playing alone and are more persistent in play (Belsky, Garduque, & Hrncir, 1984; Matas, Arend, & Sroufe, 1978).

Hay, Ross, and Goldman (1979) suggest that infants' preferred social mode of learning may be play because 19-month-old infants initiate playful interactions with strangers within four minutes of meeting them. This use of play as a means of establishing new social relationships gives support to the hypothesis that, having played initially with caregivers to whom they were attached, infants use play as a social tool to facilitate other social attachments.

|| 3. Social play with reciprocal roles assists in-
|| fants in learning how to modulate their
|| arousal level.

Being able to anticipate social responses and control the level of stimulation is a skill infants need to develop. Caregivers serve as sources of arousal and assist infants in learning how to modulate their arousal levels in response to the caregiver (Stern, 1974a.) In Shultz's study, infants whose mothers had played tickling games with them were able to anticipate more vigorous tickling and respond appropriately to the levels of vigor. The repetition of most early games assists infants in anticipating and having some control over the play (Ross & Kay, 1980).

Sutton-Smith (1979a) describes how caregivers manipulate the social play to increase excitement, especially in games in which the adult is the central actor and the child is the responder. Because caregivers provide both constant and varied kinds of stimulation, they convey both certainty and uncertainty in social play interactions. Within a safe environment, social games give infants experience in adapting to, anticipating, and controlling their own arousal levels (Lewis, 1979; Sutton-Smith, 1979a).

4. Infants' exploratory play is affected by levels of adult attention focusing.

Mothers who use strategies of focusing attention, such as pointing or demonstrating, have infants who show higher exploration levels with objects (Belsky, Goode, & Most, 1980). Belsky et al. report that when experimenters verbally recognized the mothers' attention-focusing strategies as they occurred, the mothers increased the use of these strategies. Two months later, the infants in the experimental group showed more focused exploration and more functional play.

5. Toddlers' pretense development is affected by adult interaction styles and their methods of encouraging pretend play.

Methods adults use to facilitate pretend play have been reported by many researchers (e.g., Dunn & Wooding, 1977; Fein, 1979b; Fenson, 1984; Hrncir, 1980; Miller & Garvey, 1984). Studies include ones in which adults make specific verbal suggestions (Fein & Robertson, 1975); model symbolic play (Fein, 1975b; Watson & Fischer, 1977); and present toys without making suggestions (Fein & Apfel, 1979).

Fein (1979b) reports that mothers of 12-month-olds exhibit three play interaction styles: (a) elaborative, (b) imitative, and (c) unrelated. Elaborative mothers select their child's action or an object the child is manipulating and make modifications in the same behaviors. For example, if an infant is banging a spoon, an elaborative mother might bang a stick or eat from a spoon. Imitative mothers do exactly what their children are doing, with no modification. Unrelated mothers play separately with materials and disregard what their children are doing. If they intervene at all, they do so in demanding and intrusive, rather than playful, ways.

Mothers aid their children's play with two levels of involvement: (a) joint attention and (b) joint play (Dunn & Wooding, 1977). Usually they operate at one or two levels of play above the children's level (Adler, 1982). Familiar adults can elicit more frequent and varied play (Fein & Robertson, 1975).

Mothers also assist female children in learning to portray both mother and baby roles by creating a context for the pretense, providing props, accepting the appropriateness of pretend actions with objects, expanding the play, giving explicit instructions, providing running commentary, responding to pretend actions positively, and acting as play partners who facilitate joint performances (Miller & Garvey, 1984). Mothers are less active and give less unsolicited assistance to the pretense as children's age increases. By age 3, girls show mature role-play and use pretend "motherese" and "baby talk."

Although mothers actively instruct their children, suggesting a variety of play modes, children's responses depend on their readiness level. Toddlers select the activities to include in play from their mothers' instructions and thus maintain control of the play direction (O'Connell & Bretherton, 1984). Toddlers' imitation of modeling increases as age increases (Fenson, 1984). Although adults verbally describe their play actions as they model them, most toddlers' play is action only, not accompanied by language.

● **Peer group and sibling effects**

Infants' interest in peers and their social play in group care settings has long been observed by researchers from countries such as the USSR, where group care has been common (El'konin, 1966). Because until recently infant group care settings were not common in the United States, peer play in this age group received little attention here. Since the 1970s, however, infant and toddler peer play has been studied by many American researchers. Their work supports the following conclusions:

1. Infants and toddlers enjoy the presence of other children and actively attempt to engage peers in social play interactions.

Lee (1973), Hay, Nash, and Pedersen (1983), and Bleier (1976) have demonstrated that infants are aware of peers and that early distal and proximal peer interactions such as looking, touching, smiling, crawling close, and exchanging objects are typical social strategies of infants. Vandell, Wilson, and Buchanan (1980) and Lee (1973) indicate that as early as 6 to 9 months infants initiate interactions and respond to peers.

As infants become toddlers, they play less with adults and more with one another (Finkelstein, Dent, Gallacher, & Ramey, 1978). In one infant/toddler group setting, 47% of infant interactions were with adults, but only 33% of toddler interactions were with adults. Interactions with peers increased in the toddler age period; over 50% of toddler interactions were focused on peers (Bergen, Gaynard, & Torelli, 1985). Holmberg (1980) indicates that adult-child play occurs earlier and episodes last longer than peer play because adults make the necessary adjustments to keep the interchange going. As toddler age increases, both peer and adult-child interchanges become more balanced.

Peer interaction research shows mixed results, depending on setting. Eckerman, Whatley, and Kutz (1975) found that toddlers preferred to play socially with an unfamiliar peer rather than with their mothers. Ross and Goldman (1977) also observed high levels of play interactions between unfamiliar peers. However, Stefani and Camaioni (1983) found that peer play was enhanced by familiarity of peers. Bronson (1981) described toddlers as spending more time with toys and their mothers than with peers.

Vandell & Mueller (1978) found that the familiarity of the setting influences peer interaction; toddlers are more likely to interact with peers when they are in familiar settings. Toddlers who have had a group experience show more social play interactions with their parents than do home-reared toddlers (Vandell, 1979), and those toddlers whose mothers are employed are more peer oriented (Schachter, 1981).

2. Peer play increases children's abilities to communicate with one another in ways that promote pretend play.

Garvey's (1977a) studies of peer play dyads demonstrated that children show increasing sophistication in communication about the play frame and within the play frame over the toddler and preschool age periods. As children play together they learn to use language to assume roles (e.g., "I'm the dad"); frame the play setting (e.g., "This is the car"); and act out their play role (e.g., "Good-by, I'm going to work now").

Miller and Garvey (1984) observed that girls show mothering behavior to dolls before the boys take "father" roles. Boy-girl dyads cooperate in other make-believe play, such as "eating dinner" or "going on a trip," before they play complementary family roles. Boys are more likely to be interested observers rather than show nurturing toward dolls, and they refuse the role of baby.

3. Older siblings may assist toddlers in reaching higher levels of play development.

Samuels (1980) and Dunn and Dale (1984) report that 2-year-olds explore more and exhibit more independent behavior when with an older sibling. They also show different types of pretend play with their mothers and with their siblings (Dunn & Dale, 1984). Mother-child and sibling-child dyads differ in how the play is initiated, the themes expressed, and the nature of the toddlers' participation. Most mother-child play begins with transformation of objects; sibling play often begins with the older sibling modeling a pretend game that the toddler then imitates. Most sibling-child pretend games do not involve objects.

Child gender influences the play themes; with girl toddlers, mothers and siblings do not suggest or model pretense focusing on vehicles (Dunn & Dale, 1984). Siblings of the same gender play together more positively; negative affect is more common in different-gender pairs (Dunn & Kendrick, 1981).

Mothers interact with toddlers primarily in spectator or facilitator roles, while siblings act in collaborator roles. Mother-child pretense focuses on "as if," simulates reality, and follows conventional themes. Sibling play stresses "what if," and is more imaginative and far ranging. Dunn and Dale report that less than half of 24-month-old toddlers engaged in role enactment, but that those who did exhibited that behavior only with siblings. Miller and Garvey (1984) did not observe role enactment with mothers or peers until toddlers were at least 30 months old.

It may be that siblings are especially able to increase toddlers' level of pretense; however, toddler play with older unrelated children might show similar patterns.

Interaction of Physical Environment, Social Environment, and Individual Differences

In considering factors influencing early play development, some researchers point out that a firm distinction between the social and physical environments is essentially artificial (Parke, 1978). They indicate that the influence of the physical environment is mediated by the children's caregivers, who determine the nature, amount, quality, and intensity of the stimulation from children's natural surroundings (Bradley & Caldwell, 1976a; Clarke-Stewart, 1973; White, Kaban, Shapiro, & Attanucci, 1977).

|| 1. Adult organization of the total environment affects play and cognitive development.

In studies of home environments with the Home Observation for Measurement of the Environment (HOME) inventory (Bradley & Caldwell, 1976a, 1976b; Elardo, Bradley, & Caldwell, 1975) scores on the subscale "organization of the physical and temporal environment" were related to children's IQ at age 3 (Bradley & Caldwell, 1976a). Three of the subscale measures, taken when the children were 6 months old, predicted child scores of the children at age three (Bradley & Caldwell, 1976b). These subscales reflected lack of organization in the physical environment and child's schedule, lack of appropriate play materials, and low maternal involvement with the child.

Elardo, Bradley, and Caldwell (1975) found that the HOME inventory also correlated significantly with general cognitive development as measured by Stanford-Binet scores, a finding paralleled by Wachs, Uzgiris, and Hunt (1971), who used a Piagetian measure of cognitive development.

Parke (1978) states that the amount of predictability infants encounter in the environment (i.e., how ordered and regular) is one way adults consistently mediate its impact on children. Adults also act as boundary-setters, thus influencing the range of access children have to the environment to explore its features and properties (White et al., 1977; White & Carew-Watts, 1973).

|| 2. Specific features of the environment may also interact with social contexts.

Wachs (1985), Wachs and Chan (1985), and Wachs and Gandour (1983) stress that, although adult mediation in the home is an important variable, specific factors in the physical environment do make a difference that is distinct from the mediation of caregivers. As evidence of physical context effect, they cite their work that shows little relationship between high affordance object attributes and parental interaction with 6-month-old infants. Although the physical and social interactions were related when infants were 12 months, there was no evidence to indicate that the social factors caused the results. Wachs and colleagues state that the effects of social contexts depend on the aspects of the physical environment that are being looked at, and they suggest that study should focus on specific environmental variables (e.g., level of focused attention or responsiveness of objects) rather than on global variables (e.g., low income or minority homes).

The research of Collard (1971, 1979), focusing on English home-reared and institution-reared infants, demonstrates other interactions of physical and social environment factors. In her first study, home-reared infants exhibited more exploratory responses initially and more play responses subsequently when presented with play objects than did institution-reared infants. The particular institution was physically unstimulating; infants were kept crib-bound with few toys available. There were, however, many adults interacting with the infants.

On her second visit, additional toys had been provided and children were out of the cribs, interacting with many toys. They were in a setting with 20 other infants and numerous adults. Collard found that infants' exploration had increased, but it was of short duration and stereotypic. Some infants appeared overstimulated.

In another study, Collard found that infants who were from middle-class homes had more play schemes than those from lower class homes. The middle class homes had a moderate number of varied play objects and mothers who spent time playing with the infants. Collard concludes from these studies that moderate numbers and varieties of play objects and moderate numbers of adults who interact playfully on a regular basis may produce the most play schemes in infants. Environments that allow infants to control their level of stimulation by mobility (i.e., being able to leave settings in order to moderate their arousal level) may result in higher quality of exploration and play.

3. Individual children react differently to environmental factors.

Evidence is also mounting that there are individual child differences, even in infancy, that interact with physical and social environmental effects (McCall, 1974; O'Connell & Bretherton, 1984; Vandell, Wilson, & Buchanan, 1980; Wachs, 1985). Wachs (1985) suggests that it might be possible to distinguish children who are more focused on objects from those who are more interested in social relations at an early age. He speculates that the importance of the physical versus the social environment may differ for these two types of children.

Wolf and colleagues (Wolf & Gardner, 1979; Wolf & Grollman, 1982; Wolf, Rygh, & Altshuler, 1984) indicate that these two different modes of relating to the world are evident in toddlers but that by age 3 children can use either mode. Determining infants' cognitive style and approach to the world may be helpful for designing the most appropriate environment for each child during the first 2 years of life. Cultural and language differences are also important variables that should be considered in environmental design.

Based on the information from research and practice, some suggestions for environmental design will be made; these can provide guidance in planning both home and group environments for infants and toddlers.

Guidelines for Home Play Environments

Infants and toddlers in the home must fit into adult living and working space instead of having specially designed space to meet their unique needs (Olds, 1982a). Unfortunately, many home environments are created without adult awareness of the role that the environment plays in infant and toddler develop-

ment. Such a lack of awareness can be especially detrimental to handicapped or minority infants or young children with other special needs. The first step in looking at a home environment is to analyze how to modify and adapt it so that infants' or toddlers' play needs can be met while the adults' needs are also met (Bailey & Burton, 1982). Children's needs include opportunities for exploratory play, for pretend play, and for social games.

Nonmobile infants can be exposed to sensory diversity by placing them in varied locations, such as on a mat or blanket, in an infant seat, or by carrying them in a sling. Every setting affords a wealth of things to see, both human and nonhuman. Varying surfaces where infants are placed increases their sensory experiences. Adult sensitivity to infant cues can help them to vary the stimulation appropriately. For example, adults can put an infant near a window where tree branches are being blown by the wind, creating movement and shadows, or they can position an infant on a counter near a sink and turn on the faucet. After initially allowing the infant to observe, the adult can increase the stimulation by singing, talking, allowing the child to feel the wind or water, and giving the child objects that would float on the wind or catch the water (Olds, 1982a). According to Olds (1982a), a variety of sensory stimulation helps children maintain an optimal arousal level. She suggests that techniques used with infants can also help older nonmobile handicapped children to obtain sensorimotor feedback; severely handicapped children can experience sensory deprivation because they cannot initiate sensorimotor action (Ellis, 1973).

Infants also need to practice their grasping, banging, mouthing, and other action schemes on a variety of objects. By placing objects such as mobiles, rattles, busy boxes, and common household items near enough for infants to explore, adults can encourage play development. A moderate number of objects with frequent change is better than a cluttered or empty environment. Providing a balance between self-directed free-play time and adult-child playtime is most appropriate. The home affords many opportunities for experiences that incorporate elements of free play and guided play.

Once infants become mobile, the home environment should be reexamined and rearranged to meet the mobility and exploration needs of toddlers.

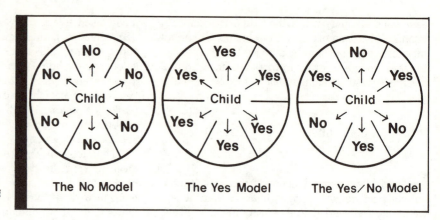

FIGURE 8–1 • Models of Social Environments

The No Model   The Yes Model   The Yes/No Model

Clearing the center of rooms encourages movement because space is needed for rolling over, creeping, pulling up, standing, and walking. Furniture that safely encourages these activities should be available. It is during this stage of movement that adults are most likely to need to modify the environment to accommodate the toddler. Because the home is designed primarily without regard for toddlers' needs, adults should try to visualize their environment through the eyes of a toddler. Three toddler world-views, which parallel Erikson's (1963) "autonomy versus shame and doubt" stage of development, are shown in Figure 8–1.

The worldviews are as follows:

1. *"No" model.* The child in this world learns that as he moves toward objects to explore or to play, he encounters painful or harmful events. For example, the lamp may fall with a crash, the child hears a loud "no," or the child is physically restrained. Some home environments look like this "no" model.
2. *"Yes" model.* The child in this world learns that the world exists for his or her discovery and exploration and there are no rules or concerns for safety that must be considered. This model is rarely encountered in the home and, if it were, it would not prepare the child for survival in the larger world.
3. *"Yes and no" model.* Realistically, the home modifications made to meet children's play

needs should form a balance: the child should be able to explore and play, but should also learn that the world has limits and rules. The child can experience this world as a challenging place that encourages play, but also as a place that requires some modification of behavior.

In order to promote a "yes and no" worldview in the child, the home environment should include some "yes" and some "no" items in every room. For example, in the kitchen, certain cabinets might be off-limits, while the one that contains the pots and pans might be available for pulling out, putting in, and banging pots. Objects such as puzzles, pop beads, and blocks (which can be gathered, stacked, knocked down, filled up, and dumped out) should be available. Adults who value children's play, who notice and comment upon the play activity, and who join in the play nurture play development in toddlers.

Because realistic objects enhance early pretense, the availability of old sets of keys or realistic plastic keys, an old phone or a realistic toy phone, and many other inexpensive household objects promotes pretend play. As the studies of adult play facilitation show, however, the most important support for pretend play is adult modeling and elaboration of pretense. In the home, adults can take advantage of the many opportunities for having pretend "birthday parties," caring for dolls, or driving cars into a "garage."

Adults can encourage toddler observation of sibling play and provide materials that promote toddler participation in sibling play. For example, making a tent with a cloth over a table enables the older child to play at "camping" with the toddler. Because one of the toddler's favorite actions is to get into enclosed spaces, being a "camper" is a role toddlers enjoy playing. Outdoor backyard play of older siblings and their friends can also include toddlers, giving them the opportunity to extend their gross motor and role-playing skills.

Because early exchange routines or social games are so important for learning the basic reciprocal structures of play, it is essential for the social environment in the home to include many opportunities for adult-child interactive games. These games require little or no equipment and relatively little time. Games can be played while the adult is fixing dinner, relaxing after work, or waiting in the doctor's office. The essential ingredient is that of enjoyment as the child gains the understanding that "This is play" (Bateson, 1956).

Guidelines for Out-of-Home Play Environments

The quality of infant and toddler play in group care settings is greatly influenced by the physical and social features of those environments. In planning an appropriate group environment for young children, educators need to reflect on the developmental range represented by the children in the setting. Because the children in such groups may range from birth to age 2½ or 3, the developmental level may go from totally dependent newborns to assertive toddlers feeling the headiness of autonomous behavior. An environment designed to support children's developmental progress across such a span must be flexible and responsive.

Ferguson (1979) points out that the physical environment for infant-toddler care must reflect the program goal of moving children toward greater personal autonomy and independence. A developmentally appropriate setting has as few barriers and constraints as possible so that exploratory play is not restricted; it includes the materials and equipment that support children's choices and strivings for autonomy.

TABLE 8-1 ● Early Childhood Educators' Priorities for Infant and Toddler Programs (from Bergen et al., 1985)	
Infants	Toddlers
Safe environment	Safe environment
Consistent nurturance	Cognitive stimulation
Reciprocal responsiveness	Autonomy/ independence
Exploration of objects	Peer interaction/play
Peer awareness	Exploration of objects and environment
Cognitive stimulation	Reciprocal responsiveness
Peer interaction/play	Consistent nurturance
Democratic guidance	Democratic guidance

Desirable out-of-home environments for non-mobile infants include most of the characteristics of good home environments; the specially designed out-of-home environments for toddlers include many of the characteristics that are required to adapt the home to toddler's play needs. For example, opportunities that encourage exploratory/practice play, pretense, and social games are all essential in the group environment. There are additional ways that the group environment can encourage play, however. The group environment affords opportunities to explore and expand the repertoire of skills that may not be available in the smaller, more physically restricted home setting. The added attraction of other infants and toddlers enables even quite young children to learn about social interaction with peers and to develop the skills needed for social play.

Adults who plan group environments must clearly identify the priority needs of the children. When early childhood educators in one center were asked to identify the developmental needs of infants and of toddlers in group environments, they listed many of the same needs for infants and for toddlers, but ranked them differently (see Table 8-1; Bergen, Gaynard, & Torelli, 1985). Identification of priorities can clarify criteria for evaluating the environmental design. All designs should balance adult nurturance with child independence and provide safe and stimulating physical and social environments.

● Providing a playful, nurturing, and responsive environment

Many programs confine nonmobile infants to small rooms where they interact only with one adult; this arrangement is not necessarily the best one even for nonmobile infants, because it may lack sufficient play opportunities. Toddlers need more space for their size than children of any other age; they should not have to spend their entire day in one small room. If a setting has only small rooms available and the children are separated into narrow age-range groups, portions of the day can be planned in which children move, or are moved, from room to room. Every room should have play materials that are appropriate for children of each age range in the group setting.

Infants and toddlers need consistency of nurturing care, but that care does not have to be provided by one adult. Instead, consistent care can be provided by a team of adults; often children develop attachments to each adult, as they do to more than one adult relative. Social game playing—peek-a-boo, hide-and-find, language and pretend games, and other reciprocal routines—encourages attachment to caregivers.

Although some children are more responsive to social game playing than others, either because they come from homes where this play is common or because they have a social, playful orientation toward the world, it is important for all infants to have the opportunity to play on a one-to-one basis with several of their caregivers so they can learn how to modulate their levels of arousal and adapt to the turn-taking rules of reciprocal play interactions. At-risk, abused, and handicapped infants must not miss these chances to play, even though their initial responses may be limited.

An environment with excitement and playfulness is very important; caregivers should not become so caught up in caregiving or teaching roles that they forget that their interactions with infants should be fun. Adult-child social play is an essential aspect of the group environment.

● Providing a safe and autonomy-fostering environment

Besides providing nurturance and reciprocal social play, infants' programs also need to have interesting physical environments for object exploration and practice play, as well as opportunities to observe, to touch, and to manipulate. Both nonmobile and mobile infants need adult responsiveness to their instrumental (i.e., achievement-oriented) attention-getting attempts; that is, adults need to help infants reach a toy, open a fastener or door, climb in the hammock, or make space for blocks or cars. This kind of help enables infants to do it themselves the next time. Attention to making the environment safe so that infants do not need to have adults hovering over them constantly lets the children make the most of opportunities to explore and engage in trial-and-error and sensory play.

Independent opportunities for exploratory play should be allowed for every infant, including those children with orientations toward the social rather than the object world. Children whose limited mobility or other physical handicaps make independent play more difficult for caregivers to arrange should be in a play environment that is adapted to make some independent play possible.

Children of both sexes should have opportunities to engage in all types of play, with all types of materials. Girls should not be discouraged from rough-and-tumble play nor boys from nurturing play. Adults should limit suggestions that direct children's play participation into "boys' " and "girls' " play. Adults can assist young children in developing gender identity by basing their comments about gender distinctions on male/female physical sexual differences, not on irrelevant criteria such as hair length or clothes. By limiting their suggestions that direct children's play participation into "boys' " or "girls' " play, adults can widen the play opportunities for every child.

The optimal physical environment for mobile infants and toddlers should respond to three developmental polarities: (a) need for independence versus need for dependence; (b) growth of motor ability versus lack of motor competence; and (c) sense of being in control versus sense of being controlled (Smith & Jaworski, 1984). Personal care facilities, well-organized materials, and personal spaces to allow withdrawal from the stimulation of the larger environment should be accessible to children to meet independence/dependence needs. Safe walking surfaces; opportunities to run, jump, and climb safely and at a variety of levels of difficulty; hard surfaces for riding toys and soft surfaces for rolling or tumbling;

places to get into, under, on, and through; and materials to carry, manipulate, and combine address motor development/lack of competence needs. The environment should also be free of attractive nuisances (e.g., electrical cords that invite pulling). To meet control needs there can be predictable access to and choice of malleable materials, responsive toys, and social activities; sufficient numbers of materials and space to allow simultaneous solitary and parallel play; and large structures and objects to promote harmonious peer interactions.

According to Olds (1982a), standard preschool furniture and structures are not appropriate for toddlers because such furniture takes up the important space for movement in the room. She suggests, instead, air mattresses, water mattresses, foam- and air-filled wedges, mats, balance beams, and ladders, and risers to climb and crawl over. She stresses that this is even more important for children with physical limitations or other special needs.

A few of the many other ways to encourage motor play include availability of toys such as pop-beads, puzzles, and small blocks that can be manipulated and gathered, put in containers, carried around, and dumped; many-faceted climbing structures that can be safely used without intense supervision; balls of many sizes and materials; and even basketball hoops made from plastic laundry baskets.

Art materials at the toddler age are primarily used as sensory play materials. Toddlers do not care about making a product. Space for messy art activity such as sand and water play should be provided, preferably in a separate room or area out of sight of the other activity areas. Prone to herding, toddlers are likely to leave the paint table and run to the climber with paint-covered hands if they can see the excitement increasing on the climber and slide.

Because the development of pretense is so important during the toddler age period, environments should encourage pretend play with objects and with adults. Sets of realistic objects, including not only the typical housekeeping items but also hats, lunchboxes, briefcases, and tools should be provided. Puppets are especially interesting to toddlers and enhance their language play as well as their pretend play abilities. Parallel pretend play is the more common kind for toddlers; there should be enough objects such as dishes, cups, and dolls for a number of toddlers to cook and feed the baby at the same time.

Adults should facilitate this pretense by unobtrusive modeling, making verbal suggestions, and taking a role as "baby" or "fireman" at times. Caregivers' ability to foster pretend play is especially important for those children who come from homes where parents don't promote this kind of play.

Books, music, clay, and other materials that encourage representational play also can add play opportunities. Sometimes adults reserve books for times when they can be there to interact and be sure that the book is not torn. Toddlers use books as playthings and enjoy carrying them in their wagons, stopping to review the pictures, reciting the names of pictured objects, "reading" a particular story, or taking books to adults to have them read.

Although toddler social game playing is primarily with adults, adults can also encourage peer tag, turn taking, and parallel games by having materials and structures such as barrels, boxes, and wagons that children can take turns getting in and out of, balls, and ball game equipment (e.g., "basketball"). Adults can often facilitate a peer initiated game by entering in briefly as the routine breaks down. They also can initiate finger-play and parallel games like "Ring-Around-the-Rosy." Some children may enjoy these games for only short periods; adults should not attempt to engage the whole group in a game or to hold children at the game when their interest wanes.

● Meeting the needs of children from varied cultural backgrounds

The physical and social environment of the out-of-home setting also must take children's cultural differences into account. Little attention has been paid to this aspect when considering environmental design. For children who come from various ethnic or sociocultural backgrounds, the language, food, music, objects to be explored, and adult interaction styles may be very different from those in their home (Laosa, 1977). Unfortunately, often the adults in the group setting are not aware of these differences or do not value them. Yet some of these differences impinge upon these children's abilities to develop their play skills in the group setting.

A few of the contrasting values found in just one setting—one with Mexican-American children—were examined by O'Neill and Levy (1981). Mexican-American families value cooperation, politeness, closeness of family, respect for authority, and obedience; these values are in contrast to the values of the Anglo-American culture. Mexican-American children's play is affected by these values. For example, when an older child is playing with blocks and a younger sibling wants to participate in the block building, the older child allows the younger to enter the play even if it disrupts the older child's plans for building. Although the older child may not want the intrusion, he or she allows the family member to be included because family closeness is a prime value in this ethnic group. The play environment should be designed to permit children to express the values of their ethnic group.

One Model of a Play Environment for Infants and Toddlers

The authors of this chapter have participated in the design of the special environments for infants and toddlers at the Matthew Lowry Early Childhood Center, at Oakland University, Rochester, Michigan. The physical and social environments were planned to encourage the play of young children, within an educational approach built upon Piagetian theory. In an article describing their early research on toddler play, conducted at the center, Sponseller and Lowry (1974) stated that the two processes discussed by Piaget—children's interactions with the physical environment and their interactions with the social environment—can be influenced by educators through environmental design. Environmental design for young children should foster these interactions. An environment incorporating elements to promote these interactions through the medium of play was designed at the Lowry Center.

● The physical environment

A floor plan adapted from the floor plans of two programs at the Lowry center is shown in Figure 8–2. The plan includes one large room, which is divided into areas by a playpen/octopus structure in the center of the room. A separate sensorimotor activity room for "messing about," and a parent/family room are other program rooms in the building. In addition there are bathrooms, a kitchen, an office, and a sleeping room. The areas that are defined by the central structure in the main room are (a) a fine motor area; (b) home area; (c) book area; (d) table/eating area; (e) gross motor area 1—Mountain and Caves social/climbing equipment; (f) gross motor area 2—blocks, trucks, pull toys; and (g) gross motor area 3—flexible space that alternates equipment, such as mats, rocking boat, hammock, gym bars, basketball hoop, or has no equipment on some days.

Because observations indicate that mobile infants and toddlers tend to carry many objects to the center of rooms and leave them, and that they are easily distracted and prone to herding, the areas defined by the structure were designed to face out from the center of the room. Adult supervision is not hampered because the dividers are low enough for them to see over. Children have numerous small places to go that are physically separated; yet they have access to all of the areas. The lowest shelves in all cabinets are too high for toddlers to gain a foothold for climbing up to the next shelf. Children are allowed to climb into the lower shelf spaces.

The sensory activity room is tiled and has a drain in the floor. It is used for sensory exploration activities with small groups of children and is easily cleaned. The social/climbing equipment—Mountains and Caves—includes ladders, platforms, tunnels, slides, and three platform levels for play. Because all infants and toddlers do not feel sleepy at the same time, the sleeping room is not designed to hold all the children at once. Children sleep as it is necessary for them to sleep. With the exception of the office and parent/family room, the other rooms are accessible to the children. If many children need to nap or if a child is sick, the parent/family room can also be used.

The outdoor play area is designed to carry the play easily into the outdoors. It is accessible and has structures with features similar to those in the indoor setting, as well as equipment that is unique to the outdoors. The sandbox and climber/slide areas are roofed so that they can be used during less than ideal weather.

The design of the physical environment affects the way adults and children act. For children, the environment provides controlled freedom with many opportunities to explore its physical properties and to engage in social play.

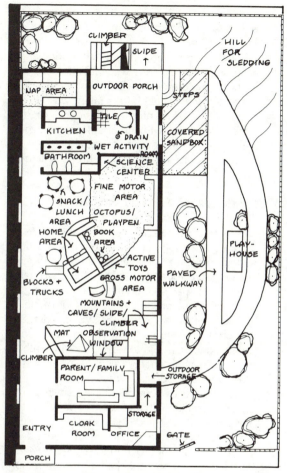

FIGURE 8–2 ● Prototype Infant/Toddler Environment

TABLE 8–2 ● Adult Roles Used Most With Infants and Toddlers in the Play Environment

Infants	Toddlers
Nurturer	Observer
Responder	Responder
Initiator	Preparer
Participator	Nurturer
Observer	Coach
Preparer	Participator
Coach	Initiator
Director	Director
Teacher	Teacher
Custodian	Custodian

children's needs, is comprised of a mix of these 10 roles:

1. The "laid back but vigilant observer," stepping in only when assistance is needed or enhancement of play seems warranted.
2. The "responder," showing sensitivity to children's cues, interest in children's activities, and warmth in meeting children's needs for attention.
3. The "preparer of the physical environment," planning activities and arranging materials so that children can pursue them with minimal adult direction.
4. The "initiator," planning, demonstrating, and directly encouraging children's play.
5. The "participator," engaging in role-play, games, and motor activity with children.
6. The "director," giving specific guidance about play safety rules or direct instruction about expected behaviors or routines.
7. The "coach," providing encouragement from the sidelines or specific help to learn a skill.
8. The "nurturer," attending to children's physical needs.
9. The "teacher," using the method of proleptic instruction, which allows the learner to set the learning conditions.
10. The "custodian," cleaning up, picking up, and putting away.

Table 8–2 shows which of these roles are used most with younger and older children in the play

● The social environment

Social interaction among children is high because the structures allow diverse parallel play, and the movable objects are varied, responsive, and accessible. Depending on the age range of children in the environment (i.e., whether young infants are included and how great the spread of the age range), the balance between social play and object-centered play varies.

Adults who work in infant-toddler centers must have a versatile repertoire of skills. The nature of adult interaction with the children, which varies with environment. With infants and younger toddlers, the roles most often taken are those of nurturer, responder, initiator, and participator. For older toddlers, roles of observer, responder, and preparer are the most common. All adults in infant and toddler environments must act as custodian at times.

Conclusion

Although all societies have recognized the importance of play in the lives of very young children, even the adults who have been most concerned about infant and toddler development have only recently become aware of the complexity of the play development process and the potential lifelong value of play experiences. Recent research evidence pointing out ways physical and social environmental factors influence play development and outlining stages of exploratory, pretense, and social game play is now providing adults who care for and teach young children with information to assist them in planning environments for play. This information can also help adults tune into the subtle and not-so-subtle messages they give that signal what play is or should be and make them recognize how social relationships, social conventions, scripts for gender and other social roles, and attitudes toward exploration of the physical object world are all influenced by play in infancy and toddlerhood. Their efforts to provide optimal play environments are of utmost importance because children's future development draws much of its direction from these early play experiences.

Questions for Discussion

1. How would you support and help a mother who was engaging in few playful interactions with her 6-month-old infant? A father with the same problem? What if their infant was 12 months old? 24 months old? A boy? A girl?
2. What individual and cultural differences might influence the kind of toddler social play observed in a group setting? In a home setting?

Environmental Design Problems

1. You have a position as a teacher of toddlers in a day-care setting that previously has had no toddler program. A meeting is set up to discuss with the director and board what you will need in terms of space requirements, equipment, and personnel for the toddler program. The center's initial plan is to include 25 children in the program with one aide, and to have two rooms, one with 15-month-old to 24-month-old toddlers and another with 24-month-old to 30-month-old toddlers. Describe what you would discuss as your priorities in environmental planning, what concerns you would raise, and what solutions you would propose in order to have a quality play environment.
2. An in-home infant program to meet the needs for play experiences for children from a minority and/or low income group (e.g., black, Mexican-American, rural poor, single parent) has been funded by a community agency. You have been asked to be the program designer. Describe how you would plan to enhance the play possibilities of these culturally diverse home environments and how you would implement the program. State what social/cultural factors you would consider in order to assure the program's success.

Suggestions for Further Reading

Bretherton, I. (Ed.) (1984). *Symbolic play: The development of social understanding.* New York: Academic Press. Presents studies of several researchers on symbolic play in very young children and discusses the implications of this research for understanding cognitive, social, and language development.

Gordon, I. (1970) *Baby learning through baby play.* New York: St. Martin's Press. Though written primarily for parents, it is valuable for caregivers in infant/toddler centers. Describes many ways play can be built into commonplace activity. Ideas are also helpful for encouraging play with handicapped children.

Smith, K. E., & Jaworski, A. P. (1984). Physical environments for toddlers in group care. *Child Care Quarterly, 13*(1), 52–61. Describes the elements necessary for the design of a toddler environment.

Sutton-Smith, B., & Sutton-Smith, S. (1974). *How to play with your children (and when not to).* New York: Hawthorn/Dutton. Gives all adults, not only parents, suggestions for playing with infants as well as with older children. Encourages adults also to respect children's time and interests.

Vandell, D. L., & Mueller, E. C. (1980). Peer play and friendships during the first two years. In H. C. Foote, A. J. Chapman, & J. R. Smith (Eds.), *Friendship and social relations in children* (pp. 181–208). London: Wiley. Gives an overview of the ways infant and toddler play begin and the factors influencing early social development.

Reality and Fantasy in Make-Believe Play

INGE BRETHERTON

"I a daddy," says a 2-year-old to his older sibling. Admittedly, the 2-year-old's understanding of the father role is rudimentary, but it is nonetheless astonishing that a toddler can even entertain the idea of being a daddy. By adopting a variety of roles and acting out role-appropriate actions with a variety of realistic or imaginary props, young children create alternative realities through play. Three important abilities are involved: the ability to step in and out of multiple roles or perspectives, the ability to playfully transform reality or engage in counterfactual thinking, and the ability to play with the play frame itself. Early precursors of these abilities emerge in babyhood, but they come truly into their own during the preschool years.

In order to reenact playful transformations of reality with other children a number of organizational skills are required. Players must make sure that their play actions are taken as nonliteral, but much more is involved than merely conveying the message "This is play" (Bateson, 1956). Once children have decided to enter the play frame, they have to become co-writers, co-directors, co-actors, and vicarious actors all rolled into one, without getting confused about which of these roles they or a co-player are momentarily adopting. Children must organize the theme, locale, role distribution, and props as well as actually enact the agreed upon story. To do so successfully, they must be able to switch roles rapidly, because the creation of make-believe plots proceeds on an invent-as-you-go principle: Negotiations about the plot alternate with acting it out. As Holly Giffin (1984) has pointed out, it is often not at all obvious that plot-planning is going on. A player who explains that he is dishing out "barbecue" to co-players sitting at the "picnic table" is sharing information about plot construction as well as acting out the role of father. At a real world picnic, it would usually not be necessary to tell family members what was being served. Director-actor role switching is more obvious when one co-player prompts another about what to say next by dropping the acting voice and whispering: "You don't say it like that, you say . . ." In addition to switching back and forth from directing to acting, players must also coordinate their enactment of complementary character roles (playing the mommy role has to be integrated with the co-player's rendering of the daddy role). Sometimes a vicarious role is added as well (talking for the "baby"). Kate Garvey (1977a) writes about a 39-month-old girl who plays the role of mother to her baby doll, the role of baby for the doll, and the role of wife to her 33-month-old husband. To cap it all, she prompts husband on how to act the father role. Because the plots tend to be quite simple, the complex conceptual juggling of roles in make-believe play is often hardly noticed by adult onlookers.

A second development concerns transformations of everyday reality. Infants' initial pretense consists of reenacting real world event schemas (e.g., drinking from cups, sleeping on pillows) outside the normal context. Later playful and sometimes fantastic transformations of reality become more and more prominent. First, young children play with who they are, taking on the feelings, mannerisms, behaviors, and appearance of another person or of an animal. In performing the parent role, a child can give the orders he or she normally has to obey. By reenacting scary events or turning them around, a child can playfully master negative feelings—becoming the hero instead of the victim. In addition to transformations of social and emotional reality, a child can alter the natural laws of time, space, and causality. If some part of the plot is not very interesting and takes too long, a child can magically contract time and space by saying "drive, drive, drive," and speed up arrival at the desired destination. If a child doesn't want to spend hours at the stove, because serving is more interesting, he can say "cooky, cooky, cooky" and the meal is done. By telling other players "You can't see me," a child can make herself or himself invisible, and in dramatically jumping off a one-foot tree stump to simulate space flight, a child can defy the laws of gravity. Likewise, players who have been shot can miraculously be brought back to life by fiat or with "special medicine," undoing the laws of causality. All this is possible because children have built up shared understandings about the real world that all participants can jointly draw on and then jointly agree to transform.

Third, preschoolers begin to play with the play frame itself. They interweave, blur, and confuse the distinction between what is play and what is reality—the distinction between map and territory (Bateson, 1955). Metacommunication serves to inform participants whether someone is performing within the acting frame, the directing frame, or the real world frame. But astonishingly, almost as soon as the map-territory distinction is understood and skillfully used, children begin to toy with it. A little boy, holding up a small matchbox car to mother, tells her that it's burning up, that it's a "real fire." He uses the world "real" to intensify the illusion of pretense. Another way in which map and territory are intertwined is by incorporating real world events into the ongoing play story: a child accidentally falls over and instead of dealing with the mishap as an event outside the play frame, the players treat it as an accident within the story, requiring ambulance and hospitalization (Wolf & Pusch, 1985). Similarly, antagonisms that may reflect real world feelings between co-players are sometimes surreptitiously incorporated into the plot. One child gleefully taunts another by saying, "I stole your cake," to which the other retorts pointedly, "It's not a cake anymore." I have observed such undercover sparring between a parent and child, too. Mother, returning into the playroom after a brief absence, observes her 4-year-old daughter turning the steering wheel of a toy dashboard and remarks, "Oh, you're a driver." Daughter, who had been angry at mother's departure, retorts haughtily, "I'm not a driver, I'm a queen," to which mother in turn replies offhandedly and contemptuously, "Queens don't drive; they have a chauffeur." Blurring of map and territory also occurs when roles are allotted to players. Popular children manage to obtain the desirable roles of mommy, daddy, or doctor, while unpopular children may have to content themselves playing the pets (Schwartzman, 1978).

Steiner (1975), a well-known linguist, wrote that "ours is the ability to gainsay and unsay the world, to image and speak it otherwise" (p. 218). Children use this ability in joint play with others, or alone with small figures; they do it just for fun, to come to terms with and master difficult, anxiety-provoking emotional events, and sometimes to get their own back at someone. But they also use it to make serious plans, consider alternative courses of action, and to communicate about these with others. Because the same propensities are used literally and nonliterally, there has been a tendency to regard pretend play as practice or pre-exercise of serious cognitive and social functions, rather than something of interest and value in its own right. This leads, as Brian Sutton-Smith (1984) has pointed out, to a sanitized view of make-believe play. I would like to suggest here that if we must look at the future implications of pretend play in childhood, it may be more profitable to think of it as the hallmark of an emerging artistic and literary ability. To do so does justice to the expressive spirit of make-believe without trying to turn it into something it is not. Such an approach could also provide the impetus for studying the developing artistic function in young children, an important topic about which we are far too ignorant.

CHAPTER NINE

Designing Play Environments for Preschool and Kindergarten Children

PATRICIA RAMSEY ● REBECCA REID

Ever since Froebel (1887) advocated a play curriculum in the "children's garden," the value of a play environment in early childhood has been recognized. Because play is so much a part of the life of children from 3 to 6, it serves many purposes as a medium for learning. During the past 20 years, however, a strange thing has happened to the early childhood play curriculum. Educators and policy makers have gradually pushed play out of the kindergarten and even, in some cases, out of the preschool.

When education is interpreted as a specified set of academic basic skills, the role of play as a medium for learning is truncated and distorted. While most early childhood programs still include some play, free and guided playtime has often been turned into directed play, work disguised as play, and work. This trend has been especially true in the kindergarten.

This chapter includes both preschool and kindergarten in order to emphasize that the kindergarten learning environment should be more similar to settings designed for other preoperational children than to elementary classrooms designed for concrete op-

erational children. The playful means of academic learning, discussed in chapter 10, also are relevant for kindergarten children who are nearing concrete operations.

First, examples of the play development of the preschool and kindergarten child are given. Then research on physical properties of the play environment, the roles of adults in facilitating play, and the effects of peers on play development is reviewed. Guidelines for designing play environments appropriate for preschool and kindergarten children are described. The chapter concludes with a model of a specific environment.

Play Development of Preschool and Kindergarten Children

According to Piaget, children of 3 to 6 are in a transitional period between the sensorimotor stage of development and the concrete operational stage of thought. During this preoperational stage, children increase their abilities to think representationally, extending the power and range of thought beyond the immediate and concrete perceptual stimuli of their environment. While sensorimotor children are limited to perceiving and manipulating objects at hand, preoperational children are able to imbue objects with symbolic meaning and thus to expand their experiences beyond manipulating and exploring physical properties. For example, sensorimotor children might explore many ways to turn a mounted steering wheel. Preoperational children first explore its physical attributes, but then expand the range of play to pretend that they are driving a spaceship, a motorboat, or a bus. This latter play may be further elaborated by incorporating other players, such as "passengers" and "ticket collectors."

Rapid growth of language accompanies this expansion of representational thought. Preschool children increase their vocabulary at a rate of nine words a day (Carey, 1977). This extraordinary rate of development leads children to experience continuously the excitement of their power to communicate. Playing with language and ways of communicating is a prominent feature of their play.

The enhanced development has psychosocial implications as well. Erikson (1963) has described this period as the "initiative versus guilt" crisis. As children become more aware of their independence, power, and efficacy, they want to experiment and have an impact on their environment; they want to make things happen and to be heard. "I am what I can imagine myself to be" is the way that Erikson (1968) has characterized the child's sense of self at this age. At the same time, the pull toward independence and power is countered by a need to be reassured of the constancy of their parents' and other caregivers' nurturance and love. Play is a means for children to safely express these strivings for independence and power.

During the preschool and kindergarten period, children's social interactions are also rapidly developing. They are shifting their focus from adults to peers. The shift from solitary and parallel play to interactive social engagement is striking during the years from 3 to 6. As children try new ways to initiate and maintain social encounters, they use play to create situations in which they can experiment with different social roles and behaviors. Shared fantasy also provides the social "glue" that enables children to maintain interactions. Often these shared fantasies follow fairly prescribed scripts in which children learn to accommodate to the perceptions and expectations of others. This social accommodation is a prelude to the ability to play competitive games with rules during the elementary school years.

Specific developmental trends in preschool and kindergarten children's play reflect the major shifts that have been described above. Some of these areas of play are skill-building (practice/constructive) play, inventive play involving pretense and language, sociodramatic play, and games with rules. Children at these ages also experience play as pure enjoyment.

● **Practice/constructive (skill-building) play**

Preschool and kindergarten children engage in a great deal of skill-building play. As their fine and gross motor skills increase, they constantly try to meet new physical challenges, as seen in the following vignette:

J. (3 years, 9 months) carefully stacks the cylinders one on top of the other. His tower is five cylinders high. He slowly places the next cylinder; the tower wobbles slightly; he is intently watching it. He gently places the sixth cylinder on top and gradually releases his hold on the cylinder. The tower remains upright; he smiles broadly. He picks up the next cylinder and more boldly puts it on top of the tower. The tower sways; J. puts his hand in front of his mouth and stares at the tower. It falls with a crash. J. looks distressed, hops slightly, and then grins broadly and claps his hands.

In this observation, J. is challenging himself to build a higher tower. His variations between tentativeness and boldness reflect Erikson's "initiative versus guilt" distinction. He wants to succeed yet is apprehensive. His reaction to the crash, showing first some distress and anxiety and then enjoyment of the noise and impact, also illustrates how children vacillate between these two polarities.

This observation also indicates the increased physical control that children have acquired by this age. Muscular control and the desire to master physical challenges are seen in many different activities such as riding a tricycle, learning to pump on the swing, climbing higher on the school jungle gym, cutting shapes carefully, learning to master glue in construction projects, and building increasingly intricate forms with interlocking table blocks. Kindergarten and older preschool children also exhibit these increased motor skills in their complex block constructions, precise representational drawings, spontaneous production of written letters and numbers, and elaborate sculptures.

● Inventive play with pretense and language

As children are increasingly able to think in terms of mental representations, they think in terms of possibilities instead of being bound by what exists. These new capabilities enable them to find new solutions and experiment with materials in ways that often defy adult constraints. The following observation illustrates this process:

P. (4 years, 6 months) and H. (4 years, 5 months) are "putting the teddy bears to bed" in the block corner. They have built a "crib" using several different kinds of blocks to form a standing railing edge. They are now confronting the problem of how to "cover" the bears. They experiment with several kinds of blocks, including squares and rectangles. After each attempt they discuss the merits of the design and express concern that they can't get the "covers to lie down." Finally they use thinner blocks and, by pressing them down hard on the bears, make the covers stay down.

These two children have an idea of the effect that they want to create and are experimenting with ways of trying to achieve it. They are not simply practicing skills, but are trying to find ways to replicate the mental images they have. This endeavor leads them to focus on the attributes of blocks and the contours of bears and the ways that these two elements interact. Because the children have an idea of the goal they want to accomplish, they keep inventing new combinations to achieve it.

Children's use of language, too, reflects the skill building and inventive aspects of play. They assiduously practice existing language skills, repeating stories, songs, and poems. As any parent or teacher knows, children's desire for multiple repetitions is impervious to adult requests to read or sing something new. At the same time, children are remarkably inventive in their use of language. As they achieve clarity of concepts, they begin to enjoy the incongruities of "topsy-turvy" statements, such as claiming that the dog says "meow" (Chukovsky, 1963). They also like to play with sound and to invent new words (Cazden, 1976).

S. (4 years, 3 months) to her teacher Linda who is giving her an occasional push on the swing, "Linda, Ginda . . . Dinda . . . Sinda . . . Kinda . . . Minda . . . Binda . . . Hey I call you Binda!" Peals of laughter.

Here the child is demonstrating her knowledge of the "right" word and the fact that it has a unique sound by varying the sounds. As often happens with this process, the child hit upon one vocal combination, "Binda," that struck her as particularly funny. Why "Binda" was funnier than "Dinda" or any of the other combinations was not apparent to the observing adult. It is likely that this word reminded the child of something that was particularly incongruous or suggestive of forbidden words. Finding humor in incongruity is a sign both of mental development and the ability to engage in "playful play" (McGhee, 1984).

● Symbolic/pretense and sociodramatic play

Pretense is the most salient aspect of preschool and kindergarten play. In this type of play children feel the power of representational thought and play out Erikson's characterization of "I am what I can imagine myself to be." During these years pretense becomes increasingly complex and imaginative. Young preschoolers are more bound in their fantasies to the actual physical properties of the objects at hand (Field, DeStefano, & Koewler, 1982). For 2- and 3-year-olds, symbolic play is usually stimulated by objects that realistically portray something of interest, such as a telephone or a truck. As children's symbolic thought develops, they are able to imbue less realistic objects with fantastic properties or even to use imaginary objects. A block can serve as a telephone or a gesture can convey answering an imaginary phone.

Sociodramatic play becomes elaborate as children broaden their awareness of social roles. Three-year-old children frequently use equipment in the housekeeping corner stereotypically—fixing food, feeding babies, and putting dolls to bed. Contrasted with this is the following observation of a group of 4-year-old boys in the housekeeping area:

Three boys (mean age 4 years, 5 months) are dressed in skirts and dresses and much costume jewelry. Dolls' underpants have been forced on to their heads, giving each of them a set of ear-like protrusions. They are vigorously stirring up food and slapping utensils on to the table. As they talk, it becomes apparent that they are "robbers" and that, while engaged in these do-mestic chores, they are busily planning their next "robbery." As they settle down to eat, the milk bottles are referred to as "beer," which they swill down with gusto and then bang the bottles down on the table.

Here the children have gone far beyond simply using the housekeeping toys and clothing in imitative fashion. Rather, they have invented a whole new script that suggests knowledge not only of domestic chores, but also of male role models and the larger social environment that includes events such as robberies. This particular theme also offers a way for the boys to be in the housekeeping area and yet play at male roles.

Sociodramatic play reflects children's increasing understanding of their cultural milieu. Four- to six-year-olds often enact characters that they have seen on television: sometimes these enactments are a blend of real life and media events, as in the follow-ing:

T. (4 years, 7 months), who comes from a home split by domestic violence and R. (3 years, 8 months) are sitting together in the library corner wearing their usual dress-up garb. As the two girls whisper intently to one another, a teacher walks by. R. looks up and announces wide-eyed, "T.'s boyfriend has a gun and he's going to shoot me!"

A. (4 years, 10 months) became She-Ra, He-man's sister, for about six months. Whenever she was called by her own name, she restated that she was She-Ra, not A. When the teacher asked her about She-Ra, A. would describe her strength and prowess. The year before, A. was Wonder Woman, holding to that identity with a similar degree of intensity.

Teachers often express concern about the domi-nance of superhero play in preschool and kinder-garten classrooms. What is the appeal of these fantastic and often aggressive figures? Children at this age are attracted to such characters for several rea-sons. First, as children struggle with issues related to power and independence, pretending to be a magi-cally powerful, invulnerable superhero is a way of reassuring oneself that one can control self as well as have an impact on others. Superhero play helps children feel self-confident and gives them access to power and prestige. Second, as children experience feelings of guilt over their newfound independence and power, and deal with the contradictions in be-havioral expectations, the unambiguous good of the superheroes and the clear evil of the antiheroes are reassuring (Kostelnik, 1983).

Because children are representing roles and events they have seen, the themes and specific en-actments of pretense differ across cultures. The psy-chological processes underlying the play are similar; the specific scenes and roles differ. Accounts of so-ciodramatic play in other countries demonstrate this (e.g., Fortes, 1976; Leacock, 1976). In the United States, regional, economic, and ethnic differences also are reflected in symbolic and constructive play, as the following example illustrates:

J. (4 years, 10 months), who lives on a dairy farm, headed for the blocks during the morning play period. He carefully constructed a barn, making sure to include the stalls for the cows. He than stacked two large cylinder blocks on top of each other and said, "That's the silo."

In a classroom of children from different cultural and class backgrounds, teachers should be aware that some of the children may not be able to un-derstand one anothers' play themes. The lack of shared fantasy themes has been cited as a contribut-ing factor in the persistence of ethnic cleavage among children (Doyle, 1976).

Sociodramatic play also provides ways for chil-dren to experiment with language, not simply in the formation of new words, but also with enactment of how people in varied roles use language. They can play the authoritative parent or teacher, the gruff truck driver, and the cooing baby. They experiment with voice tones, use of words, and communicative relationships.

Sociodramatic play also provides a safe environ-ment for initiating and maintaining social interactions.

Assigning roles (e.g., "You be the brother, OK") defines the membership of a particular social interaction. Offering to play a part (e.g., "I'll be the sister") is one way of entering groups. The use of scripts (e.g., "No, you say, 'It's time to go to bed' ") enables children to sustain the interaction by maintaining common ground rules and shared expectations. As Garvey (1974) says, social play is a "state of engagement in which the successive nonliteral behaviors of one partner are contingent on the nonliteral behaviors of the other partner" (p.. 174). These patterns help children mutually develop themes, as in the following exchange (Garvey, 1974, p. 174):

X: Dinner is ready. What do you want for dinner?

Y: Well . . .

X: Hot beef?

Y: OK, hot beef.

X: Coffee, too?

Y: No, I'm the little boy. I'll have some milk.

X: OK, you can eat now.

Y: (*Moves closer to stove to begin eating.*)

X: Kid, we're going to get some milk from the store. Come on in the dunebuggy.

Y: OK, I'm in the dunebuggy.

Here the two children accommodated to each other's introduction of themes or recognition of certain constraints (Y's not being able to drink coffee). Children do not always accommodate to one another's ideas so easily: there is often a point where the partners disagree. Sometimes the play ends if the children fail to find an acceptable compromise. However, because the scripts and rules are being generated by the players themselves during the course of the enactment, children often find ways of adjusting the story line to fit one anothers' needs. The following illustration shows how children can take the role of others and use this experience to broaden their knowledge of the social world (K.H. Rubin, 1980, pp. 75–76).

(*Two children, same sex, were playing mother and father.*)

Father: So long. I'll see ya later. It's time to go to work.

Mother: Hey! Wait for me! I gotta go to work too!

Father: Hey, my mom don't work . . . you stay here!

Mother: Well my mom works . . . lotsa womens work ya know. My mom is a perfessor at the unibersity [sic].

Father: OK, then just hurry so we won't be late. Are you sure you wanna work?

● **Games with rules**

Games with rules are more dominant in the elementary years because during preschool years adhering to rigid rules set by an outsider is difficult. Kindergartners are able to decenter sufficiently so that simple rule games can be a major source of pleasure. However, children at these ages look at rules as fluid, flexible, and easily adapted to one's immediate needs, as these examples show:

> Three boys (mean age 4 years, 6 months) are playing the "snow game," which consists of throwing snow at one another. There is a lot of activity, hilarity, and yelling. J. suddenly stops and says "We need a rule about snow in people's faces." The three stop for a minute and quickly decide that they cannot throw snow in one anothers' faces. The play then resumes with the same enthusiastic spirit.

> A group of five children (mean age 4 years, 11 months) began a spontaneous version of the game, "Are you ready, Wolf?," during outdoor play. (The game had been previously introduced by the teacher. In the original game, the wolf is asked by the others if he or she is ready. The wolf uses stall tactics such as "No, I'm brushing my teeth." Eventually, the wolf cries "Yes!" and tries to catch the others. Whoever is caught first becomes the new wolf.) In the children's spontaneous game, the wolf role was the most popular one so they decided that there could be more than one wolf. Then everyone became wolves and there was no one to chase. Faced with that problem, the children asked the teachers to be the ones who were chased. This solved the problem, and the game continued.

While children can invent rules, they have more trouble following set rules of games. Trying to get preschoolers to adhere to the rules of even simple games usually generates frustration and often leads to abandonment of the effort. They seem to do better "playing *at* games" (K.H. Rubin, 1980, p. 79) than actually following the rules of a particular game. For instance, they may go through the motions of baseball, but will allow one another many more than three strikes. They create a nonliteral derivative of the game (K.H. Rubin, 1980).

Because they have trouble adhering to the rules and seeing the implications of the rules for winning or losing, games in which children play parallel or complementary roles (e.g., "The farmer in the Dell") are more suitable than games with competitive roles in which children lose or have to be "out" (Kamii & DeVries, 1980).

Kindergarten children are more aware of rules of games than their preschool peers but do not always understand the point of the rules. They may follow the form of the rules, but not necessarily in a meaningful way, as the following joke-telling session illustrates:

(*Four children—mean age 5 years, 6 months—are sitting at snack.*)

A: Why does the chicken cross the road?

(*Pause—there is no response from others, although they look at A with interest.*)

A: (*shrieks*) To get to the other side!!

(*All four laugh with vigor; it is not clear whether they understand the joke, but they do understand that it is appropriate to laugh.*)

L: Why does the—ummm—the chair—ummm—cross the—ummm (*looking around the room*) the blocks?

(*Another pause—no response, but the others look expectant.*)

L: Ummm—to be a baby!

(*All of the children laugh gleefully.*)

The interaction continues as each child takes a turn "telling a joke" with words and phrases substituted into the format randomly rather than meaningfully, and with a responsive chorus of laughter.

Cooperative games, in which children do not have to use strategies that require outwitting or beating one another are more developmentally appropriate for these ages as well as more congruent with the social goals of most early childhood classrooms. Playing appropriate games can serve some important purposes of cognitive development during these years, because they give children practice in perspective taking and coordination of actions with others (Kamii & DeVries, 1980).

● **Pleasurable aspects of play**

Finally, it is important to consider play as a pleasurable activity for preschool and kindergarten children. In a sense play is an adverb rather than a noun or verb because almost any activity can be done "playfully." Play is often distinguished by the en-

joyment it generates. While the sources of enjoyment differ across ages and cultures, play is often accompanied by laughter, smiles, and a relaxed manner that suggests a sense of well-being and pleasure (Damon, 1983). Like their sensorimotor peers, preoperational children derive pleasure from physical and perceptual sensations and motion. They also enjoy both physical and verbal incongruities and actions that come close to "being bad." They gain pleasure from social exchange, even if it is not directed toward a particular goal. The contagion of "4- or 5-year-old silliness" is a good example of this enjoyment:

(*Three children—mean age 4 years, 7 months—are putting away pattern blocks by dumping them into a large container.*)

A: (*Picks up two pointed blocks, puts them in his ears*) I can't hear you, I've got points in my ears! (*Then he throws the blocks in the container.*)

B: (*Does and says the same thing.*)

C: (*Also copies the action and words, but his voice is louder.*)

(*All three repeat this action sequence in turn, with each one saying it louder and throwing the blocks more vigorously. All are smiling and laughing. After a second round the exchange continues.*)

A: (*yelling*) I can't hear you, I've got poop in my ears!

(*All three squeal with laughter; the teacher comes over to quiet them down.*)

For preoperational children, play provides the zone of proximal, or most appropriate, development (Vygotsky, 1967), in which they can practice their physical, linguistic, representational, and social skills. But more than simply practicing their skills, children celebrate their newfound mastery by creating imaginary environments, powerful roles, and social and physical incongruities.

Characteristics of the Physical Environment

Researchers were interested in the relationship between young children and their environments as a way to assess the quality of their play as early as the 1920s (Bott, 1928; Bridges, 1927; Farwell, 1925). Some of these early studies have become classics upon which much current practice and research are based (Johnson, 1935; Lewin, 1931; Parten, 1932; Sears, 1947). Historically, interest in a quality learning environment has followed the development of ecological psychology. Ecological psychologists suggest that the type and arrangements of content in an environment dictate how people will behave in that environment (Barker & Wright, 1955). Interactionist theorists tell us that certain properties attract children (Lewin, 1931) and that by solving the "problem of the match" (Hunt, 1961), we can provide environments that are challenging and gratifying to learners. Behaviorists have emphasized the importance of reinforcers to shape desired behaviors (Bijou, 1964). These theories have been particularly strong influences on environmental research and design.

Early childhood program designers have long focused on preparing environments that meet the needs of children. Montessori (1914/1965) developed a "prepared environment" after observing the children she planned to serve. Environments designed in the 1960s were planned to meet the needs of economically disadvantaged children, and research has demonstrated the long-term benefits of a number of these environmental designs (Lazar, Darlington, Murray, Royce, & Snipper, 1982).

Of great interest to both practitioners and researchers are the parameters of successful learning environments. As a result, much research has focused on how the physical environment affects children's play. Three general categories have been examined (Phyfe-Perkins, 1980): (a) fixed features and semi-fixed features, such as placement of doors, windows, walls, built-in cabinets, and other structures; (b) features of movable objects such as availability, amount, type, variety, complexity, and arrangement of equipment; and (c) ecological factors such as program structure, group size, and activity types.

● **Fixed and semi-fixed features**

The arrangement of these features sends a message to children as to how to behave in a given space (Proshansky & Wolfe, 1975). Researchers who have studied space organization have described some of these messages, as reflected in children's behavior:

1. Separate areas with clear boundaries enhance the quality of children's play.

Pollowy (1974) indicates that when activity areas are well-defined, child-equipment interactions increase. Semi-fixed features can be arranged to channel traffic around areas so that disruptions will be minimized yet children can see their choices (Kritchevsky, Prescott, & Walling, 1977; Osmon, 1971). Children interact more with peers and adults and spend more time in conversations and groups when carpeting and screens separate play areas (Neill, 1982). Reduction of impact noise also increases staff-initiated conversation with children.

In classrooms, the provision of closed spaces separated from open areas increases growth-producing behaviors (Fitt, 1974; Sheehan & Day, 1974). Environments with several small rooms or partitions to separate work/play areas cut down on noise levels and visual distractions. Closed spaces that provide privacy for one child or for small groups of children increase task involvement and educational achievement (Zifferblatt, 1972). A higher frequency of interactive play occurs in classrooms with partitions as compared to open spaces (Field, 1980).

Arrangement of play units affects play: When clear pathways and adequate empty spaces are not obvious to children, they are more likely to be injured or to disrupt other children's play (Kritchevsky, et al., 1977). Kritchevsky et al. indicate that the amount of uncovered surface should range from one-third to one-half of the play area. Prescott, Jones, and Kritchevsky (1972) found that quality of outdoor play space affects teachers' behavior as well as children's. High quality (i.e., uncrowded, fewer than 10 in a group, clear pathways, many play choices) space was associated with sensitive, friendly, and involved teachers and low quality (i.e., crowded, cluttered, more than 10 in a group, few play choices) space was associated with neutral, insensitive, or restrictive teachers.

Both children's and adults' responses to social cues are inhibited in environments with high noise levels (Cohen & Lezak, 1977; Weinstein & Weinstein, 1978). This inhibition may affect children's social interaction quality, because they tend to maintain focus on the activity they are engaged in and to have a slower pace when auditory distractions are present. When the separated areas and boundaries were arranged to prevent noisier activities from disrupting quieter ones, a decrease in children's activity level and an increase in cooperative behavior were observed by Sheehan and Day (1974). Prescott (1978) evaluated the softness and privacy of home and center settings and found that private places in centers were associated with softness and homelike atmosphere.

2. Most studies of crowding indicate that spatial or social crowding has negative effects on children, especially when space ratios are below 25 square feet per child.

Preiser (1972) observed that children in crowded conditions engaged in more on-looking, standing, and generally passive behavior with differentiation of activity areas blurred as spatial density increased. A decrease in aggressive play with increased social (rather than spatial) crowding was observed by Peck and Goldman (1978). This is in contrast to the decrease in rough-and-tumble play found by Smith and Connolly (1976) in high spatial density conditions. According to Smith and Connolly (1972), aggression increases under crowded conditions if there is no corresponding increase in the quality of available materials. However, Loo (1976) reports that crowding results in more frequent interruptions of activities, but less aggression. The mixed results on aggression may be explained by a study by Shapiro (1975) who reports a U-shaped threshold effect. When space per child is between 30 and 50 square feet, uninvolved behavior remains low (15% of all behavior); when the ratio is either below 30 square feet or above 50 square feet, uninvolved behavior increases (26% when space per child is below 30 square feet; 20% when space per child is above 50 square feet).

In a study of the effects of spacing of children for small group activities, Krantz and Risley (1972) found that when children sat at least two feet apart on the floor or were seated evenly around a table, as opposed to being crowded on a blanket on the floor, attentive behavior increased and disruptive behavior decreased. Pollowy (1974) notes that when floor space was increased in a preschool classroom, children showed more initiative in choosing activities on their own and increased their use of space, because they spent less time at table activities.

Both spatial density (i.e., decreasing the space available to a constant group size) and social density (i.e., an increase in the number of children rather than a decrease in space) also affect children's play. McGrew (1970) found that running behavior decreased with an increase in spatial density regardless of group size. However, social density did not affect running behavior. A decrease in social density moderated children's social interactions, resulting in more solitary behavior and fewer acts of aggression. Peck and Goldman (1978) report that an increase in social density significantly increases dramatic play for some children and on-looker behavior for others. The on-looking behavior may be stimulated by the more interesting social interactions that can be observed.

Although study results are difficult to compare because of methodological differences, they point to the possibility that there is an "optimal spatial density level." More data are needed before Loo's (1972) view that "crowdedness over a long time span may retard the development of more mature social behavior in children" (p. 379–80) can be supported. Few of these studies have directly focused on specific play behaviors; thus, the effect of crowding on higher play levels is as yet unclear.

● **Movable objects**

Researchers who have looked at movable objects have focused much of their interest on variety and complexity of toys and other play materials.

1. The types of movable objects provided in the environment strongly affect the types of play in which children engage.

Early research on the degree of structure in play materials suggested that raw materials, such as sand or clay, which are open-ended in their usage, have a higher appeal to children and are used in a greater variety of ways than are highly structured or mechanical toys that can be used in only one way (Bott, 1928; Van Alstyne, 1932).

More recent studies have supported these findings; certain kinds of materials are associated with specific types and levels of play. Rubin (1977) reports that nonsocial play occurs more than social play during painting, crayoning, Play Dough, sand, water, and puzzle activities. Functional play is observed with Play Dough, sand, and water; constructive play is more evident in painting, crayoning, and puzzle play. The greatest number of social interactions occur during housekeeping, vehicle play, reading, and number activities. Availability of art materials, sand, water, and puzzles may inhibit group and dramatic play (Rubin & Seibel, 1979). Rubin and Seibel recommend that a well-stocked dress-up corner is one of the best ways to promote social skill development, and a good selection of puzzles and blocks can promote construction and problem-solving play.

Rogers (1985) found that more group play was observed when children played with large, hollow blocks and more parallel and solitary play were associated with unit blocks. Children spent more time playing with hollow blocks and showed more frequent, positive social behaviors when using the hollow blocks.

Brenner (1976) reports that pretense is most highly correlated with block and truck areas and with the housekeeping corner. He found that two-thirds of all make-believe play occurred in those two areas. Vandenberg (1981a) reports social play to be more likely in a gross motor room than in a fine motor room, where solitary and parallel play predominate. Smith and Connolly (1972) and Smith (1974) state that the availability of larger, stationary structures increases verbal, physical, and cooperative play while the availability of movable toys increases only object manipulation and adult watching.

Early childhood educators have mixed feelings about the use of microcomputers in the classroom (e.g., Bowman, 1983; Colker, 1983), and the proliferation of this technology has raised questions about its effects on children's play choices (e.g., Fein, 1985a; Johnson, 1985; Klinzing, 1985; Lipinski, Nida, Shade, & Watson, 1984; Nieboer, 1984; Piestrup, 1981). These studies indicate that when the microcomputer is put into the setting as a free-play choice, it may disrupt the flow of activity initially but it does not make major changes in children's play patterns. For example, Fein (1985a) found that at first children were interested in mastering the commands, but then moved into an assimilation (i.e., playful) mode. She describes pretend scenarios of children using the computer that "resemble those occurring in the block corner or on the playground" (p. 50).

Most children choose to use the computer at least once (Nieboer, 1984); older children choose to play with the computer more often than younger children (Johnson, 1985). Most studies of preschool-age children show that both girls and boys select the computers with about equal frequency (Johnson, 1985; Lipinski et al., 1984). It is not used in isolation from other children; rather, children enjoy

sharing their computer experiences with peers (Swigger, Campbell, & Swigger, 1983).

Researchers who have used computer programs to teach skills (e.g., Monahan & Monahan, 1983; Piestrup, 1981) indicate that preschool children can learn reading, visual discrimination, classification, and language skills through this approach. However, many researchers caution against "drill and practice" approaches (Swigger et al., 1983). Kee (1985) reports that computers are usually used as free-play "toys" at home.

2. The number and accessibility of play materials affect the quality of play.

Gramza (1976) provided a heavy rope to children in a gross motor play area under two conditions: attached to a climbing trestle or unattached and freely accessible. The children preferred the unattached rope and the play behavior observed was more complex under that condition. Placing the climbing apparatus in the middle of the room rather than in a corner made it more accessible; children used it more and engaged more in interactive play (Witt & Gramza, 1969).

Using Kritchevsky et al.'s (1977) recommendation that there should be 2.5 play spaces (i.e., activities) per child, Getz and Berndt (1982) found increases in child participation and decreases in aggression when play spaces were increased from 1.9 to 2.9 per child. When Doke and Risley (1972) reduced the number of playthings from 24 per child to 1 per child, participation in play dropped by half. As children were limited to one play area rather than having access to several play areas, level of participation also dropped off significantly. Their recommendation is that when program materials are limited it is better to have play options for children in several areas. Smith and Connolly (1972, 1976) observed that thumb sucking, as well as levels of aggression, increases when equipment is severely limited. Johnson (1935) found a similar result with reduced outdoor play material; teasing, quarreling, and crying increased. The children also were less active.

Some researchers have found a preference among children for complex structures rather than simple ones (Gramza, Corush, & Ellis, 1972; Peck & Goldman, 1978). A more complex indoor climbing apparatus was shown to stimulate more interaction than a simpler piece (Scholtz & Ellis, 1975); however, as the novelty wore off, preference for the complex apparatus declined sharply. Scholtz and Ellis suggest that less complex structures may encourage more peer interactions because there is less for children to do on an individual basis. However, Getz and Keller (1981) found that super (i.e., complex) play structures encouraged more richly detailed cooperative play.

Fields (1979) observed children who were given a choice of two large boxes that could be entered. One was painted to look like a car; the other had an abstract pattern. Children spent more time in the realistic box and displayed more diverse pretense elements but fewer pretense themes. Themes for the abstract box were more diverse but it was used less.

3. Variety and complexity of play spaces and materials influence children's play; manipulation of the "functional complexity" (i.e., the opportunities for interaction) changes the play.

Studies of complex variables (e.g, Ellis & Scholtz, 1978; Gramza & Scholtz, 1974; Hutt, 1971) indicate that exploration and play are influenced by "functional complexity," which is the "number, variety, and quality of responses the objects are capable of eliciting and sustaining" (Ellis, 1979, pp. 158–160).

The functional complexity of computers may be a factor in the long interest spans older preschool and kindergarten children exhibit in computer play (Swigger et al., 1983). Johnson (1985) found child computer users had significantly higher levels of cognitive maturity; cognitive challenge may be an important reason for providing computers in early childhood programs.

Colker (1983) states that the characteristics of computer dimensions of responsiveness, complexity, and versatility allow three levels of use: (a) exploration, (b) fulfillment of fantasies and purposes and (c) engrossing gaming challenges. These qualities, in his view, make computers functionally complex and appropriate playthings for early educational settings. Malone (1980, 1981) states that the three dimensions of challenge, fantasy, and curiosity that computers provide are congruent with the Piagetian theory of knowledge acquisition.

Day and Sheehan (1974) investigated another type of functional complexity. They observed 14 early childhood centers and rated them according to materials provided. They concluded that the best environments provide an overlapping of materials into different areas; for example, food coloring in the water table, sand in the fingerpaint, and books in the block area. Overlapping provides for greater complexity of play and more opportunities for interaction. Kinsman and Berk (1979) overlapped the block and housekeeping areas by removing a barrier. They found that although girls had spent more time in the housekeeping area before the barrier was removed, both boys and girls spent more time in the block area when they were overlapped. Children played there twice as often as in the housekeeping area. More solitary and stereotypic activity was observed in the housekeeping area and much of it was unrelated to the materials available there. More clustered social play occurred in the block area. Kinsman and Berk judged the play as more varied and relevant in the block area because of the greater flexibility of objects. Quality of play and social involvement for girls and younger children were most enhanced by the accessibility of the combined area.

4. Presence of television at home influences play at school.

Although television is not a play material available in most half-day preschool or kindergarten programs, it is a pervasive influence in the home and is used in some day-care/preschool programs. In a review of research on effects of television, Honig (1983) cites evidence that viewing various types of television affects the prosocial behavior, aggression, gender/sex role socialization, and achievement that are exhibited in the preschool. Also, J. L. Singer and D. G. Singer (1978) found that preschool children who played imaginatively in classroom settings watched more benign family and children's programs. There is also a link between watching physical aggression on television and display of similarly aggressive play behavior afterward (Bandura, 1973; Eron, Huesmann, Lefkowitz, & Walder, 1972). Children who watch violent action-adventure stories demonstrate more aggressive behavior, but children who are initially aggressive are more likely to be affected by and to watch more such stories (Friedrich & Stein, 1973).

Perhaps the greatest concern about extensive television viewing is that preschool children are not spending that time in active play (Winn, 1977). A study by James and McCain (1982) demonstrates that preschool children turn this seemingly passive activity into active experience by using the thematic content of television in pretense. In their analysis of what "television-facilitated" play revealed in terms of themes, content, and purposes in the play exhibited in a preschool, the researchers found that although superhuman/high-action/powerful characters were portrayed most often, children also portrayed funny/silly ones, pretty/handsome ones, characters with distinctive costumes and props, and characters with easy-to-imitate behavior. Few real or cartoon animals were portrayed. Four- and five-year-olds used television content more than 3-year-olds and boys played television-inspired roles more than girls. Major themes of play included good guys/bad guys, doctor/fireman, house/family, singing/dialogue, self-announced identity, and follow-the-leader games. The researchers conclude that this play serves the same purposes as other pretend play; that is, it provides self-exploration of new behaviors, and it accomplishes social purposes (e.g., gaining attention, maintaining relationships, creating social hierarchies). Television themes also add embellishments and fun to preschool children's pretend play.

● Ecological features

Ecological features include classroom structure variables such as time sequences and intervals, balance of individual and group activities, and amount of teacher direction. These variables, too, seem to influence preschool play.

1. The length of time children are allowed to engage in free play and whether time is individually structured or blocked into group activity time may affect the quality of play.

Van Alstyne (1932) found when free play was extended from 45 minutes to 60 minutes, children spent an average of two minutes longer in each play area they visited during free play. Doke and Risley (1972) report that when the whole group was required to change activities at the same time rather than being able to move freely, there was much un-occupied time as children waited for others. While these findings suggest that the organization of time is a crucial variable, there is a paucity of research on this question.

2. The level of program structure affects children's play.

Rubin and Bryant (cited in Rubin & Seibel, 1979) compared play choices of children in a Montessori program to those of children in a "traditional" preschool. They found the Montessori program stressed more individual, task-oriented activities and allowed no time for dramatic play or group activities. In the Montessori environment, children engaged in more solitary, parallel, and constructive play. Children in the traditional nursery school engaged in more group constructive and dramatic play.

Investigating teacher-directed small group time and free-play session activities, Emmerich (1977) found that free-play sessions produced more cooperative play, compliant behavior, and peer affiliation than did the teacher-led small group sessions. Other changes over time included more autonomous achievement and higher levels of gross motor activity and fantasy play.

In summary, although numerous studies show that physical environmental factors influence play, some of the results provide a mixed picture. Clear organization of space and moderate levels of density seem to enhance play quality, but specific play behaviors may be difficult to predict. Movable objects also elicit different types of play and play themes. Only a few studies have systematically manipulated environmental variables; more of these studies are needed to clarify effects of specific objects on play. Because of the pervasive influence of physical environment factors, however, educators need to consider these potential effects in curricular planning for play.

Characteristics of the Social Environment

Research on factors in the social environment that affect play includes studies of (a) the roles of adults as facilitators of play and as trainers who attempt to increase levels of play, and (b) the effects of peers on play.

● Adults' roles in fostering play development

Parent and teacher attitudes and behavior have an influence on the play of preschool and kindergarten children. Research evidence indicates that the influences include the following:

> 1. Teachers can intervene effectively to increase children's social and pretend play skills but they need to exercise caution in order to avoid disrupting the play.

With preschool and kindergarten children, the teacher is an unequivocally central figure (Curry & Arnaud, 1984); however, relatively little research has been done on the effects of teacher behaviors on children's play. The small amount of evidence that does exist supports the idea that teachers can improve some types of play by intervention but that they need to be careful not to disrupt the play process.

Intervention programs to increase children's skills and motivation in sociodramatic and fantasy play (e.g., Freyberg, 1973; Saltz, Dixon, & Johnson, 1977; Smilansky, 1968) have produced positive results. For example, in the Freyberg study, children identified as low imaginative were trained in eight 20-minute sessions in a room with many open-ended toys such as Play Dough, blocks, and Tinkertoys. During each session, the adult enacted stories, using dolls and modeling different types of voices and sound effects. She encouraged children to join and to make up their own characters. By the end of the eight sessions, the children were initiating their own stories independently of the experimenter. The findings suggest that, when children are ready to engage in fantasy play but lack the necessary skills, this kind of direct teaching intervention is successful.

In a study of intervention with institutionalized children (Udwin, 1983), results were similar, but children with both high IQs and fantasy predispositions were most responsive to the training. A number of studies have found that relatively short "encouragement" sessions are enough to motivate and reassure children to enter into fantasy play (e.g., Fein & Stork, 1981; Saltz & Brodie, 1982), but what causes

the effect is unclear. Adult attention, rather than the specific techniques, may release skills the children already possess. Further study to clarify these findings is needed.

While adult intervention may enhance children's play in some cases, there is also evidence that it may inhibit play. In a participant observational study of children's play, Silver and Ramsey (1983) found instances when teachers disrupted the flow of play with intrusive comments, directives, or routines. Teachers' sense of timing and ideas of what should interest children sometimes may be in conflict with the play that children initiate. More indirect evidence of the possible constraining effects of teachers is found in a study by Field (1980) in which higher frequencies of fantasy play and social interactions were found in classrooms with the lowest teacher-child ratio. Furthermore, peers create their own culture, which is distinct from the teacher-oriented activities (Corsaro, 1985). Often teachers may not be aware of the specific ways in which the peer culture and the adult culture interact.

> 2. Teachers can help to create a more hospitable social environment and can assist in the integration of socially isolated children.

When modeling of affection is combined with encouragement to practice prosocial behaviors, children tend to display more affection and less aggression (Marton & Acker, 1977). Modeling of prosocial behaviors by television characters (e.g., in "Mr. Roger's Neighborhood") can also be effective (Friedrich & Stein, 1973).

In a study of social isolates at preschool, Scarlett (1980) found that these children tend to exacerbate their isolation by spending less time playing and more time watching their peers. They rarely try to influence or structure how peers behave and they spend relatively little time in imaginative dramatic play; their interactions increase when they are in small structured group situations.

Intervention methods used to improve isolated children's social play included positive reinforcement of these children's efforts to socialize, modeling appropriate social behavior, and training in social skills (e.g, Oden & Asher, 1977). These methods have had some success, particularly with older children (Oden & Asher, 1977). However, Scarlett and Ballenger (no date) point out that few positive reinforcements are effective with young isolated children. Pushing them into interactions with peers when they may lack the initiative and skills to be satisfying play partners is not effective.

Scarlett and Ballenger suggest that one way to prepare isolates for peer relations is to foster close teacher-isolate relationships in which the child is encouraged to take the initiative. Two specific techniques suggested are "mirroring," in which the teacher reflects on what the child is doing, thinking, or feeling, and co-playing, in which the teacher encourages the child to assume a leadership role by imitating the child's actions and following the child's directions. When teachers notice that a child is isolated from peers, they may want to structure small group activities that will bring the child into contact with other children in protected teacher-directed activities. Simultaneously they can use these teacher-child techniques to encourage the child to take more initiative with classmates.

3. Parental attitudes about children's play vary; some value play while others hold negative views about certain kinds of play or communicate a disinterest in their children's play development.

Brooks and Knowles (1982) found that some parents report that they respond to their children's play with imaginary companions in a neutral or discouraging way. In this study, mothers, but not fathers, associated fantasy play with deceitful behaviors. Other studies report an ambivalent attitude toward imaginary playmates.

The attitudes of parents appear to exert an influence on the development of their children's play. Smilansky (1968) identified certain aspects of parental attitudes and practices that were related to the frequency of fantasy play, finding that parents of high fantasy children attached a great deal of importance to play and provided a large number of toys and spaces for play. They often joined their children's play and allowed the children to interrupt conversations with adults. The parents of low fantasy children had opposite patterns of behavior. Other reports of research (e.g., Singer, 1973) also indicate that there can be positive and negative parental influences on imaginative play.

● **Peer group effects**

During the preschool and kindergarten years, the effects of the peer group on play behavior is primary. Each group of children has its own character, dynamics, and themes of play, but some patterns seem to be universal for the majority of this age group. Aspects of peer group composition include the following:

1. Peer relationships become more articulated and stable during the preschool and kindergarten years.

Infants and toddlers are attracted to their peers, and a few examples of tenuous friendships can be observed (Vandell & Mueller, 1978, 1980). During the preschool and kindergarten years peer interactions change from being primarily sporadic contacts to sustained friendships (Oden, 1982b). Early preschool peer relationships have been characterized as "playmateships" (Selman, 1981). Children initially select playmates on the basis of proximity and momentary attractiveness (e.g., the possession of an appealing toy). Although children may tend to play with particular classmates, they have little sense of relationships as enduring beyond the immediate interaction. However, they are intensely aware of one another at this age and attempt to adjust to the needs of peers in order to maintain contact (Curry & Arnaud, 1984).

Older preschoolers begin to form more stable friendships. Selman (1981) describes this stage as "one way assistance." Children prefer particular classmates, but remain in relationships only as long as they serve their play needs. They are more aware of one another and attuned to what interests, provokes, and pleases others (Curry & Arnaud, 1984). Gender-separate peer groups begin to be formed, especially by boys (Pitcher & Schultz, 1983); these are frequently defined by exclusion as well as inclusion (Curry & Arnaud, 1984). Skills of negotiation and compromise begin to appear.

Some children appear to "hit it off" when they first meet and are able to exchange information, resolve conflicts, and establish common ground more quickly than other types of stranger dyads (Gottman, 1983). Not surprisingly, children are more effective playmates when they are paired with a friend rather than with a stranger or disliked person. One study demonstrated that when children are paired with a preferred classmate, they talk more and with greater effectiveness than they do when they are paired with nonpreferred classmates (George & Krantz, 1981).

2. Peer familiarity is related to the quality of peer interactions and the richness of play.

In one study comparing familiar and unfamiliar pairs, more complex toy play, more social play, and more positive behaviors were observed in the familiar pairs (Doyle, Connolly, & Rivets, 1980). However, in another study (McCornack, 1982), only the younger girls and older boys were positively affected by the familiarity condition. Younger boys were not affected, and older girls interacted with unfamiliar peers more than familiar ones. In a more naturalistic setting, the social behaviors of children were studied during the first 10 weeks of school (Shea, 1981); all social behaviors increased and aggression decreased during that time. Although the findings are mixed, familiarity seems to exert a positive influence on children's social interactions. While these findings suggest that children's social skills might advance more rapidly with more intensive preschool experiences (i.e., five-day as opposed to three-day programs), there is evidence that length of time, not intensity of exposure, is the critical variable. In a 10-week study of children in five-day, three-day, and two-day programs (Shea, 1981), children's social behaviors increased at the same rate, regardless of the program they attended.

3. The quality of peer interactions varies with the social skills of individual children.

A number of recent studies (e.g., Corsaro, 1981, 1985; Putallatz & Gottman, 1981) have looked at some of the subtle ways that children's social interactions are organized, initiated, and maintained. In general, the findings suggest that popular children are ones who are able to enter groups in ways that do not disrupt play already in progress. These behaviors require that children have an insight into the way other children are thinking and feeling. These children are less likely to meet the resistance that a less popular child faces in attempting to enter a group. Peers create their own culture, which is distinct from

teacher-oriented activities (Corsaro, 1981, 1985); teachers need to be aware of this in their efforts to provide an enriching environment for young children.

Interactions of Cultural and Individual Factors with Physical and Social Environment Factors

Researchers have also explored sex, age, socioeconomic, and cultural differences in children's use of play materials, as well as the ways play assists in integrating handicapped children. Results indicate an interaction among these factors and those of the physical and social environment, as follows:

1. There are age/environment interactions both in children's fantasy and social play.

There is a correlation between age and level of social participation in play (Parten, 1932; Pellegrini, 1982a; Vandenberg, 1981a). During the preschool years, solitary play decreases and interactive play increases (Rubin, Fein & Vandenberg, 1983). These changes have been observed during a year that a particular group is together; there is also a significant increase in dramatic interactive play (Johnson & Ershler, 1981; Johnson, Ershler, & Bell, 1980).

Social play becomes more elaborate, and at the same time, children become better able to sustain interest in independent construction play. According to Rubin, Watson, and Jambor (1978) and Roper and Hinde (1978), these increases in solitary play during the late preschool and the kindergarten years reflect cognitive advancement. Older preschoolers and kindergartners exhibit increased levels of activity focused on solitary constructive play, which differs from the solitary and parallel play of younger children.

Play complexity increases with age, and the play materials available to children affect their behavior differently at different ages (Parten, 1933; Rubin, 1977; Vandenberg, 1981a). McLloyd (1983a) found that 3- to 5-year-olds' reactions to high and low structure objects differ. The high structure objects (those that direct children to certain uses, e.g., puzzles or stacking rings) increase frequency of noninteractive pretense in 3-year-olds but not in 5-year-olds. Low structure objects (those that give less direction, e.g., blocks or sand) do not increase overall levels of pretense; older children engage in more cooperative pretense than younger children with both types of objects.

Many researchers report that older children are better able to pretend with substitute objects (e.g., Elder & Pederson, 1978; Golomb, 1977; Matthews, 1977; Phillips, 1945; Pulaski, 1973). These studies report that as materials become less realistic, play themes of older children become more diverse. Specific types of fantasy play also change over time.

Older children may have more difficulty adapting to environmental changes or to material substitutions requiring flexibility of thought. Kinsman and Berk (1979) found that kindergarten children most rigidly adhered to separation of house and block areas. Golomb (1977) also found that kindergarten children made more objections to using incongruous objects in puzzle solutions. This change may reflect an increased level of classification ability in which children approaching concrete levels of operational thought apply relatively rigid categorization rules.

2. Boys and girls generally show increasingly different play patterns during the preschool and kindergarten age period; the physical and social environment of both home and school reflect and foster traditional gender/sex role behaviors.

In studies of family effects on children's play (e.g., Bright & Stockdale, 1984; MacDonald & Parke, 1984), findings suggest that there are differences between same- and cross-gender parent and child interactions both in terms of the type of play that occurs and the leadership that the child is allowed to assume. Home environments and toys provided for children of each gender also reflect sex role stereotypes (Jacklin & Maccoby, 1980; Rheingold & Cook, 1975). In a study of young children's use of toys at home (Giddings & Halverson, 1981), boys were observed playing more with vehicles and girls more with dolls. Boys also spent significantly more time watching television, whereas girls read more books or were being read to by parents.

Numerous researchers have noted gender differences in ways boys and girls relate to the same classroom environment (e.g., Clance & Dawson, 1974; Kinsman & Berk, 1979; Rubin, 1977; Shure, 1963; Vandenberg, 1981a). As early as 1933, Parten observed that girls engage more in art and less in block and vehicle play than boys. Shure and Rubin found these patterns to be similar today. Kinsman and Berk found that even with barriers removed between housekeeping and block areas, children still played in same gender groups. Both boys and girls showed higher involvement in the block area; even when boys were in the housekeeping area they showed a low level of involvement. Shure found that boys engaged mostly in associative play in the housekeeping area while girls played cooperatively. However, not all researchers have observed these patterns; Brenner (1976) reports that boys and girls use housekeeping and block areas equally often.

Boys' and girls' levels of exploratory play and make-believe are similar but boys' pretense involves more gross motor activity and uses more space (Brenner, 1976; Harper & Sanders, 1975; Pulaski, 1970). In outdoor play, boys show more pretense and their fantasy roles include running, jumping, and wrestling. Girls engage in more person fantasy and announced fantasy play; boys spend more time in object fantasy play (Field, DeStefano, & Koewler, 1982). Girls are more likely to enact domestic events that involve nurturing and caretaking and boys gravitate towards adventure themes that include aggressive figures and actions (Fein, 1981; Singer, 1973). The amount of time in dramatic play also appears to be related to gender. Girls have been observed to spend more time in solitary and parallel constructive play and less time in dramatic play than their male peers (Johnson & Ershler, 1981; Rubin, Maioni, & Hornung, 1976; Rubin, Watson, & Jambor, 1978). Type of fantasy play also varies by gender. Differences in boys' and girls' fantasy play with computers have also been reported (Kee, 1985).

Boys and girls also differ in their preferred level of structure and in the content of play they enact. Carpenter, Huston-Stein, and Baer (1978) indicate that boys are more attracted to low structure activities in which they create order and girls select more high structure activities in which they follow order or sequences already created by adults or by materials.

Pitcher and Schultz (1983) report that the peer group enforces conformity to sex role standards, especially for boys. They hypothesize that the increasing differences are due to cognitive developmental understandings of gender characteristics; however, the environments they observed apparently did not attempt to counteract the development of stereotypic behaviors.

Although many teachers express frustration at the seemingly inexorable increase in gender-typed behavior and gender cleavage that occurs during the preschool years (Greif, 1976), they may be unwittingly contributing to the problem. One series of studies (Fagot, 1978a, 1978b) revealed that teachers and children frequently rewarded gender-typed behavior and ignored or negatively reinforced cross-gender behavior. These findings concur with those in a study looking at the effects of male teachers in a preschool classroom (Lee & Wolinsky, 1973). Male and female teachers played different roles in the children's activities; male teachers were more responsive to boys engaged in male sex-typed activities than were their female colleagues.

In a study attempting to challenge sex role stereotypes, Guttentag and Bray (1976) developed a nonstereotypic curriculum for kindergartners and elementary children. They reported that kindergarten children initially saw little overlap in male and female adult roles. After the curriculum had been implemented, the children were more likely to see the advantages and possibilities of overlapped gender roles. However, both boys and girls defined boys' and men's roles narrowly (i.e., they "didn't do" certain things), while they defined girls' and women's roles more diffusely and broadly.

Children are less stereotypical about what they can do themselves than about what they say boys and girls and men and women in general can do (Guttentag & Bray, 1976). Although traditional play behaviors are usually observed in children's play during preschool and kindergarten years, kindergarten children characterize their own personalities unstereotypically. When asked what they are like, both boys and girls see themselves as strong and capable (i.e., with traditional male characteristics) and good looking, obedient, and neat (i.e., with traditional female characteristics). Guttentag and Bray say that kindergarten children are aware both of the cultural

values and the sex role stereotypes; their play reflects both of these dimensions.

3. Ethnic, socioeconomic, and familial factors are related to children's play.

While young American children tend to form rather exclusive, even if temporary, play groups, this pattern is not universal (Graves, 1974). Cross-cultural research demonstrates that children are able to learn to interact more inclusively if they are in environments that support this type of social behavior (Graves, 1974).

The ways children approach material possessions and cooperative play also seem to differ across cultures. In a comparison of Chinese and American children's use and exchange of materials (Navon & Ramsey, no date), the Chinese children were more likely to negotiate the use of materials, to compromise, and to redistribute materials to maintain equal allotments than were their American counterparts. In cross-cultural comparisons of children's competitive and cooperative behaviors, Anglo-American children have tended to be more competitive than their Mexican and Mexican-American counterparts (Madsen, 1971).

In one of the few studies of 5-year-old Mexican-American girls' sociodramatic play (Genishi & Galvan, 1985), the children exhibited language and social patterns similar to those of other children of that age. The potential effects of cultural factors need further exploration.

Ethnic differences appear to be related to choice of friends and social contact patterns in older preschool and kindergarten children. In interviews, young preschoolers often express negative cross-ethnic views, but they do not show a great deal of same-ethnic preference in their actual playmate choices (Porter, 1971; Ramsey, 1985). However, as children get older, their actual play contacts become more exclusively with same-race children (Asher, Singleton, & Taylor, 1982; Singleton & Asher, 1977).

In several studies, low socioeconomic status has been linked with low frequency of fantasy play (Feitelson & Ross, 1973; Freyberg, 1973; Rosen, 1974; Saltz, Dixon, & Johnson, 1977; Smilansky, 1968). Questions have been raised, however, about the validity of these findings (McLloyd, 1983b; Schwartz-man, 1984). They may be related to proximate variables rather than simply social class (P.K. Smith, 1983). Family characteristics other than their social class may be related to children's fantasy play. In Freyberg's (1973) study working class families of high and low fantasy children were compared. Although occupations and income levels were similar, there were differences between the home environments in the two groups of families. High fantasy children were either only children or the oldest sibling, which suggests that they had more of their parents' attention in their early years. There was also more space in these homes so that these children had more opportunity to be alone. The parents had a few more years of education and, in contrast to the parents of the low fantasy children, expressed an interest in the child's activities and an approval of imaginative play. While some of these factors, such as the number of rooms, may be directly related to income level, these results suggest that variables other than socioeconomic status are related to the frequency of fantasy play.

The differences in exhibited levels of pretense may also be due to unfamiliarity with the materials used in the school setting (Feitelson & Ross, 1973), which may explain why some children from low income families initially play in exploratory or functional ways when they begin school. The fact that brief training seems to release their ability to pretend would indicate that the competencies are there but are not exhibited (Saltz & Brodie, 1982).

4. Efforts to integrate handicapped and non-handicapped children in play yield mixed results.

A particularly difficult task for teachers has been the social integration of handicapped and nonhandicapped children. In addition to different physical appearances, handicapped children often cannot do certain activities because of their physical limitations. For young children, who are just mastering certain skills, these disabilities are salient. Informal mainstreaming of handicapped children has not always shown positive outcomes (Peck, Apolloni, Cooke & Raver, 1978). In interviews nonhandicapped preschool children described their handicapped peers disparagingly; they often assumed that their handi-

capped peers were "babies" and had become handicapped "because they were bad" (Hill, 1981).

Intervention programs have attempted to (a) train handicapped children to behave like their nonhandicapped peers and (b) train nonhandicapped children to communicate more effectively with handicapped children. When handicapped children have been reinforced for imitating the free-play behavior of their nonhandicapped classmates they did acquire some of those behaviors (Peck et al., 1978). However, their imitation was not really self-initiated play. Even with direct training, there may be limits to the extent of integrated play. Guralnick (1980; 1981) reports that mildly handicapped and nonhandicapped children interact, but that nonhandicapped children do not interact with severely handicapped children.

The second approach, training nonhandicapped children to communicate with handicapped peers, has also yielded somewhat disappointing results. In one study in which hearing peers were trained to communicate more effectively with their hearing impaired classmates, the children who underwent the training initiated fewer contacts with their hearing impaired classmates than did the children in the control group (Vandell, Anderson, Erhardt, & Wilson, 1982). However, in a study by Odom, Jenkins, Speltz, and DeKlyen (1982), a preschool curriculum specifically designed to integrate learning disabled children did successfully promote social play between handicapped and nonhandicapped children. As a result of their work, the authors cautioned that social integration between handicapped and nonhandicapped children will probably not occur without such special efforts.

Guidelines for Home Play Environments

As the discussion of home environments for infants and toddlers pointed out, homes must be shared by children and other family members; therefore, home environments cannot be shaped solely to meet preschool and kindergarten children's needs. However, parental attitudes toward their young children's play influence whether the home is a good play environment. As Smilansky (1968) suggests, children who play well live in homes where parents notice and express appreciation for their children's play by (a) playing with them and modeling playfulness; (b) purchasing toys because they believe toys will help their children learn; (c) helping children organize and display toys so they can find them easily; and (d) providing books and didactic games and modeling reading.

Research indicates that parents have a tendency to give sex-typed toys to children and decorate their rooms in stereotypic ways (Giddings & Halverson, 1981; Jacklin & Maccoby, 1980; Rheingold & Cook, 1975), but parents can counter this tendency by the toys and environments they provide. Parents need to consider carefully what message the toy and the play environments are giving to their children.

Results of research on the influence of television suggest that parents need to monitor their children's television viewing. Even if television programming is not specifically harmful to children, it does take time away from play (Honig, 1983). Children might better spend time in active play that involves them in concrete experiences. Parents are offered guidelines for monitoring and controlling their children's television viewing in family magazines (e.g., Katz, 1982), newsletters (Veit, 1983) and books (Singer, Singer, & Zuckerman, 1981).

Parents of handicapped young children usually have more concerns about their children's physical and motor development and language acquisition, rather than about their play development and need to explore (Shere & Kastenbaum, 1966). Especially if they have severely handicapped or multihandicapped children, parents may need to be taught how to play with their children (Hewitt, 1970). In England, toy lending libraries have helped parents develop ways to play with their handicapped children (Mogford, 1977). Such play may be particularly beneficial for handicapped children because they typically have difficulty entering the social mainstream.

Guidelines for Out-of Home Environments

In planning environments for preschool and kindergarten children, Osmon (1971) urges that "The relationship between the program and the group play environment should be one of 'good fit'; that is, the physical environment should give maximum support to the program goals" (p. 35). Environmental designs that fit three types of program goals are described below.

1. A *free flow* design best serves programs that focus on promoting all areas of development by encouraging children to choose from a carefully selected range of play materials. Individual adult contact with children rather than whole group instruction typifies this kind of program. Semi-fixed and movable features are placed to allow interest areas where children can choose activities. Play activities are visible and accessible to children. Furniture is flexible and allows easy movement so that large, open areas can be created as well as smaller private areas. Adults in these settings are carefully spaced around the environment. Educational programs using a setting design like this are traditional nursery school programs, British infant schools, and open kindergarten and primary classrooms.

2. A *slow paced* design places more emphasis on cognitive development although it has many features similar to those in the free flow model. Some or all of the activities have a teacher-directed component. For example, there are usually large and small group sessions as well as some free playtime. A choice of materials is available, but children are encouraged to spend a longer time at certain teacher-identified activities. According to King (1979), the teacher may call these activities play, but the children may label them work. Play areas are defined with more obvious space barriers and teachers concentrate their attention in designated areas rather than monitoring the total flow of movement. Activities are relatively quiet in the classroom although there may be active play periods elsewhere (e.g., outdoors). Programs that typically employ this design are those modeled after the High/Scope cognitive program (Hohman, Banet, & Weikart 1979), the Montessori (1973) program, and traditional kindergarten programs.

3. The *highly structured* design focuses primarily on academic skill development in areas such as language and mathematics. Play development is not a goal of these programs. Typically work periods alternate between teacher-directed sessions and individual practice periods, both of

which are designed to prepare children for the elementary school. The physical arrangement has small enclosed areas for individual or small group work and larger areas for larger group work. The most well-known preschool and kindergarten model of this type is Distar, which was designed by Bereiter and Engelman (1966). Some academically oriented kindergartens and many primary school programs have designs similar to this model.

● The indoor physical environment

Dalziel, 1972; Irwin and Bushnell (1976) and Rambusch (1982) suggest guidelines for constructing the physical portion of the play environment. These guidelines are useful for free-flow and slow-paced programs. Irwin and Bushnell map the environment along a continuum of noisy to quiet. Rambusch (1982) has developed a model incorporating a wet to dry continuum with an active to quiet continuum. This model is also advocated by Dalziel (1972). Figure 9–1 presents the Rambusch dimensions.

In addition to using these dimensions, a number of other guidelines can be drawn from the research evidence presented earlier. The ideal space per child for group environments is between 35 and 50 square feet. State licensing requirements and school codes may vary as to minimum space needed and group size as well as adult supervision ratios may also vary. Square footage should not fall below 35 square feet per child, unless the environment is highly enriched with many activities from which to choose.

The expected flow of movement in the room must be clear to children, with furniture, shelving, and partitions signaling the pathways and discouraging running, which tends to occur in large, unstructured, minimally equipped space. Sufficient floor and table or platform space for materials to be used by children should be planned.

Because children need some privacy, small places such as cubbies, nooks, large boxes, or enclosed structures should be included in the environment. Clearly defined learning areas that are spaced properly and localized by lighting encourage focused attention; however, "overlapping" (i.e., materials from different locations can be used in combination) should also be permitted. Provision of a variety of raw materials, such as sand, water, or clay, encourages complex and problem-solving play. These materials can be overlapped with art materials and wood. Housekeeping and block area combinations can diminish sex role stereotyping.

The availability of novel, plentiful, frequently rotated, and nonstereotypic sets of materials can encourage both solitary and group pretense as well as

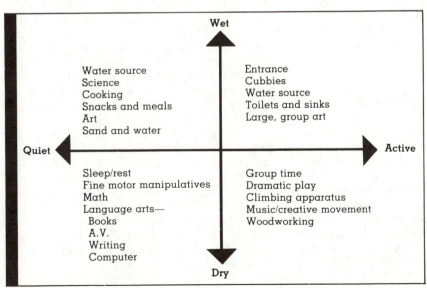

FIGURE 9–1 ● Continuum of Activities

social play and verbal interactions in general. Both realistic and nonrealistic props for family, work, and fantasy role-play are essential. They can be home-made or purchased, as long as they are strong enough to hold up to vigorous play. Blocks and other construction materials, as well as complex climbing structures, also encourage a wide range of play be-havior. Materials that encourage both gross and fine motor play (e.g., climbing structures and manipula-tive table toys) should be available. If computers are in the environment, they should be placed in a quiet quadrant of the room (e.g., near the reading area) and offered as a free-play option.

The physical environment should also be de-signed to allow mainstreaming of handicapped chil-dren. For example, one-story buildings should have ramps, and multistoried buildings should have eleva-tors. Multi-textured surfaces and bright colors can help visually impaired, mentally retarded, or neuro-logically impaired children find their way comfortably in the environment (Moore, Cohen, Oertel, & Van Ryzin, 1979).

The environment must be arranged to allow interaction of handicapped children with adults and peers (Widerstrom, 1983). To encourage interaction between handicapped and nonhandicapped chil-dren, as well as older and younger children, flexible materials that can be used by children of varied levels of ability should be provided. Social toys, such as blocks, ball, and puppets, encourage interaction. Teachers should offer materials with graded chal-lenges and paced alternatives; levels of difficulty should be obvious by the way materials are displayed (Moore, et al., 1979).

● The outdoor physical environment

In the last 20 years, there has been a great deal of interest in developing outdoor play environments that maximize not only physical/motor development but also social, emotional, and cognitive develop-ment. In order to have an interesting outdoor envi-ronment, Osmon (1971) suggests incorporating the following four areas: (a) an active area for exercising gross motor skills such as running, climbing, swing-ing, tricycle riding, and participating in group games; (b) a passive area for quiet and fine motor activities such as water and sand play, painting, looking at

books; (c) a nature area, which can be interspersed around the playground or be separate, and which can include a garden or pets; and (d) social areas that should include materials that can be used for socio-dramatic or fantasy play. Private areas are also needed outdoors (Moore, Cohen, & McGinty, 1979).

Kritchevsky, Prescott, and Walling (1977) have provided a way to evaluate variety and complexity of play spaces that is particularly relevant for outdoor play areas. *Variety* refers to the number of different activities that a play space accommodates, such as climbing, digging, riding a tricycle, running, balanc-ing, engaging in make-believe, or looking at books. *Complexity* refers to the relative capacity of a play unit to capture and hold children's interest and the relative number of children who can play there at one time. Points assigned to a play unit reflect its internal complexity as well as the number of children most likely to be found using it at one time. The levels of complexity are simple (one point), complex (four points), and super (eight points). The simple unit has only one use and no sub-parts to allow manipulation or improvisation. Examples include slides, tricycles, and rocking horses. Complex units incorporate two separate play materials that children can manipulate, integrate, or use to improvise. Some play units, such as Play Dough, paints, or classroom pets, are more novel and flexible and can be considered complex units even though these do not have sub-parts. Other examples include a water table with toys, a play stove with pots, a climber with a slide. The super unit is a complex unit offering three or more juxtaposed mate-rials. A climber with ladders and boxes, a sand area with water and digging tools, a language arts center with books, writing materials, and computer, and a listening center with record player, cassette player, and headphones are all super units.

The assignment of quality points to each level of complexity makes it possible to determine the num-ber of possible places to play per child. Kritchevsky et al. (1977) recommend clear pathways and 2.5 play spaces per child to ensure a safe movement flow. Moore, Cohen, & McGinty (1979) recommend that loose, portable objects such as building materials are needed to encourage creativity and group problem solving. Commercial and recycled materials should be available near the play area.

Handicapped children have usually found playgrounds inaccessible and thus socially isolating (Worner, 1983). Well-designed playgrounds that include access ramps, graded challenges, paced alternatives, clearly defined activity areas, and places for emotional release are recommended (Moore Cohen, Oertel, & Van Ryzin, 1979).

● **The social environment**

Because play is a spontaneous, internally generated opportunity for children to assimilate reality into their own desires and needs, adults should be facilitative as opposed to directive.

The danger is when adults intervene in play, it may lose its critical characteristics and therefore its special value. We must maintain an atmosphere of familiarity and emotional reassurance, not inhibit play by directing it, or prevent its intrinsically joyful quality through external reinforcement. (Cazden, 1976, p. 607)

Specifically, teachers can plan flexibly so that rigid schedules and routines do not disrupt the flow of play. Further, they can incorporate themes that children introduce so that teacher plans and children's ideas are mutually supportive. Teachers can support play by acknowledging the pleasure and meaning that children derive from all play, even when it is not appealing to the adult (e.g., superheroes).

In games with rules, adults often assume a more didactic role because there are specific pieces of information that most adults feel are necessary to play the game. Kamii and DeVries (1980) argue against this approach; rather, they suggest that teachers observe the ways that children play the game and then adapt the rules so that they are meaningful to the children. In this way, rules are not external constraints that children must remember and follow, but rather an intrinsically meaningful way to organize the game. They urge teachers to "reduce adult power as much as possible and encourage cooperation among children" (Kamii & DeVries, 1980, p. 204). Although teachers often have to play a major organizing role with preschool children, efforts should be made to minimize the role of adult authority and to encourage children to function as autonomously as possible. To promote more positive social interactions, teachers

can organize games to have cooperative instead of competitive goals (Orlick, 1978).

Although generally teachers should not disrupt the flow of children's play, they may need to take a more active role with children who are not engaging in developmentally appropriate play. By providing a supportive social climate and easing children into social interactions, teachers can begin to integrate these socially isolated children. To encourage children's fantasy play, teachers may want to use a variety of voices when reading stories, present short skits to the children and respond to children "in character" when they are involved in fantasy play. By modeling pretend play behaviors, teachers can convey their approval of that kind of play, which may counterbalance the neutral or disapproving attitude of some parents toward fantasy play.

Teachers can also influence the affective tone of the classroom by modeling affectionate and prosocial behaviors and using storytelling and other techniques to encourage children to practice these behaviors, which may in turn foster more prosocial and affiliative actions and reduce levels of aggression.

To provide the environment most conducive to social growth, classrooms should have a fairly even distribution of boys and girls to allow for both same- and cross-gender interactions. The curriculum and physical setting should be planned with the idea of reducing the amount of sex stereotyping and allowing for a wide range of play for both boys and girls. Props, clothing, and pictures should be selected to induce children to try out a variety of roles.

In classrooms of mixed-age children, there may be some discrepancies in how the children of different ages approach imaginative play. However, through their interactions with their older peers, younger children may learn to fantasize at a more advanced level. The presence of younger children often elicits prosocial behaviors from older children. In same-age classrooms, children may be more similar in their approaches to fantasy, but have less impetus to expand their skills.

Ideally, preschools and kindergartens should include children from a range of ethnic and socioeconomic groups. This kind of diversity enables children to learn a wider variety of interactional skills and styles. Children can become familiar with people who look, speak, and act in different ways; contacts made

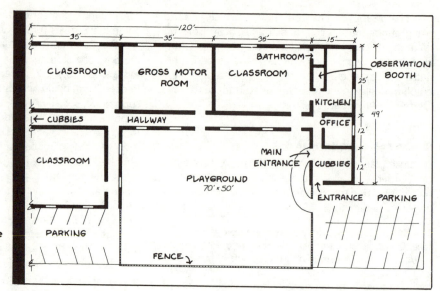

FIGURE 9–2 • Prototype Preschool/Kindergarten Environment (Within School)

in a positive environment may prevent later negative social attitudes and dispel negative assumptions that children have already acquired. Kendall (1983) and Ramsey (1987) suggest familiarizing all children with a range of ethnic groups. In mono-ethnic classrooms, this can be done with photographs and simulated experiences. In diverse groups, teachers should be aware of the significant cultural themes of the children; provision of culturally relevant material appears to foster creative play (Curry & Arnaud, 1984).

Because peer familiarity is positively associated with the quality of peer interactions and the richness of play, children benefit from prolonged contact with a consistent group of peers. Programs with stable groups of children may foster complex play more effectively than ones that have a constantly changing population of children.

Children use their most effective communication skills when they are with a preferred play partner as opposed to a nonpreferred one (George & Krantz, 1981). Teachers need to balance the need to encourage children to expand their social realms and yet allow them to develop the relationships they have already formed. For example, children might initially choose preferred play partners, then be asked to find new partners or groups for some play activities during part of each day.

Teachers can encourage specific behaviors that are associated with high peer acceptance among children. By observing ways in which children make and try to maintain contact, teachers may see ways to help them be socially successful. By providing specific coaching and by structuring social interactions, teachers can help children acquire skills to relate successfully to peers. Games that require different types of communication skills are useful in making children more aware of others' perspectives, a skill that is highly associated with group acceptance.

The promotion of positive relationships between handicapped and nonhandicapped children is particularly difficult. Although the findings from training studies have been mixed, teachers can foster more empathetic awareness of the effects of impairments with simulation exercises (e.g., the "What If You Couldn't" Program from the Boston Children's Museum). Handicapped children in the class may benefit from learning skills that will ease their social integration. Teachers can also set up situations where the negative social impact of the handicap is minimized and the special skills of the children are apparent.

Because parents often have negative views about play and either discourage or ignore it at home, teachers can further support children's play by reassuring parents about the value of play and imaginary

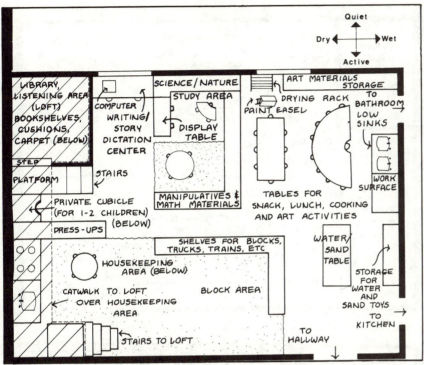

FIGURE 9–3 • Prototype Classroom

playmates in their parent-teacher conferences. By having parents visit and participate in the classroom, teachers can also model how adults can facilitate—and enjoy!—their children's play.

● One model of a play environment for preschool and kindergarten children

The model classroom and playground in Figures 9–2, 9–3, 9–4, and 9–5 represent a composite taken from programs where the authors have worked or supervised. Either the free-flow or the slow-paced program type could be implemented in this environment. It is also adaptable for day-care, preschool, and kindergarten programs.

The physical design includes the following elements: (a) 40 square feet of space per child; (b) overlapping of centers to encourage combining and experimentation with materials; (c) carpeting where noise could be a problem; (d) areas for visual, acoustical, and physical privacy (e.g., in the loft and

cubicles); (e) materials accessible at children's level; (f) play areas arranged on the wet-dry, active-quiet dimensions; (g) accessibility for handicapped children; (h) a mixture of social and solitary toys; (i) movable structures in the gross motor room that can be manipulated by children; (j) gross motor equipment that includes simple, complex, and super structures. Tables 9–1 and 9–2 list indoor and outdoor complexity levels of equipment.

The outdoor play area is over four times the size of one classroom, making it a larger space than the minimum of three times the indoor space recommended by Kritchevsky et al. (1977). Other features include (a) areas for social, active, passive, and nature play; (b) water activities near the outdoor faucet; (c) accessibility to handicapped children; (d) movable materials that can be combined and manipulated; (e) accessible storage; (f) equipment providing for a variety of fundamental movements and cardiovascular exercise; and (g) equipment that includes simple, complex, and super structures.

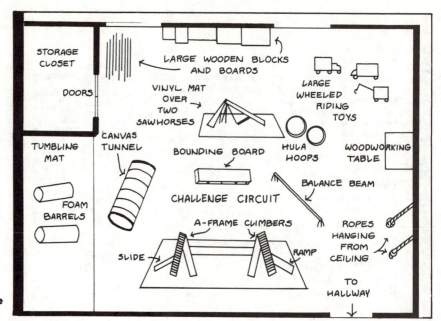

FIGURE 9–4 • Prototype Gross Motor Room

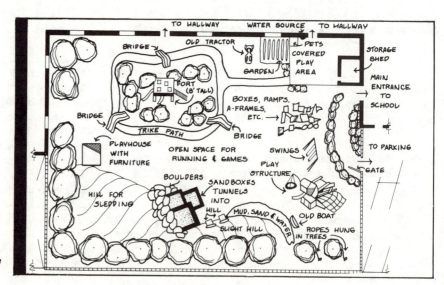

FIGURE 9–5 • Prototype Playground

TABLE 9–1 ● Complexity Level: Gross Motor Room—Indoor Play Space (from Kritchevsky, Prescott, & Walling, 1977)	
Play Units	Number of Play Spaces
Simple:	
Two wall-hanging ropes	2
Complex:	
Mat-covered sawhorses with hula hoops	4
Mat and foam barrels	4
Woodworking table with tools and wood	4
Super:	
Blocks, boards, and trucks	8
Challenge circuit	8
Total number of play spaces: 30 ÷ 2.5 = 12 children	30

TABLE 9–2 ● Complexity Level: Outdoor Play Space (from Kritchevsky, Prescott, & Walling, 1977)	
Play Units	Number of Play Spaces
Simple:	
Tricycles	6
Tunnels	2
Boat	1
Tractor	1
Rope swings	2
Swing sets	3
Complex:	
Sandbox with toys	4
Playhouse with furniture	4
Super:	
Fort	8
Large climber	8
Sand, mud, and water area	8
Boxes, ramps, and A-frame climbers	8
Total number of play spaces: 55 ÷ 2.5 = 22 children	55

Conclusions

Play is the natural learning medium for preschool and kindergarten children. As this chapter has demonstrated, play facilitates cognitive, motor, emotional, and social development. Unfortunately, it is often seen as "only fun" by some parents and educators. Early childhood educators need to protect and foster this valuable component of children's lives.

The many studies reviewed suggest that physical and social environments influence the amount and quality of play in numerous ways. Adults need to consider these variables when purchasing materials, arranging equipment and space, planning programs, hiring staff, and establishing school policies. Teachers' decisions about where children sit, whether to enter ongoing interactions, when to encourage peer play, and how to respond to individual children will all influence the day-to-day play climate of the school. Physical changes such as relocating a physical barrier, adding a rug, building an enclosed loft, or opening access to new materials can shape the play that children engage in, too.

It is of paramount importance that adults who lead children's programs maintain an appreciation and respect for children's play and that they make programming decisions in light of the effect these decisions will have on this critical aspect of children's growth.

Questions for Discussion

1. How would you explain the conflicting or mixed results reported on effects of crowding and space arrangements? What types of studies are needed to clarify these kinds of environmental effects?

2. What factors might account for the research findings that teachers both facilitate and inhibit play? What are some specific examples of both patterns that you have observed? Explain why these occurred.

Environmental Design Problems

1. You have just been hired by a local day-care center to help set up their program in a new facility. It will be located in a church basement that presents several challenges. First, it is L-shaped. Second, it is a large, wide-open space. Third, there is no water source other than the bathroom sinks; and fourth, there are no storage or display shelves in the room. How would you compensate for these drawbacks to ensure quality play with regard to the room arrangement, traffic flow, the lack of display areas for materials, and use of water for activities such as art?

2. You have been told by the director of the early childhood program where you work that the center will need to either raise its parents' fees or increase group size in each classroom. The director wants you to tell her or him how you could manage with three more children in your class of 20 without sacrificing the quality of your program. What would be your response?

3. Your class of 3- and 4-year-old children has been together for six weeks. Most of the children are beginning to form social relationships. However, you observe that one boy of 3 years, 6 months is usually playing alone. He avoids the noisier areas (e.g., gross motor and blocks) and looks at children in those areas from a safe distance, appearing to wish he could join in. What would you do if you were the teacher? What if you observed exactly the same behavior in a girl of the same age? In a 5-year-old boy or girl?

4. At a recent parent meeting, several parents voiced their concerns that "all the children do is play at the school," and they compared your program negatively to another that stresses academic skill learning. As the director of the program, what steps would you take to address their concerns?

Suggestions for Further Reading

Campbell, P. F., & Fein, G. G. (Eds.), (1984). *Young children and microcomputers—Conceptualizing the issues.* Englewood Cliffs, NJ: Prentice Hall. Contains a variety of perspectives on computer use with young children and gives practical examples of effective, playful methods.

Corsaro, W. A. (1985). *Friendship and peer culture in the early years.* Norwood, NJ: Ablex. Provides an overview of the basic trends in the development of friendship and other peer relationships, including practical suggestions for helping children become friends.

Harms, T., & Clifford, R. M. (1980). *Early childhood environment rating scale.* New York: Teachers College Press. Provides an easy-to-use instrument for evaluating early childhood environments. Designed by Frank Porter Graham Child Development Center staff, the instrument consists of a 37-item scale, which has been field tested extensively.

Kritchevsky, S., Prescott, E., & Walling, L. (1977). *Planning environments for young children: Physical space* (Revised edition). Washington, DC: National Association for the Education of Young Children. Discusses the factors of complexity in environmental design and gives examples of ways to solve environmental design problems.

Orlick, T. (1978). *The cooperative sports and game book: Challenge without competition.* New York: Pantheon. Provides ideas for cooperative games that young children can enjoy. Many of the games are appropriate for people of all ages to play together.

Ramsey, P. G. (1987). *Teaching and learning in a diverse world: Multicultural education for young children.* New York: Teachers College Press. Presents theoretical and practical ideas on multicultural education for all young children.

Singer, J. L., & Singer, D. G. (1977). *Partners in play*. New York: Harper & Row. Contains guidance for adults in helping children develop their imaginative play abilities. Includes a chapter on using television to promote growth of imaginative play.

Sprung, B. (1978). *Perspectives on non-sexist early childhood education*. New York: Teachers College Press. Gives an overview of research and practice perspectives and practical suggestions for designing non-sexist environments. Includes advice for parents and curricular materials and media ideas for teachers.

The Mental Image: A Question That Remains Open

CONSTANCE KAMII

Following is a typical "story" problem in math: "Johnny had 15 marbles at the beginning of a game but had only 10 at the end. How many did he lose?" When children read such a problem, they must evoke mental images of Johnny and his marbles to understand the situation depicted. This evocation of objects and events that are not present is known as representation. When young children begin to read, ability to evoke mental images may not seem essential, since their books usually have pictures. As pictures decrease in number, however, it becomes clear that children must be able to evoke mental images of people, objects, and actions to understand the events described with words.

Educators generally assume that mental images are a continuation of visual perception, but Piaget (1962) disagrees. Since the origin of the mental image is not well understood, I would like to sketch highlights from *Play, Dreams, and Imitation in Childhood* to clarify the nature of the mental image and raise a question about classroom practice.

All babies' thinking begins by being limited to the world of objects that are immediately present. During the second year of life, however, children become able to think about objects that are absent from their perceptual field. They thus accomplish an enormous transition from the sensorimotor intelligence of here and now to representational intelligence that extends their universe in space and time. How do they make this transition?

I wish to express appreciation to R. Long, M. Manning, and B. Wolfson of the University of Alabama at Birmingham and to D. Morgan of Louisiana Technical University for critically reading drafts of this essay.

241

It is necessary to go back to the first week of life to answer this question. To take babies' knowledge of their bottle as an example, infants begin by not knowing that there are objects in their environment. Their knowledge of the bottle is limited to what they can know with their mouths during the time their mouths are in direct contact with the nipple. If their eyes are open, they get only impressions of colors. If we made the baby touch the bottle with his or her hand, the hand would remain passive without any accommodation to the bottle, and the baby would certainly not make any relationship between what he or she knows with the mouth and what he or she can know through the sense of touch or vision.

Later, the baby begins to construct the bottle in his or her mind by coordinating what he or she knows by sucking milk, looking at the object, and touching and holding it. The construction of the object is beyond the scope of this paper; the point I wish to emphasize here is the active nature of babies' construction of their knowledge of each object. They accommodate their schemes actively to objects, and this activity results in the mutual assimilation and accommodation of previously isolated schemes, such as those of sucking, looking, and grasping.

When the baby has finally constructed some knowledge of the bottle by about 6 months of age, this knowledge is limited to the time when the bottle is actually present. The bottle does not have a permanent existence for babies until they have constructed object permanency. Object permanency is both the result of the baby's mental activity and a necessary condition for representation.

The transition from sensorimotor intelligence to representational intelligence can be found toward the latter half of the second year, when children begin to reproduce their sensorimotor schemes outside their usual, practical contexts. To refer to the example of the bottle again, babies begin to pretend to hold a bottle, tilt their heads back, and pretend to drink milk through the nipple. Since this behavior takes place without the presence of a real bottle, representation can be inferred from it. After the appearance of representation, pretend play becomes a major activity of the child for a few years.

The original French title of *Play, Dreams and Imitation* was *The Formation of the Symbol in the Child: Imitation, Play and Dreams, Images and Representation*. As this title suggests, the significance of pretend play lies in the transition from sensorimotor intelligence to representational intelligence. The child who has become able to pretend to drink out of a bottle can be said to have a mental image of the bottle. This mental image is a continuation not only of a visual scheme but also of all the other schemes through which the baby came to know the object. In short, the mental image is formed when the child thinks about an object, and this thinking is done not just visually but with all the motoric schemes involved in the child's knowing of the object.

There is complete continuity from sensorimotor schemes to representation with mental images. The image is at first not dissociated from sensorimotor schemes, and the child can think about the bottle only while pretending to drink out of it. Later, however, the child becomes able to evoke the object (i.e., to think about the object) before externally engaging in make-believe behaviors. The proof is that the child begins to announce what he or she will pretend to do before doing it. When children can make a doll drink milk out of a bottle, it can be said that their mental image is now dissociated from the sensorimotor schemes.

Piaget called the toddler's pretend play *symbolic* play (rather than *dramatic* play) because the child engaging in pretend play is using his or her own body to externalize the mental image. Children can also externalize their image with other instruments such as crayons and Play Dough or use an object to represent another object. For example, when children use a cylindrical block to represent (i.e., symbolize) a bottle, they are assimilating the block to their scheme (i.e., mental image) of a bottle. All these symbolic behaviors are made possible by the child's mental image.

The question that naturally follows is why symbolic play is such a big part of young children's lives. Piaget's explanation is that in symbolic play children relive their experiences, thereby assimilating reality to their way of thinking, their desires, and their interests. An analogy may be adults' daydreams. When we daydream, we relive our experiences, think about them, and try to master and understand them better. Children's understanding of reality likewise becomes better organized and more meaningful, and their images become more accurate as they engage in symbolic play over many years.

There are personality differences in symbolic play. Some children engage in it from morning to late afternoon at child-care centers, while others seldom pretend to do anything. There are also socioeconomic class differences in level and frequency of symbolic play (Smilansky, 1968). Lower class children's symbolic play is both less frequent and less elaborate. My question is this: What should educators do, if anything, beyond valuing children's symbolic play and providing materials in the classroom such as dolls, plates, and dress-up clothes?

Early childhood education texts usually do not distinguish between *symbolic* play and *dramatic* play, but I think the two are very different. In symbolic play, children externalize their own mental images of their own reality. In dramatic play, by contrast, they dramatize stories written by someone else. I have no doubt about the value of dramatizing stories in the classroom because dramatization helps children better understand the stories by externalizing their ideas of the events in them. Children's externalization of their own ideas about their own experiences, however, seems more problematic.

The distinction between symbolic play and dramatic play leads to very different principles of teaching. Writing about sociodramatic play without differentiating it from symbolic play, Smilansky (1968), for example, suggests "guidance in the techniques of play" (p. 87), such as "interact[ing] with the child from inside the play" and "directing the play from the outside." An example of interacting

from inside the play is the teacher acting as a nurse saying to a child who is playing a mother, "Mrs. Ohajon, here is the medicine" (while pretending to hand her something). "Give it to your baby twice a day. Now call the cab to fetch you . . . " (p. 102). An example of directing the play from the outside is suggesting to the child, "Let's take your baby to the clinic" and saying to another child acting as a nurse at the clinic, "Here is Mrs. Mizrahi with her ill baby, can you help her . . . ?" (pp. 101–102). Such interventions may improve children's techniques of sociodramatic play. However, when our aim is to strengthen children's mental images and understanding of their own reality, we refrain from this kind of intervention.

When we understand the nature of symbolic play, we also become careful not to impose our adult notions on children's pretend play. For example, if a child walks out of a pretend store without paying for the merchandise, we become careful not to teach him or her at this moment that one must pay for one's purchases. We also become careful not to impose our ideas after each field trip because young children experience a reality that is different from ours. For example, after an elaborate trip to the airport including a visit to the cockpit of an airplane, one group of children was interested only in acting out the way they flushed the toilet with a foot pedal!

Ability to evoke mental images facilitates reading comprehension, writing, and understanding of "story" problems in math. The links among these abilities and symbolic play are complex and not well understood. It seems desirable to study symbolic play in depth and its relationship to field trips, other kinds of play such as physical knowledge activities, social-economic-cultural backgrounds, and the subsequent development of academic abilities that require the evocation of mental images.

CHAPTER TEN

Designing Play Environments for Elementary-Age Children

DORIS BERGEN ● SHERRI ODEN

Except for two brief periods, in the early 1900s and again in the 1960s, the idea of play in the American elementary school has never been popular with the American public, parents, or even educators. According to Glickman (1981, 1984), a focus on play in schools has been unpopular because of a philosophical bias favoring basic skills acquisition as the purpose of education in the United States. Notable exceptions to this bias include the early play school movement, which was fostered by the work of Dewey, and the open classroom era, which was inspired by British education. Most often, the American school has been structured as a work environment reflecting the model of manufacturing industries. This "product-oriented" approach has often negated the value of play in education.

As discussed earlier, the British infant schools have focused on promoting all aspects of children's development in a setting that encourages children's choice and creativity, and promotes curricular indi-vidualization. In contrast, most American elementary schools have relegated playtime to unsupervised recess periods and overly structured, weekly physical education classes. Glickman contends that there are only two ways to bring play into the American school: (a) research on play must provide evidence that play can help teachers meet narrowly defined basic skills objectives, either immediately or through a cumulative process, or (b) the purposes of the elementary school curriculum must be enlarged to include a broader range of educational and developmental objectives, especially those that research shows are promoted by play.

The purpose of this chapter is to present information on physical and social environmental characteristics that promote play and learning in the home and in the elementary school. During middle childhood, defined here as the period from age 6 to 11, play affects children's development of problem-solving and creative thinking abilities, communicative and expressive skills, mathematical and scientific knowledge, emotional maturity, and social competencies.

First, a view of play during middle childhood is given. Then the literature discussing aspects of the physical environment that may promote academic learning through play is described. Because the play of children in this age period, either in or out of school, has not been a major topic of research, empirical evidence on effects of play in the elementary school years is limited. Therefore, the research described in this chapter is drawn from a variety of sources from which inferences regarding play-oriented learning are made.

In regard to school environments, examples of research on discovery approaches to learning and effects of open classroom approaches are reviewed for their implications for the design of play environments. The relationship of the social world of middle childhood, especially as it relates to children's peer interactions and relationships, is discussed as it affects and is affected by the characteristics of the elementary classroom. The ways children define both play and work in the classroom are also described. Finally, some inferences are drawn concerning ways that play and learning can be encouraged in middle childhood. Examples of school play and learning environments are also provided.

Play Development of Elementary-Age Children

During the elementary years, play undergoes some interesting transformations. The pervasive view that play does not belong in the school, however, has limited the types of play that have been studied and the locations where play has been observed. Recess and after-school time are commonly viewed as the times for play; playground, neighborhood, and home are the places where play primarily occurs. As stated in chapter 3, the trends in play development of elementary children are often difficult to study because of the limitations of time and place that make much of their play inaccessible to observers. Nevertheless, many types of play can be seen, even in the school classroom, lunchroom, or corridor. Elementary children engage in practice or functional play, construct-

ive play, symbolic and cooperative play, and games with rules, with games predominating as the major mode.

● Practice or functional play

A variety of gross and fine motor activities that appear very similar to earlier practice play are observable during the elementary years. Children climb up and slide down; crawl through and under; swing, twirl, jump, throw, and run. They ride bikes, roller skate, do puzzles, bounce balls, tramp through the woods, dig holes, and pound clay. They often repeat an action, with numerous variations, over and over. In the early elementary years this play seems to assist in the mastery of more complex versions of skills already learned. For example, climbing a pole and hanging upside down requires a high level of fine and gross motor coordination. By age 7 or 8, many practice play activities begin to serve as rehearsals of specific skills that will be used in games or sports, as this example illustrates:

> L. (8 years, 5 months) spends many hours throwing a basketball into the hoop fastened on the garage. He tries shots from both sides, close ones, distant ones, backward ones, one- and two-arm ones. He never seems to get enough of this play and often has to be called repeatedly to come in for dinner. Sometimes his friend, E., joins him, bringing his own ball, and they play in a parallel fashion. On the weekend, L.'s dad may also "shoot a few baskets." His dad accompanies his participation with words of encouragement and "tips" for L. The focus on "practice" continues to be the point of the play.

Rough-and-tumble play (i.e., play-fighting) is another common activity during the elementary-age period. Aldis (1975) describes many instances of this type of play; for example, fragmentary wrestling (e.g., pushing and pulling); wrestling for superior position; hitting and kicking, swimming pool dunking; and splashing, chasing, and vestibular reinforcement activities, such as swinging, sliding, spinning, and acrobatics, are all commonly observed play in the elementary years. Although boys of 6 and older engage in more vigorous, boys-only play, these types of play are also seen in girls, especially in boy-girl chasing and play-fighting (Robinson, 1978), as this anecdote illustrates:

> Recess time has just begun and the fourth graders have spilled out on to the paved, barren play area. P., J., and M., three socially popular and active girls, begin to tease two of the boys, L. and R., who started to wrestle each other as soon as they stepped from the school building. L. and R. look at each other and, with a nodded signal, L. grabs the scarf of P., who shrieks in exaggerated horror and begins to chase L. and R. The other girls join in the chase and when the boys stop and a tussle occurs, there is much laughter, screaming, and yelling. After some pushing and hitting, the girls retreat, threatening to tell the teacher about P.'s scarf being stolen. As the girls walk away, L. throws P.'s scarf after her and the boys resume their wrestling. The girls walk to the crowd of girls around the hopscotch diagram painted on the pavement to recruit some more girls, and the "girls against the boys" game escalates. By the time the bell rings, about half of the class is involved in the chasing and wrestling game.

Experimenting with new materials and combining known materials in new combinations are also important play activities. Often this exploration (i.e., finding out what the materials can do) is then transformed into functional play (i.e., finding out what the child can do with the materials). A final stage may be using the materials for problem solving or constructive play. The following anecdote describes these three stages:

> C. (7 years , 3 months) observes the electrical switches, batteries, and bulbs that are arrayed on the table, and finally gives a tentative touch to the clips on each end of the section of wire. She fastens one end to the battery and observes that nothing happens. She picks up the bulb and examines the tip and metal casing. She looks again at the wire and then attaches one end of the clip to the bulb's tip and the other to the battery and smiles as the bulb lights. After placing the clips on a variety of places on the bulb and battery,

she selects some more wires and connects them to each other, making a long circuit, which also lights the bulb. D., who has been watching C., says "We could light two bulbs." The children gather more batteries and, after about 15 minutes of experimentation, construct an elaborate circuit. C. then says, "Let's make a signal light," and the children construct a taller base and a housing for the signal, also connecting a switch to turn the light off and on.

● **Constructive play**

In school the most observable type of play is often constructive play, which involves the use of materials to make a particular product. Often these are symbolic products, such as drawings, paintings, and three-dimensional creations that represent objects (e.g., a house), ideas (e.g., friendship), or processes (e.g., war). Constructive and symbolic play can also be combined to create a poem, a dramatic production, a tape recording, or other visual or technological products, as this vignette illustrates:

> In the language arts center, there are magic markers and clear film that can be used to make filmstrips. M. (6 years, 7 months) has used these materials before, experimenting with colored markings and observing how they look when shown through the projector. When M. came into class on Monday, he excitedly told everyone about a fire that occurred over the weekend in his neighborhood, giving many details about the fire and the fire trucks. In "choice" time for the rest of the week, the fire was his topic of interest. He covered a long strip of film with "fire" of various hues and showed the glowing colors on the projector. He recorded a story of the fire on the tape recorder. At the teacher's suggestion, he played his story as he showed the filmstrip to B. He also drew pictures of fire trucks on paper, made a fire truck with the Lego blocks, and replayed the fire events.

An example of a combination of constructive and sociodramatic play is evident in this adult retrospective self-report of a favorite play activity (Bergen, 1985):

When I was in first grade, one of my favorite types of play was to build. There was a group of us who would go into the woods around our school during recess and pick up broken limbs and branches and put them together to build forts. The forts were important to protect us from being attacked... We were the "good guys" and the "bad guys" were out to destroy our stronghold. We had to cooperate. If not, we would be defeated, killed or captured... We had special guns and other weapons that no one else had. The teachers gave us a lot of freedom to play. They intervened only in dangerous situations. Usually they would watch. (p. 2).

Another type of constructive play is that of making collections (e.g., of stamps, baseball cards, or bottle caps). Collections are carefully organized and often examined; they are discussed and traded, and they are sometimes displayed. Child constructions (e.g., miniature cars or planes made from kits) are also collected and displayed.

● **Symbolic play**

Researchers and theorists have stated that for many children dramatic and sociodramatic play wane after the kindergarten year (e.g., Piaget, 1962; Rubin, Fein, & Vandenberg, 1983). Although this play may be observed less as a school activity, playground researchers report that when equipment that fosters dramatic play is included in playgrounds the incidence of sociodramatic play remains high (Frost & Strickland, 1985). Some evidence indicates that children from different cultural backgrounds may exhibit sociodramatic play at different age levels (Eiferman, 1971).

Television watching and after-school lessons or structured activities may also have replaced much of this type of play (Roberts, 1980; Winn, 1977). However, as fantasy play becomes more internalized (e.g., into reading, drawing, daydreaming), privately enacted (e.g., at home rather than at school), and miniaturized (e.g., with GI Joe or Barbie as the symbolic actors), it is more difficult to observe in public settings. Two examples of at-home pretend play reported by adults (Bergen, 1985) are illustrative of fantasy play during this age period:

I was a child in the forties during World War II. My heroes were the cowboys in the five-cent Saturday matinees of our small town. Gene Autry and Roy Rogers topped the list of favorites and were the idols we emulated. A cousin and my younger brother were my side-kicks. Gene and Roy always rode together in our imaginary world and we would trade off characters as though they were cowboy hats... The adults around us were tolerant of our play as we ranged around my cousin's farm or our big yard in town, but when it was chore time or mealtime, they called an abrupt halt to our fantasies. (p. 4)

Somewhere between the ages of 8 to 10, my favorite form of play was paper dolls. My playmate was a neighbor who was an only child. She had a room of her own so most of the time we played on her big bed with the white bedspread. The bedspread had designs of big squares and was equally divided so that she could spread out her dolls on one half and I could do the same on the other half. We would play for hours with the door shut... My favorite paper doll was Brenda Starr who had a very romantic love life. My friend and I acted out life as we thought it should be. I remember acting out anger by having the paper dolls quarrel a lot, just as my parents did, but we always ended in them making up... As I look back on our play, it was very ordinary, but while I was living it, it was exciting and fun—a kind of magic time away from everyone in our own little world. (p. 4)

Elementary-age children engage in role experimentation based on experiences that are not concrete or direct (e.g., historical or futuristic stories they have read, problem situations or travel experiences heard in adult conversation, or plots seen on television and in movies). This role-play is usually with miniature objects and it often involves constructive play as well. For example,

W. (9 years, 3 months) and V. (8 years, 9 months) are extensive readers and one of the bases of their friendship is their interest in "horse" stories. They have read every one of these that the library has and avidly share each new one that they find. Their class is studying pioneer life and the teacher has involved the children in building a replica of a frontier town. W. and V. volunteer to build the blacksmith shop and horse stables. They make clay horses, each with a name and personality. Wagons and carriages, tools for the blacksmith, and many other details are added to their section of the town. As they are creating, and after the building is completed, they spend time imagining elaborate stories that involve the horses and citizens of the town. When they have some extra time, they play out the actions of the stories with the replica animals.

Language play is an especially visible form of symbolic play in middle childhood. Kirschenblatt-Gimblett (1976), in a description of a number of ethnographic studies of speech play, demonstrates that secret codes, jokes, verbal duels, and other types of language play occur in many cultures. Sanches and Kirschenblatt-Gimblett (1976) indicate that much of elementary-age children's speech play focuses on phonological (i.e., sound) elements and includes gibberish rhymes, systematic variations in sound substitution, and puns based on sound similarities. Joking riddles that make fun of adult-child question/answer formats are common by about age 6 (Wolfenstein, 1954). By age 8 or 9, children also play with the grammatical and semantic (i.e., meaning) features and parody adult activities or values. Opie and Opie (1959) have provided an extensive catalog of English language play examples, including riddles, parody, nicknames, epithets, jeers, satire, and nonsense such as tangletalk, tongue twisters, and puns. Here are a few of the Opies' examples:

- Parody: Mary had a little lamb,
              Her father shot it dead,
              And now it goes to school with her
              Between two chunks of bread.
              (p. 90)
- Conundrum: Why did the window-box?—Because it saw the garden fence. (p. 81)
- Riddle: What goes up when the rain comes down?—An umbrella. (p. 74)
- Guile: Adam and Eve and Pinch-me
              Went down to the river to bathe.
              Adam and Eve were drowned,
              Who do you think was saved?
              (p. 59)

- Jeer: Roses are red, violets are blue,
              Onions stink, and so do you.
              (p. 48)
- Oath: Cross my heart and hope to die,
              Drop down dead if I tell a lie.
              (p. 125)

Elementary-age children enjoy secret codes and languages like "Pig Latin," and by fourth or fifth grade much recess time is spent in "just conversation," which is one of the primary play modes of adults. Another favorite form of language play is described in the following example:

J. (8 years, 8 months) and G. (8 years, 3 months) have been putting out a newspaper, "The Daily-Monthly Extra" each month in their after-school time. The paper consists of headline stories about events in their families (i.e., the death of G.'s family's canary, J.'s sister's engagement), jokes, sensationalized versions of mundane events in their school and family life, and parodies of advertisements (e.g., "Sale! Hurry to Brown's Auto to get the new Whiz car; only one million dollars!"). They type the paper on G.'s father's typewriter, make a few copies, and sell the papers for five cents to family members. A great deal of time and effort goes into each issue and they are pleased with the response of their families to the "interesting" and often humorous news.

● **Games with rules**

The flowering of games during the elementary years has been described by many researchers (e.g., Opie & Opie, 1969; Roberts, 1980; Sutton-Smith & Rosenberg, 1961). Girls play more traditional games, while boys move more and more toward sports-related activities. Although most elementary games are structured, requiring adherence to a set of determined, invariant rules, elementary children still invent spontaneous one-rule motor games that are similar to those young children enjoy, as this example demonstrates:

The boys (average age 9 years, 5 months) are in line on their way to the lunchroom. The act of going through the doorway becomes a time for play. B. pushes the door hard, then slips through without touching his body against the wall or door. He challenges A. and D. to do the same before the door closes. A. is successful but D. is bumped by the door, amid laughter. R. pushes the door hard and calls out another challenge. J. and F. successfully maneuver thorough the space before the door closes. Other boys in the line try their skill at sliding through on one push of the door. Before the challenge can escalate, the teacher directs the boys to get their food.

The majority of games at this age have an element that is lacking in the game playing of younger children—competition. Both individual and team competition is evident. Although cooperative games are less often played, cooperation is required within teams; thus success of cooperative effort is measured in the success of competition. Dominance hierarchies are also developed in play.

Games played in middle childhood, as described by the Opies (1969), include chasing, catching, seeking, hunting, racing, exerting, daring, guessing, acting, and pretending games. The Opies state that many games have characteristics more similar to ceremonies than competitions; the games serve to reassure children of their place in the social world and to give them a sense of belonging. Because much symbolic play becomes miniaturized, play with computer games and simulations, board games such as Monopoly or Clue, and card games are popular. They often combine game challenges with symbolic role enactment and fantasy plots.

In middle childhood a typical recess period at school would show the play of boys and girls as fairly similar in the primary grades but quite different in the upper elementary grades. Traditional games, cooperative games, and small group or two-person games with individual competition, such as jump rope, hopscotch, and jacks, are more often played by girls. Sports-related games, such as kickball, four-square, and tag football, are the primary games of boys. Boys and girls do play together in some sports-related games, but often these are initiated by the teacher or playground supervisor.

Peer relationships are vitally important in middle childhood. Often the relationship with a "chum" (Sullivan, 1953) is a major positive factor in navigating these transitional years, as the words of some adults who still remember illustrate (Bergen, 1986):

S. had an outgoing personality. I was shy; maybe that's why I looked to S. for friendship and guidance. S. took piano lessons, so I took them. S. took twirling lessons, so I learned. S. played the clarinet; so did I. In talking recently to S. about what she remembers about our early friendship, I was shocked with her reply. She remembers how I "made her" join 4-H and Girl Scouts and how I "talked her into" many other activities. She says I was the "idea" person. All these years I had thought of myself as merely the follower. I told her how much I had wanted to be like her and she just laughed and said it wasn't a one-way street! (p. 1)

When I was in the fifth grade, I was informed I needed glasses. I was sure glasses would make me hideous to behold and for a while my assumption seemed to be true. People I barely knew picked on me and I got into many fights, even one with a GIRL! But soon I found out that the glasses didn't seem to matter to my real friends. Having close friends that I could share my secrets with and who liked me, even with glasses, made me realize the value of friends. (p. 3).

Characteristics of the Physical Environment

Research on the ways play relates to physical features of preschool and kindergarten environments is so extensive that it could scarcely be encompassed in chapter 9, but there is a dearth of research on how the physical environment affects elementary-age children's play or how play in middle childhood affects academic and social learning. In a book giving guidelines for elementary school environments, Taylor and Vlastos (1975) comment that research on physical environmental effects on all aspects of behavior and learning during this age period is sparse. They deplore this lack of information because, in their view, classrooms are "three-dimensional textbooks" (p. 9). Research-based guidelines for design of play-oriented, three-dimensional textbooks for elementary school children must await precise analyses of physical environment effects on middle childhood play and learning. However, tangential and global research from which inferences can be made for design of play environments is available from a number of sources.

Many of the findings from research that are described in chapter 9 can also be instructive in planning environments for older children. This chapter will describe some additional factors that have been discussed in the literature, although the base of empirical research is limited. The following factors will be discussed: (a) physical materials and features of early home and school environments that may affect later or concurrent academic performance, and (b) characteristics of architectural and environmental school design that may promote playful learning.

● Materials and features of home and school environments

The ways that the early home environment influences the academic ability of elementary-age children and the influences of specific types of play materials in school settings on academic learning have been reported by some researchers, although many of these studies have methodological flaws, making them difficult to interpret. The following variables have been identified as worthy of further study:

1. The presence of various types of materials or equipment in the home (e.g., books, toys, television, computers) may have an influence on children's play at home and on their academic achievement at school.

In a review of research on early home environment effects on reading, Becher (1985) cites a number of studies indicating that the presence of books and other reading materials in the home promotes more positive attitudes and higher reading achievement in school (e.g., Teale, 1978). The types of toys played with in the home also seem to have a relationship to early reading (Thomas, 1984). Children who read early are more likely to play with reading readiness toys, such as alphabet cards, books, and language games, while later readers of equal intelligence play more with gross motor, construction, and fantasy toys. In Thomas' study, no other home environment features predicted the difference in early and later readers.

The effects of different types of commercial toys on development during middle childhood (e.g., especially actively marketed action or glamour toys that are based on television or movie characters) have not been systematically studied, although Sotamaa (1980) speculates that the commercialization and aggressive marketing of toys has had a negative influence on children's play. He states that toys are more superficially stimulating but that choices are more narrow and stereotypic. In a study on industrial product design, Sotamaa (1980) found that appearance may be used as a lure but that safety and play value may be poor. He contends that because synthetic materials (e.g., plastics) are impossible for children to transform, they leave nothing to the imagination.

The presence of television in the home has been linked to effects on academic learning. After analysis of 23 studies of television effects on academic learning of children from kindergarten to high school age, Williams, Haertel, Haertel, and Walberg (1982) report that overall, the number of hours watched is negatively related to academic achievement. Williams et al., conclude that watching less than 10 hours a week may have a slightly positive effect; beyond 10 hours a negative effect occurs. They suggest that in homes with 10 or fewer hours a week of viewing, parents may help children be selective about the programs watched. An alternate hypothesis is that more than 10 hours begins to interfere with time that might be spent on more intellectually stimulating activities (or in "just play"). Williams et al. cite Ratner et al., who report that the average weekly viewing time of 6- to 11-year-olds is 25 hours and conclude, "the negative impact of televiewing beyond 10 hours per week is clearly a matter of concern" (p. 36). This concern is not only because of its academic consequences, but also because of its play consequences.

Potential effects of computers in the home have been the topic of numerous articles (e.g., Kee, 1985; P. Smith, 1981) but little research has been reported on the relationship of home computer play to academic achievement or to social and emotional development. In a pilot study with 6- to 9-year-olds, Silvern, Williamson, and Countermine (1985) suggested videogames may provide catharsis for aggressive feelings. Informal observation and teacher reports (Porter, personal communication) suggest that the use of computers at home by some, but not all, children may widen the academic ability and experience range of children in each grade level. Thus, teachers may be less able to use whole group approaches to teach basic skills in mathematical, scientific, or language areas as middle class children's play with home computers becomes pervasive.

2. Opportunities to explore and use play-eliciting materials in schools can affect reading and language, mathematical and scientific, and artistic and creative performance.

A variety of studies have assessed the relationship of play to language and reading competence. For example, Isenberg and Jacob (1983, 1985), citing case study data, state that the integration of symbolic play materials into literacy activities in school promotes reading ability. Pellegrini (1980) agrees that young children's engagement in pretense with symbolic props predicts success in early reading, language, and writing. Yawkey (1980) reports that imaginative self-actions and play with puppets are especially helpful for 6- and 7-year-olds' language expression, and Galda (1982) states that children who play out a story rather than those who discuss stories exhibit better reading comprehension. These play influences are especially strong in primary-grade children.

Sociodramatic play props have been related not only to children's language abilities, but also to their mathematical abilities. For example, children who engaged in sociodramatic play involving mathematical concepts performed better in subsequent mathematical assessments (e.g., Yawkey, 1981; Zammerelli & Bolton, 1977). Mathematical performance has also been improved by mathematical game approaches (Rogers & Miller, 1984). Rogers and Miller hypothesize that play fosters development because children are not bored by playful practice. The consolidation of skills from playful practice opportunities also promotes transfer to other mathematical tasks. The context of mathematical game playing (i.e., whether competition is stressed) appears to affect boys and girls differentially, with boys doing better in competitive games and girls benefiting more from cooperative or neutral games (Peterson & Fennema, 1985).

The literature on mathematics instruction indicates that activity with concrete materials enhances early elementary children's mathematical problem solving (Suydam, 1984a). For example, in a longitudinal study of children from first to third grade, Carpenter and Moser (1984) found that in the earlier stages children require modeling with physical objects to solve mathematical problems. Although the majority of elementary teachers agree that concrete, manipulative materials (e.g., blocks, chips, fraction pieces) are important in elementary children's mathematical learning, only first-grade teachers report frequent use of manipulatives in mathematics (Suydam & Higgins, 1977). Teachers in grades two and up report progressively less use of concrete materials.

Computer use in elementary schools has been increasingly advocated (e.g., Wiburg & Rader, 1984); however, much computer use has focused on programs for drill and practice rather than for playful and creative engagement in learning. For example, in a review of computer use in mathematics, Suydam (1984b) states, "Few programs are designed to teach concepts or to develop problem solving techniques" (p.35). She reports that when higher order skills are promoted, advanced achievement is related to children's use of problem-solving and strategy games.

Other research evidence indicates that children who play with materials that are later applied to problem-solving tasks are better problem solvers than those given direct instruction (Vandenberg, 1978, 1980). In Vandenberg's (1980) study, 6- to 7-year-olds benefited most from the play experience. In a review of the role of play in science education, Severeide and Pizzini (1984) cite numerous studies of the influence of play with concrete materials on the development of skills and attitudes that promote flexibility and fluency of thought, which are necessary for solving scientific problems (e.g., Li, 1978; Pepler & Ross, 1981; Smith & Dutton, 1979). Most of these studies have been done with children in the age range of 4 to 7. Additional replications with older children are needed. The importance of educational games in helping children learn mathematical and scientific concepts has also been demonstrated in cross-cultural environments (Maxwell, 1983).

In observational accounts of the artistic process, Szekely (1983) and Giopulos (1979) suggest that play with many fluid materials and unstructured forms constitutes the initial phase in the development of artistic works. Szekely, who advocates a phase of "preliminary play" states that play helps children see "what is interesting about a hose, the lines of a slinky toy, or the changing lines of an extension cord. Play thus becomes a means of observing and rehearsing so that a better, more informed use of these elements can be made" (p. 19).

Giopulos characterizes play as "transformation," offering the example of the potter working with clay to describe the play process. The process involves to-and-fro movements, choices, and transcending statements as the potter manipulates the clay. Giopulos asserts, "It is through play that insight comes" (p.13). Empirical studies of the effects of preliminary play periods on children's artistic development are needed.

In sum, there is some limited support for the view that play with specific materials promotes learning in particular curricular areas. Because carefully controlled studies of these processes during middle childhood are sparse, the effects are still speculative. However, the questions are intriguing and worthy of further study.

● Architectural and environmental design characteristics that promote play

A number of authors have made suggestions about the overall design of open, play-oriented learning environments in elementary schools (e.g., David & Wright, 1975; Frank, 1958; Palmer, 1971; Rasmussen, 1958; Sotamaa, 1980; Taylor & Vlastos, 1975). Suggestions for incorporating play-oriented features into traditional classrooms have also been made (Proshansky & Wolfe, 1975). Much of this literature is based on architectural and environmental design principles drawn from observational or interview data collection methods. For example, there are observation scales for rating classroom environments on basic environmental design principles. Time-lapse film documentation of hours of classroom activity have explored children's and teachers' movement patterns; and interviews with children have identified design aspects from their perspectives (Taylor & Vlastos, 1975). Environmental designers stress the following points:

1. Environmental planning must attend both to children's characteristics and to the goals of the curriculum, if both play and learning are to be enhanced.

Observations of children's movement through space, activity levels, and multisensory involvement in learning suggest that environments should (a) be child- rather than adult-scaled, (b) have a variety of levels, (c) provide for experiences using all the senses, and (d) permit flexibility in the arrangement of space and equipment (Taylor & Vlastos, 1975). Spivack (1975) asserts that informal observational research focusing on children's behavior on a number of polar dimensions (e.g., stimulus-avoiding or stimulus-seeking, rigid or fluid, solitary or social, ritualized or open) is an essential first step in planning appropriate environments, especially for children who have special needs.

According to Proshansky and Wolfe (1975), physical environments communicate a symbolic message (i.e., what *should* happen in the environment) and a pragmatic message (i.e., what *can* happen in the environment). For example, physical isolation of the teacher's desk communicates the teacher's authority and distance; likewise, arrangement of children's desks in unmovable rows all facing the teacher's desk prevents children from engaging in playful, cooperative activity and discussion as a learning method. Getzels (1975) ties each of four views of children as learners to a particular classroom design, and summarizes the importance of the physical environment by quoting Winston Churchill, "We shape our buildings and afterwards our buildings shape us" (p. 12).

2. School environments influence aesthetic and emotional development as well as cognitive and academic development; therefore, play materials and environments must also be evaluated on those bases.

In a discussion of quality standards of playthings, Sotamaa (1980) stresses the importance of aesthetic quality. Form, material, color, and expressiveness are elements of the environment that are often not considered sufficiently in schools. Sotamaa suggests that environmental models include enduring playthings of natural materials and aesthetic excellence, in spite of the tendency of children, especially in middle childhood, to be attracted to playthings that "the selective taste of adults finds cheap and common" (p. 270).

David (1975) urges attention to "environmental literacy," which refers to (a) sensitivity to the environment on multiple levels of experience, (b) an active attitude toward the environment, and (c) the ability to modify the environment in response to needs and functions. He cites Propst (p. 174), who describes "the two intersecting planes of reality" relevant to school environments; these are (a) economic and technological concerns that dictate such things as amount of floor space and cost of various building materials, and (b) "the way the building treats its inhabitants" (p. 175). He questions whether a school building designed to "please administrators with its indestructibility and low maintenance" can also meet the "scale and personal space requirements of children" (p. 175); but he urges environmental designers to keep the needs of children in the forefront of their planning.

Because the physical environment does communicate so clearly a message about what behaviors are desired, school environments cannot effectively foster a playful approach to learning if the design elements that promote this type of learning are not present. On the other hand, any classroom can convey the message that children have choices, and teachers can arrange space, time, and materials to promote learning through play, as well as task-oriented activity.

Characteristics of the Social Environment

The relationship of play to children's social development in middle childhood has been described in chapter 5. The research literature reported here focuses on adult roles in promoting play and learning and on how the development of peer relationships is affected by social play and cooperative learning activities. Adults foster play by playing with children, by providing settings for play, and by encouraging peer and sibling play interactions. Peers construct play primarily through engagement in common activity and peer relationships, such as friendship.

● Adult roles in fostering play, learning, and peer relationships

During this age period, children's social environment continues to involve high interaction levels with family members, but it also includes other adults.

Teachers are the major out-of-family adults with whom children must build relationships and other adults, such as scout leaders or coaches, may also have influence. How children establish friendships with adults outside of their family network has not been explored.

In the elementary school years, children's relationships with teachers are highly defined by the school situation and thus may range widely, depending on the learning environment and the specific goals of the curriculum. Research on teacher effectiveness has not focused on teacher-child social relationship issues, however, but rather on teacher management of task achievement and classroom discipline (e.g., Brookover, et al., 1982). Research on methods with which adults can foster peer interactions and promote positive peer relationships in school has demonstrated that adults can affect the development of children's social skills, particularly for cooperative play activity, by encouraging play (e.g., Ladd, 1981; Oden & Asher, 1977). Parent-child and teacher-child influences include the following:

1. Although children's social world is less focused on the home during this age period, and thus parents are less involved in their children's play, parents still exert an influence on their children's play and learning.

Research on the specific nature of parents' play with elementary-age children is sparse; the research results that are reported are primarily from questionnaire data. For example, in a national study of 7- to 12-year-old children reported by Zill and Peterson (1982), approximately 60% of the parents reported they had recently bought toys or games and had played a game with their children. Although only 26% had gone with their children for a morning or afternoon in a park, 80% participated in tasks with their children such as building something or cooking. With the exception of studies of parent involvement in sports organization and management (e.g., Devereux, 1976), there are few observational studies of parent-child play interaction with children of these ages. Identification of interactional dimensions of parent-child play such as those reported in studies of early childhood would be of value in furthering understanding of the role of parents in middle childhood social development.

Research evidence is also lacking on the environmental arrangements that parents could make that would facilitate their children's play. Parents may contribute to the richness of their children's play by allowing clutter and dirt, providing materials and equipment, and giving children time for play. Chapter 11 gives some examples of this facilitation in backyard and neighborhood play. There has not been much study of the role of parents in helping their children with playmates and/or friends, either. Some studies of children who have social adjustment problems indicate that there may be early family experiences, such as parental discipline strategies, that affect social adjustment (Scarr, 1985). Clinical reports indicate that parents whose children are experiencing play difficulties may have also had interpersonal problems as children or the family as a whole may be isolated (Oden, 1982a).

2. **Teachers can promote playful approaches to learning when they are supportive, interested, responsive, and informative (i.e., when they employ a "scaffolding" approach).**

In a seminal work, Bruner (1966) described the teacher's role during children's playful discovery of logico-mathematical knowledge. Using the example of the child playing with unit blocks, he described how the teacher's interest in and encouragement of the child's discovery promotes the child's construction of mathematical knowledge. In his essay "On Learning Mathematics," Bruner (1979), discusses how the discovery process is an "active, manipulative approach to learning" (p. 100) that occurs in cycles involving conversion of what has been learned intuitively into representation (i.e., symbolic formulations). The teacher's role is to provide experiences "that cry for representation" (p. 101). This involves helping children to make sense of their intuitive operations rather than using the "premature language of mathematics," which "makes it seem that mathematics is something new rather than something the child already knows" (p. 104). Wood, Bruner, and Ross (1976) refer to this interactive relationship between teacher and children, in which children have a right to ask for various kinds of assistance and the teacher is responsive to the levels of the children's learning needs, as the process of "scaffolding." This model of teaching is often observed in teachers of very young children as they guide play (Bergen, Gaynard, & Torelli, 1985). It has not been the model used in the more formal curricula of most American elementary schools, where teacher initiatives and direction of group instruction are more typical.

Erickson (1984), in a critique of school literacy teaching methods from an anthropological perspective, compares the forms of learning found in everyday life (e.g., those identified in Rogoff and Gardner's (1984) study of parents teaching cognitive skills on shopping trips) to methods of teaching found in schools. The "fluid, interactional system" (p. 533) of these everyday learning events often does not occur in schools because children are not encouraged to shape the tasks or to negotiate the level of teacher guidance or modeling they need. Erickson urges a rethinking of the school social organization, which puts "constraints on learner choice" and makes it difficult for "teachers and students to construct cognitive scaffolding together" (p. 535).

The research on open learning environments and on specific academic skill development via play, both described in other sections of this chapter, are examples of approaches by which teachers foster learning through play. Included are curricular designs that build on children's individual interests in mastery (Block, 1984), emphasize cooperation and collaboration (Sharan, 1980; Sharan & Sharan, 1976), and encourage initiative, curiosity, and investigation (Bruner, 1979; Duckworth, 1972).

3. **Adults can use play as a medium for fostering social development as well as academic learning.**

The extensive body of intervention research indicates that more positive peer relationships can be fostered by a variety of direct adult intervention methods, including coaching social skills (e.g., Oden & Asher, 1977), modeling (e.g., Gresham & Nagel, 1980), and training in social problem solving (e.g., Shure & Spivack, 1978; Spivack & Shure, 1974). Many of these techniques involve play. For example, Oden and Asher asked children to play a game together after they were coached in social skills and encouraged to have a goal of "having fun" or making the game enjoyable for both participants to play.

As the discussion in chapter 5 indicates, for adults who wish to increase elementary children's social acceptance and foster positive peer relationships, play can function as both a diagnostic strategy and an intervention method. Rubin (1985a) followed a group of preschool children who were lacking in social skills through the second grade. He states that identifying withdrawn kindergartners through their play (i.e., children who play in solitary or parallel functional and dramatic play), and helping them to gain social play skills is important because early patterns of isolation can continue. He reports that over 60% of the isolated kindergartners identified in his study were still isolated in second grade.

Cooperative learning models also draw upon some of the principles of play to foster both learning and peer relationships. In a review of cooperative learning, Slavin (1980a; 1983) lists four major models, all of which exemplify elements that are present in play and in many games:

- *Teams-games-tournaments* (DeVries & Slavin, 1978), in which diverse student teams practice together to prepare for a team tournament.
- *Student teams-achievement divisions* (Slavin, 1978, 1980a), which features a quiz technique rather than a tournament.
- *Jigsaw* (Aronson, 1978), in which students help others prepare academically to meet their learning goals.
- *Group investigation* (Sharan & Sharan, 1976), which involves an organizational plan that allows students to select teams, choose goals, and present their findings to others.

Slavin (1980b) concludes that, although there has been some inconsistency in results, the highly structured cooperative games tend to increase basic skill learning and the open-ended games tend to improve higher order cognitive skills. All methods seem to promote positive peer relationships including friendship, self-esteem, and enjoyment of school.

If children are to develop social abilities, the school environment must provide time for both playful and task-oriented social interaction. Oden (1987) proposes that some children's lack of peer acceptance is mainly a function of inadequate curriculum planning, particularly curricula that emphasize competition and/or allow too little time or opportunity for peer interaction during academic activities. As

manager of the classroom, the teacher can provide opportunities for playful and cooperative interactions among children and can encourage the development of positive peer relationships as a goal of the curriculum. The research on children's social relationships is extensive and can offer guidance for adults who are planning playful learning environments.

● Peer group relationships and friendship development

Six- to eleven-year-old children are greatly interested in their peer relationships, and the environment of the elementary school can have a major impact on the growth and development of these relationships. Chapter 5 describes the nature of middle childhood friendships (i.e., they can be activity partnerships, play-related friendships, or they can be both). The role of play and open learning environments in friendship development in middle childhood includes the following:

1. In middle childhood, children's understanding of friend relationships, particularly close ones, is based not only on opportunities to engage in common play activities but also on sharing of resources and cooperation; however, experiences regarded by children as playful appear to be the major vehicle for friendship development.

Berndt (1981b) explored the friendship conceptions of kindergartners, third graders, and sixth graders; children at all three ages considered engagement in "play or association" as the most salient category for friendship. Ladd and Emerson (1984) interviewed first- and fourth-grade children and found that they differed in what they knew about their friends. Fourth-grade mutual friends were aware of how their friends differed from themselves while first graders described their friends as being very similar to themselves. Children at both age levels described friends' observable characteristics (i.e., what they do) as well as psychological qualities (i.e., what they are like). Differences in interactions between children who are friends or not friends show up in a variety of ways. With their friends, children are less constrained in behavior (Foot, Chapman, & Smith, 1977), more lively in competitive and cooperative tasks (Newcomb, Brady & Hartup, 1979), and more likely to engage in fantasy play (Gottman, 1983).

Thus, friendships are both promoted during play and are especially evidenced in play during the middle childhood years.

> 2. In addition to friendship, children have activity partnerships, which have interactive purposes and characteristics that are somewhat different from friendships, but they also have many similar characteristics.

Oden, Herzberger, Mangione, and Wheeler (1984), in a study differentiating relationships between friends and activity partners, found that previously unacquainted, same-age pairs of children ranging in age from 5 to 7, who played together for short play periods over a five-day time span, behaved as activity partners rather than friends. That is, their conversation was primarily activity related and they were less direct in their communication than the friendship dyads were. Compared to friendship dyads from a previous study who engaged in the same activity (Wheeler, 1981), the activity partners in the Oden et al. study were less direct, disputed more, took longer turns, and made fewer comments about their own or their partner's activity.

In a study of elementary children's conceptions of "play friends" and "work friends," Cooper and Edward (1985) found that there were few differences in the two concepts, although children became increasingly selective in their friendship choices across the age range. Younger children described work friends in more general and static terms; both older and younger children cited common interests in play and reciprocal relationship qualities for play friendship choices (e.g., she helps me and I help her).

As discussed previously by Oden (1987), there may be a developmental progression in the ability to distinguish the collaborative partnership dimension from the friendship dimension of peer relationships. The factors that determine whether and how activity partners might become friends also need further exploration. According to Oden et al. (1984), research on peer relationships has often oversimplified matters by calling all sustained peer interactions friendships. As children grow older, they become increasingly able to engage in collaborative activity relationships defined in terms of the social roles needed in a particular context, and they learn to coordinate their actions with those of others, including children who are not their special friends, toward a common purpose.

Social play and social activity directed toward task accomplishment may reflect parallel developments or they may interface in stage-related ways. At the present time, their interrelated developmental patterns are unclear.

In school contexts, activity partnerships may emerge more readily if the environment encourages peer interaction and collaboration on tasks. Cooper and Edward (1985) suggest that helping children to have close relationships with one or two friends may be a prime goal for social skills training. Assisting children to learn how to have positive social interactions with peers in both play and activity relationships may be one of the more critical educative tasks of the school.

> 3. Many individual, social, and cultural variables influence the development of peer relationships; some of these factors make the establishment of friendships and/or activity partnerships more difficult for some children.

Peer relationships are more likely to develop between children of similar ages (Hartup, 1983), gender (Lockheed & Harris, 1984), race (Ramsey, 1985), and physical size and appearance (Graziano, 1984). Average school achievers are rated more popular than below-average achievers (Austin & Draper, 1984). Children who have difficulty with peer relationships include those who are socially neglected, those who withdraw from social contact (Gottman, 1977), and those who are rejected by peers because they are overly aggressive (Dodge, 1983).

Children with peer relationship problems often believe that they are socially incompetent, that their problems are due to uncontrollable factors, that peer rejection is unchangeable, and that it is not related to their own specific inappropriate actions (Oden, 1987). Since some innate characteristics do influence peer acceptance (e.g., physical or mental handicaps), these perceptions are not totally unrealistic (Dion, 1973).

When socially unskilled children do attempt to play with peers, they are usually required to play submissive roles or they are rebuffed, thus peer encounters reinforce their poor-self concept (Rubin, 1985a). Results of intervention research with low peer status children indicates that peer acceptance can be increased, however. Because the behaviors exhibited by children who have social problems are often only slightly discrepant from the "normal range," intervention that assists the children in learning to cross over the "threshold of acceptance" may be sufficient (Oden, 1987). Gaining experience in positive peer interactions in group contexts is important to children in the middle years. Cognitively, they are capable of negotiation, competition, cooperation, and social problem solving (Damon, 1977; Piaget, 1932).

Research on cooperative learning, which uses a gamelike team approach with elementary children in either traditional or open classroom settings, has shown that in addition to academic benefits (e.g., mastery, retention, and transfer), motivation is higher with this approach. Moreover, children gain in self-esteem and in acceptance by peers, and are perceived more positively by teachers (Johnson & Johnson, 1974, 1975, 1979b). These methods have improved intergroup relations, especially between children of different ethnic groups and between mainstreamed children and other class members (Slavin, 1980b, 1980c). Whether long-term friendships can be fostered through these methods has not been determined.

Although mainstreaming studies have demonstrated that mere placement of handicapped children in regular classrooms is not sufficient to promote play and friendships between handicapped and normal peers, those that include planned play interventions often show improved peer relationships. In two studies of play with autistic and nonhandicapped elementary children, the nonautistic children went to the autistic children's class. They were told to help the autistic children to learn to play better, and they succeeded in promoting more normal play in the autistic children. The nonhandicapped children's social skills and attitude toward the handicapped children also improved (McHale, 1983; McHale & Boone, 1980).

Interactions Between the Physical and Social Environment and Other Factors

As is true of the environments discussed in earlier chapters, physical and social design factors operate interactively to affect children's behavior and learning. Parents, teachers, and peers mediate the effects of physical environment features, and developmental changes in children (e.g., age-related cognitive or gender role behavior) affect social interactions. The following points illustrate a few of these interactions:

1. Studies of home play factors that influence academic learning show that physical environment factors (e.g., the presence of books, literacy-readiness toys, time and space for play) interact with those of the social environment (e.g., parents who value play, provide models of reading, talk about children's activities).

In a review of home reading environments, Becher (1985) cites a number of studies showing that parental involvement with their children in reading books on a regular basis promotes higher reading achievement and more positive attitudes toward reading (e.g., Hoskins, 1976; Romotowski & Trepanier, 1977), and that parent-child discussion and question answering with books contributes to reading achievement (e.g., Snow, 1983; Teale, 1978). Laosa (1982) found that older siblings also influence intellectual development; for example, siblings spend a significant amount of time reading books to preschoolers. More studies of these interactions (e.g., parental-child, television-child, and computer-child) are needed.

2. Individual differences in children's cognitive or personality development interact with environmental factors.

The studies of toy preferences and academic learning point to individual differences in children that may influence their choices of materials in the environment. For example, the young children in Thomas' (1984) study who played more with reading-readiness toys were seen by their parents as more quiet and less difficult children. Whether temperamental differences influenced the children's choice of play materials or whether their interest in those materials promoted a more quiet attitude is unclear. Because parents tend to be evaluative of their children's behavior (Bacon & Ashmore, 1982), parents whose children play with quiet reading-readiness materials might react favorably to that behavior, thus reinforcing the reading-readiness play.

Children's individual cognitive developmental stages also interact with social and physical environmental variables. Hiebert (1980) concludes that logical reasoning ability and "print awareness" are more predictive of reading skill than are home environment variables. Other studies have also found reading to be related to concrete operational thinking (e.g., Becher & Wolfgang, 1977; Polk & Goldstein, 1980). Just as early language, symbolic play, and cognitive development are related in infancy, so concrete operational thought, language and reading, and play experiences with print and other literacy materials seem to be closely related in the elementary years. These relationships probably hold for other academic content areas as well. With the exception of early readers, these relationships have not been studied.

3. Although open learning environments generally have positive effects, teachers' values, curricular objectives, and management practices influence the outcomes of learning in open, play-encouraging learning environments, as well as in traditional, work-encouraging learning environments.

Unfortunately, the research comparing open and traditional elementary school environments includes many confounded variables; therefore, it is sometimes difficult to assess the effects of play in those environments. Research studies comparing global aspects of curricula differences (e.g., traditionally structured programs versus open education programs) and using tests of basic skill learning or problem-solving performance as the effectiveness measures have not demonstrated that open-design or play-encouraging environments are either more or less effective in teaching basic skills in the elementary years (e.g., Epstein & McPartland, 1979). However, in a review of the research on open versus traditional programs, Minuchin and Shapiro (1983) conclude that a wide range of positive effects are more frequently associated with the open school environments.

For example, children in open classrooms have more positive attitudes toward school (Horwitz, 1979); become more positive the longer they are in such schools (Traub, Weiss, & Fisher, 1974); have more differentiated self-concepts (Horwitz, 1979); have less gender role stereotyped and more cross-gender contact (Bianchi & Bakeman, 1978); exhibit more cooperative behavior (Horwitz, 1979); and are more autonomous (Horwitz, 1979). Hallinan (1976) reports much clearer and stable categories of popular and isolated children in traditional classrooms as compared to open classrooms. Thus it may be more difficult to help socially unskilled children to gain friends in a traditional environment, which generally has fewer opportunities for children to construct peer interaction and form relationships.

In a study of the "operating environments" of open and traditional schools that described sequences and time periods of activity in the classrooms, Gump (1975) found that children in open primary level environments used more learning sites, interacted with more adults, and were engaged in more "pupil active" and "pupil interdependent" programs. They did not spend more time on task, possibly because of the amount of time required for individual activity preparation before beginning tasks, which in these settings required them to wait until the teacher was ready for a group to begin an activity. Minuchin and Shapiro (1983) state that often "off-task" behavior is recorded in studies whenever children engage in a social interaction, thus inappropriately skewing the results toward classrooms where no social exchange is allowed. Gump found that neither open nor traditional settings allowed children many opportunities for leadership or independent responsibility. These results may be due to the teachers' management rather than to the physical settings.

Although the open environment may have many positive effects, Minuchin and Shapiro (1983) cite evidence that teachers who work in open settings but who do not value the open teaching approach "close what is open in any way they can: by walling off open areas with cabinets or bookcases (Gump, 1978), or by establishing traditional rules for behavior that restrict the social possibilities of the space and design" (p. 206). Similarly, teachers in traditional classrooms may "opt for an open program, redesigning classrooms to provide more flexibility . . . " (p. 206).

In sum, although many variables interact in the global environment of the school, environments that foster approaches to learning that involve play, discovery, and choice result in many positive outcomes, as long as teachers support those outcomes.

4. The increasing gender/sex role differences in play, friendships, activity partnerships, and other social interactions of boys and girls during middle childhood may be related to the physical and social environment of the school.

In a review of the factors involved in the role of play in the socialization process, Schwartzman (1978, 1980) cites evidence from ethnographic studies clearly showing that gender-appropriate play behavior and role distinctions are increasingly apparent in many cultures as children move through the middle childhood years. Researchers who have studied playground games in middle childhood find a limited set of common games played by both boys and girls (Rosenberg & Sutton-Smith, 1960). Given the differences in gender-based, parent-child interactions, in toys provided to boys and to girls, in teacher responses based on gender, and in peer play patterns of preschoolers, it is not surprising that gender/sex role stereotypic play and peer group separation based on gender is noted in the later elementary years. The books used in school may also promote stereotypic models of boys' and girls' play. For example, books may imply that boys play much *more* than girls (McVaigh & Johnson, 1979).

In middle childhood, boys' and girls' achievement motivation, cognitive abilities, and occupational goals become increasingly different (see Huston, 1983, for a review of these factors). Girls have lower expectancies of success and lower levels of aspiration. They fear failure more and attribute failure to their lack of ability, while boys tend to attribute their failures to external causes and their success to their ability. Children stereotype athletic, spatial, and mechanical skills as masculine, and verbal, artistic, and social skills as feminine. Differences in math performance have been noted (e.g., Fennema & Sherman, 1977). Huston comments that "differences in performance generally parallel social stereotypes" (p. 405). These stereotypes are often promoted by both school and home environments (Minuchin, 1965).

Lack of opportunities to engage in a wide range of activity and play may be related to these stereotypic differences in interests, goals, and abilities. For example, Carpenter (1983) asserts that adult encouragement of high structure activities for girls and low

structure activities for boys promotes these gender differences. She suggests that girls learn how to fit into the structures of others while boys learn to create structures of their own in play. Boys usually play less under adult direction, are encouraged to use toys that require organizing space, and play games that need rule negotiation and design. School behavior reflects these socialization expectations, with girls performing well in content areas where following arbitrary, pre-existing rules is required (e.g., reading and spelling) but less well in content areas requiring organizing and conceptualizing space and materials or exploring possibilities (e.g., science and math). Environments that encourage both genders to engage in both structured and unstructured activity can broaden all children's abilities and enhance both boys' and girls' feelings of competence (Carpenter, 1983).

Research on teachers' responses (reviewed by Minuchin & Shapiro, 1983) indicates teachers in traditional classrooms tend to reinforce differentiations (e.g., "boys line up first, then girls") and give few opportunities for boys and girls to engage in cross-gender cooperative play or work groups. On the other hand, studies of open school environments indicate that children have both more differentiated and more broadly defined self-concepts and have more cross-gender friendships in these settings (Hallinan & Tuma, 1978; Serbin, Tonick & Sternglanz, 1977). When cooperative cross-gender groups are used in an atmosphere of competition, however, they can also reinforce gender/sex role stereotypes. For example, in one study boys tended to be the leaders in cross-gender activity groups; girls indicated a preference for same-gender groups more than boys did, possibly because of this male-dominant leadership problem (Lockheed & Harris, 1984).

The complexity of the factors that influence gender-related behaviors makes it difficult to predict effects of teacher and school environments on gender/sex role behavior; however, greater knowledge of these factors can help teachers be aware of the influence of their behaviors on gender/sex-role stereotyping.

5. The contextual distinctions made by older and younger children in the elementary classroom influence their definitions of work and play and their responses to teacher-

labeled play and work activities; these distinctions may have long-term implications for how they view work and play as adults.

The studies of King (1979, 1982a, 1982b, 1982c) have demonstrated the interaction of physical and social environmental variables in children's evaluation of the climate of classrooms in regard to the distinctions between work and play. King (1979) points out that in the kindergarten, environmental signals about timing of play help to socialize children into the school's work-oriented environment. Although play is considered an acceptable activity, and the environment includes play materials such as blocks, house and doll equipment, flexible art materials, and gross and fine motor toys, children quickly learn that time for play is limited and is usually secondary to work time. Integrating the play needs of children and the work-oriented requirements of the school is a major goal of the kindergarten teacher.

According to King (1979), kindergarten children characterize the distinction between work and play primarily in terms of its social context (i.e., work is an activity required by the teacher and play is an activity chosen by the child, even when the materials and the actions are similar). For example, a math game that all children must play is labeled work but choosing to use the math materials during free time is considered play by the children. The availability of academic skill materials during times when children have choices of activity can foster their perceptions that learning these skills can also be enjoyable.

Older elementary children make distinctions between work and play on a different basis. By fifth grade children judge work and play on the basis of the "psychological context of their experience" (King, 1982c, p. 111). Activities are divided into work (i.e., required activities children think are difficult or tedious), play (i.e., either required or freely chosen activities children think are enjoyable), and "real" play (i.e., enjoyable activities done at recess or in out-of-school time). King contends that adult labeling of activities as work or play make children aware of adult perspectives that devalue play and promote work. However, children still use their own internal criteria to determine what they think are worklike or playlike learning activities. Fourth and fifth graders call academic games "play" if they enjoy them; kin-

dergartners call building with blocks "work" if an adult requires them to build.

King (1982c) contends that work and play can be integrated rather than differentiated in the classroom because the curricular activities have no intrinsic characteristics that make them work or play. Leaning contexts can be created that include both characteristics of playfulness (e.g., choices, enjoyment, imagination) and workmanship (e.g., task completion, goal orientation). Academic experiences that include dimensions of self-direction and voluntary participation can enhance both playfulness and workmanship.

An environment in which children can experience enjoyment and freedom in meeting challenges and striving at optimal capacity promotes the quality of "flow" (Csikszentmihayli, 1975). Block (1984), who has stressed the value of mastery learning, believes that making school activities more playlike will foster flow and enhance mastery. Adults who have the capacity to play intensely and to work with enjoyment are those who have been able to integrate work and play in their lives. Whether the school environment sharply differentiates between more valued work and less valued play or is designed to promote the integration of work and play will have an influence not only on children's immediate learning, but also on their attitudes toward work and play throughout life.

Guidelines for Home Environments

Although the play environments of the neighborhood and the larger community are particularly important for elementary-age children, the home continues to be an essential place for the fostering of play and learning. The time that parents and children have together to play Chinese checkers, build and fly kites, make and decorate cookie faces, talk about plans for fantasy trips into space or for mountain climbing expeditions, figure out solutions to word puzzles, and share their reading or television watching experiences is well spent. Parental provision of places where messy activities can be done without fear of censure, of old hats or clothes that can serve as costumes for a play, of display space for bottle cap collections or paintings, and of tools for digging up buried treasure are also ways that the home environment can encourage play in middle childhood.

Parents can also give children time alone so that they can daydream, explore the basement boxes, write in diaries, and just "do nothing"; parents can also allow children time to be "out" with their neighborhood friends. Finally, parents' help in planning some of their children's out-of-school time so that it includes formal group participation (e.g., in Scouts or the Girls' or Boys' Club), lessons (e.g., dance, piano, or judo), sports activities (e.g., basketball or swimming), and visits to neighborhood and community sites (e.g., museums or nature centers) is also needed. Parents must plan appropriate alternative play environments and/or well-designed arrangements for safe play at home if they will not be there when children get home from school.

According to Bergstrom (1984, p. 10), "Parents can learn to strike a delicate balance between demanding too much and providing too little" during their children's out-of-school time. By following the leads provided by their children's interests, parents can help them avoid having "empty afternoons" while also avoiding too many highly structured activities that crowd out time for play. Bergstrom suggests that parents take the lead in helping children plan portions of their time in ways that increase their proficiency in activities that they particularly enjoy, while at the same time helping them keep a broader perspective and develop versatile competencies. Many of these planned experiences may involve functional play (e.g., motor practice of sports skills); symbolic play (e.g., making up computer programs or writing and performing plays); and games-with-rules (e.g., playing kickball, red rover, or checkers).

During middle childhood, only a few elements are essential for a rich home play environment: (a) a room, yard, basement, or other space that is available for children's flexible use and in which their decisions about environmental arrangements, neatness and order, privacy, manipulation of materials, and clean-up periods are respected; (b) "loose parts," such as junk material, boxes, art paper, mechanical equipment discards, sheets and old clothes, as well as commercial play equipment that can be combined and recombined as the play demands; and (c) uninterrupted blocks of time that are available for play

and a rule that those blocks of time cannot all be spent in passive television watching.

There are only a few essential home social environmental requirements as well: (a) adults who are comfortable with children's taking charge of their play environment and who are responsive to children's requests for materials, rearrangements, and time and space needs; (b) adults who enjoy and value play with their children, who include time for parent-child interactive play, who observe and admire play creations when asked to do so, and who share their own play interests and hobbies; and (c) play friends who are welcome in the home and/or siblings who are encouraged to spend some playtime together.

As pressures for academic achievement and sports-related performance increase in our society, the physical and social environment of the home can provide an important haven for children of 6 to 11. It is the place they can retire when the competition gets too rough, a safe site for attempting projects that need practice before they can be displayed, and the location where their imaginary life can be maintained in privacy and safety. Home should be the place where children's choices and freedom in play are always respected.

Guidelines for School Environments

Most children of 6 through 11 are in the cognitive developmental stage of concrete operations (Piaget, 1952). This stage includes the ability to reason logically, solve problems by considering alternatives, and understand the perspectives of others, with the use of concrete materials as aids to thought processes. Elementary children are capable of symbolic thinking and following rules to find solutions; however, they are not yet able to reason abstractly and mentally consider a range of possible solutions to a problem. Formal rather than concrete reasoning is often required in school when children still have difficulty reasoning abstractly. Thus, they may memorize rules, definitions of concepts, and algorithmic processes in a rote fashion, conceptualizing them as what Piaget calls "verbalisms" rather than with true understanding. Because they are so adept at repeating verbalisms, they can often fool adults into thinking that they understand a concept that they really do not understand. One of the major tasks of elementary teachers is to test continually the level of understanding that children actually have. Observing their play with concrete mathematical, language, science, and other materials is a way they can determine children's level of knowledge.

Because elementary children are capable of creating unique play experiences and sharing them in collaborative endeavors, adults in the school should provide opportunities and materials geared to individual creativity and discovery, collaborative play, and the sharing of self in social play and close friendships. It is important for adults to interact with children and listen carefully to their expressions of attitudes and feelings.

Although these experiences can occur in physical environments that are not intentionally designed to promote playful learning, they are much more likely to occur in settings with open classroom approaches. Educational proponents such as Dewey (1916/1966) and the leaders of the British infant school movement have emphasized the importance of learning by doing. In the elementary school, where the critical foundation for subsequent academic learning is formed, children must gain not only the formal knowledge of reading, writing, spelling, science, mathematics, and social science, but also a love of knowledge-seeking in formal knowledge disciplines. In an educational setting that stresses individual control of one's ability to learn, master, and innovate (i.e., in a setting that promotes playful learning), the long-term love of learning is likely to be strengthened. Moreover, development of metacognition (i.e., the ability to think about thinking) is also assisted by play (Flavell, 1976, 1981). Aspects of the school physical and social environment that foster play as a medium for learning include the following:

● The physical environment

Play environments (i.e., environments in which children have opportunities to enjoy their learning, make choices, and have inner control, inner motivation, and inner reality) in the elementary school can be especially created by environmental designers or architects, or they can be created by teachers' transformations of ordinary classrooms. In either case, the same ingredients make the environment a successful one for play and learning. The basic ingredients in both of these environments are as follows:

1. *There is a rich variety of concrete materials that provide multisensory experiences.* The environment is planned so that children have many ways to gain information; opportunities to manipulate objects and elicit response variations; chances to ask and answer questions through experimenting, observing, organizing, and recording; and encouragement to relate their experiences to formal knowledge in the content fields (Taylor & Vlastos, 1975).

2. *The spatial arrangements maximize flexibility in activities.* Children have space to move about the environment, rearrange space to accommodate their activities, and keep constructions or projects for a day or week. A variety of scales and levels, hard and soft areas, quiet and noisy places, large and small spaces, types of furniture, and storage areas are provided.

3. *The environment is related to the curriculum, with learning objectives identified and experiences provided that give children opportunities to meet those learning objectives through self-directed actions and play, as well as through teacher-directed tasks and work.* Rich resource areas for reading and writing, using mathematical materials, experimenting with science, nature, and art/music activities, and engaging in social science experiences are provided. When computers are used, they are expected to foster playful, creative, and higher order thinking. Because play is valued as a curricular tool, opportunities for functional, construction, symbolic, and game play, and goals of cooperative play and learning are considered in the arrangement of materials and space.

4. *Blocks of time are provided that allow children to delve deeply into activities and explore materials in depth.* According to Palmer (1971), "liberation of time" is essential if discovery learning and play development are to occur.

5. *Beauty and order in the environment are created and maintained by the children.* The children feel ownership of their classroom because they have had a voice in planning the space and room

to exhibit their artistic and academic work. Children in the elementary school should have the opportunity to "help create their own school world" (Frank, 1958). This world may have different aesthetic standards from those of adults; children's and adults' standards should be balanced in the classroom.

● The social environment

The interactions of teacher and children are different in an environment that values playful learning. The teacher is seen less as an authority figure who requires children to learn and more as a facilitator of learning for children who are actively motivated to seek knowledge through exploration and play. The social environment fosters the development of both classroom activity partnerships and friendships. The following social environmental principles hold for play environments:

1. *The children see themselves as part of a larger social unit.* Teachers encourage children's discussion and consensus on rules for the class that make the learning environment pleasant and productive. Further, teachers promote collaborative and cooperative learning through games, constructive play, and group symbolic activities (Proshansky & Wolfe, 1975). Prosocial behavior and nonviolent conflict resolution are modeled and taught (Kreidler, 1984).

2. *The teacher and children employ a model of instruction that can be described as "scaffolding."* Children have a role in negotiating their learning. Teachers facilitate as well as direct learning activities and are responsive to children's self-initiated learning needs. Together children and teacher engage in the construction of knowledge (Wood, Bruner, & Ross, 1976).

3. *Those children who have difficulty finding friendship are given assistance by the teacher in becoming more socially skilled.* Teachers plan heterogeneous groups that include members with varied abilities and provide peer models and coaching to less accepted children. The teacher believes that fostering social and emotional development of children is an appropriate curricular objective, and that play is an appro-

priate means for meeting that objective, as well as meeting academic objectives (Oden, 1987).

● Play as a curricular tool in language arts, science, math, social sciences, and aesthetic areas

Although an in-depth discussion of methods for fostering playful learning in specific content areas is beyond the scope of this book, opportunities for building on children's creativity and imagination, role-playing abilities, and interest in games, abound in the content areas of science, mathematics, social studies, and language arts. Integration of these content areas in learning experiences for elementary-age children can provide the kind of learning that they classify as "play" (i.e., "play" but not "real play," according to King's, 1982c, definitions) because the activities are enjoyable, challenging, intellectually interesting, and they foster internal control.

For example, the curriculum unit "Voyage to the New World" (Fehrenbach & Daniel, 1984), designed for fourth to sixth graders with a range of ability levels, integrates study of European voyages of discovery with knowledge of how astronomy was used for early navigation, and links both to the "new world" of space travel. Playful activities include role-playing of historical characters and events, game playing (e.g., "Who am I," "Trivia," "The Voyage Game"), creative writing (e.g., poetry, a newspaper giving the "news" of these historical events, imaginary correspondence), mapmaking, astronomy plotting, a planetarium visit, and art activities (e.g., calligraphy, murals, ship models, flags, coats of arms). For children in grades one through three, a similarly integrated unit, "LEA on the Moon," has been designed (Fehrenbach, Greer, & Daniel, 1986). Other play-eliciting curricula include many in science (e.g., "Batteries and Bulbs," Delta Education, 1966); mathematics (e.g., "I Do, and I Understand," Nuffield Mathematics Project, 1967), and social studies (e.g., "Teaching About Spaceship Earth," Torney & Mastrude, 1972).

Language arts activities that draw on children's experiences should not be restricted to the primary grades. Both older and younger children need many opportunities to integrate their experiences through writing reports and newspapers, creating poetry, fiction, and drama, and using tape recorders, word processors, and cameras. Performance of their dramatic and musical creations, display of their artistic endeavors, and participation in unified themes of learning are all "basics" of the elementary curriculum at every grade (e.g., Beetlestone & Taylor, 1982; Berry, 1984; Graves, 1977). Even their own "folklore" can be incorporated in the learning experience (Sitton & Jeter, 1980).

Playful approaches to higher order cognitive skills such as critical thinking are also described in curricular materials (e.g., Costa, 1985). These approaches are especially important during the elementary years as children begin to be able to "play with ideas," testing their thinking and comparing it with that of their peers. Opportunities for creating playful challenges that have a comfortable level of risk are crucial during this age period and should be available at school.

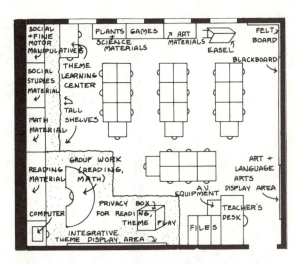

FIGURE 10–1 • Adapted Elementary Classroom (Primary), 1–3

Models of Elementary Classroom Environments

Architects have created many school designs that were supposed to foster open, child-controlled, playful, and integrated learning. These schools have only been as successful as the educators in them wanted them to be (Minuchin & Shapiro, 1983). Ultimately the climate of learning is created by the people who use an educational environment. That is why all teachers who want to include elements of playful learning in the educational environment can do so, even if their schools have traditional physical designs.

Figures 10–1 and 10–2 illustrate models of two teacher-designed environments: one at first- and the other at fourth-grade level. These environments are adapted from the classrooms of two teachers, S. Timm and B. Timm, at the Lakeside School, Pittsburg, Kansas. These environments contain most of the typical materials, equipment, and space constraints of traditional elementary classrooms; however, they have been designed so that children (a) have access to many resources, (b) can feel some control and choice, (c) can learn to work independently and cooperatively, and (d) can gain experience in integrating learning from a variety of content

fields. Even though the classrooms are of limited size, every inch of shelf space, floor space, closet space, and wall space is a planned part of the learning environment.

Because space constraints make it impossible to provide many learning centers, each classroom has rotating centers that focus on themes that integrate content from a number of areas. Floor-to-ceiling shelves are identified as resource centers, with storage on the top shelves and materials related to the week's curricular plans located on the lower accessible shelves. Space is further defined by carpets on some floor areas, private spaces (cardboard boxes or closets), desks grouped to foster cooperative learning, and furniture that is is rearranged according to changing curricular needs.

The social environment created by the teacher and children is one of cooperation, challenge, respect, and interest. According to the Timms, the social climate is "relaxed but controlled," because "children learn better when they are relaxed." Attention is paid to peer relationships and to giving children leadership opportunities. Both independent activity and group activity are planned, and boys and girls are encouraged to participate together. The grouped desks at times permit "conversation islands," especially when the class is involved in an

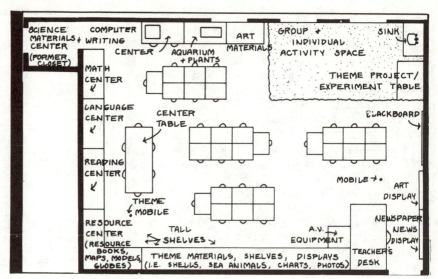

FIGURE 10–2 • Adapted Elementary Classroom (Middle Grades), 4–6

integrated project like the "sea circus," planned to culminate study of the sea (first grade) or a social science, language arts, and science integrated project of a "Hawaiian luau" (fourth grade). Humor is encouraged when it is appropriate for the activity; for example, imaginary sea animals (e.g., ones that eat "octupizza") are drawn by fourth graders, and "silly sentences" are used for practicing writing in first grade.

Integrating language arts, math, science, and social science in activity-based themes may require some additional resources, but the Timms believe that its main requirement is additional teacher time, because "you can't do all the planning at school." They maintain that teachers have to "enjoy doing this" if children are to enjoy their learning.

Although traditional classrooms can promote playful learning, specially designed environments can provide a wealth of opportunities of this type. Figure 10–3 shows a classroom architecturally designed to create a playful, open approach to learning (Taylor & Vlastos, 1975). This environment incorporates many of the ideal qualities that elementary schools should have in order to foster open learning. The number of levels, the varied textures, the well-designed private and group spaces, and the rich resources available are evident in the model plan. Taylor and Vlastos

stress that the basic design principles can be translated into many settings. The crucial variable is "a rich, ever-changing learning environment" (p. 112). The social environment provided in this architecturally designed environment is not very different from that of a teacher-designed environment. The Taylor and Vlastos environment promotes "confidence, initiative, and responsibility," as well as demonstrating to children "the very ideals of our democratic society" (p. 112).

Taylor and Preiser (no date) have developed guidelines that can be used to redesign a traditional school classroom to incorporate features similar to those in the Taylor and Vlastos (1975) plan, shown in Figure 10–3. Taylor and Preiser suggest "generic learning zones" that vary from active to passive, quiet to noisy, and vertical to horizontal. They include (a) entry, (b) work, (c) storage systems, (d) display/museum, (e) graphic arts, (f) technology, (g) living things, (h) research/library, and (i) soft/home-like zones. A zone for the teacher and a transition zone between indoors and outdoors are also recommended. Figure 10–4 shows a traditional classroom redesigned by Vlastos, which follows these guidelines. All four of the environmental models (Figures 10–1 through 10–4) are designed to foster an integration of play, work, and learning.

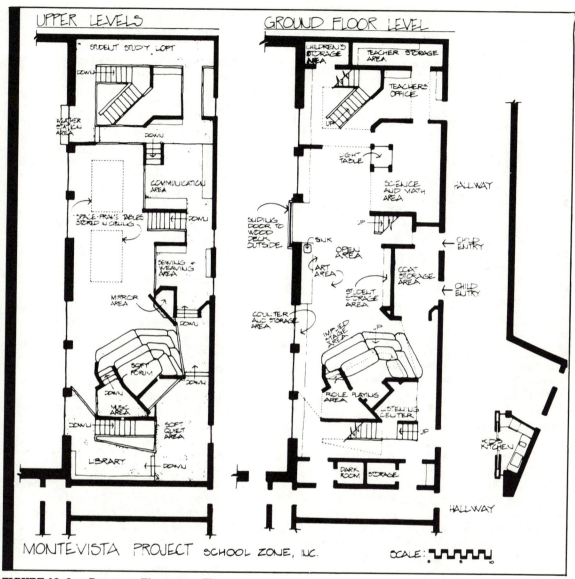

FIGURE 10–3 • Prototype Elementary Classroom

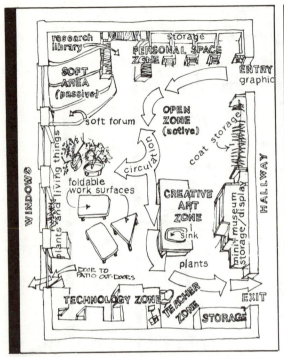

FIGURE 10–4 • Adapted Elementary Classroom (Drawing by George Vlastos, School Zone, Inc., Architect)

Conclusion

Environments for children in the elementary grades have often been rigid, bland, unattractive, and unimaginative. Thus, they have not encouraged children to use all of their senses in their search for knowledge, to dream of possibilities, to create and solve problems, or to develop cooperative modes of learning. Although "basic" skills learning is certainly an essential focus of the school, it should not be the only focus. Educators, administrators, parents, and the larger community must keep in mind the importance of rich and varied learning experiences that can be mastered and integrated through playful means. Children's needs for play should be recognized as part of curricular planning. The importance of their developing peer relationships should also be considered in education design. Children should have opportunities to learn how to integrate and transform their work and to achieve required tasks by using all of their capabilities, including their play abilities.

Questions for Discussion

1. Given what we know about children's stages of play development, what should be the teacher's role in encouraging cross-gender play in middle childhood?
2. Should a 6-year-old child who seems to prefer to play alone in the classroom or on the playground and to be happy playing alone be encouraged to change? Why or why not? Is he or she capable of changing social status? What about a 9-year-old? How does the social adjustment of 6- or 9-year-olds who play alone compare to that of 4-year-olds who engage primarily in solitary play?

Play Activity Problems

1. You are teaching second grade in a school that has a limited number of manipulative materials, a small school library, and traditional classroom furniture and equipment in each classroom. The materials presently available include workbooks for every child in reading, spelling, writing, math, and social studies. There are sets of two basal reader series, and math, social studies, and science textbooks. There is an old science kit on the top shelf of the closet and a computer that you must share with the first grade. Your principal tells you that you can spend $300 for curriculum materials. Describe what you would purchase, make, or obtain without cost and how you would rearrange the furniture and equipment to turn your classroom into a play and learning environment.
2. An architect is visiting your school to get ideas for a new school building that will house third through fifth graders. List the 10 high-priority suggestions you would give the architect and give a reason why each suggestion would be important to include in a school that will be designed as a play and learning environment. List five behaviors that a teacher would need to exhibit in order to promote children's social and intellectual development in that environment.

Suggestions for Further Reading

Bergstrom, J. M. (1984). *School's out—now what?* Berkeley, CA: Ten Speed Press. Provides many suggestions for out-of-school time, especially for children whose parents are both still at work when school is out. Also gives a philosophy that balances parental concern with children's use of time and children's need for choice and independence in play.

Blau, R., Brady, E. H., Bucher, I., Hiteshew, B., Zavitkovsky A., & Zavitkowsky, D. (1977). *Activities for school-age child care.* Washington, DC: National Association for the Education of Young Children. Gives an overview of after-school child-care and suggests a range of play activities that elementary-age children would enjoy in any setting (i.e., home, school, or after-school child-care).

Cartledge, G., & Milburn, J. F. (Eds.) (1986). *Teaching social skills to children: Innovative approaches.* (2nd ed.). New York: Pergamon Press. Describes research-based techniques that have been effective in helping children to learn better social interaction and play patterns.

Fehrenbach, C. R., Greer, F. S., & Daniel, T. B. (1986). LEA on the moon. *Science and Children, 25*(5), 15–17. Gives an example of an integrated approach to language arts and science for primary grade children.

Gottman, J. M. (1983). How children become friends. *Monographs of the Society for Research in Child Development, 44*(3, Serial No. 201). Provides an overview of the processes by which children become friends.

Kreidler, W. J. (1984). *Creative conflict resolution.* Glenview, IL: Scott, Foresman. Contains interesting and effective methods for creating a classroom climate that promotes negotiation, cooperation, and peer understanding. Helps children learn a philosophy of problem solving through peace-promoting rather than aggressive means.

Oden, S. (1986). Developing social skills instruction for peer interaction. In G. Cartledge & J. F. Milburn (Eds.), *Teaching social skills to children: Innovative approaches* (2nd ed., pp. 246–269). New York: Pergamon Press. Gives research-based but practical suggestions for teachers and other adults to use in helping children to improve their social skills.

Newman, J. (Ed.) (1985). *Whole language: Theory in use.* Portsmouth, NH: Heinemann. Provides information on approaches to language, reading, and writing that use playful "whole language" experiences.

Schools Council. (1971). *Informal schools in Britain today.* New York: Citation Press. Includes a series of books on aspects of informal education (e.g., *Space, time and grouping; Reading and writing; Music*) that give a picture of how teachers plan and operate in an open setting.

Taylor, A. P., & Vlastos, G. (1975). *School zone, learning environments for children.* New York: Van Nostrand Reinhold. Provides a rationale, guidelines, and practical suggestions for creating or transforming one classroom or an entire school into a rich, inviting play and learning environment. Also includes suggestions for outdoor play environments.

The Computer in the Play Environment

ANNE E. PORTER

How can computers and robots (i.e., computers designed for movement) be integrated appropriately into early childhood play environments? While the pros and cons of their inclusion continue to be debated, the ultimate impact of these potential "playthings" is unknown. As adults plan ways of incorporating the computer into the home or school setting, they must be clear about two basic points: First, interaction with the computer requires computer programs. Although young children may write simple "Logo" type programs, their experience with the computer environment is primarily dependent upon programs written by adults. Second, although the presence of computers may have some specific effects on environments, their impact is affected by and related to the total physical, social, emotional, and cognitive environment of the home or school setting.

The first point implies that adults who write, sell, and purchase computer programs may have theoretical views that could lead them at one extreme to use the computer to teach drill and practice exercises or alternatively to promote playful experiences fostering higher levels of thought, creativity, fantasy, and sociability. The implication of the second point is that the characteristics of the total environment, as reflections of these adults' perspectives, will greatly affect how children interact with and learn from the computer.

It is fascinating to note the differences in various adults' reactions when they observe children's interest in computers. Those who view play as a learning medium and those who see play as an immature and inconsequential pastime see the role of computers for children very differently. Adults not necessarily knowledgeable about play neverthe-less readily recognize the power they are ob-serving and their first reaction often is to try to harness that power to control children's learning. They envision 3-year-olds recogniz-ing the alphabet, identifying symbols for words and quantities, or matching complex diagrams. They don't realize that these are such low level cognitive skills that even a computer can master them. The person who understands the learning that can come from play approaches the uses of computers very differently. For example, here are the words of a preschool teacher:

While using a program with children, notice how they are bringing other curriculum areas to the computer. For example, some children use com-puter programs that make sounds to make their own music rather than repeating the routine pro-gram. Notice how easily they pick up computer "lingo," such as "get back to the menu," and how they learn the sequences for loading, the letters they need to recognize in order to program, and concepts such as left and right. Watch the motor skills that they exercise while using the keyboard and the joystick. Observe the children's social skills. How do they help each other? Do they share computer time and space? How independent of adult help do they become? (Daniels, 1985)

This teacher had no previous experience with computers, but as she learned about them through her observations, she became intrigued with the possibilities and the at-tractions that computers had for children. This is an example of what can happen in an environment that consistently supports a view of play as a medium for learning. The staff in this teacher's school is chosen and educated to exemplify this trust in children's active seeking of knowledge. Further, the environ-ment is arranged to make playful learning possible. The setting is open and accessible, rich in a variety of materials and equipment, and supportive of both individual and group play. In a social environment that encourages child initiative and choice of activities, the computer is seen as just another play choice in that environment. The children think they are playing, and the teacher thinks they are learning (King, 1979), and of course, they are doing both. The question remains, what are they learning?

Children learn from their interactions with the physical and social environment. From people children learn about acting and being acted upon, and how they can influ-ence others' actions and reactions. Because of the nature of the social world, they also learn that social interaction is not totally predict-able. The physical environment provides a different set of lessons. When it is acted upon, natural laws bring about consistent outcomes. Children's interactions with their physical and social environments provide them with different sets of information. The unique learning from the computer is gained from its blending of these two types of experiences: (a) the responsiveness and variation in ability to control and influence responses that is characteristic of the social world; and (b) the predictable and consistent interactions learned from the physical world. Because children can make the computer respond as they wish, they get a feeling of power. But with that power comes responsibility. If the computer doesn't respond as they expect it to, because of their past experience with its consistency, they are more likely to consider the possibility that they are responsible for the computer's unanticipated responses.

Another aspect of computer experience is related to the interaction of the realms of development—physical, social, emotional, and cognitive. The computer may encourage a higher level of interaction by allowing assimilation of abstract concepts such as sequences or classifications at a symbolically "semi" concrete level. Images on the screen are a step away from the concrete physical environment; they can't be touched or held and manipulated. But children can act on them and control them. Sometimes there appears to be a "dance" between computer and child that is similar to the dance described by Brazelton (1978) when he observed the interaction patterns of mothers and children. In this exchange routine, one of the participants (i.e., the computer) never gets tired. Through the two-dimensional images on the screen, children learn about the process of manipulating ideas in this environment, integrating all developmental realms. This bridge between the concrete and the abstract worlds may help children learn to manipulate ideas, assimilating and consolidating knowledge of these two world (Fein, 1985a).

If computers are used to force the introduction of abstract symbol systems, however, the playfully constructed bridge evaporates. Then the ABC's and the 123's will be as meaningless to children drilled by the computer as to those drilled by dittos or flash cards. Because play actively engages the imagination and encourages the creation of new possibilities, those children who have the opportunity to engage their imagination in active computer play with ideas may develop deeper understandings of concepts and greater creativity and flexibility of thought. Because children also use the computer as a social mediator (Swigger, Campbell, & Swigger, 1983), their experience may foster social skills such as cooperation and reciprocal turn taking as well. Even if higher levels of integrated development are not the ultimate outcomes of computer play, however, the computer can be enjoyed as a plaything if adults provide the environment that supports its use as another choice, among many, for play.

CHAPTER ELEVEN

Designing Special Play Environments

DORIS BERGEN ● LAURA GAYNARD ● EVELYN HAUSSLEIN

Because play is pervasive in the lives of children, every environment they inhabit has the potential to be a play environment. The previous chapters in this section have described how the play and learning of children of different ages can be promoted in the home and in formal educational environments. There are many other environments—city streets, neighborhood vacant lots, community parks and playgrounds, rural fields and forests—that can be play settings for children. Museums and shopping malls, video arcades and after-school clubs, zoos, and beaches are all potential sites for play. So are hospitals, rehabilitation centers, out-patient clinics, and intervention programs for the multihandicapped. The value of play in promoting the development of effective coping skills and preventing developmental delays is especially important in some of these environments.

Although the scope of this book does not permit a detailed discussion of all of these environments, this chapter will focus on two types of special play envi-

ronments: (a) play settings that all children encounter in their neighborhood and community, including public parks and playgrounds; and (b) environments for children with special needs, including programs for multihandicapped and hospitalized children. In all of these environments, children's developmental needs must be considered if good play opportunities are to be available. In the environments for special needs children, designers must also be able to make adaptations in space arrangements, equipment, and materials to increase the children's chances of realizing their play potential.

Beckwith (1982), one of the major designers of children's playgrounds, observes that "Kids play up to the limit of their abilities" (p. 61). This is true whether they are urban children who have few natural environments for play, multihandicapped children, or children with either temporary or chronic illnesses. Play is valuable for all of them and environments can be designed that foster "rich play" (Bruner, 1983).

The Neighborhood and Community as Play Environments

While the play of very young children typically centers around the home, as children grow older, their play territory becomes wider and more varied. The street, the neighborhood, the park, the playground, and the broader community hold many opportunities for play. The value of play in these environments is that it presents increasingly diverse and complex opportunities for challenge. The secret clubs and special language codes that serve both to include and to exclude players, the elaborated fantasy play in the backyard fort or tree house, the confrontations of riddling and jeering, the risk taking of skate boarding and tree climbing, and the arguments in informal games of stick ball and kick-the-can are means by which children stretch their physical, social, and intellectual abilities and test their courage. Because play in these settings has not been extensively studied, its relationship to other areas of development has been only minimally investigated by social science researchers. The effects of play have been explored by artists, however, as the poet Dylan Thomas (1954) so vividly illustrates:

Though it was only a little park, it held within its borders of old tall trees, notched with our names and shabby from our climbing, as many secret places, caverns and forests, prairies, and deserts, as a country somewhere at the end of the sea.

And though we would explore it one day, armed and desperate, from end to end, from the robbers' den to the pirates' cabin, the highwayman's inn to the cattle ranch, or the hidden room in the undergrowth, where we held beetle races, and lit the wood fires and roasted potatoes and talked about Africa, and the makes of motor cars, yet still the next day, it remained as unexplored as the Poles—a country just born and always changing. . . .

Behind the school was a narrow lane where only the oldest and boldest threw pebbles at windows, scuffled and boasted, fibbed about their relations—

"My father's got a chauffeur."

"What's he want a chauffeur for? He hasn't got a car."

"My father's the richest man in the town."

"My father's the richest man in Wales."

"My father owns the world."

And swapped gob-stoppers for slings, old knives for marbles, kite string for foreign stamps.

The lane was always the place to tell your secrets; if you did not have any, you invented them. Occasionally now I dream that I am turning out of school into the lane of confidences when I say to the boys of my class, "At last, I have a real secret."

"What is it—what is it?"

"I can fly."

And when they do not believe me, I flap my arms and slowly leave the ground only a few inches at first, then gaining air until I fly waving my cap level with the upper windows of the school, peering in until the mistress at the piano screams and the metronome falls to the ground and stops, and there is no more time . . .

The memories of childhood have no order, and no end (pp. 4–5, 10–11).

● Characteristics of play in neighborhood and community

Berg and Medrich (1980) state that the neighborhood "defines a social universe" (p. 320). The range of this universe is marked by physical boundaries of major streets or other safety factors, features of the terrain, and by parental limits. Younger children stay closer to home than older ones; boys usually cover a wider range than girls (Anderson & Tindall, 1972; Roberts, 1980). The patterns of play in small towns and rural areas differ from those in urban settings. The whole town may be part of the play environment for child residents of small towns; rural children may be more likely to play with siblings because of the distances between farms and to use the natural environment as the play world (McCollum, 1964).

City children may have little exposure to natural environments unless these are provided in vacant lots, parks, and ecologically designed playgrounds. The city environment may also foster competitiveness in play and challenge-play among groups (Beckwith, 1982; Berg & Medrich, 1980; Wallach, 1983). Research on factors that influence children's play in urban and suburban settings indicates that these environments have constraints that may make play difficult (e.g., Berg & Medrich, 1980; Cooper, 1970; Lynch, 1977). For example, urban redevelopment projects have made little provision for children's play, and park grass is often off limits for playing.

Children are major "consumers" of neighborhoods; their ability to develop relationships to informal support networks and to community resources is related to their social emotional functioning during middle childhood (Bryant, 1985). Therefore, the qualities of their neighborhood environments can affect both their play and friendship development.

In a study of middle childhood play in four neighborhoods, Berg and Medrich (1980) identified the environmental factors that influence play patterns: (a) terrain, built environment, and land use; (b) access to play space; (c) social interaction opportunities; and (d) safety and mobility. Children who live in hilly, less densely populated areas where residences are separated from commercial areas are constrained by lack of level play sites and access to sidewalk or safe street areas for play. They have few opportunities for informal friendship and are dependent on parents for transportation to varied play settings and to friends' homes. Those in high child-density flat areas with commercial sections interwoven with residences are more independent and have more group play activities. Their friends are in close proximity and cover a wide age range, including adults. However, safety concerns are greater in these neighborhoods.

Access to play space, especially "unmanaged" play space, is difficult to find in any neighborhood. Public parks or play areas are often not considered by children as their space, because of the presence of adults and teenagers, and because they are often not designed with child-culture needs in mind (Sutton-Smith, 1980). Children seek undeveloped open spaces such as vacant lots unless they have backyards in which they are allowed to dig and build. They especially value unplanned areas they discover; unfortunately, these are often glass-strewn lots or garbage-filled streams. Streets provide play opportunities for many children even though traffic must be constantly monitored. Berg and Medrich (1980) state that streets are "generally more exciting than a myriad of other play spaces" (p. 341), possibly because they are more responsive and hold more opportunities for effective actions (i.e., street play).

Access to other children is a very important environmental variable. Since adults often prefer residential settings with low child-density, children's and parents' preferred residence locations may not be in agreement. Personal and traffic safety concerns affect the range of accessible play spaces and children's mobility. In the low density suburban areas, chil-

dren's mobility depends on parents; in the inner city, distances to designed play spaces are also often long and there is neither private transportation nor safe public transportation.

After review of over 30 studies of neighborhood play, Moore (1985) concludes that children's favorite play spaces are paved areas (i.e., streets, sidewalks), front yards and porches, open public spaces, and backyards. He states that less than 15% of children's outdoor time is spent in designated playgrounds because children prefer and use "informal neighborhood spaces [with] . . . natural features and everyday urban features . . . more than specially built areas" (p. 175).

The world of children's play usually observed by adults has been the "sanitized" (i.e., rationalized and civilized) play of home or school settings (Sutton-Smith, 1985). This play, the kind that has been most studied by researchers, presents an incomplete picture of the play phenomenon. The group play of children in neighborhood streets and community fields, parks, and playgrounds "is a world of power politics, incredible struggle, aggression, sexuality, parody, regression" (p. 14). When play is observed in schools and other adult supervised settings, these social power dimensions are muted. Even young children have already learned that aggressive acts in play do not meet with adult approval (Getz & Berndt, 1982). By elementary age, children reserve much of their most intense play for the times when they are unsupervised by adults (Foster, 1974; Knapp & Knapp, 1976; Foley & McGuire, 1981; Opie & Opie, 1969).

Adults' involvement in children's neighborhood and community play takes a number of forms. Often they act primarily as restrictors of unorganized play. Prohibiting playing in the street, preventing digging in the dirt around the ornamental trees, and labeling manipulations of the environment as vandalism or misuse communicate to children the message that they should stay out of adult life (Aaron & Winawer, 1965). Effects of adult involvement may be positive or negative. Playground designers often advocate more adult involvement (e.g., Moore, 1985, and Allen, 1968, encourage adult playground supervisors and facilitators). However, some researchers on children's street and neighborhood play hold the view that adults teaching traditional games will destroy the "culture of childhood" (Opie & Opie, 1969; Roberts, 1980). The presence of adult observers may also affect the length and nature of elementary children's spontaneous play (Coakley, 1980). For example, by making public what children view as private, they may shorten the length and alter the themes of play.

Although many adults may not be active supporters of their children's free play, they often become intensely involved in Little League or other sports (Beckwith, 1982). Critics have pointed to problems in spending playtime in adult-directed sports (Devereux, 1976; Underwood, 1978). According to Coakley (1980), the developmental implications of organized sports differ from those of informal games, symbolic play, and spontaneous physical play. Instead of being child controlled, allowing expressive, empathetic, and experimental responses and fostering peer interpersonal skills and rule negotiation, organized sports are adult controlled, emphasize following standardized rules, encourage rigidity of behavior, and require unquestioning acceptance of adult authority. Moreover, children often see sports practice as serious (i.e., work) rather than playful.

Because most environments are built to meet adults' needs, these environments can deter children from meeting their play needs (Wallach, 1983). The value of informal play in neighborhood and community settings is rarely recognized by adults. Berg and Medrich (1980) conclude that children succeed in playing in spite of these constraints but "only their energy, imagination, and perseverance make it possible for them to define an acceptable play environment" (p. 343).

● Improving neighborhood and community play environments

By helping their children to make choices among athletic, cultural, community, outdoor, and religious activities, to develop special interests, and to visit new places in the community, parents can assist them to develop their own interests and gain attachments outside of the family circle (Bergstrom, 1984). Coakley (1980) urges adults to encourage children's participation in all types of play activities, including symbolic play, physically oriented free play, and informal games, in addition to organized sports.

Whether these activities are viewed as play or work by children depends on a number of factors: (a) whether the child's interest is the impetus for the activity; (b) whether the purpose is to enjoy the experience or to achieve an external standard of performance; and (c) whether the child is feeling in control of decisions about level of participation in the activity. In planning activities for children, the impact of environmental complexity and novelty (i.e., "load" as defined by Mehrabian, 1976) must be considered. A balance between high and low load environments is crucial if children are to feel neither bored nor pressured during their out-of-school time.

Parents are not the only ones who should be concerned with promoting good play environments for children, however. It is beginning to be recognized as a responsibility of the entire community. San Francisco has passed legislation requiring provision of facilities for children's care as part of their master downtown plan (Section 314). A collaborative effort of the City of Seattle, the Junior League, and the YMCA has resulted in the Kidsplace Project, which is designed to address the needs of children within the community environment. Both Seattle and San Francisco have conducted surveys to find out from children how cities can be better places for them. Boston has also developed an "open city" project that utilizes the public transportation system (Zien, 1974).

City planning can include planning play space; this space can be on rooftops, vacant lots, and closed streets, as well as in parks or special playgrounds (Aaron & Winawer, 1965; Frost, 1985). Moore (1985, pp. 179–180) urges that communities should develop an environmental policy for play spaces that gives attention to the "whole fabric of children's play in urban, suburban, and rural environments" and includes a linkage network that provides safe play on the way to and from play areas. Plans for revising or building new neighborhood and community environments can take into account the needs of all citizens, not just those of adults. In some communities children as well as adults have been involved in planning and designing parks (Vance, 1982).

A range of special environments, such as museums, playgrounds, and neighborhood clubs, designed to minimize physically dangerous and socially harmful elements and to allow children to feel in control should be available. Special paths for bike games and theater sites for acting can be assigned, and mobile playgrounds can move to a variety of sites (Bengtsson, 1970). Children's museums (e.g., Boston Children's Museum and the Philadelphia "Please Touch Museum") have been effectively designed as play environments, encouraging sensory experiences, manipulation of objects and materials, and active thinking and imagining. Unfortunately, many play environments planned by adults are based on adult criteria (e.g., adult aesthetic criteria, easy maintenance, durability, cost-effectiveness) rather than children's criteria (e.g., diversity, complexity, flexibility, challenge). Adult memory of their own childhood may even cause them to provide space for games that are no longer played (Wallach, 1983). Good neighborhood and community play environments designed for children must include space in which the entire culture of childhood can flourish. If such environments are not available, however, children will continue to use whatever resources they have to maintain that culture (Berg & Medrich, 1980; Opie & Opie, 1969; Roberts, 1980; Sutton-Smith, 1985).

The Park and Playground as Play Environments

One type of community planned environment for play is that of the public park and playground. During the past 100 years in the United States, the importance of public play environments has been alternately stressed and ignored. The design of these play spaces has also varied over time as a function of the goals of the playground developers. For example, in the early part of the century, concern for providing activity for immigrant youth in cities prompted the building of play areas with space for organized games and sports; during the thirties and forties, concern for durability made nonmovable concrete structures popular in playground design (Wortham, 1985). On the whole, however, most playgrounds have not changed much in design in the entire 100-year period (Ellis, 1973; Wallach, 1983). The following vignette provides a glimpse of playground activity on traditional playground equipment.

A., J., B., and R. (ages 7 to 8½) are near the high slide. A. goes up and slides down. R., J., and B. follow; they all repeat, laugh. Now A. has

a box. He gets it to the top of the slide and positions the box. He steps in it and pushes off. He slides down, laughing; brakes himself at bottom and runs back to the ladder. A. gets to the top and positions the box; he steps in. B. steps in behind him and tries to sit. The box begins to tear. They push off. The box tears more; they reach bottom laughing. A larger group is gathering. A. and R. tear the box apart and flatten it. They both try to carry the box to the top of the slide. With some pulling, they get it to the top. A. positions the cardboard like a toboggan. R. and B. get on. J. squeezes on in back. Down they go laughing. More want to try. Back up they go. Five boys try to get on cardboard. The last boy has only his feet on it. Down they go. A. seems to be the leader; he is always in front.

● Characteristics of traditional playground environments

American traditional park and playground designs have been severely criticized for being dangerous, one-dimensional, unimaginative, nonresponsive to children's actions, haphazardly planned, and unstimulating (e.g., Beckwith, 1982; Dattner, 1969; Ellis, 1973; Frost, 1985; Moore, 1985; Parnell & Ketterson, 1980). Many playgrounds are used only sporadically and briefly by children (Wade, 1968). Playgrounds have high injury rates, with falls from equipment accounting for most of the severe injuries (Consumer Products Safety Commission, 1975).

Beckwith (1982) explains that "children find most playgrounds boring" (p. 60). When the equipment is lacking in interest children begin to use it in risk-taking ways. For example, they may walk up the slide instead of sliding down, twirl or twist the swing chains, sit backwards on the teeter-totter, or hang by one foot on the climber. Many accidents result from children's attempts to make the equipment interesting and challenging (Dattner, 1969; Moore, 1985; Wallach, 1983). It is the nature of play to involve the creation of variations on themes. Wallach contends that children will always seek additional challenge because once they have explored the equipment they "have nothing more to learn from it" unless they seek playful challenge (p. 37). Contemporary adult life-styles that children observe on television have many high-risk elements that children want to emulate. For example, popular adult play includes sky diving, hang gliding, and balloon sailing.

Younger children's play needs have not often been a major focus of public park and playground design; usually one small section of these sites is reserved for young children. It contains the traditional equipment of slides, swings, and sandbox, requiring close adult supervision. Traditional playgrounds have also not been accessible to handicapped children. The lack of concern for the play needs of these children has resulted in a void in playground design and construction.

● **Characteristics of nontraditional parks and playgrounds**

According to Frost (1985), a new playground movement is under way. Due to backlash against emphasis on narrow cognitive concerns, renewed interest in other areas of development has emerged. Also, the problems with traditional American designs and the influence of European playground design have promoted the development of new playground types. A number of options have been proposed and implemented to alleviate the problems of traditional playgrounds. These include (a) adventure or "junk" playgrounds, modeled after those that have been in operation in Europe since the 1940s; (b) designer playgrounds, usually built in urban areas by child-focused architects or environmental designers; (c) creative playgrounds, developed by combining elements of traditional, adventure, and environmental designs into a comprehensive play environment; (d) play parks, planned as sections of large public parks; (e) environmental parks, designed to preserve natural and ecological elements; and (f) playgrounds specially designed for handicapped children. The nontraditional playground designs have the following features:

Adventure playgrounds. Adventure playgrounds are adult-supervised play areas where children of a wide range of ages can "develop their own ideas of play" (Allen, 1968, p. 55). Using their imaginations, appropriate tools, and a variety of raw materials, children can build and tear down, create, and explore pretend play and games as they wish (Bengtsson, 1972). Often cooking and gardening are also en-

couraged. The object of these playgrounds is to give city children experiences comparable to those available to rural children. Most of these programs have been started by parents and communities on land not yet built upon or inappropriate for building. The playgrounds are usually fenced, have storage sheds for tools, some indoor play space, and regular hours of use. Adult leaders are present during the time when the manipulative parts of the playground are open. Ball playing areas and sections for parents and young children are accessible at any hour. Flexibility of use is the prime design criterion. Such playgrounds can accommodate children from toddler age to late teens and are usually open at hours when elementary-age children can attend, too.

Initially begun by Sorensen in Denmark in 1940, these playgrounds have continued to be extremely popular in Denmark, Sweden, and England; however, only 25 cities in the United States have such playgrounds (Vance, 1982). These playgrounds meet all criteria for good design except that they are often perceived by adults as unattractive "junk" areas. Also, there have been concerns about safety and reluctance to provide adult leadership. Safety concerns appear to be unwarranted; although minor accidents occur frequently, Lady Allen of Hurtwood reports that no deaths or major injuries occurred in England over a 10-year period (Allen, 1968). The safety record of this type of playground in America is better than that for traditional playgrounds and for aquatic and sports programs (Vance, 1982). Creating an adventure playground usually involves getting the community together to find land and provide start-up materials. The most workable governing committee seems to be one drawn from voluntary organizations and public agencies in the community. Although the cost of starting an adventure playground is reasonable, providing adult leadership has been a problem in the United States because many communities are not willing to provide funds for such positions. The role of the adult leaders is crucial to the success of adventure playgrounds; thus, if the organizations or agencies that begin the programs are not committed to providing this leadership, the playgrounds become inoperable. In Europe, this commitment is provided by government and volunteer partnerships.

Designer playgrounds. Designer playgrounds are formal play areas that have been designed by professional architects or environmental planners. A number of these professionals have worked with communities to plan neighborhood parks in inner city areas, play areas within city parks, and play sculptures in civic center locations (e.g., Dattner, 1969; Ellison, 1974; Friedberg, 1979; Joyner, 1976). Although the aesthetics are excellent and the playground structures are usually safe, the structures are fixed ones without movable parts; there are no loose or malleable materials in the settings. Because most are in busy public areas, they have been designed to discourage vandalism and theft. Some of them have been well used by children but, in other cases, they are less popular because children have little control or sense of effectance. Usually they are visited for brief periods by a continually changing stream of children. Intensive evaluations of use have not been conducted for most of these playgrounds (Moore, Cohen, Oertel, & Van Ryzin, 1979).

Creative playgrounds.   Creative playgrounds are ones usually created by parents or other community members in consultation with a playground designer (e.g., Beckwith, 1982). They often serve as a middle ground between commercial/traditional playgrounds and adventure playgrounds. The semiformal and eclectic nature of the playgrounds can make them very flexible and filled with variety. In addition to commercial equipment, they have constructed structures, water, sand, and loose parts for building and manipulating. Art, gardening, and animals are often included. They meet most criteria of good design but may, like adventure playgrounds, involve the problem of messiness. This cooperative design approach has been particularly effective in transforming existing traditional school playgrounds because the builders draw upon the existing elements, adapt the structures and add new elements, structures, and materials to increase the variety and flexibility of the environment while still holding costs down.

Play parks.   Play parks are also common in Europe. They are comprehensive play spaces that have been designed within public parks. The play parks in Sweden are accessible to children at all times but the manipulative materials needing supervision are only available when the playground leader is there. These parks typically provide some of the features of adventure, designer, and creative playgrounds within the public park setting. They attempt to meet the needs of a wide age range, combining places for adults to meet, sports fields, and playgrounds for various age levels (Bengtsson, 1970).

Environmental parks.   Environmental parks focus on the natural setting and ecological materials. They attempt to replicate natural settings and include replicas of meadow, river, and forest environments, nature trails, natural materials to explore and manipulate, as well as abundant plant and animal life (Gibson, 1978). There are few parks in urban areas that are completely devoted to natural environmental design; however, natural features are sometimes included in portions of adventure, designer, or creative park designs. The federal and state park systems, which preserve the natural environment, also provide many play opportunities for children and families. Camping activities are sometimes included in school curricula; these activities are often conducted at natural or designed environmental parks. Because preservation of the natural environment is stressed, adult leadership and learning of appropriate and inappropriate manipulations of the materials in the environment are necessary. Thus, these play areas do not allow children to manipulate the environment in ways that involve permanent changes.

Special needs playgrounds.   Special needs playgrounds are designed specifically to ameliorate the constraints that children with handicapping conditions often face in regular playgrounds. Such areas would, for example, feature ramps to accommodate wheelchairs and crutches. Playgrounds designed for the handicapped typically draw upon recognized principles of good design; thus, they are often effective sites for normally developing young children as well. Principles of design include a flow of activity options, variety of size and configuration of space; clear multiple cues and boundaries for activities; developmentally appropriate skill demands; loose parts that include both structured and unstructured products; a range of ambiguous and defined spaces; order and consistency; variety in sensorimotor and locomotor experiences; clear points of performance completion; retreats from activity; opportunities for emotional expression; safety; and adequate supervision (Moore, Cohen, Oertel, & Van Ryzin 1979). Plans developed by New York City provide for integration of handicapped and able-bodied children in one playground setting (Department of Housing and Urban Development, 1976).

● Research on children's play in parks and playgrounds

Although studies on children's park and playground behaviors are still not extensive, research in the last 15 years has provided some evidence regarding children's preferences for certain types of equipment and comparisons of the types of play that occur in different types of playgrounds. Studies of playground preferences indicate that although all children like to have trees, grass, and flowers, they express a diversity of needs when asked what equipment they would like (Moore & Bond, 1975). Based on observations, children spend more time on unified or linked structures than separated ones (Bruya, 1985); prefer play modes that support more than one type of play (Myers, 1985; Naylor, 1985); select single-use items on the basis of movement opportunities (Brown, 1980; Naylor, 1985); choose items that have novelty, challenge, and complexity (Callecod, 1974); and show more imaginative play in closed space units (Krudiner, 1978). For example, climbers that have ramps, slides, and bridges linking units and that include open and closed sections are usually very popular complex structures. The single-use items that are usually most popular are swings.

There are age and gender differences as well. For example, infants prefer less enclosed spaces than toddlers (Steele & Nauman, 1985); kindergartners prefer equipment that fosters dramatic play more than first and second graders do (Frost & Strickland, 1985). Compared to girls, boys frequent public playgrounds more often (Naylor, 1985); engage in more gross motor play (Campbell & Frost, 1985); cover more play area; and prefer equipment accommodating larger groups (Myers, 1985). Choice of activity also differs; for example, boys prefer ball games; girls prefer swings (Myers, 1985). Comparisons of the various types of playgrounds indicate that at adventure playgrounds children develop more friendships (Rittenhouse, 1974); play for longer time periods (Hayward, Rothenberg, & Beasley, 1974); visit more regularly (Hayward et al., 1974); play with wider age ranges and in more cross-gender groups (Cooper, 1970); and spend more time in cognitive

play (Hayward et al., 1974). Children also indicate a preference for adventure playgrounds (Hayward et al., 1974).

Research shows that at traditional playgrounds, by contrast, there are relatively greater numbers of children who require adult supervision; and children play for shorter time periods, visit less frequently, engage in more gross motor play; and engage in less social play than at other types of playgrounds (Hayward et al., 1974). Play at designer and creative playgrounds tends to have characteristics of both adventure and traditional, depending on which types of structures, equipment, and materials are available. For example, if "loose parts" are available the play pattern is more like that of adventure playgrounds, and if complex structures are present the time of play is longer than that observed at traditional playgrounds.

In a series of studies comparing traditional to creative playgrounds, Frost and colleagues (Campbell & Frost, 1985; Frost & Campbell, 1985; Frost & Strickland, 1985) indicate that children engaged in a wider range of activities and preferred the action-oriented and multiple-function equipment at the creative playground, but that there are differences in preference with age level. For example, first and second graders play on swings more than kindergartners, and older children play more on the outside rather than inside of structures (Frost & Strickland, 1985).

● Improving park and playground environments

Based on suggestions of playground designers and research evidence, criteria for good playground design include provision of: (a) a wide variety of play opportunities; (b) equipment and materials that are appropriate for children at many developmental levels; (c) flexibility of use of equipment and materials; (d) possibilities for making changes in the environment; (e) opportunities for challenge and risk taking; and (f) safety within minimally hazardous settings.

For example, Beckwith (1982) states that playgrounds can provide challenge without hazards; that is, children should not be exposed to hidden danger but should be able to see challenges and choose to take risks. Soft surfaces and durability of equipment combined with possibilities for challenges to balance and increase coordination, flexibility, and strength can provide this mix. He advocates connected play events, with clear and interesting paths between play units. There should be equipment that accommodates several children at once, such as wide slides and movable equipment; and all sites should have loose materials.

Wallach (1983) stresses that playgrounds should be designed for a developmental range of capabilities. There should be many choices (e.g., to play alone or with others, to go up or down, to be active or passive) and opportunities for children to learn about failure in a safe way. Playgrounds should also provide social experiences and enhance self-image. Technology should be included in play spaces (e.g., electronic games, computers, and props for space "adventures"). Equipment should be durable and safe, and children should be involved in planning activities.

Research gives support to the playground designers who are advocating environments that (a) allow children to meet their arousal-seeking needs by finding their optimal level of stimulation (Ellis, 1973); (b) are appropriate for a range of developmental levels (Beckwith, 1982); and (c) encourage variety and choice (Frost et al., 1985). Because so many specific plans for playground design are available in recent books, no one model of playground design will be described in detail here. Models that fit the criteria of each playground type can be adapted to fit the needs of children of different ages, the goals of the playground developers, and the requirements of the terrain and social setting. Designs for playgrounds for handicapped children are also available in numerous publications. Some of these books are listed in suggestions for further reading.

Play Environments for Multihandicapped Children

All children have to interact with their environment in order to develop their capabilities. Children with physical, cognitive, social, and emotional disabilities, developmental delays, or illness are no exception. Play interactions with the objects in the physical environment are especially important for these children. They also must have opportunities for interaction with adults and other children in order to learn ways

to affect their social environment. However, constraints due to their disabilities often make playful physical and social interactions with the environment difficult to achieve. The challenge in environmental design for children with special needs is to create opportunities for them to have playful interactions and to experience enjoyment of a world that accommodates to their physical limitations. They can enjoy play, as this example shows:

> K. (4 years, 9 months) has cerebral palsy and is confined to a wheelchair. She has the use of one hand, is mentally retarded, and although she understands what is said to her, her expressive language is unintelligible. K. is in her wheelchair at the water table with three other 4-year-olds. The water table has two levels, one high enough for the wheelchair arms to slide under the table so that she can lean up on the edge of the table and immerse her arms completely in the water. The water flows from one level to the other and is automatically pumped back up to the higher level. The play begins with the children pouring water from containers into the water table, but soon progresses to splashing at one another. The interaction escalates between K. and her peers, resulting in giggles and finally laughter. J. (age 4 years, 3 months), who is standing with braces, manipulates a water pump to spray water up in the air. He quickly looks around to see who will notice and what adult reaction will be. When no negative reactions occurs, he repeats the experiments with great pleasure.

Children with severe and/or multiple handicapping conditions have a desire to play that is as intense as that of normal children (Aaron & Winawer, 1965; McCollum, 1975). If they have difficulty initiating play interactions with the environment, they may become chronically frustrated and encounter sensory deprivation (Ellis, 1973). Unfortunately, through the eyes of the adults around them, life seems to be very serious for children who have so much to learn and so many things preventing or delaying that learning. Research reported in special education literature usually puts emphasis on how adults should teach rather than how children learn. It often focuses on how behaviors that are called play can be modeled or reinforced to increase language learning (e.g., Sherman, Shapiro, & Glassman, 1983; Copeland, Reiner, & Jirkovsky, 1984), social skills (e.g., Bradtke, Kirkpatrick, & Rosenblatt, 1972), or performance of cognitive tasks (e.g., Hopper & Wambold, 1978). There appears to be little understanding of the need for pleasure and playfulness in children and adults and little appreciation of the value of play as a learning medium for overall development.

Play that has the elements of inner control and free choice is especially valuable for special needs children for two reasons: (a) It allows safe risk taking; and (b) it permits peer interactions and friendships to develop (McCollum, 1975). The value of a well-designed environment that allows special needs children to take risks and make choices is important because they have few opportunities to select their own challenges. They are often so protected by adults or constrained by the physical barriers of equipment or structures that they have little opportunity to test themselves. Also, so much of their time is allotted to physical, speech, or other therapy that they need time to choose what they want to do.

Play in a carefully designed environment provides them with challenging motor activity (Enseki & Ahern, 1980). For example, children may try to climb to a platform or other higher structure if falling would only result in a drop of six or twelve inches or a plop into pillows. Similarly, taking the risk of trying on a pretend role as a princess, a monster, a truck driver, or an astronaut is made possible if pretend materials are accessible to children in wheelchairs and space is provided for a "motorcade," a "chase," a "highway," or a "launching pad."

The value of play as a means of encouraging peer interaction is also extremely high because physical constraints often prevent the social give-and-take that most children experience in play. Social play abilities (e.g., spontaneous sharing and turn taking, considering another child's viewpoint and adapting one's own role behavior to keep the play going, and recognizing peer signals that "this is play") are not gained through adult-directed learning sessions. Lack of social experiences and, consequently, social skills, prevents many special needs children from learning the joy of peer play (McCollum, 1975). Often handicapped children's only source of social play is within the family because they are given few opportunities to play in the neighborhood (McEvoy & McConkey, 1983). Social play deprivation may have long lasting negative consequences on social development, leaving special needs children with an additional disability that could affect their coping skills throughout their life span.

● Characteristics of multihandicapped children's play

The forms of play that can be fostered in multihandicapped children are dependent on the level and complexity of their disabilities. Many children will not achieve play levels above those described in chapter 8. Even if children remain at an infant or toddler developmental level, however, the play possibilities that are realized in adult-infant social routines and games, peer observation and contact, and early pretense interactions of normally developing infants and toddlers are certainly appropriate for special needs children. Exploratory play, using whatever sensory and physical capabilities the children have, will account for much of the play activity. Social routines/games can be particularly helpful to visually impaired multihandicapped children (Rogow, 1984).

Research on parent-child play indicates that the severity and type of handicap influence the quality of play. For example, parent and sibling play with mentally handicapped children is similar to play with normal infants (McEvoy & McConkey, 1983); parent play with visually impaired infants differs from play with normal infants in levels of verbal interaction, attending, and initiation of play (Rogers & Puchalski, 1984a).

Because engaging in these types of play is essential for all children, efforts to make them available to special needs children can have important implications for their overall development. Bradtke, Kirkpatrick, and Rosenblatt (1972) describe how adult "intensive" motor and verbal play with severely handicapped children can improve their social interaction. They stress that adults must exhibit humor, flexibility, and empathy if such play is to generalize to interactions with peers. Parents of handicapped children report enjoying play with their infants; however, they do not seem to change their play styles as their children grow older as parents of normally developing children do (McEvoy & McConkey, 1983).

Thus, the children may have less opportunity to learn higher level play skills.

Many special needs children are capable of achieving a preschool level of play, but the type and severity of disability affects the play level that can be achieved. Chapters 6 and 9 describe the mixed results of mainstreaming multihandicapped children in play environments and give examples of environmental adaptations that can facilitate integration of special needs children into regular classroom or playground settings. Although multihandicapped children's sensorimotor/practice play, constructive play, and early pretense may be delayed, they can usually find parallel play opportunities and they enjoy observing and imitating other children.

The higher levels of pretend play, such as sociodramatic play, are often difficult for mentally retarded, language delayed, or emotionally disturbed children because they require role enactment abilities. Cooperative play thus may be out of the range of some of these children (Brophy & Stone-Zukowski, 1984). Multihandicapped children may not participate in neighborhood play with other children, either because of parental overprotectiveness or peer avoidance (McEvoy & McConkey, 1983). They are not easily accepted as playmates by peers, especially if their handicaps are severe (Brophy & Stone-Zukowski, 1984; Karnes & Lee, 1979). Acceptance of children with some types of handicaps seems to depend on whether they have other handicaps as well; for example, the play patterns of deaf children with no other handicaps are similar to those of normal peers (Meadow, 1984), but multihandicapped children experience more difficulty in social adjustment.

It is at this point in play development that some children become social isolates because they do not have the social and pretend skills to engage in cooperative symbolic play. Research is beginning to address the issue of early social isolation (Rubin, 1985); information gained from this research may eventually give adults suggestions for enhancing social play for multihandicapped children. Simple games, with adult support and rule reminders, can be played by many children who have physical or intellectual deficits. Even in the home, the higher levels of play are rarely initiated by parents although siblings of multihandicapped children sometimes engage them in symbolic play (McEvoy & McConkey, 1983). Because some

multihandicapped children are capable of reaching symbolic play levels (Rogers & Puchalski, 1984b), adults, siblings, and peers should encourage such play.

Play levels achieved depend in large part on the nature of their disability. Children whose intellectual functioning is in the normal range can engage in symbolic play and games (e.g., computer simulations or LOGO) even if extensive physical disabilities prevent participation in games or sports requiring physical skill (Maddux & Cummings, 1984; Wall, 1984). If the communication and motor abilities of children with cerebral palsy or other physical disabilities can be enhanced through computers and other technological devices, these children can participate in play (Behrmann & Lahm, 1983; Meyers, 1984). Children whose mental capacities are below age level can participate in physically oriented games and sports with great enjoyment, as the Special Olympics demonstrates.

Play environments that foster whatever levels of play that children with disabilities can achieve are important for their later success. Play will be important throughout their lives. While the focus on developing work skills in special needs adolescents and adults is certainly essential, the development of their play skills is equally valuable if they are to acquire social coping and enjoy life to the greatest extent possible.

● Improving play environments for multihandicapped children

Olds (1979) indicates that a well-designed play environment for special needs children should be similar to that for other children and should be one in which children feel comfortable, in control of themselves, and able to be active. She lists five elements that should be considered in adapting environments for special needs children: location, boundaries, activity surfaces, storage, and mood. The location of play activities for special needs children is important because access may be a problem and because the level of stimulation must be appropriate. There should be protected areas and quiet spaces for solitary play, as well as areas that encourage activity and interaction with other children.

Boundaries that define locations while at the

same time provide access are necessary. These may be low walls, platforms of gradually graded levels, variations in color and texture of surfaces, focused lighting, and ceiling height differentiation. Activity surfaces are usually low tables or the floor. However, adaptations such as having drafting tables that are adjustable in angle and height make these activities accessible to children in standing braces or wheelchairs. The boundary platforms may also serve as surfaces for play (e.g., for building with blocks or putting a puzzle together).

Storage needs are similar to those of other environments except that they may be more extensive to accommodate a variety of adaptive equipment. For example, wheelchair storage may be needed. Play materials should be arranged so that they are accessible to special needs children; such accessibility encourages their independent choice of playthings and their active involvement with other children. The teacher should not always transport play materials from shelf to child; children need to be able to do this themselves to increase their sense of competence and independence. Finally, the mood of play areas can be conveyed by colors (e.g., quiet or loud), textures (e.g., soft or hard), and shapes (e.g., open or closed). Olds (1979) comments that running water, fish moving in tanks, and light drifting through plants all set the mood in adult public spaces. Equal care should be given to mood setting for children who need help reading the cues for appropriate behavior.

Prosthetic aids that increase mobility provide much assistance for peer play (Mueller & Bergstrom, 1982). Devices that improve locomotion (e.g., scooter boards, walkers, and ramps); that encourage upright posture (e.g., corner or other special seats, and standing boards or braces); and that enhance safety (e.g., protective helmets) greatly foster multi-handicapped children's opportunities for play. Structural designs that promote certain types of play can be built; for example, wheelchair basketball can be played on circle-walled courts, which cause the ball to rebound into the center, and climbers with many handles and supports can make gross motor play easier (Aaron & Winawer, 1965). Tables with a central pedestal leg facilitate small muscle play on table surfaces. In general, the principles advocated by designers of outdoor playgrounds for handicapped children (e.g., Allen, 1968; Dept. of Housing and Urban Development, 1976; Moore et al., 1979) are appropriate for home and indoor classroom design as well. Most importantly, environments adapted to meet the needs of the handicapped often "humanize" the environment for everyone (Ostroff, 1978; Ostroff & Tomashiro, 1976).

Play Environments for Hospitalized Children

Illness and hospitalization constitute major stresses in development and are likely to effect a profound change in children's life-styles and behavior (King & Ziegler, 1981; Newman & Lind, 1980; Petrillo & Sanger, 1980). Hospitalized children face separation from family, friends, home, and daily routines. They are placed in a foreign environment where they are overwhelmed with new and often frightening sights, sounds, and sensations, and confront a large number of unfamiliar people, some of whom inflict discomfort and pain. Child-patients are usually uncomfortable and in pain due to disease or injury, and often experience fears of mutilation as well as confusion caused by exposure to a unique environment and experiences not previously confronted (King & Ziegler, 1981). In this situation, play serves many important purposes for child-patients, families, and hospital personnel.

Play in hospital contexts functions to optimize children's developmental processes and facilitate learning. Because development does not cease when children become ill and need to be hospitalized, it is important for the hospital staff to provide age-appropriate play activities for child-patients of all ages. Children can participate in these activities while in their beds or in the hospital playroom, when they are not involved in medical procedures. Developmentally appropriate play offers child-patients the cognitive, sensory, perceptual, and social stimulation they need for continued developmental progress (Adams, 1976; Oremland & Oremland, 1973; Petrillo & Sanger, 1980; Thompson & Stanford, 1981).

Play in hospitals also offers child-patients important distraction from pain, discomfort, fear, and anxiety (Azarnoff, 1974; Beyer & Byers, 1985; Klinzing & Klinzing, 1977; McCaffery, 1977). Children's participation in enjoyable, playful pursuits before, after, and sometimes during, uncomfortable and painful medical experiences, can reduce the overall stress and trauma of hospitalization; further, children have less time and energy to focus on the negative aspects of their situation (Petrillo & Sanger, 1980; Thompson & Stanford, 1981). For example, children who can play Atari right up to the time they are anesthetized for an operation may be distracted from frightening thoughts of the impending surgery, and may therefore be more relaxed, compliant, and require fewer physical restraints and less medication (Byers, 1972; Clatworthy, 1981; Senn, 1945). This type of playful activity also leaves child-patients with positive associations regarding hospitalization and medical personnel, which can decrease children's anxiety and fear on subsequent hospital admissions.

Play is a comfortable, familiar medium that soothes and consoles child-patients and reassures parents and family members that their children are still the same people they observed playing at home (Azarnoff & Flegal, 1975; Chan, 1980; Harding, 1977). Being able to participate in familiar play activities lessens the stress caused by displacement into a foreign, frightening environment. As parents and family members are able to interact with their children through familiar play media, they are reassured to see normal play behaviors that have been diminished or absent since their children have been ill.

Play in hospitals also tends to motivate children to comply with health care plans and procedures and to stimulate depressed or frightened children (Brooks, 1973; Chan, 1980; Harding, 1977; Schwartz, Albino, & Tedesco, 1983). When child-patients are aware that they will be able to resume their play in some capacity (e.g., engaging in finger painting, petting the rabbit, playing a game with peers, or participating in cooking activities), it is easier for them to tolerate medical regimes because they have something to look forward to. This play also gives child-patients the important message that life will continue after procedures and serves as an incentive for complying with children's medical care (e.g., "after you take your medication you can come to the playroom").

Additional values of play in hospitals involve both intercommunication and intracommunication of child-patients. Play enhances intercommunication between patients, staff, and family members in sev-

eral ways. Observing children's play can enable hospital personnel to more accurately diagnose and care for child-patients (David, 1973; Green, 1974). Depressed, frightened, or withdrawn children often fail to exhibit their full range of abilities during medical examinations. Once engaged in play, however, they may demonstrate behaviors and abilities not previously observed by hospital professionals. Observation of these behaviors is crucial for accurate diagnosis and the development of effective care plans.

Play also establishes and maintains relationships between the staff and pediatric patients. Relating to child-patients through play promotes the development of trust between children and the hospital staff and leads to subsequent supportive and therapeutic relationships (Fosson & deQuan, 1984; Klinzing & Klinzing, 1977; Menezes, 1980). Through play and games, staff can establish initial positive contacts and develop supportive, working relationships with the children and family members. Then, at subsequent stress points the children and family members are better able to depend on these previously established relationships for support, guidance, and communication (Chan, 1980; Skipper & Leonard, 1968; Wolfer & Visintainer, 1975).

Enhanced communication through play among child-patients, staff, and family members also assists the early detection and correction of misconceptions children and family members may have concerning illness, injury, and hospitalization. Fears and fantasies can be explored in playful ways and children can be reassured and educated regarding the reality of hospital experiences. For example, a child may bandage a teddy bear by wrapping the bear's head entirely so that the bear's eyes, ears, mouth, and nose are completely covered. This might be an indication that the child fears this may happen during his or her hospital stay. If staff members observe this, they can explain that the child will not experience that type of bandaging at any point during hospitalization (Axline, 1947; David, 1973; Moustakas 1953/1973; Wolfgang & Bolig, 1979).

Play promotes intracommunication by helping children, as they play, to reorganize their experience and thought to make meaning of their life (Erikson, 1963; Piaget, 1954). Facilitating the organization of thought and experience is especially important for children in strange, frightening, and painful environments. Child-patients are often so overwhelmed by new sensory input that they are unable to process adequately the incoming information. Repetitive playing-out of their hospital experiences helps them to accommodate to the unfamiliar medical situation (Erickson, 1958). As children become active participants in the playing-out of a situation recently experienced in a passive manner, they gain an increased sense of competence and mastery of the once frightening and traumatic situation (Derrick, Bachman, & Parker, 1982; Erickson, 1958; Freud, 1952; Letts, Stevens, Coleman, & Kettner, 1983; Newman & Lind, 1980; Wolfgang & Bolig, 1979).

The following vignette gives an example of the therapeutic use of medical play:

J. (4 years, 6 months) was admitted to the hospital for pneumonia and needed to receive respiratory therapy several times a day. A portion of this therapy involved patting J. on his sides, back, and chest in a a painless manner to loosen matter in his lungs. The first time J. received this treatment he cried and screamed and had to be restrained because he had no idea what was happening and perceived that someone was beating on him. Subsequent to the first treatment he was given an opportunity to handle and manipulate the soft percussers used to pat his body. J. was encouraged to give his stuffed dog respiratory therapy and to perform the same on his mother. Soon he was patting himself with the percussers and explaining to the hospital staff why he needed such therapy. When J. received his second treatment several hours later, he calmly complied with the therapists' requests, needed no restraints, and animatedly visited with parents and therapists during the procedure about why he needed respiratory therapy.

The play that J. had engaged in following the first treatment facilitated his education and understanding of the situation. This play enhanced his feelings of control and gave him the opportunity to experience actively what he had previously been subjected to as a passive victim.

Play also functions to increase child-patients' feelings of control in an environment where they have little control over their experiences and bodies. Pediatric patients are forced to undergo uncomfortable and painful experiences, lose privacy, relinquish control over what and when they eat, and may even lose control over bodily functions. Through play children can gain increased control by making choices. Choices that may appear trivial in other contexts become very important therapeutic choices in the hospital environment (e.g., "Do you want to play in your room or the playroom?" "What game would you like to play?" "Do you want to go first or should I?" "Do you want to take your medication before or after you play the game?"). These choices give child-patients a sense of control over some aspect of their lives, which is highly important for maintaining a sense of self-worth and increasing their feelings of mastery (Derrick et al., 1982; Menezes, 1980; Thompson & Stanford, 1981).

● Characteristics of play in the hospital environment

There are two broad forms of play used in hospital settings: (a) developmental play and (b) medical play. Developmental play is similar to play found in other environments. This form of play meets child-patients' developmental needs, encourages peer group interaction, and offers opportunities to engage in familiar and comfortable behaviors. Because of the age range of children served by pediatric settings (0 to 18 years of age) and the wide variety of needs exhibited by child-patients, a hospital play/activity program must offer both structured and unstructured equipment and supplies to meet the fine and gross motor needs of all ages of children, as well as the cognitive, social, and emotional needs of child-patients (Goldberger, 1984). Each play program must take into account and compensate for the effects of medical procedures and physical disabilities on performance in each of these areas.

All children need to experience as many successes as possible throughout their developmental years (Satir, 1972); it is especially important for child-patients to have such opportunities in abundance. Pediatric patients experience extreme loss of control through the processes of disease and injury; this is compounded by institutionalization (Beuf, 1979). Because such a loss of control can have devastating effects on children's self-esteem (Riffee, 1981), providing meaningful play experiences for child-patients is very important. Developmentally appropriate materials that challenge children without incurring undue frustration should be in every hospital play program (Goldberger, 1984; Newman & Lind, 1980).

Medical play, the second form of play, is specific to health care settings and particularly tailored to meet the special needs of hospitalized children (Goldberger, 1984; Petrillo & Sanger, 1980). The common characteristic of all medical play is the use of pretend or actual medical equipment and the focus on medical and hospital-related themes.

The aims of most medical play are twofold: (a) to help children integrate medical experiences in a meaningful and nonthreatening manner, thus reducing the trauma of hospitalization; and (b) to educate and prepare children for impending hospitalization experiences. All medical play is based on theory and research stating that actively mastering a passively experienced situation through repetition on or with another subject or object expresses and alleviates fears, confusion, and frustrations (Clatworthy, 1981; Erikson, 1951; Erickson, 1958; Freud, 1952; Letts et al., 1983; Schwartz et al., 1983; Thompson & Stanford, 1981; Wolfgang & Bolig, 1979). Through the manipulation of medical equipment with dolls, stuffed animals, and puppets, child-patients may act out and gain mastery over the frightening and unfamiliar experiences encountered in a hospital setting.

Many hospitals include this play in the activity rooms by arranging a hospital or medical play area similar to housekeeping and other dramatic play areas typical of out-of-hospital settings. Child-sized medical equipment and attire is combined with actual medical materials to simulate a hospital environment. Dolls or stuffed animals and puppets serve as the patients, or children take turns playing the patient roles. In this way children are able to engage themselves in medical play in a safe environment if they choose, exploring individual themes and terminating the play at will.

Hospital staff supervise medical play to encourage children to pursue their own themes; to detect and correct misconceptions; to gain information about idiosyncratic fears and fantasies; and to edu-

cate pediatric patients regarding their hospital experiences. In this way medical play functions as a diagnostic and educational tool as well as a vehicle for self-expression and mastery (Azarnoff, 1974; Chan, 1980; Harding, 1977; Knudsen, 1975).

Older children benefit from simple exposure to and handling of medical equipment as well as the examination of medical models and anatomically correct dolls. Through the exposure to and use of these concrete materials older child-patients gain increased understanding of medical procedures and also gain mastery over unfamiliar and frightening hospital experiences as they learn why and how equipment is used. Anatomically correct dolls and models offer concrete visual and tactile aids to facilitate the education of child-patients by allowing them to explore in three dimensions the how and why of their medical experiences. Both the education and understanding enhanced by medical play and activity decrease the anxiety experienced by pediatric patients through the increased sense of control that accompanies understanding and knowledge (David, 1973; Knudsen, 1975; Ritchie, 1979; Schwartz et al., 1983; Visintainer & Wolfer, 1975).

Medical play is often used as an integral part of general preparation with child-patients. Many hospitals sponsor preadmission tours during which children gain exposure to medical equipment and areas, learn about possible future hospital experiences, explore medical materials, and engage in dramatic medical play. The preparation and education children gain via these programs reduce anxiety during hospitalization and alleviate the post-discharge distress often experienced by pediatric patients (King & Ziegler, 1981; O'Meara, McAuliffe, Motherway, & Dunleavy, 1983; Schreier & Kaplan 1983).

Medical play can also help prepare individual patients for specific procedures. The staff members may use dolls or puppets to show child-patients what they will see, hear, smell, feel, and taste during a medical procedure. As the staff member explains the procedure, the doll or puppet demonstrates how the medical equipment will be used and what the experience will be like for the child. Then the child is encouraged to perform the procedure on the doll or puppet to gain a greater sense of understanding and knowledge. This experience allows the staff member to correct misconceptions and alleviate fears expressed by child-patients (Droske & Francis, 1981; Letts et al., 1983; Petrillo & Sanger, 1980).

To aid in the process of effective medical play, age-appropriate materials should be available to every pediatric patient. All material should be safe, be presented as nonthreateningly as possible, and be appropriate for the child's age and experience. Medical play should offer choices between real and pretend items since some patients may find the realism of the actual equipment too threatening while other patients need the reality of using real medical materials to gain the full educational and therapeutic benefit of hospital play (Goldberger, 1984).

Medical equipment can also be included in many activities such as crafts and games. For example, children enjoy painting with paint-filled syringes or surgical sponges, making finger casts, using medical equipment in water play, blowing up and decorating surgical gloves, or making mobiles with various medical supplies. Doing body tracings, making murals related to hospital themes, or shooting at targets with water-filled syringes are additional ways of incorporating medical experiences in a variety of playful, educational activities. Using medical materials in these nonthreatening and enjoyable ways helps children to familiarize themselves with the equipment and to feel more comfortable and less frightened with such objects. It also allows children to exercise active control over supplies that may have been employed in treatments, thus fulfilling the therapeutic role discussed earlier.

● **Overcoming constraints on play in hospitals**

There are both physical constraints and social constraints that must be considered in designing play environments for hospitalized children. Most children who are hospitalized face some physical limitations. They may require bed rest, although this is much less frequently prescribed now than in the days of rheumatic fever wards. However, they may need to stay in bed because of effects of chemotherapy or may be isolated because of infection or susceptibility to infections from others. The lack of stimuli and loss of frequent interaction with others produced by isolating conditions often leads to depression and to loss of interest in play. For other child-patients, mobility is limited by the presence of IV's in a limb during part of a hospitalization, and many other child-patients have casts, surgical dressings, or are confined to wheelchairs even when they are allowed to be in a room with other children.

Hospital staff have usually realized the need for children to play and to socialize regardless of physical constraints, and thus they consider it important to make the effort required to encourage children to walk while pulling an IV pole behind, to manipulate a wheelchair, or to play while on a stretcher. The playroom design must allow children to play freely and in a self-directed manner. Usually, the patients are wheeled in or assisted to a table or easel, where their play is limited to what is put on or near the table. Open shelves with a range of toys or activities accessible to children help encourage feelings of mastery and control as well as choice. Because storage space is always at a premium, toys are sometimes locked away out of sight or must be brought from other locations. Having some open and accessible play materials in the playroom is a necessity. A play structure that has built-in space can meet the storage space needs and allow choices for children of different ages and mobility (Olds, 1978; 1979).

Careful design of a play space requires creativity, skill, and collaboration between hospital staff and designer (Cotton & Geraty, 1984). For example, one creative design allows infants and their parents to relax and interact on waterbeds in the hospital playrooms. Traditional floor toys such as blocks and trucks often have been neglected in hospital playrooms, not only because the play tends to be at table height, but also because there is frequently little floor space for those patients able to sit on the floor. However, toddlers, in particular, need a protected, preferably carpeted space for floor play (Olds, 1982a, 1982b). A raised platform or a separate space behind banquette or Plexiglas walls can serve this purpose. Older preschoolers need some space to ride bikes or push trucks without being run over.

Elementary-age children also need to play. A separate space or well-defined area where their activities and games of longer duration can continue without interruption from younger children usually helps them feel the playroom is not only for babies. Often having storage space to put projects that are not finished when medical need interrupts playtime demonstrates the value of play best to elementary-age patients. Older children may not admit their interest in play other than sports or educational games, and may be embarrassed to be with younger patients in other than the helping role. Adolescents and older elementary patients are frequently given either separate space or separate hours in a common space to allow them to feel some ownership of the playroom. Patients of all ages need the outlet for their emotions that play and peer interaction allow.

For those children who are not mobile, play activities must be provided at bedside. Infants confined to bed need interesting and colorful visual and tactile stimulation that must be varied daily and chosen with appropriate age and developmental needs in mind. Mirrors, cradles, gyms, busy boxes, objects with varied textures and sounds, and mobiles are important toys on an infant floor. Unfortunately, common choices for infant toys are nonresponsive stuffed animals, and adults may often turn on the television just for auditory stimulation, resulting in another passive and potentially irritating stimulus.

Children on bedrest also need play. Those that cannot be moved should have a way to make the environment more personal and less institutional. A space or bulletin board on which to display cards and pictures of home and family can make a hospital bed space more like a child's room. Personalizing space by decorating the beds as each child chooses can create a brighter, more enjoyable living area. The biggest constraint to an institutional environment is often the staff's feelings that space cannot be adapted. Play activity specialists who understand the children's developmental need can assist in adapting the bedroom environment for play. Two beds in a room can be moved to allow for a nerf ball game. Patients in casts can be protected by plastic sheets to allow water play or messy paint play. Punch balls or balloons can hang from traction beds to allow an active outlet for pent-up energy and angry emotions. Accommodations must be made to allow active play and peer interaction to occur outside of the hospital playroom.

Pediatric divisions of hospitals tend to be organized by ages of children or by diagnosis (i.e., medical, surgical, orthopedic, psychiatric). This type of organization depends on the size of the pediatric division and the philosophy determining priority of psycho-social and medical care needed. Sometimes children from age 1 to 18 are included in one playroom. That range of children, with their families and visitors, cannot all find space for age-appropriate play. In other hospitals children within a 5- to 8-year age span are in separate playrooms even though they may have similar physical or medical constraints. The kind of play engaged in is determined both by the ages of children and the physical limitations of the setting. The challenge facing child life specialists or play activity therapists in hospitals is both to overcome the physical constraints and to encourage social interaction in a constantly changing group of children of different ages. The group available to come to a playroom on any given day changes according to the medical needs of each patient and the continually changing hospital census. On one day there may be five toddlers eager to play with blocks and trucks and two 6-year-olds at the easel. The next day the toddlers may be discharged, in surgery, or undergoing tests, and the population of the playroom and the nature of interaction are different. There may be one toddler, lonely for his friends, two 6-year-olds trying to decide whether to let a newly arrived 7-year-old play with them, and an 11-year-old wishing he could be with teenagers. This changing configuration in the population often means that guided play is more appropriate than free play.

In addition to the changing social mix, there are constant interruptions in the playtime available to children. Children are in hospitals primarily because of medical needs; thus, the schedules of the medical personnel and various tests that child-patients must undergo have higher priority than play and may interrupt and intrude upon the time for play. Hospital staff must help children understand the reality of the hospital schedule and at the same time reserve some time and space for children's play. Daily collaborative planning between the play and nursing staff is beneficial; sometimes there may be a whole morning or a whole day allowed for respite from diagnostic tests, but this is not usually the case. As a consequence, children have little control over the amount of playtime available.

Hospital staff need to respect the play space; intrusive procedures and medical checkups should not occur there. Children should be able to know that when they go to the playroom they can relax and enjoy a respite from the often stressful hospital routines. If play is interrupted, there should be sufficient warning. This concept of a safe playroom encourages freedom of expression in play and other social interactions.

Play has been accepted as an integral part of many pediatric floors for over 25 years because of its vital role in helping children get well. In the eyes of many doctors and nurses play is more appropriate in the hospital than school work. This positive attitude toward play is different from that found in the school environment, where play is often dichotomized from children's school work. However, just as schools should recognize children's need to play, so should hospitals recognize children's need to continue doing their schoolwork, which is an important part of their life outside the hospital. The hospital environment that promotes children's play and children's work also promotes children's health.

Although play is allowed and encouraged in many hospitals, many medical personnel still do not really understand the value of play for developmental learning. The responsibilities of hospital child life specialists include not only providing appropriate play environments for children, but also communicating information about the value of play to the rest of the hospital staff.

● One model of a hospital play environment

The model environment described here is adapted from that of the Association for the Care of Children's Health Child Life Project and the Phoenix Children's Hospital. It also draws on the play environment design of the Alfred I. DuPont Institute, Wilmington, Delaware. This play (i.e., child life) program model can serve a pediatric unit of approximately 80 beds. It includes one child life coordinator, four child life specialists, and two child life assistants.

The staff plan. The coordinator is responsible for child life administration work such as representing the program at hospital meetings, making community contacts, arranging for special events (e.g., holiday parties for child-patients, visits from entertainers, celebrities), and serving as a liaison between the child life program and other hospital departments and personnel. The child life specialists establish contact with each child and family upon admission to the

hospital to begin the supportive relationship with the child-patient. They develop a psychosocial care plan for each child to ensure that individual needs are met.

One of the key roles played by the child life staff is to offer children and families a consistent relationship throughout the hospital experience. In an environment where children encounter many new people and experiences each day and often must move from room to room to accommodate the ever-changing hospital population, it is important that one person remains constant and supportive. The child life specialists are soon recognized by child-patients as familiar advocates who will support them and serve as liaisons between the children and the medical world.

Child life specialists educate and prepare children and family members for hospital routines, procedures, and impending surgeries. They provide therapeutic play during preparatory activities as well as during the postprocedural period. Child life specialists also support child-patients during other stress points of hospitalization (e.g., during diagnostic tests, anesthesia, etc.) and offer support to family members by orienting them to the hospital environment and engaging them in therapeutic conversation. Advocating for patient rights and acting as liaisons between families and the hospital system are also ways child life specialists provide assistance to families.

The child life specialists supervise the child life assistants, who are primarily responsible for planning, supervising and maintaining the playroom areas. The playroom is open from 10:00 a.m. to 12:30 p.m. each day and children are encouraged to eat their lunch in the playroom between 12:30 and 1:00 p.m. A quiet rest time is enforced between 1:00 and 2:30 p.m. and then the playroom is reopened between 2:30 and 5:00 in the afternoon. Following determination of the child-patients' needs by the child life specialists, those children who are able to participate in playroom activities are invited to do so. Children are brought to the playroom by nurses, parents, or child life staff. Those children not able to participate in playroom activities because of physical restrictions (e.g., bedrest, extreme illness, infection susceptibility) are attended to at bedside by the child life specialists, who perform the majority of the individual care, education, preparation, and family support.

A well-trained volunteer group aids the child life staff in attending to the needs of all patients by assisting in playroom and bedside care. Often volunteers rock infants to console them, support the child

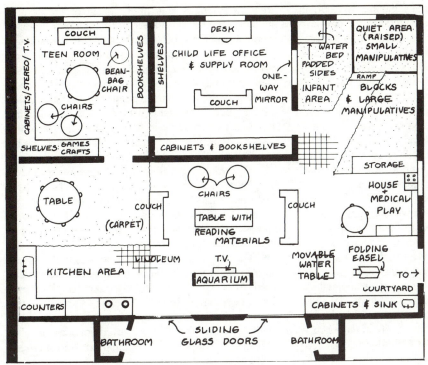

FIGURE 11-1 • Prototype Hospital Play Environment

life assistants in the playroom, or engage patients in bedside activities such as playing games or reading stories. Because no child life personnel are available on weekends and evenings, volunteers extend the play program to these times by planning and implementing various activities such as showing movies, organizing games, and monitoring mobile book and toy carts.

Due to the wide age range of hospitalized children (birth to 18 years) the playroom is designed to accommodate the interests and needs of all developmental levels. The child life assistants take the age range into consideration when planning the playroom curriculum, making sure there will be some activity of interest for children of each age. The age range factor coupled with the ever-changing hospital population demands a great deal of creativity and flexibility of those working with hospitalized children. Child life personnel must be able to change plans and activities at a moment's notice and must have readily available a variety of materials and ideas to meet the needs of a diverse group of children.

Physical and social features of the environment. A diagram of the playroom is presented in Figure 11–1. This design is very similar to designs of other child-centered environments that facilitate the play and activity of children, with some minor accommodations specific to the needs of hospitalized children.

The facility has a wide entrance, which allows ample space for wheelchairs and beds to be pushed in and out. This is especially important for child-patients who are in traction for long periods of time and unable to get out of bed but who need the stimulation offered by a change of environment, play activities, and contact with peers. The toilets are located close to the playroom for easy and quick access, but do not take up valuable playroom space. In the middle of the playroom is an aquarium and a sitting area specifically designed to accommodate parents who accompany their children to the playroom. This area allows the parents to maintain close proximity to their children yet to relax in a comfortable environment, read, watch TV, or visit with other parents. They can feel assured that their children are safe and enjoying themselves and at the same time get a break from supervising and entertaining them. Parents also have an opportunity to gain support from other parents who accompany their children to the playroom.

Behind the sitting area is a child life office and supply room with a one-way mirror for the observation of child-patients by hospital staff. This opportunity to observe children while they are relaxed and involved in the pleasurable pursuits of play offers staff additional information regarding the patients' behavior and medical condition. The window facilitates the observation of children in a nonobtrusive manner. No window is on the other side of the office in order to preserve the privacy of adolescents. The teen activity room is a place where adolescents can come to gain peer contact and a break from the intrusive hospital environment. Because of the developmental needs of adolescents, there is an added emphasis on privacy in the teen space. The teen area includes comfortable seating; a table for game playing, eating, or lounging; a TV and stereo; and cabinets that allow free choice of arts-and-crafts materials, games, books, and magazines. A "For Teens Only" sign is posted at the entrance to the teen area to formalize the philosophy that teens need a place of their own to relax and enjoy themselves.

Next to the teen room is a kitchen area shared by all ages. The two spaces are divided by a half-wall and windows. Curtains can be drawn by teens to add to the privacy of their space. The eating/cooking area includes a table and chairs, a stove, oven, refrigerator, sink, and storage space. When not used for cooking, this area is used for messy activities by all ages. Cooking and eating experiences are important for all hospitalized children due to the nurturing aspects inherent in food preparation and eating; this has special therapeutic benefits for hospitalized children who often feel battered by painful and uncomfortable hospital routines, procedures, and operations. Food preparation increases feelings of independence and control for patients of all ages.

The cooking/eating area is also used by the middle childhood (i.e., 7 to 11) age group for arts, crafts, and game playing when it is not in use for other purposes. This gives the elementary-age children a place to play that is separated from young children while also allowing teens to maintain their own space.

The area to the right of the sitting area is similar to other environments designed for infants and young children. This space includes quiet and active areas, a dramatic play area, space for messy and sensory activities, and an infant exploration area. A medical play corner is included because hospitalized children demonstrate a strong need to participate frequently and repetitively in therapeutic dramatic play related to their medical experiences. The space allotted for the areas in the playroom accommodates traction beds, intravenous poles, and wheelchairs. There is little variation in floor levels because of the constraints imposed on most hospitalized children by wheelchairs, IV's, and other medical equipment.

The water bed is relaxing and soothing for many hospitalized infants and toddlers. The small size of the bed makes it easy to move children on and off the mattress, and the padded area around the outside makes it a comfortable place for staff and parents to sit and watch the infants and toddlers.

The playroom has a large doorway to the courtyard to open the play area to the outside when desired. After being in a hospital for any length of time the opportunity to breathe "real air" and to feel the warmth of sunshine is very therapeutic for many pediatric patients. This area is used for various play activities for preschool, kindergarten, and elementary-age children, as a gathering area for teens, and a place for cookouts and picnics for patients of all ages and their families.

The activities planned for hospitalized children are similar to those planned for other child-centered environments. Emphasis is on open-ended, process-oriented activities to offer child-patients as many choices as possible during play and to encourage children to express themselves freely as a counter experience to the lack of choice and control inherent in hospital settings. Activities are planned that allow safe and appropriate expression of feelings of anxiety, fear, and anger. Aggression activities are offered daily (e.g., target shooting with syringes, making and pounding salt dough, bean bag throwing). Many sensory and messy activities are included in the curriculum because of the soothing effects these activities offer and the affective expression they encourage.

Older children are encouraged to participate in sensory and art activities and in a wide variety of card and board games. These games offer excellent vehicles for staff to use in developing relationships with older children and teens. They also serve as a nonthreatening way for staff to engage patients in therapeutic conversation about their hospital experiences, fears, and wishes.

An obvious use of the playroom is to encourage socialization among child-patients, peers, and family members. Children can easily feel isolated in hospitals, and the playroom offers them a place to interact with peers in a relatively normal environment. This peer contact is therapeutic for children who can share feelings and thoughts with other child-patients regarding their common hospital experiences. Parents also gain support from interaction with other parents by discussing concerns and needs related to the hospitalization of their children.

The following description is of a typical day in a hospital playroom: Several parents are relaxing and talking in the seating area. On the water bed an infant is being soothed by a volunteer gently rocking the mattress. Several preschoolers are engaged in easel painting and water play, and a number of young children are relaxing in the quiet area listening to a story being read by another volunteer. The child life assistant is involved in sensory stimulation with an infant on an infant mat. Another child life assistant is supervising several children in the medical corner engaged in pretend play, attending to the needs of a sick teddy bear. In the kitchen area elementary-age children are preparing their lunch while other child-patients of the same age are engrossed in board games and putting puzzles together. In the teen room several adolescents are listening to music, playing chess or checkers, and talking about their hospital experiences as well as other aspects of their lives. Out in the courtyard a volunteer supervises several children in traction beds who have been rolled outside to gain the therapeutic benefits of the fresh air and sunshine; they are engaged in a game of volleyball with an inflatable punching bag. On other days there may be more or fewer patients taking advantage of the hospital play space, depending on the characteristics of the changing population, but child life staff maintains the same playroom hours each day so that supervised play/activity time is available to all child-patients and families during their hospital experience.

Conclusion

Children's play occurs in every environment that they occupy. The quality, diversity, and content of that play varies, however, depending on the richness of the play opportunities, the safety of the setting, and the nature of adult facilitation and interaction. In the neighborhood and community children need to feel that their play is important and that the environment welcomes their participation. At specially designed parks and playgrounds, children need safe but challenging equipment, natural materials that can be manipulated, and appropriate levels of supervision and help from adults.

In environments for children with handicapping conditions, equipment and designs that promote their active involvement and give opportunities for social interaction are essential. In hospitals, environments should encourage children not only to meet their developmental play needs, but also to use play to deal with the trauma of their medical experiences. Such environments promote both health and growth.

This chapter and the others in this book have stressed the value of play as a learning medium that promotes every area of children's development. Play is essential for children in every type of life circumstance. In that sense, every environment is a special one if it promotes children's optimal play development and learning.

Questions for Discussion

1. How can a neighborhood environment or a playground environment be designed to meet the play needs of children of all age levels while also recognizing adult concerns for safety and order?
2. What are some of the important play development issues that adults must keep in mind when planning an environment to promote the play of multihandicapped children? Hospitalized children? How are these issues similar and how are they different for children in these two groups? For children not experiencing deficits or trauma?

Play Activities Problem

1. As the city planner, you have been asked to suggest an overall plan for meeting the play needs of children in your community of 50,000. Presently the city has two traditional playgrounds in parks, an outdoor swimming

pool, 20 vacant lots that were reclaimed for nonpayment of taxes, and a tot lot at a shopping center. The community is an industrial one, with two very hazardous traffic areas. Residents are not currently supportive of a tax increase. There may be the possibility of getting a $5,000 pilot project grant. How can you design a comprehensive but relatively inexpensive plan? What resources would you draw upon to implement the plan?

2. As the director of a program for multihandicapped or for hospitalized children (select one), you have been operating in one room of a school or hospital. The room is typical of other rooms in your setting, having some built-in storage space, tables and chairs, materials you have designed to adapt the space for the children's needs, and a few donated items of special equipment. You have been notified that the facility now also has the room across the hall available and that $7,000 has been provided to make this wing of the building into a more appropriate special unit. How will you arrange the space? What will you buy or build with the money? How will the new design better meet your program goals (specify what those goals are)?

Suggestions for Further Reading

Azarnoff, P., & Flegal, S. (1975). *A pediatric play program*. Springfield, IL: Charles C Thomas. A small but useful book that has become a classic in the field of child life. Gives practical suggestions for setting up a hospital play program.

Derrick, S., Bachman, K., & Parker, S. (1982). *Hospitalized children: Play and play activities*. Lake Mills, IA: Graphic Publishing. A small book offering a good overview of the theoretical background of play in hospitals, the research conducted in the area, and some concrete suggestions for implementing play with hospitalized children.

Frost, J. L., & Sunderlin, S. (Eds.). (1985). *When children play*. Wheaton, MD: Association for Childhood Education International. Presents a wealth of the latest research on playgrounds and other play spaces for children from infancy to elementary age. Includes playground plans and equipment suggestions.

Lindheim, R., Glaser, H. H., & Coffin, C. (1972). *Changing hospital environments for children*. Cambridge, MA: Harvard University Press. Advises pediatricians, architects, and administrators on how to design environments for hospitalized children.

Lindquist, I. (1977). *Therapy through play*. London: Arlington Books. Presents case studies and practical suggestions for providing therapeutic play experiences in hospitals. Gives an empathetic view of the need for play of children with a number of specific handicapping conditions.

Moore, G., Cohen, U., & McGinty, T. (1979). *Planning and design guidelines: Childcare centers and outdoor play environments*. Milwaukee: University of Wisconsin, Milwaukee Center for Architecture and Urban Planning Research. Describes environmental design principles that are especially useful for these settings but can also be used as guidelines for any setting for children.

Moore, G., Cohen, U., Oertel, J., & Van Ryzin, L. (1979). *Designing environments for handicapped children: A design guide and case study*. New York: Educational Facilities Laboratories. Presents ideas for adapting play spaces and designing new spaces for children with handicaps. The guidelines are applicable to settings for all children.

Olds, A. R. (1979). Designing developmentally optimal classrooms for children with special needs. In S. Meisels (Ed.), *Special education and development perspectives of young children with special needs* (pp. 91–138). Baltimore: University Park Press. Provides many useful suggestions for developing effective and attractive special education classrooms.

Olds, A. R. (1982b). *Humanizing the pediatric hospital environment. Adaptive Environments Conference Papers*, 59–72. Boston: Adaptive Environments. Demonstrates how principles of environmental design can be applied to pediatric settings.

Rudolph, N. (1974). *Workyards*. New York: Teachers College Press. Although called "workyards" rather than "play yards," this book gives many ideas on setting up "adventure" type playgrounds in the United States. Includes ways to mobilize communities to get their involvement and support.

Play, Technology, and the Authentic Self

DORIS BERGEN

"What is REAL?" asked the Rabbit one day, when they were lying side by side near the nursery fender, before Nana came to tidy the room. "Does it mean having things that buzz inside you and a stick-out handle?"

"Real isn't how you are made," said the Skin Horse. "It's a thing that happens to you. When a child loves you for a long, long time, not just to play with, but REALLY loves you, then you become Real."

"Does it hurt?" asked the Rabbit.

"Sometimes," said the Skin Horse, for he was always truthful. "When you are Real you don't mind being hurt."

"Does it happen all at once, like being wound up," he asked, "or bit by bit?"

"It doesn't happen all at once," said the Skin Horse. "You become. It takes a long time. That's why it doesn't often happen to people who break easily, or have sharp edges, or who have to be carefully kept. Generally, by the time you are Real, most of your hair has been loved off, and your eyes drop out and you get loose in the joints and very shabby. But these things don't matter at all, because once you are Real you can't be ugly, except to people who don't understand." (Bianco, 1926, pp. 16–17).

The Velveteen Rabbit: Or How Toys Become Real (Bianco, 1926) has always been one of my favorite stories. As a child, I remember reading it over and over, partly because it was one of the books I owned. (Although I think libraries are wonderful, there has always been something very special to me about the books I owned.) But also, the question of realness—of authenticity—captures for me the dilemma of human existence, which is, I think, how to become—and to stay—"real."

The search for authenticity has always been part of the human quest for personal meaning; however, in our technological age, with all the things that "buzz inside" and "break easily," some people think we are more in danger than ever of not becoming "real." Our society often seems to encourage the superficial fad, the artificial material, and the official front. Our technology sometimes directs minds and efforts toward interaction with things not persons, toward abstractions not concreteness, and toward events that "happen all at once" not things that "take a long time."

The social context has always been a major influence on human authenticity, of course. From infancy on, all of us are required to begin differentiating our inner world from the outer "real" world, as defined first by parents, siblings, and other relatives; then by teachers and peers; then by significant others, spouses, one's own children, friends, colleagues, bosses, and the other humans met in person or through media in communities, nations, and continents.

They insist that we learn to separate fantasy from "reality," accept the cognitive and social conventions of how things "really" are, and come to believe the common wisdom that says it is "real work," not play, that counts. As we learn to perform the roles we are assigned by the socialization forces in our environment, we sometimes forget that they are roles—often ones we have been pressed into accepting but not ones we would have chosen. They may not comfortably fit our authentic selves but rather leave us feeling diminished and unreal.

Our interactions with the physical world of reality also shape us—form and structure, time and space, matter and energy, even atom and particle—often appear to be more real than our playful fantasies and our dreams. Sometimes our encounters with the technological world may leave us feeling distant and alone, out of control of our lives, and, as robots become more humanlike, even fearing that we will be increasingly unable to distinguish "what is real."

So how do we become real in a technological age?

The same playful qualities that saved humans from the vagaries of primitive existence and that have brought us into this present complex society can help us to find and preserve our realness in the future. As Ellis points out earlier in this book, play may be our major adaptive tool for dealing with the future, as it has been for surviving the past. Bateson (1955, 1956) has suggested that being able to manipulate reality in play confirms our grasp on other realities. And, in an earlier essay, Bretherton explains that it is the fact that children have "shared understandings about the real world" that makes it possible for them to agree to transform that world in their play. The "problem" of play, as I see it, is that few consider play to be real. Its *nonliterality* is often interpreted to mean *nonreality*. But, as Sheehan (1975) reminds us, "play . . . is the most real thing . . . " (p. 184).

When children engage in play, trying out practice skills, trying on pretend roles, trying to live by game rules, they can learn much about their authentic selves. By testing the limits of their abilities in the self-imposed activities of play, they can find out who they are and realize what they can become. Unfortunately, there are also times (e.g., under adult or peer pressure) when they learn in play to narrow their perspectives and to deny who they really are because of what society wants them to be. It is important that as children learn to individuate, classify, accept, and come to terms with socially identified realities, they don't lose the opportunity to "become real" in the process.

How can play help them (and us) to "become real?"

First, play enables us to distinguish text and context and thus, to keep our perspective on reality and our sense of inner control. We can test a wide range of roles and risk playing those that are most authentic for ourselves. We can create and revise the play frame of our lives so that we can play these authentic roles comfortably and joyously. We can communicate with others within and without of the social context; and thus negotiate for ourselves better texts for performing our roles. We can use play as a finetuning device to stay in touch with our most intense and personal feelings and thoughts. And we can bend the reality of the present social and physical world to imagine and to plan for the world of the future.

Second, play can provide a medium for linking technological learning and our self-knowledge-seeking. To adapt to the world of the next century, with its as yet unimagined human, scientific, and technological possibilities, we have to be able to think in "as if" and "what if" ways. In our concern about possible negative effects of technology, I think we have often ignored its play and self-enhancement potential, which can help us in our search for realness. For example, computer networks are demonstrating that technology can connect the mind and heart and leave the irrelevant characteristics of the body—gender, physical appearance, race, handicaps—behind, thus opening up a new world of play and communication of "unencumbered" ideas and feelings.

Play also serves as a medium for technological conquest, as the simulations that prepare adults for space flight, the models used to "play through" the planned flight experiences, and even the risk taking "what if" attitudes of the astronauts demonstrate. In the same way that play provided a medium for invention in other centuries, it encourages the thinking and dreaming that are needed for survival now. Perhaps, in the future, war games will be played on a computer or in a stadium with symbolic weapons so that we can even leave the crazy "reality" of war's pain and destruction behind us.

Finally, play is the medium through which we can learn to risk the pain and the joy of realness. Children know this intuitively and, underneath our layers of sophistication and socialization, so do we. Play helps us learn that becoming real involves risk taking and willingness to be hurt, get shabby, and become loose in the joints. In our search for realness, we may have to follow new scripts, discarding or revising the scripts we rehearsed and memorized in childhood. We may be required to face dark and scary visions and thoughts or give up tightly held areas of control to experience what Herron and Sutton-Smith (1971) call "voluntary disequilibrium" as a price for movement. And we may even need to acknowledge that many of our social maneuvers and our work goals, which seem to be such serious business, are games after all.

A playful attitude toward life allows us to keep in touch with ourselves while we examine, accept, manipulate, and integrate our many realities. Once we learn to do that, we can even reframe and integrate the realities of our work with those of our play, and experience the joyful "flow" that comes from this holistic authenticity (Csikszentmihayli, 1979). Then, perhaps we will be more able to help children to experience and develop their authenticity in both their play and their work.

As we open ourselves up to the "as ifs" and "what ifs" in our futures, transform our work into play and our play into work as the need arises, and see beyond our props, roles, and appearances to embrace our realness—even those parts of us that are a bit worn and shabby—we will convey to children our knowledge that a life playfully and actively lived is worth the risk. We will know (as the Toys know) that "once you are Real, you can't be ugly, except to people who don't understand."

Epilogue: How to Begin

I wrote this summary of the perspective underlying my book at the time I wrote the Preface and the Introduction, because it seemed that I needed to know where the ending place was going to be in order to stay on the road to get there. Now that we have reached the end of the book, I hope you have gained some knowledge of this perspective, which includes the following beliefs:

1. Parents, teachers, educational administrators, psychologists, child life specialists, and policy makers should be aware, not only of the ways that play relates to children's early learning and development, but also of its role in promoting many of the competencies needed by citizens in contemporary American society.
2. All people who care for and teach children should be knowledgeable about research on play development and on the relationship of play to cognitive, social, emotional, physical, language, moral, and gender/sex role development and should be able to communicate this knowledge to others.
3. To promote play development and to use play pedagogically or therapeutically, practitioners must be able to apply this information by knowing how to design play-enhancing physical environments and to use play-facilitating techniques that enhance development and learning.
4. Students who plan to enter professions that focus on children's care and education must understand the ways in which play has been studied and have experience with play research methods, so they will be able to evaluate the effectiveness of their environments and/or curriculum and the progress of children's play development within these settings.

These beliefs are ones I hope you will take with you as you end your experience with this book. But because I believe this will not be the end for you but just the beginning, I am including one final suggestion to you (and to all of us) on How to Begin:

T: Let's pretend that I am a writer who has helped you to learn more about play . . . And let's pretend that you are a student who wants to try out some of the ideas you learned in this book . . .

(The others join in . . .)

A: Let's pretend I am a teacher who understands how to use play as a curricular tool . . .

B: And let's pretend I am a center director who has ideas about play to share with parents and caregivers of infants . . .

C: And let's pretend I am a child life specialist who has skills to develop a play program . . .

D: I'll be an administrator who believes I should share my knowledge of play with my board . . .

E: I'll be a psychologist who knows how to study about play development . . .

All: Let's get the ideas and materials we need . . . let's find the right places to start . . . let's arrange our space . . . And now let us Begin . . .

References

Aaron, D., & Winawer, B. P. (1965). *Child's play: A creative approach to play spaces for today's children.* New York: Harper & Row.

Abrahams, R. D. (1962). Playing the dozens. *Journal of American Folklore, 75,* 209–220.

Abrahams, R. D. (Ed.). (1969). *Jump-rope rhymes: A dictionary.* Austin: University of Texas Press.

Adams, M. A. (1976). The hospital play program: Helping children with serious illness. *American Journal of Orthopsychiatry, 46,* 416–424.

Adler, L. (1982). *Mother-toddler interaction: Content, style, and relations to symbolic development.* Unpublished doctoral dissertation, Rutgers University, New Brunswick, NJ.

Ainsworth, M. D. S. (1969). Object relations dependency and attachment: A theoretical review of the infant-mother relationship, *Child Development, 40,* 969–1025.

Ainsworth, M. D. S. (1972). Attachment and dependency: A comparison. In J. Gewirtz (Ed.), *Attachment and dependency* (pp. 97–137). Washington, DC: Halstead Press.

Ainsworth, M. D. S. (1973). The development of infant-mother attachment. In B. Caldwell & H. Riccutti (Eds.), *Review of child development research* (Vol. 3, pp. 1–94). Chicago: University of Chicago Press.

Ainsworth, M. D. S. (1974). Infant-mother attachment and social development: Socialization as a product of recip-rocal responsiveness to signals. In M. Richards (Ed.), *The integration of the child into the social world* (pp. 99–135). New York: Cambridge University Press.

Ainsworth, M. D. S. (1979). Infant-mother attachment. *American Psychologist, 34,* 932–937.

Aldis, O. (1975). *Play fighting.* New York: Academic Press.

Alexander, F. (1958). A contribution to the theory of play. *Psychoanalytic Quarterly, 27,* 175–193.

Allen, K. E., Turner, K. D., & Everett, P. M. (1970). A behavior modification classroom for Head Start children with problem behaviors. *Exceptional Children, 37*(2), 119–129.

Allen, K. E., Hart, B. M., Buell, J. S., Harris, F. R., & Wolf, M. M. (1964). Effects of social reinforcement on isolate behavior of a nursery school child. *Child Development, 35,* 511–518.

Allen of Hurtwood, Lady. (1968). *Planning for play.* London: Thames & Hudson.

Ames, L. B. (1937). The sequential patterning of prone progression in the human infant. *Genetic Psychology Monograph, 19,* 409–460.

Ammar, H. (1954). *Growing up in an Egyptian village.* London: Routledge & Kegan Paul.

Anderson, J., & Tindall, M. (1972). The concept of home range: New data for the study of territorial behavior. In W. J. Mitchell (Ed.), *Environmental design: Research and* practice. (pp. 1.1.1–1.1.7) Washington, DC: Environmental Design Research Associates.

Anderson, R. C., & Pearson, P. D. (1984). A schema-theoretic view of basic processes in reading. In P. D. Pearson, R. Barr, M. L Kamil, & P. Mosenthal (Eds.), *Handbook of reading research* (pp. 255–291). New York: Longman.

Anisfield, M. (1984). *Language development from birth to three.* Hillsdale, NJ: Erlbaum.

Arco, C. (1983). Pacing of playful stimulation to young infants: Similarities and differences in maternal and paternal communication. *Infant Behavior and Development, 6*(2), 223–228.

Arend, R., Grove, F. L., & Sroufe, L. A. (1979). Continuity of individual adaptation from infancy to kindergarten: A predictive study of ego-resiliency and curiosity in preschoolers. *Child Development, 50*(4), 950–959.

Arlow, J. A. (1977). Affects and the psychoanalytic situation. *International Journal of Psychoanalysis, 58,* 158–170.

Arnaud, S. H. (1971). Polish for play's tarnished reputation. In G. Engstrom (Ed.), *Play: The child strives toward self-realization* (pp. 5–12). Washington, DC: National Association for the Education of Young Children.

Arnaud, S. H., & Curry, N. E. (Producers). (1974). *The facilitation of children's dramatic play* [Film]. New York: Campus Film Distributors.

Aronson, E. (1978). *The jigsaw classroom.* Beverly Hills, CA: Sage.

Ashby, W. R. (1960). *Design for a brain: The origin of adaptive behavior.* (2nd Ed.). New York: Wiley.

Asher, S. R., & Gottman, J. M. (1981). *The development of children's friendships.* New York: Cambridge University Press.

Asher, S. R., Singleton, L. C., & Taylor, A. R. (1982). *Acceptance versus friendship: A longitudinal study of racial integration.* Paper presented at the Annual Meeting of the American Educational Research Association, New York.

Ashton, E. (1983). Measures of play behavior: The influence of sex-role stereotyped children's books. *Sex Roles, 9*(1), 43–47.

Athey, I. (1971). Language models and reading. *Reading Research Quarterly, 7*(1), 16–110.

Austin, A. M., & Draper, D. C. (1984). The relationship among peer acceptance, social impact, and academic achievement in middle childhood. *American Educational Research Journal, 21,* 597–604.

Ausubel, D. P. (1968). *Educational psychology: A cognitive view.* New York: Holt, Rinehart & Winston.

Ausubel, D. P., Sullivan, E. V., & Ives, S. W. (1980). *Theory and problems of child development* (3rd ed.). New York: Grune & Stratton.

Axline, V. (1947). *Play therapy.* New York: Ballantine Books.

Azarnoff, P. (1974). Mediating the trauma of serious illness and hospitalization in childhood. *Children Today, 3*(4), 12–17.

Azarnoff, P., & Flegal, S. (1975). *A pediatric play program.* Springfield, IL: Charles C Thomas.

Bach, G. R. (1946). Father-fantasies and father-typing in father-separated children. *Child Development, 17,* 63–80.

Bacon, M. K., & Ashmore, R. D. (1982). The role of categorization in the socialization process: How parents and older siblings cognitively organize child behavior. In L. M. Laosa & I. E. Sigel (Eds.), *Families as learning environments for children* (pp. 301–341). New York: Plenum Press.

Baer, D. M. (1967). *Recent examples of behavior modification in preschool settings.* Paper presented at the Ninth Annual Institute for Clinical Psychology, University of Kansas, Lawrence.

Bailey, L., & Slee, P. T. (1984). A comparison of play interactions between non-disabled and disabled children and their mothers: A question of style. *Australia and New Zealand Journal of Developmental Disabilities, 10*(1), 5–10.

Bailey, R. A., & Burton, E. C. (1982). *The dynamic self: Activities to enhance infant development.* St. Louis: C. V. Mosby.

Bakeman, R., & Adamson, L. B. (1984). Coordinating attention to people and objects in mother-infant and peer-infant interaction. *Child Development, 55,* 1278–1289.

Bandura, A. (1969). *Principles of behavior modification.* New York: Holt, Rinehart & Winston.

Bandura, A. (1973). *Aggression: Social learning analysis.* Englewood Cliffs, NJ: Prentice-Hall.

Bandura, A. (1977). *Social learning theory.* Englewood Cliffs, NJ: Prentice-Hall.

Barbarin, O. A., & Chesler, M. A. (1984). Relationships with the medical staff and aspects of satisfaction with care expressed by parents of children with cancer. *Journal of Community Health, 9,* 302–313.

Barbero, G. (1984). Children with recurrent hospitalization: A problem of disabled children, parents, and physicians. *Developmental and Behavioral Pediatrics, 5*(6), 319–324.

Barker, R. G., & Wright, H. F. (1955). *Midwest and its children.* New York: Harper & Row.

Barnard, C. P., & Corrales, R. G. (1979). *The theory and technique of family therapy.* Springfield, IL: Charles C Thomas.

Barnes, G. M. (1981). Solitary play: Social immaturity or autonomous achievement striving? *Australian Journal of Early Childhood, 6*(3), 12–15.

Barnett, L., & Kleiber, D. A. (1984). Playfulness and the early play environment. *Journal of Genetic Psychology, 144*(2), 153–164.

Barnett, M. A., King, L. M., Howard, J. A., & Dino, G. A. (1980). Empathy in young children: Relation to parents, empathy, affection and emphasis on the feelings of others. *Developmental Psychology, 16,* 243–244.

Basch, M. F. (1976). The concept of affect: A re-examination. *Journal of the American Psychoanalytic Association, 24*(4), 759–777.

Bateson, G. (1955). A theory of play and fantasy. *American Psychiatric Association Research Reports, 2,* 39–51.

Bateson, G. (1956). The message "This is play." In B. Schaffner (Ed.), *Group processes: Transactions of the second conference* (pp. 145–241). New York: Josiah Macy, Jr. Foundation.

Baumgartner, A. (1983). *My daddy might have loved me: Student perceptions of differences between being male and being female.* Denver, CO: Institute for Equality in Education.

Baumrind, D. (1966). Effects of authoritative control on child behavior. *Child Development, 37,* 887–907.

Baumrind, D. (1971). Current patterns of parental authority. *Developmental Psychology Monograph, 4* (1, Pt. 2).

Baumrind, D. (1973). The development of instrumental competence through socialization. In A. D. Pick (Ed.), *Minnesota Symposium on Child Psychology* (Vol. 7, pp. 3–46). Minneapolis: University of Minnesota Press.

Baumrind, D. (1980). New directions in socialization research. *American Psychologist, 35*(7), 639–652.

Bayley, N. (1935). The development of motor abilities during the first three years. *Monographs of the Society for Research in Child Development,* (1), 26–61.

Becher, R. M. (1985). Parent involvement and reading achievement: A review of research and implications for practice. *Childhood Education, 62*(1) 44–50.

Becher, R. M., & Wolfgang, C. (1977). An exploration of the relationship between symbolic representation in dramatic play and art and the cognitive and reading readiness levels of kindergarten children. *Psychology in the Schools, 14*(3), 377–381.

Beckman, P. J. (1983). The relationship between behavioral characteristics of children and social interaction in an integrated setting. *Journal of the Division for Early Childhood, 7,* 69–77.

Beckman, P. J., & Kohl, F. L. (1984). The effects of social and isolate toys on the interactions and play of integrated and nonintegrated groups of preschoolers. *Education and Training of the Mentally Retarded, 19*(3), 169–174.

Beckwith, J. (1982). It's time for creative play. *Parks and Recreation, 17*(9), 58–62, 89.

Beckwith, L. (1985). Parent-child interaction and social-emotional development. In C. C. Brown & A. W. Gottfried (Eds.), *Play interactions: The role of toys and parental involvement in children's development* (pp. 152–159). Skillman, NJ: Johnson & Johnson.

Beckwith, L., Cohen, S. E., Kopp, C. B., Parmelee, A. H., & Marcy, T. (1976). Caregiver-infant interaction and early cognitive development in preterm infants. *Child Development, 47,* 579–587.

Beeson, B. S., & Williams, R. A. (1985). The persistence of sex differences in the play of young children. In J. L. Frost & S. Sunderlin (Eds.), *When children play* (pp. 39–42). Wheaton, MD: Association for Childhood Education International.

Beetlestone, J., & Taylor, C. (1982). Linking science and drama at school. *Impact of Science on Society, 32*(4), 473–480.

Behrmann, M., & Lahm, L. (1983). *Critical learning: Multiply handicapped babies get on-line.* Paper presented at the Council for Exceptional Children National Conference on the Use of Microcomputers in Special Education, Hartford, CT.

Bell, R. Q. (1971). Stimulus control of parent or caretaker behavior by offspring. *Developmental Psychology, 4,* 61–72.

Belsky, J. (1977). *Mother-infant interaction at home and in the laboratory: The effects of context.* Paper presented at the Biennial Meeting of the Society for Research in Child Development, New Orleans.

Belsky, J., Garduque, L., & Hrncir, E. (1984). Assessing performance, competence, and executive capacity in infant play: Relations to home environment and security of attachment. *Developmental Psychology, 20*(3), 418–426.

Belsky, J., Goode, M., & Most, R. G. (1980). Maternal stimulation and infant exploratory competence: Cross-sectional, correlational, and experimental analysis. *Child Development, 51,* 1163–1178.

Belsky, J., & Most, R. (1981). From exploration to play: A cross-sectional study of infant free play behavior. *Developmental Psychology, 17,* 630–639.

Bem, S. L. (1976). Probing the promise of androgyny. In A. Kaplan & J. P. Bean (Eds.), *Beyond sex-role stereotypes: Readings toward a psychology of androgyny* (pp. 47–62). Boston: Little, Brown.

Bem, S. L. (1981). Gender schema theory: A cognitive account of sex typing. *Psychological Review, 88,* 354–364.

Bem, S. L. (1983). Gender schema theory and its implications for child development: Raising gender-aschematic children in a gender-schematic society. *Signs: Journal of Women in Culture and Society, 8,* 598–616.

Bengtsson, A. (1970). *Environmental planning for children's play.* New York: Praeger.

Bengtsson, A. (Ed.). (1972). *Adventure playgrounds.* New York: Praeger.

Benjamin, J. (1961). Some developmental observations relating to the theory of anxiety. *Journal of the American Psychoanalytic Association, 9,* 652–668.

Bereiter, C. (1972). Moral alternatives to education. *Interchange, 3,* 25–41.

Bereiter, C., & Engelmann, S. (1966). *Teaching disadvantaged children in the preschool.* Englewood Cliffs, NJ: Prentice-Hall.

Berg, M., & Medrich, E. A. (1980). Children in four neighborhoods: The physical environment and its effect on play and play patterns. *Environment and Behavior, 12*(3), 320–348.

Bergen, D. (1984). [Review of *Boys and girls at play: The development of sex roles*]. *Journal of Education, 166*(1), 111–116.

Bergen, D. (1985, 1986). *Memories of play.* (Nos. 1 & 2) Unpublished manuscripts. Pittsburg State University, Pittsburg, KS.

Bergen, D., Gaynard, L., & Torelli, L. (1985). *The influence of the culture of an infant/toddler center on peer play behavior: Informant and observational perspectives.* Des Moines, IA: Midwest Association for the Education of Young Children. (ERIC Document Reproduction Service No. ED 257 580)

Bergstrom, J. M. (1984). *School's out—Now what?* Berkeley, CA: Ten Speed Press.

Berlyne, D. E. (1960). *Conflict, arousal and curiosity.* New York: McGraw-Hill.

Berlyne, D. E. (1966). Curiosity and exploration. *Science, 153,* 25–33.

Berlyne, D. E. (1969). Laughter, humor and play. In G. Lindzey & E. Aronson (Eds.), *The handbook of social psychology* (Vol. 3, pp. 795–852). Reading, MA: Addison-Wesley.

Berlyne, D. E. (1970). Children's reasoning and thinking. In P. H. Mussen (Ed.), *Carmichael's manual of child psychology* (pp. 939–981). New York: Wiley.

Berman, P. W., Stoan, V. L., & Goodman, V. (1979). *Development of sex differences in response to an infant and to the caretaker role.* Paper presented at the biennial meeting of the Society for Research in Child Development, San Francisco.

Berndt, T. J. (1981a). Effects of friendship on prosocial intentions and behavior. *Child development, 52,* 636–643.

Berndt, T. J. (1981b). Relations between social cognition, nonsocial cognition, and social behavior: The case of friendship. In J. H. Flavell & L. Ross (Eds.), *Social cognitive development* (pp. 176–199). New York: Cambridge University Press.

Berndt, T. J. (1982). Fairness and friendship. In K. H. Rubin & H. S. Ross (Eds.), *Peer relationships and social skills in childhood* (pp. 253–278). New York: Springer-Verlag.

Berne, E. (1964). *Games people play.* New York: Grove Press.

Berry, P. (1984). Playing with print. *Australian Journal of Reading, 7*(2), 71–74.

Beth-Halachmy, S. B. (1980). Elementary school children's play behavior during school recess periods. In P. F. Wilkinson (Ed.), *In celebration of play* (pp. 135–142). New York: St. Martin's Press.

Beuf, A. H. (1979). *Biting off the bracelet.* Philadelphia: University of Pennsylvania Press.

Beyer, J. E., & Byers, M. (1985). Knowledge of pediatric pain: The state of the art. *Children's Health Care, 13*(4), 150–159.

Bianchi, B. D., & Bakeman, R. (1978). Sex-typed affiliation preferences observed in preschoolers: Traditional and open school differences. *Child Development, 49,* 910–912.

Bianco, M. W. (1926). *The velveteen rabbit: Or how toys become real.* Garden City, NY: Doubleday.

Bigelow, B. L. (1977). Children's friendship expectations: A cognitive developmental study. *Child Development, 48,* 246–253.

Bijou, S. W. (1964). An empirical concept of reinforcement and a functional analysis of child behavior. *Journal of Genetic Psychology, 104,* 215–223.

Birns, B., & Sternglanz, S. H. (1983). Sex-role socialization: Looking back and looking ahead. In M. B. Liss (Ed.), *Social and cognitive skills: Sex roles and children's play* (pp. 235–251). New York: Academic Press.

Blau, R., Brady, E. H., Bucher, I., Hiteshew, B., Zavitkovsky, A., & Zavitkovsky, D. (1977). *Activities for school-age child care.* Washington, DC: National Association for the Education of Young Children.

Blehar, M. C., Lieberman, A. F., & Ainsworth, M. D. S. (1977). Early face-to-face interaction and its relation to later infant-mother attachment. *Child Development, 48,* 182–194.

Bleier, M. (1976). *Social behaviors among one-year-olds in a playgroup.* Unpublished doctoral dissertation, Boston University.

Bloch, M. N. (1984). Play materials: Considerations from a West African setting. *Childhood Education, 60*(5), 345–348.

Block, J. H. (1979). Another look at sex differentiation in the socialization behavior of mothers and fathers. In J. Sherman & F. L. Denmark (Eds.), *Psychology of women: Future directions of research* (pp. 29–85). New York: Psychological Dimensions.

Block, J. H. (1983). Differential premises arising from differential socialization of the sexes: Some conjectures. *Child Development, 54,* 1335–1354.

Block, J. H. (1984). Making school learning activities more playlike: Flow and mastery learning. *The Elementary School Journal, 85*(1), 65–75.

Block, J. H., & Block, J. (1980). The role of ego-control and ego-resiliency in the organization of behavior. In W. A. Collins (Ed.), *Minnesota Symposium on Child Psychology: Vol. 13. Development of cognition, affect, and social relations* (pp. 39–101). Hillsdale, NJ: Erlbaum.

Bloom, B. (1964). *Stability and change in human characteristics.* New York: Wiley.

Bloom, L., & Lahey, M. (1978). *Language development and language disorders.* New York: Wiley.

Blurton-Jones, N. G. (1972). Categories of child-child interaction. In N. G. Blurton-Jones (Ed.), *Ethological studies of child behavior* (pp. 97–129). New York: Cambridge University Press.

Blurton-Jones, N. G., & Konner, M. J. (1973). Sex differences in behavior of London and Bushman children. In R. P. Michael & J. H. Crook (Eds.), *Comparative ecology and behaviour of primates* (pp. 689–750). London: Academic Press.

Borke, H. (1971). Interpersonal perception of young children: Egocentrism or empathy? *Developmental Psychology, 5,* 263–269.

Bott, H. (1928). Observations of play activities in the nursery school. *Genetic Psychology Monographs, 4,* 44–88.

Bower, T. G. R. (1982). *Development in infancy* (2nd ed.). San Francisco: W. H. Freeman.

Bowlby, J. (1969). *Attachment and loss: Vol. 1. Attachment.* New York: Basic Books.

Bowlby, J. (1973). *Attachment and loss: Vol. 2. Separation, anxiety and anger.* New York: Basic Books.

Bowman, B. T. (1983). *Do computers have a place in preschools?* Paper presented at the meeting of the New Mexico Association for the Education of Young Children, Albuquerque.

Bradley, R. H., & Caldwell, B. (1976a). Early home environment and changes in mental test performance in children from 6 to 36 months. *Developmental Psychology, 12,* 93–97.

Bradley, R. H., & Caldwell, B. (1976b). The relation of infants' home-environments to mental test performance at 54 months: A follow-up study. *Child Development, 47,* 1172–1174.

Bradtke, L., Kirkpatrick, W., & Rosenblatt, K. (Eds.). (1972). Intensive play: A technique for building affective behaviors in profoundly mentally retarded young children. *Education and Training of the Mentally Retarded, 7*(1), 8–13.

Brazelton, T. B. (1978). Early parent-infant reciprocity. In J. K. Gardner (Ed.), *Readings in developmental psychology* (pp. 71–78). Boston: Little, Brown.

Brazelton, T. B., & Als, H. (1979). Four early stages in the development of mother-infant interaction. *Psychoanalytic Study of the Child, 34,* 349–370.

Brazelton, T. B., Koslowski, B., & Main, M. (1974). The origins of reciprocity: The early mother-infant interaction. In M. Lewis & L. A. Rosenblum (Eds.), *The effect of the infant on its caregiver* (pp. 49–77). New York: Wiley.

Breger, L., Hunter, I., & Cane, R. W. (1971). *The effect of stress on dreams.* New York: International Universities Press.

Brenner, C. (1974). On the nature and development of affects: A unified theory. *Psychoanalytic Quarterly, 4,* 532–556.

Brenner, M. (1976). *The effects of sex, structure, and social interaction of preschoolers' make-believe in a naturalistic setting.* Master's thesis, University of Illinois. (ERIC Document Reproduction Service No. ED 128 103) Urbana-Champaign, IL

Bretherton, I. (1984a). Representing the social world in symbolic play: Reality and fantasy. In I. Bretherton (Ed.), *Symbolic play: The development of social understanding* (pp. 1–43). New York: Academic Press.

Bretherton, I. (Ed.). (1984b). *Symbolic play: The development of social understanding.* New York: Academic Press.

Bretherton, I., O'Connell, B., Shore, C., & Bates, E. (1984). The effect of contextual variation on symbolic play: Development from 20 to 28 months. In I. Bretherton (Ed.), *Symbolic play: The development of social understanding* (pp. 271–298). New York: Academic Press.

Brewster, A. (1982). The chronically ill child's conception of illness. *Pediatrics, 69*(3), 355–362.

Brewster, P. G. (1953). *American nonsinging games.* Norman: University of Oklahoma Press.

Bridges, K. M. B. (1927). Occupational interests in three year old children. *Pedagogical Seminary, 34,* 415–423.

Brierley, M. (1937). Affects in theory and practice. *International Journal of Psychoanalysis, 18,* 256–268.

Bright, M. C., & Stockdale, D. F. (1984). Mothers', fathers' and preschool children's interactive behaviors in a play setting. *Journal of Genetic Psychology, 144*(2), 219–232.

Britt, S. H., & Janus, S. (1941). Toward a social psychology of human play. *The Journal of Social Psychology, 13,* 351–384.

Bronson, W. C. (1981). *Toddlers' behaviors with age-mates: Issues of interaction, cognition, and affect.* Norwood, NJ: Ablex.

Brookover, W. B., Beamer, L., Efthim, H., Hathaway, D., Lezotte, L., Miller, S., Passalacqua, J., & Tornatzky, L. (1982). *Creating effective schools.* Holmes Beach, FL: Learning Publications.

Brooks, M. (1973). Programmed play complements care. *Hospitals, 47*(15), 78–87.

Brooks, M., & Knowles, D. (1982). Parents' views of children's imaginary companions. *Child Welfare, 61*(1), 25–33.

Brooks-Gunn, J., & Lewis, M. (1982). Development of play behavior in handicapped and normal infants. *Topics in Early Childhood Special Education, 2*(3), 14–27.

Brophy, K., & Stone-Zukowski, D. (1984). Social and play behaviour of special needs and non-special needs toddlers. *Early Child Development and Care, 13*(2), 137–154.

Brown, F. L., Amos, J. R., & Mink, O. G. (1975). *Statistical concepts: A basic program.* New York: Harper & Row.

Brown, P. (1980). Fitness and play. In P. F. Wilkinson (Ed.), *In celebration of play* (pp. 282–295). New York: St. Martin's Press.

Brown, R., & Bellugi, U. (1964). Three processes in the child's acquisition of syntax. *Harvard Educational Review, 34,* 133–151.

Bruner, J. S. (1966). *Toward a theory of instruction.* Cambridge, MA: Harvard University Press.

Bruner, J. S. (1970). The growth and structure of skills. In K. Connolly (Ed.), *Mechanisms of motor skill development* (pp. 63–91). New York: Academic Press.

Bruner, J. S. (1972). The nature and uses of immaturity. *American Psychologist, 27*(8), 687–708.

Bruner, J. S. (1979). *On knowing.* Cambridge, MA: Harvard University Press.

Bruner, J. S. (1982). The organization of action and the nature of the adult-infant transaction. In E. Z. Tronick (Ed.), *Social interchange in infancy: Affect, cognition, and communication* (pp. 23–35). Baltimore: University Park Press.

Bruner, J. S. (1983). Play, thought, and language. *Peabody Journal of Education, 60*(3), 60–69.

Bruner, J. S., Jolly, A., & Sylva, K. (Eds.). (1976). *Play: Its role in development and evolution.* New York: Basic Books.

Bruner, J. S., & Sherwood, V. (1976). Peek-a-boo and the learning of rule structures. In J. S. Bruner, A. Jolly & K. Sylva, (Eds.), *Play: Its role in development and evolution* (pp. 277–285). New York: Basic Books.

Bruya, L. D. (1985). The effect of play structure format differences on the play behavior of preschool children. In J. L. Frost & S. Sunderlin (Eds.), *When children play* (pp. 115–121). Wheaton, MD: Association for Childhood Education International.

Bryant, B. (1985). The neighborhood walk: Sources of support in middle childhood. *Monographs of the Society for Research in Child Development, 50*(3, Serial No. 210).

Buhler, C. (1935). *From birth to maturity.* London: Routledge & Kegan Paul.

Bull, N. J. (1969). *Moral judgment from childhood to adolescence.* Beverly Hills, CA: Sage.

Burns, C. (1984). The hospitalization experience in single parent families. *Nursing Clinics of North America, 10*(2), 285–293.

Burstein, S., & Meichenbaum, D. (1979). The work of worrying in children undergoing surgery. *Journal of Abnormal Child Psychology, 7*(2), 121–132.

Bushell, D., Jr. (1973). *Classroom behavior: A little book for teachers.* Englewood Cliffs, NJ: Prentice-Hall.

Byers, M. L. (1972). Play interviews with a five year old boy. *Nursing Journal, 4*(2), 133–141.

Caillois, R. (1961). *Man, play and games.* New York: Free Press.

Callecod, R. L. (1974). *Play preferences of selected grade-school children on varying types of playground equipment.* Unpublished master's thesis, University of Illinois: Urbana-Champaign, IL.

Campbell, P. F. & Fein, G. G. (Eds.). (1984). *Young children and microcomputers: Conceptualizing the issues.* Englewood Cliffs, NJ: Prentice Hall.

Campbell, P. F., & Schwartz, S. S. (1984). Microcomputers in the preschool: Children, parents and teachers. In P. F. Campbell & G. G. Fein (Eds.), *Young children and microcomputers: Conceptualizing the issues* pp. 45–59. Englewood Cliffs, NJ: Prentice Hall.

Campbell, S. D., & Frost, J. L. (1985). The effects of playground type on the cognitive and social play behaviors of grade two children. In J. L. Frost & S. Sunderlin (Eds.), *When children play* (pp. 81–89). Wheaton, MD: Association for Childhood Education International.

Capell, M. (1967). Games and the mastery of helplessness. In R. Slovenko & J. A. Knight (Eds.), *Motivation in play, games and sports* (pp. 39–54). Springfield, IL: Charles C Thomas.

Capella, J. N. (1981). Mutual influence in expressive behavior: Adult-adult and infant-adult dyadic interaction. *Psychological Bulletin, 89*(1), 101–132.

Caplan, F., & Caplan, T. (1973). *The power of play.* New York: Anchor Press/Doubleday.

Carey, S. (1977). The child as word-learner. In M. Halle, J. Bresnan, & G. A. Miller (Eds.), *Linguistic theory and psychological reality* (pp. 264–293). Cambridge, MA: MIT Press.

Carpenter, C., Huston-Stein, A., & Baer, D. (1978). *The relation of children's activity preferences to sex-typed behavior.* Paper presented at the annual meeting of the American Psychological Association, Toronto. (ERIC Document Reproduction Service No. ED 160 952)

Carpenter, J. (1983). Activity structure and play: Implications for socialization. In M. B. Liss (Ed.), *Social and cognitive skills: Sex roles and children's play* (pp. 117–145). New York: Academic Press.

Carpenter, T. P., & Moser, J. M. (1984). The acquisition of addition and subtraction concepts in grades one through three. *Journal for Research in Mathematics Education, 15*(3), 179–202.

Cartledge, C. J., & Krauser, E. L. (1963). Training first-grade children in creative thinking under quantitative and qualitative motivation. *Journal of Educational Psychology, 54*, 295–299.

Cartledge, G., & Millburn, J. F. (Eds.). (1986). *Teaching social skills to children: Innovative approaches* (2nd ed.). New York: Pergamon Press.

Casby, M. W., & Ruder, K. F. (1983). Symbolic play and early language development in normal and mentally retarded children. *Journal of Speech and Hearing Research, 26*(3), 404–411.

Cassell, S. (1965). Effect of brief puppet therapy upon the emotional response of children undergoing cardiac catheterization. *Journal of Consulting Psychology, 29*(1), 1–8.

Castell, R. (1970). Effect of familiar and unfamiliar environments on proximity behavior of young children. *Journal of Experimental Child Psychology, 9*(3), 342–347.

Cazden, C. B. (1968). The acquisition of noun and verb inflections. *Child Development, 39*, 433–448.

Cazden, C. B. (1976). Play with language and metalinguistic awareness. In J. S. Bruner, A. Jolly & K. Sylva (Eds.), *Play: Its role in development and evolution* (pp. 603–608). New York: Basic Books.

Chafel, J. A. (1984). Social comparisons by young children in classroom contexts. *Early Child Development and Care, 14*, 109–124.

Chaille, C. (1978). The child's conceptions of play, pretending and toys: Sequences and structural parallels. *Human Development, 21*, 201–210.

Chaille, C., & Young, P. (1980). Some issues linking research on children's play and education: Are they "only playing"? *International Journal of Early Childhood, 12*(2), 52–56.

Chan, J. (1980). Preparation for procedures and surgery through play. *Paedeatrician, 9*, 210–219.

Chandler, M. J., & Greenspan, S. (1972). Ersatz egocentrism: A reply to H. Borke. *Developmental Psychology, 7*, 104–106.

Chesler, M. A. & Barbarin, O. A. (1984). Relating to medical staff: How parents of children with cancer see the issues. *Health and Social Work, 9*(1), 49–65.

Cheyne, J. A. & Rubin, K. H. (1983). Playful precursors of problem-solving in preschoolers. *Developmental Psychology, 19*(4), 577–584.

Chodorow, N. (1974). Family structure and feminine personality. In M. Z. Rosaldo & L. Lamphere (Eds.), *Woman, culture, and society* (pp. 43–66). Stanford, CA: Stanford University Press.

Christie, J. F. (1980a). Play for cognitive growth. *Elementary School Journal, 81*, 115–118.

Christie, J. F. (1980b). The cognitive significance of children's play: A review of selected research. *Journal of Education, 62*(4), 23–33.

Christie, J. F. (1982). Sociodramatic play training. *Young Children, 37*(4), 25–32.

Christie, J. F., & Johnsen, E. P. (1983). The role of play in social-intellectual development. *Review of Educational Research, 53*(1), 93–115.

Chukovsky, K. (1963). *From two to five.* Berkeley, CA: University of California Press.

Cicchetti, D. (1985a). Caregiver-infant interaction: The study of maltreated infants. In C. C. Brown & A. W. Gottfried (Eds.), *Play interactions: The role of toys and parental involvement in children's development* (pp.107–113). Skillman, NJ: Johnson & Johnson.

Cicchetti, D. (1985b). *Parent-infant interaction.* Paper presented at Plenary Session of National Clinical Infant Conference, Washington, D.C.

Clance, P. R., & Dawson, F. B. (1974). *Sex differences in spatial play behavior of six-year-olds.* Georgia State University; Atlanta, GA. (ERIC Document Reproduction Service No. ED 160 952)

Clarke-Stewart, K. A. (1973). Interactions between mothers and their young children: Characteristics and consequences. *Monographs of the Society of Research in Child Development, 38*(6–7, Serial No. 153)

Clarke-Stewart, K. A. (1977). *The father's impact on mother and child.* Paper presented at the meeting of the Society for Research in Child Development, New Orleans.

Clarke-Stewart, K. A., & Hervey, C. M. (1981). Longitudinal relations in repeated observations of mother-child interactions from 1 to 2½ years. *Developmental Psychology, 17,* 127–145.

Clarke-Stewart, K. A., VanderStoep, L. P., & Killian, G. A. (1979). Analysis and replication of mother-child relations at two years of age. *Child Development, 50,* 777–793.

Clatworthy, S. (1981). Therapeutic play: Effects on hospitalized children. *Children's Health Care, 9*(4), 108–113.

Clune, C., Paolella, J. M., & Foley, J. M. (1979). Free-play behavior of atypical children: An approach to assessment. *Journal of Autism and Developmental Disorders, 9,* 61–72.

Coakley, J. (1980). Play, games, and sport: Development implications for young people. *Journal of Sport Behavior, 3,* 99–118.

Coates, G. (1974). *Alternative learning environments.* Stroudsburg, PA. Dowden, Hutchinson, & Ross.

Coates, S., Lord, M., & Jakabovics, E. (1975). Field dependence-independence, social-nonsocial play, and sex differences. *Perceptual and Motor Skills, 40,* 195–202.

Cohen, S., & Lezak, A. (1977). Noise and inattentiveness to social cues. *Environment and Behavior, 9*(4), 559–572.

Cohen, U., Moore, G. T., & McGinty, T. (1978). *Environments for play and child care.* Milwaukee: University of Wisconsin, Milwaukee Center for Architecture and Urban Planning Research.

Coleman, M., Skeen, P. (1985). Play, games, and sport: Their use and misuse. *Childhood Education, 61,* 192–198.

Colker, L. (1983). *Computers and play.* Paper presented at the Conference on the Young Child and Computers, Building the future together, Columbus, OH. (ERIC Document Reproduction Service No. ED 251 173)

Collard, R. (1971). Exploratory and play behaviors of infants reared in an institution and in lower and middle-class homes. *Child Development, 42,* 1003–1015.

Collard, R. (1979). Exploration and play. In B. Sutton-Smith (Ed.), *Play and learning* (pp. 45–56). New York: Gardner Press.

Combs, M. L. & Arezzo-Slaby, D. (1977). Social skills training with children. In B. B. Lahey & A. E. Kazdin (Eds.), *Advances in clinical child psychology* (Vol. 1, pp. 161–201). New York: Plenum Press.

Condon, W. S., & Sander, L. W. (1974). Synchrony demonstrated between movements of the neonate and adult speech. *Child Development, 65,* 456–462.

Connolly, J. A. (1981). *The relationship between social pretend play and social competence in preschoolers: Correlational and experimental studies.* Unpublished doctoral dissertation, Concordia University, Montreal.

Connolly, J. A., & Doyle, A. B. (1984). Relation of social fantasy play to social competence in preschoolers. *Developmental Psychology, 20*(5), 797–806.

Consumer Products Safety Commission. (1975). *Hazard analysis: Playground equipment.* Washington, DC: Bureau of Epidemiology.

Cooper, A. Y., Ruggles, T., & LeBlanc, J. M. (1979). *Teaching techniques for increasing the positive social interactions of disruptive children.* Paper presented at the meeting of the Council for Exceptional Children, Dallas.

Cooper, C. C. (1970). Adventure playgrounds. *Landscape Architecture, 61,* 18–29.

Cooper, C., & Edward, D. (1985). Playfriends and workfriends: Developmental patterns in the meaning and function of children's friendships. In J. L. Frost & S. Sunderlin (Eds.), *When children play* (pp. 67–71). Wheaton, MD: Association for Childhood Education International.

Copeland, A. P., Reiner, E. M., & Jirkovsky, A. M. (1984). Examining a premise underlying self-instructional techniques. *Cognitive Therapy and Research, 8*(6), 619–629.

Copple, C. E., Cocking, R. R., & Matthews, W. S. (1984). Objects, symbols, and substitutes: The nature of the cognitive activity during symbolic play. In T. D. Yawkey & A. D. Pellegrini (Eds.), *Child's play: Developmental and applied* (pp. 105–123). Hillsdale, NJ: Erlbaum.

Corbin, C. B. (1976). *Becoming physically educated in the elementary school.* Philadelphia: Lea & Febiger.

Corsaro, W. (1979). Young children's conception of status and role. *Sociology of Education, 52,* 46–59.

Corsaro, W. A. (1981). Friendship in the nursery school: Social organization in a peer environment. In S. R. Asher & J. M. Gottman (Eds.), *The development of children's friendships* (pp. 207–241). New York: Cambridge University Press.

Corsaro, W. A. (1985). *Friendship and peer culture in the early years.* Norwood, NJ: Ablex.

Costa, A. L. (1985). *Developing minds: A resource book for teaching thinking.* Alexandria, VA: Association for Supervision and Curriculum Development.

Cotton, N. S., & Geraty, R. G. (1984). Therapeutic space design: Planning an inpatient children's unit. *American Journal of Orthopsychiatry, 54*(4), 624–636.

Coury, K., & Wolfgang, C. (1984). An overview of the measurement methods of toy and play preference studies. *Early Child Development and Care, 14* (3-4), 217–232.

Cowan, P. A. (1982). The relationship between emotional and cognitive development. In D. Cicchetti & P. Hesse (Eds.), *New directions in child development: Emotional development.* (No. 16, 49–81.) San Francisco: Jossey-Bass.

Craft, M., Wyatt, N., & Sandell, B. (1985). Behavior and feeling changes in siblings of hospitalized children. *Clinical Pediatrics, 24,*(7), 374–378.

Cramer, P., & Hogan, K. A. (1975). Sex differences in verbal and play fantasy. *Developmental Psychology, 11*(2), 145–154.

Cratty, B. J. (1979). *Perceptual and motor development in infants and children.* Englewood Cliffs, NJ: Prentice-Hall.

Cratty, B. J. (1982). Motor development in early childhood: Critical issues for researchers in the 1980s. In B. Spodek (Ed.), *Handbook of research in early childhood education* (pp. 27–46). New York: Free Press.

Crawley Films, Ltd. (Producer). (1956). *Children's play.* [Film]. Del Mar, CA: McGraw-Hill Films.

Crawley, S. B., & Chan, K. S. (1982). Developmental changes in free-play behavior of mildly and moderately retarded preschool-age children. *Education and Training of the Mentally Retarded, 17*(3), 234–238.

Crawley, S. B., Rogers, P., Freidman, S., Jacabbo, M., Criticos, A., Richardson, L., & Thompson, M. (1978). Developmental changes in the structure of mother-infant play. *Developmental Psychology, 14,* 30–36.

Crawley, S. B., & Sherrod, K. G. (1984). Parent-infant play during the first year of life. *Infant behavior and development, 7,* 65–73.

Crothers, B., & Paine, R. (1960). *The natural history of cerebral palsy.* Cambridge, MA: Harvard University Press.

Csikszentmihayli, M. (1975). *Beyond boredom and anxiety.* San Francisco: Jossey-Bass.

Csikszentmihayli, M. (1979). The concept of flow. In B. Sutton-Smith (Ed.), *Play and learning* (pp. 257–274). New York: Gardner Press.

Curry, N. (1986). *The feeling child: Affective development reconsidered.* New York: Haworth.

Curry, N., & Arnaud, S. H. (1974). Cognitive implications in children's spontaneous role play. *Theory and Practice, 13*(4), 273–277.

Curry, N., & Arnaud, S. H. (1982). Dramatic play as a degenerative aid in the preschool. In M. Frank (Ed.), *The puzzling child* (pp. 37–48). New York: Haworth.

Curry, N., & Arnaud, S. H. (1984). Play in developmental preschool settings. In T. D. Yawkey & A. D. Pellegrini (Eds.), *Child's play: Developmental and applied* (pp. 273–290). Hillsdale, NJ: Erlbaum.

Curtis, S. R. (1982). *Joy of movement in early childhood.* New York: Teachers College Press.

Dale, E. (Ed.). (1972). *Building a learning environment.* Bloomington, IN: Phi Delta Kappa.

Dalziel, S. (1972). *Spaces in open places.* Cortland, NY: SUNY at Cortland. Project Change. (EPDA-OE Grant No. 23-92A)

Damon, W. (1977). *The social world of the child.* San Francisco: Jossey-Bass.

Damon, W. (1983). *Social and personality development.* New York: Norton.

Damon, W., & Hart, D. (1982). The development of self-understanding from infancy through adolescence. *Child Development, 53,* 841–864.

Daniel, J. H., Hampton, R. L., & Newberger, E. H. (1983). Child abuse and accidents in black families: A controlled comparative study. *American Journal of Orthopsychiatry, 53*(4), 645–653.

Daniels, N. (1985). *Somerset early childhood center staff training program.* Unpublished manuscript. Troy, MI.

Dansky, J. L., & Silverman, I. W. (1973). Effects of play on associative fluency in pre-school children. *Developmental Psychology, 9,* 38–43.

Darwin, C. (1965). *The expressions of the emotions in man and animals.* Chicago: University of Chicago Press. (Original work published 1872)

Dattner, R. (1969). *Design for play.* Stamford, CT: Reinhold.

David, N. (1973). Play: A nursing diagnostic tool. *Maternal-Child Nursing Journal, 4,* 49–56.

David, T. G. (1975). Environmental literacy. In T. G. David & B. D. Wright (Eds.), *Learning environments* (pp. 161–179). Chicago: University of Chicago Press.

David, T. G., & Wright, B. D. (Eds.). (1975). *Learning environments.* Chicago: University of Chicago Press.

Davidson Films, Inc. (Producer). (1974). *Child's play and the real world.* [Film]. San Anselmo, CA: Sterling Education Films, Inc.

Day, D., & Sheehan, R. E. (1974). Elements of a better preschool. *Young Children, 30*(1), 15–23.

Delacato, C. (1959). *The treatment and prevention of reading problems.* Springfield, IL: Charles C Thomas.

DeLoache, J. S., Sugarman, S., & Brown, A. L. (1985). The development of error correction strategies in young children's manipulative play. *Child Development, 56,* 928–939.

Delta Education. (1966). *Elementary science study: Batteries and bulbs.* Nashua, NH.

Demarest, D. C., Hooke, J. F., & Erickson, M. T. (1984). Preoperative intervention for the reduction of anxiety in pediatric surgery patients. *Children's Health Care, 12*(4), 179–184.

Department of Housing and Urban Development. (1976). *A playground for all children: Book 1. User groups and site selection.* (DHHS Publications No. NYC DCP 76-02) Washington, DC: U. S. Government Printing Office.

Derrick, S., Bachman, K., & Parker, S. (1982). *Hospitalized children: Play and play activities.* Lake Mills, IA: Graphic Publishing.

Desmond, R. J., Singer, J. L., Singer, D. G., Calam, R., & Colimore, K. (1985). Family mediation patterns and television viewing. Young children's use and grasp of the medium. *Human Communication Research, 11*(4), 461–480.

DeStefano, C. T. & Mueller, E. C. (1982). Environmental determinants of peer social activity in 18-month-old males. *Infant Behavior and Development, 5,* 175–183.

Devereux, E. C. (1976). Backyard versus little league baseball: The impoverishment of children's games. In D. M. Landers (Ed.), *Social problems in athletics* (pp. 37–56). Urbana: University of Illinois Press.

DeVries, D. L., & Slavin, R. E. (1978). Teams-games-tournaments. *Journal of Research and Development in Education, 12,* 28–38.

DeVries, R. (1969). Constancy of generic identity in the years three to six. *Monographs of the Society for Research in Child Development, 34* (Serial No. 127).

DeVries, R. (1970). The development of role-taking as reflected by behavior of bright, average, and retarded children in a social guessing game. *Child Development, 41,* 759–770.

Dewey, J. (1966). *Democracy and education.* New York: Free Press. (Original work published 1916)

Dion, K. K. (1973). Young children's stereotyping of facial attractiveness. *Developmental Psychology, 9,* 183–188.

DiPietro, J. A. (1981). Rough and tumble play: A function of gender. *Developmental Psychology, 17*(1), 50–58.

Dodge, K. A. (1983). Behavioral antecedents of peer social status. *Child Development, 54,* 1386–1399.

Doke, L. A., & Risley, T. R. (1972). The organization of day care environments: Required vs. optional activities. *Journal of Applied Behavioral Analysis, 5,* 405–420.

Downing, J. (1969). The perception of linguistic structures in learning to read. *British Journal of Educational Psychology, 39*(3), 267–271.

Downs, A. C., & Langlois, J. H. (1977). *Mother and peer influences on children's sex-role play behaviors.* Austin, TX: Hogg Foundation for Mental Health. (ERIC Document Reproduction Service No. ED 146 475)

Doyle, A. B., Connolly, J., & Rivest, L. P. (1980). The effect of playmate familiarity on the social interactions of young children. *Child Development, 51*, 217–223.

Doyle, P. H. (1976). The differential effects of multiple and single niche play activities on interpersonal relations among preschoolers. In B. A. Tindall (Ed.), *The anthropological study of play: Problems and prospects* (pp. 189–197). Cornwall, NY: Leisure Press.

Droske, S., & Francis, S. (1981). *Pediatric diagnostic procedures.* New York: Wiley.

Duckworth, E. (1972). The having of wonderful ideas. *Harvard Educational Review, 42,* 217–231.

Dunn, J., & Dale, N. (1984). I a Daddy: 2-year-old's collaboration in joint pretend with sibling and with mother. In I. Bretherton (Ed.), *Symbolic play: The development of social understanding* (pp. 131–158). New York: Academic Press.

Dunn, J., & Kendrick, C. (1981). Social behavior of young siblings in the family context: Differences between same-sex and different-sex dyads. *Child Development, 52,* 1265–1273.

Dunn, J., & Wooding, C. (1977). Play in the home and its implications for learning. In B. Tizard & D. Harvey (Eds.), *Biology of play* (pp. 45–58). London: Heinemann.

Dyson-Hudson, R., & Van Dusen, R. (1972). Food sharing among young children. *Ecology of food and nutrition, 1,* 319–324.

Eckerman, C. O., & Whatley, J. L. (1977). Toys and social interaction between infant peers. *Child Development, 48,* 1645–1656.

Eckerman, C. O., Whatley, J. L., & Kutz, S. L. (1975). Growth of social play with peers during the second year of life. *Developmental Psychology, 11*(1), 42–49.

Eckert, H. M. (1973). Age changes in motor skills. In G. L. Rarick (Ed.), *Physical activity: Human growth and development* (pp. 155–175). New York: Academic Press.

Eiferman, R. R. (1971). Social play in childhood. In R. E. Herron & B. Sutton-Smith (Eds.), *Child's play* (pp. 270–297). New York: Wiley.

Eimas, P. (1974). Linguistic processing of speech by young infants. In R. L. Schiefelbusch & L. L. Lloyd (Eds.), *Language perspectives* (pp. 55–74). Baltimore: University Park Press.

Eisenberg-Berg, N., & Mussen, P. (1978). Empathy and moral development in adolescents. *Developmental Psychology, 14,* 185–186.

Eisenberg, N., Tryon, K., & Cameron, E. (1984). The relation of preschoolers' peer interaction to their sex-typed toy choices. *Child Development, 55,* 1044–1050.

Ekman, P., & Friesen, W. V. (1975). *Unmasking the face.* Englewood Cliffs, NJ: Prentice-Hall.

Ekman, P., & Friesen, W. V. (1978). *Facial action coding system.* Palo Alto, CA: Consulting Psychologists Press.

Ekman, P., Friesen, W., & Ellsworth, P. (1972). *Emotion in the human face: Guidelines for research and an integration of findings.* New York: Pergamon.

Ekman, P., Roper, G., & Hager, J. C. (1980). Deliberate facial movement. *Child Development, 51,* 886–891.

Elardo, R., Bradley, R., & Caldwell, B. (1975). The relation of infants' home environments to mental test performance from 6 to 36 months: A longitudinal analysis. *Child Development, 46,* 71–76.

Elder, J. L., & Pederson, D. R. (1978). Preschool children's use of objects in symbolic play. *Child Development, 49,* 500–504.

Elkind, D. (1981). *Children and adolescents: Interpretive essays on Jean Piaget* (3rd ed.). New York: Oxford University Press.

Elkind, D. (1986). Formal education and early childhood education: An essential difference. *Phi Delta Kappan, 67*(9), 631–636.

El'konin, D. B. (1966). Symbolics and its functions in the play of children. *Soviet Education, 8,* 35–41.

Ellis, M. J. (1973). *Why people play.* Englewood Cliffs, NJ: Prentice-Hall.

Ellis, M. J. (1979). The complexity of objects and peers. In B. Sutton-Smith (Ed.), *Play and learning* (pp. 157–174). New York: Gardner Press.

Ellis, M. J., & Scholtz, G. (1978). *Activity and play of children.* Englewood Cliffs, NJ: Prentice-Hall.

Ellison, G. (1974). *Play structures.* Pasadena, CA: Pacific Oaks College.

Emde, R., Gaensbauer, T., & Harmon, R. (1976). Emotional expression in infancy: A biobehavioral study. *Psychological Issues, Monograph Series, Vol. 10, Monograph #37,* New York: International Universities Press.

Emde, R. N. (1980). Toward a psychoanalytic theory of affect. In S. Greenspan & G. Pollock (Eds.), *The course of life: Psychoanalytic contributions toward understanding personality development and early childhood* (pp. 63–112). Washington, DC: Mental Health Study Center, National Institute of Mental Health.

Emde, R. N. (1983). The pre-representational self and its affective core. *The Psychoanalytic Study of the Child, 38,* 165–207.

Emde, R., Swedberg, J., & Suzuki, B. (1975). Human wakefulness and biological rhythms after birth. *Archives of General Psychiatry, 32,* 780–783.

Emmerich, W. (1977). Evaluating alternative models of development: An illustrative study of preschool personal-social behaviors. *Child Development, 48,* 1401–1410.

Enseki, C., & Ahern, K. (1980, November). Environments of all children. *Access Information Bulletin.*

Enslein, J. P., & Fein, G. G. (1981). Temporal and cross-situational stability of children's social and play behavior. *Developmental Psychology, 17,* 760–776.

Epstein, H. T. (1978). Growth spurts during brain development: Implications for educational policy and practice. In J. S. Chall & A. F. Mirsky (Eds.), *77th National Society for the Study of Education Yearbook: Education and the brain* (pp. 343–370). Chicago: University of Chicago Press.

Epstein, J. L., & McPartland, J. M. (1979). Authority structures. In H. J. Walberg (Ed.), *Educational environments and effects* (pp. 293–310). Berkeley, CA: McCutchan.

Erickson, F. (1958). Play interview for 4 year old hospitalized children. *Monograph of the Society for Research in Child Development, 23*(3, Serial No. 69).

Erickson, F. (1984). School literacy, reasoning, and civility: An anthropologist's perspective. *Review of Educational Research, 54*(4), 525–546.

Erikson, E. H. (1950). *Childhood and society* (1st ed.). New York: Norton.

Erikson, E. H. (1951). Sex differences in the play configurations of American pre-adolescents *American Journal of Orthopsychiatry, 21,* 667–692.

Erikson, E. H. (1963). *Childhood and society* (2nd ed.). New York: Norton.

Erikson, E. H. (1968). *Identity, youth and crisis.* New York: Norton.

Erikson, E. H. (1977). *Toys and reasons.* New York: Norton.

Eron, L. D., Huesmann, L. R., Lefkowitz, M. H., & Walder, L. O. (1972). Does television violence cause aggression? *American Psychologist, 27,* 253–262.

Escalona, S. K. (1968). *The roots of individuality. Normal patterns of development in infancy.* Chicago: Aldine.

Escalona, S. K., & Heider, G. (1959). *Prediction and outcome. A study of child development.* New York: Basic Books.

Espenschade, A. S. (1960). The contributions of physical activity to growth. *Research Quarterly, 31,* 351–364.

Facilitation of children's dramatic play. (1975) [Film]. Scarsdale, NY: Campus Film Distributors, Inc.

Fagot, B. I. (1974). Sex differences in toddlers' behavior and parental reaction. *Developmental Psychology, 10,* 554–558.

Fagot, B. I. (1978a). *Sex determined consequences of different play styles in early childhood.* Bethesda, MD: National Institutes of Health. (ERIC Document Reproduction Service No. ED 170 055)

Fagot, B. I. (1978b). *The consequences of same-sex, cross-sex, and androgynous preferences.* Bethesda, MD: National Institutes of Health. (ERIC Document Reproduction Service No. ED 160 967)

Fagot, B. I. (1981). Continuity and change in play styles as a function of sex of child. *International Journal of Behavioral Development, 4*(1), 37–43.

Fagot, B. I. (1984a). Teacher and peer reactions to boys' and girls' play styles. *Sex Roles, 11,* 691–702.

Fagot, B. I. (1984b). The consequents of problem behaviors in toddler children. *Journal of Abnormal Child Psychology, 12,* 385–895.

Fagot, B. I. (1985). Changes in thinking in early sex role development. *Developmental Review, 5,* 85–98.

Fagot, B. I., Hagen, R., Leinbach, M. D., & Kronsberg, S. (1985). Differential reactions to assertive and communicative acts of toddler boys and girls. *Child Development, 56,* 1499–1505.

Fagot, B. I., & Littman, I. (1975). Stability of sex role and play interests from preschool to elementary school. *Journal of Psychology, 89,* 285–292.

Fagot, B. I., & Patterson, G. R. (1969) An "in vivo" analysis of reinforcing contingencies for sex role behaviors in the preschool child. *Developmental Psychology, 1,* 563–568.

Fait, H., & Kupferes, H. (1976). A study of two motor achievement tests and their implications in planning physical education activities for the mentally retarded. *American Journal of Mental Deficiency, 64,* 729–732.

Fantz, R. L. (1966). Pattern discrimination and selective attention as determinants of perceptual development from birth. In A. H. Kidd & J. L. Rivoire (Eds.), *Perceptual development in children* (pp. 143–172). New York: International Universities Press.

Farwell, L. (1925). Reactions of kindergarten, first and second grade children to constructive play materials. *Genetic Psychology Monographs, 8,* (5, Serial No. 6).

Fehrenbach, C., & Daniel, B. (1984). *Voyage to the new world.* Pittsburg, KS: Pittsburg State University.

Fehrenbach, C. R., Greer, F. S., & Daniel, T. B. (1986). LEA on the moon. *Science and Children, 25*(5), 15–17.

Fein, G. G. (1975a). Children's sensitivity to social contexts at 18 months of age. *Developmental Psychology, 11*(6), 853–854.

Fein, G. G. (1975b). A transformational analysis of pretending. *Developmental Psychology, 11*(3), 291–296.

Fein, G. G. (1979a). Play and the acquisition of symbols. In L. Katz (Ed.), *Current topics in early childhood education* (pp. 195–225). Norwood, NJ: Ablex.

Fein, G. G. (1979b). Play with actions and objects. In B. Sutton-Smith (Ed.), *Play and learning* (pp. 69–82). New York: Gardner Press.

Fein, G. G. (1981). Pretend play: An integrative review. *Child Development, 52,* 1095–1118.

Fein, G. G. (1984). The self-building potential of preschool play or "I got a fish all by myself." In T. D. Yawkey & A. D. Pellegrini (Eds.), *Child's play: Developmental and applied* (pp. 125–170). Hillsdale, NJ: Erlbaum.

Fein, G. G. (1985a). Learning in play: Surfaces of thinking and feeling. In J. L. Frost & S. Sunderlin (Eds.), *When children play* (pp. 45–53). Wheaton, MD: Association for Childhood Education International.

Fein, G. G. (1985b). The affective psychology of play. In C. C. Brown & A. W. Gottfried (Eds.), *Play interactions: The role of toys and parental involvement in children's development.* (pp. 19–28). Skillman, NJ: Johnson & Johnson.

Fein, G. G., & Apfel, N. (1979). Some preliminary observations on knowing and pretending. In N. Smith & M. Franklin (Eds.), *Symbolic functioning in childhood* (pp. 87–100). Hillsdale, NJ: Erlbaum.

Fein, G. G., Johnson, D., Kosson, N., Stork, L., & Wasserman, L. (1975). Sex stereotypes and preferences in the toy choices of 20-month old boys and girls. *Developmental Psychology, 11*(4), 527–528.

Fein, G. G., & Robertson, A. R. (1975). *Cognitive and social dimensions of pretending in two-year-olds.* Detroit: Merrill-Palmer Institute. (ERIC Document Reproduction Service No. ED 119 806)

Fein, G. G., & Schwartz, P. M. (1982). Developmental theories in early education. In B. Spodek (Ed.), *Handbook of research in early childhood education* (pp. 82–104). New York: Free Press.

Fein, G. G., & Stork, L. (1981). Sociodramatic play: Social class effects in integrated preschool classrooms. *Journal of Applied Developmental Psychology, 2,* 267–279.

Feitelson, D., & Ross, G. S. (1973). The neglected factor—play. *Human Development, 16,* 202–223.

Fennema, E., & Sherman, J. (1977). Sex-related differences in math achievement, spatial visualization, and affective factors. *American Educational Research Journal, 14,* 51–71.

Fenson, L. (1984). Developmental trends for action and speech in pretend play. In I. Bretherton (Ed.), *Symbolic play: The development of social understanding* (pp. 249–270). New York: Academic Press.

Fenson, L., Kagan, J., Kearsley, R. B., & Zelazo, P. R. (1976). The developmental progression of manipulative play in the first two years. *Child Development, 47,* 232–235.

Fenson, L., & Ramsay, D. S. (1980). Decentration and integration of the child's play in the second year. *Child Development, 51,* 171–178.

Ferguson, J. (1979). Creating growth-producing environments for infants and toddlers. In E. Jones (Ed.), *Supporting the growth of infants, toddlers, and parents* (pp. 13–25). Pasadena, CA: Pacific Oaks College.

Feshbach, N. D. (1974). The relationship of child-rearing factors to children's aggression, empathy, and related positive and negative social behaviors. In J. de Witt & W. W. Hartup (Eds.), *Determinants and origins of aggressive behavior* (pp. 427–436). The Hague: Mouton.

Feshbach, N. D. (1978). Studies of empathic behavior in children. In B. A. Mahler (Ed.), *Progress in experimental personality research* (Vol. 8, pp. 1–47). New York: Academic Press.

Field, T. M. (1979). Games parents play with normal and high-risk infants. *Child Psychiatry and Human Development, 10,* 41–48.

Field, T. M. (1980). Preschool play: Effects of teacher/child ratios and organization of classroom space. *Child Study Journal, 10(3),* 191–205.

Field, T. M. (1982). Affective displays of high-risk infants during early interactions. In T. M. Field & A. Fogel (Eds.), *Emotion and early interaction* (pp. 101–125). Hillsdale, NJ: Erlbaum.

Field, T., DeStefano, L., & Koewler, J. (1982). Fantasy play of toddlers and preschoolers. *Developmental Psychology, 18,* 503–508.

Field, T., & Fogel, A. (Eds.). (1982). *Emotions and early interaction.* Hillsdale, NJ: Erlbaum.

Field, T., Roseman, S., DeStefano, L., & Koewler, J. (1982). The play of handicapped preschool children with handicapped and non-handicapped peers in integrated and nonintegrated situations. *Topics in Early Childhood Special Education, 2(3),* 28–38.

Fields, W. (1979). *Imaginative play of four year old children as a function of toy realism.* Unpublished master's thesis, Merrill-Palmer Institute, Detroit.

Fine, G. (1980). The natural history of preadolescent friendship groups. In H. C. Foot, A. J. Chapman, & J. R. Smith (Eds.), *Friendship and social relations in children* (pp. 293–320). New York: Wiley.

Fine, G. (1981). Friends, impression management and preadolescent behavior. In S. R. Asher and J. M. Gottman (Eds.), *The development of children's friendships* (pp. 29–52). Cambridge, England: Cambridge University Press.

Finkelstein, N., Dent, C., Gallacher, K., & Ramey, C. (1978). Social behavior of infants and toddlers in a day-care environment. *Developmental Psychology, 14,* 257–262.

Fischer, J., & Fischer, A. (1963). The New Englanders of Orchard Town, U.S.A. In B. Whiting (Ed.), *Six cultures: Studies of child rearing* (pp. 869–1010). New York: Wiley.

Fitt, S. (1974). The individual and his environment. *School Review, 82(4),* 617–620.

Flavell, J. H. (1976). Metacognitive aspects of problem solving. In I. B. Resnick (Ed.), *The nature of intelligence* (pp. 231–235). Hillsdale, NJ: Erlbaum.

Flavell, J. H. (1977). *Cognitive development.* Englewood Cliffs, NJ: Prentice-Hall.

Flavell, J. H. (1981). Cognitive monitoring. In W. P. Dixon (Ed.), *Children's oral communication skills* (pp. 35–60). New York: Academic Press.

Flavell, J. H. (1982). On cognitive development. *Child Development, 53,* 1–10.

Fling, S., & Manosevitz, M. (1972). Sex typing in nursery school children's play interests. *Developmental Psychology, 7(2),* 146–152.

Foley, G. (1986). Emotional development of children with handicaps. In N. E. Curry (Ed.), The feeling child: Affective development reconsidered (pp. 57–73). New York: Haworth Press.

Foley, M., & McGuire, D. (1981). Cognitive skills and street activity. *Urban Education, 16(1),* 13–36.

Foot, H. C., Chapman, A. J., & Smith, J. R. (1977). Friendship and social responsiveness in boys and girls. *Journal of Personality and Social Psychology, 35,* 401–411.

Foot, H. C., Chapman, A. J., & Smith, J. R. (1980). Patterns of interaction in children's friendships. In H. C. Foot, A. J. Chapman, & J. R. Smith (Eds.), *Friendship and social relations in children* (pp. 267–289). New York: Wiley.

Forman, G. E., & Hill, F. (1980). *Constructive play: Applying Piaget in the preschool.* Monterey, CA: Brooks/Cole.

Fortes, M. (1976). Social and psychological aspects of education in Taleland. In J. S. Bruner, A. Jolly, K. Sylva (Eds.), *Play: Its role in development and evolution* (pp. 474–483). New York: Basic Books.

Fosson, A., & deQuan, M. M. (1984). Reassuring and talking with hospitalized children. *Children's Health Care, 13,* 37–46.

Foster, H. L. (1974). *Ribbin', jivin', and playin' the dozens: The unrecognized dilemma of inner city schools.* Cambridge, MA: Ballinger.

Fraiberg, S. (1959). *The magic years.* New York: Scribner.

Fraiberg, S. (1974). Blind infants and their mothers: An examination of the sign system. In M. Lewis & L. A. Rosenblum (Eds.), *The effect of the infant on its caregiver* (pp. 215–232). New York: Wiley.

Frank, A. (1958). Organization and arrangement for middle grades. In M. Rasmussen (Ed.), *Space, arrangeme[nt] beauty in school* (pp. 10–11). Washington, DC: Associa[tion] for Childhood Education International.

Freud, A. (1928). *Introduction to the techniq[ue of] analysis.* New York: Nervous & Mental Disease[.]

Freud, A. (1952). The role of bodily illness in the mental life of children. In R. S. Eissler, A. Freud, H. Hartmann, & E. Kris (Eds.), *The psychoanalytic study of the child* (Vol. 8, pp. 69–81). New York: International Universities Press.

Freud, A (1965). *Normality and pathology in childhood.* New York: International Universities Press.

Freud, S. (1923–1924). The ego and the id. In *The standard edition of the complete psychological works of Sigmund Freud* (Vol. 19, pp. 3–66). London: Hogarth Press.

Freud, S. (1926). Inhibitions, symptoms and anxiety. In *The standard edition of the complete psychological works of Sigmund Freud* (Vol. 20, pp. 75–175). London: Hogarth Press.

Freud, S. (1961). *Beyond the pleasure principle.* New York: Norton. (Original work published 1920)

Freud, S. (1962). On the grounds for detaching a particular syndrome from neurasthenia under the description "Anxiety Neurosis." In *The standard edition of the complete psychological works of Sigmund Freud* (Vol. 3, pp. 87–139). London: Hogarth Press. (Original work published 1895)

Freyberg, J. T. (1973). Increasing the imaginative play of urban disadvantaged kindergarten children through systematic training. In J. L. Singer (Ed.), *The child's world of make-believe: Experimental studies of imaginative play* (pp. 129–155). New York: Academic Press.

Frick, S., & Deplo, E. (1984). Play to reduce anxiety in children after bone marrow aspiration. *Journal of the Association of Pediatric Oncology Nurses, 1*(4), 17–18.

Friedberg, M. P. (1969). *Playgrounds for city children.* Wheaton, MD: Association for Childhood Education International.

Friedrich, L. K., & Stein, A. H. (1973). Aggressive and prosocial television programs and the natural behavior of preschool children. *Monographs of the Society for Research in Child Development, 38* (4, Serial No. 151).

Friedrich, L. K., & Stein, A. H. (1975). Prosocial television and young children: The effects of verbal labeling and role playing on learning and behavior. *Child Development, 46,* 27–28.

Frodi, A., & Lamb, M. (1980). Child abuser's responses to infant smiles and cries. *Child Development, 51,* 238–241.

Froebel, F. (1887). *The education of man.* New York: Appleton-Century.

Frost, J. L. (1985). The American playground movement. In J. L. Frost & S. Sunderlin (Eds.), *When children play* (pp. 165–171). Wheaton, MD: Association for Childhood Education International.

Frost, J. L., & _____. (1985). Equipment _____ conventional and creative _____ underlin (Eds.), *When* _____ n, MD: Association for _____

_____ 985). Equipment choices _____ In J. L. Frost & S. Sun- _____ p. 93–103). Wheaton, _____ cation International. _____ ds.). (1985). *When chil-* _____ n of Childhood Educa- _____

_____ knowledge: Theoretical _____ rentice-Hall.

Furth, H. J. (1980). *The world of grown-ups: Children's conceptions of society.* New York: Elsevier.

Furth, H. J., & Wachs, H. (1974). *Thinking goes to school.* New York: Oxford University Press.

Gaensbauer, T. (1982). The differentiation of discrete affects: A case report. *Psychoanalytic study of the child, 37,* 29–66.

Gaensbauer, T., & Emde, R. N. (1973). Wakefulness and feeding in human newborns. *Archives of General Psychiatry 28,* 894–987.

Gagne, R. M. (1968). Contributions of learning to human development. *Psychological Review, 75,* 177–191.

Gagne, R. M. (1977). *The conditions of learning* (3rd ed.). New York: Holt, Rinehart & Winston.

Galda, L. (1982). Playing about a story: Its impact on comprehension. *The Reading Teacher, 36*(1), 52–55.

Gallahue, D. L. (1982). *Understanding motor development in children.* New York: Wiley.

Garai, J. E., & Scheinfield, A. (1968). Sex differences in mental and behavioral traits. *Genetic Psychology Monographs, 77,* 169–299.

Garvey, C. (1974). Some properties in social play. *Merrill-Palmer Quarterly, 20,* 163–180.

Garvey, C. (1977a). *Play.* Cambridge, MA: Harvard University Press.

Garvey, C. (1977b). Play with language. In B. Tizard & D. Harvey (Eds.), *Biology of play* (pp. 74–99). London: Heinemann.

Garvey, C. (1979). Communicational controls in social play. In B. Sutton-Smith (Ed.), *Play and learning* (pp. 109–125). New York: Gardner Press.

Garvey, C., & Berndt, R. (1977). Organization of pretend play. *JSAS Catalog of Selected Documents in Psychology, 7,* (MS. No. 1589).

Gay, L. R. (1976). *Educational research: Competencies for analysis and application.* Columbus, OH: Charles E. Merrill.

Genishi, C., & Galvan, J. (1985). Getting started: Mexican-American preschoolers initiating dramatic play. In J. L. Frost & S. Sunderlin (Eds.), *When children play* (pp. 23–31). Wheaton, MD: Association for Childhood Education International.

George, S. W., & Krantz, M. (1981). The effects of preferred play partnership on communication adequacy. *The Journal of Psychology 109*(2) 245–253.

Gershner, V. T., & Moore, L. (1985). Girl play: Sex segregation in friendships and play patterns of preschool girls. In J. L. Frost & S. Sunderlin (Eds.), *When children play* (pp. 319–323). Wheaton, MD: Association for Childhood Education International.

Getz, S. K., & Berndt, E. G. (1982). A test of a method for quantifying amount, complexity, and arrangement of play resources in the preschool classroom. *Journal of Applied Developmental Psychology, 3,* 295–305.

Getz, S. K., & Keller, C. A. (1981). *Play material complexity: Effects on the quality and structure of preschool play within groups graduated by size.* Manuscript submitted for publication.

Getzels, J. W. (1975). Images of the classroom and visions of the learner. In T. G. David & B. D. Wright (Eds.), *Learning environments* (pp. 1–14). Chicago: University of Chicago Press.

Gewirtz, J. L. (1965). The cause of infant smiling in four child-rearing environments in Israel. In B. M. Foss (Ed.), *Determinants of infant behavior* (Vol. 3, pp. 205–248). London: Methuen.

Gibbons, M., & Boren, H. (1985). Stress reduction. *Nursing Clinics of North America, 20,* 83–101.

Gibson, D. G. (1978, May). Down the rabbit hole: A special environment for preschool learning. *Landscape Architecture, 68,* 211–216.

Giddings, M., & Halverson, C. F. (1981). Young children's use of toys in home environments. *Family Relationships, 30,* 69–74.

Giffin, H. (1984). The coordination of meaning in the creation of a shared make-believe reality. In I. Bretherton (Ed.), *Symbolic play: The development of social understanding.* (pp. 73–100) Orlando, FL: Academic Press.

Gilligan, C. (1977). In a different voice: Women's conception of the self and of morality. *Harvard Educational Review, 47*(4) 481–517.

Gilmore, J. B. (1966). The role of anxiety and cognitive factors in children's play behavior. *Child Development, 37,* 397–416.

Gilmore, J. B. (1971). Play: A special behavior. In. R. E. Herron & B. Sutton-Smith (Eds.), *Child's play* (pp. 343–355). New York: Wiley.

Ginsburg, B., Sywulak, A., & Cramer, T. (1984). Beyond behavior modification: Client centered therapy with retarded children. *Academic Psychology Bulletin, 6*(3), 321–334.

Giopulos, P. (1979). Play as transformation: A potter's world. *Art Education, 32*(7), 12–14.

Glassow, R. B., & Kruse, P. (1960). Motor performance of girls age 6 to 14 years. *Research Quarterly, 31*(3), 426–433.

Glickman, C. D. (1981). Play and the school curriculum: The historical context. *Journal of Research and Development in Education, 14*(3), 1–10.

Glickman, C. (1984). Play in the public school settings: A philosophical question. In T. Yawkey & A. D. Pellegrini (Eds.), *Child's play: Developmental and applied* (pp. 255–271). New Jersey: Erlbaum.

Goldberg, S., & Lewis, M. (1969). Play behavior in the year-old infant: Early sex differences. *Child Development, 40,* 21–32.

Goldberger, J. (1984). The use of toys with hospitalized children. *Children's Environments Quarterly, 2*(3), 57–62.

Golden, D. B. (1983). Play therapy for hospitalized children. In C. E. Schaeffer & K. J. O'Connor (Eds.), *Handbook of play therapy* (pp. 213–233). New York: Wiley.

Golomb, C. (1977). Symbolic play: The role of substitutions in pretense and puzzle games. *British Journal of Educational Psychology, 47,* 175–186.

Goodson, B. D., & Greenfield, P. M. (1975). The search for structural principles in children's manipulative play: A parallel with linguistic development. *Child Development, 46,* 734–746.

Gordon, I. (1970). *Baby learning through baby play.* New York: St. Martin's Press.

Gottman, J. M. (1977). Toward a definition of social isolation in children. *Child Development, 48,* 513–517.

Gottman, J. M. (1983). How children become friends. *Monographs of the Society for Research in Child Development, 44* (3, Serial No. 201).

Gottman, J. M., & Parkhurst, J. T. (1980). A developmental theory of friendship and acquaintanceship process. In W. A. Collins (Ed.), *Minnesota symposia on child psychology: Vol. 13. Development of cognition, affect, and social relations* (pp. 197–253). Hillsdale, NJ: Erlbaum.

Gould, R. (1972). *Child studies through fantasy.* New York: Quadrangle Books.

Graham, D. (1972). *Moral learning and development: Theory and research.* New York: Wiley.

Graham, G., Holt-Hale, S. A., McEwen, T., & Parker, M. (1980). Children moving: A reflective approach to teaching physical education. Palo Alto, CA: Mayfield.

Gramza, A., Corush, J., & Ellis, M. (1972). Children's play on trestles of differing complexity: A study of play equipment design. *Journal of Leisure Research, 4,* 303–311.

Gramza, A. (1976). Responses to manipulability of a play object. *Psychological Reports, 38,* 1109–1110.

Gramza, A., & Scholtz, G. (1974). Children's responses to visual complexity in a play setting. *Psychological Reports, 35,* 895–899.

Graves, D. H. (1977). Writing and the self: An examination of the writing processes of seven year old children. In G. Pine & A. Boy (Eds.), *Learner centered teaching* (pp. 171-191). Denver, CO: Love.

Graves, N. B. (1974). *Inclusive versus exclusive interaction styles in Polynesian and European classrooms.* Paper presented at the annual meeting of the Society for Research in Child Development, Denver, CO.

Graziano, W. G. (1984). A developmental approach to social exchange processes. In J. C. Masters & K. Yarkin-Levin (Eds.), *Boundary areas in social and developmental psychology* (pp. 161–193). New York: Academic Press.

Green, A. (1977). Conceptions of affects. *International Journal of Psycho-Analysis, 58,* 129–156.

Green, C. S. (1974). Understanding children's needs through therapeutic play. *Nursing, 4,* 31–32.

Greenfield, P. M., Nelson, K., & Saltzman, E. (1972). The development of rule-bound strategies for manipulating seriated cups: A parallel between action and grammar. *Cognitive Psychology, 3,* 291–310.

Greenspan, S., & Greenspan, N. T. (1985). *First feelings: Milestones in the emotional development of the child.* New York: Viking.

Greif, E. B. (1976). Sex role playing in pre-school children. In J. S. Bruner, A. Jolly & K. Sylva (Eds.), *Play: Its role in development and evolution* (pp. 385–391). New York: Basic Books.

Gresham, F. M. (1981). Social skills training with handicapped children: A review. *Review of Educational Research, 51,* 139–171.

Gresham, F. M. & Nagel, R. J. (1980). Social skills training with children: Responsiveness to modeling and coaching as a function of peer orientation. *Journal of Consulting and Clinical Psychology, 18,* 718–729.

Griffiths, R. (1935). *Imagination in early childhood.* London: Kagen, Paul, French & Trubner.

Groos, K. (1901). *The play of man.* New York: Appleton.

Guerney, L. (1976). Filial therapy used as a treatment method for disturbed children. *Evaluation, 3,* 34–35.

Guerney, L. (1979). Play therapy with learning disabled children. *Journal of Clinical Child Psychology, 8*(3), 242–244.

Guilford, J. P. (1967). *The nature of human intelligence.* New York: McGraw-Hill.

Gump, P. V. (1975). Operating environments in schools of open and traditional design. In T. G. David & B. D. Wright (Eds.), *Learning environments* (pp. 49–67). Chicago: University of Chicago Press.

Gump, P. V. (1978). School environments. In I. Altman & J. F. Wohwill (Eds.), *Children and the environment* (pp. 131–174). New York: Plenum Press.

Gump, P. V., & Sutton-Smith, B. (1955). The "it" role in children's games. *The Group, 17,* 3–8.

Guralnick, M. J. (1980). Social interactions among preschool children. *Exceptional Children, 46*(4), 248–253.

Guralnick, M. J. (1981). The social behavior of preschool children at different developmental levels: Effects of group composition. *Journal of Experimental Child Psychology, 31,* 115–130.

Guralnick, M. J., & Groom, J. M. (1985). Correlates of peer-related social competence of developmentally delayed preschool children. *American Journal of Mental Deficiency, 90*(2), 140–150.

Guralnick, M. J., & Weinhouse, E. (1983). Child-child social interactions: An analysis of assessment instruments for young children. *Exceptional Children, 50*(3), 268–271.

Guralnick, M. J., & Weinhouse, E. (1984). Peer-related social interactions of developmentally delayed young children: Development and characteristics. *Developmental Psychology, 20*(5), 815–827.

Guttentag, M., & Bray, H. (1976). *Undoing sex stereotypes: Research and resources for educators.* New York: McGraw-Hill.

Hall, G. S. (1920). *Youth.* New York: Appleton.

Hall, J. A., & Halberstadt, A. G. (1980). Masculinity and femininity in children: Development of the children's personal attributes questionnaire. *Developmental Psychology, 16,* 270–280.

Hallinan, M. T. (1976). Friendship patterns in open and traditional classrooms. *Sociology of Education, 49,* 254–265.

Hallinan, M. T., & Tuma, N. B. (1978). Classroom effects on change in children's friendships. *Sociology of Education, 51,* 270–282.

Halverson, C. F., & Waldrop, M. F. (1973). The relations of mechanically recorded activity level to varieties of preschool play behavior. *Child Development, 44,* 678–681.

Halverson, C. F., & Waldrop, M. F. (1976). Relations between preschool activity and aspects of intellectual and social behavior at age 7½. *Developmental Psychology, 12,* 107–112.

Harding, V. (1977). The importance of play for children in hospital. *Nursing Mirror, 133*(3), 46–48.

Harms, T., & Clifford, R. M. (1980). *Early childhood environment rating scale.* New York: Teachers College Press.

Harper, L. V., & Sanders, K. M. (1975). Preschool children's use of space: Sex differences in outdoor play. *Developmental Psychology, 11,* 119.

Harter, S. (1983). Developmental perspectives on the self-system. In E. M. Hetherington (Ed.), & P. H. Mussen (Series Ed.) *Handbook of child psychology: Vol. 4. Socialization, personality, and social development* (4th ed., pp. 276–385). New York: Wiley.

Hartmann, H. (1958). *Ego psychology and the problem of adaptation.* New York: International Universities Press.

Hartup, W. W. (1975). The origins of friendship. In M. Lewis & L. Rosenblum (Eds.), *Friendship and peer relations* (pp. 11–26). New York: Wiley.

Hartup, W. W. (1976). Peer interaction and the behavioral development of the individual child. In E. Schopler & R. Reichler (Eds.), *Psychopathology and child development* (pp. 203–218). New York: Plenum Press.

Hartup, W. W. (1983). Peer relations. In E. M. Hetherington (Ed.), & P. H. Mussen (Series Ed.), *Handbook of child psychology: Vol. 4. Socialization, personality, and social development* (pp. 103–196). New York: Wiley.

Havighurst, R. J. (1972). *Developmental tasks and education* (3rd ed.). New York: David McKay.

Hay, D. F. (1979). Cooperative interactions and sharing between very young children and their parents. *Developmental Psychology, 5*(6), 647–653.

Hay, D. F., Nash, A., & Pedersen, J. (1983). Interaction between six-month-old peers. *Child Development, 54,* 557–562.

Hay, D. F., Ross, H. S., & Goldman, B. D. (1979). Social games in infancy. In B. Sutton-Smith (Ed.), *Play and learning* (pp. 83–107). New York: Gardner Press.

Hayward, D., Rothenburg, M., & Beasley, R. (1974). Children's play and urban playground environments: A comparison of traditional, contemporary, and adventure playground types. *Environment and Behavior, 6*(2), 131–168.

Henderson, B. (1984). The social context of exploratory play. In T. Yawkey & A. D. Pellegrini (Eds.), *Child's play: Developmental and applied* (pp. 171–201). Hillsdale, NJ: Erlbaum.

Herron, R. E., & Sutton-Smith, B. (1971). *Child's play.* New York: Wiley.

Hershorn, M., & Rosenbaum, A. (1985). Children of marital violence: A closer look at the unintended victims. *American Journal of Orthopsychiatry, 55*(2), 260–266.

Hesse, P., & Cicchetti, D. (1982). Perspectives on an integrated theory of emotional development. In D. Cicchetti & P. Hesse (Eds.) *New directions for child development: Vol. 16. Emotional development.* (No. 16, 3–48.) San Francisco: Jossey-Bass.

Hetherington, E. M. (1972). Effects of father absence on personality development in adolescent daughters. *Developmental Psychology, 7,* 313–326.

Hetherington, E. M., Cox, M., & Cox, R. (1979). Play and social interaction in children following divorce. *Journal of Social Issues, 35*(4), 26–49.

Hetherington, E. M. (Ed.), & Mussen, P. H. (Series Ed.). (1983). *Handbook of child psychology: Vol. 4. Socialization, personality, and social development.* New York: Wiley.

Hewitt, S. (1970). *The family and the handicapped child.* London: Allen & Unwin.

Hiebert, E. H. (1980). The relationship of logical reasoning ability, oral language comprehension, and home experiences to preschool children's print awareness. *Journal of Reading Behavior, 12*(4), 313–323.

Higginbotham, D. J., & Baker, B. M. (1981). Social participation and cognitive play differences in hearing impaired and normally hearing preschoolers. *Volta Review, 83,* 135–149.

Higginbotham, D. J., Baker, B. M., & Neill, R. D. (1980). Assessing the social participation and cognitive play abilities of hearing-impaired preschoolers. *Volta Review, 82,* 261–269.

Hill, D. F. (1981). *Children's understanding of their handicapped peers.* Paper presented at the annual meeting of the American Psychological Association, Los Angeles.

Hill, P. M., & McCune-Nicolich, L. (1981). Pretend play and patterns of cognition in Down's syndrome children. *Child Development, 52,* 611–617.

Hodapp, R. M., & Goldfield, E. C. (1983). The use of mother-infant games as therapy with delayed children. *Early Child Development and Care, 13*(1), 17–32.

Hodapp, R. M., Goldfield, E. C., & Boyatzis, C. J. (1984). The use and effectiveness of maternal scaffolding in mother-infant games. *Child Development, 55,* 772–781.

Hoffman, M. L. (1982). The measurement of empathy. In C. E. Izard (Ed.), *Measuring emotions in infants and children* (pp. 279–296). New York: Cambridge University Press.

Hohman, M., Banet, B., & Weikart, D. (1979). *Young children in action: A manual for preschool educators.* Ypsilanti, MI: High/Scope.

Holland, J. G. (1971). *The use of a computer for programmed instruction presentation of a pre-school classification program.* Paper presented at the meeting of the American Educational Research Association, New York. (ERIC Document Reproduction Service No. ED 056 510)

Holmberg, M. C. (1980). The development of social interchange patterns from12 to 42 months. *Child Development, 51,* 448–456.

Honig, A. S. (1983). Research in review: Television and young children. *Young Children, 38*(4), 63–76.

Honig, A. S. (1986). Research in review: Stress and coping in children. *Young Children, 41*(4), 50–63.

Hopper, C., & Wambold, C. (1978). Improving the independent play of severely retarded children. *Education and Training of the Mentally Retarded, 13*(1), 42–46.

Horne, B. M., & Philleo, C. P. (1942). A comparative study of the spontaneous play activities of normal and mentally defective children. *The Journal of Genetic Psychology, 61,* 33–46.

Horwitz, R. A. (1979). Psychological effects of the "open classroom." *Review of Educational Research, 49,* 71–86.

Hoskins, K. F. (1976). *Effects of home reading experiences on academic readiness for kindergarten children.* Unpublished doctoral dissertation, University of Missouri, Columbia.

Hovell, M. F., Bursick, J. H., Sharkey, R., & McClure, J. (1978). An evaluation of elementary students' voluntary physical activity during recess. *Research Quarterly, 49*(4), 460–474.

Howes, C., & Rubenstein, J. A. (1978). *Peer play and the effect of the inanimate environment.* Washington, DC: Eastern Psychological Association. (ERIC Document Reproduction Service No. ED 163 323)

Hrncir, E. J. (1980, April). *Adult facilitation of pretend play in two-year-olds.* Paper presented at the annual meeting of the American Educational Research Association. Boston, MA.

Hubbell, R. D. (1977). On facilitating spontaneous talking in young children. *Journal of Speech and Hearing Disorders, 42,* 216–231.

Hughes, H. M., & Barad, S. J. (1983). Psychological functioning of children in a battered women's shelter: A preliminary investigation. *American Journal of Orthopsychiatry, 53*(3), 525–531.

Hughes, M. C. (1982). Chronically ill children in groups: Recurrent issues and adaptations. *American Journal of Orthopsychiatry, 52*(4), 704–711.

Huizinga, J. (1950). *Home Ludens: A study of the play-element in culture.* London: Routledge & Kegan Paul.

Hulme, I., & Lunzer, E. A. (1966). Play, language, and reasoning in subnormal children. *Journal of Child Psychology and Psychiatry, 7,* 107–123.

Hunt, J. M. (1961). *Intelligence and experience.* New York: Ronald Press.

Hunt, J. M. (1981). The epigenesis of intrinsic motivation and early cognitive learning. In M. Kaplan-Sanoff & R. Magid (Eds.), *Exploring early childhood: Theory and practice* (pp. 23–41). New York: Macmillan.

Hursh, D. E., & House, D. J. (1983). Designing environments for handicapped persons: The evaluation of a play unit. *Exceptional Education Quarterly, 4*(2), 54–66.

Huston, A. C. (1983). Sex-typing. In E. M. Hetherington (Ed.), & P. H. Mussen (Series Ed.), *Handbook of child psychology: Vol. 4. Socialization, personality, and social development,* (pp. 387–468). New York: Wiley.

Hutt, C. (1971). Exploration and play in children. In R. E. Herron & B. Sutton-Smith (Eds.), *Child's play* (pp. 231–251). New York: Wiley. (Reprinted from *Symposium of the Zoological Society of London 18,* 61–81)

Hutt, C. (1979). Exploration and play. (#2). In B. Sutton-Smith (Ed.), *Play and learning* (pp. 175–194). New York: Gardner Press.

Hutt, C., & Hutt, S. J. (1977). Heart rate variability—The adaptive consequences of individual differences and state changes. In N. Blurton-Jones & V. Reynolds, (Eds.), *Human behavior and adaptation* (pp. 171–189). London: Taylor & Francis.

Iano, R. P. (1971). Learning deficiency versus developmental conceptions of mental retardation. *Exceptional Children, 12,* 301–310.

Inhelder, B., Lezine, I., Sinclair, H., & Stambak, M. (1972). Less debuts de la function symbolique. *Archives de Psychologie, 41,* 187–243.

Inhelder, B., & Piaget, J. (1964). *The early growth of logic in the child.* New York: Norton.

Irwin, D. M., & Bushnell, M. M. (1976). Replant your learning garden. *Day Care and Early Education, 3,* 33–46.

Isaacs, L. D. (1980). Effects of ball size, ball color, and preferred color on catching by young children. *Perceptual and Motor Skills, 51*(2) 583–586.

Isaacs, S. (1933). *Social development in young children.* New York: Schocken.

Isaacs, S. (1966). *Intellectual growth in young children.* New York: Schocken (Original work published 1930)

Isenberg, J., & Jacob, E. (1983). Literacy and symbolic play: A review of the literature. *Childhood Education, 59*(4), 272–274.

Isenberg, J., & Jacob, E. (1985). Playful literacy activities and learning: Preliminary observations. In J. L. Frost & S. Sunderlin (Eds.), *When children play* (pp. 17–23). Wheaton, MD: Association for Childhood Education International.

Iwanga, M. (1973). Development of interpersonal play structures in 3, 4 and 5 year old children. *Journal of Research and Development in Education, 6,* 71–82.

Izard, C. (1971). *The face of emotion.* New York: Meredith.

Izard, C. (1972). *Patterns of emotions. A new analysis of anxiety and depression.* New York: Academic Press.

Izard, C. (1980). The emergence of emotions and the development of consciousness in infancy. In J. M. Davidson, & R. J. Davidson, (Eds.), *The Psychobiology of consciousness* (pp. 193–216). New York: Plenum Press.

Izard, C. (1982). Measuring emotions in human development. In C. E. Izard (Ed.), *Measuring emotions in infants and children* (pp. 3–18). New York: Cambridge University Press.

Jacklin, C., & Maccoby, E. (1980). *The pinks and the blues* [Television program aired by KERA, PBS]. Dallas, Texas.

Jacklin, C. N., Maccoby, E., & Dick, A. E. (1973). Barrier behaviors and toy preference: Sex differences (and their absence) in the year old child. *Child Development, 44,* 196–200.

Jacobs, L. B. (1965). *Using literature with young children.* New York: Teachers College Press.

Jacobson, E. (1964). *The self and the object world.* New York: International Universities Press.

Jakobson, R. (1968). *Child language, aphasia, and phonological universals.* The Hague: Mouton.

N. C., & McCain, T. A. (1982). Television games ms, themes and uses. *Journal* 00.

ogical stress. New York: Wiley.

, R. (1976). An observation 's imaginative doll play. *Journal* chiatry, 17, 180–197.

. R. (1977). *Curriculum design:* hysical education teaching-learn- ican Alliance for Health, Physical

Johnson, D. L., Breckenridge, J. N., & McGowan, R. J. (1984). Home environment and early cognitive development in Mexican-American children. In A. W. Gottfried (Ed.), *Home environment and early cognitive development: Longitudinal research.* (pp. 151–195) New York: Academic Press.

Johnson, D. W., & Johnson, R. T. (1974). Instructional structure: Cooperative, competitive or individualistic. *Review of Educational Research, 44,* 213-240.

Johnson, D. W., & Johnson, R. T. (1975). *Learning together and alone.* Englewood Cliffs, NJ: Prentice-Hall.

Johnson, D. W., & Johnson, R. T. (1979a). Conflict in the classroom: Controversy and learning. *Review of Education Research, 49,* 51–70.

Johnson, D. W., & Johnson, R. T. (1979b). *Structuring cooperative learning: The 1979 handbook.* Minneapolis, MN: Cooperative Network.

Johnson, H. M. (1928). *Children in the nursery school.* New York: Day.

Johnson, J. (1984). Foreword. In T. Yawkey and A. Pellegrini (Eds.), *Child's play: Developmental and applied* (pp. xi-xiii). Hillsdale, NJ: Lawrence Erlbaum.

Johnson, J., & Ershler, J. (1981). Developmental trends in preschool play as a function of classroom setting and child gender. *Child Development, 52,* 95–104.

Johnson, J., Ershler, J., & Bell, C. (1980). Play behavior in a discovery-based and a formal education preschool program. *Child Development, 51,* 271–274.

Johnson, J. E. (1985). Characteristics of preschoolers interested in microcomputers. *Journal of Educational Research, 78*(5), 299–305.

Johnson, M. M. (1975). Fathers, mothers and sex typing. *Sociological Inquiry, 45,* 15–26.

Johnson, M. W. (1935). The effect of behavior of variation in the amount of play equipment. *Child Development, 6,* 56–68.

Johnson, P., & Stockdale, F. (1975). Effects of puppet therapy on palmar sweating test of hospitalized children. *The Johns Hopkins Medical Journal, 137,* 1–5.

Johnston, M. K., Kelley, C. S., Harris, F. R., & Wolf, M. M. (1966). An application of reinforcement principles to development of motor skills of a young child. *Child Development, 37,* 379–387.

Jones, T. D. (1939). The development of certain motor skills and play activities in young children. *Child Development, Monographs* No. 26. New York: Teachers College, Columbia University.

Josselyn, I. (1955). *The happy child.* New York: Random House.

Joyner, L. (1976). The changing playscape. *Southern Living, 11,* 51–55.

Kaczmarek, L. A., & Dell, A. G. (1981). Designing instructional activities for young handicapped children. *Journal for the Division of Early Childhood, 2,* 74–83.

Kagan, J. (1971). *Change and continuity in infancy.* New York: Wiley.

Kagan, J., Kearsley, R. B., & Zelazo, P. R. (1978). *Infancy: Its place in human development.* Cambridge, MA: Harvard University Press.

Kamii, C., & DeVries, R. (1978). *Physical knowledge in preschool education.* Englewood Cliffs, NJ: Prentice-Hall.

Kamii, C., & DeVries, R. (1980). *Group games in early education: Implications of Piaget's theory.* Washington, DC: National Association for the Education of Young Children.

Kaplan-Sanoff, M., & Kletter, E. F. (1985). The developmental needs of abused children: Classroom strategies. *Beginnings, 2*(3), 15–19.

Kardos, E., & Peto, A. (1956). Contributions to the theory of play. *The British Journal of Medical Psychology, 29,* 100–112.

Karnes, M., & Lee, R. C. (1979). Mainstreaming in the preschool. In L. Katz, *Current topics in early childhood education* (Vol. 2, pp. 13–42). Norwood, NJ: Ablex.

Katz, E., Kellerman, J., & Siegel, S. (1980). Behavioral distress in children with cancer undergoing medical procedures: Developmental considerations. *Journal of Consulting and Clinical Psychology, 48*(3), 356–365.

Katz, L. G. (1982). TV and your preschooler. *Parents' Magazine, 57,* 92.

Kawin, E. (1934). The function of toys in relation to child development. *Child Education, 11*(3), 122–133.

Kee, D. W. (1985). Computer play. In C. C. Brown & A. W. Gottfried (Eds.), *Play interactions: The role of toys and parental involvement in children's development* (pp. 53–60). Skillman, NJ: Johnson & Johnson.

Kegan, R. (1982). *The evolving self.* Cambridge, MA: Harvard University Press.

Keil, F. (1979). *Semantic and conceptual development.* Cambridge, MA: Harvard University Press.

Kendall, F. (1983). *Diversity in the classroom: A multicultural approach to the education of young children.* New York: Teachers College Press.

Keogh, J. F. (1977). The study of movement skill development. *Quest* (Monograph No. 28), 76–88.

Keogh, J. F. (1978). Movement outcomes as conceptual guidelines in the perceptual-motor maze. *Journal of Special Education, 12*(3), 321–329.

Kephart, N. (1960). *The slow learner in the classroom.* Columbus, OH: Charles E. Merrill.

Kernberg, O. (1975). *Borderline conditions and pathological narcissism.* New York: Jason Aronson.

Kernberg, O. (1980). *Internal world and external reality.* New York: Aronson.

King, J., & Ziegler, S. (1981). The effects of hospitalization on children's behavior: A review of the literature. *Children's Health Care, 10,* 20–28.

King, N. (1979). Play: The kindergartners' perspective. *Elementary School Journal, 80*(2), 81–87.

King, N. (1982a). Children's play as a form of resistance in the classroom. *Journal of Education, 164*(4), 320–329.

King, N. (1982b). School uses of materials traditionally associated with children's play. *Theory and Research in Social Education, 10*(3), 17–27.

King, N. (1982c). Work and play in the classroom. *Social Education, 46*(2), 110–113.

Kinsman, C., & Berk, L. (1979). Joining the block and housekeeping areas: Changes in play and social behavior. *Young Children, 35*(7), 66–75.

Kirk, S. (1958). *Early education of the mentally retarded.* Urbana: University of Illinois Press.

Kirschenblatt-Gimblett, B. (Ed.). (1976). *Speech play.* Philadelphia: University of Pennsylvania Press.

Kirschenblatt-Gimblett, B. (1979). Speech play and verbal art. In B. Sutton-Smith (Ed.), *Play and learning* (pp. 219–238). New York: Gardner Press.

Klahr, D., & Wallace, J. G. (1970). An information processing analysis of some Piagetian experimental tasks. *Cognitive Psychology, 1*(4), 358–387.

Klein, M. (1932). *The psychoanalysis of children.* New York: Evergreen, Grove Press.

Klein, M. (1955). The psychoanalytic play technique. *American Journal of Orthopsychiatry, 25,* 223–237.

Klinger, E. (1970). *The structure and function of fantasy.* New York: Wiley.

Klinnert, M., Campos, J. J., Sorce, J., Emde, R. N., & Svejda, M. (1983). Emotions and behavior regulators: Social referencing in infancy. In R. Plutchik & H. Kellerman (Eds.), *Emotion: Theory, research, and experience: Vol. 2. Emotions in early development* (pp. 57–86). New York: Academic Press.

Klinzing, D. G. (1985). *A study of the behavior of children in a preschool equipped with computers.* Paper presented at the annual meeting of the American Educational Research Association, Chicago. (ERIC Document Reproduction Service No. ED 255 320)

Klinzing, R., & Klinzing, D. G. (1977). *The hospitalized child.* Englewood Cliffs, NJ: Prentice-Hall.

Knapp, M., & Knapp, H. (1976). *One potato, two potato . . . The secret education of American children.* New York: Norton.

Knafl, K., & Dixon, D. (1984). The participation of fathers in their children's hospitalization. *Comprehensive Pediatric Nursing, 1,* 269–281.

Knudsen, K. (1975). Play therapy: Preparing the young child for surgery. *Nursing Clinics of North America, 10,* 679–686.

Kohlberg, L. K. (1966). A cognitive-developmental analysis of children's sex-role concepts and attitudes. In E. E. Maccoby (Ed.), *The development of sex differences* (pp. 82–172). Stanford, CA: Stanford University Press.

Kohlberg, L. K. (1976). Moral stages and moralization; The cognitive-developmental approach. In T. Lickona (Ed.), *Moral development and behavior* (pp. 31–53). New York: Holt, Rinehart & Winston.

Kohlberg, L. K., & Mayer, R. (1972). Development as the aim of education. *Harvard Educational Review, 42,* 449–496.

Kohut, H. (1971). *The analysis of the self.* New York: International Universities Press.

Kohut, H. (1977). *The restoration of the self.* New York: International Universities Press.

Koplow, L. (1985). Premature competence in young children: A false declaration of independence. *Beginnings, 2*(3), 8–11.

Kostelnik, M. J. (1983). Living with superman. *Two-to-Twelve, 1*(5), 6–9.

Krantz, P., & Risley, T. (1972). *The organization of group care environments: Behavioral ecology in the classroom.* Lawrence: The University of Kansas. (ERIC Document Reproduction Service No. ED 078-915)

Krasnor, L. R., & Pepler, D. J. (1980). The study of children's play: Some suggested future directions. In K. H. Rubin (Ed.), *New directions in child development: Children's play* (No. 3, pp. 85–96). San Francisco: Jossey-Bass.

Kravitz, R. I.; & Driscoll, J. M. (1983). Expectations for childhood development among child-abusing and nonabusing parents. *American Journal of Orthopsychiatry, 53*(2), 336–344.

Kreidler, W. J., (1984). *Creative conflict resolution.* Glenview, IL: Scott, Foresman.

Kreitler, H., & Kreitler, S. (1976). *Cognitive orientation and behavior.* New York: Springer-Verlag.

Kretschmer, R. (1972). *A study to assess the play activities and gesture output of hearing handicapped preschool children.* (Project No. 45-2901). Washington, D.C.: U. S. Department of Health, Education and Welfare, Office of Education, Bureau of the Handicapped.

Kritchevsky, S., Prescott, E., & Walling, L. (1977). *Planning environments for young children: Physical space* (Rev. ed.). Washington, DC: National Association for the Education of Young Children.

Krown, S. (1974). *Threes and fours go to school.* Englewood Cliffs, NJ: Prentice-Hall.

Krudiner, W. P. (1978). The effects of encapsulation on preschool children's imaginative play. Unpublished master's thesis, University of Illinois, Urbana.

Kuhn, D. (1972). Mechanisms of change in the development of cognitive structures. *Child Development, 43,* 833–844.

Kuhn, D., Nash, S. C., & Brucken, L. (1978). Sex role concepts of two- and three-year-olds. *Child Development, 49,* 445–451.

Laban, R. (1948). *Modern educational dance.* London: Macdonald & Evans.

Laban, R., & Lawrence, F. (1947). *Effort.* London: Unwin Brothers.

LaBerge, D., & Samuels, S. J. (1974). Toward a theory of automatic processing in reading. *Cognitive Psychology, 6,* 293–323.

Ladd, G. W. (1981). Effectiveness of a social learning method for enhancing children's social interaction and peer acceptance. *Child Development, 52,* 171–178.

Ladd, G. W., & Emerson, E. S. (1984). Shared knowledge in children's friendships. *Developmental Psychology, 20,* 932–940.

Ladd, G. W., & Oden, S. (1979). The relationship between peer acceptance and children's ideas about helpfulness. *Child Development, 50,* 402–408.

Lamb, M. E. (1977). Father-infant and mother-infant interaction in the first year of life. *Child Development, 48,* 167–181.

Lamb, M. E. (1981). The role of the father: An overview. In M. E. Lamb (Ed.), *The role of the father in child development* (2nd ed., pp. 1–61). New York: Wiley.

Langlois, J. H., & Downs, A. G. (1980). Mothers, fathers, and peers as socialization agents of sex-typed play behavior in young children. *Child Development, 51,* 1237–1247.

Laosa, L. M. (1977). Socialization, education and continuity: The importance of the sociocultural context. *Young Children, 32*(5), 21–27.

Laosa, L. M. (1982). Families as facilitators of children's intellectual development: A causal analysis. In L. M. Laosa & I. E. Sigel (Eds.), *Families as learning environments for children* (pp. 1–45). New York: Plenum Press.

Lazar, I., Darlington, R., Murray, H., Royce, J., & Snipper, A. (1982). Lasting effects of early education. *Monographs of the Society for Research in Child Development,* 47, (2–3, Serial No. 195).

Leacock, E. (1976). At play in African villages. In J. S. Bruner, A. Jolly, & K. Sylva (Eds.), *Play: Its role in development and evolution* (pp. 466–473). New York: Basic Books.

Leahey, M. L. (1984). Finding from research on divorce: Implications for professionals' skill development. *American Journal of Orthopsychiatry, 54*(2), 298–317.

Lee, L. (1973, August). *Social encounters of infants: The beginnings of popularity.* Paper presented at the International Society for the Study of Behavioral Development, Ann Arbor, MI.

Lee, P. C., & Wolinsky, A. L. (1973). Male teachers of young children: A preliminary empirical study. *Young Children, 28*(6), 342–352.

Lefever, H. G. (1981). Playing the dozens: A mechanism for social control. *Phylan, 42*(1), 73–85.

Lehman, H. C., & Witty, P. A. (1927). *The psychology of play activities.* New York: A. S. Barnes.

Lepper, M. R., & Greene, D. (1975). Turning play into work: Effects of adult surveillance and extrinsic motivation. *Journal of Personality and Social Psychology, 31,* 479–486.

Lerner, H. E. (1974). Early origins of envy and devaluation of women: Implications for sex-role stereotypes. *Bulletin of the Menninger Clinic, 38,* 538–553.

Letts, M., Stevens, L., Coleman, J., & Kettner, R. (1983). Puppetry and doll play as an adjunct to pediatric orthopedics. *Journal of Pediatric Orthopedics, 3,* 605–609.

Lever, J. (1976). Sex differences in the games children play. *Social Problems, 23*(4), 478–487.

Lever, J. (1978). Sex differences in the complexity of children's play and games. *American Sociological Review, 43,* 471–483.

Levin, H., & Wardwell, E. (1962). The research uses of doll play. *Psychological Bulletin, 59,* 27–56.

Levy, A. K. (1984). The language of play: The role of play in language development. A review of literature. *Early Child Development and Care, 17,* 49–62.

Levy, L., & Gottlieb, J. (1984). Learning disabled and non-LD children at play. *Remedial and Special Education, 5*(6), 43–50.

Lewin, K. (1931). Environmental forces in child behavior and development. In C. Murchison (Ed.), *A handbook of child psychology* (pp. 94–127). Worcester, MA: Clark University Press.

Lewis, M. (1963). *Language, thought and personality.* New York: Basic Books.

Lewis, M. (1979). The social determination of play. In B. Sutton-Smith (Ed.), *Play and learning* (pp. 23–33). New York: Gardner Press.

Lewis, M., & Brooks-Gunn, J. (1979). *Social cognition and the acquisition of self.* New York: Plenum Press.

Lewis, M., & Michaelson, L. (1983). *Children's emotions and moods.* New York: Plenum Press.

Lewis, M., & Rosenblum, L. (Eds.). (1974). *The effect of the infant on its caregiver.* New York: Wiley.

Li, A. K. F. (1978). Effects of play on novel responses in kindergarten children. *The Alberta Journal of Educational Research, 23,* 31–36.

Li, A. K. F. (1983). Pleasurable aspects of play in enhancing young handicapped children's relationships with parents and peers. *Journal of the Division for Early Childhood, 7,* 87–92.

Lieberman, A. F. (1977). Preschoolers' competence with a peer: Relations with attachment and peer experiences. *Child Development, 48,* 1277–1287.

Lieberman, J. N. (1965). Playfulness and divergent thinking: An investigation of their relationship at the kindergarten level. *The Journal of Genetic Psychology, 107*(2), 219–224.

Lieberman, J. N. (1977). *Playfulness: Its relationship to imagination and creativity.* New York: Academic Press.

Linder, T. W. (1982). Pleasurable play: Its value for handicapped infants and their parents. *The Journal for Special Educators, 19*(1), 59–68.

Lindheim, R., Glaser, H. H., & Coffin, C. (1972). *Changing hospital environments for children.* Cambridge, MA: Harvard University Press.

Lindquist, I. (1977). *Therapy through play.* London: Arlington Books Ltd.

Linford, A., Jeanrenaud, C., Karlsson, K, Witt, P., & Linford, M. (1971). A computerized analysis of characteristics of Down's Syndrome and normal children's free play patterns. *Journal of Leisure Research, 3,* 44–52.

Lipinski, J. M., Nida, R. E., Shade, D. D., & Watson, J. A. (1984). *Competence, gender, and preschooler's free play choices when a microcomputer is present in the classroom.* Greensboro,NC: Family Research Center. (ERIC Document Reproduction Service No. ED 243 609)

Liss, M. B. (Ed.). (1983). *Social and cognitive skills: Sex roles and children's play.* New York: Academic Press.

Lockheed, M. E., & Harris, A. M. (1984). Cross-sex collaborative learning. *American Educational Research Journal, 21,* 275–294.

Loevinger, J. (1976). *Ego development: Conceptions and theories.* San Francisco: Jossey-Bass.

Lombardino, L. J., & Sproul, C. J. (1984). Patterns of correspondence and non-correspondence between play and language in developmentally delayed preschoolers. *Education and Training of the Mentally Retarded, 19*(1), 5–14.

Longo, J., Harvey, A., Wilson, S., & Deni, R. (1982). Toy play, play tempo and reaction to frustration in infants. *Perceptual and Motor Skills, 55*(1), 239–242.

Loo, C. M. (1972). The effects of spatial density on the social behavior of children. *Journal of Applied Social Psychology, 2,* 372–381.

Loo, C. M. (1976). *The effects of spatial density on behavior styles of children.* Paper presented at the annual meeting of the American Psychological Association, Washington, D.C.

Lorenz, K. (1976). Psychology and phylogeny. In J. S. Bruner, A. Jolly, & K. Sylva (Eds.) *Play: Its role in development and evolution* (pp. 84–95). New York: Basic Books.

Lovell, K., Hoyle, H. W., & Siddall, M. C. (1968). A study of some aspects of the play and language of young children with delayed speech. *Journal of Child Psychology and Psychiatry, 9,* 41–50.

Lowe, M. (1975). Trends in the development of representational play in infants from one to three years: An observational study. *Journal of Child Psychology and Psychiatry, 16,* 33–47.

Lowenfeld, M. (1935). *Play in childhood.* London: Victor Gallancz.

Luchins, A. S., & Luchins, E. H. (1968). New experimental attempts at preventing mechanization in problem solving. In P. C. Wason & P. N. Johnson (Eds.), *Thinking and reasoning* (pp. 50–79). Baltimore: Penguin.

Lunzer, E. A. (1959). Intellectual development in the play of young children. *Educational Review, 11*(3), 205–217.

Lynch, K. (Ed.). (1977). *Growing up in cities.* Cambridge, MA: MIT Press.

MacCarthy, D. & MacKeith, R. (1985). A parent's voice. *Archives of Diseases of Childhood, 60*(2), 179–181.

Maccoby, E., & Jacklin, C. (1974). *The psychology of sex differences.* Stanford, CA: Stanford University Press.

Maccoby, E. E., & Martin, J. A. (1983). Socialization in the context of the family: Parent-child interaction. In E. M. Hetherington (Ed.), & P. H. Mussen (Series Ed.). *Handbook of child psychology: Vol. 4. Socialization, personality, and social development,* (pp. 1–102). New York: Wiley.

MacDonald, K., & Parke, R. D. (1984). Bridging the gap: Parent-child play interaction and peer interactive competence. *Child Development, 55*(4), 1265–1277.

Mackworth, N. H. (1965). Originality. *American Psychologist, 20,* 51–66.

Maddux, C. D., & Cummings, R. E. (1984). LOGO is for all children: Learning with the turtle. *The Exceptional Parent, 14*(4), 15–19.

Madsen, M. C. (1971). Developmental and cross-cultural differences in the cooperative and competitive behavior of young children. *Journal of Cross-Cultural Psychology, 2,* 365–371.

Mahler, M. S., Pine, F., & Bergman, A. (1975). *The psychological birth of the human infant: Symbiosis and individuation.* New York: Basic Books.

Maier, H. (1969). *Three theories of child development.* New York: Harper & Row.

Maier, N. R. F. (1940). The behavior mechanisms concerned with problem solving. *Psychological Review, 47,* 43–58.

Malone, T. W. (1980). *What makes things fun to learn? A study of intrinsically motivating computer games.* Palo Alto, CA: Xerox, Palo Alto Research Center.

Malone, T. W. (1981). Toward a theory of intrinsically motivating instruction. *Cognitive Science, 4,* 333–369.

Marcus, D. E., & Overton, W. F. (1978). The development of cognitive gender constancy and sex role preferences. *Child Development, 49* 434–444.

Martlew, M., Connolly, K., & McLeod, C. (1978). Language use, role and context in a five-year-old. *Journal of Child Language, 5,* 81–99.

Marton, J. P., & Acker, L. E. (1977). *Measurement and facilitation of affectionate behaviour in the play of young children.* British Columbia: University of Victoria. (ERIC Document Reproduction Service, No. ED 143 428)

Matas, L., Arend, R. A., & Sroufer, L. A. (1978). Continuity of adaption in the second year of life; The relationship between quality of attachment and later competence. *Child Development, 49,* 547–556.

Matthews, W. (1977). Modes of transformation in the initiation of fantasy play. *Developmental Psychology, 13,* 212–216.

Matthews, W. (1981). Sex-role perception, portrayal, and preference in the fantasy play of young children. *Sex Roles: A Journal of Research,* 7(10), 979–987.

Matthews, W. S., Beebe, S., & Bopp, M. (1980). Spatial perspective-taking and pretend play. *Perceptual and Motor Skills,* 5(1), 49–50.

Matthews, W. S., & Matthews, R. J. (1982). Eliminating operational definitions: A paradigm case approach to the study of fantasy play. In D. J. Pepler & K. H. Rubin (Eds.), *The play of children: Current theory and research* (pp. 21–30). Basel, Switzerland: Karger AG.

Maxwell, W. (1983). Games children play. *Educational Leadership,* 40(6), 39–41.

McCaffery, M. (1977). Pain relief for the child. *Pediatric Nursing,* 4(4), 11–16.

McCall, R. (1974). Exploratory manipulation and play in the human infant. *Monographs of the Society for Research in Child Development, 39,* (2, Serial No. 155).

McCall, R. (1979). Stages in play development between zero and two years of age. In B. Sutton-Smith (Ed.), *Play and learning* (pp. 35–44). New York: Gardner Press.

McClenaghan, B. A., & Gallahue, D. L. (1978). *Fundamental movement: A developmental and remedial approach.* Philadelphia: W. B. Saunders.

McCollum, A. T. (1975). *The chronically ill child.* New Haven, CT: Yale University Press.

McCollum, E. V. (1964). *From Kansas farm boy to scientist: The autobiography of Elmer Verner McCollum.* Lawrence: University of Kansas Press.

McConkey, R., & Jeffree, D. (1980). Developing children's play. *Forward Trends,* 7(2), 21–23.

McCornack, B. L. (1982). Effects of peer familiarity on play behavior in preschool children. *The Journal of Genetic Psychology, 141,* 225–232.

McCune, L. (1985). Play-language relationships and symbolic development. In C. C. Brown & A. W. Gottfried (Eds.), *Play interactions: The role of toys and parental involvement in chldren's development* (pp. 38–45). Skillman, NJ: Johnson & Johnson.

McCune-Nicolich, L. (1981). Toward symbolic functioning: Structure of early pretend games and potential parallels with language. *Child Development, 52,* 785–797.

McCune-Nicolich, L., & Bruskin, C. (1982). Combinatorial competency in play and language. In D. J. Pepler & K. H. Rubin (Eds.), *The play of children: Current theory and research* (pp. 30–45). Basel, Switzerland: Karger AG.

McCune-Nicolich, L., & Carroll, S. (1981). Development of symbolic play: Implications for the language specialist. *Topics in Language Disorders,* 2(1), 1–15.

McCune-Nicolich, L., & Fenson, L. (1984). Methodological issues in studying early pretend play. In T. Yawkey & A. D. Pellegrini (Eds.), *Child's play: Developmental and applied* (pp. 81–104). Hillsdale, NJ: Erlbaum.

McDermott, J. (1968). Parental divorce in early childhood. *American Journal of Psychiatry, 124,* 118–126.

McEvoy, J., & McConkey, R. (1983). Play activities of mentally handicapped children at home and mothers' perception of play. *International Journal of Rehabilitation Research,* 6(2), 143–151.

McGhee, P. E. (1984). Play, incongruity, and humor. In T. Yawkey & A. D. Pellegrini (Eds.), *Child's play: Developmental and applied* (pp. 219–236). Hillsdale, NJ: Erlbaum.

McGraw, M. B. (1935). *Growth: A study of Johnny and Jimmy.* New York: Appleton-Century Crofts.

McGrew, P. L. (1970). Social and spacial density effects on spacing behavior of preschool children. *Journal of Child Psychology and Psychiatry, 11,* 197–205.

McGrew, W. C. (1972). *An ethological study of children's behaviour.* London: Academic Press.

McGuinness, K. (1982). *Design tools for adapting environments.* Boston: Adaptive Environments.

McHale, S. M. (1983). Social interactions of autistic and nonhandicapped children during free play. *American Journal of Orthopsychiatry,* 53(1), 81–91.

McHale, S. M., & Boone, W. (1980). Play between autistic and nonhandicapped children: An innovative approach to mainstreaming. *Pointer,* 24(3), 28–32.

McKeever, P. (1983). Siblings of chronically ill children: A literature review with implications for research and practice. *American Journal of Orthopsychiatry,* 53(2), 209–218.

McLloyd, V. C. (1983a). The effects of the structure of play objects on the pretend play of low-income preschool children. *Child Development, 54,* 626–635.

McLloyd, V. C. (1983b). Class, culture, and pretend play: A reply to Sutton-Smith and Smith. *Developmental Review, 3,* 11–17.

McTigue, D. J., & Pinkham, J. (1978). Association between children's dental behavior and play behavior. *ASDC Journal of Dentistry for Children,* 45(3), 218–226.

McVaigh, B. L., & Johnson, M. F. K. (1979). Who plays, and why, in picture books. *The Elementary School Journal, 80*(1), 24–28.

Mead, G. H. (1934). *Mind, self and society.* Chicago: University of Chicago Press.

Mead, M. (1975). *Growing up in New Guinea.* New York: Morrow.

Meadow, K. P. (1984). Social adjustment of preschool children: Deaf and hearing, with and without other handicaps. *Topics in Early Childhood Special Education, 3*(4), 27–39.

Mehrabian, A. (1976). *Public places and private spaces: The psychology of work, play, and living environments.* New York: Basic Books.

Meltzer, N., & Herse, R. (1969). The boundaries of written words as seen by first graders. *Journal of Reading Behavior, 1,* 3–14.

Menezes, L. (1980). Innovative programs in a health care setting. *Social Work in Health Care, 6*(1), 101–105.

Menninger, K. (1942). *Love against hate.* New York: Harcourt.

Menyuk, P. (1974). Early development of receptive language: From babbling to words. In R. L. Schiefelbusch & L. L. Lloyd (Eds.), *Language perspectives* (pp. 213–236). Baltimore: University Park Press.

Meyer, B. (1980). The development of girls' sex-role attitudes. *Child Development, 51,* 508–514.

Meyers, L. F. (1984). Use of microprocessors to initiate language use in young non-oral children. *The Exceptional Parent, 14*(4), 19–25.

Millar, S. (1968). *The psychology of play.* Baltimore: Penguin.

Miller, P., & Garvey, C. (1984). Mother-baby role play: Its origins in social support. In I. Bretherton (Ed.), *Symbolic play: The development of social understanding* (pp. 101–130). New York: Academic Press.

Milne, A. A. (1924). *When we were very young.* New York: E. P. Dutton.

Milne, A. A. (1927). *Now we are six.* New York: E. P. Dutton.

Minuchin, P. P. (1965). Sex-role concepts and sex typing in childhood as a function of school and home environments. *Child Development, 36,* 1033–1048.

Minuchin, P. P., & Shapiro, E. K. (1983). The school as a context for social development. In E. M. Hetherington (Ed.), & P. H. Mussen (Series Ed.). *Handbook of child psychology: Vol. 4. Socialization, personality, and social development* (pp. 197–274). New York: Wiley.

Mischell, W., & Mischell, H. (1976). A cognitive social learning approach to morality and self regulation. In T. Lickona (Ed.), *Moral development and behavior* (pp. 84–107). New York: Holt, Rinehart & Winston.

Mitchell, E. D., & Mason, B. (1948). *The theory of play.* New York: A. S. Barnes.

Mogford, K. (1977). The play of handicapped children. In B. Tizard & D. Harvey (Eds.), *Biology of play* (pp. 170–184). London: Heinemann.

Monahan, B. D., & Monahan, T. A. (1983). *Compute first: Read and write later.* (ERIC Document Reproduction Service No. ED 226 357)

Montessori, M. (1965). *Dr. Montessori's own handbook.* New York: Schocken. (Original work published in 1914)

Montessori, M. (1973). *The Montessori method.* Cambridge, MA: Bentley.

Moore, G. T. (1980). The application of research to the design of therapeutic play environments for exceptional children. In W. Cruickshank (Ed.), *Approaches to learning* (pp. 201–229). Syracuse, NY: Syracuse University Press.

Moore, G. T. (1985). State of the art in play environment. In J. L. Frost & S. Sunderlin (Eds.), *When children play* (pp. 171–192). Wheaton, MD: Association for Childhood Education International.

Moore, G. T., Cohen, U., & McGinty, T. (1979). *Planning and design guidelines: Childcare centers and outdoor play environments.* Milwaukee: University of Wisconsin, Milwaukee Center for Architecture and Urban Planning Research.

Moore, G. T., Cohen, U., Oertel, J., & Van Ryzin, L. (1979). *Designing environments for handicapped children: A design guide and case study.* New York: Educational Facilities Laboratories.

Moore, J. B., & Bond, A. W. (1975). Playgrounds: An experience center for elementary physical education. *Journal of Physical Education and Recreation, 46*(1), 21–23.

Moore, R. C. (1974). Anarchy zone: Kids' needs and school yards. *School Review, 82,* 621–645.

Morris, G. (1976). Effects ball and background color have upon the catching performance of elementary school children. *Research Quarterly, 47,* 409–416.

Morse, P. (1974). Infant speech: A preliminary model. In R. L. Schiefelbusch & L. L. Lloyd (Eds.), *Language perspectives* (pp. 19–54). Baltimore: University Park Press.

Moss, H. A., & Robson, K. (1968). *The role of protest behavior in the development of mother-infant attachment.* Paper presented at the Meeting of the American Psychological Association, San Francisco.

Moustakas, C. (1973). *Children in play therapy* (Rev. ed.). New York: Jason Aronson. (Original work published in 1953)

Mueller, E. C., & Bergstrom, J. (1982). Fostering peer relations in young normal and handicapped children. In K. Borman (Ed.), *The social life of children in a changing society* (pp. 191–215). New York: Plenum Press.

Mueller, E. C., Brenner, J. (1977). The origins of social skills and interaction among playgroup toddlers. *Child Development, 48*(3), 854–861.

Mueller, E. C., & Lucas, T. (1975). A developmental analysis of peer interaction among toddlers. In M. Lewis & L. Rosenblum (Eds.), *Peer relations* (pp. 223–257). New York: Wiley.

Murphy, L. (1962). *The widening world of childhood.* New York: Basic Books.

Murrow, L., & Murrow, C. (1972). *Children come first: The inspired work of English primary schools.* New York: Harper & Row.

Mussen, P. H., & Eisenberg-Berg, N. (1977). *Roots of caring, sharing and helping.* San Francisco: Freeman.

Myers, G. D. (1985). Motor behavior of kindergartners during physical education and free play. In J. L. Frost & S. Sunderlin (Eds.), *When children play* (pp. 151–157). Wheaton, MD: Association for Childhood Education International.

Nadelman, L. (1970). Sex identity in London children: Memory, knowledge, and preference tests. *Human Development, 13,* 28–42.

Nadelman, L. (1974). Sex identity in American children. *Developmental Psychology, 10,* 413–417.

Navon, R., & Ramsey, P. G. (no date). *A comparison of Chinese and U.S. children's possession and exchange of materials.* Manuscript submitted for publication.

Naylor, H. (1985). Design for outdoor play: An observational study. In J. L. Frost & S. Sunderlin (Eds.), *When children play* (pp. 103–114). Wheaton, MD: Association for Childhood Education International.

Neill, S. (1982). Experimental alterations in playroom layout and their effect on staff and child behavior. *Educational Psychology, 2*(2), 103–109.

Nelson, K. (1981). Social cognition in a script framework. In J. H. Flavell & L. Ross (Eds.), *Social cognitive development: Frontiers and possible futures* (pp. 97–118). New York: Cambridge University Press.

Nelson, K., & Seidman, S. (1984). Playing with scripts. In I. Bretherton (Ed.), *Symbolic play: The development of social understanding* (pp. 45–72). New York: Academic Press.

Nemerowicz, G. M. (1979). *Children's perceptions of gender and work roles.* New York: Praeger.

Neumann, E. A. (1971). *The elements of play.* New York: MSS Information Corp.

Newberger, C. M., & Cook, M. A. (1983). Parental awareness and child abuse: A cognitive-developmental analysis of urban and rural samples. *American Journal of Orthopsychiatry, 53*(3), 512–524.

Newcomb, A. F., Brady, J. E., & Hartup, W. W. (1979). Friendship and incentive condition as determinants of children's task-oriented behavior. *Child Development, 50,* 878–881.

Newcombe, N., Rogoff, G., & Kagan, J. (1977). Developmental changes in recognition memory for pictures of objects and scenes. *Developmental Psychology, 13,* 337–341.

Newman, J. (Ed.) (1985). *Whole language: Theory in use.* Portsmouth, NH: Heinemann.

Newman, L., & Lind, J. (1980). The child in the hospital: Early stimulation and therapy through play. *Paediatrician, 9,* 147–150.

Newson, E., & Newson, J. (1979). *Toys and playthings in development and education.* New York: Pantheon Books.

Nicolich, L. M. (1977). Beyond sensorimotor intelligence: Assessment of symbolic maturity through analysis of pretend play. *Merrill-Palmer Quarterly, 23*(2) 89–99. thesis, Oakland University, Rochester, MI. (ERIC Document Reproduction Service No. ED 234 898)

Nuffield Mathematics Project. (1967). *I do, and I understand.* Edinburgh: W. & R. Chambers.

O'Brien, M. (1980). *Sex differences in toy and activity preferences of toddlers.* Unpublished master's thesis, University of Kansas.

O'Connell, B., & Bretherton, I. (1984). Toddlers' play, alone and with mother: The role of maternal guidance. In I. Bretherton (Ed.), *Symbolic play: The development of social understanding* (pp. 337–369). New York: Academic Press.

O'Connor, R. D. (1972). Relative efficacy of modeling, shaping, and the combined procedures for modification of social withdrawal. *Journal of Abnormal Psychology, 77*(3), 327–334.

Oden, S. (1982a). The applicability of social skills training research. *Child and Youth Services, 5,* 75–89.

Oden, S. (1982b). Peer relationship development in childhood. In L. G. Katz (Ed.), *Current topics in early childhood education* (Vol. 4, pp. 87–117). Norwood, NJ: Ablex.

Oden, S. (1986). Developing social skills instruction for peer interaction. In G. Cartledge & J. F. Milburn (Eds.), *Teaching social skills to children: Innovative approaches* (2nd ed., pp. 246–269). New York: Pergamon Press.

Oden, S. (1987). Alternate perspectives on children's peer relationships. In T. D. Yawkey & J. E. Johnson (Eds.), *Integrative processes and socialization: Early to middle childhood.* Hillsdale, NJ: Erlbaum.

Oden, S., & Asher, S. R. (1977). Coaching children in social skills for friendship making. *Child Development, 48,* 495–506.

Oden, S., Herzberger, S. D., Mangione, P. L., & Wheeler, V. A. (1984). Children's peer relationships: An examination of social processes. In J. C. Masters & K. Yarkin-Levin (Eds.), *Boundary areas in social and developmental psychology* (pp. 78–107). New York: Academic Press.

Odom, S. L. (1981). The relationship of play to developmental level in mentally retarded, preschool children. *Education and Training of the Mentally Retarded, 16*(2), 136–141.

Odom, S. L., Jenkins, J. R., Speltz, M. L., & De Klyen, M. (1982). Promoting social integration of young children at risk for learning disabilities. *Learning Disability Quarterly, 5*(4), 379–387.

Ogbu, J. U. (1981). Origins of human competence: A cultural-ecological perspective. *Child Development, 52,* 413–429.

Olds, A. (1978). Psychological considerations in humanizing the physical environment of pediatric outpatient and hospital settings. In E. Gellert (Ed.), *Psychological aspects of pediatric care* (pp. 111–131). Orlando, FL: Grune & Stratton.

Olds, A. R. (1979). Designing developmentally optimal classrooms for children with special needs. In S. Meisels (Ed.), *Special education and development perspectives of young children with special needs* (pp. 91–138). Baltimore: University Park Press.

Olds, A. R. (1982a). Designing play environments for children under three. *Topics in Early Childhood Special Education, 2*(3), 87–95.

Olds, A. R. (1982b). *Humanizing the pediatric hospital environment. Adaptive Environments Conference Papers* (pp. 59–72). Boston: Adaptive Environments.

Olson, M. R. (1983). A study of the exploratory behavior of legally blind and sighted preschoolers. *Exceptional Children, 50*(2), 130–138.

O'Meara, K., McAuliffe, M., Motherway, D., & Dunleavy, M. (1983). Preadmission programs: Development, implementation and evaluation. *Children's Health Care, 11*(4), 137–141.

O'Neill, S., & Levy, L. (1981). *Simple justice: A case for mainstreaming the severely emotionally handicapped bilingual preschool child.* Paper presented at the annual meeting of the Council for Exceptional Children, New Orleans.

Opie, I. & Opie, P. (1959). *The lore and language of school children.* London: Clarendon Press.

Opie, I., & Opie, P. (1969). *Children's games in streets and playgrounds.* London: Clarendon Press.

Oremland, E. K., & Oremland, J. D. (1973). *The effects of hospitalization on children: Models for their care.* Springfield, IL: Charles C Thomas.

Orlick, T. (1978). *The cooperative sports and games book: Challenge without competition.* New York: Pantheon.

Osmon, F. L. (1971). *Patterns for designing children's centers.* New York: Educational Facilities Laboratories.

Ostroff, E. (1978). *Humanizing environments: A primer.* Cambridge, MA: The Ford Guild.

Ostroff, E., & Tomashiro, R. (1976). *Transforming institutions with play, arts, environmental design.* Amherst: University of Massachusetts, School of Education.

Ott, J. N. (1973). *Health and light.* New York: Simon & Schuster.

Overton, W., & Jackson, J. (1973). The representation of imagined objects in action sequences: A developmental study. *Child Development, 44,* 309–314.

Palmer, R. (1971). *Space, time and grouping.* New York: Citation Press.

Papandropoulou, I., & Sinclair, H. (1974). What is a word? Experimental study of children's ideas on grammar. *Human Development, 17*(4), 241–258.

Parke, R. D. (1978). Children's home environment: Social and cognitive affects. In I. Altman & J. Wohlwill (Eds.), *Human behavior and the environment: Vol. 3. Children and the environment* (pp. 33–81). New York: Plenum Press.

Parnell, K., & Ketterson, P. (1980). What should a playground offer? *The Elementary School Journal, 80*(5), 232–238.

Parry, M. (1972). Infant's responses to novelty in familiar and unfamiliar settings. *Child Development, 43,* 233–237.

Parsons, T. (1970). *Social structure and personality.* New York: Free Press.

Parten, M. (1932). Social participation among pre-school children. *Journal of Abnormal and Social Psychology, 27,* 243–269.

Parten, M. (1933). Social play among preschool children. *Journal of Abnormal and Social Psychology, 28,* 136–147.

Peck, C. A., Apolloni, T., Cooke, T. P., & Raver, S. A. (1978). Teaching retarded preschoolers to imitate the free play behavior of nonretarded classmates: Trained and generalized effects. *The Journal of Special Education, 12*(2) 195–207.

Peck, J., & Goldman, R. (1978). *The behaviors of kindergarten children under selected conditions in the social and physical environment.* Paper presented at the annual meeting of the American Educational Research Association. Toronto. (ERIC Document Reproduction Service No. ED 152 436)

Pellegrini, A. D. (1980). The relationship between kindergartners' play and achievement in pre-reading, language, and writing. *Psychology in the Schools, 17*(4), 530–535.

Pellegrini, A. D. (1981). Speech play and language development in young children. *Journal of Research and Development in Education, 14*(13), 75–80.

Pellegrini, A. D. (1982a). Development of preschoolers' social cognitive play behaviors. *Perceptual and Motor Skills, 55,* 1109–1110.

Pellegrini, A. D. (1982b). Preschoolers' generation of cohesive text in two play contexts. *Discourse Processes, 5,* 101–107.

Pellegrini, A. D. (1984a). The effects of exploration and play on young children's associative fluency: A review and extension of training studies. In T. D. Yawkey & A. D. Pellegrini (Eds.), *Child's play: Developmental and applied* (pp. 237–253). Hillsdale, NJ: Erlbaum.

Pellegrini, A. D. (1984b). Training teachers to assess children's play. *Journal of Education for Teaching, 10*(3), 233–241.

Peller, L. E. (1952). Models of children's play. *Mental Hygiene, 36* 66–83.

Peller, L. E. (1954). Libidinal phases, ego development and play. *Psychoanalytic Study of the Child, 9,* 178–199.

Pepler, D., & Ross, H. S. (1981). The effects of play on convergent and divergent problem-solving. *Child development, 52,* 1202–1210.

Pepler, D., & Rubin, K. H. (1982). Current issues in the study of children's play. *Human Development, 25*(6), 443–447.

Perry, D. G., & Bussey, K. (1979). The social learning theory of sex differences: Imitation is alive and well. *Journal of Personality and Social Psychology, 37,* 1699–1712.

Perry, D. G., Bussey, K., & Redman, J. (1977). Reward-induced decreased play effects: Reattribution of motivation, competing responses or avoiding frustration. *Child Development, 48,* 1369–1374.

Peterson, P. L., & Fennema, E. (1985). Effective teaching, student engagement in classroom activities, and sex-related differences in learning mathematics. *American Educational Research Journal, 22*(3), 309–335.

Petrillo, M., & Sanger, S. (1980). *Emotional care of hospitalized children.* Philadelphia: Lippincott.

Pfeffer, C. R. (1979). Clinical observations of play of hospitalized suicidal children. *Suicide and Life Threatening Behavior, 9*(4), 235–244.

Phillips, R. (1945). Doll play as a function of the realism of the materials and the length of the experimental session. *Child Development, 16,* 123–143.

Phyfe-Perkins, E. (1980). Children's behavior in preschool settings: The influence of the physical environment. In L. G. Katz (Ed.), *Current topics in ea* (Vol. 3, pp. 91–125). Norwood, NJ:

Piaget, J. (1926). *Language and* London: Routledge & Kegan Paul.

Piaget, J. (1932). *The moral jud* York: Free Press.

Piaget, J. (1952). *The origins of* New York: International Universities

Piaget, J. (1954). *The construction of reality in the child.* New York: Basic Books.

Piaget, J. (1962). *Play, dreams and imitation in childhood.* New York: Norton.

Piaget, J. (1966). Response to Brian Sutton-Smith. *Psychological Review, 73,* 111–112.

Piaget, J. (1972). Some aspects of operations. In M. W. Piers (Ed.), *Play and development* (pp. 15–27). New York: W. W. Norton.

Piaget, J., & Inhelder, B. (1956). *The child's conception of space.* New York: Norton.

Piers, M. (Ed.). (1972). *Play and development.* New York: Norton.

Piestrup, A. M. (1981). *Preschool children use Apple II to test reading skills program.* Portola Valley, CA: Advanced Learning Technology. (ERIC Document Reproduction Service No. ED 202 476)

Pinskton, E. M., Reese, N. M., LeBlanc, J. M., & Baer, D. M. (1973). Independent control of a child's aggression and peer interaction by contingent teacher attention. *Journal of Applied Behavior Analysis, 6,* 115–124.

Pitcher, E. G., & Schultz, L. H. (1983). *Boys and girls at play: The development of sex roles.* South Hadley, MA: Praeger.

Plutchik, R. (1983). Emotions in early development: A psychoevolutionary approach. In R. Plutchik & H. Kellerman (Eds.), *Emotion: Theory, research, and experience: Vol. 2. Emotions in early development* (pp. 221–257). New York: Academic Press.

Polk, C. L. H., & Goldstein, D. (1980). Early reading and concrete operations. *The Journal of Psychology, 106,* 111–116.

Pollowy, A. M. (1974). The child in the physical environment: A design problem. In G. Coates (Ed.), *Alternative learning environments* (pp. 370–381). Stroudsburg, PA: Dowden, Hutchinson & Ross.

Polya, G. (1971). *How to solve it* (2nd Ed.). Princeton, NJ: Princeton University Press.

Porter, J. D. (1971). *Black child, white child.* Cambridge, MA: Harvard University Press.

Power, T. G., & Parke, R. D. (1980). Play as a context for early learning: Lab and home analyses. In I. E. Sigel & L. J. Laosa (Eds.), *Families as learning environments for children* (pp. 147–178). New York: Plenum Press.

Power, T. G., & Parke, R. D. (1983). Patterns of mother and father play with their 8-month-old infant: A multiple analysis approach. *Infant Behavior, 6,* 453–459.

Preiser, W. F. E. (1972). Work in progress: The behavior of nursery school children under different spatial densities. *Man Environment Systems, 2,* 247–250.

Prescott, E. (1978). Is day care as good as a good home? *Young Children, 33*(2), 13–19.

Prescott, E., Jones, E., & Kritchevsky, S. (1972). *Day care as a child rearing environment, 2.* Washington, DC: National Association for the Education of Young Children.

Proshansky, E., & Wolfe, M. (1975). The physical setand open education. In T. G. David & B. D. Wright *Learning environments* (pp. 31–48). Chicago: UniChicago Press.

Prugh, D. G., Staub, E. M., Sands, H. H., Kirchbaum, R. M., & Leniham, E. (1953). A study of the emotional reactions of children and families to hospitalization and illness. *American Journal of Orthopsychiatry, 23,* 70–106.

Pulaski, M. (1970). Play as a function of toy structure and fantasy predisposition. *Child Development, 41,* 531–537.

Pulaski, M. A. (1973). Toys and imaginative play. In J. L. Singer (Ed.), *The child's world of make-believe: Experimental studies of imaginative play* (pp. 74–103). New York: Academic Press.

Putallatz, M., & Gottman, J. M. (1981). Social skills and group acceptance. In S. R. Asher & J. M. Gottman (Eds.), *The development of children's friendships* (pp. 116–149). New York: Cambridge University Press.

Quilitch, H., & Risley, T. R. (1973). The effects of play materials on social play. *Journal of Applied Behavior Analysis, 6,* 573–578.

Quinn, J. M. & Rubin, K. H. (1984). The play of handicapped children. In T. Yawkey & A. Pellegrini (Eds.), *Child's play: Developmental and applied* (pp. 63–80). Hillsdale, NJ: Erlbaum.

Radke-Yarrow, M. R., & Zahn-Waxler, C. (1976). Dimensions and correlates of prosocial behaviors in young children. *Child Development, 47,* 118–125.

Radke-Yarrow, M. R., Zahn-Waxler, C., & Chapman, M. (1983). Children's prosocial dispositions and behavior. In E. M. Hetherington (Ed.), & P. H. Mussen (Series Ed.). *Handbook of child psychology: Vol. 4. Socialization, personality, and social development.* New York: Wiley.

Radler, D. H., & Kephart, N. C. (1960). *Success through play.* New York: Harper & Row.

Rambusch, N. (1982). Organization of environments. In D. T. Streets (Ed.), *Administering daycare and preschool programs* (pp. 71–87). Boston: Allyn & Bacon.

Ramsey, P. G. (1985). *Early ethnic socialization in a mono-racial community.* Paper presented at the biennial meeting of the Society for Research in Child Development, Toronto.

Ramsey, P. G. (1987). *Teaching and learning in a diverse world: Multicultural education for young children.* New York: Teachers College Press.

Rangell, L. (1967). Psychoanalysis, affects and the "human core". On the relationship of psychoanalysis to the behavioral sciences. *The Psychoanalytic Quarterly, 36,* 172–202.

Rapaport, D. (1953). On the psychoanalytic theory of affect. *International Journal of Psycho-Analysis, 34,* 177–198.

Rarick, G. L., & Larsen, G. L. (1958). Observations on frequency and intensity of isometric muscular effect in developing static muscular strength in post-pubescent males. *Research Quarterly, 29,* 333–411.

Rasmussen, M. (Ed.). (1958). *Space, arrangement, beauty in school.* Washington, DC: Association for Childhood Education International.

Redl, F. (1959). The impact of game ingredients on children's play behavior. In B. Schaeffner (Ed.), *Group processes* (pp. 33–81). New York: Josiah Macy Jr., Foundation.

Rheingold, H. L. (1979, March). *Helping by two-year-old children.* Paper presented at the biennial meeting of the Society for Research in Child Development, San Francisco.

Rheingold, H. L., & Cook, K. V. (1975). The contents of boys' and girls' rooms as an index of parents' behavior. *Child Development, 46*, 459–463.

Rheingold, H. L., & Eckerman, C. (1970). The infant separates himself from his mother. *Science, 168*, 78–93.

Rheingold, H. L., Hay, D. F., & West, M. J. (1976). Sharing in the second year of life. *Child Development, 47*, 1148–1158.

Richardson, S. A., & Royce, J. (1968). Race and physical handicap in children's preference for other children. *Child Development, 39*, 467–480.

Riffee, D. M. (1981). Self-esteem changes in hospitalized school-age children. *Nursing Research, 30*(2), 94–97.

Riguet, C. B., Taylor, N. D., Benaroya, S., & Klein, L. S. (1981). Symbolic play in autistic, Down's, and normal children of equivalent mental age. *Journal of Autism and Developmental Disorders, 11*(4), 439–448.

Ritchie, J. A. (1979). Preparation of toddlers and preschool children for hospital procedures. *The Canadian Nurse, 75*, 30–32.

Rittenhouse, A. M. (1974). Measuring the impact. *Parks and Recreation, 9*, 24–26.

Roberts, A. (1980). *Out to play: The middle years of childhood*. Aberdeen, Scotland: Aberdeen University Press.

Roberts, J. M., & Foreman, M. L. (1971). Riddles: Expressive models of interrogation. *Ethnology, 10*, 509–533.

Roberts, J. M. & Sutton-Smith, B. (1962). Child training and game involvement. *Ethnology, 2*, 166–185.

Robertson, J. (1958). *Young children in hospitals*. New York: Basic Books.

Robertson, J. (1961) (Director) *Two year-old goes to the hospital* [Film]. New York: New York University.

Robinson, C. (1978). Sex-typed behavior in children's spontaneous play. *The Association for the Anthropological Study of Play Newsletter, 4*, 14–17.

Robinson, C. A. (1985). Double bind: A dilemma for parents of chronically ill children. *Pediatric Nursing, 11*(2), 112–115.

Robinson, E. S. (1920). The compensatory function of make believe play. *Psychological Review, 27*, 429–439.

Rogers, C. (1942). *Counseling and psychotherapy*. Boston: Houghton-Mifflin.

Rogers, D. L. (1985). Relationships between block play and the social development of young children. *Early Child Development and Care, 20*, 245–261.

Rogers, P. J., & Miller, J. V. (1984). Playway mathematics: Theory, practice and some results. *Educational Research, 26*(3), 200–207.

Rogers, S. J., & Puchalski, C. B. (1984a). Development of symbolic play in visually impaired young children. *Topics in Early Childhood Special Education, 3*(4), 57–63.

Rogers, S. J., & Puchalski, C. B. (1984b). Social characteristics of visually impaired infants' play. *Topics in Early Childhood Special Education, 3*(4), 52–56.

Rogoff, B., & Gardner, W. (1984). Adult guidance of cognitive development. In B. Rogoff & J. Love (Eds.), *Everyday cognition: Its development in social context* (pp. 95–116). Cambridge, MA: Harvard University Press.

Rogow, S. M. (1984). The uses of social routines to facilitate communication in visually impaired and multihandicapped children. *Topics in Early Childhood Special Education, 3*(4), 64–70.

Rohwer, W. (1971). Prime time for education: Early childhood or adolescence? *Harvard Educational Review, 41*, 316–342.

Romotowski, J. H., & Trepanier, M. L. (1977). *Examining and influencing the home reading behaviors of young children*. Dearborn, MI (ERIC Document Reproduction Service No. ED 195-938).

Roper, R., & Hinde, R. A. (1978). Social behavior in a play group: Consistency and complexity. *Child Development, 49*, 570–579.

Rosen, C. E. (1974). The effects of sociodramatic play on problem solving behavior among culturally disadvantaged children. *Child Development, 45*, 920–927.

Rosenberg, B. G., & Sutton-Smith, B. (1960). A revised conception of masculine-feminine differences in play activities. *Journal of Genetic Psychology, 96*, 165–170.

Rosenblatt, D. (1977). Developmental tasks in infants' play. In B. Tizard & D. Harvey (Eds.), *Biology of Play* (pp. 33–34). London: Heinemann.

Ross, H. S. (1974). The influence of novelty and complexity on exploratory behavior in 12-month-old infants. *Journal of Experimental Child Psychology, 17*(3), 436–451.

Ross, H. S., & Goldman, B. D. (1977). Establishing new social relations in infancy. In T. Alloway, L. Krames, & P. Pliner (Eds.), *Advances in the study of communication and affect: Vol. 3. Attachment behaviors* (pp. 61–79). New York: Plenum Press.

Ross, H. S., & Kay, D. A. (1980). The origins of social games. In K. H. Rubin (Ed.), *New directions for child development: Children's play* (No. 9, pp. 17–31). San Francisco: Jossey-Bass.

Roswal, G., & Frith, G. H. (1980). The children's developmental play program: Physical activity designed to facilitate the growth and development of mildly handicapped children. *Education and Training of the Mentally Retarded, 15*(4), 322–324.

Rubin, K. H. (1977). Play behaviors of young children. *Young Children, 32*(6), 16–24.

Rubin, K. H. (1980). Fantasy play: Its role in the development of social skills and social cognition. In K. H. Rubin (Ed.), *New directions for child development: Children's play* (No. 9, 69–84). San Francisco: Jossey-Bass.

Rubin, K. H. (1982a). Early play theories revisited: Contributions to contemporary research and theory. In D. J. Pepler & K. H. Rubin (Eds.), *The play of children: Current theory and research* (pp. 4–14). Basel, Switzerland: Karger AG.

Rubin, K. H.. (1982b). Nonsocial play in preschoolers: Necessarily evil? *Child Development, 53*, 651–657.

Rubin, K. H. (1985a). Play, peer interaction, and social development. In C. C. Brown & A. W. Gottfried (Eds.), *Play interactions: The role of toys and parental involvement in children's development* (pp. 88–96). Skillman, NJ: Johnson & Johnson.

Rubin, K. H. (1985b). *The play observation scale (POS)* (Revised ed.). Waterloo, Ontario: University of Waterloo.

Rubin, K. H., Daniels-Beerness, T., & Hayvren, M. (1982). Correlates of peer acceptance and rejection in early childhood. *Canadian Journal of Behavioral Science, 14*, 338–349.

Rubin, K. N., Fein, G. G., Vandenberg, B. (1983). Play. In E. M. Hetherington (Ed.) & P. H. Mussen (Series Ed.), *Handbook of child psychology: Vol. 4. Socialization, personality, and social development* (pp. 698–774). New York: Wiley.

Rubin, K. H., & Hayvren, M. (1981). The social and cognitive play of preschool-aged children differing with regard to sociometric status. *Journal of Research and Development in Education, 14*(3), 116–122.

Rubin, K. H., & Krasnor, L. R. (1980). Changes in the play behaviors of preschoolers: A short-term longitudinal investigation. *Canadian Journal of Behavioral Science, 12*, 278–282.

Rubin, K. H., & Maioni, T. L. (1975). Play preference and its relationship to egocentrism, popularity, and classification skills in preschoolers. *Merrill-Palmer Quarterly, 21*(3), 171–179.

Rubin, K. H., Maioni, T. L., & Hornung, M. (1976). Free play behaviors in middle and lower class preschoolers: Parten and Piaget revisited. *Child Development, 47*, 414–419.

Rubin, K. H., & Pepler, D. J. (1982). Children's play: Piaget's views reconsidered. *Contemporary Educational Psychology, 7*(3), 289–299.

Rubin, K. H., & Seibel, G. (1979). *The effects of ecological setting on the cognitive and social play behaviors of preschoolers*. Paper presented at the annual meeting of the American Educational Research Association, San Francisco. (ERIC Document Reproduction Service No. ED 168 691)

Rubin, K. H., Watson, K., & Jambor, T. (1978). Free play behaviors in preschool and kindergarten children. *Child Development, 49*, 534–536.

Rudolph, N. (1974). *Workyards*. New York: Teachers College Press.

Sachs, J. (1980). The role of adult-child play in language development. In K. H. Rubin (Ed.), *New directions in child development: Children's play* (No. 9, pp. 33–48). San Francisco: Jossey-Bass.

Sack, N. H., Mason, R., & Higgins, J. E. (1985). The single-parent family and abusive child punishment. *American Journal of Orthopsychiatry, 55*(2), 252–259.

Saltz, E., & Brodie, J. (1982). Pretend-play: Training in childhood: A review and critique. In D. J. Pepler & K. H. Rubin (Eds.), *The play of children: Current theory and research* (pp. 97–113). Basel, Switzerland: Karger AG.

Saltz, E., Dixon, D., & Johnson, H., (1977). Training disadvantaged preschoolers on various fantasy activities: Effects on cognitive functioning and impulse control. *Child Development, 48*, 367–380.

Saltz, E., & Johnson, J. (1974). Training for thematic-fantasy play in culturally disadvantaged children: Preliminary results. *Journal of Educational Psychology, 66*, 623–630.

Samuels, H. (1980). The effect of an older sibling on infant locomotor exploration of a new environment. *Child Development, 51*, 607–609.

Sanches, M., & Kirschenblatt-Gimblett, B. (1976). Children's traditional speech play and child language. In B. Kirschenblatt-Gimblett (Ed.), *Speech play* (pp. 65–110). Philadelphia: University of Pennsylvania Press.

Sander, L. (1975). Infant and caretaking environment: Investigation and conceptualization of adaptive behavior in a system of increasing complexity. In E. J. Anthony (Ed.), *Explorations in child psychiatry* (pp. 129–166). New York: Plenum Press.

Sanders, K., & Harper, L. (1976). Free play fantasy behavior in preschool children: Relations among gender, age, season and location. *Child Development, 47*, 1182–1185.

Saracho, O. N. (1983). Assessing cognitive style in young children. *Studies in Educational Evaluation, 8*, 229–236.

Saracho, O. N. (1985). Young children's play behaviors and cognitive styles. *Early Child Development and Care, 22*(1), 1–18.

Saracho, O. N. (1986). Play and young children's learning. In B. Spodek (Ed.), *Today's kindergarten: Exploring the knowledge base, expanding the curriculum* (pp. 91–109). New York: Teachers College Press.

Saracho, O. N. & Spodek B. (1986). Cognitive style and children's learning: Individual variations in cognitive processes. In L. G. Katz (Ed.), *Current topics in early childhood education* (Vol. 6, pp. 177–194). Norwood, NJ: Ablex

Sarbin, T. R. (1962). A preface to a psychological analysis of the self. In C. Goodman & K. J. Gergan (Eds.), *The self in social interaction* (pp. 179–188). New York: Wiley.

Sarner, M. (1978, June). Growing up old. *Canadian Weekend Magazine*, 3–5.

Sarnoff, C. (1976). *Latency*. New York: Aronson.

Satir, V. (1967). *Conjoint family therapy*. Palo Alto, CA: Science & Behavior Books.

Satir, V. (1972). *Peoplemaking*. Palo Alto, CA: Science and Behavior Books.

Sawin, D. B. (1980). *A field study of children's reactions to distress in their peers*. Unpublished manuscript. Austin, TX: University of Texas.

Scarlett, W. G. (1980). Social isolation from agemates among nursery school children. *Journal of Child Psychology and Psychiatry, 21*, 231–240.

Scarlett, W. G., & Ballenger, C. (no date). *When children fail to find friends*. Unpublished manuscript.

Scarr, S. (1985). Constructing psychology. Making facts and fables of our times. *American Psychologist, 40*, 499–512.

Schachter, F. F. (1981). Toddlers with employed mothers. *Child Development, 52*, 958–964.

Schaefer, C., & Millman, H. (1980). *Therapies for children*. San Francisco: Jossey-Bass.

Schafer, R. (1964). The clinical analysis of affects. *Journal of the American Psychoanalytic Association, 12*, 275–299.

Schaffer, H. R., & Emerson, P. E. (1964). *The development of social attachments in infancy (Monographs of the Society for Research in Child Development, 29*(3, Serial No. 94).

Schank, R., & Abelson, R. (1977). Scripts, plans, and knowledge. In P. Johnson-Laird & P. Wason (Eds.), *Thinking: Reading in cognitive science* (pp. 421–432). New York: Cambridge University Press.

Schiller, F. (1954). *On the aesthetic education of man*. New Haven, CT: Yale University Press. (Original work published 1875)

Schlosberg, H. (1947). The concept of play. *Psychological Review, 54*, 229–231.

Schmale, A. H. (1964). A genetic view of affects: With special references to the genesis of helplessness and hopelessness. *Psychoanalytic Study of the Child, 19,* 287–310.

Schneider-Rosen, K., & Cicchetti, D. (1984). The relationship between affect and cognition in maltreated infants: Quality of attachment and the development of visual self-recognition. *Child Development, 55,* 648–658.

Schoggen, P., & Schoggen, M. (1985). Play, exploration, and density. In J. F. Wohlwill & W. VanVliet (Eds.), *Habitats for children: The impacts of density* (pp. 77–95). Hillsdale, NJ: Erlbaum.

Scholtz, G., & Ellis, M. (1975). Repeated exposure to objects and peers in a play setting. *Journal of Experimental Child Psychology, 19,* 448–455.

Schools Council. (1971). *Informal schools in Britain today.* New York: Citation Press.

Schreier, A., & Kaplan, D. (1983). The effectiveness of a preoperation preparation program in reducing anxiety in children. *Children's Health Care, 11*(4), 142–148.

Schurr, E. (1980). *Movement experiences for children: A humanistic approach to elementary school physical education.* Englewood Cliffs, NJ: Prentice-Hall.

Schwartz, B. H., Albino, J. E., & Tedesco, L. A. (1983). Effects of psychological preparation on children hospitalized for dental operations. *Journal of Pediatrics, 102*(4), 634–638.

Schwartzman, H. (1978). *Transformations: The anthropology of children's play.* New York: Plenum Press.

Schwartzman, H. B. (1979). The sociocultural context of play. In B. Sutton-Smith (Ed.), *Play and learning* (pp. 239–255). New York: Gardner Press.

Schwartzman, H. B. (1980). *Play and culture.* West Point, NY: Leisure Press.

Schwartzman, H. B. (1984). Imaginative play: Deficit or difference? In T. D. Yawkey & A. D. Pellegrini (Eds.), *Child's play: Developmental and applied* (pp. 49–62). Hillsdale, NJ: Erlbaum.

Scott, S. (1985). What works for abused children: Environments and activities. *Beginnings, 2*(3), 20–22.

Scribner, S., & Cole, M. (1973). Cognitive consequences of formal and informal education. *Science, 182,* 553–559.

Sears, R. R. (1947a). Child psychology. In W. Dennis (Ed.), Current trends in psychology (pp. 50–74). Pittsburgh, PA: University of Pittsburgh Press.

Sears, R. R. (1947b). Influence of methodological factors on doll play performance. *Child Development, 18,* 190–197.

Sears, R. R. (1950). Relation of fantasy aggression to interpersonal aggression. *Child Development, 21*(1), 5–6.

Sears, R. R. (1961). Relationship of early social experience to aggression in middle childhood. *Journal of Abnormal and Social Psychology, 63*(3), 466–492.

Sears, R. R., Maccoby, E., & Levin, H. (1957). *Patterns of child rearing.* New York: Harper & Row.

Sears, R. R., Rau, L., & Alpert, R. (1965). *Identification and child rearing.* Stanford, CA: Stanford University.

Sears, R. R., & Whitney, J. W. (1953). Some child-rearing antecedents of aggression and dependency in young children. *Genetic Psychology Monographs, 47,* 135–236.

Selman, R. L. (1976). Social-cognitive understanding: A guide to educational and clinical practice. In T. Lickona (ED.), *Moral development and behavior* (pp. 299–316). New York: Holt, Rinehart, & Winston.

Selman, R. L. (1981). The child as a friendship philosopher. In S. R. Asher and J. M. Gottman, (Eds.), *The development of children's friendships* (pp. 242–272). New York: Cambridge University Press.

Senn, M. J. E. (1945). Emotional aspects of convalescence: Fulfillment of child's emotional needs is factor in physical as well as psychological recovery. *Child, 10,* 24.

Serbin, L. A., Tonick, I. J., & Sternglanz, S. H. (1977). Shaping cooperative cross-sex play. *Child Development, 48,* 924–929.

Severeide, R. C., & Pizzini, E. L. (1984). The role of play in science. *Science and Children, 21*(8), 58–61.

Shantz, C. U. (1975). The development of social cognition. In E. M. Hetherington (Ed.), *Review of child development research: Vol. 5* (pp. 257–323). Chicago: University of Chicago Press.

Shantz, C. U. (1983). Social cognition. In J. H. Flavell & E. M. Markham (Eds.), P. H. Mussen (Series Ed.), *Handbook of child psychology: Vol. 3. Cognitive development* (pp. 495–555).

Shapiro, S. (1975). Preschool ecology: A study of three environmental variables. *Reading Improvement, 12,* 236–241.

Sharan, S. (1980). Cooperative learning in small groups: Recent methods and effects on achievement, attitudes, and ethnic relations. *Review of Educational Research, 50*(2), 241–271.

Sharan, S., & Sharan, Y. (1976). *Small group teaching.* Englewood Cliffs, NJ: Educational Technology Publications.

Shea, J. D. (1981). Changes in interpersonal distances and categories of play behavior in the early weeks of preschool. *Developmental Psychology, 17,* 417–425.

Sheehan, G. A. (1975). *Dr. Sheehan on running.* Mountain View, CA: World.

Sheehan, R., & Day, D. (1974). Is open space just empty space? *Day Care and Early Education, 3,* 10–13, 47.

Shere, E., & Kastenbaum, R. (1966). Mother-child interactions and cerebral palsy: Environmental and psychosocial obstacles to cognitive development. *Genetic Psychology Monographs, 73*(2).

Sherman, M., Shapiro, T., & Glassman, M. (1983). Play and language in developmentally disordered preschoolers: A new approach to classification. *Journal of the American Academy of Child Psychiatry, 22,* 511–524.

Shimada, S., Kai, Y., & Sano, R. (1981). Development of symbolic play in late infancy. *RIEEC Research Bulletin, 17,* Tokyo, Japan: Gakugi University.

Shirley, M. M. (1931). *The first two years.* Minneapolis: University of Minnesota Press.

Shotwell, J., Wolf, D., & Gardner, H. (1979). Exploring early symbolization: Styles of achievement. In B. Sutton-Smith (Ed.), *Play and learning* (pp. 127–156). New York: Gardner Press.

Shotwell, J.. Wolf, D., & Gardner, H. (1980). Styles of achievement in early symbol use. In M. Foster & S. Brandes (Eds.), *Symbol as sense: New approaches to the analysis of meaning* (pp. 175–199). New York: Academic Press.

Shultz, T. R. (1979). Play as arousal modulation. In B. Sutton-Smith (Ed.), *Play and learning* (pp. 7–22). New York: Gardner Press.

Shure, M. B. (1963). The psychological ecology of a nursery school. *Child Development, 34,* 979–992.

Shure, M. B., & Spivack, G. (1978). *Problem-solving techniques in childrearing.* San Francisco: Jossey-Bass.

Siedentop, D., Herkowitz, J., & Rink, J. (1984). *Elementary physical education methods.* Englewood-Cliffs, NJ: Prentice-Hall.

Silver, P. G., & Ramsey, P. G. (1983). Participant observation: Broadening points of view. *Early Child Development and Care, 10,* 147–156.

Silvern, S. B. Williamson, P. A., & Countermine, T. A. (1985). Videogame play and social behavior: Preliminary findings. In J. L. Frost, & S. Sunderlin (Eds.). *When children play* (pp. 279–282). Wheaton, MD: Association for Childhood Education.

Simeonsson, R., Grunewald, K., & Scheiner, A. (1978). Normalization and Piagetian theory. In R. Weizmann (Ed.), *Piagetian theory and the helping professions: Vol. 1. Emphasis: Social work and psychological services* (pp. 290–298). Proceedings from the Seventh Interdisciplinary Seminar. Los Angeles: University of Southern California.

Simon, J., & Larson, C. (1985). Detecting experience with violence: The uses of play interviews. *Beginnings, 2*(3), 12–15.

Simon, T., & Smith, P. K. (1985). A role for play in children's problem-solving: Time to think again. In J. L. Frost & S. Sunderlin (Eds.), *When children play* (pp. 55–61). Wheaton, MD: Association for Childhood Education International.

Sinclair, H. (1970). The transition from sensorimotor to symbolic activity. *Interchange, 1,* 119–126.

Singer, D. G., & Revenson, R. A. (1978). *A Piaget primer: How a child thinks.* New York: New American Library.

Singer, D. G., & Rummo, J. (1973). Ideational creativity and behavioral style in kindergarten aged children. *Developmental Psychology, 8,* 154–161.

Singer, D. G., & Singer, J. L. (1977). *Partners in play.* New York: Harper & Row.

Singer, D. G., & Singer, J. L. (1978). *Some correlates of imaginative play in preschoolers.* Paper presented at the annual meeting of the American Psychological Association, Toronto. (ERIC Document Reproduction Service No. ED 174 302)

Singer, D. G., & Singer, J. L. (1981). Television and the developing imagination of the child. *Journal of Broadcasting, 25*(4), 373–387.

Singer, D. G., & Singer, J. L. (1984). Parents as mediators of the child's television environment. *Educational Media International, 4,* 7–11.

Singer, D. G., & Singer, J. L. (1985). *Make believe: Games and activities to foster imaginative play in young children.* Glenview, IL: Scott, Foresman.

Singer, D. G., Singer, J. L., & Zuckerman, D. (1981). *Teaching television: How to use television to your child's advantage.* New York: Dial.

Singer, J. L. (1973). *The child's world of make-believe: Experimental studies of imaginative play.* New York: Academic Press.

Singer, J. L. (1977). Imagination and make-believe play in early childhood: Some educational implications. *Journal of Mental Imagery, 1,* 127–144.

Singer, J. L. (1984). *The human personality.* San Diego: Harcourt Brace Jovanovich.

Singer, J. L. (1985). Transference and the human condition: A cognitive-affective perspective. *Psychoanalytic Psychology, 2*(3), 189–219.

Singer, J. L., & Singer, D. G. (1976). Imaginative play and pretending in early childhood: Some experimental approaches. In A. Davis (Ed.), *Child personality and psychopathology: Current topics* (Vol. 3, pp. 69–112). New York: Wiley.

Singer, J. L., & Singer, D. G. (1978). *Television-viewing and imaginative play in preschoolers: A developmental and parent-intervention study.* (Progress Report No. 2). New Haven, CT: Yale University. (ERIC Document Reproduction Service No. ED 168 576)

Singer, J. L., & Singer, D. G. (1979). The value of the imagination. In B. Sutton-Smith (Ed.), *Play and learning* (pp. 195–218). New York: Gardner Press.

Singer, J. L., & Singer, D. G. (1983). Psychologists look at television: Cognitive, developmental, personality and social policy implications. *American Psychologist, 38,* 826–834.

Singer, J. L., Singer, D. G., & Rapaczynski, W. (1984). Family patterns and television-viewing as predictors of children's beliefs and aggression. *Journal of Communication, 34,* 73–89.

Singer, J. L., & Streiner, B. F. (1966). Imaginative content in the dreams and fantasy play of blind and sighted children. *Perceptual and Motor Skills, 22,* 475–482.

Singleton, L. C., & Asher, S. R. (1977). Peer preferences and social interaction among third-grade children in an integrated school district. *Journal of Educational Psychology, 69,* 330–336.

Sitton, T., & Jeter, J. (1980, March). Discovering children's folklore. *Teacher, 97*(6), 58–61.

Skinner, B. F. (1974). *About behaviorism.* New York: Knopf.

Skipper, J. K., & Leonard, R. C. (1968). Children, stress, and hospitalization: A field experiment. *Journal of Health and Social Behavior, 9*(4), 274–287.

Slavin, R. E. (1978). Student teams and achievement divisions. *Journal of Research and Development in Education, 12,* 39–49.

Slavin, R. E. (1980a). *Using student team learning.* Baltimore: Johns Hopkins University, Center for Social Organization of Schools.

Slavin, R. E. (1980b). Cooperative learning. *Review of Educational Research, 71,* 381–387.

Slavin, R. E. (1980c). Cooperative learning in teams: State of the art. *Educational Psychologist, 15*(2), 93–111.

Slavin, R. E. (1983). *Cooperative learning.* New York: Longman.

Smilansky, S. (1968). *The effects of sociodramatic play on disadvantaged preschool children.* New York: Wiley.

Smith, A. B. (1983). Sex differences in activities in early childhood centres. *New Zealand Journal of Psychology, 12*(2), 74–81.

Smith, C., & Lloyd, B. (1978). Maternal behavior and perceived sex of infant: Revisited. *Child Development, 49,* 1263–1265.

Smith, K. E., & Jaworski, A. P. (1984). Physical environments for toddlers in group care. *Child Care Quarterly, 13*(1), 52–61.

Smith, P. (1981). The impact of computerization on children's toys and games. *Journal of Children in Contemporary Society, 14*(1), 73–82.

Smith, P. K. (1973). Temporal clusters and individual differences in the behavior of preschool children. In R. P. Michael & J. H. Crook (Eds.), *Comparative ecology and behaviour of primates* (pp. 751–798). London: Academic Press.

Smith, P. K. (1974). Aspects of the playground environment. In D. Canter & T. Lee (Eds.), *Psychology and the built environment* (pp. 56–62). Tonbridge, Kent, England: Architecture Press.

Smith, P. K. (1977). Social and fantasy play in young children. In B. Tizard & D. Harvey (Eds.), *Biology of play* (pp. 123–145). London: Heinemann.

Smith, P. K. (1981). A comparison of the effects of fantasy play tutoring and skills tutoring in nursery classes. *International Journal of Behavioral Development, 4*(4), 421–441.

Smith, P. K. (1983). Differences or deficits? The significance of pretend and sociodramatic play. *Developmental Review, 3,* 6–10.

Smith, P. K., & Connolly, K. J. (1972). Patterns of play and social interaction in pre-school children. In N. B. Jones (Ed.), *Ethological studies of child behavior* (pp. 65–95). New York: Cambridge University Press.

Smith, P. K., & Connolly, K. J. (1976). Social and aggressive behavior in preschool children as a function of crowding. *Social Science Information, 16,* 601–620.

Smith, P. K., & Daglish, L. (1977). Sex differences in infant and parent behavior. *Child Development, 48,* 1250–1254.

Smith, P. K., & Dutton, S. (1979). Play and training in direct and innovative problem solving. *Child Development, 50,* 830–836.

Smith, P. K., & Vollstedt, R. (1985). On defining play: An empirical study of the relationship between play and various play criteria. *Child Development, 56,* 1042–1050.

Snow, C. E. (1983). Literacy and language: Relationships during the preschool years. *Harvard Educational Review, 55,* 165–189.

Sokal, R. R. (1974). Classification: Purposes, principles, progress, prospects. *Science, 185,* 1115–1123.

Solomon, J. (1951). Therapeutic use of play. In H. H. Anderson & G. L. Anderson (Eds.), *Introduction to Projective Techniques,* pp. 639–661. New York: Prentice-Hall.

Sotamaa, Y. (1980). Criteria for children's playthings and play environments. In P. Wilkinson (Ed.), *In celebration of play* (pp. 257–273). New York: St. Martin's Press.

Speers, R. W. (1975). Variations in separation individuation and implications for play ability and learning. In D. Bergma (Ed.), *The infant at risk* (pp. 77–100). New York: Intercontinental Medical Book Corporation.

Spencer, H. (1954). *Principles of psychology* (Vol. 2). New York: Appleton. (Original work published in 1873.)

Spidell, R. A. (1985). *Preschool teachers' interventions in children's play.* Unpublished doctoral dissertation, University of Illinois, Urbana-Champaign.

Spitz, R. (1945). Hospitalism: An inquiry into the genesis of psychiatric conditions in early childhood. *Psychoanalytic Study of the Child, 1,* 53–74.

Spitz, R. A. (1959). *A genetic field theory of ego formation: Its implications for pathology.* New York: International Universities Press.

Spitz, R., & Cobliner, W. (1965). *The first year of life.* New York: International Universities Press.

Spivack, G., & Shure, M. (1974). *Social adjustment of young children: A cognitive approach to solving real-life problems.* San Francisco: Jossey-Bass.

Spivack, M. (1975). The exceptional environment: Strategies for design. In T. G. David & B. D. Wright (Eds.), *Learning environments* (pp. 121–139). Chicago: University of Chicago Press.

Spivack, M., & Tamer, J. (1981). *Light and color: A designer's guide.* Washington, DC: American Institute of Architects Press.

Spodek, B., Saracho, O. N., & Davis, M. (1987). *Foundations of early childhood education: Teaching three-, four-, and five-year-olds.* Englewood Cliffs, NJ: Prentice-Hall.

Sponseller, D. B. (Ed.). (1974). *Play as a learning medium.* Washington, DC: National Association for the Education of Young Children.

Sponseller, D. B. (1982). Play and early education. In B. Spodek (Ed.), *Handbook of research in early childhood education* (pp. 215–241). New York: Free Press.

Sponseller, D. B., & Jaworski, A. P. (1979). *Social and cognitive complexity in young children's play: A longitudinal analysis.* Paper presented at the meeting of the American Educational Research Association, San Francisco. (ERIC Document Reproduction Service No. ED 171 416)

Sponseller, D. B., & Lowry, M. (1974). Designing a play environment for toddlers. In D. B. Sponseller (Ed.), *Play as a learning medium* (pp. 81–106). Washington, DC: National Association for the Education of Young Children.

Sprung, B. (1978). *Perspectives on non-sexist early childhood education.* New York: Teachers College Press.

Sroufe, L. A. (1979). Socioemotional development. In J. Osofsky (Ed.), *Handbook of infant development* (pp. 426–516). New York: Wiley.

Sroufe, L. A., & Wunsche, J. P. (1972). The development of laughter in the first year of life. *Child Development, 43,* 1326–1344.

Stanley, S. (1969). *Physical education: A movement orientation.* Toronto: McGraw-Hill.

Steele, C., & Nauman, M. (1985). Infants' play on outdoor play equipment. In J. L. Frost & S. Sunderlin (Eds.), *When children play* (pp. 121–129). Wheaton, MD: Association for Childhood Education International.

Stefani, L., & Camaioni, L. (1983). Effects of familiarity on peer interaction in the first year of life. *Early Child Development and Care, 11*(1), 45–54.

Stein, A., & Friederich, L. K. (1972). Television content and young children's behavior. In J. P. Murray, E. A. Rubenstein, & G. A. Comstock (Eds.), *Television and social behavior: Vol. 2. Television and social learning* (pp. 202–317). Washington, DC: U. S. Government Printing Office.

Steiner, G. (1975). *After Babel: Aspects of language and translation*. New York: Oxford University Press.

Sterling, E., Sterling, T., & McIntyre, D. (1983). New health hazards in sealed buildings: Findings from recent research. *American Institute of Architects Journal, 4,* 64–67.

Sterman, M. B., & Hoppenbrouwers, T. (1971). The development of sleep waking and rest-activity patterns from fetus to adult in man. In M. B. Sterman, D. J. McGinty, & A. Adinolfi (Eds.), *Brain development and behavior* (pp. 203–517). New York: Academic Press.

Stern, D. (1971). A micro-analysis of mother-infant interaction: Behavior regulating social contact between a mother and her 3½ month old twins. *Journal of American Academy of Child Psychiatry, 10,* 501–517.

Stern, D. N. (1974a). The goal and structure of mother-infant play. *Journal of the American Academy of Child Psychiatry, 13,* 402–421.

Stern, D. N. (1974b). Mother and infant at play: The dyadic interaction involving facial, vocal, and gaze behaviors. In M. M. Lewis & L. Rosenblum (Eds.), *The effect of the infant on its caregiver* (pp. 187–213). New York: Wiley.

Stern, D. N. (1977). *The first relationship*. Cambridge, MA: Harvard University Press.

Stillwell, J. L. (1987). *Making and using creative play equipment*. Champaign, IL: Human Kinetics.

Stillwell, J. L., & Stockard, J. R. (1983). *Fitness exercises for children*. New York: Leisure Press.

Stocking, H., & Arezzo, P. (1979). *Helping kids make friends*. Allen, TX: Argus Communications.

Stockinger Forys, S. K., & McCune-Nicolich, L. (1984). Shared pretend: Sociodramatic play at three years of age. In I. Bretherton (Ed.), *Symbolic play: The development of social understanding* (pp. 159–193). New York: Academic Press.

Stoneman, Z., Brody, G. H., & Abbott, D. (1983). In-home observations of young Down syndrome children with their mothers and fathers. *American Journal of Mental Deficiency, 87*(6), 591–600.

Strain, P. S. (1975). Increasing social play of severely retarded preschoolers with sociodramatic activities. *Mental Retardation, 13,* 7–9.

Strain, P. S., & Wiegerink, R. (1976). The effects of sociodramatic activities on social interaction among behaviorally disordered preschool children. *Journal of Special Education, 10*(1), 71–75.

Strayer, J. (1980). A naturalistic study of empathic behaviors and their relation to affective states and perspective-taking skills in preschool children. *Child Development, 51,* 815–822.

Strayer, J. (1983). *Emotional and cognitive components of children's empathy*. Paper presented to the Society for Research in Child Development, Detroit.

Sugarman, S. (1983). *Children's early thought: Development in classification*. New York: Cambridge University Press.

Sullivan, H. S. (1953). *The interpersonal theory of psychiatry*. New York: Norton.

Susman, E. J., Trickett, P. K., Iannotti, R. J., Hollenbeck, B. E., & Zahn-Waxler, C. (1985). Child-rearing patterns in depressed, abusive, and normal mothers. *American Journal of Orthopsychiatry, 55*(2), 237–259.

Sutton-Smith, B. (1967). The role of play in cognitive development. *Young Children, 6,* 364–369.

Sutton-Smith, B. (1976). A developmental structural account of riddles. In B. Kirschenblatt-Gimblett (Ed.), *Speech play* (pp. 111–119). Philadelphia: University of Pennsylvania Press.

Sutton-Smith, B. (1979a). Epilogue: Play as performance. In B. Sutton-Smith (Ed.), *Play and learning* (pp. 295–322). New York: Gardner Press.

Sutton-Smith, B. (1979b). Introduction. In B. Sutton-Smith (Ed.), *Play and learning* (pp. 1–6). New York: Gardner Press.

Sutton-Smith, B. (1979c). Overview: Play or flow. In B. Sutton-Smith (Ed.), *Play and learning* (pp. 275–294). New York: Gardner Press.

Sutton-Smith, B. (Ed.). (1979d). *Play and learning*. New York: Gardner Press.

Sutton-Smith, B. (1980). Children's play: Some sources of play theorizing. In K. H. Rubin (Ed.), *New directions for child development: Children's play* (No. 9, pp. 1–16). San Francisco: Jossey-Bass.

Sutton-Smith, B. (1984). Recreation as folly's parody. *The Association for the Anthropological Study of Play Newsletter, 10,* 4–13.

Sutton-Smith, B. (1985). Play research: State of the art. In J. L. Frost & S. Sunderlin (Eds.), *When children play* (pp. 9–16). Wheaton, MD: Association for Childhood Education International.

Sutton-Smith, B., & Kelly-Byrne, D. (1984). The phenomenon of bipolarity in play theories. In T. D. Yawkey & A. D. Pellegrini (Eds.), *Child's play: Developmental and applied* (pp. 29–48). Hillsdale, NJ: Erlbaum.

Sutton-Smith, B., & Rosenberg, J. (1961). Sixty years of historical change in games of American children. *Journal of American Folklore, 74,* 17–46.

Sutton-Smith, B., & Savasta, M. (1972, April). *Sex differences in play and power*. Paper presented at the annual meeting of the Eastern Psychological Association, Washington, DC.

Sutton-Smith, B., & Sutton-Smith, S. (1974). *How to play with your children (and when not to)*. New York: Hawthorn/Dutton.

Suydam, M. N. (1984a). Manipulative materials. *Arithmetic Teacher, 31*(5), 27.

Suydam, M. N. (1984b). Microcomputers in mathematics instruction. *Arithmetic Teacher, 32,* 35.

Suydam, M. N., & Higgins, J. L. (1977). *Activity-based learning in elementary school mathematics instruction: Recommendations from research*. Washington, DC: National Institute of Education. (ERIC Document Reproduction Service No. ED 144 840)

Swigger, K. M., Campbell, J., & Swigger, B. K. (1983, January/February). Preschool children's preferences for different types of CAI programs. *Educational Computer Magazine,* 38–40.

Switzky, H. N., Ludwig, L., & Haywood, H. C. (1979). Exploration and play in retarded and nonretarded preschool children: Effects of object complexity and age. *American Journal of Mental Deficiency, 83,* 637–644.

Switzky, H. N., Rotatori, A., Miller, T., & Freagon, S. (1979). The development model and its implication for assessment and instruction for the severely/profoundly handicapped. *Mental Retardation, 17,* 167–170.

Sylva, K. (1977). Play and learning. In B. Tizard & D. Harvey (Eds.), *Biology of play* (pp. 59–73). London: Heinemann.

Sylva, K., Bruner, J. S., & Genova, P. (1976). The role of play in the problem solving of children 3–5 years old. In J. S. Bruner, A. Jolly, & K. Sylva (Eds.), *Play: Its role in development and evolution* (pp. 244–257). New York: Basic Books.

Szekely, G. (1983). Preliminary play in the art class. *Art Education, 36*(6), 18–24.

Taenzer, S. F., Cermak, C., & Hanlon, R. C. (1981). Outside the therapy room: A naturalistic approach to language intervention. *Topics in Learning and Learning Disabilities, 1*(2), 41–46.

Tait, P. (1972a). A description analysis of the play of young blind children. *Education of the Visually Handicapped, 4,* 12–15.

Tait, P. (1972b). Behavior of young blind children in a controlled play session. *Perceptual and Motor Skills, 34,* 963–969.

Tait, P. (1972c). Play and the intellectual development of blind children. *New Outlook for the Blind, 66*(10), 361–369.

Taylor, A., & Preiser, W. F. E (undated). *Activity based design of applied classroom environments.* Albuquerque: University of New Mexico, Institute of Environmental Education.

Taylor, A. P., & Vlastos, G. (1975). *School zone, learning environments for children.* New York: Van Nostrand Reinhold.

Teale, W. H. (1978). Positive environments for learning to read: What studies of early readers tell us. *Language Arts, 55,* 922–931.

Tenny, Y. H. (1973). *The child's conception of organization and recall: The development of cognitive strategies.* Unpublished doctoral dissertation. Cornell University, Ithaca, NY.

Terman, L. (1926). *Genetic studies of genius (Vol. 1).* Palo Alto, CA: Stanford University Press.

Terrell, B. Y., Schwartz, R. G., Prelock, P. A., & Messick, C. K. (1984). Symbolic play in normal and language-impaired children. *Journal of Speech and Hearing Research, 27,* 424–429.

Thomas, A., & Chess, S. (1977). *Temperament and development.* New York: Brunner/Mazel.

Thomas, B. (1984). Early toy preferences of four-year-old readers and nonreaders. *Child Development, 55,* 424–430.

Thomas, D. (1954). *Quite early one morning.* New York: James Laughlin.

Thompson, R. A., & Lamb, M. E. (1983). Security of attachment and stranger sociability in infancy. *Developmental Psychology, 19,* 184–191.

Thompson, R. G., & Stanford, G. (1981). *Child life in hospitals.* Springfield, IL: Charles C Thomas.

Thompson, S. K. (1975). Gender labels and early sex role development. *Child Development, 46,* 339–347.

Tilton, J. T., & Ottinger, D. R. (1964). Comparison of the toy play behavior of the autistic retarded and normal child. *Psychological Reports, 15,* 967.

Tipps, S. (1981). Play and the brain: Relationships and reciprocity. *Journal of Research and Development in Education, 14*(3), 19–29.

Tizard, B., Philips, J., & Plewis, I. (1976a). Play in preschool centers: Effects on play of the child's social class and of the educational orientation of the center. *Journal of Child Psychology and Psychiatry, 17*(4), 265–274.

Tizard, B., Philips, J., & Plewis, I. (1976b). Play in preschool centers: Play measures and their relation to age, sex, and IQ. *Journal of Child Psychology and Psychiatry, 17,* 251–264.

Tizard, B., Philips, J., & Plewis, I. (1976c). Staff behavior in preschool centers. *Journal of Child Psychology and Psychiatry, 17*(1), 21–23.

Toffler, A. (1980). *The third wave.* New York: William Morrow.

Tolpin, M. (1971). On the beginning of a cohesive self. *Psychoanalytic study of the child, 26,* 316–352.

Tomkins, S. (1962–1963). *Affect, imagery, consciousness (2 Vols.).* New York: Springer-Verlag.

Tomkins, S., & McCarter, R. (1964). What and where are the primary affects? Some evidence for a theory. *Perceptual and Motor Skills, 18,* 119–158.

Torney, J. V., & Mastrude, P. (1972). *Teaching about spaceship earth: A role-playing experience for the middle grades.* New York: Center for War/Peace Studies.

Torrance, E. P. (1965). *Rewarding creative behavior.* Englewood Cliffs, NJ: Prentice-Hall.

Torrance, E. P. (1966). *Torrance tests of creative thinking.* Princeton, NJ: Personnel Press.

Traub, R. E., Weiss, J., & Fisher, C. W. (1974). Studying openness in education: An Ontario example. *Journal of Research and Development in Education, 8,* 47–59.

Trevarthen, C. (1977). Descriptive analyses of infant communicative behavior. In H. R. Schaffer (Ed.), *Studies in mother-infant interaction* (pp. 227–270). London: Academic Press.

Turiel, E. (1975). The development of social concepts. In D. DePalma & J. Foley (Eds.), *Moral development* (pp. 7–37). Hillsdale, NJ: Erlbaum.

Turiel, E. (1977). The development of concepts of social structure. In J. Glick & R. A. Clarke-Stewart (Eds.), *Personality and social development* (Vol. 1, pp. 25–107). New York: Gardner Press.

Turiel, E. (1978). Social regulations and domains of social concepts. In W. Damon (Ed.), *New directions in child development: Social cognition* (No. 1, pp. 45–74). San Francisco: Jossey-Bass.

Turner, V. (Ed.) (1984). *Celebration: Studies in festivity and ritual.* Washington, DC: Smithsonian Press.

Udwin, O. (1983). Imaginative play training as an intervention method with institutionalized preschool children. *British Journal of Educational Psychology, 53,* 32–39.

Underwood, J. (1978). Taking the fun out of a game. In R. Martens (Ed.), *Joy and sadness in children's sports* (pp. 50–64). Champaign, IL: Human Kinetics.

Ungerer, J. A., & Sigman, M. (1981). Symbolic play and language comprehension in autistic children. *Journal of the American Academy of Child Psychiatry, 20*(2), 318–337.

Ungerer, J. A., & Sigman, M. (1984). The relation of play and sensorimotor behavior to language in the second year. *Child Development, 55*, 1448–1455.

Uzgiris, I., & Hunt, J. McV. (1975). *Assessment in infancy.* Urbana: University of Illinois Press.

Van Alstyne, D. (1932). *Play behavior and choice of play materials of preschool children.* Chicago: University of Chicago Press.

Vance, B. (1982). Adventure playgrounds: The American experience. *Parks and Recreation, 17*(9), 67–70.

Vance, T. F., & McCall, L. T. (1934). Children's preferences among play materials as determined by the method of paired comparisons of pictures. *Child Development, 5*, 267–277.

Vandell, D. L. (1979). Effects of a playgroup experience on mother-son and father-son interaction. *Developmental Psychology, 35*(4), 379–385.

Vandell, D. L., Anderson, L. D., Ehrhardt, G., & Wilson, K. S. (1982). Integrating hearing and deaf preschoolers: An attempt to enhance hearing children's interactions with deaf peers. *Child Development, 53*, 1354–1363.

Vandell, D. L., & Mueller, E. C. (1978). *Individual differences in early social interactions with peers.* Dallas, University of Dallas; Boston, Boston University. (ERIC Document Reproduction Service No. ED 153 736)

Vandell, D. L., & Mueller, E. C. (1980). Peer play and friendships during the first two years. In H. C. Foot, A. J. Chapman, & J. R. Smith (Eds.), *Friendships and social relations in children* (pp. 181–208). London: Wiley.

Vandell, D. L., Wilson, K. S., & Buchanan, R. (1980). Peer interaction in the first year of life: An examination of its structure, content, and sensitivity to toys. *Child Development, 51*, 481–488.

Vandenberg, B. (1978). Play and development from an ethological perspective. *American Psychologist, 33*, 724–738.

Vandenberg, B. (1980). Play, problem-solving and creativity. In K. H. Rubin (Ed.), *New directions in child development: Children's play* (No. 9, pp. 49–68). San Francisco: Jossey-Bass.

Vandenberg, B. (1981a). Environmental and cognitive factors in social play. *Journal of Experimental Child Psychology, 31*, 169–175.

Vandenberg, B. (1981b). The role of play in the development of insightful tool-using strategies. *Merrill-Palmer Quarterly, 27*, 97–109.

Vandenberg, B. (1982). Play: A concept in need of a definition. In D. J. Pepler & K. H. Rubin (Eds.), *The play of children: Current theory and research* (pp. 15–21). Basel, Switzerland: Karger AG.

Veit, M. (1983). Children and television: Should we pull the plug? *Two to twelve, 1*(5), 3–6.

Visintainer, M. A., & Wolfer, J. A. (1975). Psychological preparation for surgical pediatric procedures: The effect on children's and parents' stress reduction. *Pediatrics, 56*, 187–195.

Von Glascoe, C. A. (1980). The work of playing redlight. In H. B. Schwartzman (Ed.), *Play and culture* (pp. 228–231). West Point, NY: Leisure Press.

Vygotsky, L. (1962). *Thought and language.* Cambridge, MA: MIT Press.

Vygotsky, L. (1967). Play and the role of mental development in the child. *Soviet Psychology, 5*, 6–18.

Wachs, T. (1976). Utilization of a Piagetian approach in the investigation of early experience effects: A research strategy and some illustrative data. *Merrill-Palmer Quarterly, 22*, 11–29.

Wachs, T. D. (1985). Home stimulation and cognitive development. In C. C. Brown & A. W. Gottfried (Eds.), *Play interactions: The role of toys and parental involvement in children's development* (pp. 142–152). Skillman, NJ: Johnson & Johnson.

Wachs, T. D., & Chan, A. (1985). *Physical and social environment correlates of three aspects of 12 month language functioning.* Paper presented at the meeting of the Society for Research in Child Development, Toronto.

Wachs, T. D., & Gandour, M. (1983). Temperament, environment and 6 months cognitive intellectual development. *International Journal of Behavioral Development, 6*, 135–152.

Wachs, T., Uzgiris, I., & Hunt, J. McV. (1971). Cognitive development in infants of different age levels and from different environmental backgrounds: An exploratory investigation. *Merrill-Palmer Quarterly, 17*, 283–317.

Wade, G. R. (1968). *A study of free play patterns of elementary school age children on playground equipment.* Unpublished master's thesis, Pennsylvania State University, University Park.

Wade, M., Ellis, M., & Bohrer, R. (1973). Biorhythms in the activity of children during free play. *Journal of the Experimental Analysis of Behavior, 20*, 155–162.

Waelder, R. (1933). The psychoanalytic theory of play. *Psychoanalytic Quarterly, 2*, 208–224.

Walberg, H. J. (Ed.). (1979). *Educational environments and effects.* Berkeley, CA: McCutchan.

Wall, N. (1984). Microcomputer activities and occupational therapy. *The Exceptional Parent, 14*(4), 25–28.

Wallach, F. (1983). Play in the age of technology. *Parks and Recreation, 18*(4), 36–38, 63.

Wallach, M. A., & Kogan, N. (1965). *Modes of thinking in young children: A study of the creativity-intelligence distinction.* New York: Holt, Rinehart & Winston.

Wallerstein, J. S. (1983). Children of divorce: The psychological tasks of the child. *American Journal of Orthopsychiatry, 53*(2), 230–243.

Wallerstein, J. S. (1984). Children of divorce: Preliminary report of a ten-year follow-up of young children. *American Journal of Orthopsychiatry, 54*(3), 444–458.

Wallerstein, J. S., & Kelly, J. B. (1981). *Surviving the breakup: How children and parents cope with divorce.* New York: Basic Books.

Waltman, A. (1955). Concepts of play therapy techniques. *American Journal of Orthopsychiatry, 25*(4), 771–783.

Warren, S. F., & Rogers-Warren, A. K. (1980). Current perspectives on language remediation. *Education and Treatment of Children, 3,* 133–152.

Wason, P. C., & Johnson, P. N. (1968). *Thinking and reasoning.* Baltimore: Penguin.

Wason, P. C., & Johnson-Laird, P. N. (1972). *Psychology of reasoning: Structure and content.* Cambridge, MA: Harvard University Press.

Waters, E., Wippman, J., & Sroufe, L. A. (1979). Attachment, positive affect and competence in the peer group: Two studies in construct validation. *Child Development, 50,* 821–829.

Watson, J. B. (1914). *Behavior, an introduction to comparative psychology.* New York: Holt, Rinehart & Winston.

Watson, J. S., & Ramey, C. T. (1972). Reactions to response-contingent stimulation in early infancy. *Merrill-Palmer Quarterly, 18,* 219–227.

Watson, M. W., & Fischer, K. W. (1977). A developmental sequence of agent use in late infancy. *Child Development, 48,* 828–836.

Watson, M. W., & Fischer, K. W. (1980). Development of social roles in elicited and spontaneous behavior during the preschool years. *Developmental Psychology, 16,* 483–494.

Webster's New Collegiate Dictionary. (1980). Springfield, MA: G. & C. Merriam.

Webster's New World Dictionary: Second College Edition. (1972). New York: World.

Wehman, P. (1975). Establishing play behaviors in mentally retarded youth. *Rehabilitation Literature, 36,* 238–246.

Wehman, P. (1977). *Helping the mentally retarded acquire play skills.* Springfield, IL: Charles C Thomas.

Weiner, B. J., Ottinger, D. R., & Tilton, J. R. (1969). Comparison of toy play behavior of autistic, retarded and normal children: A reanalysis. *Psychological Reports, 25,* 223–227.

Weiner, E. A., & Weiner, B. J. (1974). Differentiation of retarded and normal children through toy play analysis. *Multivariate Behavioral Research, 9,* 245–252.

Weininger, O. (1979). *Play and education: The basic tool for early childhood learning.* Springfield, IL: Charles C Thomas.

Weininger, O. (1983). Play and the hospitalized child. *Canadian Counsellor, 17*(2), 67–74.

Weinraub, M., & Frankel, J. (1977). Sex differences in parent-infant interaction during free play, departure and separation. *Child Development, 48,* 1240–1249.

Weinstein, C., & Weinstein, N. (1978). *The effect of noise in an open space school on reading comprehension.* Paper presented at the annual meeting of the American Educational Research Association, Toronto. (ERIC Document Reproduction Service No. ED 154 357).

Weir, R. (1966). Some questions on the child's learning of phonology. In F. Smith & G. A. Miller, *The genesis of language: A psycholinguistic approach* (pp. 153–172). Cambridge, MA: MIT Press.

Wenckstern, S., & Weizmann, F., & Leenaars, A. A. (1984). Temperament and tempo of play in eight-month-old infants. *Child Development, 55*(4), 1195–1199).

Wertsch, J. (1979). From social interaction to higher psychological processes. *Human Development, 22,* 1–22.

Westby, C. E. (1980). Assessment of cognitive and language abilities through play. *Language, Speech, and Hearing Services in School, 11*(3), 154–168.

Wheeler, V. A. (1981). *Reciprocity between first-grade friend and nonfriend classmates in a conflict-of-interest situation.* Unpublished doctoral dissertation, University of Rochester, Rochester, NY.

White, B. (1975). *The first three years of life.* Englewood Cliffs, NJ: Prentice-Hall.

White, B. L., & Carew-Watts, J. (1973). *Experience and environment: Major influences on the development of the young child.* (Vol. 1). Englewood Cliffs, NJ: Prentice-Hall.

White, B. L., & Kaban, B. T. (1978). *Experience and environment: Major influences on the development of the young child* (Vol. 2). Englewood Cliffs, NJ: Prentice-Hall.

White, B. L., Kaban, B., Shapiro, B., & Attanucci, J. (1977). Competence and experience. In I. Uzgiris & F. Weizmann (Eds.), *The structuring of experience* (pp. 115–152). New York: Plenum Press.

White, R. W. (1959). Motivation reconsidered: The concept of competence. *Psychological Review, 6,* 297–333.

Whiteman, M. (1967). Children's conceptions of psychological causality. *Child Development, 38,* 143–155.

Wiburg, K., & Rader, B. (1984). Computers are elementary. *Arithmetic Teacher, 31*(5), 18–22.

Widerstrom, A. (1983). How important is play for handicapped children? *Childhood Education, 60,* 39–49.

Williams, P. A., Haertel, E. H., Haertel, G. D., & Walberg, H. J. (1982). The impact of leisure-time television on school learning: A research synthesis. *American Educational Research Journal, 19*(1), 19–50.

Williams, R. (1980, February). *Symbolic play in young, language handicapped and normal speaking children.* Paper presented at the International Conference on Piaget and the Helping Professions, Los Angeles.

Wing, L., Gould, J., Yeates, S., & Brierley, L. (1977). Symbolic play in severely retarded and in autistic children. *Journal of Child Psychology and Psychiatry, 18*(2), 167–178.

Winn, M. (1977). *The plug-in drug.* New York: Viking.

Winnicott, D. (1971). *Playing and reality.* New York: Basic Books.

Witt, P., & Gramza, A. (1969). *Position effects in play equipment preferences of nursery school children.* Urbana, IL: Children's Research Center.

Wohlwill, J. (1984). Relationships between exploration and play. In T. Yawkey & A. D. Pellegrini (Eds.), *Child's play: Developmental and applied* (pp. 143–170). Hillsdale, NJ: Erlbaum.

Wolf, D. (Ed.). (1979). *New directions in child development: Early symbolization.*(No. 3). San Francisco: Jossey-Bass.

Wolf, D., & Gardner, H. (1979). Style and sequence in early symbolic play. In M. Franklin & N. Smith (Eds.), *New directions in child development: Early symbolization.* (No. 3, pp. 117–138). Hillsdale, NJ: Erlbaum.

Wolf, D., & Grollman, S. H. (1982). Ways of playing: Individual differences in imaginative style. In D. J. Pepler K. H. Rubin (Eds.), *The play of children: Current theor research,* pp. 46–64. Basel, Switzerland: Karger AG.

Wolf, D. P., & Pusch, J. (1985). The origins of autonomous texts in play boundaries. In L. Galda & A. Pellegrini (Eds.), *Play, language, and stories: The development of children's literate behavior* (pp. 63–77). Norwood, NJ: Ablex.

Wolf, D. P., Rygh, J., & Altshuler, J. (1984). Agency and experience: Actions and states in play narratives. In I. Bretherton (Ed.), *Symbolic play: The development of social understanding* (pp. 195–218). New York: Academic Press.

Wolfenstein, M. (1954). *Children's humor: A psychological analysis.* Glencoe, IL: Free Press.

Wolfer, J. A., & Visintainer, M. A. (1975). Pediatric surgical patients' and parents' stress responses and adjustment. *Nursing Research, 24*(4), 244–255.

Wolff, P. H. (1969). The natural history of crying and other vocalizations in early infancy. In B. Foss (Ed.), *Determinants of infant behavior* (Vol. 4, pp. 81–109). New York: Wiley.

Wolfgang, C. H. (1977). *Helping aggressive and passive preschoolers through play.* Columbus, OH: Charles E. Merrill.

Wolfgang, C. H. (1985). Preschool children's preferences for gender-stereotyped play materials. In J. L. Frost & S. Sunderlin (Eds.), *When children play* (pp. 273–279). Wheaton, MD: Association for Childhood Education International.

Wolfgang, C. H., & Bolig, R. (1979). Play techniques for helping preschool children under stress. *Children's Health Care, 7*(3), 3–10.

Wood, B., Bruner, J. S., & Ross, G. (1976). The role of tutoring in problem solving. *Journal of Child Psychology and Psychiatry, 17,* 89–100.

Worner, P. (1983). Meeting the playground challenge. *Exceptional Parent, 13*(2), 14–16, 18–20.

Wortham, S. C. (1985). A history of outdoor play 1900–1985: Theories of play and play environments. In J. L. Frost & S. Sunderlin (Eds.), *When children play* (pp. 3–8). Wheaton, MD: Association for Childhood Education International.

Wurtman, R. J. (1975). The effects of light on the human body. *Scientific American, 233*(1), 68–77.

Yando, R., Seitz, V., & Zigler, E. (1978). *Imitation: A developmental perspective.* Hillsdale, NJ: Erlbaum.

Yardley, A. (1973). *Young children learning series: Exploration and language; Reaching out; Discovering the physical world; Senses and sensitivity.* New York: Citation Press.

Yarrow, L., Rubenstein, J., & Pedersen, F. (1975). *Infant and environment.* Washington, DC: Hemisphere Publishing Corp.

Yarrow, M. R., & Waxler, C. Z. (1976). Dimensions and correlates of prosocial behavior in young children. *Child Development, 47,* 118–125.

Yawkey, T. (1980). An investigation of imaginative play and aural language development in young children, five, six and seven. In P. F. Wilkinson (Ed.), *In celebration of play: An integrated approach to play and child development* (pp. 85–99). New York: St. Martin's Press.

Yawkey, T. (1981). Sociodramatic play effects on mathematical learning and adult ratings of playfulness in five years olds. *Journal of Research and Development in Education, 14*(3), 30–39.

Youniss, J. (1978). The nature of social development: A conceptual discussion of cognition. In H. McGurk (Ed.), *Issues in childhood social development* (pp. 203–227). London: Methuen.

Youniss, J. (1980). *Parents and peers in social development.* Chicago: University of Chicago Press.

Youniss, J., & Volpe, J. (1978). A relational analysis of children's friendships. In W. Damon (Ed.), *New directions in child development: Social cognition* (No. 1, pp. 1–22). San Francisco: Jossey-Bass.

Zahn-Waxler, C. (1980). *Young children's responses to the emotions of others.* Workshop presented at International Conference on Infant Studies, New Haven, CT.

Zahn-Waxler, C., Radke-Yarrow, M., & King, R. A. (1979). Child rearing and children's prosocial initiations toward victims of distress. *Child Development, 50,* 319–330.

Zammarelli, J., & Bolton, N. (1977). The effects of play on mathematical concept formation. *British Journal of Educational Psychology, 47*(36), 155–161.

Zaporozhets, A. V., & El'konin, D. B. (1971). *Psychology of preschool children.* Cambridge, MA: MIT Press.

Zeller, J. (1985). *A methodology for the identification of specific motor deficits in young children.* Unpublished doctoral dissertation, Harvard University, Cambridge, MA.

Zien, J. (1974). Children in transit: The open city project. In G. Coates, *Alternative learning environments* (pp. 256–273). Stroudsburg, PA: Dowden, Hutchinson, & Ross.

Zifferblatt, S. M. (1972). Architecture and human behavior: Toward increased understanding of a functional relationship. *Educational Technology, 12,* 54–57.

Zigler, E. (1966). Mental retardation: Current issues and approaches. In L. W. Hoffman & M. L. Hoffman (Eds.), *Review of child development research* (Vol. 2, pp. 107–168). New York: Russell Sage Foundation.

Zill, N. & Peterson, J. L. (1982). Learning to do things without help. In L. M. Laosa & I. E. Sigel (Eds.), *Families as learning environments for children* (pp. 343–374). New York: Plenum Press.

Index

Subject Index